Short Fiction
& Critical Contexts

Edited by
Eric Henderson & Geoff Hancock

OXFORD
UNIVERSITY PRESS

OXFORD
UNIVERSITY PRESS

8 Sampson Mews, Suite 204, Don Mills, Ontario, M3C 0H5
www.oupcanada.com

Oxford University Press is a department of the University of Oxford.
It furthers the University's objective of excellence in research, scholarship,
and education by publishing worldwide in

Oxford New York

Auckland Cape Town Dar es Salaam Hong Kong Karachi
Kuala Lumpur Madrid Melbourne Mexico City Nairobi
New Delhi Shanghai Taipei Toronto

With offices in

Argentina Austria Brazil Chile Czech Republic France Greece
Guatemala Hungary Italy Japan Poland Portugal Singapore
South Korea Switzerland Thailand Turkey Ukraine Vietnam

Oxford is a trade mark of Oxford University Press
in the UK and in certain other countries

Published in Canada
by Oxford University Press

Library and Archives Canada Cataloguing in Publication

Short fiction & critical contexts : a short reader / [edited by] Eric Henderson & Geoff Hancock.

ISBN 978-0-19-542993-0

1. College readers. 2. English language—Rhetoric—Problems, exercises, etc.
3. Short stories, English. I. Henderson, Eric II. Hancock, Geoff

PN6120.2.S55 2009   808'.0427   C2009-902386-5

Cover image: Eric Cator/www.ericcator.com

Oxford University Press is committed to our environment. This book is printed on
Forest Stewardship Council certified paper, harvested from a responsibly managed forest,
which contains a minimum of 20% post-consumer waste.

Printed on 20% recycled paper

trees were saved for our forests

Preserving our environment

Oxford University Press chose to print the pages of this
book on recycled paper and saved these resources[1]:

energy	water	greenhouse gases	solid waste
2 million BTUs	12,494 L	311 kg	91 kg

Printed by **Webcom Inc.** on
Legacy Lightweight Opaque 20% post-consumer waste.

FSC
www.fsc.org

MIX
Paper from
responsible sources
FSC® C004071

[1]Estimates were made using the Environmental Defense Paper Calculator.

Printed and bound in Canada.

2 3 4 -- 13 12 11

Contents

Preface   vii

Introduction   xi

Part I   Short Fiction   1

EDGAR ALLAN POE   3
 *The Masque of the Red
 Death*   4

CHARLOTTE PERKINS GILMAN   9
 The Yellow Wallpaper   10

STEPHEN CRANE   23
 A Mystery of Heroism   24

EDITH WHARTON   31
 A Journey   32

E. PAULINE JOHNSON   41
 The Derelict   42

JAMES JOYCE   47
 A Painful Case   48

FRANZ KAFKA   55
 A Report to an Academy   56

J.G. SIME   63
 An Irregular Union   64

D.H. LAWRENCE   71
 Tickets, Please   72

KATHERINE MANSFIELD   82
 The Stranger   83

MORLEY CALLAGHAN   93
 A Predicament   94

ERNEST HEMINGWAY   97
 The Capital of the World   98

MARCEL AYMÉ   107
 *The Walker-Through-
 Walls*   108

HEINRICH BÖLL   116
 My Sad Face   117

SINCLAIR ROSS   122
 The Runaway   123

ETHEL WILSON   135
 The Window   136

MARGARET LAURENCE   146
 The Loons   147

ITALO CALVINO   156
 The Origin of the Birds   157

CLARK BLAISE   165
 Eyes   166

ANGELA CARTER   171
 The Company of Wolves   172

MAVIS GALLANT   180
 Between Zero and One   181

ELIZABETH SPENCER   196
 The Girl Who Loved Horses   197

MARGARET ATWOOD   211
 Happy Endings   212

JORGE LUIS BORGES   216
 Shakespeare's Memory   217

JOSE DALISAY, JR   224
 Heartland   225

AMY HEMPEL   235
 Nashville Gone to Ashes   236

BHARATI MUKHERJEE   242
 The Lady from Lucknow   243

RAYMOND CARVER   250
  Feathers   251

ALICE MUNRO   266
  Pictures of the Ice   267

DIANE SCHOEMPERLEN   280
  Antonyms of Fiction   281

MICHAEL DOUGAN   285
  Black Cherry   287

SHANI MOOTOO   290
  Out on Main Street   291

EDWIDGE DANTICAT   299
  Children of the Sea   300

GREG HOLLINGSHEAD   312
  The People of the Sudan   313

BARBARA GOWDY   327
  We So Seldom Look on Love   328

HARUKI MURAKAMI   338
  The Seventh Man   339

TIMOTHY TAYLOR   350
  Smoke's Fortune   351

RICHARD VAN CAMP   358
  Sky Burial   359

THOMAS KING   366
  A Short History of Indians in Canada   367

SHYAM SELVADURAI   370
  The Demoness Kali   371

Part II   Documents & Dialogues   387

A. Prologue: The Need for Narrative

Fourteen Ways of Looking at a Classic   389
Italo Calvino, from 'Why Read the Classics?'

The Need for Narrative   390
Robert Fulford, from 'Gossip, Literature, and the Fictions of the Self'

The Qualities of an Outstanding Story   392
Thomas Gullason, from 'What Makes a "Great" Short Story Great?'

B. The Art of the Short Story

The Single Effect   395
Edgar Allan Poe, from 'Review of *Twice-Told Tales*'

Rendering 'Reality'   396
Henry James, from 'The Art of Fiction'

Codifying the Short Story   398
Brander Matthews, from *The Philosophy of the Short-Story*

Fiction's Appeal   399
Joseph Conrad, from Preface to *The Nigger of the Narcissus*

Rendering Experience   402
Virginia Woolf, from 'Modern Fiction'

The Morality of the Short Story 403
Elizabeth Bowen, from Introduction to *The Faber Book of Modern Short Stories*

Exploring 'Storyness' through Metaphor 405
Julio Cortázar, from 'Some Aspects of the Short Story'

C. Genre and the Short Story

The Novel and the Short Story 409
Edith Wharton, from *The Writing of Fiction*

Steven Millhauser, from 'The Ambition of the Short Story' 410

Greg Hollingshead, from 'Short Story vs Novel' 412

The Lyric and the Short Story 414
Eileen Baldeshwiler, from 'The Lyric Short Story: The Sketch of a History'

D. Epiphany and the Short Story

The Joycean Epiphany 417
James Joyce, from *Stephen Hero*

Against Epiphany 418
Philip Stevik, from Introduction to *Anti-Story: An Anthology of Experimental Fiction*

Moving Toward Disillusionment 419
Thomas M. Leitch, from 'The Debunking Rhythm of the American Short Story'

Significant Omissions 420
Cynthia J. Hallett, from 'Minimalism and the Short Story'

E. Reality, Fantasy, and the Short Story

The Grotesque 423
Flannery O'Connor, from 'Aspects of the Grotesque in Southern Fiction'

The Fantastic 424
Tzvetan Todorov, from *The Fantastic: A Structural Approach to a Literary Genre*

The 'Tale' 425
Angela Carter, from Afterword to *Fireworks: Nine Stories in Various Disguises*

Magic Realism 426
Geoff Hancock, from *Magic Realism and Canadian Literature: Essays and Stories*

Fantasy, Reality, and Metafiction 428
Linda Hutcheon, from 'Actualizing Narrative Structures: Detective Plot, Fantasy, Games, and the Erotic'

F. The Writer's Tools

Character 431
Frank O'Connor, from
Introduction to *The Lonely Voice*

Language 432
Raymond Carver, from 'On
Writing'

Plot and Form 434
Eudora Welty, from 'The Reading
and Writing of Short Stories'

Style 435
Mavis Gallant, from 'What Is
Style?'

Symbol and Theme 438
Flannery O'Connor, from 'The
Nature and Aim of Fiction'

Voice 439
Katherine Mansfield, Letter to
Richard Murry

G. The Short Story and Its
Practitioners

Charlotte Perkins Gilman 441
Charlotte Perkins Gilman,
'Why I Wrote "The Yellow
Wallpaper"'

Anton Chekhov 442
Anton Chekhov, from *Letters
1888–99*

Stephen Crane 444
Stephen Crane, from 'Letters
to a Friend About His Ambition,
His Art, and His Views of Life'

Native Fiction 445
Thomas King, from Introduction
to *All My Relations: An Anthology
of Contemporary Canadian Native
Fiction*

**Literature of the South Asian
Diaspora** 449
Shyam Selvadurai, from
'Introducing Myself in the
Diaspora'

Dialogues
Interview with Alice Munro,
from *Canadian Writers at
Work: Interviews with Geoff
Hancock* 453

Interview with Bharati
Mukherjee, from *Canadian
Writers at Work: Interviews with
Geoff Hancock* 456

Interview with Shani Mootoo,
from Maya Khankoje, 'To Bend
but not to Bow' 458

H. Epilogue: Writer and
Reader

How to Read Well 461
Vladimir Nabokov, from 'Good
Readers and Good Writers'

In Praise of Reading 465
Alberto Manguel, from 'Endpaper
Pages'

The Need for a Reader 470
Margaret Atwood, from
'Communion: Nobody to
Nobody: The Eternal Triangle'

Part III   A Brief Handbook of Short Fiction Terms and Concepts 479

Acknowledgements 497

Preface

Short Fiction & Critical Contexts: A Compact Reader has been designed, first, as a resource for courses in which short fiction is studied, either exclusively or with other genres. With forty stories and forty selections about fiction, this anthology can be used in introductory literature courses or more advanced ones where theory and practice are complementary goals. Its strong focus on multicultural writing would make it suitable in cultural studies courses. As a literary companion, it could also be used in creative writing courses.

This anthology represents a wide range of stories spanning 170 years of innovation and experimentation. Although canonical authors are well represented, many of the stories are not the usual selections, marking a departure from other anthologies by introducing students to new works by familiar authors. As well, many authors appear here for the first time in an anthology of this kind. In all, we tried to choose a diverse yet balanced group of authors. In addition to Canada, the United States, and Great Britain, the following countries are represented: Argentina, Czech Republic, France, Germany, Haiti, India, Ireland, Italy, Japan, New Zealand, the Philippines, Sri Lanka, and Trinidad. Approximately half of the stories are by women, and three are by Aboriginal authors. Although the best literature transcends its writer's era, contemporary writers often speak with immediacy to today's student readers. Twelve writers in this anthology were born post-World War II, and four were born post-1960.

In the post-war period, new perspectives and techniques reinvigorated short fiction; new ways of writing led to new ways of reading. *Short Fiction & Critical Contexts* confronts these challenges through story introductions: 'brief biographies' encapsulate facts for quick reference while the prose sections situate authors and stories within important critical contexts, clarifying and foregrounding literary terms and concepts applicable to the author, story, and age. These matters are discussed in further detail in the remaining sections of the anthology, 'Dialogues & Documents' and 'A Brief Handbook of Short Fiction Terms and Concepts.'

'Documents & Dialogues' serves as a complement to the story introductions, enabling stories to be studied within a range of critical viewpoints. Seventeen authors in this section are represented by stories in the anthology, while others are short story writers, literary critics, or theorists who explore a diversity of topics. We were guided by several criteria in our choice of essays, from canonical status—such as that of the critical writing of Edgar Allan Poe, Henry James, Joseph Conrad, Virginia Woolf, Elizabeth Bowen, Frank O'Connor, and Flannery O'Connor—to the unique perspective on issues relevant to the study of short fiction. Organized into eight subsections for practical classroom use, essay topics include the need for narrative; the art of the short story; short fiction as a genre; the evolution of the epiphany; 'non-realistic' writing; the conventions of short fiction; the goals and ideals of several writers; and the aesthetics of reading in a complex relationship between reader, writer, and text.

The handbook section of the anthology includes over 100 terms and explains concepts frequently encountered in today's short fiction. Many entries give stories from the anthology as concrete examples of the term being defined and direct readers to relevant essays or excerpts in the 'Dialogues & Documents' section. The story introductions, essays, and handbook give students the tools to successfully read and analyze all stories in this anthology and, we hope, to invigorate their future reading of short fiction.

For any compact anthology, inclusion implies exclusion, and it has been necessary to omit information on general writing and research skills, as well as formats and other guidelines for writing literary essays. Ample resources for these topics exist in older anthologies and composition textbooks, in style guides, and in reliable online resources. Instructors wishing to utilize them have many options, including the companion website for this anthology (http://www. oupcanada.com/higher_education/companion/literature/9780195429930. html), which has been customized for its users.

Acknowledgements

We wish, first, to gratefully acknowledge Oxford University Press Canada president David Stover for his commitment to this project from the very beginning. Our appreciation extends particularly to developmental editor Peter Chambers for his competent care, patience, and enthusiasm, and to copyeditor Janna Green whose insightful editorial suggestions made this a better book. The constructive comments of anonymous reviewers occasioned a great many deliberations and some significant changes.

Several colleagues at the University of Victoria offered valuable input at different stages in the process: Adrienne Williams Boyarin, Michael Cullen, Misao Dean, Claire McKenzie, Andrew Murray, Richard Pickard, and Harb Sanghara. Special thanks to lion-hearted Nanny who kept things in perspective for me. Above all, the advice, support, and love of my family has been a vital and sustaining force in this project as in every project I undertake.–E.H.

Writing his *Natural History* in 77 AD, Pliny and his colleagues consulted over 2,000 volumes and up to 400 authors. Likewise our experience sifting selections for this compact anthology of short fiction. As we considered the nature of stories, we revelled in the infinity of short forms, in new critical approaches, and in writers and scholars who reinvigorate this most varied genre. Thanks of a personal nature for suggestions, hints, ideas, and supportive friendship through an evolving process go to Dr Madeline Sonik, Robert Newland, Michael Fox, Dean Dougherty, Matt Willems, and Dr Glenda Guest. I thank the staff of the Stratford Public Library for their resources, including the literary web via Internet and interlibrary loans. Most profound thanks go to Gay Allison and Meagan Allison-Hancock, who help me live creatively. –G.H.

Introduction:
A Story of Subversion

During the 170 years represented by the short stories in *Short Fiction & Critical Contexts*, assumptions about fiction have often been challenged, and the short fiction genre has undergone many changes. Rooted in Romanticism, the artistic miniature known as a short story evokes myth, mysteries, and strangeness. Short fiction evolved at precise historical moments of transition, and its writers have recorded, celebrated, or foretold these moments. These 'shock points' include the weakening of religion by science; the rise of American nationalism; the decline of the aristocracy in nineteenth-century Europe; new discoveries in science, psychology, and social and economic theory; the trauma and aftermath of World War I; the technology revolution; and post-colonialism, multiculturalism, and new nationalism. Throughout its flexible and evolving history, the modern short story has remained a resistant form, so elusive that extensive scholarship continues to seek a suitable definition. Neither novel nor poetry, yet sharing elements of both, the short story is unique in its variety of forms.

The characteristics of stories derive from history, and to neglect traditions is to neglect their rich diversity. Threads of their origins are woven through even the most modern story because storytelling is as ancient as human culture. Yet classifications falter. Tale, fable, legend, prose poem, sketch—scholars debate their slippery traits and characteristics. In the narrative tradition, folktales and story cycles recur early, then were rediscovered by post-colonial writers who saw their potential to challenge and critique colonial and contemporary politics and culture. The ancient and medieval tales in *The Arabian Nights*, the fourteenth-century stories in Boccaccio's *The Decameron* and Geoffrey Chaucer's *The Canterbury Tales*, and the fairy tales collected by seventeenth-century Charles Perrault and those by the nineteenth-century Brothers Grimm are all part of the rich tradition of modern stories. By comparison, novels developed in the sixteenth and seventeenth centuries as part of European written culture; their length and detailed descriptions enabled them to make powerful commentaries on society. During the eighteenth century Age of Enlightenment, reason, logic, and scientific and mathematical thinking prevailed, and novelists increasingly trained their lens on the social relations of their characters. Yet in essence the story is not social criticism. Fairy tales carried wild memories of

demons, nightmares, revenge, and the supernatural. While stories may over-
lap novels with elements of protest, social conscience, and communal identities, their differences—word count and unity of effect—indicate that short
story understanding lies elsewhere. By nature, as Irish short story writer Frank
O'Connor suggested in his 1962 study of the form, stories are individualistic,
anti-communal, and visionary.

Differing from the novel meant departing from the novel's characteristic
realism, which partially explains the visionary nature of stories. Specifically,
stories less typically portray the lives of the middle class depicted in novels;
they are outside the urban industrial capitalist experience. Though O'Connor
originally meant the Irish, his view of short fiction speaks for outsiders, exiles, the lonely, women, minorities, or voices recovered from oppression and
marginalization. In contrast to the novel, then, a literary story is concentrated,
intense, subtle, and suggestive. Because something in a character's life is revealed, a story deals with the core of an individual in conflict. Stories present a
moment in time, described as slice-of-life, frozen moment, fleeting sensation,
fragmentary impression, a powerful image, or even, as one critic noted (drawing from quantum physics), a vibrating energy pattern. Perfect for depicting
breakdown or randomness, stories are the art of shaping conflict or crisis. This
'crisis,' sometimes called a complication, may or may not be resolved within
the story.

Yet defining a short story remains an elusive task. Dramatic structures and
lengths are as varied as authorial perceptions. How long is a story? How short?
Some of Anton Chekhov's stories exceed 10,000 words, though many critics
would consider this length a novella. Ernest Hemingway's shortest story is only
six sad words ('For sale. Baby shoes. Never worn.') Consumer magazine editorial guidelines after the 1850s determined that the average length of a story
was 2,500 words, that is, as filler between advertisements. Classic explanations
of definition and length are undermined by postmodern variants and contradictions. In addition to length what makes scholarly definitions difficult is the
lack of clear divisions or categories within the form: stories may be realistic
or non-realistic with a continuum that glides between them. In the realistic
story, the author's techniques are invisible, language is descriptive, characters
have a psychology and motivation, and the plot moves from cause to effect.
By contrast, the 'non-realistic' story calls attention to its devices and mixes in
the improbable and unlikely. In such stories, says philosopher and storyteller
William Gass, a character may simply be 'an object of perception in a carefully
designed lexical adventure.'

In America and France, the quest for national identity inevitably followed
independence. In the years immediately after the American Revolution (1775–
83), the earliest published stories were Gothic narratives, moral Oriental tales,
and didactic American character sketches modelled after those by English and
European writers. Yet even this early in its development, the short story in the

United States incorporated elements from other genres and recombined them in new ways. Washington Irving adapted German legends to feature American characters and settings in his stories 'Rip Van Winkle' and 'The Legend of Sleepy Hollow' (*The Sketch Book of Geoffrey Crayon, Gent.* [1820]). Nathaniel Hawthorne, whose forebears were Puritans, manipulated history and atmosphere to create stories of old New England that owed much to ancient fables, allegories, and morality tales. The modern short story, however, dates from Edgar Allan Poe. Considered the founder of science fiction, detective fiction, and horror fiction, he defined the rules and laid down the requirements of the short story, especially its characteristic unity of effect. Blending traditions and his own obsessions, he declared a good story must be unusual, original, and strange, an apt description of his own *Tales of the Grotesque and Arabesque* (1840).

Insurrection, revolution, and war are part of the story's heritage. The bloody terror of the French Revolution (1789–99) led to secular literature and the end of aristocratic privilege. French literary forms such as *contes, récits,* and *nouvelles* (the terms are not always clearly defined even by the French, although *contes* refers to fanciful tales from the oral tradition) are considered forerunners of the modern story. Though fairy tales are usually considered stories for children, the French *conte de fees* were seventeenth-century fairy tales for adults. As literary works, these tales, revised and crafted by professional writers, were as popular in France as fantasy stories are today. Historically, oral storytelling was told by women, their names long forgotten, except for one who stands for them all: Mother Goose. Though women were barred from many levels of society, in the mid-seventeenth century, literary salons were popular. Here, men and women could discuss the preoccupations of the day and tell stories. Fairy tales were especially well regarded. Tales of wicked tyrants, stormy settings, and unified crowds could easily critique the royal court; their subversive subtexts enabled them to get past court censors. At the end of the twentieth century, these stories were reclaimed by a new generation of fantastic story writers.

In the history of short stories, Americans and Europeans are linked. Poe's ideas that inner sensations and emotional reactions were more potent than description became enormously influential in France. Symbolist poet Charles Baudelaire declared Poe a Frenchman lost in America. Yet as influential as Poe was in France, France's Guy de Maupassant (1850–93) created a sensation in the United States. De Maupassant's stories came to New Orleans around 1883, where they were translated for the local newspapers and eventually found their way to New York. Several books of stories, nation-wide reviews, excerpts, and newspaper publications followed. Influential editors looked for stories that followed de Maupassant's model. In his essay 'The Philosophy of the Short Story' (1884), Brander Matthews proclaimed him among the world's great artists. Unfortunately, many writers ignored de Maupassant's complexly structured stories, preferring those with trick, plot reversal, or surprise endings—now called

'O. Henry endings,' after the writer who overused the technique. Yet Matthews's thoughts on short stories established the first conceptual steps in a new tradition. In 1901, influenced by Poe's dictums and de Maupassant's techniques, he wrote the first formal principles—drawing attention to symmetry of design as essential in defining a tradition; he did much to restore Poe's American reputation.

With Poe's unity of effect as a guide, interest in the short story spread almost worldwide. Though it was established in America by the 1840s, and in France, Germany, and Russia by the 1860s, interest did not develop in Great Britain until the 1880s. Mass market magazines like *Blackwoods*, *The Penny Magazine*, and *The Strand* were devoted to simple or sensational aspects of the form, including ghost stories, 'true' adventures, and sentimental sketches. Literary agents and American expatriate authors such as Henry James suggested writing stories to leading British authors.

But literary thought also changed with the publications of Charles Darwin and, later, Sigmund Freud. From Darwin emerged an uncertainty about the world which began to appear in fiction. In Victorian literary thought, Darwin's ideas permeated even non-scientific culture. His *On the Origin of Species* (1859) and *The Descent of Man* (1871) proposed new ways of perceiving the world. He challenged religious orthodoxy and political ideas about how humans behave with such concepts as survival of the fittest, natural selection, and experimental thought. Since it seemed untruthful to dwell on idealized human traits, writers turned to everyday actions among ordinary people, using an accumulation of realistic detail. American economist Thorstein Veblen applied Darwin's ideas to society, helping shape the literary school of naturalism, an outgrowth of realism that saw humans as victims of large oppressive forces. Another kind of determinism was introduced by Sigmund Freud, influencing modernists as dissimilar as James Joyce and D.H. Lawrence, though the focus on psychological states antedated Freud in the works of Poe and psychological realists like Henry James.

In Russia, the poverty-stricken doctor Anton Chekhov (1860–1904) studied Charles Darwin carefully. Darwin's approach to natural sciences was a great influence on Chekhov and the French 'naturalists.' Sometimes called a 'scientific impressionist,' Chekhov was as influential as Poe and de Maupassant in reshaping the short story. As a physician he had a professional interest in the scientific writings of the late nineteenth and early twentieth centuries. His subjects are carefully observed. From the naturalist writings of de Maupassant, Chekhov learned brevity, poetic lyricism, and unplotted dramatic action. Unlike Poe, whose unity of effect was contrived from details put into a story, Chekhov intentionally left things out. Instead of exposition, development, and dénouement, Chekhov eliminated plot. He reshaped the structure of his stories (an estimated 600 or more) with themes, metaphors, and strong images that contributed to meanings. Chekhov's stories have a mood of disillusionment or disappointment. His characters display frustration, lack of communication, and obsession, their failures reflected through the use of understatement. Chekhov's innovative stories, which often eliminated beginnings and endings, were sometimes called 'pre-stories.' These 'anti-plots' led to the works of James Joyce, Katherine Mansfield, Ernest Hemingway, and Raymond Carver. Though he was close friends with the great novelist Leo Tolstoy, Chekhov reduced omniscient authorial narration to the protagonist's consciousness, a great technical development for short stories.

From 1882 to 1913 a remarkable period in Paris became known as 'La Belle Epoque,' or 'the beautiful time.' Characterized by new artistic forms, it also began the worldwide spread of a common popular culture—some 45 million people migrated from or to the holdings of the colonial powers, cross-exchanging identities and cultural ideas. In the visual arts, Impressionist and Expressionist painters defied conventions with sensory jolts of pure colour. In literature, a large affluent middle class and mass literacy led to popular magazines and newspapers. Along with de Maupassant, playwright Henrik Ibsen and novelist Émile Zola pushed naturalism and realism to explore taboo subjects, including sex, crime, poverty, civic corruption, and repressed psychology. Frank, often shocking, literary portrayals of everyday life led to the literary modernism of James Joyce, Franz Kafka, and D.H. Lawrence. Parisian radical experiments in all the arts would profoundly affect the post-war generations of writers.

From his experiences in Italy, Switzerland, and Paris, the Irish modernist James Joyce saw that the details of ordinary life held substructures and intertextual possibilities within realism. Critic Hugh Kenner calls Joyce's achievement 'double writing,' with every word a shimmering haze of other words, places, myths, and meanings. Before Joyce, a writer's subject determined the style—Joyce's subject was style. After *Dubliners* (1914), the commonplace became unique. In short fiction, epiphanic revelations and unity of development moved the story away from 'mimetic realism' as modernists rebelled against the conventions of Edwardian and Victorian fiction. Controlled narrative language, apparently simple and free of rhetoric and sentiment, was rich with subtext, patterns, and images. This experiment in realism changed the tone and manner of telling fiction. Titles, beginnings, and endings became crucial to an understanding of an author's intention. Subtle details and fragments directed readers to meanings.

Idyllic recollections of La Belle Epoque masked the war industries of the colonial powers. While Impressionism, Expressionism, and Cubism became artistic conventions, the 'joyless gaiety' of profiteering, poverty, and disenchantment led to trauma, depression, or the politics of non-identity. With World War I's poison gas, trenches, machine guns, barbed wire, and tanks came a brooding sense of mechanized society, fragmentation, questions of identity, and isolation from society and nature. Literary impressionism considers how meaning is derived from metaphors or precise descriptions of passing sensations. By 1918, though, even the nature of language changed, taking on ironic undertones: the phrase 'all quiet on the western front' (and the later Vietnam-era 'friendly fire' and the Gulf War expression 'smart bombs') meant the opposite.

As a result of these changes, a new creative principle, the artistic fragment, became the hallmark of the modernist short story and antecedent of minimalism. Painter Pablo Picasso, living through both world wars, called modern art 'a sum of destructions.' With history in ruins, recollection was often expressed as fragments of thought. Literary heroes, once capable of action, became passive victims of circumstance. Ernest Hemingway, a shell-shocked war veteran, would learn from war correspondent Stephen Crane, who revealed meaninglessness in clichés of courage, honour and glory, that uncertainty was truer than assurance.

Of course, fiction is also a commodity, and this was particularly true in the two decades following World War I. The economic basis of short story publishing divided itself into three types of publications according to the type of paper they were printed on. The classiest and highest-paying publications, with large circulations, had expensive lifestyle advertising; printed on laminated paper they were known as 'slicks.' At the other end of the scale were so-called pulps, printing comics, westerns, crime, and horror stories on cheap paper. The tiniest market of all were the so-called literary magazines, published in small book-like editions, sometimes as a university quarterly, but more often privately subsidized by passionate editors and authors. Because of small circulations, non-commercial and non-profit status, short life spans, and various print formats often known only to special interest groups of writers and readers, these crucial publications were sometimes called 'little' magazines. The success of these publications created a fissure between so-called popular and literary fiction, one suggesting misleadingly that commercial success and literary value are mutually exclusive.

In the years between the two world wars, Poe's sense of shifting perspectives continued with Franz Kafka, whose inner depictions of the loss of self epitomized feelings of alienation and, often, paranoia. With the displacement of the self, some writers, like Morley Callaghan, looked outward and confronted the failure of religious, moral, or social structures. Later, French existentialists Jean-Paul Sartre and Albert Camus looked inward at the bared human soul and its quest for authenticity. Though the story in North America and England briefly retreated to a conservative realism after World War II, modernist experiments continued as a literary underground in the small presses and literary magazines. Latin Americans of Jorge Luis Borges's generation were experimenting with forms, techniques, and avant-garde principles as early as the 1940s and came in contact with the French avant-garde in the 1950s. From 1916 to the 1950s, Canada had a small but important little magazine culture. The 1949–51 Royal (or Massey) Commission paved the way for the Canada Council for the Arts (1957). By the mid-1960s and Canada's centenary, small magazines and literary presses grew by the dozens and then hundreds in every area of Canada, an important resource for a generation of poets and short story writers. In Canada, the little literary magazine edited by Robert Weaver and William Toye, *The Tamarack Review* (1956–82), began publishing the earliest stories of Alice Munro.

As the world continued to change, so did fiction. Writers reacted to the events that shaped their lives. Technology transformed the last four decades of the twentieth century, just as the first questioning of mechanized and urban society suggested the postmodern decades in the future. From then on, literature was defined by the technology that shaped each era, be it telegraph and telephone, railways and automobiles, airpower, or nuclear energy and electronics. The effects of technology now gave rise to the 'new' modernism, to uncertainty, to global immigration, and the end of cultural isolation. The technology of World War II gave way to the strange combination of nuclear physics and cheap assault rifles which ended up in colonial wars twenty years later. A method of army supply lines became the template for the twenty-first century's Big Box corporate culture. As the large superpowers divested themselves of their colonies, the quest for a national literature could be found in short stories—Canadian fiction, Australian fiction, Filipino or Mexican fiction. In Canada, Australia, and other post-Empire 'new nations,' questions of identity arose. Women's rights, anticipated by Americans Charlotte Perkins Gilman and Edith Wharton, appeared in Canadian fiction as early as the 1920s. Within realism were different ways to understand representation. *Canadian Fiction Magazine* (1971–98) was devoted exclusively to experimental short stories. Beyond aesthetics, short fiction proffered cautions against the limitations of certain ways of thinking, living an inauthentic life, and compromising basic beliefs.

The sixty-year period between the post-war Baby Boom and the twenty-first-century Generation-X opened up diverse possibilities for short fiction writers. In much of the eighteenth and nineteenth centuries, meaning was provided by the author as an omniscient, pre-eminent commentator. By the early twentieth century, however, perceptions within the text determined readings. Now the focus shifted to the reading of a work and its images, patterns, and themes. In a world of uncertainty, contemporary authors entangled in mass

media, pop culture, or unfathomable urban and historical experiences provided a brooding and distrustful undertone to many short stories. Against a
backdrop of sweeping social and technological change, long-held views crum-
bled. In the 1960s came the youth and civil rights movements, anti-war sentiment, and an unprecedented view of 'the blue planet' from the vantage point
of the moon. A new generation of readers avidly read the fiction of 'hip' anti-
establishment writers such as American Kurt Vonnegut, a major influence on
Haruki Murakami. With Vonnegut, science fiction and fantasy became mainstream, bridging the gap between popular and literary fiction. Other American
writers, like John Barth and Donald Barthelme, found renewal in parodying
traditional styles and techniques. In Canada, Margaret Laurence, Alice Munro,
and Margaret Atwood began long careers as novelists and short story writers
that would gain them international stature.

Many cultures are in the process of 'becoming,' with groups who lack a unified tradition emigrating from other countries. In some emerging literatures,
short stories explore issues in the lives of ordinary people. In the Caribbean,
writers describe cross influences. The social impact of translation in a closed
society like China introduced new literary techniques, trends, and Western
thoughts such as the conflict between individuals and collectives. South Africa
has two Nobel laureates in Nadine Gordimer and J.M. Coetzee; with the end
of apartheid, some black South African story writers, with eleven languages,
censorship, limited access to printed media, and political oppression, chose to
publish in English. Yet many take pride in traditional Afrikaans. As a former
US territory, American English was imposed on the Philippines. Writers now
wonder whether they should return to one of a hundred local languages. As
these nations mature, the short story often questions realism versus experiment
and asks: is nationalism over? Insightful scholarly methodologies expanded the
boundaries of short fiction, and personal essays on writing led to deeper understanding of an author's works. The popularity of creative writing courses
generated innovative collections, how-to handbooks, and new interest in short
stories.

As a subversive form, the story is oddly double: the world depicted and the
meaning revealed, suggested, hinted. In the post-colonial phase of short fiction, the centre and the periphery switched places. The first stirrings of fiction
beyond empire appear in a 'nationalist phase' of former colonies cleverly described by writer Pico Iyer in a 1993 *Time* magazine article (borrowing a title
from *Star Wars*) as 'the empire writes back.' Various multiculturalism policies
in Canada and former imperial colonies led to a new form of cohesion called
multicultural publishing. A new internationalism emerged from a combination
of small local publishing houses and literary magazines as well as a new interest in translations, exposing readers to new perspectives. The essential qualities
of short fiction were also re-evaluated. Italo Calvino, Heinrich Böll, and Jorge
Luis Borges, among others, suggest in their 'anti-realistic' works that personal

visions matter—not everything can be explained, and not everything is scientific, be it atom smashing or genetic engineering. A story is a snapshot, not a movie. Short stories, then, become the means of a personal pursuit to know the world. In such a world, 'reality' is an exception to the laws of short fiction. Borges said that short inquiries or 'inquisitions' were the purpose of stories. Calvino suggested a new poetic of the story: replace classic ideas with lightness, quickness, exactness, consistency, and visibility.

Once again, the tradition of short fiction was reshaped. Marginality, always an aspect of short fiction (O'Connor made it the premise for his study), found perfect expression in national allegories. In the new geo-politics of short fiction, non-Western nations shaped world affairs. On a social level, personal expressions long suppressed produced potent stories—those of indigenous groups known as the Fourth World, as well as graphic artists, and gay, lesbian, or transgendered writers. In a complex world, the always subversive short story confronted its opposite, excess: too much history, government, corporations, commercialism, dishonest philosophies, and inauthentic lives.

By the twenty-first century, consumer technologies replaced producer technologies with cell phones, hand-held devices, games, and giant screen HDTV that provided access to unusual places and peoples. In the global communication world, the threat of the 'matrix' (a simulated, artificially created reality, a term suggested by a trilogy of popular movies) is real. Fiction merged with media studies as the expressive qualities of image while text and comics evolved into movies, hypertext, and game theory, all promising areas of research into cultural hybrids and cultural trends. This combination created not only new audiences but also a new awareness of the relationship between writer and reader.

Along with these new forms and relationships, writers like Pauline Johnson and J.G. Sime were reclaimed from the past, and new perspectives on established authors such as Sinclair Ross, Angela Carter, and Ernest Hemingway suggested new insights into the creation of the self. Even the nature of the writer was redefined, in some cases as a strong solo voice and in others as a communal storyteller articulating for those who cannot. In a full circle of the persistence of short forms came the revival of fabulist and magical tales, breakaway styles often retold in a post-colonial or anti-capitalist stance or as some other form of debate. If there is a crisis of meaning, it will be expressed in short stories.

Every story has a moment of distress, a moment that can't quite be understood, but in this moment, the inner world of the self is revealed. Tone, menace, tension, and allusions all carry meaning. If the story has a 'flattened arc' (no clear beginning or end), the reader needs to reflect or ponder blanks, gaps, implications, or metaphors. 'True endings' are found in these re-readings, not in the formal conclusion to a story. Readers enlarge the possibilities of the fiction as they engage in a conversation with the text and remain open to the 'unwritten.'

Rooted in humanity, the multiple heritages of the elusive and subversive short story defy definition. Despite a century of approaches and scholarly and authorial debate, despite science, psychology, and electronic networks, the short story remains a persistent mystery. Reason cannot always bridge fiction's intuitive gap between what is said and what is meant. Some generations need magic and marvellous events; others need small narratives of family and relationships. Still others require national allegories and political awareness. Even today, some writers see the world through the consciousness of a character, while others challenge not only the conventions of narratives but even the act of reading. Though writers cannot capture reality, they can explore the poetics of consciousness, imagination, and process. With no consensus on generic traits, a fiction of openness has unlimited possibilities.

Yet no matter how innovative in ideas, trends, styles, or subjects, stories are how we communicate, how we share who we are. Against a backdrop of transformations, the story evolves and eludes, a subversive form that trivializes the large events of history, claims importance for the insignificant, and cares about lonely characters. Each generation finds in a story a 'moment' or renewal, a 'version of reality' that, be it allegory, epiphany, or graphic fiction, questions traditional values and meanings and explores new possibilities of interpreting the world. The vitality of short fiction depends upon patterns, not plot, perceptions, or descriptions. The hidden wisdom within every story is the result of the details noticed, and somehow, as we pay attention to the seemingly insignificant, an effect becomes a truth. In uniting individuals into one community, stories are true to their roots. In this way, short story writers embrace the mystery of the world. The writers celebrated in this anthology invite you to explore the mysteries of their worlds.

G.H., Stratford, ON
E.H., Victoria, BC

Part I

Short Fiction

Edgar Allan Poe

Brief Biography

- Born in Boston in 1809; lives in England 1815–20.
- Parents are actors; father deserts family; mother dies of tuberculosis when Poe is four.
- Raised by John Allan, a wealthy merchant, who later disowns and disinherits him because of Poe's gambling debts.
- In 1836 marries his thirteen-year-old cousin, Virginia, who dies in 1847.
- Sells 'The Fall of the House of Usher' for ten dollars.
- Dedicates 'The Raven' to English poet Elizabeth Barrett Browning. Without copyright protection, Poe earns nothing from the poem.
- Dies in 1849, four days after being found on the Baltimore streets.
- On his deathbed, repeatedly cries out for Reynolds, an obscure Antarctic explorer who inspired his 1838 novel *The Narrative of Arthur Gordon Pym*.

Creator of timeless horror stories, the detective story, and early science fiction, the unhappy genius Edgar Allan Poe continues to fascinate. His portrayal of obsessive mental states and theories of short fiction anticipate twentieth-century psychology and aesthetics.

Poe attended and was expelled from the University of Virginia for gambling debts and was later court-martialled from West Point for neglecting duties. After marrying his cousin Virginia (in an unconsummated marriage of convenience, claims biographer Wolf Mankowitz), he moved from Boston to Philadelphia, where he lived with his wife and her mother (Poe's aunt). Heavy drinking and occasional opium use contributed to the increasing instability of his life. When reality proved uncertain and overwhelming, he found solace in fiction drawn from Romantic and Gothic traditions.

Though he rated the 'Beauty' of poetry higher than the 'Truth' of fiction, Poe wrote seventy major stories and worked as an editor on popular magazines. As an editor, he reviewed books on science, classical history, navigation, and phrenology, which he often used in his allusive fiction. However, his intemperance and a quarrelsome nature made it hard for him to maintain a job, and he moved from magazine to magazine. Poe's literary standards were high, and in spite of publishing his own stories in these magazines, he described them as full of 'contemptible pictures, fashion-plates, and love tales.' His first collection of stories, *Tales of the Grotesque and Arabesque* (1840), sold poorly. But the success of the poem 'The Raven' (1845) secured his last editor's job in New York with a nearly bankrupt paper.

Poe's final days are a mystery. In the months following his wife's death, he was frequently intoxicated. Mysteriously, he was found dying in a Baltimore gutter on 3 October 1849; cause of his death is variously suggested as alcohol intoxication, robbery, or a beating by political press gangs.

Poe's harsh critical reviews of fellow writers and parodies of their works earned him many enemies. One in particular, his first biographer, Rev. Rufus Wilmot Griswold—who was jealous of and hated Poe—forged his manuscripts and smeared his reputation in America. In France, however, Charles Baudelaire considered Poe's investigation 'of the secret chambers of his mind' a great leap for nineteenth-century consciousness. Julio Cortázar said, 'Poe's genius was doctor to his sick soul.' Biographer David Ketterer sees Poe as a major influence on French symbolist poetry, as well as later critical trends such as structuralism. A century and a half after Poe's death, recent developments in science, literary theory, cinema, comics, cryptography, psychoanalysis, and hypertexts show his enduring critical and popular influence.

Like Jorge Luis Borges, Poe was fascinated with ancient books and obscure subjects. He felt 'strangeness was an essential part of beauty'; for example, 'The Masque of the Red Death' features exotic trappings and elements of the grotesque.

Master of 'the pre-established design,' he taught the next century of writers the importance of the opening sentence or narrative hook—the end is in the beginning. With the end (the dénouement) in mind he creates 'novel and vivid' images.

'The Masque of the Red Death' has been read in various ways—from a moral tale of a ruler's accountability to an allegory to a solemn meditation on time and death. It might have been inspired by an incident at a Paris ball when a reveller dressed as the personification of cholera. The story has even been read autobiographically. One biographer suggests that the story's source was an incident in which Poe's wife burst a blood vessel while singing in 1842. Poe's age, not unlike ours, was haunted by the spectre of diseases, especially cholera and tuberculosis. The latter terrified Poe, who lost both his mother and wife to the disease.

See Edgar Allan Poe, from 'Review of *Twice-Told Tales*,' p. 395; see also Brander Matthews, from 'The Philosophy of the Short-Story,' p. 398.

The Masque of the Red Death

The 'Red Death' had long devastated the country. No pestilence had ever been so fatal, or so hideous. Blood was its Avatar and its seal—the redness and the horror of blood. There were sharp pains, and sudden dizziness, and then profuse bleeding at the pores, with dissolution. The scarlet stains upon the body and especially upon the face of the victim, were the pest ban which shut him out from the aid and from the sympathy of his fellowmen. And the whole seizure, progress, and termination of the disease, were the incidents of half an hour.

But the Prince Prospero was happy and dauntless and sagacious. When his dominions were half depopulated, he summoned to his presence a thousand hale and light-hearted friends from among the knights and dames of his court, and with these retired to the deep seclusion of one of his castellated abbeys. This was an extensive and magnificent structure, the creation of the prince's own eccentric yet august taste. A strong and lofty wall girdled it in. This wall had gates of iron. The courtiers, having entered, brought furnaces and massy hammers and welded the bolts. They resolved to leave means neither of ingress or egress to the sudden impulses of despair or frenzy from within. The abbey was amply provisioned. With such precautions the courtiers might bid defiance to contagion. The external world could take care of itself. In the meantime it was folly to grieve, or to think. The prince had provided all the appliances of pleasure. There were buffoons, there were improvisatori, there were ballet-dancers, there were musicians, there was Beauty, there was wine. All these and security were within. Without was the 'Red Death.'

It was toward the close of the fifth or sixth month of his seclusion, and while the pestilence raged most furiously abroad, that the Prince Prospero entertained his thousand friends at a masked ball of the most unusual magnificence.

It was a voluptuous scene, that masquerade. But first let me tell of the rooms in which it was held. There were seven—an imperial suite. In many palaces, however, such suites form a long and straight vista, while the folding doors slide back nearly to the walls on either hand, so that the view of the whole extent is scarcely impeded. Here the case was very different; as might have been expected from the duke's love of the *bizarre*. The apartments were so irregularly disposed that the vision embraced but little more than one at a time. There was a sharp turn at every twenty or thirty yards, and at each turn a novel effect. To the right and left, in the middle of each wall, a tall and narrow Gothic window looked out upon a closed corridor which pursued the windings of the suite. These windows were of stained glass whose colour carried in accordance with the prevailing hue of the decorations of the chamber into which it opened. That at the eastern extremity was hung, for example, in blue—and vividly blue were its windows. The second chamber was purple in its ornaments and tapestries, and here the panes were purple. The third was green throughout, and so were the casements. The fourth was furnished and lighted with orange—the fifth with white—the sixth with violet. The seventh apartment was closely shrouded in black velvet tapestries that hung all over the ceiling and down the walls, falling in heavy folds upon a carpet of the same material and hue. But in this chamber only, the colour of the windows failed to correspond with the decorations. The panes here were scarlet—a deep blood colour. Now in no one of the seven apartments was there any lamp or candelabrum, amid the profusion of golden ornaments that lay scattered to and fro or depended from the roof. There was no light of any kind emanating from lamp or candle within the suite of chambers. But in the corridors that followed the suite, there stood, opposite to each window a heavy tripod, bearing a brazier of fire, that projected its rays through the tinted glass and so glaringly illumined the room. And thus were produced a multitude of gaudy and fantastic appearances. But in the western or black chamber the effect of the fire-light that streamed upon the dark hangings through the blood-tinted panes, was ghastly in the extreme, and produced so wild a look upon the countenances of those who entered, that there were few of the company bold enough to set foot within its precincts at all.

It was in this apartment, also, that there stood against the western wall, a gigantic clock of ebony. Its pendulum swung to and fro with a dull, heavy, monotonous clang; and when the minute-hand made the circuit of the face, and the hour was to be stricken, there came from the brazen lungs of the clock a sound which was clear and loud and deep and exceedingly musical, but of so peculiar a note and emphasis that, at each lapse of an hour, the musicians of the orchestra were constrained to pause, momentarily, in their performance, to hearken to the sound; and thus the waltzers perforce ceased their evolutions; and there was a brief disconcert of the whole gay company; and, while the chimes of the clock yet rang, it was observed that the giddiest grew pale, and the more aged and sedate passed their hands over their brows as if in confused revery or meditation. But when the echoes had fully ceased, a light laughter at once pervaded the assembly; the musicians looked at each other and smiled as if at their own nervousness and folly, and made whispering vows, each to the other, that the next chiming of the clock should produce in them no similar emotion; and then, after the lapse of sixty minutes (which embrace three thousand and six hundred seconds of the Time that flies), there came yet another chiming of the clock, and then were the same disconcert and tremulousness and meditation as before.

But, in spite of these things, it was a gay and magnificent revel. The tastes of the duke were peculiar. He had a fine eye for colours and effects. He disregarded the *decora* of mere fashion. His plans were bold and fiery, and his conceptions glowed with barbaric lustre. There are some who would have thought him mad. His followers felt that he was not. It was necessary to hear and see and touch him to be *sure* that he was not.

He had directed, in great part, the moveable embellishments of the seven chambers, upon occasion of this great *fête*; and it was his own guiding taste which had given character to the masqueraders. Be sure they were grotesque. There were much glare and glitter and piquancy and phantasm—much of what has been since seen in 'Hernani.' There were arabesque figures with unsuited limbs and appointments. There were delirious fancies such as the madman fashions. There were much of the beautiful, much of the wanton, much of the *bizarre*, something of the terrible, and not a little of that which might have excited disgust. To and fro in the seven chambers there stalked, in fact, a multitude of dreams. And these—the dreams—writhed in and about, taking hue from the rooms, and causing the wild music of the orchestra to seem as the echo of their steps. And, anon, there strikes the ebony clock which stands in the hall of the velvet. And then, for a moment, all is still, and all is silent save the voice of the clock. The dreams are stiff-frozen as they stand. But the echoes of the chime die away— they have endured but an instant—and a light, half-subdued laughter floats after them as they depart. And now again the music swells, and the dreams live, and writhe to and fro more merrily than ever, taking hue from the many-tinted windows through which stream the rays from the tripods. But to the chamber which lies most westwardly of the seven, there are now none of the maskers who venture; for the night is waning away; and there flows a ruddier light through the blood-coloured panes; and the blackness of the sable drapery appals; and to him whose foot falls upon the sable carpet, there comes from the near clock of ebony a muffled peal more solemnly emphatic than any which reaches *their* ears who indulge in the more remote gaieties of the other apartments.

But these other apartments were densely crowded, and in them beat feverishly the heart of life. And the revel went whirlingly on, until at length there commenced the sounding of midnight upon the clock. And then the music ceased, as I have told; and the evolutions of the waltzers were quieted; and there was an uneasy cessation of all things as before. But now there were twelve strokes to be sounded by the bell of the clock; and thus it happened, perhaps, that more of thought crept, with more of time, into the meditations of the thoughtful among those who revelled. And thus, too, it happened, perhaps, that before the last echoes of the last chime had utterly sunk into silence, there were many individuals in the crowd who had found leisure to become aware of the presence of a masked figure which had arrested the attention of no single individual before. And the rumour of this new presence having spread itself whisperingly around, there arose at length from the whole company a buzz, or murmur, expressive of disapprobation and surprise—then, finally, of terror, of horror, and of disgust.

In an assembly of phantasms such as I have painted, it may well be supposed that no ordinary appearance could have excited such sensation. In truth the masquerade license of the night was nearly unlimited; but the figure in question had out-Heroded Herod, and gone beyond the bounds of even the prince's indefinite decorum. There are chords in the hearts of the most reckless which cannot be touched without emotion. Even with the utterly lost, to whom life and death are equally jests, there are matters of which no jest can be made. The whole company, indeed, seemed now deeply to feel in the costume and bearing of the stranger neither wit nor propriety existed. The figure was tall and gaunt, and shrouded from head to foot in the habiliments of the grave. The mask which concealed the visage was made so nearly to resemble the countenance of a stiffened corpse that the closest scrutiny must have had difficulty in detecting the cheat. And yet all this might have been endured, if not approved, by the mad revellers around. But the mummer had gone so far as to assume the type of the Red Death. His vesture was dabbled in *blood*—and his broad brow, with all the features of the face, was besprinkled with the scarlet horror.

When the eyes of Prince Prospero fell upon this spectral image (which with a slow and solemn movement, as if more fully to sustain its *rôle*, stalked to and fro among the waltzers) he was seen to be convulsed, in the first moment with a strong shudder either of terror or distaste; but, in the next, his brow reddened with rage.

'Who dares?' he demanded hoarsely of the courtiers who stood near him—'who dares insult us with this blasphemous mockery? Seize him and unmask him—that we may know whom we have to hang at sunrise, from the battlements!'

It was in the eastern or blue chamber in which stood the Prince Prospero as he uttered these words. They rang throughout the seven rooms loudly and clearly—for the prince was a bold and robust man, and the music had become hushed at the waving of his hand.

It was in the blue room where stood the prince, with a group of pale courtiers by his side. At first, as he spoke, there was a slight rushing movement of this group in the direction of the intruder, who at the moment was also near at hand, and now, with deliberate and stately step, made closer approach to the speaker. But from a certain nameless awe with which the mad assumptions of the mummer had inspired the whole party, there were found none who put forth hand to seize him; so that, unimpeded, he passed within a yard of the prince's person; and, while the vast assembly, as if with one impulse, shrank from the centres of the rooms to the walls, he made his way uninterruptedly, but with the same solemn and measured step which had distinguished him from the first, through the blue chamber to the purple—through the purple to the green—through the green to the orange—through this again to the white—and even thence to the violet, ere a decided movement had been made to arrest him. It was then, however, that the Prince Prospero, maddening with rage and the shame of his own momentary cowardice, rushed hurriedly through the six chambers, while none followed him on account of a deadly terror that had seized upon all. He bore aloft a drawn dagger, and had approached, in rapid impetuosity, to within three or four feet of the retreating figure, when the latter, having attained the extremity of the velvet apartment, turned suddenly and confronted his pursuer. There was a sharp cry—and the dagger dropped gleaming upon the sable carpet, upon which, instantly afterwards, fell prostrate in death the Prince Prospero. Then, summoning the wild courage of despair, a throng of the revellers at once threw themselves into the black apartment, and, seizing the mummer, whose tall figure stood erect and motionless within the shadow of the ebony clock, gasped in unutterable horror at finding the grave-cerements and corpse-like mask which they handled with so violent a rudeness, untenanted by any tangible form.

And now was acknowledged the presence of the Red Death. He had come like a thief in the night. And one by one dropped the revellers in the blood-bedewed halls of their revel, and died each in the despairing posture of his fall. And the life of the ebony clock went out with that of the last of the gay. And the flames of the tripods expired. And Darkness and Decay and the Red Death held illimitable dominion over all.

1842

Charlotte Perkins Gilman

Brief Biography

* Born in 1860 in Hartford, CT.
* Father deserts the family; she is raised in poverty by her emotionally distant mother.
* A great-niece of Harriet Beecher Stowe, author of *Uncle Tom's Cabin*, to whom she credits her zeal for social service.
* In 1894 divorces her first husband and later marries George Gilman, whose views on a marriage of equals reflect her own.
* Writes 'The Yellow Wallpaper' in two days in 39.5°C temperatures in Pasadena, CA.
* Diagnosed with breast cancer, commits suicide by chloroform in 1935.

American Charlotte Perkins Gilman is known today primarily as the feminist author of 'The Yellow Wallpaper' (1892), but this undervalues her originality and genius as a revolutionary writer, lecturer, and social reformer. Gilman published poetry and novels and founded a magazine, *The Forerunner*. As its only writer, she contributed hundreds of essays and fiction excerpts concerned with the social issues of her day. Her only equal as a prolific author and social critic in the United States was Mark Twain.

In *Women and Economics* (1898), her most enduring book, Gilman wrote that the 'worst evils under which [women] suffer . . . are but the result of certain arbitrary conditions of [their] own adoption,' arguing that women need economic independence to achieve full equality with men. In an era of 'domestic ideology' that considered a woman's place to be the home and a man's place the public domain, she, like the 'New Women,' or Suffragettes, advocated that men and women perform housework. She also held progressive views on birth control, divorce, and euthanasia.

In 1888 Gilman separated from her husband and moved to California, supporting herself and her daughter, Katharine, by touring the lecture circuit and by running a boarding house. After the divorce, amid charges that she was an 'unnatural mother,' she let her husband retain custody of Katharine. In her autobiography, she explained that the decision was the result of a conscious three-way arrangement among herself, her former husband, and his second wife (a close friend of Gilman's). Like Katherine Mansfield or Edith Wharton, the 'new woman' at the turn of the century drew upon her intelligence in making radical reforms.

In a well-known essay, Gilman described the composition of 'The Yellow Wallpaper.' Gilman wrote that after the birth of her daughter she 'suffered from a severe and continuous nervous breakdown tending to melancholia.' Her husband and friends suggested she consult the fashionable physician S. Weir Mitchell, a specialist in women's nervous disorders. He recommended that she take the 'rest cure' under his direction. After one month, she was sent home with instructions to restrict herself to 'two hours' intellectual life a day. And never touch pen, brush, or pencil as long as [she lived].'

A life devoid of interaction and creativity worked no better for Gilman than for the narrator of 'The Yellow Wallpaper,' which was written as a warning against the 'rest cure.' But the story is much more than a cautionary tale: behind the increasingly obsessive journal entries describing a woman's descent into madness lies a broad critique of gender roles that provide the foundations of the patriarchal social structure of Gilman's time. 'The Yellow Wallpaper' received only a lukewarm reception on publication, with some reviewers complaining that it was poorly written and too gloomy. It was neglected for three decades. Since the 1960s, though, it has been praised as an exceptionally crafted story and studied as a seminal work of feminism.

See Charlotte Perkins Gilman, 'Why I Wrote "The Yellow Wallpaper"', p. 441.

The Yellow Wallpaper

It is very seldom that mere ordinary people like John and myself secure ancestral halls for the summer.

A colonial mansion, a hereditary estate, I would say a haunted house and reach the height of romantic felicity—but that would be asking too much of fate!

Still I will proudly declare that there is something queer about it.

Else, why should it be let so cheaply? And why have stood so long untenanted?

John laughs at me, of course, but one expects that.

John is practical in the extreme. He has no patience with faith, an intense horror of superstition, and he scoffs openly at any talk of things not to be felt and seen and put down in figures.

John is a physician, and *perhaps*—(I would not say it to a living soul, of course, but this is dead paper and a great relief to my mind)—*perhaps* that is one reason I do not get well faster.

You see, he does not believe I am sick! And what can one do?

If a physician of high standing, and one's own husband, assures friends and relatives that there is really nothing the matter with one but temporary nervous depression—a slight hysterical tendency—what is one to do?

My brother is also a physician, and also of high standing, and he says the same thing.

So I take phosphates or phosphites—whichever it is—and tonics, and air and exercise, and journeys, and am absolutely forbidden to 'work' until I am well again.

Personally, I disagree with their ideas.

Personally, I believe that congenial work, with excitement and change, would do me good.

But what is one to do?

I did write for a while in spite of them; but it *does* exhaust me a good deal—having to be so sly about it, or else meet with heavy opposition.

I sometimes fancy that in my condition, if I had less opposition and more society and stimulus—but John says the very worst thing I can do is to think about my condition, and I confess it always makes me feel bad.

So I will let it alone and talk about the house.

The most beautiful place! It is quite alone, standing well back from the road, quite three miles from the village. It makes me think of English places that you read about, for there are hedges and walls and gates that lock, and lots of separate little houses for the gardeners and people.

There is a *delicious* garden! I never saw such a garden—large and shady, full of box-bordered paths, and lined with long grape-covered arbors with seats under them.

There were greenhouses, but they are all broken now.

There was some legal trouble, I believe, something about the heirs and co-heirs; anyhow, the place has been empty for years.

That spoils my ghostliness, I am afraid, but I don't care—there is something strange about the house—I can feel it.

I even said so to John one moonlight evening, but he said what I felt was a draught, and shut the window.

I get unreasonably angry with John sometimes. I'm sure I never used to be so sensitive. I think it is due to this nervous condition.

But John says if I feel so I shall neglect proper self-control; so I take pains to control myself—before him, at least, and that makes me very tired.

I don't like our room a bit. I wanted one downstairs that opened onto the piazza and had roses all over the window, and such pretty old-fashioned chintz hangings! But John would not hear of it.

He said there was only one window and not room for two beds, and no near room for him if he took another.

He is very careful and loving, and hardly lets me stir without special direction.

I have a schedule prescription for each hour in the day; he takes all care from me, and so I feel basely ungrateful not to value it more.

He said he came here solely on my account, that I was to have perfect rest and all the air I could get. 'Your exercise depends on your strength, my dear,' said he, 'and your food somewhat on your appetite; but air you can absorb all the time.' So we took the nursery at the top of the house.

It is a big, airy room, the whole floor nearly, with windows that look all ways, and air and sunshine galore. It was nursery first, and then playroom and gymnasium, I should judge, for the windows are barred for little children, and there are rings and things in the walls.

The paint and paper look as if a boys' school had used it. It is stripped off—the paper—in great patches all around the head of my bed, about as far as I can reach, and in a great place on the other side of the room low down. I never saw a worse paper in my life. One of those sprawling, flamboyant patterns committing every artistic sin.

It is dull enough to confuse the eye in following, pronounced enough constantly to irritate and provoke study, and when you follow the lame uncertain curves for a little distance they suddenly commit suicide—plunge off at outrageous angles, destroy themselves in unheard-of contradictions.

The color is repellent, almost revolting: a smouldering unclean yellow, strangely faded by the slow-turning sunlight. It is a dull yet lurid orange in some places, a sickly sulphur tint in others.

No wonder the children hated it! I should hate it myself if I had to live in this room long.

There comes John, and I must put this away—he hates to have me write a word.

We have been here two weeks, and I haven't felt like writing before, since that first day.

I am sitting by the window now, up in this atrocious nursery, and there is nothing to hinder my writing as much as I please, save lack of strength.

John is away all day, and even some nights when his cases are serious.

I am glad my case is not serious!

But these nervous troubles are dreadfully depressing.

John does not know how much I really suffer. He knows there is no reason to suffer, and that satisfies him.

Of course it is only nervousness. It does weigh on me so not to do my duty in any way!

I meant to be such a help to John, such a real rest and comfort, and here I am a comparative burden already!

Nobody would believe what an effort it is to do what little I am able—to dress and entertain, and order things.

It is fortunate Mary is so good with the baby. Such a dear baby!

And yet I *cannot* be with him, it makes me so nervous.

I suppose John never was nervous in his life. He laughs at me so about this wallpaper!

At first he meant to repaper the room, but afterward he said that I was letting it get the better of me, and that nothing was worse for a nervous patient than to give way to such fancies.

He said that after the wallpaper was changed it would be the heavy bedstead, and then the barred windows, and then that gate at the head of the stairs, and so on.

'You know the place is doing you good,' he said, 'and really, dear, I don't care to renovate the house just for a three months' rental.'

'Then do let us go downstairs,' I said. 'There are such pretty rooms there.'

Then he took me in his arms and called me a blessed little goose, and said he would go down cellar, if I wished, and have it whitewashed into the bargain.

But he is right enough about the beds and windows and things.

It is as airy and comfortable a room as anyone need wish, and, of course, I would not be so silly as to make him uncomfortable just for a whim.

I'm really getting quite fond of the big room, all but that horrid paper.

Out of one window I can see the garden—those mysterious deep-shaded arbors, the riotous old-fashioned flowers, and bushes and gnarly trees.

Out of another I get a lovely view of the bay and a little private wharf belonging to the estate. There is a beautiful shaded lane that runs down there from the house. I always fancy I see people walking in these numerous paths and arbors, but John has cautioned me not to give way to fancy in the least. He says that with my imaginative power and habit of story-making, a nervous weakness like mine is sure to lead to all manner of excited fancies, and that I ought to use my will and good sense to check the tendency. So I try.

I think sometimes that if I were only well enough to write a little it would relieve the press of ideas and rest me.

But I find I get pretty tired when I try.

It is so discouraging not to have any advice and companionship about my work. When I get really well, John says we will ask Cousin Henry and Julia down for a long visit; but he says he would as soon put fireworks in my pillow-case as to let me have those stimulating people about now.

I wish I could get well faster.

But I must not think about that. This paper looks to me as if it *knew* what a vicious influence it had!

There is a recurrent spot where the pattern lolls like a broken neck and two bulbous eyes stare at you upside down.

I get positively angry with the impertinence of it and the everlastingness. Up and down and sideways they crawl, and those absurd unblinking eyes are everywhere. There is one place where two breadths didn't match, and the eyes go all up and down the line, one a little higher than the other.

I never saw so much expression in an inanimate thing before, and we all know how much expression they have! I used to lie awake as a child and get more entertainment and terror out of blank walls and plain furniture than most children could find in a toy-store.

I remember what a kindly wink the knobs of our big old bureau used to have, and there was one chair that always seemed like a strong friend.

I used to feel that if any of the other things looked too fierce I could always hop into that chair and be safe.

The furniture in this room is no worse than inharmonious, however, for we had to bring it all from downstairs. I suppose when this was used as a playroom they had to take the nursery things out, and no wonder! I never saw such ravages as the children have made here.

The wallpaper, as I said before, is torn off in spots, and it sticketh closer than a brother—they must have had perseverance as well as hatred.

Then the floor is scratched and gouged and splintered, the plaster itself is dug out here and there, and this great heavy bed, which is all we found in the room, looks as if it had been through the wars.

But I don't mind it a bit—only the paper.

There comes John's sister. Such a dear girl as she is, and so careful of me! I must not let her find me writing.

She is a perfect and enthusiastic housekeeper, and hopes for no better profession. I verily believe she thinks it is the writing which made me sick!

But I can write when she is out, and see her a long way off from these windows.

There is one that commands the road, a lovely shaded winding road, and one that just looks off over the country. A lovely country, too, full of great elms and velvet meadows.

This wallpaper has a kind of sub-pattern in a different shade, a particularly irritating one, for you can only see it in certain lights, and not clearly then.

But in the places where it isn't faded and where the sun is just so—I can see a strange, provoking, formless sort of figure that seems to skulk about behind that silly and conspicuous front design.

There's sister on the stairs!

Well, the Fourth of July is over! The people are all gone, and I am tired out. John thought it might do me good to see a little company, so we just had Mother and Nellie and the children down for a week.

Of course I didn't do a thing. Jennie sees to everything now.

But it tired me all the same.

John says if I don't pick up faster he shall send me to Weir Mitchell in the fall.

But I don't want to go there at all. I had a friend who was in his hands once, and she says he is just like John and my brother, only more so!

Besides, it is such an undertaking to go so far.

I don't feel as if it was worthwhile to turn my hand over for anything, and I'm getting dreadfully fretful and querulous.

I cry at nothing, and cry most of the time.

Of course I don't when John is here, or anybody else, but when I am alone.

And I am alone a good deal just now. John is kept in town very often by serious cases, and Jennie is good and lets me alone when I want her to.

So I walk a little in the garden or down that lovely lane, sit on the porch under the roses, and lie down up here a good deal.

I'm getting really fond of the room in spite of the wallpaper. Perhaps *because* of the wallpaper.

It dwells in my mind so!

I lie here on this great immovable bed—it is nailed down, I believe—and follow that pattern about by the hour. It is as good as gymnastics, I assure you. I start, we'll say, at the bottom, down in the corner over there where it has not been touched, and I determine for the thousandth time that I *will* follow that pointless pattern to some sort of a conclusion.

I know a little of the principle of design, and I know this thing was not arranged on any laws of radiation, or alternation, or repetition, or symmetry, or anything else that I ever heard of.

It is repeated, of course, by the breadths, but not otherwise.

Looked at in one way, each breadth stands alone; the bloated curves and flourishes—a kind of 'debased Romanesque' with delirium tremens—go waddling up and down in isolated columns of fatuity.

But, on the other hand, they connect diagonally, and the sprawling outlines run off in great slanting waves of optic horror, like a lot of wallowing sea-weeds in full chase.

The whole thing goes horizontally, too, at least it seems so, and I exhaust myself trying to distinguish the order of its going in that direction.

They have used a horizontal breadth for a frieze, and that adds wonderfully to the confusion.

There is one end of the room where it is almost intact, and there, when the crosslights fade and the low sun shines directly upon it, I can almost fancy radiation after all—the interminable grotesque seems to form around a common center and rush off in headlong plunges of equal distraction.

It makes me tired to follow it. I will take a nap, I guess.

I don't know why I should write this.

I don't want to.

I don't feel able.

And I know John would think it absurd. But I *must* say what I feel and think in some way—it is such a relief!

But the effort is getting to be greater than the relief.

Half the time now I am awfully lazy, and lie down ever so much. John says I mustn't lose my strength, and has me take cod liver oil and lots of tonics and things, to say nothing of ale and wine and rare meat.

Dear John! He loves me very dearly, and hates to have me sick. I tried to have a real earnest reasonable talk with him the other day, and tell him how I wish he would let me go and make a visit to Cousin Henry and Julia.

But he said I wasn't able to go, nor able to stand it after I got there; and I did not make out a very good case for myself, for I was crying before I had finished.

It is getting to be a great effort for me to think straight. Just this nervous weakness, I suppose.

And dear John gathered me up in his arms, and just carried me upstairs and laid me on the bed, and sat by me and read to me till it tired my head.

He said I was his darling and his comfort and all he had, and that I must take care of myself for his sake, and keep well.

He says no one but myself can help me out of it, that I must use my will and self-control and not let any silly fancies run away with me.

There's one comfort—the baby is well and happy, and does not have to occupy this nursery with the horrid wallpaper.

If we had not used it, that blessed child would have! What a fortunate escape! Why, I wouldn't have a child of mine, an impressionable little thing, live in such a room for worlds.

I never thought of it before, but it is lucky that John kept me here after all; I can stand it so much easier than a baby, you see.

Of course I never mention it to them any more—I am too wise—but I keep watch for it all the same.

There are things in that wallpaper that nobody knows about but me, or ever will.

Behind that outside pattern the dim shapes get clearer every day.

It is always the same shape, only very numerous.

And it is like a woman stooping down and creeping about behind that pattern. I don't like it a bit. I wonder—I begin to think—I wish John would take me away from here!

It is so hard to talk with John about my case, because he is so wise, and because he loves me so.

But I tried it last night.

It was moonlight. The moon shines in all around just as the sun does.

I hate to see it sometimes, it creeps so slowly, and always comes in by one window or another.

John was asleep and I hated to waken him, so I kept still and watched the moonlight on that undulating wallpaper till I felt creepy.

The faint figure behind seemed to shake the pattern, just as if she wanted to get out.

I got up softly and went to feel and see if the paper *did* move, and when I came back John was awake.

'What is it, little girl?' he said. 'Don't go walking about like that—you'll get cold.'

I thought it was a good time to talk, so I told him that I really was not gaining here, and that I wished he would take me away.

'Why, darling!' said he. 'Our lease will be up in three weeks, and I can't see how to leave before.

'The repairs are not done at home, and I cannot possibly leave town just now. Of course, if you were in any danger, I could and would, but you really are better, dear, whether you can see it or not. I am a doctor, dear, and I know. You are gaining flesh and color, your appetite is better, I feel really much easier about you.'

'I don't weigh a bit more,' said I, 'nor as much; and my appetite may be better in the evening when you are here but it is worse in the morning when you are away!'

'Bless her little heart!' said he with a big hug. 'She shall be as sick as she pleases! But now let's improve the shining hours by going to sleep, and talk about it in the morning!'

'And you won't go away?' I asked gloomily.

'Why, how can I, dear? It is only three weeks more and then we will take a nice little trip of a few days while Jennie is getting the house ready. Really, dear, you are better!'

'Better in body perhaps—' I began, and stopped short, for he sat up straight and looked at me with such a stern, reproachful look that I could not say another word.

'My darling,' said he, 'I beg of you, for my sake and for our child's sake, as well as for your own, that you will never for one instant let that idea enter your mind! There is nothing so dangerous, so fascinating, to a temperament like yours. It is a false and foolish fancy. Can you not trust me as a physician when I tell you so?'

So of course I said no more on that score, and we went to sleep before long. He thought I was asleep first, but I wasn't, and lay there for hours trying to decide whether that front pattern and the back pattern really did move together or separately.

On a pattern like this, by daylight, there is a lack of sequence, a defiance of law, that is a constant irritant to a normal mind.

The color is hideous enough, and unreliable enough, and infuriating enough, but the pattern is torturing.

You think you have mastered it, but just as you get well under way in following, it turns a back-somersault and there you are. It slaps you in the face, knocks you down, and tramples upon you. It is like a bad dream.

The outside pattern is a florid arabesque, reminding one of a fungus. If you can imagine a toadstool in joints, an interminable string of toadstools, budding and sprouting in endless convolutions—why, that is something like it.

That is, sometimes!

There is one marked peculiarity about this paper, a thing nobody seems to notice but myself, and that is that it changes as the light changes.

When the sun shoots in through the east window—I always watch for that first long, straight ray—it changes so quickly that I never can quite believe it.

That is why I watch it always.

By moonlight—the moon shines in all night when there is a moon—I wouldn't know it was the same paper.

At night in any kind of light, in twilight, candlelight, lamplight, and worst of all by moonlight, it becomes bars! The outside pattern, I mean, and the woman behind it is as plain as can be.

I didn't realize for a long time what the thing was that showed behind, that dim sub-pattern, but now I am quite sure it is a woman.

By daylight she is subdued, quiet. I fancy it is the pattern that keeps her so still. It is so puzzling. It keeps me quiet by the hour.

I lie down ever so much now. John says it is good for me, and to sleep all I can.

Indeed he started the habit by making me lie down for an hour after each meal.

It is a very bad habit, I am convinced, for you see, I don't sleep.

And that cultivates deceit, for I don't tell them I'm awake—oh, no!

The fact is I am getting a little afraid of John.

He seems very queer sometimes, and even Jennie has an inexplicable look.

It strikes me occasionally, just as a scientific hypothesis, that perhaps it is the paper!

I have watched John when he did not know I was looking, and come into the room suddenly on the most innocent excuses, and I've caught him several times *looking at the paper!* And Jennie too. I caught Jennie with her hand on it once.

She didn't know I was in the room, and when I asked her in a quiet, a very quiet voice, with the most restrained manner possible, what she was doing with the paper, she turned around as if she had been caught stealing, and looked quite angry—asked me why I should frighten her so!

Then she said that the paper stained everything it touched, that she had found yellow smooches on all my clothes and John's and she wished we would be more careful!

Did not that sound innocent? But I know she was studying that pattern, and I am determined that nobody shall find it out but myself!

Life is very much more exciting now than it used to be. You see, I have something more to expect, to look forward to, to watch. I really do eat better, and am more quiet than I was.

John is so pleased to see me improve! He laughed a little the other day, and said I seemed to be flourishing in spite of my wallpaper.

I turned it off with a laugh. I had no intention of telling him it was *because* of the wallpaper—he would make fun of me. He might even want to take me away.

I don't want to leave now until I have found it out. There is a week more, and I think that will be enough.

I'm feeling so much better!

I don't sleep much at night, for it is so interesting to watch developments; but I sleep a good deal during the daytime.

In the daytime it is tiresome and perplexing.

There are always new shoots on the fungus, and new shades of yellow all over it. I cannot keep count of them, though I have tried conscientiously.

It is the strangest yellow, that wallpaper! It makes me think of all the yellow things I ever saw—not beautiful ones like buttercups, but old, foul, bad yellow things.

But there is something else about that paper—the smell! I noticed it the moment we came into the room, but with so much air and sun it was not bad. Now we have had a week of fog and rain, and whether the windows are open or not, the smell is here.

It creeps all over the house.

I find it hovering in the dining-room, skulking in the parlor, hiding in the hall, lying in wait for me on the stairs.

It gets into my hair.

Even when I go to ride, if I turn my head suddenly and surprise it—there is that smell!

Such a peculiar odor, too! I have spent hours in trying to analyze it, to find what it smelled like.

It is not bad—at first—and very gentle, but quite the subtlest, most enduring odor I ever met.

In this damp weather it is awful. I wake up in the night and find it hanging over me.

It used to disturb me at first. I thought seriously of burning the house—to reach the smell.

But now I am used to it. The only thing I can think of that it is like is the *color* of the paper! A yellow smell.

There is a very funny mark on this wall, low down, near the mopboard. A streak that runs round the room. It goes behind every piece of furniture, except the bed, a long, straight, even *smooch*, as if it had been rubbed over and over.

I wonder how it was done and who did it, and what they did it for. Round and round and round—round and round and round—it makes me dizzy!

I really have discovered something at last.

Through watching so much at night, when it changes so, I have finally found out.

The front pattern *does* move—and no wonder! The woman behind shakes it!

Sometimes I think there are a great many women behind, and sometimes only one, and she crawls around fast, and her crawling shakes it all over.

Then in the very bright spots she keeps still, and in the very shady spots she just takes hold of the bars and shakes them hard.

And she is all the time trying to climb through. But nobody could climb through that pattern—it strangles so; I think that is why it has so many heads.

They get through, and then the pattern strangles them off and turns them upside down, and makes their eyes white!

If those heads were covered or taken off it would not be half so bad.

I think that woman gets out in the daytime!

And I'll tell you why—privately—I've seen her!

I can see her out of every one of my windows!

It is the same woman, I know, for she is always creeping, and most women do not creep by daylight.

I see her in that long shaded lane, creeping up and down. I see her in those dark grape arbors, creeping all around the garden.

I see her on that long road under the trees, creeping along, and when a carriage comes she hides under the blackberry vines.

I don't blame her a bit. It must be very humiliating to be caught creeping by daylight!

I always lock the door when I creep by daylight. I can't do it at night, for I know John would suspect something at once.

And John is so queer now that I don't want to irritate him. I wish he would take another room! Besides, I don't want anybody to get that woman out at night but myself.

I often wonder if I could see her out of all the windows at once.

But, turn as fast as I can, I can only see out of one at one time.

And though I always see her, she *may* be able to creep faster than I can turn! I have watched her sometimes away off in the open country, creeping as fast as a cloud shadow in a wind.

If only that top pattern could be gotten off from the under one! I mean to try it, little by little.

I have found out another funny thing, but I shan't tell it this time! It does not do to trust people too much.

There are only two more days to get this paper off, and I believe John is beginning to notice. I don't like the look in his eyes.

And I heard him ask Jennie a lot of professional questions about me. She had a very good report to give.

She said I slept a good deal in the daytime.

John knows I don't sleep very well at night, for all I'm so quiet!

He asked me all sorts of questions, too, and pretended to be very loving and kind.

As if I couldn't see through him!

Still, I don't wonder he acts so, sleeping under this paper for three months.

It only interests me, but I feel sure John and Jennie are affected by it.

Hurrah! This is the last day, but it is enough. John is to stay in town over night, and won't be out until this evening.

Jennie wanted to sleep with me—the sly thing; but I told her I should undoubtedly rest better for a night all alone.

That was clever, for really I wasn't alone a bit! As soon as it was moonlight and that poor thing began to crawl and shake the pattern, I got up and ran to help her.

I pulled and she shook. I shook and she pulled, and before morning we had peeled off yards of that paper.

A strip about as high as my head and half around the room.

And then when the sun came and that awful pattern began to laugh at me, I declared I would finish it today!

We go away tomorrow, and they are moving all my furniture down again to leave things as they were before.

Jennie looked at the wall in amazement, but I told her merrily that I did it out of pure spite at the vicious thing.

She laughed and said she wouldn't mind doing it herself, but I must not get tired.

How she betrayed herself that time!

But I am here, and no person touches this paper but Me—not *alive!*

She tried to get me out of the room—it was too patent! But I said it was so quiet and empty and clean now that I believed I would lie down again and sleep all I could, and not to wake me even for dinner—I would call when I woke.

So now she is gone, and the servants are gone, and the things are gone, and there is nothing left but that great bedstead nailed down, with the canvas mattress we found on it.

We shall sleep downstairs tonight, and take the boat home tomorrow.

I quite enjoy the room, now it is bare again.

How those children did tear about here!

This bedstead is fairly gnawed!

But I must get to work.

I have locked the door and thrown the key down into the front path.

I don't want to go out, and I don't want to have anybody come in, till John comes.

I want to astonish him.

I've got a rope up here that even Jennie did not find. If that woman does get out, and tries to get away, I can tie her!

But I forgot I could not reach far without anything to stand on!

This bed will *not* move!

I tried to lift and push it until I was lame, and then I got so angry I bit off a little piece at one corner—but it hurt my teeth.

Then I peeled off all the paper I could reach standing on the floor. It sticks horribly and the pattern just enjoys it! All those strangled heads and bulbous eyes and waddling fungus growths just shriek with derision!

I am getting angry enough to do something desperate. To jump out of the window would be admirable exercise, but the bars are too strong even to try.

Besides I wouldn't do it. Of course not. I know well enough that a step like that is improper and might be misconstrued.

I don't like to *look* out of the windows even—there are so many of those creeping women, and they creep so fast.

I wonder if they all come out of that wallpaper as I did?

But I am securely fastened now by my well-hidden rope—you don't get *me* out in the road there!

I suppose I shall have to get back behind the pattern when it comes night, and that is hard!

It is so pleasant to be out in this great room and creep around as I please!

I don't want to go outside. I won't, even if Jennie asks me to.

For outside you have to creep on the ground, and everything is green instead of yellow.

But here I can creep smoothly on the floor, and my shoulder just fits in that long smooch around the wall, so I cannot lose my way.

Why, there's John at the door!

It is no use, young man, you can't open it!

How he does call and pound!

Now he's crying to Jennie for an axe.

It would be a shame to break down that beautiful door!

'John, dear!' said I in the gentlest voice. 'The key is down by the front steps, under a plantain leaf!'

That silenced him for a few moments.

Then he said, very quietly indeed, 'Open the door, my darling!'

'I can't,' said I. 'The key is down by the front door under a plantain leaf!' And then I said it again, several times, very gently and slowly, and said it so often that he had to go and see, and he got it of course, and came in. He stopped short by the door.

'What is the matter?' he cried. 'For God's sake, what are you doing!'

I kept on creeping just the same, but I looked at him over my shoulder.

'I've got out at last,' said I, 'in spite of you and Jane. And I've pulled off most of the paper, so you can't put me back!'

Now why should that man have fainted? But he did, and right across my path by the wall, so that I had to creep over him every time!

1892

Stephen Crane

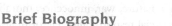

Brief Biography

- Born in 1871 in Newark, NJ, to religious parents, the youngest of fourteen children.
- Lives in New York City; becomes a war correspondent and travels to Mexico, Cuba, and Europe.
- Following its initial appearance as a newspaper serial, *The Red Badge of Courage* is published as a book in 1895 and brings him critical acclaim.
- His poetry anticipates free verse; changes style and techniques with each book.
- Befriended by H.G. Wells, Henry James, and Joseph Conrad, who may have used aspects of Crane in his novel *Lord Jim* (1900).
- An iconoclast, Crane lives his last few years with a former brothel madam until his death from tuberculosis and malaria in 1900 at age twenty-eight.

In many ways, the short life of Stephen Crane was stranger than his fiction. An apathetic student, he chafed under academic regimen. Though he might have become a professional athlete, he was forbidden to play baseball by his stern father, a Methodist minister. Unlike many writers, Crane's call came not from literature but from observing the lives of real people reacting to the tragedies and trivialities around them. From his bohemian life in New York City as a freelance journalist and his association with petty criminals and prostitutes, he gathered the material for his first novel (self-published under a pseudonym), *Maggie: A Girl of the Streets* (1893), a pioneering social-realist portrayal of a young girl who descends into prostitution and suicide.

Though Crane had never served in the military, his most famous novel, *The Red Badge of Courage* (1895), astonished readers with its emotional accuracy. Factual detail, such as the names of real places and people, is noticeably absent from this novel; instead, Crane, who was twenty-four, interviewed war veterans and studied popular historical sources in order to present a 'soldier's eye view' of the American Civil War. Through understatement, an ironic tone, and an impressionistic use of imagery—all characteristic of Crane's style—he conveyed the confusion and conflicting emotions of a young recruit. He returned to this setting in 'A Mystery of Heroism,' published after he had toured the American West and Mexico as a newspaper correspondent, accumulating material for future stories. His travels and adventures resulted in more than one hundred stories and sketches. Indeed, according to his early editor, Carl Van Doren, short fiction was Crane's natural medium: 'His gifts were his intense perception and realization of what he had briefly seen or imagined, his bright freedom from dragging illusions . . . his mastery of lightning images.' Crane was one of the first in a line of early twentieth-century reporter-writers, like Ernest Hemingway and

Morley Callaghan, whose writing targeted significant detail while avoiding judgment and sentimentality.

Obsessed with danger, he went as a correspondent to the Greco-Turkish and Spanish-American wars. In 1897, he joined a group of insurgents bound for Cuba in the ammunition-laden steamship *Commodore*. The ship sank two days out of Jacksonville, FL—drifting for thirty hours in a dingy with three of the crew inspired his famous story 'The Open Boat.' Crane's ability to transmute the raw material of lived experience served him well in his short fiction, which typically shows ordi-nary men under extraordinary circum-stances. These experiences seldom change Crane's characters, but they enable him to explore the concepts that fascinated him: nature, war, innocence, morality, and so-cial responsibility. Heroism also intrigued him; from its soldier's unaccountable need to risk his life for water to the puzzle of its concluding words, 'A Mystery of Hero-ism' resonates with unanswered questions about heroism and human behaviour.

See Stephen Crane, from 'Letters to a Friend About His Ambition, His Art, and His Views of Life,' p. 444.

A Mystery of Heroism

The dark uniforms of the men were so coated with dust from the incessant wrestling of the two armies that the regiment almost seemed a part of the clay bank which shielded them from the shells. On the top of the hill a battery was arguing in tremendous roars with some other guns, and to the eye of the infan-try the artillerymen, the guns, the caissons, the horses, were distinctly outlined upon the blue sky. When a piece was fired, a red streak as round as a log flashed low in the heavens, like a monstrous bolt of lightning. The men of the battery wore white duck trousers, which somehow emphasized their legs; and when they ran and crowed in little groups at the bidding of the shouting officers, it was more impressive than usual to the infantry.

Fred Collins, of A Company, was saying: 'Thunder! I wisht I had a drink. Ain't there any water round here?' Then somebody yelled: 'There goes th' bugler!'

As the eyes of half the regiment swept in one machine-like movement, there was an instant's picture of a horse in a great convulsive leap of a death-wound and a rider leaning back with a crooked arm and spread fingers before his face. On the ground was the crimson terror of an exploding shell, with fibres of flame that seemed like lances. A glittering bugle swung clear of the rider's back as fell headlong the horse and the man. In the air was an odour as from a con-flagration.

Sometimes they of the infantry looked down at a fair little meadow which spread at their feet. Its long green grass was rippling gently in a breeze. Beyond it was the grey form of a house half torn to pieces by shells and by the busy axes of soldiers who had pursued firewood. The line of an old fence was now dimly marked by long weeds and by an occasional post. A shell had blown the well-house to fragments. Little lines of grey smoke ribboning upward from some embers indicated the place where had stood the barn.

From beyond a curtain of green woods there came the sound of some stupendous scuffle, as if two animals of the size of islands were fighting. At a distance there were occasional appearances of swift-moving men, horses, batteries, flags, and with the crashing of infantry volleys were heard, often, wild and frenzied cheers. In the midst of it all Smith and Ferguson, two privates of A Company, were engaged in a heated discussion which involved the greatest questions of the national existence.

The battery on the hill presently engaged in a frightful duel. The white legs of the gunners scampered this way and that way, and the officers redoubled their shouts. The guns, with their demeanours of stolidity and courage, were typical of something infinitely self-possessed in this clamour of death that swirled around the hill.

One of a 'swing' team was suddenly smitten quivering to the ground, and his maddened brethren dragged his torn body in their struggle to escape from this turmoil and danger. A young soldier astride one of the leaders swore and fumed in his saddle and furiously jerked at the bridle. An officer screamed out an order so violently that his voice broke and ended the sentence in a falsetto shriek.

The leading company of infantry regiment was somewhat exposed, and the colonel ordered it moved more fully under the shelter of the hill. There was the clank of steel against steel.

A lieutenant of the battery rode down and passed them, holding his right arm carefully in his left hand. And it was as if this arm was not at all a part of him, but belonged to another man. His sober and reflective charger went slowly. The officer's face was grimy and perspiring, and his uniform was tousled as if he had been in direct grapple with an enemy. He smiled grimly when the men stared at him. He turned his horse toward the meadow.

Collins, of A Company, said: 'I wisht I had a drink. I bet there's water in that there ol' well yonder!'

'Yes; but how you goin' to git it?'

For the little meadow which intervened was now suffering a terrible onslaught of shells. Its green and beautiful calm had vanished utterly. Brown earth was being flung in monstrous handfuls. And there was a massacre of the young blades of grass. They were being torn, burned, obliterated. Some curious fortune of the battle had made this gentle little meadow the object of the red hate of the shells, and each one as it exploded seemed like an imprecation in the face of a maiden.

The wounded officer who was riding across this expanse said to himself: 'Why, they couldn't shoot any harder if the whole army was massed here!'

A shell struck the grey ruins of the house, and as, after the roar, the shattered wall fell in fragments, there was a noise which resembled the flapping of shutters during a wild gale of winter. Indeed, the infantry paused in the shelter of the bank appeared as men standing upon a shore contemplating a madness of the sea. The angel of calamity had under its glance the battery upon the hill. Fewer white-legged men laboured about the guns. A shell had smitten one of the pieces, and after the flare, the smoke, the dust, the wrath of this blow were gone, it was possible to see white legs stretched horizontally upon the ground. And at that interval to the rear where it is the business of battery horses to stand with their noses to the fight, awaiting the command to drag their guns out of the destruction, or into it, or wheresoever these incomprehensible humans demanded with whip and spur—in this line of passive and dumb spectators, whose fluttering hearts yet would not let them forget the iron laws of man's control of them—in this rank of brute-soldiers there had been relentless and hideous carnage. From the ruck of bleeding and prostrate horses, the men of the infantry could see one animal raising its stricken body with its forelegs and turning its nose with mystic and profound eloquence toward the sky.

Some comrades joked Collins about his thirst. 'Well, if yeh want a drink so bad, why don't yeh go git it?'

'Well, I will in a minnet, if yeh don't shut up!'

A lieutenant of artillery floundered his horse straight down the hill with as little concern as if it were level ground. As he galloped past the colonel of the infantry, he threw up his hand in swift salute. 'We've got to get out of that,' he roared angrily. He was a black-bearded officer, and his eyes, which resembled beads, sparkled like those of an insane man. His jumping horse sped along the column of infantry.

The fat major, standing carelessly with his sword held horizontally behind him and with his legs far apart, looked after the receding horseman and laughed. 'He wants to get back with orders pretty quick, or there'll be no batt'ry left,' he observed.

The wise young captain of the second company hazarded to the lieutenant-colonel that the enemy's infantry would probably soon attack the hill, and the lieutenant-colonel snubbed him.

A private in one of the rear companies looked out over the meadow, and then turned to a companion and said, 'Look there, Jim!' It was the wounded officer from the battery, who some time before had started to ride across the meadow, supporting his right arm carefully with his left hand. This man had encountered a shell, apparently, at a time when no one perceived him, and he could now be seen lying face downward with a stirruped foot stretched across the body of his dead horse. A leg of the charger extended slantingly upward, precisely as stiff as a stake. Around this motionless pair the shells still howled.

There was a quarrel in A Company. Collins was shaking his fist in the faces of some laughing comrades. 'Dern yeh! I ain't afraid t' go. If yeh say much, I will go!'

'Of course, yeh will! You'll run through that there medder, won't yeh?'

Collins said, in a terrible voice: 'You see now!'

At this ominous threat his comrades broke into renewed jeers.

Collins gave them a dark scowl, and went to find his captain. The latter was conversing with the colonel of the regiment.

'Captain,' said Collins, saluting and standing at attention—in those days all trousers bagged at the knees—'Captain, I want t' get permission to go git some water from that there well over yonder!'

The colonel and the captain swung about simultaneously and stared across the meadow. The captain laughed. 'You must be pretty thirsty, Collins?'

'Yes, sir, I am.'

'Well—ah,' said the captain. After a moment, he asked, 'Can't you wait?'

'No, sir.'

The colonel was watching Collins's face. 'Look here, my lad,' he said, in a pious sort of voice—'Look here, my lad'—Collins was not a lad—'don't you think that's taking pretty big risks for a little drink of water?'

'I dunno,' said Collins uncomfortably. Some of the resentment toward his companions, which perhaps had forced him into this affair, was beginning to fade. 'I dunno w'ether 'tis.'

The colonel and the captain contemplated him for a time.

'Well,' said the captain finally.

'Well,' said the colonel, 'if you want to go, why, go.'

Collins saluted. 'Much obliged t' yeh.'

As he moved away the colonel called after him. 'Take some of the other boys' canteens with you, an' hurry back, now.'

'Yes, sir, I will.'

The colonel and the captain looked at each other then, for it had suddenly occurred that they could not for the life of them tell whether Collins wanted to go or whether he did not.

They turned to regard Collins, and as they perceived him surrounded by gesticulating comrades, the colonel said: 'Well, by thunder! I guess he's going.'

Collins appeared as a man dreaming. In the midst of the questions, the advice, the warnings, all the excited talk of his company mates, he maintained a curious silence.

They were very busy in preparing him for his ordeal. When they inspected him carefully, it was somewhat like the examination that grooms give a horse before a race; and they were amazed, staggered, by the whole affair. Their astonishment found vent in strange repetitions.

'Are yeh sure a-goin'?' they demanded again and again.

'Certainly I am,' cried Collins at last, furiously.

He strode sullenly away from them. He was swinging five or six canteens by their cords. It seemed that his cap would not remain firmly on his head, and often he reached and pulled it down over his brow.

There was a general movement in the compact column. The long animal-like thing moved slightly. Its four hundred eyes were turned upon the figure of Collins.

'Well, sir, if that ain't th' derndest thing! I never thought Fred Collins had the blood in him for that kind of business.'

'What's he goin' to do, anyhow?'

'He's goin' to that well there after water.'

'We ain't dyin' of thirst, are we? That's foolishness.'

'Well, somebody put him up to it, an' he's doin' it.'

'Say, he must be a desperate cuss.'

When Collins faced the meadow and walked away from the regiment, he was vaguely conscious that a chasm, the deep valley of all prides, was suddenly between him and his comrades. It was provisional, but the provision was that he return as a victor. He had blindly been led by quaint emotions, and laid himself under an obligation to walk squarely up to the face of death.

But he was not sure that he wished to make a retraction, even if he could do so without shame. As a matter of truth, he was sure of very little. He was mainly surprised.

It seemed to him supernaturally strange that he had allowed his mind to manoeuvre his body into such a situation. He understood that it might be called dramatically great.

However, he had no full appreciation of anything, excepting that he was actually conscious of being dazed. He could feel his dulled mind groping after the form and colour of this incident. He wondered why he did not feel some keen agony of fear cutting his sense like a knife. He wondered at this, because human expression had said loudly for centuries that men should feel afraid of certain things, and that all men who did not feel this fear were phenomena—heroes.

He was, then, a hero. He suffered that disappointment which we would all have if we discovered that we were ourselves capable of those deeds which we most admire in history and legend. This, then, was a hero. After all, heroes were not much.

No, it could not be true. He was not a hero. Heroes had no shames in their lives, and, as for him, he remembered borrowing fifteen dollars from a friend and promising to pay it back the next day, and then avoiding that friend for ten months. When, at home, his mother had aroused him for the early labour of his life on the farm, it had often been his fashion to be irritable, childish, diabolical; and his mother had died since he had come to the war.

He saw that, in this matter of the well, the canteens, the shells, he was an intruder in the land of fine deeds.

He was now about thirty paces from his comrades. The regiment had just turned its many faces toward him.

From the forest of terrific noises there suddenly emerged a little uneven line of men. They fired fiercely and rapidly at distant foliage on which appeared little puffs of white smoke. The spatter of skirmish firing was added to the thunder of the guns on the hill. The little line of men ran forward. A colour-sergeant fell flat with his flag as if he had slipped on ice. There was hoarse cheering from this distant field.

Collins suddenly felt that two demon fingers were pressed into his ears. He could see nothing but flying arrows, flaming red. He lurched from the shock of this explosion, but he made a mad rush for the house, which he viewed as a man submerged to the neck in a boiling surf might view the shore. In the air little pieces of shell howled, and the earthquake explosions drove him insane with the menace of their roar. As he ran the canteens knocked together with a rhythmical tinkling.

As he neared the house, each detail of the scene became vivid to him. He was aware of some bricks of the vanished chimney lying on the sod. There was a door which hung by one hinge.

Rifle bullets called forth by the insistent skirmishers came from the far-off bank of foliage. They mingled with the shells and the pieces of shells until the air was torn in all directions by hootings, yells, and howls. The sky was full of fiends who directed all their wild rage at his head.

When he came to the well, he flung himself face downward and peered into its darkness. There were furtive silver glintings some feet from the surface. He grabbed one of the canteens and, unfastening its cap, swung it down by the cord. The water flowed slowly in with an indolent gurgle.

And now, as he lay with his face turned away, he was suddenly smitten with the terror. It came upon his heart like the grasp of claws. All the power faded from his muscles. For an instant he was no more than a dead man.

The canteen filled with a maddening slowness, in the manner of all bottles. Presently he recovered his strength and addressed a screaming oath to it. He leaned over until it seemed as if he intended to try to push water into it with his hands. His eyes as he gazed down into the well shone like two pieces of metal, and in their expression was a great appeal and a great curse. The stupid water derided him.

There was the blaring thunder of a shell. Crimson light shone through the swift-boiling smoke and made a pink reflection on part of the wall of the well. Collins jerked out his arm and canteen with the same motion that a man would use in withdrawing his head from a furnace.

He scrambled erect and glared and hesitated. On the ground near him lay the old well bucket, with a length of rusty chain. He lowered it swiftly into the well. The bucket struck the water and then, turning lazily over, sank. When, with hand reaching tremblingly over hand, he hauled it out, it knocked often against the walls of the well and spilled some of its contents.

In running with a filled bucket, a man can adopt but one kind of gait. So, through this terrible field over which screamed practical angels of death, Collins ran in the manner of a farmer chased out of a dairy by a bull.

His face went staring white with anticipation—anticipation of a blow that would whirl him around and down. He would fall as he had seen other men fall, the life knocked out of them so suddenly that their knees were no more quick to touch the ground than their heads. He saw the long blue line of the regiment, but his comrades were standing looking at him from the edge of an impossible star. He was aware of some deep wheel-ruts and hoofprints in the sod beneath his feet.

The artillery officer who had fallen in this meadow had been making groans in the teeth of the tempest of sound. These futile cries, wrenched from him by his agony, were heard only by shells, bullets. When wild-eyed Collins came running, this officer raised himself. His face contorted and blanched from pain, he was about to utter some great beseeching cry. But suddenly his face straightened, and he called: 'Say, young man, give me a drink of water, will you?'

Collins had no room amid his emotions for surprise. He was mad from the threats of destruction.

'I can't!' he screamed, and in his reply was a full description of his quaking apprehension. His cap was gone and his hair was riotous. His clothes made it appear that he had been dragged over the ground by the heels. He ran on.

The officer's head sank down, and one elbow crooked. His foot in its brass-bound stirrup still stretched over the body of his horse, and the other leg was under the steed.

But Collins turned. He came dashing back. His face had now turned grey, and in his eyes was all terror. 'Here it is! here it is!'

The officer was as a man gone in drink. His arm bent like a twig. His head drooped as if his neck were of willow. He was sinking to the ground, to lie face downward.

Collins grabbed him by the shoulder. 'Here it is. Here's your drink. Turn over. Turn over, man, for God's sake!'

With Collins hauling at his shoulder, the officer twisted his body and fell with his face turned toward that region where lived the unspeakable noises of the swirling missiles. There was the faintest shadow of a smile on his lips as he looked at Collins. He gave a sigh, a little primitive breath like that from a child.

Collins tried to hold the bucket steadily, but his shaking hands caused the water to splash all over the face of the dying man. Then he jerked it away and ran on.

The regiment gave him a welcoming roar. The grimed faces were wrinkled in laughter.

His captain waved the bucket away. 'Give it to the men!'

The two genial, skylarking young lieutenants were the first to gain possession of it. They played over it in their fashion.

When one tried to drink, the other teasingly knocked his elbow. 'Don't Billie! You'll make me spill it,' said the one. The other laughed.

Suddenly there was an oath, the thud of wood on the ground, and a swift murmur of astonishment among the ranks. The two lieutenants glared at each other. The bucket lay on the ground, empty.

1895

Edith Wharton

Brief Biography

- Born in 1862 in New York City to a distinguished English-Dutch family.
- Marries in 1885 and in 1902 moves into 'The Mount,' a thirty-five-room Massachusetts estate she helped design.
- In 1905, publishes *The House of Mirth*, her first New York novel; writes more than forty books.
- In 1921 is the first woman to win the Pulitzer Prize (for *The Age of Innocence*) and in 1923 becomes the first woman to receive an honorary Doctor of Letters degree from Yale University.
- Several years after an affair with a journalist, divorces her husband and lives as an expatriate in southern France where she dies in 1937.

Edith Wharton was born Edith Newbold Jones, the scion of an established and wealthy New York family (the showy wealth of a maiden aunt gave rise to the expression 'keeping up with the Joneses'). Wharton's socialite mother, like many Victorian-age elite, considered artists as disreputable as manual labourers—but less useful. In her autobiography, *A Backward Glance* (1934), Wharton said, 'None of my relations ever spoke to me of my books, either to praise or blame—they simply ignored them.' Her husband, Teddy Wharton, whom she married out of filial duty, had no interest in literature; her friendships with (mostly male) writers and intellectuals sustained her creatively.

Early on, the conflict between the expectations of high society and literary ambition took their toll, and Wharton was treated for physical and mental ailments during the 1890s. Her biographers debate whether she was an incest survivor, and literary historians disagree whether she, like Charlotte Perkins Gilman, underwent S. Weir Mitchell's drastic 'rest cure.'

Wharton began her literary career as a short story writer, but after finishing her first novel in 1902, she took the advice of close friend and fellow writer Henry James to 'do New York,' producing *The House of Mirth*, a best-selling novel about a young woman victimized by the city's 'genteel' society. Her later New York novels, *The Custom of the Country* (1913) and

The Age of Innocence (1920), were satirical novels of manners. She often wrote about the wealthy, but *Ethan Frome* (1911) is a grim naturalistic work set in impoverished rural New England. As well as her successful novels, she published over eighty short stories, many on controversial topics: sexual passion and adultery, divorce, euthanasia, and the supernatural.

Like Crane and Hemingway, Wharton was a war correspondent, visiting frontline troops. Following World War I, during which she tirelessly organized relief efforts in France, her literary reputation—though not her popularity—faded. With decidedly non-American literary forebears, like nineteenth-century novelists Gustave Flaubert and Leo Tolstoy, she was often viewed as representing pre-war conservatism; she was openly disdainful of some of the aims of modernism. Nor was her reputation enhanced by her focus on the popular market, particularly high-paying women's magazines. But feminist critics have reexamined Wharton's literary merit and stress her independence in overcoming the obstacles of an unfortunate marriage, as well as her sharp observations of social change, including early twentieth-century technology. In her essay 'Telling a Short Story,' she argued that the short story's epiphany was an aesthetic illumination, 'a shaft of sunlight driven into the heart of experience.'

Wharton's women, such as the unnamed narrator in the disturbing 'A Journey,' often have fears and anxieties about marriage, social conditioning, repressed sexuality, class and gender roles, and finances. As the woman and sick husband return to New York from the American West the story's protagonist reflects on how her husband's illness has disrupted her marriage: he resents her health, and she resents caregiving. Wharton's diction—'sepulchral,' 'dreary,' 'meaningless'—suggests their estrangement. Certainly, 'A Journey' is as expertly crafted around a single effect as even Poe could have wished.

See Edith Wharton, from '*The Writing of Fiction,*' p. 409.

A Journey

As she lay in her berth, staring at the shadows overhead, the rush of the wheels was in her brain, driving her deeper and deeper into circles of wakeful lucidity. The sleeping car had sunk into its night silence. Through the wet windowpane she watched the sudden lights, the long stretches of hurrying blackness. Now and then she turned her head and looked through the opening in the hangings at her husband's curtains across the aisle. . . .

She wondered restlessly if he wanted anything and if she could hear him if he called. His voice had grown very weak within the last months and it irritated him when she did not hear. This irritability, this increasing childish petulance seemed to give expression to their imperceptible estrangement. Like two faces looking at one another through a sheet of glass they were close together, almost touching, but they could not hear or feel each other: the conductivity between them was broken. She, at least, had this sense of separation, and she fancied sometimes that she saw it reflected in the look with which he supplemented his failing words. Doubtless the fault was hers. She was too impenetrably healthy to be touched by the irrelevancies of disease. Her self-reproachful tenderness was tinged with the sense of his irrationality: she had a vague feeling that there was a purpose in his helpless tyrannies. The suddenness of the change had found her so unprepared. A year ago their pulses had beat to one robust measure; both had the same prodigal confidence in an exhaustless future. Now their energies no longer kept step: hers still bounded ahead of life, pre-empting unclaimed regions of hope and activity, while his lagged behind, vainly struggling to over-take her.

When they married, she had such arrears of living to make up: her days had been as bare as the whitewashed schoolroom where she forced innutri-tious facts upon reluctant children. His coming had broken in on the slumber of circumstance, widening the present till it became the encloser of remotest chances. But imperceptibly the horizon narrowed. Life had a grudge against her: she was never to be allowed to spread her wings.

At first the doctors had said that six weeks of mild air would set him right; but when he came back this assurance was explained as having of course in-cluded a winter in a dry climate. They gave up their pretty house, storing the wedding presents and new furniture, and went to Colorado. She had hated it there from the first. Nobody knew her or cared about her; there was no one to wonder at the good match she had made, or to envy her the new dresses and the visiting cards which were still a surprise to her. And he kept grow-ing worse. She felt herself beset with difficulties too evasive to be fought by so direct a temperament. She still loved him, of course; but he was gradually, undefinably ceasing to be himself. The man she had married had been strong, active, and gently masterful: the male whose pleasure it is to clear a way through the material obstructions of life; but now it was she who was the protector, he who must be shielded from importunities and given his drops or his beef juice though the skies were falling. The routine of the sickroom bewildered her; this punctual administering of medicine seemed as idle as some uncomprehended religious mummery.

There were moments, indeed, when warm gushes of pity swept away her instinctive resentment of his condition, when she still found his old self in his eyes as they groped for each other through the dense medium of his weakness. But these moments had grown rare. Sometimes he frightened her: his sunken expressionless face seemed that of a stranger; his voice was weak and hoarse; his thin-lipped smile a mere muscular contraction. Her hand avoided his damp soft skin, which had lost the familiar roughness of health: she caught herself furtively watching him as she might have watched a strange animal. It fright-ened her to feel that this was the man she loved; there were hours when to tell him what she suffered seemed the one escape from her fears. But in general she judged herself more leniently, reflecting that she had perhaps been too long alone with him, and that she would feel differently when they were at home again, surrounded by her robust and buoyant family. How she had rejoiced when the doctors at last gave their consent to his going home! She knew, of course, what the decision meant; they both knew. It meant that he was to die; but they dressed the truth in hopeful euphemisms, and at times, in the joy of preparation, she really forgot the purpose of their journey, and slipped into an eager allusion to next year's plans.

At last the day of leaving came. She had a dreadful fear that they would never get away; that somehow at the last moment he would fail her; that the doctors held one of their accustomed treacheries in reserve; but nothing happened. They drove to the station, he was installed in a seat with a rug over his knees and a cushion at his back, and she hung out of the window waving unregretful farewells to the acquaintances she had really never liked till then.

The first twenty-four hours had passed off well. He revived a little and it amused him to look out of the window and to observe the humors of the car. The second day he began to grow weary and to chafe under the dispassionate stare of the freckled child with the lump of chewing gum. She had to explain to the child's mother that her husband was too ill to be disturbed: a statement received by that lady with a resentment visibly supported by the maternal sentiment of the whole car. . . .

That night he slept badly and the next morning his temperature frightened her: she was sure he was growing worse. The day passed slowly, punctuated by the small irritations of travel. Watching his tired face, she traced in its contractions every rattle and jolt of the train, till her own body vibrated with sympathetic fatigue. She felt the others observing him too, and hovered restlessly between him and the line of interrogative eyes. The freckled child hung about him like a fly; offers of candy and picture books failed to dislodge her: she twisted one leg around the other and watched him imperturbably. The porter, as he passed, lingered with vague proffers of help, probably inspired by philanthropic passengers swelling with the sense that 'something ought to be done'; and one nervous man in a skull cap was audibly concerned as to the possible effect on his wife's health.

The hours dragged on in a dreary inoccupation. Towards dusk she sat down beside him and he laid his hand on hers. The touch startled her. He seemed to be calling her from far off. She looked at him helplessly and his smile went through her like a physical pang.

'Are you very tired?' she asked.

'No, not very.'

'We'll be there soon now.'

'Yes, very soon.'

'This time tomorrow—'

He nodded and they sat silent. When she had put him to bed and crawled into her own berth she tried to cheer herself with the thought that in less than twenty-four hours they would be in New York. Her people would all be at the station to meet her—she pictured their round unanxious faces pressing through the crowd. She only hoped they would not tell him too loudly that he was looking splendidly and would be all right in no time: the subtler sympathies developed by long contact with suffering were making her aware of a certain coarseness of texture in the family sensibilities.

Suddenly she thought she heard him call. She parted the curtains and listened. No, it was only a man snoring at the other end of the car. His snores had a greasy sound, as though they passed through tallow. She lay down and tried to sleep. . . . Had she not heard him move? She started up trembling. . . . The silence frightened her more than any sound. He might not be able to make her hear—he might be calling her now. . . . What made her think of such things? It was merely the familiar tendency of an overtired mind to fasten itself on the most intolerable chance within the range of its forebodings. . . . Putting her head out, she listened: but she could not distinguish his breathing from that of the other pairs of lungs about her. She longed to get up and look at him, but she knew the impulse was a mere vent for her restlessness, and the fear of disturbing him restrained her. . . . The regular movement of his curtain reassured her, she knew not why; she remembered that he had wished her a cheerful good night; and the sheer inability to endure her fears a moment longer made her put them from her with an effort of her whole sound-tired body. She turned on her side and slept.

She sat up stiffly, staring out at the dawn. The train was rushing through a region of bare hillocks huddled against a lifeless sky. It looked like the first day of creation. The air of the car was close, and she pushed up her window to let in the keen wind. Then she looked at her watch: it was seven o'clock, and soon the people about her would be stirring. She slipped into her clothes, smoothed her disheveled hair and crept to the dressing room. When she had washed her face and adjusted her dress she felt more hopeful. It was always a struggle for her not to be cheerful in the morning. Her cheeks burned deliciously under the coarse towel and the wet hair about her temples broke into strong upward tendrils. Every inch of her was full of life and elasticity. And in ten hours they would be at home!

She stepped to her husband's berth: it was time for him to take his early glass of milk. The window shade was down, and in the dusk of the curtained enclosure she could just see that he lay sideways, with his face away from her. She leaned over him and drew up the shade. As she did so she touched one of his hands. It felt cold. . . .

She bent closer, laying her hand on his arm and calling him by name. He did not move. She spoke again more loudly; she grasped his shoulder and gently shook it. He lay motionless. She caught hold of his hand again: it slipped from her limply, like a dead thing. A dead thing?

Her breath caught. She must see his face. She leaned forward, and hurriedly, shrinkingly, with a sickening reluctance of the flesh, laid her hands on his shoulders and turned him over. His head fell back; his face looked small and smooth; he gazed at her with steady eyes.

She remained motionless for a long time, holding him thus; and they looked at each other. Suddenly she shrank back: the longing to scream, to call out, to fly from him, had almost overpowered her. But a strong hand arrested her. Good God! If it were known that he was dead they would be put off the train at the next station—

In a terrifying flash of remembrance there arose before her a scene she had once witnessed in traveling, when a husband and wife, whose child had died in the train, had been thrust out at some chance station. She saw them standing on the platform with the child's body between them; she had never forgotten the dazed look with which they followed the receding train. And this was what would happen to her. Within the next hour she might find herself on the platform of some strange station, alone with her husband's body. . . . Anything but that! It was too horrible—She quivered like a creature at bay.

As she cowered there, she felt the train moving more slowly. It was coming then—they were approaching a station! She saw again the husband and wife standing on the lonely platform; and with a violent gesture she drew down the shade to hide her husband's face.

Feeling dizzy, she sank down on the edge of the berth, keeping away from his outstretched body, and pulling the curtains close, so that he and she were shut into a kind of sepulchral twilight. She tried to think. At all costs she must conceal the fact that he was dead. But how? Her mind refused to act: she could not plan, combine. She could think of no way but to sit there, clutching the curtains, all day long. . . .

She heard the porter making up her bed; people were beginning to move about the car; the dressing-room door was being opened and shut. She tried to rouse herself. At length with a supreme effort she rose to her feet, stepping into the aisle of the car and drawing the curtains tight behind her. She noticed that they still parted slightly with the motion of the car, and finding a pin in her dress she fastened them together. Now she was safe. She looked round and saw the porter. She fancied he was watching her.

'Ain't he awake yet?' he inquired.

'No,' she faltered.

'I got his milk all ready when he wants it. You know you told me to have it for him by seven.'

She nodded silently and crept into her seat.

At half-past eight the train reached Buffalo. By this time the other passengers were dressed and the berths had been folded back for the day. The porter, moving to and fro under his burden of sheets and pillows, glanced at her as he passed. At length he said: 'Ain't he going to get up? You know we're ordered to make up the berths as early as we can.'

She turned cold with fear. They were just entering the station.

'Oh, not yet,' she stammered. 'Not till he's had his milk. Won't you get it, please?'

'All right. Soon as we start again.'

When the train moved on he reappeared with the milk. She took it from him and sat vaguely looking at it: her brain moved slowly from one idea to another, as though they were steppingstones set far apart across a whirling flood. At length she became aware that the porter still hovered expectantly.

'Will I give it to him?' he suggested.

'Oh, no,' she cried, rising. 'He—he's asleep yet, I think—'

She waited till the porter had passed on; then she unpinned the curtains and slipped behind them. In the semiobscurity her husband's face stared up at her like a marble mask with agate eyes. The eyes were dreadful. She put out her hand and drew down the lids. Then she remembered the glass of milk in her other hand: what was she to do with it? She thought of raising the window and throwing it out; but to do so she would have to lean across his body and bring her face close to his. She decided to drink the milk.

She returned to her seat with the empty glass and after a while the porter came back to get it.

'When'll I fold up his bed?' he asked.

'Oh, not now—not yet; he's ill—he's very ill. Can't you let him stay as he is? The doctor wants him to lie down as much as possible.'

He scratched his head. 'Well, if he's *really* sick—'

He took the empty glass and walked away, explaining to the passengers that the party behind the curtains was too sick to get up just yet.

She found herself the center of sympathetic eyes. A motherly woman with an intimate smile sat down beside her.

'I'm real sorry to hear your husband's sick. I've had a remarkable amount of sickness in my family and maybe I could assist you. Can I take a look at him?'

'Oh, no—no, please! He mustn't be disturbed.'

The lady accepted the rebuff indulgently.

'Well, it's just as you say, of course, but you don't look to me as if you'd had much experience in sickness and I'd have been glad to assist you. What do you generally do when your husband's taken this way?'

'I—I let him sleep.'

'Too much sleep ain't any too healthful either. Don't you give him any medicine?'

'Y—yes.'

'Don't you wake him to take it?'

'Yes.'

one out and ate it. The dry crumbs choked her, and she hastily swallowed a little brandy from her husband's flask. The burning sensation in her throat acted as a counterirritant, momentarily relieving the dull ache of her nerves. Then she felt a gently-stealing warmth, as though a soft air fanned her, and the swarming fears relaxed their clutch, receding through the stillness that enclosed her, a stillness soothing as the spacious quietude of a summer day. She slept.

Through her sleep she felt the impetuous rush of the train. It seemed to be life itself that was sweeping her on with headlong inexorable force—sweeping her into darkness and terror, and the awe of unknown days. —Now all at once everything was still—not a sound, not a pulsation. . . . She was dead in her turn, and lay beside him with smooth upstaring face. How quiet it was!—and yet she heard feet coming, the feet of the men who were to carry them away. . . . She could feel too—she felt a sudden prolonged vibration, a series of hard shocks, and then another plunge into darkness: the darkness of death this time—a black whirlwind on which they were both spinning like leaves, in wild uncoiling spirals, with millions and millions of the dead. . . .

She sprang up in terror. Her sleep must have lasted a long time, for the winter day had paled and the lights had been lit. The car was in confusion, and as she regained her self-possession she saw that the passengers were gathering up their wraps and bags. The woman with the false braids had brought from the dressing room a sickly ivy plant in a bottle, and the Christian Scientist was reversing his cuffs. The porter passed down the aisle with his impartial brush. An impersonal figure with a gold-banded cap asked for her husband's ticket. A voice shouted 'Baiggage express!' and she heard the clicking of metal as the passengers handed over their checks.

Presently her window was blocked by an expanse of sooty wall, and the train passed into the Harlem tunnel. The journey was over; in a few minutes she would see her family pushing their joyous way through the throng at the station. Her heart dilated. The worst terror was past. . . .

'We'd better get him up now, hadn't we?' asked the porter, touching her arm.

He had her husband's hat in his hand and was meditatively revolving it under his brush.

She looked at the hat and tried to speak; but suddenly the car grew dark. She flung up her arms, struggling to catch at something, and fell face downward, striking her head against the dead man's berth.

1899

E. Pauline Johnson

Brief Biography

- Born on the Six Nations Reserve near Brantford, ON, in 1861.
- Daughter of a Mohawk chief and a cultured Englishwoman.
- Reads widely in the works of English 'masters' while absorbing stories from her Mohawk grandfather.
- Entertains audiences with her public performances in North America and England.
- Is the first Native poet to have her work published in Canada and, at the time of her death from cancer in 1913, is one of Canada's most popular poets.
- Funeral is attended by city dignitaries; all flags at half-mast. Her memorial in Stanley Park, Vancouver, is the city's only monument honouring a Canadian writer in the twentieth century.

Emily Pauline Johnson, inheritor of two racial traditions, was known in her lifetime foremost as a performer and poet. For seventeen years beginning in 1892, she toured Canada, the United States, and England, reciting her poetry and dramatizing her stories on public stages, in church halls, and at private homes. She toured under her Mohawk ancestral name, Tekahionwake ('double life'). Her costume exemplified this duality: to satisfy the cravings of the upper classes for the exotic, she performed the first half of her recital in an elegant white gown, the second half in traditional fringed buckskin dress, with a hunting knife, bear claw necklace, and one of her grandfather's scalps.

The tours began as an economic expedient after the death of her father, a chief and prominent figure on the reserve where she was born. Although the performances allowed Johnson to earn her livelihood while calling attention to ennobling Native values and traits, her highly theatrical performances ultimately sapped her strength and limited her literary output. In 1909 she retired to Vancouver where she was befriended by Squamish chief Joseph Capilano (whom she had met in England), whose oral narratives she retold as a popular series for a Vancouver newspaper; in 1911, they were collected as *Legends of Vancouver*.

Academics often denigrated her as merely 'popular,' undermining her self presentation as the 'Indian princess.' They pointed to her father's acculturation to white values and Johnson's limited contact with Native peoples throughout her life. Since the mid-1990s, however, scholars have reconsidered her complete literary output (which includes poems, short stories, children's fiction, and essays); feminist and post-colonial perspectives position her as a figure of resistance, examining her roles as Aboriginal advocate and 'New Woman.' Her critique of white hegemony and religious intolerance emerge with clarity in much of her short fiction, published posthumously in the collection *The Moccasin Maker* (1913). In the ironically titled 'As It Was in the Beginning,' the young female narrator is taken away from her family by the local 'Blackcoat.' Stripped of her traditional clothes and forbidden to speak her native Cree, she is indoctrinated into Christianity but still deemed a 'caged animal' and unmarriageable by the hypocritical missionary. In 'The Derelict,' Johnson chooses as her protagonist a white man of divided loyalties who is in love with a 'half-breed,' dramatizing a complex moral dilemma through starkly contrastive scenes and settings.

Vancouver writer Ethel Wilson, who witnessed a Johnson recital when she was ten years old, summed up Johnson's life: '[She] pursued a path of her own making, and did this with integrity.'

The Derelict

Cragstone had committed what his world called a crime—an inexcusable offence that caused him to be shunned by society and estranged from his father's house. He had proved a failure.

Not one of his whole family connections could say unto the others, 'I told you so,' when he turned out badly.

They had all predicted that he was born for great things, then to discover that they had overestimated him was irritating, it told against their discernment, it was unflattering, and they thought him inconsiderate.

So, in addition to his failure, Cragstone had to face the fact that he had made himself unpopular among his kin.

As a boy he had been the pride of his family, as a youth, its hope of fame and fortune; he was clever, handsome, inventive, original, everything that society and his kind admired, but he criminally fooled them and their expectations, and they never forgave him for it.

He had dabbled in music, literature, law, everything—always with semi-success and brilliant promise; he had even tried the stage, playing the Provinces for an entire season; then, ultimately sinking into mediocrity in all these occupations, he returned to London, a hopelessly useless, a pitiably gifted man. His chilly little aristocratic mother always spoke of him as 'poor, dear Charles.' His brothers, clubmen all, graciously alluded to him with, 'deuced hard luck, poor Charlie.' His father never mentioned his name.

Then he went into 'The Church,' sailed for Canada, idled about for a few weeks, when one of the great colonial bishops, not knowing what else to do with him, packed him off north as a missionary to the Indians.

And, after four years of disheartening labor amongst a semi-civilized people, came this girl Lydia into his life. This girl of the mixed parentage, the English father, who had been swept northward with the rush of lumber trading, the Chippewa mother, who had been tossed to his arms by the tide of circumstances. The girl was a strange composition of both, a type of mixed blood, pale, dark, slender, with the slim hands, the marvellously beautiful teeth of her mother's people, the ambition, the small tender mouth, the utter fearlessness of the English race. But the strange, laughless eyes, the silent step, the hard sense of honor, proclaimed her far more the daughter of red blood than of white.

And, with the perversity of his kind, Cragstone loved her; he meant to marry her because he knew that he should not. What a monstrous thing it would be if he did! He, the shepherd of this half-civilized flock, the modern John Baptist; he, the voice of the great Anglican Church crying in this wilderness, how could he wed with this Indian girl who had been a common serving-maid in a house in Penetanguishene, and been dismissed therefrom with an accusation of theft that she could never prove untrue? How could he bring this reproach upon the Church? Why, the marriage would have no precedent; and yet he loved her, loved her sweet, silent ways, her listening attitudes, her clear, brown, consumptive-suggesting skin. She was the only thing in all the irksome mission life that had responded to him, had encouraged him to struggle anew for the spiritual welfare of this poor red race. Of course, in Penetanguishene they had told him she was irreclaimable, a thief, with ready lies to cover her crimes; for that very reason he felt tender towards her, she was so sinful, so pathetically human.

He could have mastered himself, perhaps, had she not responded, had he not seen the laughless eyes laugh alone for him, had she not once when a momentary insanity possessed them both confessed in words her love for him as he had done to her. But now? Well, now only this horrible tale of theft and untruth hung between them like a veil; now even with his arms locked about her, his eyes drowned in hers, his ears caught the whispers of calumny, his thoughts were perforated with the horror of his Bishop's censure, and these things rushed between his soul and hers, like some bridgeless deep he might not cross, and so his lonely life went on.

And then one night his sweet humanity, his grand, strong love rose up, battled with him, and conquered. He cast his pharisaical ideas, and the Church's 'I am better than thou,' aside forever; he would go now, tonight, he would ask her to be his wife, to have and to hold from this day forward, for better, for worse, for—

A shadow fell across the doorway of his simple home; it was August Beaver, the trapper, with the urgent request that he would come across to French Island at once, for old 'Medicine' Joe was there, dying, and wished to see the minister. At another time Cragstone would have felt sympathetic, now he was only irritated; he wanted to find Lydia, to look in her laughless eyes, to feel her fingers in his hair, to tell her he did not care if she were a hundred times a thief, that he loved her, loved her, loved her, and he would marry her despite the Church, despite—

'Joe, he's near dead, you come now?' broke in August's voice. Cragstone turned impatiently, got his prayer-book, followed the trapper, took his place in the canoe, and paddled in silence up the bay.

The moon arose, large, limpid, flooding the cabin with a wondrous light, and making more wan the features of a dying man, whose fever wasted form lay on some lynx skins on the floor.

Cragstone was reading from the Book of Common Prayer the exquisite service of the Visitation of the Sick. Outside, the loons clanged up the waterways, the herons called across the islands, but no human things ventured up the wilds. Inside, the sick man lay, beside him August Beaver holding a rude lantern, while Cragstone's matchless voice repeated the Anglican formula. A spasm, an uplifted hand, and Cragstone paused. Was the end coming even before a benediction? But the dying man was addressing Beaver in Chippewa, whispering and choking out the words in his death struggle.

'He says he's bad man,' spoke Beaver. A horrible, humorous sensation swept over Cragstone; he hated himself for it, but at college he had always ridiculed death-bed confessions; but in a second that feeling had vanished, he bent his handsome, fair face above the copper-colored countenance of the dying man. 'Joe,' he said, with that ineffable tenderness that had always drawn human hearts to him; 'Joe, tell me before I pronounce the Absolution, how you have been "bad"?'

'I steal three times,' came the answer. 'Oncet horses, two of them from farmer near Barrie. Oncet twenty fox-skins at North Bay; station man he in jail for those fox-skins now. Oncet gold watch from doctor at Penetanguishene.' The prayer-book rattled from Cragstone's hands and fell to the floor.

'Tell me about this watch,' he mumbled.

'How did you come to do it?'

'I liffe at the doctor's; I take care his horse, long time; old River's girl, Lydia, she work there too; they say she steal it; I sell to trader, the doctor he nefer know, he think Lydia.'

Cragstone was white to the lips. 'Joe,' he faltered, 'you are dying; do you regret this sin, are you sorry?'

An indistinct 'yes' was all; death was claiming him rapidly.

But a great, white, purified love had swept over the young clergyman. The girl he worshipped could never now be a reproach to his calling, she was proved blameless as a baby, and out of his great human love arose the divine calling, the Christ-like sense of forgiveness, the God-like forgetfulness of injury and suffering done to his and to him, and once more his soft, rich voice broke the stillness of the Northern night, as the Anglican absolution of the dying fell from his lips in merciful tenderness:

'O Lord Jesus Christ, who hath left power to His Church to absolve all sinners who truly repent and believe in Him, of His great mercy forgive thee thine offences, and by His authority committed to me I absolve thee from all thy sins in the name of the Father, and of the Son, and of the Holy Ghost. Amen.'

Beaver was holding the lantern close to the penitent's face; Cragstone, kneeling beside him, saw that the end had come already, and, after making the sign of the Cross on the dead Indian's forehead, the young priest arose and went silently out into the night.

The sun was slipping down into the far horizon, fretted by the inimitable wonder of islands that throng the Georgian Bay; the blood-colored skies, the purpling clouds, the extravagant beauty of a Northern sunset hung in the west like the trailing robes of royalty, soundless in their flaring, their fading; soundless as the unbroken wilds which lay bathed in the loneliness of a dying day.

But on the color-flooded shore stood two, blind to the purple, the scarlet, the gold, blind to all else save the tense straining of the other's eyes; deaf to nature's unsung anthem, hearing only the other's voice. Cragstone stood transfixed with consternation. The memory of the past week of unutterable joy lay blasted with the awfulness of this moment, the memory of even that first day—when he had stood with his arms about her, had told her how he had declared her reclaimed name far and wide, how even Penetanguishene knew now that she had suffered blamelessly, how his own heart throbbed suffocatingly with the honor, the delight of being the poor means through which she had been righted in the accusing eyes of their little world, and that now she would be his wife, his sweet, helping wife, and she had been great enough not to remind him that he had not asked her to be his wife until her name was proved blameless, and he was great enough not to make excuse of the resolve he had set out upon just when August Beaver came to turn the current of his life.

But he had other eyes to face to-night, eyes that blurred the past, that burned themselves into his being—the condemning, justly, and righteously indignant eyes of his Bishop—while his numb heart, rather than his ears, listened to the words that fell from the prelate's lips like curses on his soul, like the door that would shut him forever outside the holy place.

'What have you done, you pretended servant of the living God? What use is this you have made of your Holy Orders? You hear the confessions of a dying man, you absolve and you bless him, and come away from the poor dead thief to shout his crimes in the ears of the world, to dishonor him, to be a discredit to your calling. Who could trust again such a man as you have proved to be—faithless to himself, faithless to his Church, faithless to his God?'

But Cragstone was on the sands at his accuser's feet. 'Oh! my Lord,' he cried, 'I meant only to save the name of a poor, mistrusted girl, selfishly, perhaps, but I would have done the same thing just for humanity's sake had it been another to whom injustice was done.' 'Your plea of justice is worse than weak; to save the good name of the living is it just to rob the dead?'

The Bishop's voice was like iron.

'I did not realize I was a priest, I only knew I was a *man*,' and with these words Cragstone arose and looked fearlessly, even proudly, at the one who stood his judge.

'Is it not better, my Lord, to serve the living than the dead?'

'And bring reproach upon your Church?' said the Bishop, sternly.

It was the first thought Cragstone ever had of his official crime; he staggered under the horror of it, and the little, dark, silent figure, that had followed them unseen, realized in her hiding amid the shadows that the man who had lifted her into the light was himself being thrust down into irremediable darkness. But Cragstone only saw the Bishop looking at him as from a supreme height, he only felt the final stinging lash in the words: 'When a man disregards the most sacred offices of his God, he will hardly reverence the claims of justice of a simple woman who knows not his world, and if he so easily flings his God away for a woman, just so easily will he fling her away for other gods.'

And Lydia, with eyes that blazed like flame, watched the Bishop turn and walk frigidly up the sands, his indignation against this outrager of the Church declaring itself in every footfall.

Cragstone flung himself down, burying his face in his hands. What a wreck he had made of life! He saw his future, loveless, for no woman would trust him now; even the one whose name he had saved would probably be more unforgiving than the Church; it was the way with women when a man abandoned God and honor for them; and this nameless but blackest of sins, this falsity to one poor dying sinner, would stand between him and heaven forever, though through that very crime he had saved a fellow being. Where was the justice of it?

The purple had died from out the western sky, the waters of the Georgian Bay lay colorless at his feet, night was covering the world and stealing with inky blackness into his soul.

She crept out of her hiding-place, and, coming, gently touched his tumbled fair hair; but he shrank from her, crying: 'Lydia, my girl, my girl, I am not for a good woman now! I, who thought you an outcast, a thief, not worthy to be my wife, tonight I am not an outcast of man alone, but of God.'

But what cared she for his official crimes? She was a woman. Her arms were about him, her lips on his; and he who had, until now, been a portless derelict, who had vainly sought a haven in art, an anchorage in the service of God, had drifted at last into the world's most sheltered harbor—a woman's love.

But, of course, the Bishop took away his gown.

1913

James Joyce

Brief Biography

- Born in Dublin in 1882; eldest of twelve children, ten survived.
- In 1904 leaves Ireland for self-imposed exile in Europe.
- Opposes marriage institution and lives common-law with Nora Barnacle before marrying in 1931.
- In 1917, undergoes first eye operation; is frequently blind for weeks at a time from at least eleven operations for chronic glaucoma over the next fifteen years.
- In 1933 US court rules *Ulysses* not pornographic.
- Irish dramatist-novelist Samuel Beckett was Joyce's secretary.
- Terrified of dogs and thunderstorms.
- Dies after ulcer surgery in Zürich in 1941.

Once censored, attacked, rejected, and misunderstood, James Joyce is now considered by many the most influential twentieth-century writer. His heavy-drinking father was a failed distiller and unemployed tax collector. His mother struggled to maintain a facade of success only to die young at age forty-four. Joyce studied modern languages at a Jesuit college but rejected Catholic teachings in his first novel.

After graduation, Joyce moved to Paris, but returned to Dublin upon his mother's impending death. He agonized over his inability to pray at her deathbed, an incident portrayed in two of his books. He left Ireland again, this time to teach English in the busy port city of Trieste (then part of Austria-Hungary, now Croatia), near the Italian border. During his lifetime, he experienced poverty, his daughter's schizophrenia, painful eye surgeries and blindness, family quarrels, and critical indifference. Though he made only four return trips to Ireland—leaving his native land for a life 'of silence, exile, and cunning'—Irish politics were central to his writings. As an Irishman writing in English, he was able to reveal a new language hidden 'in the language of the colonizers' through literary allusions and wordplay.

In 1904, inspired by Norwegian playwright Henrik Ibsen and Irish poet W.B. Yeats, Joyce began writing the stories that would become his only short story collection, *Dubliners*. The book wasn't published until 1914, delayed a decade because the printer felt that Joyce insulted the British monarchy. His autobiographical first novel, *A Portrait of the Artist as a Young Man*, appeared in serial form that same year; in 1916, it was published as a book. In 1915, he completed his play, *Exiles*. Fascinated by the risqué, he said the poems in *Chamber Music* (1907) were inspired by the sound of a prostitute urinating into a pot.

Joyce's family moved to Zürich during the war while he wrote his dense 'stream of consciousness' novel, *Ulysses*. The 'Bloomsday' (16 June 1904, named after its central character, Leopold Bloom) described in the novel is celebrated today in Dublin and other cities. After the war, Ezra Pound suggested that Joyce move to Paris. *Ulysses* was banned as obscene in England

and America, but the Parisian bookseller Sylvia Beach published the novel from her famous store, Shakespeare & Co., in 1922. Joyce's last book, seventeen years in writing, was the most celebrated avant-garde project ever written, *Finnegans Wake* (1939). His business manager, Paul Leon, saved Joyce's papers and belongings just ahead of the occupation of Paris during World War II.

Each of Joyce's painstakingly revised works forges new directions for creative writing. A Joycean story is shaped so that allusion, tone, and every detail suggest a deeper meaning. His much-debated short story term 'epiphany' changed the way stories were written. Instead of a plot resolution, the story rested on a moment of revelation, often failure, deception, or disappointment. Other modernists, such as Virginia Woolf and Katherine Mansfield, argued the concept of the epiphany, questioning whether it was a single moment or a series of little 'moments of being,' as the latter believed. Was it for the character or the reader? In 'A Painful Case,' the epiphany may relate more immediately to the reader's perception of Duffy as pitiful, trapped in disillusionments which he cannot perceive.

See James Joyce, 'Epiphany,' from *Stephen Hero*, p. 417; see also Virginia Woolf, from 'Modern Fiction,' p. 402, and Cynthia J. Hallett, from 'Minimalism and the Short Story,' p. 420.

A Painful Case

Mr James Duffy lived in Chapelizod because he wished to live as far as possible from the city of which he was a citizen and because he found all the other suburbs of Dublin mean, modern, and pretentious. He lived in an old sombre house and from his windows he could look into the disused distillery or upwards along the shallow river on which Dublin is built. The lofty walls of his uncarpeted room were free from pictures. He had himself bought every article of furniture in the room: a blank iron bedstead, an iron washstand, four cane chairs, a clothes-rack, a coal-scuttle, a fender and irons and a square table on which lay a double desk. A bookcase had been made in an alcove by means of shelves of white wood. The bed was clothed with white bed-clothes and a black and scarlet rug covered the foot. A little hand-mirror hung above the washstand and during the day a white-shaded lamp stood as the sole ornament of the mantelpiece. The books on the white wooden shelves were arranged from below upwards according to bulk. A complete Wordsworth stood at one end of the lowest shelf and a copy of the *Maynooth Catechism*, sewn into the cloth cover of a notebook, stood at one end of the top shelf. Writing materials were always on the desk. In the desk lay a manuscript translation of Hauptmann's *Michael Kramer*, the stage directions of which were written in purple ink, and a little sheaf of papers held together by a brass pin. In these sheets a sentence was inscribed from time to time and, in an ironical moment, the headline of an advertisement for *Bile Beans* had been pasted on to the first sheet. On lifting the lid of the desk a faint fragrance escaped—the fragrance of new cedarwood pencils or of a bottle of gum or of an over-ripe apple which might have been left there and forgotten.

Mr Duffy abhorred anything which betokened physical or mental disorder. A mediæval doctor would have called him saturnine. His face, which carried the entire tale of his years, was of the brown tint of Dublin streets. On his long and rather large head grew dry black hair and a tawny moustache did not quite cover an unamiable mouth. His cheekbones also gave his face a harsh character; but there was no harshness in the eyes which, looking at the world from under their tawny eyebrows, gave the impression of a man ever alert to greet a redeeming instinct in others but often disappointed. He lived at a little distance from his body, regarding his own acts with doubtful side-glances. He had an odd autobiograpical habit which led him to compose in his mind from time to time a short sentence about himself containing a subject in the third person and a predicate in the past tense. He never gave alms to beggars and walked firmly, carrying a stout hazel.

He had been for many years cashier of a private bank in Baggot Street. Every morning he came in from Chapelizod by tram. At midday he went to Dan Burke's and took his lunch—a bottle of lager beer and a small trayful of arrowroot biscuits. At four o'clock he was set free. He dined in an eating-house in George's Street where he felt himself safe from the society of Dublin's gilded youth and where there was a certain plain honesty in the bill of fare. His evenings were spent either before his landlady's piano or roaming about the outskirts of the city. His liking for Mozart's music brought him sometimes to an opera or a concert: these were the only dissipations of his life.

He had neither companions nor friends, church nor creed. He lived his spiritual life without any communion with others, visiting his relatives at Christmas and escorting them to the cemetery when they died. He performed these two social duties for old dignity's sake but conceded nothing further to the conventions which regulate the civic life. He allowed himself to think that in certain circumstances he would rob his bank but, as these circumstances never arose, his life rolled out evenly—an adventureless tale.

One evening he found himself sitting beside two ladies in the Rotunda. The house, thinly peopled and silent, gave distressing prophecy of failure. The lady who sat next him looked round at the deserted house once or twice and then said:

—What a pity there is such a poor house to-night! It's so hard on people to have to sing to empty benches.

He took the remark as an invitation to talk. He was surprised that she seemed so little awkward. While they talked he tried to fix her permanently in his memory. When he learned that the young girl beside her was her daughter he judged her to be a year or so younger than himself. Her face, which must have been handsome, had remained intelligent. It was an oval face with strongly marked features. The eyes were very dark blue and steady. Their gaze began with a defiant note but was confused by what seemed a deliberate swoon of the pupil into the iris, revealing for an instant a temperament of great sensibility. The pupil reasserted itself quickly, this half-disclosed nature fell again under the reign of prudence, and her astrakhan jacket, moulding a bosom of a certain fulness, struck the note of defiance more definitely.

He met her again a few weeks afterwards at a concert in Earlsfort Terrace and seized the moments when her daughter's attention was diverted to become intimate. She alluded once or twice to her husband but her tone was not such as to make the allusion a warning. Her name was Mrs Sinico. Her husband's great-great-grandfather had come from Leghorn. Her husband was captain of a mercantile boat plying between Dublin and Holland; and they had one child.

Meeting her a third time by accident he found courage to make an appointment. She came. This was the first of many meetings; they met always in the evening and chose the most quiet quarters for their walks together. Mr Duffy, however, had a distaste for underhand ways and, finding that they were compelled to meet stealthily, he forced her to ask him to her house. Captain Sinico encouraged his visits, thinking that his daughter's hand was in question. He had dismissed his wife so sincerely from his gallery of pleasures that he did not suspect that anyone else would take an interest in her. As the husband was often away and the daughter out giving music lessons Mr Duffy had many opportunities of enjoying the lady's society. Neither he nor she had had any such adventure before and neither was conscious of any incongruity. Little by little he entangled his thoughts with hers. He lent her books, provided her with ideas, shared his intellectual life with her. She listened to all.

Sometimes in return for his theories she gave out some fact of her own life. With almost maternal solicitude she urged him to let his nature open to the full; she became his confessor. He told her that for some time he had assisted at the meetings of an Irish Socialist Party where he had felt himself a unique figure amidst a score of sober workmen in a garret lit by an inefficient oil-lamp. When the party had divided into three sections, each under its own leader and in its own garret, he had discontinued his attendances. The workmen's discussions, he said, were too timorous; the interest they took in the question of wages was inordinate. He felt that they were hard-featured realists and that they resented an exactitude which was the product of a leisure not within their reach. No social revolution, he told her, would be likely to strike Dublin for some centuries.

She asked him why did he not write out his thoughts. For what, he asked her, with careful scorn. To compete with phrasemongers, incapable of thinking consecutively for sixty seconds? To submit himself to the criticisms of an obtuse middle class which entrusted its morality to policemen and its fine arts to impresarios?

He went often to her little cottage outside Dublin; often they spent their evenings alone. Little by little, as their thoughts entangled, they spoke of subjects less remote. Her companionship was like a warm soil about an exotic. Many times she allowed the dark to fall upon them, refraining from lighting the lamp. The dark discreet room, their isolation, the music that still vibrated in their ears united them. This union exalted him, wore away the rough edges of his character, emotionalised his mental life. Sometimes he caught himself listening to the sound of his own voice. He thought that in her eyes he would ascend to an angelical stature; and, as he attached the fervent nature of his companion more and more closely to him, he heard the strange impersonal voice which he recognised as his own, insisting on the soul's incurable loneliness. We cannot give ourselves, it said: we are our own. The end of these discourses was that one night during which she had shown every sign of unusual excitement, Mrs Sinico caught up his hand passionately and pressed it to her cheek.

Mr Duffy was very much surprised. Her interpretation of his words disillusioned him. He did not visit her for a week; then he wrote to her asking her to meet him. As he did not wish their last interview to be troubled by the influence of their ruined confessional they met in a little cakeshop near the Parkgate. It was cold autumn weather but in spite of the cold they wandered up and down the roads of the Park for nearly three hours. They agreed to break off their intercourse: every bond, he said, is a bond to sorrow. When they came out of the Park they walked in silence towards the tram; but here she began to tremble so violently that, fearing another collapse on her part, he bade her good-bye quickly and left her. A few days later he received a parcel containing his books and music.

Four years passed. Mr Duffy returned to his even way of life. His room still bore witness of the orderliness of his mind. Some new pieces of music encumbered the music-stand in the lower room and on his shelves stood two volumes by Nietzsche: *Thus Spake Zarathustra* and *The Gay Science*. He wrote seldom in the sheaf of papers which lay in his desk. One of his sentences, written two months after his last interview with Mrs Sinico, read: Love between man and man is impossible because there must not be sexual intercourse and friendship between man and woman is impossible because there must be sexual intercourse. He kept away from concerts lest he should meet her. His father died; the junior partner of the bank retired. And still every morning he went into the city by tram and every evening walked home from the city after having dined moderately in George's Street and read the evening paper for dessert.

One evening as he was about to put a morsel of corned beef and cabbage into his mouth his hand stopped. His eyes fixed themselves on a paragraph in the evening paper which he had propped against the water-carafe. He replaced the morsel of food on his plate and read the paragraph attentively. Then he drank a glass of water, pushed his plate to one side, doubled the paper down before him between his elbows and read the paragraph over and over again. The cabbage began to deposit a cold white grease on his plate. The girl came over to him to ask was his dinner not properly cooked. He said it was very good and ate a few mouthfuls of it with difficulty. Then he paid his bill and went out.

He walked along quickly through the November twilight, his stout hazel stick striking the ground regularly, the fringe of the buff *Mail* peeping out of a side-pocket of his tight reefer over-coat. On the lonely road which leads from the Parkgate to Chapelizod he slackened his pace. His stick struck the ground less emphatically and his breath, issuing irregularly, almost with a sighing sound, condensed in the wintry air. When he reached his house he went up at once to his bedroom and, taking the paper from his pocket, read the paragraph again by the failing light of the window. He read it not aloud, but moving his lips as a priest does when he reads the prayers *Secreto*. This was the paragraph:

DEATH OF A LADY AT SYDNEY PARADE
A PAINFUL CASE

Today at the City of Dublin Hospital the Deputy Coroner (in the absence of Mr Leverett) held an inquest on the body of Mrs Emily Sinico, aged forty-three years, who was killed at Sydney Parade Station yesterday evening. The evidence showed that the deceased lady, while attempting to cross the line, was knocked down by the engine of the ten o'clock slow train from Kingstown, thereby sustaining injuries of the head and right side which led to her death.

James Lennon, driver of the engine, stated that he had been in the employment of the railway company for fifteen years. On hearing the guard's whistle he set the train in motion and a second or two afterwards brought it to rest in response to loud cries. The train was going slowly.

P. Dunne, railway porter, stated that as the train was about to start he observed a woman attempting to cross the lines. He ran towards her and shouted but, before he could reach her, she was caught by the buffer of the engine and fell to the ground.

A juror—You saw the lady fall?

Witness—Yes.

Police Sergeant Croly deposed that when he arrived he found the deceased lying on the platform apparently dead. He had the body taken to the waiting-room pending the arrival of the ambulance.

Constable 57E corroborated.

Dr Halpin, assistant house surgeon of the City of Dublin Hospital, stated that the deceased had two lower ribs fractured and had sustained severe contusions of the right shoulder. The right side of the head had been injured in the fall. The injuries were not sufficient to have caused death in a normal person. Death, in his opinion, had been probably due to shock and sudden failure of the heart's action.

Mr H. B. Patterson Finlay, on behalf of the railway company, expressed his deep regret at the accident. The company had always taken every pre- caution to prevent people crossing the lines except by the bridges, both by placing notices in every station and by the use of patent spring gates at level crossings. The deceased had been in the habit of crossing the lines late at night from platform to platform and, in view of certain other circum- stances of the case, he did not think the railway officials were to blame.

Captain Sinico, of Leoville, Sydney Parade, husband of the deceased, also gave evidence. He stated that the deceased was his wife. He was not in Dublin at the time of the accident as he had arrived only that morning from Rotterdam. They had been married for twenty-two years and had lived happily until about two years ago when his wife began to be rather intemperate in her habits.

Miss Mary Sinico said that of late her mother had been in the habit of going out at night to buy spirits. She, witness, had often tried to reason with her mother and had induced her to join a league. She was not at home until an hour after the accident.

The jury returned a verdict in accordance with the medical evidence and exonerated Lennon from all blame.

The Deputy Coroner said it was a most painful case, and expressed great sympathy with Captain Sinico and his daughter. He urged on the railway company to take strong measures to prevent the possibility of similar accidents in the future. No blame attached to anyone.

Mr Duffy raised his eyes from the paper and gazed out of his window on the cheerless evening landscape. The river lay quiet beside the empty distillery and from time to time a light appeared in some house on the Lucan road. What an end! The whole narrative of her death revolted him and it revolted him to think that he had ever spoken to her of what he held sacred. The threadbare phrases, the inane expressions of sympathy, the cautious words of a reporter won over to conceal the details of a commonplace vulgar death attacked his stomach. Not merely had she degraded herself; she had degraded him. He saw the squalid tract of her vice, miserable and malodorous. His soul's companion! He thought of the hobbling wretches whom he had seen carrying cans and bottles to be filled by the barman. Just God, what an end! Evidently she had been unfit to live, without any strength of purpose, an easy prey to habits, one of the wrecks on which civilisation has been reared. But that she could have sunk so low! Was it possible he had deceived himself so utterly about her? He remembered her outburst of that night and interpreted it in a harsher sense than he had ever done. He had no difficulty now in approving of the course he had taken.

As the light failed and his memory began to wander he thought her hand touched his. The shock which had first attacked his stomach was now attacking his nerves. He put on his overcoat and hat quickly and went out. The cold air met him on the threshold; it crept into the sleeves of his coat. When he came to the public-house at Chapelizod Bridge he went in and ordered a hot punch.

The proprietor served him obsequiously but did not venture to talk. There were five or six working-men in the shop discussing the value of a gentleman's estate in County Kildare. They drank at intervals from their huge pint tumblers and smoked, spitting often on the floor and sometimes dragging the sawdust over their spits with their heavy boots. Mr Duffy sat on his stool and gazed at them, without seeing or hearing them. After a while they went out and he called for another punch. He sat a long time over it. The shop was very quiet. The proprietor sprawled on the counter reading the *Herald* and yawning. Now and again a tram was heard swishing along the lonely road outside.

As he sat there, living over his life with her and evoking alternately the two images in which he now conceived her, he realised that she was dead, that she had ceased to exist, that she had become a memory. He began to feel ill at ease. He asked himself what else could he have done. He could not have carried on a comedy of deception with her; he could not have lived with her openly. He had done what seemed to him best. How was he to blame? Now that she was gone he understood how lonely her life must have been, sitting night after night alone in that room. His life would be lonely too until he, too, died, ceased to exist, became a memory—if anyone remembered him.

It was after nine o'clock when he left the shop. The night was cold and gloomy. He entered the Park by the first gate and walked along under the gaunt trees. He walked through the bleak alleys where they had walked four years before. She seemed to be near him in the darkness. At moments he seemed to feel her voice touch his ear, her hand touch his. He stood still to listen. Why had he withheld life from her? Why had he sentenced her to death? He felt his moral nature falling to pieces.

When he gained the crest of the Magazine Hill he halted and looked along the river towards Dublin, the lights of which burned redly and hospitably in the cold night. He looked down the slope and, at the base, in the shadow of the wall of the Park, he saw some human figures lying. Those venal and furtive loves filled him with despair. He gnawed the rectitude of his life; he felt that he had been outcast from life's feast. One human being had seemed to love him and he had denied her life and happiness: he had sentenced her to ignominy, a death of shame. He knew that the prostrate creatures down by the wall were watching him and wished him gone. No one wanted him; he was outcast from life's feast. He turned his eyes to the grey gleaming river, winding along towards Dublin. Beyond the river he saw a goods train winding out of Kingsbridge Station, like a worm with a fiery head winding through the darkness, obstinately and laboriously. It passed slowly out of sight; but still he heard in his ears the laborious drone of the engine reiterating the syllables of her name.

He turned back the way he had come, the rhythm of the engine pounding in his ears. He began to doubt the reality of what memory told him. He halted under a tree and allowed the rhythm to die away. He could not feel her near him in the darkness nor her voice touch his ear. He waited for some minutes listening. He could hear nothing: the night was perfectly silent. He listened again: perfectly silent. He felt that he was alone.

1914

Franz Kafka

Brief Biography

- Born in Prague in 1883, the only surviving son of German-speaking Jewish parents.
- His often dry tone derives from a day job as insurance officer writing reports on industrial accidents; writes fiction at night.
- Obsessed with diet fads, hygiene, and swimming.
- Twice leaves his bride at the altar and finally ends their engagement.
- With seven slim books, is considered a promising avant-garde writer in his lifetime.
- Dies of tuberculosis in 1924.

Despite lifelong feelings of inadequacy, Franz Kafka, like James Joyce, is a key figure in modernism. The Kafkas were a middle-class Jewish family surrounded by German Protestants. But unlike the young Joyce, conventional religion did not play a major role in Kafka's youth. Rather, the family devotions revolved around his father, a large and tyrannical presence. 'From your armchair you ruled the world,' Kafka wrote in his undelivered sixty-page 'Letter to His Father' (1919). 'You were capable . . . of running down the Czechs, and then the Germans, and then the Jews . . . and finally nobody was left except yourself.' This long, confessional letter foretells the authority figures in his fiction.

Kafka's frustrations and self-doubts also resulted from his failure to form significant relationships with women. Though he frequented brothels (and like Joyce was fascinated by pornography), he was repulsed by sex and afraid of the intimacy of marriage. His neurotic relationships with the meaningful women in his life were sustained by hundreds of letters. He also may have had an obsessive-compulsive disorder. He lived at home for most of his life and developed tuberculosis in 1917, forcing him to retire from his job.

Kafka published only a few stories in his lifetime, including 'The Metamorphosis,' a novella about a man who wakes up as a giant beetle and tries to treat the situation as a minor inconvenience. The transformation in the story can be read metaphorically as the father–son struggle in his own life. Kafka's flat, lucid prose, completely at odds with the fantastic or emotionally charged situation, became his trademark style. The word 'Kafkaesque' has entered the language, suggesting the nightmarish, distorted world his characters (often simply named K) inhabit. In a famous remark to his friend Max Brod, he said, 'A book must be the axe for the frozen sea within us.' Brod ignored Kafka's deathbed request to destroy all of his unpublished manuscripts; instead, he edited them and published three unfinished novels (*The Trial*, 1925; *The Castle*, 1926; and *Amerika*, 1927) as well as many other stories.

After World War II, several commentators saw in Kafka's fiction a foreshadowing of the modern totalitarian state and dehumanized bureaucracies. Common scholarly approaches include Freudian and existential readings, while others explore Kafka's relation to Jewish folklore, popular culture, or the modernist city. American poet W.H. Auden said that '[Kafka's] predicament is the predicament of modern man'; other groups—absurdists, surrealists, and magic realists—have seen him as a kindred spirit or literary forebear. Haruki Murakami entitled one of his novels *Kafka on the Shore* as a tribute.

'A Report to an Academy,' published during Kafka's life, has been treated as an allegory of the Jewish-European assimilation experience; however, Kafka rejected this as he did all 'definitive' readings of his works. A blend of pathos and satire, the story owes something to Part IV of Jonathan Swift's *Gulliver's Travels*. According to Kafka authority Walter Sokel, his genius lies in his remarkable use of metaphors—many of isolation or the difficulty of communication—to suggest possible meaning and to fuse the world of his fiction to the external world.

A Report to an Academy

Honored members of the Academy!

You have done me the honor of inviting me to give your Academy an account of the life I formerly led as an ape.

I regret that I cannot comply with your request to the extent you desire. It is now nearly five years since I was an ape, a short space of time, perhaps, according to the calendar, but an infinitely long time to gallop through at full speed, as I have done, more or less accompanied by excellent mentors, good advice, applause, and orchestral music, and yet essentially alone, since all my escorters, to keep the image, kept well off the course. I could never have achieved what I have done had I been stubbornly set on clinging to my origins, to the remembrances of my youth. In fact, to give up being stubborn was the supreme commandment I laid upon myself; free ape as I was, I submitted myself to that yoke. In revenge, however, my memory of the past has closed the door against me more and more. I could have returned at first, had human beings allowed it, through an archway as wide as the span of heaven over the earth, but as I spurred myself on in my forced career, the opening narrowed and shrank behind me; I felt more comfortable in the world of men and fitted it better; the strong wind that blew after me out of my past began to slacken; today it is only a gentle puff of air that plays around my heels; and the opening in the distance, through which it comes and through which I once came myself, has grown so small that, even if my strength and my willpower sufficed to get me back to it, I should have to scrape the very skin from my body to crawl through. To put it plainly, much as I like expressing myself in images, to put it plainly: your life as apes, gentlemen, insofar as something of that kind lies behind you, cannot be farther removed from you than mine is from me. Yet everyone on earth feels a tickling at the heels; the small chimpanzee and the great Achilles alike.

But to a lesser extent I can perhaps meet your demand, and indeed I do so with the greatest pleasure. The first thing I learned was to give a handshake; a handshake betokens frankness; well, today now that I stand at the very peak of my career, I hope to add frankness in words to the frankness of that first handshake. What I have to tell the Academy will contribute nothing essentially new, and will fall far behind what you have asked of me and what with the best will in the world I cannot communicate—nonetheless, it should indicate the line an erstwhile ape has had to follow in entering and establishing himself in the world of men. Yet I could not risk putting into words even such insignificant information as I am going to give you if I were not quite sure of myself and if my position on all the great variety stages of the civilized world had not become quite unassailable.

I belong to the Gold Coast. For the story of my capture I must depend on the evidence of others. A hunting expedition sent out by the firm of Hagenbeck— by the way, I have drunk many a bottle of good red wine since then with the leader of that expedition—had taken up its position in the bushes by the shore when I came down for a drink at evening among a troop of apes. They shot at us; I was the only one that was hit; I was hit in two places.

Once in the cheek; a slight wound; but it left a large, naked, red scar which earned me the name of Red Peter, a horrible name, utterly inappropriate, which only some ape could have thought of, as if the only difference between me and the performing ape Peter, who died not so long ago and had some small local reputation, were the red mark on my cheek. This by the way.

The second shot hit me below the hip. It was a severe wound, it is the cause of my limping a little to this day. I read an article recently by one of the ten thousand windbags who vent themselves concerning me in the newspapers, saying: my ape nature is not yet quite under control; the proof being that when visitors come to see me, I have a predilection for taking down my trousers to show them where the shot went in. The hand which wrote that should have its fingers shot away one by one. As for me, I can take my trousers down before anyone if I like; you would find nothing but a well-groomed fur and the scar made—let me be particular in the choice of a word for this particular purpose, to avoid misunderstanding—the scar made by a wanton shot. Everything is open and aboveboard; there is nothing to conceal; when the plain truth is in question, great minds discard the niceties of refinement. But if the writer of the article were to take down his trousers before a visitor, that would be quite another story, and I will let it stand to his credit that he does not do it. In return, let him leave me alone with his delicacy!

After these two shots I came to myself—and this is where my own memories gradually begin—between decks in the Hagenbeck steamer, inside a cage. It was not a four-sided barred cage; it was only a three-sided cage nailed to a locker; the locker made the fourth side of it. The whole construction was too low for me to stand up in and too narrow to sit down in. So I had to squat with my knees bent and trembling all the time, and also, since probably for a time I wished to see no one, and to stay in the dark, my face was turned toward the locker while the bars of the cage cut into my flesh behind. Such a method of confining wild beasts is supposed to have its advantages during the first days of captivity, and out of my own experiences I cannot deny that from the human point of view this is really the case.

But that did not occur to me then. For the first time in my life I could see no way out; at least no direct way out; directly in front of me was the locker, board fitted close to board. True, there was a gap running right through the boards which I greeted with the blissful howl of ignorance when I first discovered it, but the hole was not even wide enough to stick one's tail through and not all the strength of an ape could enlarge it.

I am supposed to have made uncommonly little noise, as I was later informed, from which the conclusion was drawn that I would either soon die or if I managed to survive the first critical period would be very amenable to training. I did survive this period. Hopelessly sobbing, painfully hunting for fleas, apathetically licking a coconut, beating my skull against the locker, sticking out my tongue at anyone who came near me—that was how I filled in time at first in my new life. But over and above it all only the one feeling: no way out. Of course what I felt then as an ape I can represent now only in human terms, and therefore I misrepresent it, but although I cannot reach back to the truth of the old ape life, there is no doubt that it lies somewhere in the direction I have indicated.

Until then I had had so many ways out of everything, and now I had none. I was pinned down. Had I been nailed down, my right to free movement would not have been lessened. Why so? Scratch your flesh raw between your toes, but you won't find the answer. Press yourself against the bar behind you till it nearly cuts you in two, you won't find the answer. I had no way out but I had to devise one, for without it I could not live. All the time facing that locker—I should certainly have perished. Yet as far as Hagenbeck was concerned, the place for apes was in front of a locker—well then, I had to stop being an ape. A fine, clear train of thought, which I must have constructed somehow with my belly, since apes think with their bellies.

I fear that perhaps you do not quite understand what I mean by 'way out.' I use the expression in its fullest and most popular sense—I deliberately do not use the word 'freedom.' I do not mean the spacious feeling of freedom on all sides. As an ape, perhaps, I knew that, and I have met men who yearn for it. But for my part I desired such freedom neither then nor now. In passing: may I say that all too often men are betrayed by the word freedom. And as freedom is counted among the most sublime feelings, so the corresponding disillusionment can be also sublime. In variety theaters I have often watched, before my turn came on, a couple of acrobats performing on trapezes high in the roof. They swung themselves, they rocked to and fro, they sprang into the air, they floated into each other's arms, one hung by the hair from the teeth of the other. 'And that too is human freedom,' I thought, 'self-controlled movement.' What a mockery of holy Mother Nature! Were the apes to see such a spectacle, no theater walls could stand the shock of their laughter.

No, freedom was not what I wanted. Only a way out; right or left, or in any direction; I made no other demand; even should the way out prove to be an illusion; the demand was a small one, the disappointment could be no bigger. To get out somewhere, to get out! Only not to stay motionless with raised arms, crushed against a wooden wall.

Today I can see it clearly; without the most profound inward calm I could never have found my way out. And indeed perhaps I owe all that I have become to the calm that settled within me after my first few days in the ship. And again for that calmness it was the ship's crew I had to thank.

They were good creatures, in spite of everything. I find it still pleasant to remember the sound of their heavy footfalls which used to echo through my half-dreaming head. They had a habit of doing everything as slowly as possible. If one of them wanted to rub his eyes, he lifted a hand as if it were a drooping weight. Their jests were coarse, but hearty. Their laughter had always a gruff bark in it that sounded dangerous but meant nothing. They always had something in their mouths to spit out and did not care where they spat it. They always grumbled that they got fleas from me; yet they were not seriously angry about it, they knew that my fur fostered fleas, and that fleas jump; it was a simple matter of fact to them. When they were off duty some of them often used to sit down in a semicircle around me; they hardly spoke but only grunted to each other; smoked their pipes, stretched out on lockers; smacked their knees as soon as I made one slightest movement; and now and then one of them would take a stick and tickle me where I liked being tickled. If I were to be invited today to take a cruise on that ship I should certainly refuse the invitation, but just as certainly the memories I could recall between its decks would not all be hateful.

The calmness I acquired among these people kept me above all from trying to escape. As I look back now, it seems to me I must have had at least an inkling that I had to find a way out or die, but that my way out could not be reached through flight. I cannot tell now whether escape was possible, but I believe it must have been; for an ape it must always be possible. With my teeth as they are today I have to be careful even in simply cracking nuts, but at that time I could certainly have managed by degrees to bite through the lock of my cage. I did not do it. What good would it have done me? As soon as I had poked out my head I should have been caught again and put in a worse cage; or I might have slipped among the other animals without being noticed, among the pythons, say, who were opposite me, and so breathed out my life in their embrace; or supposing I had actually succeeded in sneaking out as far as the deck and leaping overboard I should have rocked for a little on the deep sea and then been drowned. Desperate remedies. I did not think it out in this human way, but under the influence of my surroundings I acted as if I had thought it out.

I did not think things out; but I observed everything quietly. I watched these men go to and fro, always the same faces, the same movements, often it seemed to me there was only the same man. So this man or these men walked about unimpeded. A lofty goal faintly dawned before me. No one promised me that if I became like them the bars of my cage would be taken away. Such promises for apparently impossible contingencies are not given. But if one achieves the impossible, the promises appear later retrospectively precisely where one had looked in vain for them before. Now, these men in themselves had no great attraction for me. Had I been devoted to the aforementioned idea of freedom, I should certainly have preferred the deep sea to the way out that suggested itself in the heavy faces of these men. At any rate, I watched them for a long time before I even thought of such things, indeed, it was only the mass weight of my observations that impelled me in the right direction.

It was so easy to imitate these people. I learned to spit in the very first days. We used to spit in each other's faces; the only difference was that I licked my face clean afterwards and they did not. I could soon smoke a pipe like an old hand; and if I also pressed my thumb into the bowl of the pipe, a roar of appreciation went up between decks; only it took me a very long time to understand the difference between a full pipe and an empty one.

My worst trouble came from the schnapps bottle. The smell of it revolted me; I forced myself to it as best I could; but it took weeks for me to master my repulsion. This inward conflict, strangely enough, was taken more seriously by the crew than anything else about me. I cannot distinguish the men from each other in my recollection, but there was one of them who came again and again, alone or with friends, by day, by night, at all kinds of hours; he would post himself before me with the bottle and give me instructions. He could not understand me, he wanted to solve the enigma of my being. He would slowly uncork the bottle and then look at me to see if I had followed him; I admit that I always watched him with wildly eager, too eager attention; such a student of humankind no human teacher ever found on earth. After the bottle was uncorked he lifted it to his mouth; I followed it with my eyes right up to his jaws; he would nod, pleased with me, and set the bottle to his lips; I, enchanted with my gradual enlightenment, squealed and scratched myself comprehensively wherever scratching was called for; he rejoiced, tilted the bottle, and took a drink; I, impatient and desperate to emulate him, befouled myself in my cage, which again gave him great satisfaction; and then, holding the bottle at arm's length and bringing it up with a swing, he would empty it at one draught, leaning back at an exaggerated angle for my better instruction. I, exhausted by too much effort, could follow him no farther and hung limply to the bars, while he ended his theoretical exposition by rubbing his belly and grinning.

After theory came practice. Was I not already quite exhausted by my theoretical instruction? Indeed I was; utterly exhausted. That was part of my destiny. And yet I would take hold of the proffered bottle as well as I was able; uncork it, trembling; this successful action would gradually inspire me with new energy; I would lift the bottle, already following my original model almost exactly; put it to my lips and—and then throw it down in disgust, utter disgust, although it was empty and filled only with the smell of the spirit, throw it down on the floor in disgust. To the sorrow of my teacher, to the greater sorrow of myself; neither of us being really comforted by the fact that I did not forget, even though I had thrown away the bottle, to rub my belly most admirably and to grin.

Far too often my lesson ended in that way. And to the credit of my teacher, he was not angry; sometimes indeed he would hold his burning pipe against my fur, until it began to smolder in some place I could not easily reach, but then he would himself extinguish it with his own kind, enormous hand; he was not angry with me, he perceived that we were both fighting on the same side against the nature of apes and that I had the more difficult task.

What a triumph it was then both for him and for me, when one evening before a large circle of spectators—perhaps there was a celebration of some kind, a gramophone was playing, an officer was circulating among the crew—when on this evening, just as no one was looking, I took hold of a schnapps bottle that had been carelessly left standing before my cage, uncorked it in the best style, while the company began to watch me with mounting attention, set it to my lips without hesitation, with no grimace, like a professional drinker, with rolling eyes and full throat, actually and truly drank it empty; then threw the bottle away, not this time in despair but as an artistic performer; forgot, indeed, to rub my belly; but instead of that, because I could not help it, because my senses were reeling, called a brief and unmistakable 'Hallo!' breaking into human speech, and with this outburst broke into the human community, and felt its echo: 'Listen, he's talking!' like a caress over the whole of my sweat-drenched body.

I repeat: there was no attraction for me in imitating human beings; I imitated them because I needed a way out, and for no other reason. And even that triumph of mine did not achieve much. I lost my human voice again at once; it did not come back for months; my aversion for the schnapps bottle returned again with even greater force. But the line I was to follow had in any case been decided, once for all.

When I was handed over to my first trainer in Hamburg I soon realized that there were two alternatives before me: the Zoological Gardens or the variety stage. I did not hesitate. I said to myself: do your utmost to get onto the variety stage; the Zoological Gardens means only a new cage; once there, you are done for.

And so I learned things, gentlemen. Ah, one learns when one has to; one learns when one needs a way out; one learns at all costs. One stands over oneself with a whip; one flays oneself at the slightest opposition. My ape nature fled out of me, head over heels and away, so that my first teacher was almost himself turned into an ape by it, had soon to give up teaching and was taken away to a mental hospital. Fortunately he was soon let out again.

But I used up many teachers, indeed, several teachers at once. As I became more confident of my abilities, as the public took an interest in my progress and my future began to look bright, I engaged teachers for myself, established them in five communicating rooms, and took lessons from them all at once by dint of leaping from one room to the other.

That progress of mine! How the rays of knowledge penetrated from all sides into my awakening brain! I do not deny it: I found it exhilarating. But I must also confess: I did not overestimate it, not even then, much less now. With an effort which up till now has never been repeated I managed to reach the cultural level of an average European. In itself that might be nothing to speak of, but it is something insofar as it has helped me out of my cage and opened a special way out for me, the way of humanity. There is an excellent idiom: to fight one's way through the thick of things; that is what I have done, I have fought through the thick of things. There was nothing else for me to do, provided always that freedom was not to be my choice.

As I look back over my development and survey what I have achieved so far, I do not complain, but I am not complacent either. With my hands in my trouser pockets, my bottle of wine on the table, I half lie and half sit in my rocking chair and gaze out of the window: if a visitor arrives, I receive him with propriety. My manager sits in the anteroom; when I ring, he comes and listens to what I have to say. Nearly every evening I give a performance, and I have a success that could hardly be increased. When I come home late at night from banquets, from scientific receptions, from social gatherings, there sits waiting for me a half-trained little chimpanzee and I take comfort from her as apes do. By day I cannot bear to see her; for she has the insane look of the bewildered half-broken animal in her eye; no one else sees it, but I do, and I cannot bear it.

On the whole, at any rate, I have achieved what I set out to achieve. But do not tell me that it was not worth the trouble. In any case, I am not appealing for any man's verdict, I am only imparting knowledge, I am only making a report. To you also, honored Members of the Academy, I have only made a report.

1919   Translated by Willa and Edwin Muir

J. G. Sime

Brief Biography

- Born in Scotland in 1868.
- A Canadian modernist, is inspired partly by playwright and family acquaintance George Bernard Shaw, and becomes intrigued by 'New Woman' debate.
- Moves to Montreal in 1907.
- In 1916 publishes a housekeeping guide for single working women.
- Publishes *Sister Woman* in 1919, which puzzles reviewers and sells poorly.
- Dies in Great Britain in 1958.

As an Anglo-Scottish immigrant, Jessie Georgina Sime was ideally positioned to observe and write about the changing world she saw around her when she arrived in Montreal in 1907. Instead of the pioneers or farmers traditionally depicted in Canadian fiction of the Edwardian era, she observed the immigrants and workers of urban Canada. Twelve years later, she published some of these observations in *Sister Woman*, stories about working women—clerks, secretaries, seamstresses, factory and domestic workers, and even prostitutes—forging lives of tenuous independence in an increasingly urbanized and industrialized society. Remarkably prescient, she even suggested that the telephone does not necessarily make communications easier.

Both of Sime's parents were writers, and she was raised among books and educated at a woman's college in London; she briefly studied singing in Berlin. While working as a receptionist for an Edinburgh gynaecologist, Sime met Walter Chipman, a Canadian medical student. She continued this association after she immigrated to Canada, forming a lifelong relationship as his mistress, which she described as 'an irregular union' because she supported herself. As Chipman was, by this time, an established obstetrician-gynaecologist and had married into a wealthy Montreal family, the relationship could not be openly acknowledged. According to Sandra Campbell, Sime's romantic experiences fostered sympathy for her displaced female characters, whose 'double' lives she portrayed with candour and empathy. Phyllis Redmayne, in 'An Irregular Union,' is one of several characters in

Sister Woman forced into duplicity and compromise due to the hypocritical standards applied to women during the second decade of the twentieth century.

In spite of Sime's emotional marginalization and immigrant experience, she entered into the intellectual life of Montreal, then Canada's largest city. Like American writer Charlotte Perkins Gilman, Sime lectured and wrote criticism. She was also active in several literary organizations. She returned to Great Britain after World War II, dying before she could witness the social revolution of the 1960s and 1970s that raised many of the gender and socialization issues that she had addressed prophetically in her fiction.

The twenty-eight stories in *Sister Woman* are not only remarkable for their urban realism but also notable for their form, the short story cycle, which would be perfected by later story writers such as Alice Munro, Margaret Laurence, and many others. The stories are framed by a brief Prologue and briefer Epilogue in which a female writer and an insensitive male listener discuss what 'women want'; the stories themselves proffer an answer to the question. The man's somewhat dismissive 'That's all you have to say' in the Epilogue seeks to inscribe the 'woman question' as 'simple,' provoking the woman's response: 'Why, I'm not even started yet.'

Many of the stories, such as 'An Irregular Union,' centre on male–female relations, juxtaposing the price of self-actualized independence against the emotional costs of adhering to restrictive social and sexual codes. Like those of fellow Montrealer Mavis Gallant two decades later, Sime's stories, written during wartime (when women were the mainstay of the economy), even embraced the possibility of emancipation by excluding men. Yet Gerald Lynch, an authority on Canadian story cycles, argues that Sime's socialist politics and attack on the patriarchy led to decades of neglect. Collectively, the diversity and tonal subtleties of the stories in *Sister Woman* reveal that the answer to the 'woman question' is anything but simple.

An Irregular Union

Phyllis Redmayne sat in her little room that was drawing-room and dining-room and study and bedroom all in one. It was a pretty little room—pretty in spite of its not costing very much. It had its dining-table and its plain chair close up to the table, its easy-chair, its cot-bed masquerading as a couch in the day-time; it had its pillow or two covered in silk, and a vase of flowers; and, in the best light the room could give, close up by the little high window that looked out straight on the sky, it had its inevitable typewriter. Phyllis Redmayne was the ubiquitous Business Girl of our time, and she earned the money she lived on by the sweat of her brain.

But just at the moment she wasn't looking at her typewriter, or thinking of it, or working at all. She sat in her chair close up by the table and she looked at the telephone. She looked at it and she looked at it; her eyes were fixed on it, and the eyes of her mind were fixed on it too. She was just sitting there thinking of the telephone. She was longing for it to speak.

It is a bad business waiting for a letter, but it is a worse business to wait for the telephone. The telephone is there before you—it may be going to speak any minute; and minute after minute passes by and changes slowly into hour after hour—and it doesn't speak. And you sit and look and long. And when the bell goes clang at last and you take the receiver in your hand—most likely it's the wrong number or someone you don't want to speak to or some triviality or other. You just say what you have to say and hang the receiver up, and you sit there again, sick at heart, waiting.

When that has happened to you over and over again you grow, not so much accustomed to it, perhaps, as patient—passive—resigned; but that attitude of mind doesn't come all at once. You only grow like that with the years. And this was the first time Phyllis Redmayne had had to sit and watch the telephone— sick with impatience and apprehension and unable to ring up and ask what she longed to know. It was the first time she had had to sit with her heart torn with anxiety—and just wait. It is currently said that waiting comes easy to women. I wonder why that is currently said.

The thing that Phyllis Redmayne was waiting for was a telephone message to say whether the man she cared for was better or worse. He was in hospital, this man she cared for, and once every day she had a message, not from him but from his nurse—just a professional bulletin of his condition—a calm, noncommittal: 'Mr Radcliffe is rather better to-day,' or 'Mr Radcliffe has had a bad night and is not quite so well,' as the case might be. And then the telephone rang off. And Phyllis Redmayne had that much to live on till the same time to-morrow.

That isn't a very easy proposition when you are young and not used to wait—and when you care very much. And Phyllis cared—she cared very much indeed; in fact, she didn't care for very much else except for this man who lay in hospital ill and away from her. She had just one idea of happiness in life and that was to be with him, to be with him always, to take care of him and to be taken care of by him—to look after his interests—to work for him—to be close beside him all the time and help . . . and to have him there being helped, and at the same time looking after her and sheltering her and protecting her. As you see, there was nothing at all new or original about Phyllis Redmayne and her views. She was just the old traditional woman clothed in a Business Woman's garb. For all that was unexpected in her ideas, her typewriter might just as well have been a kitchen stove—or a cradle. She looked on Dick Radcliffe as Eve looked on Adam. She thought the same old things that women always have thought, though she gained her own living and imagined she was independent and free and modern and all the rest of it.

Dick was the head of the office where she worked—he was her 'bawss,' as the girls in the office called it. And she was what people call his mistress. There was nothing new in their relation—nothing whatever. It was the same old thing. He had seen her and seen that she was pretty—and she had seen him and seen that he was strong. The rest followed. What *was* a little bit new perhaps—or the way that Phyllis looked at it was new—was that though she gave herself very willingly and went on and on giving herself, she took nothing in exchange. I mean that she went on earning her own livelihood and supporting herself just as she had done before the episode—the episode was something over and above in her life, as it were, just as it was in Dick's. In plain words, she didn't take any money for the gift of herself.

It is a queer thing how a little practical fact like that can make an old episode seem new—a new thing in the history of the world; and that Phyllis Redmayne felt as she did only goes to show how this present-day life of ours is based and rooted on money. The little insignificant fact that she was able to 'keep herself,' as it is called, changed for her the whole complexion of her love episode. It gave her confidence and self-respect. She could feel with perfect accuracy that she was not a 'kept woman.' She had years of supporting herself behind her and she had every justification for feeling that in the years to come she would always be able to go on making ends meet. She could feel, in one word, independent—and it is extraordinary how deep into a woman's soul that desire for independence goes, when once she has had a taste of it. If Phyllis Redmayne had been Phyllis Radcliffe I doubt not at all that she would have felt quite differently. The fact of being a wife, of sharing house and home, bed and board, changes the most independent woman's point of view. She feels then that she can go shares with a good conscience—the children that are in the back of every woman's mind, children who will bear their father's name when they come, make that all right. But in the relation that Phyllis Redmayne bore to Dick Radcliffe—it is different. There is a sensitiveness—a lack of security perhaps—on the woman's side. She isn't a wife, and however much she may protest that she doesn't want to be, there are moments when she almost certainly does want it very much; and then, besides that—well, besides that, there is the tradition of centuries past and gone to fight against; there are all those thousands—millions—of women who *have* been 'kept women'—mistresses and women who have borne harder and more contemptuous names than that . . . they have to be taken into consideration. And a Business Woman, a modern Business Woman, working for herself, quiet and decent in her life, independent, doesn't want to be mixed up with things like that. No, she doesn't—she doesn't. She feels herself different and she *is*: different. Why, Phyllis Redmayne would hardly take even a present—the most she would accept were little valueless things at the rarest intervals. Though she wouldn't allow it even to herself, this uncertainty of her relation to Dick Radcliffe got on her nerves at times.

Just at times. She was at the period of loving him so much that nothing else seemed to matter. And when life was going on its normal lines, nothing *did* matter except that she could see him day after day—work with him—help him with that active, trained brain of hers; and see him sometimes too in the little home she had got together with her own money—her very own earnings. There was something rare and wonderful in having a little home where she could welcome him as her treasured guest. It was something that nearly made up—that sometimes far more than made up—for their not living and sharing a home together.

When things were going normally Phyllis dwelt entirely and always on the good side of their relation. She looked consistently on what is called the 'bright side.' She hardly admitted to herself that the shield had a reverse that wasn't quite so bright. Remember she was young. And their relation to one another was young too. The fear of the possible child, of Dick's tiring of her, the possibility of his caring for some other woman as well as for her, the dread of detection—of sickness . . . of all these possibilities none had pressed on her yet. She simply basked in love. Dick manifestly did care for her and she—she cared for nothing in the whole world but him; the world, indeed, hardly seemed to her to exist at all, except just as it revolved round Dick Radcliffe as its axis. There was joy in going to the office—there was infinite joy in the knowledge that she was useful . . . and she knew that she was: and there was joy unspeakable in welcoming him home sometimes—making him free of her little domain—spreading it out for his acceptance—preparing little fêtes for him. What was there in the world to worry about or to regret? Nothing.

And now Dick was ill. He wasn't ill so that he was going to die. No—not ill like that at all. But he was ill, and pretty sick too, laid low, suffering—and she wasn't able to be beside him and take care of him. He was in hospital, as the New World way is, and he had a special nurse, two special nurses, in fact—one for the day and another for the night—and she, Phyllis, who would have given ten years of her life to be near him, was shut out, shut out absolutely, not even able to take the receiver off the telephone and call up and ask how he was.

It was while Phyllis sat at the table with her eyes on the telephone that the first doubt of her way of life entered into her mind. She had thought—thought sometimes a little defiantly perhaps—that theirs was the better way of life. Such a union could never grow 'stuffy,' she would say to herself—she had read Edward Carpenter, and she borrowed the word from him. She had dwelt on all the advantages of their union. Dick was free. She was free. Nothing bound them together but their love, and if that were to fail they were free to part. But away back in—well, in her heart, I suppose it was—she said to herself at the same time that nothing could ever make them *want* to part. They were one and they would stay one. Sometimes she would tell Dick how free he was, impress it on him: 'If ever you choose another woman, if you grow tired of me,' she would say to him, 'you are free. You're absolutely quite free, Dick. I sha'n't say a thing.' But even as she said these things, and she honestly thought she said them sincerely, something within her said: 'He never will want another woman. Why should he? Aren't you his friend as well as everything else? Can't you satisfy his brain as well as his heart—why should he *want* to part from you . . .?'

She had been very happy for those last three years. Yes, she had been happy. Hardly a doubt had assailed her about anything. She had just taken the moment as it passed, enjoyed it, made the most of it, caressed it almost sometimes—and then taken the next moment as it came along. She was happy in her work—happy, perhaps, rather in her usefulness to Dick—and she was happy in her little home. She was young enough and strong enough to be able to cope with her double work, the working of her brain at the office and the working of her hands at home. But most of all she was happy because in her love for Dick she was carried wholly, utterly out of herself. She never thought of herself; she hardly knew that such a person as Phyllis Redmayne existed. For her, Dick was the Great Reality, and her whole life was her gift to him. I have said that, in spite of her brain and her modernity, she was just the old, old thing.

But now as she sat with her eyes fixed on the telephone the first doubt assailed her. She took on that road her first step—that costs. She sat there longing with all her soul to know about the man she loved; and she couldn't know. She just had to sit and wait. Twenty-four hours had passed since she heard last. Of all those hours she had merely slept uneasily two or three; all the rest she had spent—longing is a weak word for it. She had yearned and craved to know how he was. She would have prayed if she had had the least idea that she would get an answer. She thought of telepathy and she felt it was a fraud—she longed to project her spirit and it wouldn't go. There was nothing for it but to wait, harrowed and devoured by anxiety. He wasn't going to die—she said that over and over to herself; but for all that he was ill—suffering—and she wasn't beside him. Phyllis Redmayne felt it wasn't fair.

Yes, that was how she felt. She said to herself as she sat there that there was nothing wrong in what she craved. She didn't want to worry him, to bother him, to show him love at the wrong time. She merely wanted to be beside him, to tend him, to read his slightest gesture so as to be of use—*that* was what she wanted, just to be of use. And when she thought of the nurses being with him, giving him intimate care, touching him, raising him, looking after him in the sleepless watches of the night—when she thought of this and visualised it, her hands clenched under the table and she felt the hot tears rising to her eyes. That was *her* place—it was her place to be with him. It was her privilege to lose her sleep so that she might soothe him. It was her right—yes, it was her right to tire herself, to wear her body out, if need be, that he might have one moment's rest and peace. Why should he be given over to indifferent paid nurses when she, *she* would give anything, anything in the world, just to be allowed to tend him?

What she felt to be the injustice of the world came on Phyllis Redmayne all of a sudden as she sat in her little room. It was growing late. The sun was away past her window now, and that meant that it would soon be evening. Why were they so late in ringing her up to-night? Was it possible that they had forgotten her—if so, was she to sit there another twenty-four hours waiting? Or was it possible—was it possible that he—that something had happened . . . her hand went out towards the receiver. Could it be—oh, could it be, that the doctors were wrong, that he was seriously ill, that he might—*die*? Phyllis Redmayne felt her heart leap—and then she felt a sickness—she felt grey. . . .

After all, it wasn't as if she was asking anything *wrong*. She only wanted to know—and she mightn't ring up and ask. Suddenly the secrecy of the thing struck her as horrible—hateful. She felt that she loathed it—she wanted to go up to the hospital openly and boldly, just as she was, and demand that she should be let in to nurse her—Her what? If she went up to the hospital and demanded to be allowed in to nurse her lover it wouldn't advance her cause much.

It began to dawn on her dimly, the mess she was in. There was nothing wrong in the relation itself—that she would swear. No wife that ever was could look on her husband with eyes more loving than those with which Phyllis Redmayne looked on Dick Radcliffe. And—she kept saying it to herself as she sat there—there was no question of money between them. There was nothing sordid in their relation. She earned her bread as she had earned it before she ever knew that a Dick Radcliffe lived in the world. She was true to him with every shred of her. She wasn't his only in her body; she *was* his in all her heart and soul. She was devoted to him. She—she adored him. The only thing that was wrong about it all was that she had to keep it a secret, and to keep it an effectual secret she had to tell lies. She had to act lies too. Her life was more or less a lie—but that was all anyone could bring against her. And she wasn't lying for any advantage of her own . . . it was just to keep the bare bread and butter coming in that she had to lie. She felt that she was justified—yes, she felt that down to the nethermost depths of her soul. And at the same time she knew that the world would not call her justified, and dimly, reluctantly, almost against her better judgment, she felt that the world had something on its side. There was no harm in her loving him. There could be no harm just in her wanting to be beside him now that he was sick. In longing to be of use to the man she loved, was she not proving herself to be a woman? Yet she couldn't go to him—he would be furious with her if she went and gave him away; and the world, the little bit of it with which she came into daily contact, would never forgive her if she were to give it away. There would be no one to stick up for her at all—not one person that she knew could be made to understand that she, Dick Radcliffe's mistress, had kept her self-respect, that she was an independent creature—she detested the word mistress, and she didn't feel that it applied to her . . . and yet she knew that it *did* apply to her and that her poor, pitiful little plea about earning her own livelihood and keeping herself decently wouldn't have any weight with anyone at all anywhere. As she sat there gazing at the telephone she felt like Athanasius against the world—and the world looked big and heavy.

What if he were ill—seriously ill? What then? How long was she supposed to go on sitting there just waiting for a message? If they went on forgetting her might there not come a time when she would be justified in going and—not demanding at all—just asking—pleading—begging for some scrap of news? Would it be possible that they would shut her out if he—if he—was *dying*? . . .

Suddenly the telephone cried and clanged. It was speaking. Phyllis Redmayne gave a great start and she took the receiver in her hand, and in a vague, uncertain way she was astounded to feel that her hand was shaking so that it would hardly hold the receiver in its fingers. She put the other hand up to steady it; she pressed the receiver to her ear. 'Yes,' she said. And then she repeated it. 'Yes, hello!' she said again. She hardly knew that dim, unsteady voice. 'Mr Radcliffe a-asks me to 'phone you up and say he's feeling some better to-night. He guesses he'll sit up to-morrow for a spell . . .' That was the message. Phyllis Redmayne's heart gave a great leap—it leaped up nearly into her mouth, and when she tried to speak she could hardly get the words out for breathlessness. 'Is his temperature normal to-night? Is he tired?' The questions poured out as water gushes out of the neck of a bottle when the cork is removed. 'How did he sleep last night? Do you think he seems like sleeping now? Is he eating? Can he talk? Is he able to—?'

Phyllis Redmayne hung the receiver up. Everything that she had thought and feared as she sat waiting dropped again out of sight, out of touch, out of thought. Dick was better! He wasn't so very, very ill. He wouldn't die—what nonsense! The doctors were right, of course, he wasn't in any danger of dying, not even thinking of it. And as this certainty flooded Phyllis Redmayne's being, nothing else in the world seemed to matter. She was carried out of herself once more. Love spread its broad, strong wings and lifted her up—lifted her up above herself—above what the world might think or mightn't think. As she sat there looking at the telephone that had brought her the good news her heart seemed to swell in love and gratitude. She felt happy. She felt blessed. What if she couldn't be beside him? Wasn't he being taken care of and looked after so that he would be given back to her well and strong again? She felt that she had far, far more than she deserved. Mistress seemed to her the loveliest word in the language. Oh yes, she was Dick's mistress, and soon he would be well and able to come to her. She glanced round her little room, wondering how she could beautify it for his coming. There passed rapidly, tenderly through her mind the little meal she would give him to eat. She would welcome him soon—see him sitting there again—watch him eat. She would be able to see with her own eyes what havoc sickness had wrought in him—she would be able to touch and feel him—she could kiss him as he sat there and be sure that he was no spirit but dear flesh and blood.

She looked out through her little window at the early evening sky. She sat watching the lovely evening clouds going their majestic peaceful way. And suddenly—no one could be more surprised than she herself—she laid her head down on her two outstretched arms—and she sobbed and sobbed.

1919

D. H. Lawrence

Brief Biography

- Born in 1885, near Nottingham, England; son of a coal miner.
- 1908–1911 teaches school and experiences early success as a writer.
- Elopes with Frieda Weekley (née von Richthofen), who is married with three children.
- In 1913 publishes *Sons and Lovers*, an autobiographical novel.
- *The Rainbow* (1915) is banned, beginning Lawrence's long battle against censorship.
- In the 1920s travels throughout Europe, Australia, Mexico, and the United States.
- Refusing further treatment for tuberculosis, dies at home in 1930.

David Herbert Lawrence represents a controversial voice of modernism. A prolific writer in spite of many illnesses, he has been both disparaged and valorized since his death in 1930 from tuberculosis. His literary influence is narrower than James Joyce's, and feminist critics have criticized his portrayal of women. Lawrence's prose has been viewed as unwieldy—especially if set beside the spare elegance of Joyce's *Dubliners*—yet Lawrence's stylistic 'excess' is usually the result of deliberate craftsmanship: he sought to replicate the complexities of the psyche in his writing and used techniques like verbal repetition and incantatory rhythms to suggest unconscious process. Curiously, he and Joyce (the other 'banned writer') disliked each other's writings.

But Lawrence did not write fictional prose exclusively. He also published poetry, plays, travel writing, and literary criticism. His *Studies in Classic American Literature* (1923) features perceptive commentaries on nineteenth-century American writers, including Edgar Allan Poe and Herman Melville, much underrated at that time. Lawrence's letters are often mentioned among his finest achievements.

Introduced to psychoanalysis by Frieda Weekley in 1912, Lawrence (like many modernists) followed the new discipline, only to dismiss it a decade later in his proposed three-volume 'new psychologies.' His autobiographical novel, *Sons and Lovers*, describes a classic Freudian Oedipus complex drawn from Lawrence's co-dependent relationship with his mother. In a 1912 letter to his editor, Edward Garnett, he wrote about his novel: 'The son loves the mother—all the sons hate and are jealous of the father.' Lawrence later disagreed with Freud, thinking psychoanalysis 'encouraged self-centredness and fear of life and one's emotions.'

Lawrence's loss of religious faith and distrust of science led to his 'belief in the blood,' a combination of intuition and life force energies, as well as his interest in ancient culture such as Aztec blood sacrifices. His belief in mystic balance inspired his greatest novels, *The Rainbow* (1915) and *Women in Love* (1920). Mysticism is at the centre of his controversial novel, *Lady Chatterley's Lover*, but its frank language and descriptions precluded its publication in Great Britain by Penguin Books, until a landmark court case in 1960 overturned the obscenity law.

Lawrence's unconventional lifestyle and anarchical views on such subjects as bisexual eroticism made him many enemies, though he formed enduring literary friendships with Katherine Mansfield and Aldous Huxley. In 1919, he and Frieda left England (in 1917, he had been expelled from Cornwall as a possible spy; his marriage to a German who was cousin of the notorious flying ace 'Red Baron' von Richthofen caused suspicion). On a self-described 'savage pilgrimage' that would take him to many countries, he searched unsuccessfully for the stability to pursue his art.

Primal energies are always close to the surface in Lawrence's fiction, even in the early description of the female conductors of a Midlands tramline in 'Tickets, Please.' The subtle transformation from unsettling comedy to revenge story owes something to its wartime setting, a time when women began to occupy public positions and when the shortage of eligible men enabled 'impudent' young cads like John Thomas Raynor to prevail in their sexual conquests. However, to help universalize his theme, Lawrence drew on Euripedes' *The Bacchae*, a classical Greek tragedy in which a group of women take revenge on King Pentheus of Thebes, who has prohibited the worship of the fertility god Dionysius.

Tickets, Please

There is in the Midlands a single-line tramway system which boldly leaves the county town and plunges off into the black, industrial countryside, up hill and down dale, through the long ugly villages of workmen's houses, over canals and railways, past churches perched high and nobly over the smoke and shadows, through stark, grimy cold little market-places, tilting away in a rush past cinemas and shops down to the hollow where the collieries are, then up again, past a little rural church, under the ash trees, on in a rush to the terminus, the last little ugly place of industry, the cold little town that shivers on the edge of the wild, gloomy country beyond. There the green and creamy coloured tram-car seems to pause and purr with curious satisfaction. But in a few minutes—the clock on the turret of the Cooperative Wholesale Society's Shops gives the time— away it starts once more on the adventure. Again there are the reckless swoops downhill, bouncing the loops: again the chilly wait in the hill-top market-place: again the breathless slithering round the precipitous drop under the church: again the patient halts at the loops, waiting for the outcoming car: so on and on, for two long hours, till at last the city looms beyond the fat gas-works, the narrow factories draw near, we are in the sordid streets of the great town, once more we sidle to a standstill at our terminus, abashed by the great crimson and cream-coloured city cars, but still perky, jaunty, somewhat dare-devil, green as a jaunty sprig of parsley out of a black colliery garden.

To ride on these cars is always an adventure. Since we are in war-time, the drivers are men unfit for active service: cripples and hunchbacks. So they have the spirit of the devil in them. The ride becomes a steeple-chase. Hurray! we have leapt in a clear jump over the canal bridges—now for the four-lane corner. With a shriek and a trail of sparks we are clear again. To be sure, a tram often leaps the rails—but what matter! It sits in a ditch till other trams come to haul it out. It is quite common for a car, packed with one solid mass of living people, to come to a dead halt in the midst of unbroken blackness, the heart of nowhere on a dark night, and for the driver and the girl conductor to call, 'All get off— car's on fire!' Instead, however, of rushing out in a panic, the passengers stolidly reply: 'Get on—get on! We're not coming out. We're stopping where we are. Push on, George.' So till flames actually appear.

The reason for this reluctance to dismount is that the nights are howlingly cold, black, and windswept, and a car is a haven of refuge. From village to village the miners travel, for a change of cinema, of girl, of pub. The trams are desperately packed. Who is going to risk himself in the black gulf outside, to wait perhaps an hour for another tram, then to see the forlorn notice 'Depot Only,' because there is something wrong! Or to greet a unit of three bright cars all so tight with people that they sail past with a howl of derision. Trams that pass in the night.

This, the most dangerous tram-service in England, as the authorities themselves declare, with pride, is entirely conducted by girls, and driven by rash young men, a little crippled, or by delicate young men, who creep forward in terror. The girls are fearless young hussies. In their ugly blue uniform, skirts up to their knees, shapeless old peaked caps on their heads, they have all the *sang-froid* of an old non-commissioned officer. With a tram packed with howling colliers, roaring hymns downstairs and a sort of antiphony of obscenities upstairs, the lasses are perfectly at their ease. They pounce on the youths who try to evade their ticket-machine. They push off the men at the end of their distance. They are not going to be done in the eye—not they. They fear nobody— and everybody fears them.

'Hello, Annie!'

'Hello, Ted!'

'Oh, mind my corn, Miss Stone. It's my belief you've got a heart of stone, for you've trod on it again.'

'You should keep it in your pocket,' replies Miss Stone, and she goes sturdily upstairs in her high boots.

'Tickets, please.'

She is peremptory, suspicious, and ready to hit first. She can hold her own against ten thousand. The step of that tram-car is her Thermopylae.

Therefore, there is a certain wild romance aboard these cars—and in the sturdy bosom of Annie herself. The time for soft romance is in the morning, between ten o'clock and one, when things are rather slack: that is, except market-day and Saturday. Thus Annie has time to look about her. Then she often hops off her car and into a shop where she has spied something, while the driver chats in the main road. There is very good feeling between the girls and the drivers. Are they not companions in peril, shipments aboard this careering vessel of a tram-car, forever rocking on the waves of a stormy land.

Then, also, during the easy hours, the inspectors are most in evidence. For some reason, everybody employed in this tram-service is young: there are no grey heads. It would not do. Therefore the inspectors are of the right age, and one, the chief, is also good-looking. See him stand on a wet, gloomy morning, in his long oil-skin, his peaked cap well down over his eyes, waiting to board a car. His face is ruddy, his small brown moustache is weathered, he has a faint impudent smile. Fairly tall and agile, even in his waterproof, he springs aboard a car and greets Annie.

'Hello, Annie! Keeping the wet out?'

'Trying to.'

There are only two people in the car. Inspecting is soon over. Then for a long and impudent chat on the foot-board, a good, easy, twelve-mile chat.

The inspector's name is John Thomas Raynor—always called John Thomas, except sometimes, in malice, Coddy. His face sets in fury when he is addressed, from a distance, with this abbreviation. There is considerable scandal about John Thomas in half a dozen villages. He flirts with the girl conductors in the morning, and walks out with them in the dark night, when they leave their tram-car at the depot. Of course, the girls quit the service frequently. Then he flirts and walks out with the newcomer: always providing she is sufficiently attractive, and that she will consent to walk. It is remarkable, however, that most of the girls are quite comely, they are all young, and this roving life aboard the car gives them a sailor's dash and recklessness. What matter how they behave when the ship is in port. Tomorrow they will be aboard again.

Annie, however, was something of a Tartar, and her sharp tongue had kept John Thomas at arm's length for many months. Perhaps, therefore, she liked him all the more: for he always came up smiling, with impudence. She watched him vanquish one girl, then another. She could tell by the movement of his mouth and eyes, when he flirted with her in the morning, that he had been walking out with this lass, or the other, the night before. A fine cock-of-the-walk he was. She could sum him up pretty well.

In this subtle antagonism they knew each other like old friends, they were as shrewd with one another almost as man and wife. But Annie had always kept him sufficiently at arm's length. Besides, she had a boy of her own.

The Statutes fair, however, came in November, at Bestwood. It happened that Annie had the Monday night off. It was a drizzling ugly night, yet she dressed herself up and went to the fair ground. She was alone, but she expected soon to find a pal of some sort.

The roundabouts were veering round and grinding out their music, the side shows were making as much commotion as possible. In the cocoanut shies there were no cocoanuts, but artificial war-time substitutes, which the lads declared were fastened into the irons. There was a sad decline in brilliance and luxury. None the less, the ground was muddy as ever, there was the same crush, the press of faces lighted up by the flares and the electric lights, the same smell of naphtha and a few fried potatoes, and of electricity.

Who should be the first to greet Miss Annie on the showground but John Thomas. He had a black overcoat buttoned up to his chin, and a tweed cap pulled down over his brows, his face between was ruddy and smiling and handy as ever. She knew so well the way his mouth moved.

She was very glad to have a 'boy.' To be at the Statutes without a fellow was no fun. Instantly, like the gallant he was, he took her on the Dragons, grim-toothed, round-about switchbacks. It was not nearly so exciting as a tram-car actually. But, then, to be seated in a shaking, green dragon, uplifted above the sea of bubble faces, careering in a rickety fashion in the lower heavens, whilst John Thomas leaned over her, his cigarette in his mouth, was after all the right style. She was a plump, quick, alive little creature. So she was quite excited and happy.

John Thomas made her stay on for the next round. And therefore she could hardly for shame repulse him when he put his arm round her and drew her a little nearer to him, in a very warm and cuddly manner. Besides, he was fairly discreet, he kept his movement as hidden as possible. She looked down, and saw that his red, clean hand was out of sight of the crowd. And they knew each other so well. So they warmed up to the fair.

After the dragons they went on the horses. John Thomas paid each time, so she could but be complaisant. He, of course, sat astride on the outer horse— named 'Black Bess'—and she sat sideways, towards him, on the inner horse— named 'Wildfire.' But of course John Thomas was not going to sit discreetly on 'Black Bess,' holding the brass bar. Round they spun and heaved, in the light. And round he swung on his wooden steed, flinging one leg across her mount, and perilously tipping up and down, across the space, half lying back, laughing at her. He was perfectly happy; she was afraid her hat was on one side, but she was excited.

He threw quoits on a table, and won for her two large, pale-blue hat-pins. And then, hearing the noise of the cinemas, announcing another performance, they climbed the boards and went in.

Of course, during these performances pitch darkness falls from time to time, when the machine goes wrong. Then there is a wild whooping, and a loud smacking of simulated kisses. In these moments John Thomas drew Annie towards him. After all, he had a wonderfully warm, cosy way of holding a girl with his arm, he seemed to make such a nice fit. And, after all, it was pleasant to be so held: so very comforting and cosy and nice. He leaned over her and she felt his breath on her hair; she knew he wanted to kiss her on the lips. And, after all, he was so warm and she fitted in to him so softly. After all, she wanted him to touch her lips.

But the light sprang up; she also started electrically, and put her hat straight. He left his arm lying nonchalantly behind her. Well, it was fun, it was exciting to be at the Statutes with John Thomas.

When the cinema was over they went for a walk across the dark, damp fields. He had all the arts of love-making. He was especially good at holding a girl, when he sat with her on a stile in the black, drizzling darkness. He seemed to be holding her in space, against his own warmth and gratification. And his kisses were soft and slow and searching.

So Annie walked out with John Thomas, though she kept her own boy dangling in the distance. Some of the tram-girls chose to be huffy. But there, you must take things as you find them, in this life.

There was no mistake about it, Annie liked John Thomas a good deal. She felt so rich and warm in herself whenever he was near. And John Thomas really liked Annie, more than usual. The soft, melting way in which she could flow into a fellow, as if she melted into his very bones, was something rare and good. He fully appreciated this.

But with a developing acquaintance there began a developing intimacy. Annie wanted to consider him a person, a man; she wanted to take an intelligent interest in him, and to have an intelligent response. She did not want a mere nocturnal presence, which was what he was so far. And she prided herself that he could not leave her.

Here she made a mistake. John Thomas intended to remain a nocturnal presence; he had no idea of becoming an all-round individual to her. When she started to take an intelligent interest in him and his life and his character, he sheered off. He hated intelligent interest. And he knew that the only way to stop it was to avoid it. The possessive female was aroused in Annie. So he left her.

It is no use saying she was not surprised. She was at first startled, thrown out of her count. For she had been so *very* sure of holding him. For a while she was staggered, and everything became uncertain to her. Then she wept with fury, indignation, desolation, and misery. Then she had a spasm of despair. And then, when he came, still impudently, on to her car, still familiar, but letting her see by the movement of his head that he had gone away to somebody else for the time being, and was enjoying pastures new, then she determined to have her own back.

She had a very shrewd idea what girls John Thomas had taken out. She went to Nora Purdy. Nora was a tall, rather pale, but well-built girl, with beautiful yellow hair. She was rather secretive.

'Hey!' said Annie, accosting her; then softly, 'Who's John Thomas on with now?'

'I don't know,' said Nora.

'Why tha does,' said Annie, ironically lapsing into dialect. 'Tha knows as well as I do.'

'Well, I do, then,' said Nora. 'It isn't me, so don't bother.'

'It's Cissy Meakin, isn't it?'

'It is, for all I know.'

'Hasn't he got a face on him!' said Annie. 'I don't half like his cheek. I could knock him off the foot-board when he comes round at me.'

'He'll get dropped-on one of these days,' said Nora.

'Ay, he will, when somebody makes up their mind to drop it on him. I should like to see him taken down a peg or two, shouldn't you?'

'I shouldn't mind,' said Nora.

'You've got quite as much cause to as I have,' said Annie. 'But we'll drop on him one of these days, my girl. What? Don't you want to?'

'I don't mind,' said Nora.

But as a matter of fact, Nora was much more vindictive than Annie.

One by one Annie went the round of the old flames. It so happened that Cissy Meakin left the tramway service in quite a short time. Her mother made her leave. Then John Thomas was on the *qui-vive*. He cast his eyes over his old flock. And his eyes lighted on Annie. He thought she would be safe now. Besides, he liked her.

She arranged to walk home with him on Sunday night. It so happened that her car would be in the depôt at half past nine: the last car would come in at 10.15. So John Thomas was to wait for her there.

At the depôt the girls had a little waiting-room of their own. It was quite rough, but cosy, with a fire and an oven and a mirror, and table and wooden chairs. The half dozen girls who knew John Thomas only too well had arranged to take service this Sunday afternoon. So, as the cars began to come in, early, the girls dropped into the waiting-room. And instead of hurrying off home, they sat around the fire and had a cup of tea. Outside was the darkness and lawlessness of wartime.

John Thomas came on the car after Annie, at about a quarter to ten. He poked his head easily into the girls' waiting-room.

'Prayer-meeting?' he asked.

'Ay,' said Laura Sharp. 'Ladies only.'

'That's me!' said John Thomas. It was one of his favourite exclamations.

'Shut the door, boy,' said Muriel Baggaley.

'On which side of me?' said John Thomas.

'Which tha likes,' said Polly Birkin.

He had come in and closed the door behind him. The girls moved in their circle, to make a place for him near the fire. He took off his great-coat and pushed back his hat.

'Who handles the teapot?' he said.

Nora Purdy silently poured him out a cup of tea.

'Want a bit o' my bread and drippin'?' said Muriel Baggaley to him.

'Ay, give us a bit.'

And he began to eat his piece of bread.

'There's no place like home, girls,' he said.

They all looked at him as he uttered this piece of impudence. He seemed to be sunning himself in the presence of so many damsels.

'Especially if you're not afraid to go home in the dark,' said Laura Sharp.

'Me! By myself I am.'

They sat till they heard the last tram come in. In a few minutes Emma Houselay entered.

'Come on, my old duck!' cried Polly Birkin.

'It *is* perishing,' said Emma, holding her fingers to the fire.

'But—I'm afraid to, go home in, the dark,' sang Laura Sharp, the tune having got into her mind.

'Who're you going with tonight, John Thomas?' asked Muriel Baggaley, coolly.

'Tonight?' said John Thomas. 'Oh, I'm going home by myself tonight—all on my lonely-O.'

'That's me!' said Nora Purdy, using his own ejaculation.

The girls laughed shrilly.

'Me as well, Nora,' said John Thomas.

'Don't know what you mean,' said Laura.

'Yes, I'm toddling,' said he, rising and reaching for his overcoat.

'Nay,' said Polly. 'We're all here waiting for you.'

'We've got to be up in good time in the morning,' he said, in the benevolent official manner.

They all laughed.

'Nay,' said Muriel. 'Don't leave us all lonely, John Thomas. Take one!'

'I'll take the lot, if you like,' he responded gallantly.

'That you won't either,' said Muriel, 'Two's company; seven's too much of a good thing.'

'Nay—take one,' said Laura. 'Fair and square, all above board, and say which.'

'Ay,' cried Annie, speaking for the first time. 'Pick, John Thomas; let's hear thee.'

'Nay,' he said. 'I'm going home quiet tonight. Feeling good, for once.'

'Whereabouts?' said Annie. 'Take a good 'un, then. But tha's got to take one of us!'

'Nay, how can I take one,' he said, laughing uneasily. 'I don't want to make enemies.'

'You'd only make *one*,' said Annie.

'The chosen *one*,' added Laura.

'Oh, my! Who said girls!' exclaimed John Thomas, again turning, as if to escape. 'Well—good-night.'

'Nay, you've got to make your pick,' said Muriel. 'Turn your face to the wall, and say which one touches you. Go on—we shall only just touch your back— one of us. Go on—turn your face to the wall, and don't look, and say which one touches you.'

He was uneasy, mistrusting them. Yet he had not the courage to break away. They pushed him to a wall and stood him there with his face to it. Behind his back they all grimaced, tittering. He looked so comical. He looked around uneasily.

'Go on!' he cried.

'You're looking—you're looking!' they shouted.

He turned his head away. And suddenly, with a movement like a swift cat, Annie went forward and fetched him a box on the side of the head that sent his cap flying and himself staggering. He started round.

But at Annie's signal they all flew at him, slapping him, pinching him, pulling his hair, though more in fun than in spite or anger. He, however, saw red. His blue eyes flamed with strange fear as well as fury, and he butted through the girls to the door. It was locked. He wrenched at it. Roused, alert, the girls stood round and looked at him. He faced them, at bay. At that moment they were rather horrifying to him, as they stood in their short uniforms. He was distinctly afraid.

'Come on, John Thomas! Come on! Choose!' said Annie.

'What are you after? Open the door,' he said.

'We shan't—not till you've chosen!' said Muriel.

'Chosen what?' he said.

'Chosen the one you're going to marry,' she replied.

He hesitated a moment.

'Open the blasted door,' he said, 'and get back to your senses.' He spoke with official authority.

'You've got to choose!' cried the girls.

'Come on!' cried Annie, looking him in the eye. 'Come on! Come on!'

He went forward, rather vaguely. She had taken off her belt, and swinging it, she fetched him a sharp blow over the head with the buckle end. He sprang and seized her. But immediately the other girls rushed upon him, pulling and tearing and beating him. Their blood was now thoroughly up. He was their sport now. They were going to have their own back, out of him. Strange, wild creatures, they hung on him and rushed at him to bear him down. His tunic was torn right up the back, Nora had hold at the back of his collar, and was actually strangling him. Luckily the button burst. He struggled in a wild frenzy of fury and terror, almost mad terror. His tunic was simply torn off his back, his shirt-sleeves were torn away, his arms were naked. The girls rushed at him, clenched their hands on him and pulled at him: or they rushed at him and pushed him, butted him with all their might: or they struck him wild blows. He ducked and cringed and struck sideways. They became more intense.

At last he was down. They rushed on him, kneeling on him. He had neither breath nor strength to move. His face was bleeding with a long scratch, his brow was bruised.

Annie knelt on him, the other girls knelt and hung on to him. Their faces were flushed, their hair wild, their eyes were all glittering strangely. He lay at last quite still, with face averted, as an animal lies when it is defeated and at the mercy of the captor. Sometimes his eye glanced back at the wild faces of the girls. His breast rose heavily, his wrists were torn.

'Now, then, my fellow!' gasped Annie at length. 'Now then—now—'

At the sound of her terrifying, cold triumph, he suddenly started to struggle as an animal might, but the girls threw themselves upon him with unnatural strength and power, forcing him down.

'Yes—now, then!' gasped Annie at length.

And there was a dead silence, in which the thud of heart-beating was to be heard. It was a suspense of pure silence in every soul.

'Now you know where you are,' said Annie.

The sight of his white, bare arm maddened the girls. He lay in a kind of trance of fear and antagonism. They felt themselves filled with supernatural strength.

Suddenly Polly started to laugh—to giggle wildly—helplessly—and Emma and Muriel joined in. But Annie and Nora and Laura remained the same, tense, watchful, with gleaming eyes. He winced away from these eyes.

'Yes,' said Annie, in a curious low tone, secret and deadly. 'Yes! You've got it now! You know what you've done, don't you? You know what you've done.'

He made no sound nor sign, but lay with bright, averted eyes, and averted, bleeding face.

'You ought to be *killed*, that's what you ought,' said Annie, tensely. 'You ought to be *killed*.' And there was a terrifying lust in her voice.

Polly was ceasing to laugh, and giving long-drawn Oh-h-hs and sighs as she came to herself.

'He's got to choose,' she said vaguely.

'Oh, yes, he has,' said Laura, with vindictive decision.

'Do you hear—do you hear?' said Annie. And with a sharp movement, that made him wince, she turned his face to her.

'Do you hear?' she repeated, shaking him.

But he was quite dumb. She fetched him a sharp slap on the face. He started, and his eyes widened. Then his face darkened with defiance, after all.

'Do you hear?' she repeated.

He only looked at her with hostile eyes.

'Speak!' she said, putting her face devilishly near his.

'What?' he said, almost overcome.

'You've got to *choose!*' she cried, as if it were some terrible menace, and as if it hurt her that she could not exact more.

'What?' he said, in fear.

'Choose your girl, Coddy. You've got to choose her now. And you'll get your neck broken if you play any more of your tricks, my boy. You're settled now.'

There was a pause. Again he averted his face. He was cunning in his over-throw. He did not give in to them really—no, not if they tore him to bits.

'All right, then,' he said, 'I choose Annie.' His voice was strange and full of malice. Annie let go of him as if he had been a hot coal.

'He's chosen Annie!' said the girls in chorus.

'Me!' cried Annie. She was still kneeling, but away from him. He was still ly-ing prostrate, with averted face. The girls grouped uneasily around.

'Me!' repeated Annie, with a terrible bitter accent.

Then she got up, drawing away from him with strange disgust and bitterness. 'I wouldn't touch him,' she said.

But her face quivered with a kind of agony, she seemed as if she would fall. The other girls turned aside. He remained lying on the floor, with his torn clothes and bleeding, averted face.

'Oh, if he's chosen—' said Polly.

'I don't want him—he can choose again,' said Annie, with the same rather bitter hopelessness.

'Get up,' said Polly, lifting his shoulder. 'Get up.'

He rose slowly, a strange, ragged, dazed creature. The girls eyed him from a distance, curiously, furtively, dangerously.

'Who wants him?' cried Laura, roughly.

'Nobody,' they answered, with contempt. Yet each one of them waited for him to look at her, hoped he would look at her. All except Annie, and something was broken in her.

He, however, kept his face closed and averted from them all. There was a silence of the end. He picked up the torn pieces of his tunic, without knowing what to do with them. The girls stood about uneasily, flushed, panting, tidying their hair and their dress unconsciously, and watching him. He looked at none of them. He espied his cap in a corner, and went and picked it up. He put it on his head, and one of the girls burst into a shrill, hysteric laugh at the sight he presented. He, however, took no heed, but went straight to where his overcoat hung on a peg. The girls moved away from contact with him as if he had been an electric wire. He put on his coat and buttoned it down. Then he rolled his tunic-rags into a bundle, and stood before the locked door, dumbly.

'Open the door, somebody,' said Laura.

'Annie's got the key,' said one.

Annie silently offered the key to the girls. Nora unlocked the door.

'Tit for tat, old man,' she said. 'Show yourself a man, and don't bear a grudge.'

But without a word or sign he had opened the door and gone, his face closed, his head dropped.

'That'll learn him,' said Laura.

'Coddy!' said Nora.

'Shut up, for God's sake!' cried Annie fiercely, as if in torture.

'Well, I'm about ready to go, Polly. Look sharp!' said Muriel.

The girls were all anxious to be off. They were tidying themselves hurriedly, with mute, stupefied faces.

1922

Katherine Mansfield

Brief Biography

- Born in 1888 in Wellington, New Zealand.
- Name is pseudonym of Kathleen Beauchamp.
- Father, later knighted, is chairman of the Bank of New Zealand.
- Her uninhibited view of sexuality leads her to reject the middle-class values of her family and live her adult life among other artists in Europe.
- Serves as model for Gudrun in D.H. Lawrence's *Women in Love*.
- Recently discovered correspondence suggests gonorrhea, not tuberculosis, as cause of death at age thirty-four at a mystic retreat in France.
- Husband J. Middleton Murry destroys many of her papers and letters after her death.

Considered a minor literary figure at first—a mere Anton Chekhov imitator, 'a literary outsider from a little land with no history'—Katherine Mansfield transformed the short story, influencing many writers who followed. Instead of a straight sequence of events in a well-rounded narration, her style is closer to lyric poetry. Her stories (118 in five volumes) are a slow buildup of asides, stray thoughts, and seemingly inconsequential and disconnected moments. The isolated moment, of illumination or changed per-ception, is often presented in an oblique or open-ended manner that defies closure.

The most traumatic event of Mansfield's life was the death of her brother, 'blown to bits,' she wrote, by a defective hand grenade in 1915. While her earlier stories have a satirical edge, her later tone is more elegiac. Her stories have a curious 'doubleness' of meaning and subversiveness of intention. The trauma, dislocations, and collapse of social structures during World War I influenced her major themes. Only fragments were worthwhile, she wrote. Unlike the Joycean single moment or epiphany, she preferred mini-epiphanies, glimpses or fragments, a series of myriad impressions or even associations stirred up in the reader.

Sometimes called a literary impressionist, Mansfield redefined marginality. Her writings, often autobiography transformed, insinuate at exile, the oppression of women, sexual identity, colonialism, class ideology, psychoanalysis, and emerging internationalism in literature. Her unpredictable angle of vision—she studied the interaction of stories and other art forms, such as painting, cinema, and music—became a new way of seeing. Her forlorn characters are misfits, spinsters, exiles, minorities, servants, or exploited women who become central to the intensity of her short fiction. Yet the lightness of her touch, her subtle shifts of point of view, and the often sheer beauty of her prose moved short fiction from nineteenth-century Victorian and Edwardian certainties of individualism into the modernist era of flaws and weaknesses.

Her late story, 'The Stranger' (1921), may have been inspired by her reading of James Joyce's 'The Dead.' The story certainly suggests Mansfield's own pessimistic views on marriage after two unfaithful husbands and a miscarriage. Mansfield's biographer Claire Tomalin suggests that she was a repressed lesbian—Mansfield frequently called her lifelong schoolfriend, Ida Constance Baker, her 'faithful wife.' As J.G. Sime also explores in 'An Irregular Union,' in the 1920s women's emerging feminist awareness demanded equality and more dynamic roles in relationships.

See Katherine Mansfield, 'Letter to Richard Murry,' p. 439.

The Stranger

It seemed to the little crowd on the wharf that she was never going to move again. There she lay, immense, motionless on the grey crinkled water, a loop of smoke above her, an immense flock of gulls screaming and diving after the galley droppings at the stern. You could just see little couples parading—little flies walking up and down the dish on the grey crinkled tablecloth. Other flies clustered and swarmed at the edge. Now there was a gleam of white on the lower deck—the cook's apron or the stewardess, perhaps. Now a tiny black spider raced up the ladder on to the bridge.

In the front of the crowd a strong-looking, middle-aged man, dressed very well, very snugly in a grey overcoat, grey silk scarf, thick gloves and dark felt hat, marched up and down twirling his folded umbrella. He seemed to be the leader of the little crowd on the wharf and at the same time to keep them together. He was something between the sheep-dog and the shepherd.

But what a fool—what a fool he had been not to bring any glasses! There wasn't a pair of glasses between the whole lot of them.

'Curious thing, Mr Scott, that none of us thought of glasses. We might have been able to stir 'em up a bit. We might have managed a little signalling. *Don't*

hesitate to land. Natives harmless. Or: *A welcome awaits you. All is forgiven.*
What? Eh?'

Mr Hammond's quick, eager glance, so nervous and yet so friendly and con-
fiding, took in everybody on the wharf, roped in even those old chaps lounging
against the gangways. They knew, every man-jack of them, that Mrs Hammond
was on that boat, and he was so tremendously excited it never entered his head
not to believe that this marvellous fact meant something to them too. It
warmed his heart towards them. They were, he decided, as decent a crowd
of people—Those old chaps over by the gangways, too—fine, solid old chaps.
What chests—by Jove! And he squared his own, plunged his thick-gloved hands
into his pockets, rocked from heel to toe.

'Yes, my wife's been in Europe for the last ten months. On a visit to our eldest
girl, who was married last year. I brought her up here, as far as Crawford, myself.
So I thought I'd better come and fetch her back. Yes, yes, yes.' The shrewd grey
eyes narrowed again and searched anxiously, quickly, the motionless liner. Again
his overcoat was unbuttoned. Out came the thin, butter-yellow watch again, and
for the twentieth—fiftieth—hundredth time he made the calculation.

'Let me see, now. It was two fifteen when the doctor's launch went off. Two
fifteen. It is now exactly twenty-eight minutes past four. That is to say, the doctor's been gone two hours and thirteen minutes. Two hours and thirteen minutes! Whee-ooh!' He gave a queer little half-whistle and snapped his watch to
again. 'But I think we should have been told if there was anything up—don't
you, Mr Gaven?'

'Oh, yes, Mr Hammond! I don't think there's anything to—anything to worry about,' said Mr Gaven, knocking out his pipe against the heel of his shoe. 'At
the same time—'

'Quite so! Quite so!' cried Mr Hammond. 'Dashed annoying!' He paced
quickly up and down and came back again to his stand between Mr and Mrs
Scott and Mr Gaven. 'It's getting quite dark, too,' and he waved his folded umbrella as though the dusk at least might have had the decency to keep off for a
bit. But the dusk came slowly, spreading like a slow stain over the water. Little
Jean Scott dragged at her mother's hand.

'I wan' my tea, mammy!' she wailed.

'I expect you do,' said Mr Hammond. 'I expect all these ladies want their
tea.' And his kind, flushed, almost pitiful glance roped them all in again. He
wondered whether Janey was having a final cup of tea in the saloon out there.
He hoped so; he thought not. It would be just like her not to leave the deck. In
that case perhaps the deck steward would bring her up a cup. If he'd been there
he'd have got it for her—somehow. And for a moment he was on deck, standing
over her, watching her little hand fold round the cup in the way she had, while
she drank the only cup of tea to be got on board. . . . But now he was back here,
and the Lord only knew when that cursed Captain would stop hanging about
in the stream. He took another turn, up and down, up and down. He walked as

far as the cab-stand to make sure his driver hadn't disappeared; back he swerved again to the little flock huddled in the shelter of the banana crates. Little Jean Scott was still wanting her tea. Poor little beggar! He wished he had a bit of chocolate on him.

'Here, Jean!' he said. 'Like a lift up?' And easily, gently, he swung the little girl on to a higher barrel. The movement of holding her, steadying her, relieved him wonderfully, lightened his heart.

'Hold on,' he said, keeping an arm round her.

'Oh, don't worry about *Jean*, Mr Hammond!' said Mrs Scott.

'That's all right, Mrs Scott. No trouble. It's a pleasure. Jean's a little pal of mine, aren't you, Jean?'

'Yes, Mr Hammond,' said Jean, and she ran her finger down the dent of his felt hat.

But suddenly she caught him by the ear and gave a loud scream. 'Lo–ok, Mr Hammond! She's moving! Look, she's coming in!'

By Jove! So she was. At last! She was slowly, slowly turning round. A bell sounded far over the water and a great spout of steam gushed into the air. The gulls rose; they fluttered away like bits of white paper. And whether that deep throbbing was her engines or his heart Mr Hammond couldn't say. He had to nerve himself to bear it, whatever it was. At that moment old Captain Johnson, the harbour-master, came striding down the wharf, a leather portfolio under his arm.

'Jean'll be all right,' said Mr Scott. 'I'll hold her.' He was just in time. Mr Hammond had forgotten about Jean. He sprang away to greet old Captain Johnson.

'Well, Captain,' the eager, nervous voice rang out again, 'you've taken pity on us at last.'

'It's no good blaming me, Mr Hammond,' wheezed old Captain Johnson, staring at the liner. 'You got Mrs Hammond on board, ain't yer?'

'Yes, yes!' said Hammond, and he kept by the harbour-master's side. 'Mrs Hammond's there. Hul-lo! We shan't be long now!'

With her telephone ring-ringing, the thrum of her screw filling the air, the big liner bore down on them, cutting sharp through the dark water so that big white shavings curled to either side. Hammond and the harbour-master kept in front of the rest. Hammond took off his hat; he raked the decks—they were crammed with passengers; he waved his hat and bawled a loud, strange 'Hul-lo!' across the water, and then turned round and burst out laughing and said something—nothing—to old Captain Johnson.

'Seen her?' asked the harbour-master.

'No, not yet. Steady—wait a bit!' And suddenly, between two great clumsy idiots—'Get out of the way there!' he signed with his umbrella—he saw a hand raised—a white glove shaking a handkerchief. Another moment, and—thank God, thank God!—there she was. There was Janey. There was Mrs Hammond, yes, yes, yes—standing by the rail and smiling and nodding and waving her handkerchief.

'Well, that's first class—first class! Well, well, well!' He positively stamped. Like lightning he drew out his cigar-case and offered it to old Captain Johnson. 'Have a cigar, Captain! They're pretty good. Have a couple! Here'—and he pressed all the cigars in the case on the harbour-master—'I've a couple of boxes up at the hotel.'

'Thanks, Mr Hammond!' wheezed old Captain Johnson.

Hammond stuffed the cigar-case back. His hands were shaking, but he'd got hold of himself again. He was able to face Janey. There she was, leaning on the rail, talking to some woman and at the same time watching him, ready for him. It struck him, as the gulf of water closed, how small she looked on that huge ship. His heart was wrung with such a spasm that he could have cried out. How little she looked to have come all that long way and back by herself! Just like her, though. Just like Janey. She had the courage of a—And now the crew had come forward and parted the passengers; they had lowered the rails for the gangways.

The voices on shore and the voices on board flew to greet each other.

'All well?'

'All well.'

'How's mother?'

'Much better.'

'Hullo, Jean!'

'Hillo, Aun' Emily!'

'Had a good voyage?'

'Splendid!'

'Shan't be long now!'

'Not long now.'

The engines stopped. Slowly she edged to the wharfside.

'Make way there—make way—make way!' And the wharf hands brought the heavy gangways along at a sweeping run. Hammond signed to Janey to stay where she was. The old harbour-master stepped forward; he followed. As to 'ladies first,' or any rot like that, it never entered his head.

'After you, Captain!' he cried genially. And, treading on the old man's heels, he strode up the gangway on to the deck in a bee-line to Janey, and Janey was clasped in his arms.

'Well, well, well! Yes, yes! Here we are at last!' he stammered. It was all he could say. And Janey emerged, and her cool little voice—the only voice in the world for him—said,

'Well, darling! Have you been waiting long?'

No; not long. Or, at any rate, it didn't matter. It was over now. But the point was, he had a cab waiting at the end of the wharf. Was she ready to go off? Was her luggage ready? In that case they could cut off sharp with her cabin luggage and let the rest go hang until tomorrow. He bent over her and she looked up with her familiar half-smile. She was just the same. Not a day changed. Just as he'd always known her. She laid her small hand on his sleeve.

'How are the children, John?' she asked.

(Hang the children!) 'Perfectly well. Never better in their lives.'

'Haven't they sent me letters?'

'Yes, yes—of course! I've left them at the hotel for you to digest later on.'

'We can't go quite so fast,' said she. 'I've got people to say goodbye to—and then there's the Captain.' As his face fell she gave his arm a small understanding squeeze. 'If the Captain comes off the bridge I want you to thank him for having looked after your wife so beautifully.' Well, he'd got her. If she wanted another ten minutes—As he gave way she was surrounded. The whole first-class seemed to want to say good-bye to Janey.

'Good-bye, *dear* Mrs Hammond! And next time you're in Sydney, I'll *expect* you.'

'Darling Mrs Hammond! You won't forget to write to me, will you?'

'Well, Mrs Hammond, what this boat would have been without you!'

It was as plain as a pikestaff that she was by far the most popular woman on board. And she took it all—just as usual. Absolutely composed. Just her little self—just Janey all over; standing there with her veil thrown back. Hammond never noticed what his wife had on. It was all the same to him whatever she wore. But today he did notice that she wore a black 'costume'—didn't they call it?—with white frills, trimmings he supposed they were, at the neck and sleeves. All this while Janey handed him round.

'John, dear!' And then: 'I want to introduce you to—'

Finally they did escape, and she led the way to her stateroom. To follow Janey down the passage that she knew so well—that was so strange to him; to part the green curtains after her and to step into the cabin that had been hers gave him exquisite happiness. But—confound it!—the stewardess was there on the floor, strapping up the rugs.

'That's the last, Mrs Hammond,' said the stewardess, rising and pulling down her cuffs.

He was introduced again, and then Janey and the stewardess disappeared into the passage. He heard whisperings. She was getting the tipping business over, he supposed. He sat down on the striped sofa and took his hat off. There were the rugs she had taken with her; they looked good as new. All her luggage looked fresh, perfect. The labels were written in her beautiful little clear hand—'Mrs John Hammond.'

'Mrs John Hammond! He gave a long sigh of content and leaned back, crossing his arms. The strain was over. He felt he could have sat there for ever sighing his relief—the relief of being rid of that horrible tug, pull, grip on his heart. The danger was over. That was the feeling. They were on dry land again.

But at that moment Janey's head came round the corner.

'Darling—do you mind? I just want to go and say good-bye to the doctor.'

Hammond started up. 'I'll come with you.'

'No, no!' she said. 'Don't bother. I'd rather not. I'll not be a minute.'

And before he could answer she was gone. He had half a mind to run after her; but instead he sat down again.

Would she really not be long? What was the time now? Out came the watch; he stared at nothing. That was rather queer of Janey, wasn't it? Why couldn't she have told the stewardess to say goodbye for her? Why did she have to go chasing after the ship's doctor? She could have sent a note from the hotel even if the affair had been urgent. Urgent? Did it—could it mean that she had been ill on the voyage—she was keeping something from him? That was it! He seized his hat. He was going off to find that fellow and to wring the truth out of him at all costs. He thought he'd noticed just something. She was just a touch too calm—too steady. From the very first moment—

The curtains rang. Janey was back. He jumped to his feet.

'Janey, have you been ill on this voyage? You have!'

'Ill?' Her airy little voice mocked him. She stepped over the rugs, came up close, touched his breast, and looked up at him.

'Darling,' she said, 'don't frighten me. Of course I haven't! Whatever makes you think I have? Do I look ill?'

But Hammond didn't see her. He only felt that she was looking at him and that there was no need to worry about anything. She was here to look after things. It was all right. Everything was.

The gentle pressure of her hand was so calming that he put his over hers to hold it there. And she said:

'Stand still. I want to look at you. I haven't seen you yet. You've had your beard beautifully trimmed, and you look—younger, I think, and decidedly thinner! Bachelor life agrees with you.'

'Agrees with me!' He groaned for love and caught her close again. And again, as always, he had the feeling he was holding something that never was quite his—his. Something too delicate, too precious, that would fly away once he let go.

'For God's sake let's get off to the hotel so that we can be by ourselves!' And he rang the bell hard for someone to look sharp with the luggage.

Walking down the wharf together she took his arm. He had her on his arm again. And the difference it made to get into the cab after Janey—to throw the red-and-yellow striped blanket round them both—to tell the driver to hurry because neither of them had had any tea. No more going without his tea or pouring out his own. She was back. He turned to her, squeezed her hand, and said gently, teasingly, in the 'special' voice he had for her: 'Glad to be home again, dearie?' She smiled; she didn't even bother to answer, but gently she drew his hand away as they came to the brighter streets.

'We've got the best room in the hotel,' he said. 'I wouldn't be put off with another. And I asked the chambermaid to put in a bit of a fire in case you felt chilly. She's a nice, attentive girl. And I thought now we were here we wouldn't bother to go home tomorrow, but spend the day looking round and leave the morning after. Does that suit you? There's no hurry, is there? The children will have you soon enough. . . . I thought a day's sight-seeing might make a nice break in your journey—eh, Janey?'

'Have you taken the tickets for the day after?' she asked.

'I should think I have!' He unbuttoned his overcoat and took out his bulging pocket-book. 'Here we are! I reserved a first-class carriage to Salisbury. There it is—'Mr *and* Mrs John Hammond,' I thought we might as well do ourselves comfortably, and we don't want other people butting in, do we? But if you'd like to stop here a bit longer—?'

'Oh, no!' said Janey quickly. 'Not for the world! The day after tomorrow, then. And the children—'

But they had reached the hotel. The manager was standing in the broad, brilliantly lighted porch. He came down to greet them. A porter ran from the hall for their boxes.

'Well, Mr Arnold, here's Mrs Hammond at last!'

The manager led them through the hall himself and pressed the elevator-bell. Hammond knew there were business pals of his sitting at the little hall tables having a drink before dinner. But he wasn't going to risk interruption; he looked neither to the right nor the left. They could think what they pleased. If they didn't understand, the more fools they—and he stepped out of the lift, un-locked the door of their room, and shepherded Janey in. The door shut. Now, at last, they were alone together. He turned up the light. The curtains were drawn; the fire blazed. He flung his hat on to the huge bed and went towards her.

But—would you believe it!—again they were interrupted. This time it was the porter with the luggage. He made two journeys of it, leaving the door open in between, taking his time, whistling through his teeth in the corridor. Hammond paced up and down the room, tearing off his gloves, tearing off his scarf. Finally he flung his overcoat on to the bedside.

At last the fool was gone. The door clicked. Now they *were* alone. Said Hammond: 'I feel I'll never have you to myself again. These cursed people! Janey'—and he bent his flushed, eager gaze upon her—'let's have dinner up here. If we go down to the restaurant we'll be interrupted, and then there's the confounded music' (the music he'd praised so highly, applauded so loudly last night!). 'We shan't be able to hear each other speak. Let's have something up here in front of the fire. It's too late for tea. I'll order a little supper, shall I? How does the idea strike you?'

'Do, darling!' said Janey. 'And while you're away—the children's letters—'

'Oh, later on will do!' said Hammond.

'But then we'd get it over,' said Janey. 'And I'd first have time to—'

'Oh, I needn't go down!' explained Hammond. 'I'll just ring and give the order . . . you don't want to send me away, do you?'

Janey shook her head and smiled.

'But you're thinking of something else. You're worrying about something,' said Hammond. 'What is it? Come and sit here—come and sit on my knee before the fire.'

'I'll just unpin my hat,' said Janey, and she went over to the dressing-table. 'A-ah!' She gave a little cry.

'What is it?'

'Nothing, darling. I've just found the children's letters. That's all right! They will keep. No hurry now!' She turned to him, clasping them. She tucked them into her frilled blouse. She cried quickly, gaily: 'Oh, how typical this dressing-table is of you!'

'Why? What's the matter with it?' said Hammond.

'If it were floating in eternity I should say "John!"' laughed Janey, staring at the big bottle of hair tonic, the wicker bottle of eau-de-Cologne, the two hairbrushes, and a dozen new collars tied with pink tape. 'Is this all your luggage?'

'Hang my luggage!' said Hammond; but all the same he liked being laughed at by Janey. 'Let's talk. Let's get down to things. Tell me'—and as Janey perched on his knees he leaned back and drew her into the deep, ugly chair—'tell me you're really glad to be back, Janey.'

'Yes, darling, I am glad,' she said.

But just as when he embraced her he felt she would fly away, so Hammond never knew— never knew for dead certain that she was as glad as he was. How could he know? Would he ever know? Would he always have this craving— this pang like hunger, somehow, to make Janey so much part of him that there wasn't any of her to escape? He wanted to blot out everybody, everything. He wished now he'd turned off the light. That might have brought her nearer. And now those letters from the children rustled in her blouse. He could have chucked them into the fire.

'Janey,' he whispered.

'Yes, dear?' She lay on his breast, but so lightly, so remotely. Their breathing rose and fell together.

'Janey!'

'What is it?'

'Turn to me,' he whispered. A slow, deep flush flowed into his forehead. 'Kiss me, Janey! You kiss me!'

It seemed to him there was a tiny pause—but long enough for him to suffer torture—before her lips touched his, firmly, lightly—kissing them as she always kissed him, as though the kiss— how could he describe it?—

confirmed what they were saying, signed the contract. But that wasn't what he wanted; that wasn't at all what he thirsted for. He felt suddenly, horribly tired.

'If you knew,' he said, opening his eyes, 'what it's been like waiting today. I thought the boat never would come in. There we were, hanging about. What kept you so long?'

She made no answer. She was looking away from him at the fire. The flames hurried— hurried over the coals, flickered, fell.

'Not asleep, are you?' said Hammond, and he jumped her up and down.

'No,' she said. And then: 'Don't do that, dear. No; I was thinking. As a matter of fact,' she said, 'one of the passengers died last night—a man. That's what held us up. We brought him in—I mean, he wasn't buried at sea. So, of course, the ship's doctor and the shore doctor—'

'What was it?' asked Hammond uneasily. He hated to hear of death. He hated this to have happened. It was, in some queer way, as though he and Janey met a funeral on their way to the hotel.

'Oh, it wasn't anything in the least infectious!' said Janey. She was speaking scarcely above her breath. 'It was *heart*.' A pause. 'Poor fellow!' she said. 'Quite young.' And she watched the fire flicker and fall. 'He died in my arms,' said Janey.

The blow was so sudden that Hammond thought he would faint. He couldn't move; he couldn't breathe. He felt all his strength flowing—flowing into the big dark chair, and the big dark chair held him fast, gripped him, forced him to bear it.

'What?' he said dully. 'What's that you say?'

'The end was quite peaceful,' said the small voice. 'He just'—and Hammond saw her lift her gentle hand—'breathed his life away at the end.' And her hand fell.

'Who—else was there?' Hammond managed to ask.

'Nobody. I was alone with him.'

Ah, my God, what was she saying! What was she doing to him! This would kill him! And all the while she spoke:

'I saw the change coming and I sent the steward for the doctor, but the doctor was too late. He couldn't have done anything, anyway.'

'But—why *you*, why *you*?' moaned Hammond.

At that Janey turned quickly, quickly searched his face.

'You don't *mind*, John, do you?' she asked. 'You don't—It's nothing to do with you and me.'

Somehow or other he managed to shake some sort of smile at her. Somehow or other he stammered: 'No—go—on, go on! I want you to tell me.'

'But, John darling—'

'Tell me, Janey!'

'There's nothing to tell,' she said, wondering. 'He was one of the first-class passengers. I saw he was very ill when he came on board. . . . But he seemed to be so much better until yesterday. He had a severe attack in the afternoon—excitement—nervousness, I think, about arriving. And after that he never recovered.'

'But why didn't the stewardess—'

'Oh, my dear—the stewardess!' said Janey. 'What would he have felt? And besides . . . he might have wanted to leave a message . . . to—'

'Didn't he?' muttered Hammond. 'Didn't he say anything?'

'No, darling, not a word!' She shook her head softly. 'All the time I was with him he was too weak . . . he was too weak even to move a finger. . . .'

Janey was silent. But her words, so light, so soft, so chill, seemed to hover in the air, to rain into his breast like snow.

The fire had gone red. Now it fell in with a sharp sound and the room was colder. Cold crept up his arms. The room was huge, immense, glittering. It filled his whole world. There was the great blind bed, with his coat flung across it like some headless man saying his prayers. There was the luggage, ready to be carried away again, anywhere, tossed into trains, carted on to boats.

'He was too weak. He was too weak to move a finger.' And yet he died in Janey's arms. She—who'd never—never once in all these years—never on one single solitary occasion—

No; he mustn't think of it. Madness lay in thinking of it. No, he wouldn't face it. He couldn't stand it. It was too much to bear!

And now Janey touched his tie with her fingers. She pinched the edges of the tie together.

'You're not—sorry I told you, John darling? It hasn't made you sad? It hasn't spoilt our evening—our being alone together?'

But at that he had to hide his face. He put his face into her bosom and his arms enfolded her.

Spoilt their evening! Spoilt their being alone together! They would never be alone together again.

1922

Morley Callaghan

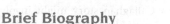

Brief Biography

- Born in 1903 to Irish Roman Catholic parents.
- Amateur boxer.
- Befriends Ernest Hemingway in Toronto in 1920 and again in Paris in 1928, where he knocks Hemingway down in a boxing match that has become legendary. The CBC miniseries *Hemingway vs Callaghan* (2003) explores this match and their relationship.
- In 1933 begins studies with theologian Jacques Maritain at St Michael's College, Toronto.
- For over sixty years is a popular CBC radio, TV, and magazine personality, commenting on books, writers, and curiosities in a variety of 'table talks.'
- Son Barry Callaghan is a prolific novelist, poet, essayist, journalist, and publisher.
- Dies in 1990.

Morley Callaghan was born in Toronto and trained as a lawyer. As a student working on the *Toronto Star*, he first met Ernest Hemingway, who encouraged him to pursue fiction instead of law. Though Callaghan never practised law, he went on to become Canada's first 'professional' writer. In 1929 he visited Paris, where he joined Hemingway and other 'ex-pat' writers F. Scott Fitzgerald, John Dos Passos, Sherwood Anderson, and James Joyce, part of a group famously named 'a lost generation' by Gertrude Stein. But unlike many 'ex-pats,' Callaghan was critical of James Joyce's enforced absence from Ireland. Callaghan 'rejected exile' and returned to Toronto for a long career as a novelist and public personality.

A religious writer in a non-religious time, he wrote the trilogy *Such Is My Beloved* (1934), *They Shall Inherit the Earth* (1935), and *More Joy in Heaven* (1937). Influenced by Hemingway's spare style, Callaghan is sometimes called a moral re-alist for his tone of doubt and social criticism. His characters often need to examine their essential selves. His first novel, *Strange Fugitive* (1928), was banned for its amoral main character. Often, he fell out of public favour, too liberal for some, too conservative for others.

In Callaghan's work, the city, not the farm or wilderness, emerges as the focus. Unusual for the 1930s, he set his realistic prose fictions in a clearly defined Toronto with identifiable landmarks, such as King and Yonge (a major intersection). The emerging 'urban experience' or 'multicultural space,' which Callaghan considered a 'moral space,' corresponds to a major shift away from Northrop Frye's 'garrison mentality,' which pits Canadians against a hostile wilderness. For Callaghan, conflict arises from social problems, temptation, and the desire for personal salvation.

Unlike the rural Depression-era writer, such as Sinclair Ross, Callaghan wrote of crime and urban decadence. Critic Robin Mathews considers him 'a new colonialist' in his embrace of American literary models. Yet his search for non-British forms of expression and syntax place him among the first English-Canadian post-colonial writers to reflect Canada's place in North American culture and its radical differences from the English social system. Writing about prostitutes, gangsters, and drunkards, Callaghan revealed 'displaced perspectives' on 'Toronto the Good' that were a counterbalance to prevailing public opinion.

Though his deceptively plain style has been criticized, Callaghan's well-crafted stories, like Heinrich Böll's, found an audience in radio and newspapers. A typical Callaghan story might involve a simple misunderstanding or a slightly absurd situation like the confessional incident in 'A Predicament.' This minor complication quickly escalates into the larger one of interwar doubts, loss of faith, and the end of priestly power as the centre of moral authority.

A Predicament

Father Francis, the youngest priest at the cathedral, was hearing confessions on a Saturday afternoon. He stepped out of the confessional to stretch his legs a moment and walked up the left aisle toward the flickering red light of the Precious Blood, mystical in the twilight of the cathedral. Father Francis walked back to the confessional, because too many women were waiting on the penitent bench. There were not so many men.

Sitting again in the confessional, he said a short prayer to the Virgin Mary to get in the mood for hearing confessions. He wiped his lips with his handkerchief, cleared his throat, and pushed back the panel, inclining his ear to hear a woman's confession. The panel slid back with a sharp grating noise. Father Francis whispered his ritual prayer and made the sign of the cross. The woman hadn't been to confession for three months and had missed mass twice for no good reason. He questioned her determinedly, indignant with this woman who had missed mass twice for no good reason. In a steady whisper he told her the story of an old woman who had crawled on the ice to get to mass. The woman hesitated, then told about missing her morning prayers . . . 'Yes, my child yes, my child . . .' 'And about certain thoughts . . .' 'Now, about these thoughts; let's look at it in this way . . .' He gave the woman absolution and told her to say the beads once for her penance.

Closing the panel on the women's side, he sat quietly for a moment in the darkness of the confessional. He was a young priest, very interested in confessions.

Father Francis turned to the other side of the confessional, pushing back the panel to hear some man's confession. Resting his chin on his hand after making the sign of the cross, he did not bother trying to discern the outline of the head and shoulders of the man kneeling in the corner.

The man said in a husky voice: 'I wanna get off at the corner of King and Yonge Street.'

Father Francis sat up straight, peering through the wire work. The man's head was moving. He could see his nose and his eyes. His heart began to beat unevenly. He sat back quietly.

'Cancha hear me, wasamatter, I wanna get off at King and Yonge,' the man said insistently, pushing his nose through the wire work.

On the man's breath there was a strong smell of whiskey. Father Francis nervously slid the panel back into position. As the panel slid into place he knew it sounded like the closing of doors on a bus. There he was hearing confessions, and a drunken man on the other side of the panel thought him a conductor on a bus. He would go into the vestry and tell Father Marlow.

Father Francis stepped out of the confessional to look around the cathedral. Men and women in the pews and on the penitents' benches wondered why he had come out of the confessional twice in the last few minutes when so many were waiting. Father Francis wasn't feeling well, that was the trouble. Walking up the aisle, he rubbed his smooth cheek with his hand, thinking hard. If he had the man thrown out he might be a tough customer and there would be a disturbance. There would be a disturbance in the cathedral. Such a disturbance would be sure to get in the papers. Everything got in the papers. There was no use telling it to anybody. Walking erectly he went back to the confessional. Father Francis was sweating.

Rubbing his shoulder-blades uneasily against the back of the confessional, he decided to hear a woman's confession. It was evading the issue—it was a compromise, but it didn't matter; he was going to hear a woman's confession first.

The woman, encouraged by many questions from Father Francis, made an extraordinarily good confession, though sometimes he did not seem to be listening very attentively. He thought he could hear the man moving. The man was drunk—drunkenness, the over-indulgence of an appetite, the drunken state. Scholastic psychology. Cardinal Mercier's book on psychology had got him through the exam at the seminary.

'When you feel you're going to tell a lie, say a short prayer to Mary the mother of God,' he said to the woman.

'Yes, father.'

'Some lies are more serious than others.'

'Yes, father.'

'But they are lies just the same.'

'I tell mostly white lies,' she said.

'They are lies, lies, lies, just the same. They may not endanger your soul, but they lead to something worse. Do you see?'

'Yes, father.'

'Will you promise to say a little prayer every time?'

Father Francis could not concentrate on what the woman was saying. But he wanted her to stay there for a long time. She was company. He would try and concentrate on her. He could not forget the drunken man for more than a few moments.

The woman finished her confession. Father Francis, breathing heavily, gave her absolution. Slowly he pushed back the panel—a street-car, a conductor swinging back the doors on a street-car. He turned deliberately to the other side of the confessional, but hesitated, eager to turn and hear another confession. It was no use—it couldn't go on in that way. Closing his eyes he said three 'Our Fathers' and three 'Hail, Marys,' and felt much better. He was calm and the man might have gone.

He tried to push back the panel so it would not make much noise, but moving slowly, it grated loudly. He could see the man's head bobbing up, watching the panel sliding back.

'Yes, my son,' Father Francis said deliberately.

'I got to get off at King and Yonge,' the man said stubbornly.

'You better go, you've got no business here.'

'Say, there, did you hear me say King and Yonge?'

The man was getting ugly. The whiskey smelt bad in the confessional. Father Francis drew back quickly and half closed the panel. That same grating noise. It put an idea into his head. He said impatiently: 'Step lively there; this is King and Yonge. Do you want to go past your stop?'

'All right, brother,' the man said slowly, getting up clumsily.

'Move along now,' Father Francis said authoritatively.

'I'm movin'; don't get so huffy,' the man said, swinging aside the curtains of the confessional, stepping out to the aisle.

Father Francis leaned back in the confessional and nervously gripped the leather seat. He began to feel very happy. There were no thoughts at all in his head. Suddenly he got up and stepped out to the aisle. He stood watching a man going down the aisle swaying almost imperceptibly. The men and women in the pews watched Father Francis curiously, wondering if he was really unwell because he had come out of the confessional three times in a half-hour. Again he went into the confessional.

At first Father Francis was happy hearing the confessions, but he became restive. He should have used shrewd judgment. With that drunken man he had gone too far, forgotten himself in the confessional. He had descended to artifice in the confessional to save himself from embarrassment.

At the supper-table he did not talk much to the other priests. He had a feeling he would not sleep well that night. He would lie awake trying to straighten everything out. The thing would first have to be settled in his own conscience. Then perhaps he would tell the bishop.

1929

Ernest Hemingway

Brief Biography

- Born in 1899 in Oak Park, IL.
- Nicknamed 'Papa.'
- Ambulance driver during World War I; injured by shrapnel while rescuing wounded soldier.
- Marries four times; has decade-long secret friendship with actress Marlene Dietrich.
- Types standing at a lectern—claims no boxer ever sat.
- Wins Pulitzer Prize in 1952 for *The Old Man and the Sea* and Nobel Prize for Literature in 1954, but is injured in two African plane crashes and cannot attend ceremonies.
- His father, two children, one granddaughter, and Hemingway (by shotgun in 1961) commit suicide.
- Loves six-toed cats; leaves provision in his will that dozens of descendants be protected in his former Key West, FL, home.

Born in a suburb of Chicago, Hemingway famously derided its 'wide lawns and narrow minds.' According to some biographers, his domineering mother dressed him as a little girl and called him Ernestine. But his physician father insisted on manly pursuits: hunting, fishing, and boxing.

Reporting for the *Kansas City Star*, Hemingway learned the virtues of 'short sentences and short paragraphs,' which led to his famous minimalist style. His goal, 'to write one true sentence,' to convey 'the exact instant of experience,' was a revelation in the era of three-volume Edwardian novels. In 1920, he worked for the *Toronto Star*, where he befriended fellow amateur boxer Morley Callaghan. As the *Star*'s Paris reporter (1920–24), he met the 'lost generation' of expatriate American artists, Gertrude Stein, F. Scott Fitzgerald, and Ezra Pound, along with Pablo Picasso and James Joyce, who influenced his sense of the city as a place of exile and disillusionment. Wounded by shrapnel and dis-

traught by his father's suicide by shooting, along with the destructive drinking of Fitzgerald, Hemingway wrote stories dominated by the certainty of death.

He wrote *The Sun Also Rises* (1926) in six weeks and the semi-autobiographical war novel *A Farewell to Arms* (1929)—including two dozen possible endings—from memory after losing his suitcase, as well as a classic collection, *Forty-Nine Stories* (1938). He disliked traditional structure, preferring a 'zero ending' or a continuation of his characters' fates. Scholars suggest that his impressionistic style was influenced by painter Paul Cézanne, as well as nineteenth-century Russian authors and the Civil War fictions of Stephen Crane. Though his influence waned for many years, writers such as Heinrich Böll and Raymond Carver endorsed his 'iceberg theory' of omission and his ideas regarding 'the non-hero' and 'writing with grace under pressure.'

Creating an image of the writer as hero, Hemingway participated in the Spanish

Civil War and claimed to have thrown grenades into a bunker during the D-Day invasion of France in 1944, a violation of the Geneva Convention for war correspondents. His personal life, however, was far from heroic. Hemingway suffered from hereditary bipolar disorder, insomnia (scholarship now suggests post-traumatic stress), and alcoholism. Electroshock therapy to improve his manic disorder led to amnesia, depression, and, eventually, suicide. Four broken marriages and a lifetime of injuries have caused scholars to challenge his 'construction of self.'

Hemingway was an authority on bullfighting after seeing 1,500 fights and writing his non-fiction account of bullfighting in *Death in the Afternoon* (1932).

'The Capital of the World,' which was performed as a ballet in 1953, appears to be a simple initiation story of an unmentored boy who naively dreams of greatness as a matador. But by using an omniscient point of view, Hemingway avoids relating the simple pathos of failure, extending his canvas to encompass more than his protagonist and the listless characters at the pension: he draws attention to the destructive ideologies—romantic, socialistic, and religious—of pre-war Madrid, 'the capital of the world.'

See Thomas M. Leitch, from 'The Debunking Rhythm of the American Short Story,' p. 419, and Cynthia J. Hallett, from 'Minimalism and the Short Story,' p. 420.

The Capital of the World

Madrid is full of boys named Paco, which is the diminutive of the name Francisco, and there is a Madrid joke about a father who came to Madrid and inserted an advertisement in the personal columns of *El Liberal* which said: PACO MEET ME AT HOTEL MONTANA NOON TUESDAY ALL IS FORGIVEN PAPA and how a squadron of Guardia Civil had to be called out to disperse the eight hundred young men who answered the advertisement. But this Paco, who waited on table at the Pension Luarca, had no father to forgive him, nor anything for the father to forgive. He had two older sisters who were chambermaids at the Luarca, who had gotten their place through coming from the same small village as a former Luarca chambermaid who had proven hardworking and honest and hence given her village and its products a good name; and these sisters had paid his way on the auto-bus to Madrid and gotten him his job as an apprentice waiter. He came from a village in a part of Extramadura where conditions were incredibly primitive, food scarce, and comforts unknown and he had worked hard ever since he could remember.

He was a well built boy with very black, rather curly hair, good teeth and a skin that his sisters envied, and he had a ready and unpuzzled smile. He was fast on his feet and did his work well and he loved his sisters, who seemed beautiful and sophisticated; he loved Madrid, which was still an unbelievable place, and he loved his work which, done under bright lights, with clean linen, the wearing of evening clothes, and abundant food in the kitchen, seemed romantically beautiful.

There were from eight to a dozen other people who lived at the Luarca and ate in the dining room but for Paco, the youngest of the three waiters who served at table, the only ones who really existed were the bull fighters.

Second-rate matadors lived at that pension because the address in the Calle San Jeronimo was good, the food was excellent and the room and board was cheap. It is necessary for a bull fighter to give the appearance, if not of prosperity, at least of respectability, since decorum and dignity rank above courage as the virtues most highly prized in Spain, and bull fighters stayed at the Luarca until their last pesetas were gone. There is no record of any bull fighter having left the Luarca for a better or more expensive hotel; second-rate bull fighters never became first rate; but the descent from the Luarca was swift since anyone could stay there who was making anything at all and a bill was never presented to a guest unasked until the woman who ran the place knew that the case was hopeless.

At this time there were three full matadors living at the Luarca as well as two very good picadors, and one excellent banderillero. The Luarca was luxury for the picadors and the banderilleros who, with their families in Seville, required lodging in Madrid during the Spring season; but they were well paid and in the fixed employ of fighters who were heavily contracted during the coming season and the three of these subalterns would probably make much more apiece than any of the three matadors. Of the three matadors one was ill and trying to conceal it; one had passed his short vogue as a novelty; and the third was a coward.

The coward had at one time, until he had received a peculiarly atrocious horn wound in the lower abdomen at the start of his first season as a full matador, been exceptionally brave and remarkably skillful and he still had many of the hearty mannerisms of his days of success. He was jovial to excess and laughed constantly with and without provocation. He had, when successful, been very addicted to practical jokes but he had given them up now. They took an assurance that he did not feel. This matador had an intelligent, very open face and he carried himself with much style.

The matador who was ill was careful never to show it and was meticulous about eating a little of all the dishes that were presented at the table. He had a great many handkerchiefs which he laundered himself in his room and, lately, he had been selling his fighting suits. He had sold one, cheaply, before Christmas and another in the first week of April. They had been very expensive suits, had always been well kept and he had one more. Before he had become ill he had been a very promising, even a sensational, fighter and, while he himself could not read, he had clippings which said that in his debut in Madrid he had been better than Belmonte. He ate alone at a small table and looked up very little.

The matador who had once been a novelty was very short and brown and very dignified. He also ate alone at a separate table and he smiled very rarely and never laughed. He came from Valladolid, where the people are extremely serious, and he was a capable matador; but his style had become old-fashioned before he had ever succeeded in endearing himself to the public through his virtues, which were courage and a calm capability, and his name on a poster would draw no one to a bull ring. His novelty had been that he was so short that he could barely see over the bull's withers, but there were other short fights, and he had never succeeded in imposing himself on the public's fancy.

Of the picadors one was a thin, hawk-faced, gray-haired man, lightly built but with legs and arms like iron, who always wore cattle-men's boots under his trousers, drank too much every evening and gazed amorously at any woman in the pension. The other was huge, dark, brown-faced, good-looking, with black hair like an Indian and enormous hands. Both were great picadors although the first was reputed to have lost much of his ability through drink and dissipation, and the second was said to be too headstrong and quarrelsome to stay with any matador more than a single season.

The banderillero was middle-aged, gray, cat-quick in spite of his years and, sitting at the table he looked a moderately prosperous business man. His legs were still good for this season, and when they should go he was intelligent and experienced enough to keep regularly employed for a long time. The difference would be that when his speed of foot would be gone he would always be frightened where now he was assured and calm in the ring and out of it.

On this evening everyone had left the dining room except the hawk-faced picador who drank too much, the birthmarked-faced auctioneer of watches at the fairs and festivals of Spain, who also drank too much, and two priests from Galicia who were sitting at a corner table and drinking if not too much certainly enough. At that time wine was included in the price of the room and board at the Luarca and the waiters had just brought fresh bottles of Valdepeñas to the tables of the auctioneer, then to the picador and, finally, to the two priests.

The three waiters stood at the end of the room. It was the rule of the house that they should all remain on duty until the diners whose tables they were responsible for should all have left, but the one who served the table of the two priests had an appointment to go to an Anarcho-Syndicalist meeting and Paco had agreed to take over his table for him.

Upstairs the matador who was ill was lying face down on his bed alone. The matador who was no longer a novelty was sitting looking out of his window preparatory to walking out to the café. The matador who was a coward had the older sister of Paco in his room with him and trying to get her to do something which she was laughingly refusing to do. This matador was saying 'Come on, little savage.'

'No,' said the sister. 'Why should I?'

'For a favor.'

'You've eaten and now you want me for dessert.'

'Just once. What harm can it do?'

'Leave me alone. Leave me alone, I tell you.'

'It is a very little thing to do.'

'Leave me alone, I tell you.'

Down in the dining room the tallest of the waiters, who was overdue at the meeting, said 'Look at those black pigs drink.'

'That's no way to speak,' said the second waiter. 'They are decent clients. They do not drink too much.'

'For me it is a good way to speak,' said the tall one. 'There are the two curses of Spain, the bulls and the priests.'

'Certainly not the individual bull and the individual priest,' said the second waiter.

'Yes,' said the tall waiter. 'Only through the individual can you attack the class. It is necessary to kill the individual bull and the individual priest. All of them. Then there are no more.'

'Save it for the meeting,' said the other waiter.

'Look at the barbarity of Madrid,' said the tall waiter. 'It is now half-past eleven o'clock and these are still guzzling.'

'They only started to eat at ten,' said the other waiter. 'As you know there are many dishes. That wine is cheap and these have paid for it. It is not a strong wine.'

'How can there be solidarity of workers with fools like you?' asked the tall waiter.

'Look,' said the second waiter who was a man of fifty. 'I have worked all my life. In all that remains of my life I must work. I have no complaints against work. To work is normal.'

'Yes, but the lack of work kills.'

'I have always worked,' said the older waiter. 'Go on to the meeting. There is no necessity to stay.'

'You are a good comrade,' said the tall waiter. 'But you lack all ideology.'

'*Mejor si me falta eso que el otro*,' said the older waiter (meaning it is better to lack that than work). 'Go on to the *mitin*.'

Paco had said nothing. He did not yet understand politics but it always gave him a thrill to hear the tall waiter speak of the necessity for killing the priests and the Guardia Civil. The tall waiter represented to him revolution and revolution also was romantic. He himself would like to be a good catholic, a revolutionary, and have a steady job like this, while, at the same time, being a bullfighter.

'Go on to the meeting, Ignacio,' he said. 'I will respond for your work.'

'The two of us,' said the older waiter.

'There isn't enough for one,' said Paco. 'Go on to the meeting.'

'*Pues, me voy*,' said the tall waiter. 'And thanks.'

In the meantime, upstairs, the sister of Paco had gotten out of the embrace of the matador as skilfully as a wrestler breaking a hold and said, now angry, 'These are the hungry people. A failed bullfighter. With your ton-load of fear. If you have so much of that, use it in the ring.'

'That is the way a whore talks.'

'A whore is also a woman, but I am not a whore.'

'You'll be one.'

'Not through you.'

'Leave me,' said the matador who, now, repulsed and refused, felt the naked-ness of his cowardice returning.

'Leave you? What hasn't left you?' said the sister. 'Don't you want me to make up the bed? I'm paid to do that.'

'Leave me,' said the matador, his broad good-looking face wrinkled into a contortion that was like crying. 'You whore. You dirty little whore.'

'Matador,' she said, shutting the door. 'My Matador.'

Inside the room the matador sat on the bed. His face still had the contortion which, in the ring, he made into a constant smile which frightened those people in the first rows of seats who knew what they were watching. 'And this,' he was saying aloud. 'And this. And this.'

He could remember when he had been good and it had only been three years before. He could remember the weight of the heavy gold-brocaded fight-ing jacket on his shoulders on that hot afternoon in May when his voice had still been the same in the ring as in the café, and now he sighed along the point-dripping blade at the place in the top of the shoulders where it was dusty in the short-haired black hump of muscle above the wide, wood-knocking, splintered-tipped horns that lowered as he went in to kill, and how the sword pushed in as easy as into a mound of stiff butter with the palm of his hand pushing the pommel, his left arm crossed low, his left shoulder forward, his weight on his left leg, and then his weight wasn't on his leg. His weight was on his lower belly and as the bull raised his head the horn was out of sight in him and he swung over on it twice before they pulled him off it. So now when he went in to kill, and it was seldom, he could not look at the horns and what did any whore know about what he went through before he fought? And what had they been through that laughed at him? They were all whores and they knew what they could do with it.

Down in the dining room the picador sat looking at the priests. If there were women in the room he stared at them. If there were no women he would stare with enjoyment at a foreigner, *un inglés*, but lacking women or strangers, he now stared with enjoyment and insolence at the two priests. While he stared the birth-marked auctioneer rose and folding his napkin went out, leaving over half the wine in the last bottle he had ordered. If his accounts had been paid up at the Luarca he would have finished the bottle.

The two priests did not stare back at the picador. One of them was saying, 'It is ten days since I have been here waiting to see him and all day I sit in the ante-chamber and he will not receive me.'

'What is there to do?'

'Nothing. What can one do? One cannot go against authority.'

'I have been here for two weeks and nothing. I wait and they will not see me.'

'We are from the abandoned country. When the money runs out we can return.'

'To the abandoned country. What does Madrid care about Galicia? We are a poor province.'

'One understands the action of our brother Basilio.'

'Still I have no real confidence in the integrity of Basilio Alvarez.'

'Madrid is where one learns to understand. Madrid kills Spain.'

'If they would simply see one and refuse.'

'No. You must be broken and worn out by waiting.'

'Well, we shall see. I can wait as well as another.'

At this moment the picador got to his feet, walked over to the priests' table and stood, gray-headed and hawk-faced, staring at them and smiling.

'A torero,' said one priest to the other.

'And a good one,' said the picador and walked out of the dining room, gray-jacketed, trim-waisted, bow-legged, in tight breeches over his high-heeled cattleman's boots that clicked on the floor as he swaggered quite steadily, smiling to himself. He lived in a small, tight, professional world of personal efficiency, nightly alcoholic triumph, and insolence. Now he lit a cigar and tilting his hat at an angle in the hallway went out to the café.

The priests left immediately after the picador, hurriedly conscious of being the last people in the dining room, and there was no one in the room now but Paco and the middle-aged waiter. They cleared the tables and carried the bottles into the kitchen.

In the kitchen was the boy who washed the dishes. He was three years older than Paco and was very cynical and bitter.

'Take this,' the middle-aged waiter said, and poured out a glass of the Valdepeñas and handed it to him.

'Why not?' the boy took the glass.

'Tu, Paco?' the older waiter asked.

'Thank you,' said Paco. The three of them drank.

'I will be going,' said the middle-aged waiter.

'Good night,' they told him.

He went out and they were alone. Paco took a napkin one of the priests had used and standing straight, his heels planted, lowered the napkin and with head following the movement, swung his arms in the motion of a slow sweeping veronica. He turned and advancing his right foot slightly, made the second pass, gained a little terrain on the imaginary bull and made a third pass, slow, perfectly timed and suave, then gathered the napkin to his waist and swung his hips away from the bull in a media-veronica.

The dishwasher, whose name was Enrique, watched him critically and sneeringly.

'How is the bull?' he said.

'Very brave,' said Paco. 'Look.'

Standing slim and straight he made four more perfect passes, smooth, elegant, and graceful.

'And the bull?' asked Enrique standing against the sink, holding his wine glass and wearing his apron.

'Still has lots of gas,' said Paco.

'You make me sick,' said Enrique.

'Why?'

'Look.'

Enrique removed his apron and citing the imaginary bull he sculptured four perfect, languid gypsy veronicas and ended up with a rebolera that made the apron swing in a stiff arc past the bull's nose as he walked away from him.

'Look at that,' he said. 'And I wash dishes.'

'Why?'

'Fear,' said Enrique. '*Miedo*. The same fear you would have in a ring with a bull.'

'No,' said Paco. 'I wouldn't be afraid.'

'*Leche!*' said Enrique. 'Everyone is afraid. But a torero can control his fear so that he can work the bull. I went in an amateur fight and I was so afraid I couldn't keep from running. Everyone thought it was very funny. So would you be afraid. If it wasn't for fear every bootblack in Spain would be a bullfighter. You, a country boy, would be frightened worse than I was.'

'No,' said Paco.

He had done it too many times in his imagination. Too many times he had seen the horns, seen the bull's wet muzzle, the ear twitching, then the head go down and the charge, the hoofs thudding and the hot bull pass him as he swung the cape, to recharge as he swung the cape again, then again, and again, and again, to end winding the bull around him in his great media-veronica, and walk swingingly away, with bun hairs caught in the gold ornaments of his jacket from the close passes; the bull standing hypnotized and the crowd applauding. No, he would not be afraid. Others, yes. Not he. He knew he would not be afraid. Even if he ever was afraid he knew that he could do it anyway. He had confidence. 'I wouldn't be afraid,' he said.

Enrique said, '*Leche*,' again.

Then he said, 'If we should try it?'

'How?'

'Look,' said Enrique. 'You think of the bull but you do not think of the horns. The bull has such force that the horns rip like a knife, they stab like a bayonet, and they kill like a club. Look,' he opened a table drawer and took out two meat knives. 'I will bind these to the legs of a chair. Then I will play bull for you with the chair held before my head. The knives are the horns. If you make those passes then they mean something.'

'Lend me your apron,' said Paco. 'We'll do it in the dining room.'

'No,' said Enrique, suddenly not bitter. 'Don't do it, Paco.'

'Yes,' said Paco. 'I'm not afraid.'

'You will be when you see the knives come.'

'We'll see,' said Paco. 'Give me the apron.'

At this time, while Enrique was binding the two heavy-bladed razor-sharp meat knives fast to the legs of the chair with two soiled napkins holding the half of each knife, wrapping them tight and then knotting them, the two chambermaids, Paco's sisters, were on their way to the cinema to see Greta Garbo in 'Anna Christie.' Of the two priests, one was sitting in his underwear reading his breviary and the other was wearing a nightshirt and saying the rosary. All the bullfighters except the one who was ill had made their evening appearance at the Café Fornos, where the big, dark-haired picador was playing billiards, the short serious matador was sitting at a crowded table before a coffee and milk, along with the middle-aged banderillero and other serious workmen.

The drinking, gray-headed picador was sitting with a glass of cazalas brandy before him staring with pleasure at a table where the matador whose courage was gone sat with another matador who had renounced the sword to become a banderillero again, and two very houseworn-looking prostitutes.

The auctioneer stood on the street corner talking with friends. The tall waiter was at the Anarcho-Syndicalist meeting waiting for an opportunity to speak. The middle-aged waiter was seated on the terrace of the Café Alvarez drinking a small beer. The woman who owned the Luarca was already asleep in her bed, where she lay on her back with the bolster between her legs; big, fat, honest, clean, easy-going, very religious and never having ceased to miss or pray daily for her husband, dead, now, twenty years. In his room, alone, the matador who was ill lay face down on his bed with his mouth against a handkerchief.

Now, in the deserted dining room, Enrique tied the last knot in the napkins that bound the knives to the chair legs and lifted the chair. He pointed the legs with the knives on them forward and held the chair over his head with the two knives pointing straight ahead, one on each side of his head.

'It's heavy,' he said. 'Look, Paco. It is very dangerous. Don't do it.' He was sweating.

Paco stood facing him, holding the apron spread, holding a fold of it bunched in each hand, thumbs up, first finger down, spread to catch the eye of the bull.

'Charge straight,' he said. 'Turn like a bull. Charge as many times as you want.'

'How will you know when to cut the pass?' asked Enrique.

'It's better to do three and then a media.'

'All right,' said Paco. 'But come straight. Huh, torito! Come on, little bull!'

Running with head down Enrique came toward him and Paco swung the apron just ahead of the knife blade as it passed close in front of his belly and as it went by it was, to him, the real horn, white-tipped, black, smooth, and as Enrique passed him and turned to rush again it was the hot, blood-flanked mass of the bull that thudded by, then turned like a cat and came again as he swung the cape slowly. Then the bull turned and came again and, as he watched the onrushing point, he stepped his left foot two inches too far forward and the knife did not pass, but had slipped in as easily as into a wineskin and there was a hot scalding rush above and around the sudden inner rigidity of steel and Enrique shouting. 'Ay! Ay! Let me get it out! Let me get it out!' and Paco slipped forward on the chair, the apron cap still held, Enrique pulling on the chair as the knife turned in him, in him, Paco.

The knife was out now and he sat on the floor in the widening warm pool.

'Put the napkin over it. Hold it!' said Enrique. 'Hold it tight. I will run for the doctor. You must hold in the hemorrhage.'

'There should be a rubber cup,' said Paco. He had seen that used in the ring.

'I came straight,' said Enrique, crying. 'All I wanted was to show the danger.'

'Don't worry,' said Paco, his voice sounding far away. 'But bring the doctor.'

In the ring they lifted you and carried you, running with you, to the operating room. If the femoral artery emptied itself before you reached there they called the priest.

'Advise one of the priests,' said Paco, holding the napkin tight against his lower abdomen. He could not believe that this had happened to him.

But Enrique was running down the Carrera San Jeromino to the all-night first-aid station and Paco was alone, first sitting up, then huddled over, then slumped on the floor, until it was over, feeling his life go out of him as dirty water empties from a bathtub when the plug is drawn. He was frightened and he felt faint and he tried to say an act of contrition and he remembered how it started but before he had said, as fast as he could, 'Oh, my God, I am heartily sorry for having offended Thee who art worthy of all my love and I firmly resolve . . . ,' he felt too faint and he was lying face down on the floor and it was over very quickly. A severed femoral artery empties itself faster than you can believe.

As the doctor from the first-aid station came up the stairs accompanied by a policeman who held on to Enrique by the arm, the two sisters of Paco were still in the moving picture palace of the Gran Via, where they were intensely disappointed in the Garbo film, which showed the great star in miserable low surroundings when they had been accustomed to see her surrounded by great luxury and brilliance. The audience disliked the film thoroughly and were protesting by whistling and stamping their feet. All the other people from the hotel were doing almost what they had been doing when the accident happened, except that the two priests had finished their devotions and were preparing for sleep, and the gray-haired picador had moved his drink over to the table with the two houseworn prostitutes. A little later he went out of the café with one of them. It was the one for whom the matador who had lost his nerve had been buying drinks.

The boy Paco had never known about any of this nor about what all these people would be doing on the next day and on other days to come. He had no idea how they really lived, nor how they ended. He did not even realize they ended. He died, as the Spanish phrase has it, full of illusions. He had not had time in his life to lose any of them, nor even, at the end, to complete an act of contrition.

He had not even had time to be disappointed in the Garbo picture which disappointed all Madrid for a week.

1936

Marcel Aymé

Brief Biography

- Born in 1902, is raised in rural France.
- Lives through Nazi occupation of Paris (1940–44).
- Fiercely independent, he rejects membership in prestigious French Academy as well as the Legion of Honour.
- Work is neglected for years because of his politics.
- Once dismissed as 'merely' a children's writer; his children's books are allegories or parables.
- Dies in 1967; a memorial statue of a man walking through a wall is raised in Montmartre; Toronto's *Theatre passe muraille* (1967) is named after his famous story.
- More than a dozen film versions of his work exist; 1991 film *Uranus*, directed by Claude Berri, challenges the myth of resistance and collaboration.

The son of a blacksmith in rural Burgundy, France, Aymé was the youngest of six children. He studied mathematics and medicine, but the 1919 Spanish flu outbreak ended his student days. He worked as a soldier, bricklayer, insurance salesman, and journalist. A long illness in 1929 confined him to bed, where he began writing about rural France; later, he lived in Montmartre in

Paris. He dedicated himself entirely to literature, film scripts, and theatre following the success of *The Green Mare* (1933), a dark satire on sexuality.

Difficult to categorize, Marcel Aymé was denounced and blacklisted for his political views. A pre-war Communist, he was critical of the left, of dominant existentialist intellectuals such as Jean-Paul Sartre and Albert Camus, and of a government allied with Americans. Finally, he became a self-proclaimed anarchist. In his novel *Uranus* (1948), he concluded that American Liberation did more damage to France with bombs and imported culture than the Nazis did. He also criticized the French Resistance as overrated, hypocritical, and dishonest, a public rebuke to President de Gaulle's post-war myth of France as a unanimous resistance nation.

Controversial cultural politics of French writers during and after World War II continue to be argued, sifted, and, some say, manipulated. The occupation, resistance, and aftermath—called the Dark Years—are frequently revised with furious realignments of competing political groups. Many filmmakers, including Louis Malle, François Truffaut, Claude Chabrol, and Max Ophüls, have tried to understand the 'survivor's guilt' of this period. Criticized for forty years, Aymé was variously accused of being a communist, a collaborator, a fascist, an anarchist, and even an anti-Semite (for supporting two friends, novelist Louis-Ferdinand Céline and film critic Robert Brassilach,

who was shot for treason). Though never criminally charged, he was also seriously compromised because he wrote for the Vichy (collaboration) newspaper, *La Gerbe*, the only paper permitted by the Nazis. Yet Aymé claimed that freedom and responsibility involved individual choice and, like Heinrich Böll, was critical of what he called 'the politics of memory.' In many oppressive regimes, fiction is disguised as parable to pass the censors and to provide relief in stark circumstances. Many readers suggest that Aymé expressed subversive ideas by using both humour and a politically non-committal stance.

Drawing from the 'non-mimetic' and revolutionary tradition of French writers François Rabelais, Jean de La Fontaine, Voltaire, and Charles Perrault, Aymé's work is reminiscent of the 'moving between worlds' stories of Julio Cortázar, who translated Aymé into Spanish; the fantastic creations of Italo Calvino; and the folk traditions explored by Angela Carter. More playful than Franz Kafka, Aymé applies the key word 'tyranny' to France's bureaucracy and civil service supportive of Nazi Germany. For example, by calling himself 'The Werewolf,' the protagonist of 'The Walker-Through-Walls' alludes to superstitions and imaginative freedoms of pre-Catholic France. The simple, clear premise of this story lends itself to various readings beyond a critique of bureaucracy; through images of restriction, persecution, and surveillance it even hints at the idea of wartime France as entrapped.

The Walker-Through-Walls

There lived in Montmartre, on the third floor of No. *75bis*, Rue d'Orchampt, an excellent man named Dutilleul who possessed the singular gift of being able to walk through walls without experiencing any discomfort. He wore *pince-nez* and a little black beard, and he was a third-grade clerk in the Ministry of Registration. In winter he went by bus to his office, and in summer he went on foot, under his bowler-hat.

Dutilleul had just entered his forty-third year when his especial aptitude was revealed to him. One evening, having been caught by a brief failure of the electricity in the vestibule of his small bachelor apartment, he fumbled for a moment in the darkness, and when the lights went on again found himself on the third-floor landing. Since his front door was locked on the inside the incident caused him to reflect, and despite the protests of his reason he resolved to go in as he had come out, by walking through the wall. This strange attainment, which seemed to correspond to none of his aspirations, preyed slightly on his mind, and on the following day, a Saturday, he took advantage of the weekend to call on a neighbouring doctor and put the case to him. The doctor, after convincing himself of the truth of his story, discovered upon examination that the cause of the trouble lay in the helicoidal hardening of the strangulatory wall of the thyroid vesicle. He prescribed a regime of intensive exertion, and, at the rate of two cachets a year, the absorption into the system of tetravalent reintegration powder, a mixture of rice flour, and centaur's hormones.

After taking the first cachet Dutilleul put the rest away in a drawer and thought no more about them. As for the intensive exertion, his work as a civil servant was ordered by custom which did not permit of any excess; neither did his leisure hours, which were devoted to the daily paper and his stamp collection, call for any unreasonable expenditure of energy. So that at the end of a year his knack of walking through walls remained unimpaired; but he never made use of it, except inadvertently, having little love of adventure and being non-receptive to the lures of the imagination. It did not even occur to him to enter his own apartment otherwise than by the door, after duly turning the key in the lock. Perhaps he would have grown old in his sedate habits, without ever being tempted to put his gift to the test, had not an extraordinary event suddenly occurred to revolutionise his existence. M. Mouron, the head of his sub-section at the ministry, was transferred to other duties and replaced by a M. Lécuyer, who was brisk of speech and wore a small military moustache. From the first day this newcomer manifested the liveliest disapproval of the *pince-nez* which Dutilleul wore attached to a short chain, and of his little black beard, and he elected to treat him as a tiresome and not over-clean elderly encumbrance. Worst of all, he saw fit to introduce into the work of his sub-section certain far-reaching reforms which were well calculated to trouble the peace of mind of his subordinate. Dutilleul was accustomed to begin his letters with the following formula: 'With reference to your esteemed communication of the such-and-such instant, and having regard to our previous exchange of letters on this subject, I have the honour to inform you . . .' For which M. Lécuyer proposed to substitute a more trans-Atlantic form of words: 'Yours of the such-and-such. I beg to state . . .' Dutilleul could not accustom himself to this epistolary terseness. Despite himself he reverted with a machine-like obstinacy to the traditional form, thereby incurring the increasing animosity of his superior. The atmosphere of the Ministry of Registration became almost oppressive to him. He went apprehensively to work in the morning, and at night, after going to bed, he would often lie brooding for as much as a quarter of an hour before falling asleep.

Outraged by a reactionary stubbornness which threatened to undermine the success of his reforms, M. Lécuyer relegated Dutilleul to a small and sombre room, scarcely more than a cupboard, next door to his own office. It was entered by a low, narrow door giving on to the corridor, and which bore in capital letters the legend: 'BACK FILES.' Dutilleul resignedly acquiesced in this unprecedented humiliation, but when he read some more than usually sanguinary story in his newspaper he found himself dreaming that M. Lécuyer was the victim.

One day his chief burst into his cupboard brandishing a letter and bellowing: 'This must be done again! I insist upon your rewriting this unspeakable document which is a disgrace to my sub-section!'

Dutilleul was about to protest, but in a voice of thunder M. Lécuyer informed him that he was a routine-besotted mole, and crumpling the letter flung it in his face. Dutilleul was a modest man, but proud. Left alone in his cupboard he felt his temperature rising, and suddenly he was seized with an inspiration. Leaving his seat he passed into the wall between his chief's room and his own, but he did so with caution, so that only his head emerged on the other side. M. Lécuyer, seated again at his desk, his pen still quivering, was in the act of striking out a comma from the text of a letter submitted by a subordinate for his approval, when he heard the sound of a cough in his room. Looking up he perceived with unspeakable dismay the head of Dutilleul, seemingly affixed to the wall like a trophy of the chase. But this head was alive. Through the *pince-nez*, with their length of chain, the eyes glared balefully at him. What is more, the head spoke.

'Sir,' it said, 'you are a scoundrel, a blockhead, and a mountebank.'

M. Lécuyer, his mouth gaping with horror, had difficulty in withdrawing his gaze from the apparition. At length he heaved himself out of his chair, plunged into the corridor and flung open the door of the cupboard. Dutilleul, pen in hand, was seated in his accustomed place, in an attitude of tranquil and devoted industry. M. Lécuyer stared at him for some time in silence, and then, after muttering a few words, returned to his office. Scarcely had he resumed his seat than the head again appeared on the wall.

'Sir, you are a scoundrel, a blockhead, and a mountebank.' In the course of that day alone the terrifying head manifested itself twenty-three times, and on the following days it appeared with a similar frequency. Having acquired a certain skill at the game, Dutilleul was no longer content merely to abuse his chief. He uttered obscure threats, for example proclaiming in a sepulchral voice punctuated with truly demoniac laughter:

'The werewolf is here, the end is near! (*laughter*). Flesh creeps and terror fills the air! (*laughter*).'

Hearing which, the unhappy sub-section chief grew yet more pale, yet more breathless, while the hairs stood rigid on his head and the sweat of anguish trickled down his spine. During the first day he lost a pound in weight. In the course of the ensuing week, besides almost visibly melting away, he developed a tendency to eat soup with a fork and to greet the guardians of the law with a military salute. At the beginning of the second week an ambulance called at his dwelling and bore him off to a mental home.

Being thus delivered from the tyranny of M. Lécuyer, Dutilleul could return to his cherished formula—'With reference to your esteemed communication of the such-and-such . . .' Yet he was not satisfied. There was now a yearning in him, a new, imperious impulse which was nothing less than the need to walk through walls. It is true that he had ample opportunities of doing so, in his apartment for example, of which he did not neglect to avail himself. But the man possessing brilliant gifts cannot long be content to squander them on trifles. Moreover, the act of walking through a wall cannot be said to constitute an end in itself. It is a mere beginning, the start of an adventure calling for an outcome, a realisation—calling, in short, for a reward. Dutilleul was well aware of this. He felt an inner need to expand, a growing desire to fulfil and surpass himself, and a restless hankering which was in some sort the call of the other side of the wall. But an objective, alas, was lacking. He sought inspiration in his daily paper, particularly in the columns devoted to politics and sport, both of which seemed to him commendable activities; but perceiving finally that these offered no outlet for persons capable of walking through walls, he fell back on the crime columns, which proved to be rich in suggestion.

Dutilleul's first burglary took place in a large credit establishment on the right bank of the Scine. After passing through a dozen walls and partitions he thrust his hand into a number of strong-boxes, filled his pockets with banknotes and before leaving signed his crime in red chalk, using the pseudonym of 'The Werewolf,' adorned with a handsome flourish which was reproduced in all the papers next day. By the end of a week 'The Werewolf' had achieved an extraordinary celebrity. The heart of the public went out unreservedly to this phenomenal burglar who so prettily mocked the police. He drew attention to himself each night by a fresh exploit carried out at the expense, now of a bank, now of a jeweller's shop or of some wealthy individual. In Paris, as in the provinces, there was no woman with romance in her heart who had not a fervent desire to belong body and soul to the terrible Werewolf. After the theft of the famous Burdigala diamond and the robbing of the Crédit Municipal, which occurred during the same week, the enthusiasm of the crowd reached the point of delirium. The Minister of the Interior was compelled to resign, dragging with him in his fall the Minister of Registration. Nevertheless, Dutilleul, now one of the richest men in Paris, never failed to arrive punctually at the office, and was spoken of as a candidate for the *palmes académiques*. And every morning, at the Ministry of Registration, he had the pleasure of hearing his colleagues discuss his exploits of the previous night. 'This Werewolf,' they said, 'is a stupendous fellow, a superman, a genius.' Hearing such praise, Dutilleul turned pink with embarrassment and behind the *pince-nez* his eyes shone with friendship and gratitude. A day came when the atmosphere of sympathy so overwhelmed him that he felt he could keep the secret no longer. Surveying with a last twinge of shyness the group of his colleagues arrayed round a newspaper containing an account of the robbery of the Banque de France, he said in a diffident voice: 'As a matter of fact, *I'm* the Werewolf.' The confession was received with a huge and interminable burst of laughter, and the nickname of 'Werewolf' was at once mockingly bestowed on him. That evening, at the time of leaving the ministry, he was the object of endless pleasantries on the part of his fellow-workers, and life seemed to him less rosy.

A few days later the Werewolf allowed himself to be caught by a police patrol in a jeweller's shop on the Rue de la Paix. He had inscribed his signature on the safe and was singing a drinking-song while smashing windows with a massive gold tankard. It would have been a simple matter for him to escape by merely slipping through a wall, but everything leads one to suppose that he wished to be arrested, probably for the sole purpose of confounding the colleagues whose incredulity had so mortified him. These were indeed greatly astonished when the newspapers next day published Dutilleul's picture on the front page. They bitterly regretted having underrated their inspired *confrère*, and did him homage by growing little beards. Some of them, carried away by remorse and admiration, went so far as to try to get their hands on the wallets or watches of their friends and relations.

It may well be considered that to allow oneself to be caught by the police in order to impress a few colleagues is to display an extreme frivolity unworthy of an eminent public figure; but the apparent exercise of free-will plays little part in a resolution of this kind. In sacrificing his liberty Dutilleul thought he was yielding to an arrogant desire for revenge, whereas in fact he was merely following the ineluctable course of his destiny. No man who walks through walls can consider his career even moderately fulfilled if he has not had at least one taste of prison. When Dutilleul entered the precincts of the Santé he had a feeling of being the spoilt child of fortune. The thickness of the walls was to him a positive delight. On the very day following his incarceration the warders discovered to their stupefaction that he had driven a nail into the wall of his cell and had hung from it a gold watch belonging to the prison Governor. He either could not or would not disclose how the article had come into his possession. The watch was restored to its owner and the next day was again found at the bedside of the Werewolf, together with the first volume of *The Three Musketeers*, borrowed from the Governor's library. The whole staff of the prison was on edge. The warders complained, moreover, of receiving kicks on the bottom coming from some inexplicable source. It seemed that the walls no longer had ears but had feet instead. The detention of the Werewolf had lasted a week when the Governor, entering his office one morning, found the following letter on his desk:

'Sir:

With reference to our interview of the 17th instant, and having regard to your general instruction of May 15th of last year, I have the honour to inform you that I have just concluded my perusal of *The Three Musketeers*, Vol. II, and that I propose to escape tonight between 11.25 p.m. and 11.35 p.m.

I beg to remain, Sir,

With expressions of the deepest respect,

Your obedient servant,

The Werewolf.'

Despite the extremely close watch kept upon him that night, Dutilleul escaped at 11.30. The news, when it became known to the public on the following day, occasioned an outburst of tremendous enthusiasm. Nevertheless, Dutilleul, having achieved another burglary which set the seal on his popularity, seemed to have little desire to hide himself and walked freely about Montmartre without taking any precautions. Three days after his escape he was arrested in the Café du Rêve on the Rue Clignancourt, where he was drinking a *vin blanc citron* with a few friends.

Being taken back to the Santé and secured behind triple locks in a gloomy dungeon, the Werewolf left it the same evening and passed the night in the guest-room of the Governor's apartment. At about nine the next morning he rang for his *petit déjeuner* and allowed himself to be captured in bed, without offering any resistance, by the warders summoned for the purpose. The outraged Governor caused a special guard to be posted at the door of his cell and put him on bread and water. Towards midday he went out and had lunch at a neighbouring restaurant, and, having finished his coffee, telephoned the Governor as follows:

'My dear Governor, I am covered with confusion. When I left the prison a short time ago I omitted to take your wallet, so that I am now penniless in a restaurant. Will you be so good as to send someone to pay my bill?'

The Governor hurried to the spot in person, and so far forgot himself as to utter threats and abuse. Wounded in his deepest feelings, Dutilleul escaped the following night, never to return. This time he took the precaution of shaving his black tuft of beard and substituting hornrimmed spectacles for the *pince-nez* and chain. A sports cap and a suit of plus-fours in a loud check completed his transformation. He established himself in a small apartment in the Avenue Junot where, during the period preceding his first arrest, he had installed a part of his furniture and the possessions which he most valued. The notoriety attaching to his name was beginning to weary him, and since his stay in the Santé he had become rather blasé in the matter of walking through walls. The thickest, the proudest of them seemed to him no more than the flimsiest of screens, and he dreamed of thrusting his way into the very heart of some massive pyramid. While meditating on the project of a trip to Egypt he lived the most tranquil of lives, divided between his stamp collection, the cinema, and prolonged strolls about Montmartre. So complete was his metamorphosis that, clean-shaven and hornrimmed-spectacled, he passed his best friends in the street without being recognised. Only the painter, Gen Paul, whom no detail escaped of any change in the physiognomy of an old resident of the quarter, succeeded in the end in penetrating his disguise. Finding himself face to face with Dutilleul at the corner of the Rue de l'Abreuvoir, he could not restrain himself from remarking in his crude slang:

'*Dis donc, je vois que tu t'es miché en gigolpince pour tétarer ceux de la sûrepige*'—which roughly means, in common speech: 'I see you've got yourself up like a man of fashion to baffle the inspectors of the Sûreté.'

'Ah!' murmured Dutilleul. 'So you've recognised me!'

He was perturbed by this and resolved to hasten his departure for Egypt. But it was on the afternoon of this very day that he fell in love with a ravishing blonde whom he twice encountered in the Rue Lepic, at a quarter of an hour's interval. He instantly forgot his stamp collection, Egypt and the Pyramids. The blonde, for her part, had gazed at him with considerable interest. Nothing stirs the imagination of the young women of the present day more than plusfours and horn-rimmed spectacles: they have a flavour of film scripts, they set one dreaming of cocktails and Californian nights. Unfortunately the lady— so Dutilleul was informed by Gen Paul—was married to a violent and jealous man. This suspicious husband, who himself led a dissolute life, regularly forsook his wife between the hours of ten at night and four in the morning; but before doing so he locked her in her bedroom and padlocked all the shutters. During the daytime he kept a close eye on her, even going so far on occasions as to follow her as she went along the streets of Montmartre.

'Always snooping, you see. He's one of those coarse-minded so-and-so's that don't stand for anyone poaching on their preserves.'

But Gen Paul's warning served only to inflame Dutilleul's ardour. Encountering the young woman in the Rue Tholozé on the following day, he boldly followed her into a *crémerie*, and while she was awaiting her turn to be served he told her of his respectful passion and that he knew all—the villainous husband, the locked door, and the padlocked shutters—but that he proposed nevertheless to visit her that same evening. The blonde flushed scarlet while the milk-jug trembled in her hand. Her eyes melting with tenderness she murmured weakly: 'Alas, Monsieur, it is impossible.'

On the evening of that glorious day, towards ten o'clock, Dutilleul was at his post in the Rue Norvins, keeping watch on a solid outer wall behind which was situated a small house of which he could see nothing except the weather-cock and the chimney-stack. A door in this wall opened and a man emerged who, after locking it carefully behind him, went down the hill towards the Avenue Junot. Dutilleul waited until he saw him vanish in the far distance at the turn of the road, after which he counted ten. Then he darted forward, skipped lightly with an athlete's stride into the wall, and running through all obstacles penetrated into the bedroom of the beautiful captive. She received him with transports of delight and they made love till an advanced hour.

The next day Dutilleul had the vexation to suffer from a severe headache. It was a matter of no importance, and he had no intention of failing to keep his rendezvous for so little. However, chancing to discover a few cachets scattered at the bottom of a drawer, he swallowed one in the morning and another in the afternoon. By the evening his headache was bearable, and his state of exaltation caused him to forget it. The young woman was awaiting him with all the impatience to which her recollections of the previous evening had given rise, and that night they made love until three in the morning. Upon his departure, as he passed through the inner and outer walls of the house, Dutilleul had a sense of unaccustomed friction at his hips and shoulders. However, he did not think this worthy of any particular attention. Only when he came to penetrate the surrounding wall did he become definitely aware of a feeling of resistance. He seemed to be moving in a substance that was still fluid, but which was thickening so that it seemed to gain in consistency with every movement that he made. Having succeeded in thrusting the whole of his body into the thickness of the wall, he found that he could no longer progress, and in terror he recalled the two cachets he had taken during the day. These cachets, which he had mistaken for aspirin, had in reality contained the tetravalent reintegration powder prescribed by the doctor a year before. The medicine, aided by his intensive exertions, was suddenly having its intended effect.

Dutilleul was, as it were, petrified in the interior of the wall. He is there to this day, incorporated in the stone. Night-birds descending the Rue Norvins at the hour when the clamour of Paris has died down, may sometimes hear a stifled voice seeming to come from beyond the tomb, which they take to be the moaning of the wind as it whistles at the crossroads of the Butte. It is Werewolf Dutilleul mourning for his glorious career and his too-brief love. Occasionally on a winter's night the painter, Gen Paul, taking down his guitar, ventures forth into the echoing solitude of the Rue Norvins to console the unhappy prisoner with a song; and the notes, flying from his benumbed fingers, pierce to the heart of the stone like drops of moonlight.

1943

Heinrich Böll

Brief Biography

- Born near Cologne, Germany, in 1917.
- Serves in Wehrmacht in Europe during World War II; wounded four times.
- POW in American prisons in 1945; influenced by Hemingway paperback in prison library.
- Called 'the conscience of the nation.'
- Wins Nobel Prize for Literature in 1972.
- Dies in 1985.
- Heinrich Böll Foundation is formed in 1996, a worldwide organization dedicated to furthering his ideals.

Winning the Nobel Prize for Literature scarcely suggests the obstacles Heinrich Böll overcame to become Germany's most important post-war author. Post-war Germany is sometimes called Zero Hour, the mythic beginning of a new nation. As part of this new beginning, Böll joined several authors in *Gruppe 47* (Group 47) who tried to reshape society with a new sense of history and identity conveyed through a revitalized literary language.

Philosopher-novelist Jean-Paul Sartre influenced Böll's sense of 'literature as commitment.' Böll's earlier fiction describes how war affects ordinary citizens; his later works represent a new Democratic Germany, though in the Soviet Union his best-selling books were seen as a denunciation of capitalism. His novel *Billiards at Half Past Nine* (1959) details the bombing of a famous abbey, symbolic of post-war disillusionment and spiritual emptiness. *The Lost Honour of Katarina Blum* (1974) is a veiled criticism of the right-wing press and police for a slanderous smear campaign against him. Similar to Morley Callaghan in his Catholic moral vision, Böll was a fierce critic of politicians, clergy, and journalists who manipulated

the truth or failed to warn their public of political dangers. Among the first to join the Green Party of Europe, he opposed the Soviet Union in Hungary and Czechoslovakia, the Berlin Wall, and the neutron bomb. He was critical of the two German societies: consumerist West Germany was 'Americanized'; East Germany, as part of the Soviet bloc and therefore a dictatorship, was 'Stalinized' or 'Sovietized.'

Böll was the first non-Jewish German writer to write against 'the official' silence of the Holocaust. Depicting 'trash and grime,' his work has been labelled 'the literature of rubble.' His stories of soldiers, non-conformists, refugees, dissidents, and the unemployed ran counter to 'official histories.' The sad-faced man confronts an ideology. But as Böll wrote, 'The dignity of the individual was always sacred.'

Because the German publishing industry was destroyed and 'all connections were cut off,' Böll wrote in a simple, direct style. In this new Germany, he had to be direct and specific; any attempt at literary style was distrusted. Many of his works were published in newspapers or broadcast as radio plays, so he modulated his prose through tone, be it ironic or anguished, bureaucratic or outraged, desperate or optimistic. In one satirical story, a young broadcaster collects audio tape snippets of a ranting spiritualist's 'silences' or breath pauses, 'dead air' that he splices together and plays back.

'False ideas of the past can meet no ideas in the present,' Böll wrote. He saw the military as self-destructive and political power as abused. In 'My Sad Face,' human freedom is his main concern. Post-war Germany brought about a 'crisis of masculinity,' but men who lost 'the best years of their lives' by war could be saved by a light-hearted attitude and adherence to firm ethical principles.

My Sad Face

While I was standing on the dock watching the seagulls, my sad face attracted the attention of a policeman on his rounds. I was completely absorbed in the sight of the hovering birds as they shot up and swooped down in a vain search for something edible: the harbor was deserted, the water greenish and thick with foul oil, and on its crusty film floated all kinds of discarded junk. Not a vessel was to be seen, the cranes had rusted, the freight sheds collapsed; not even rats seemed to inhabit the black ruins along the wharf, silence reigned. It was years since all connection with the outside world had been cut off.

I had my eye on one particular seagull and was observing its flight. Uneasy as a swallow sensing thunder in the air, it usually stayed hovering just above the surface of the water, occasionally, with a shrill cry, risking an upward sweep to unite with its circling fellows. Had I been free to express a wish, I would have chosen a loaf of bread to feed to the gulls, crumbling it to pieces to provide a white fixed point for the random flutterings, to set a goal at which the birds could aim, to tauten this shrill flurry of crisscross hovering and circling by hurling a piece of bread into the mesh as if to pull together a bunch of strings. But I was as hungry as they were, and tired, yet happy in spite of my sadness because it felt good to be standing there, my hands in my pockets, watching the gulls and drinking in sadness.

Suddenly I felt an official hand on my shoulder, and a voice said, 'Come along now!' The hand tugged at my shoulder, trying to pull me round, but I did not budge, shook it off, and said quietly, 'You're nuts.'

'Comrade,' the still-invisible one told me, 'I'm warning you.'

'Sir,' I retorted.

'What d'you mean, "sir"?' he shouted angrily. 'We're all comrades.'

With that he stepped round beside me and looked at me, forcing me to bring back my contentedly roving gaze and direct it at his simple, honest face: he was as solemn as a buffalo that for twenty years has had nothing to eat but duty.

'On what grounds . . . ' I began.

'Sufficient grounds,' he said. 'Your sad face.'

I laughed.

'Don't laugh!' His rage was genuine. I had first thought he was bored, with no unlicensed whore, no staggering sailor, no thief or fugitive to arrest, but now I saw he meant it: he intended to arrest me.

'Come along now!'

'Why?' I asked quietly.

Before I realized what was happening, I found my left wrist enclosed in a thin chain, and instantly I knew that once again I had had it. I turned toward the swerving gulls for a last look, glanced at the calm gray sky, and tried with a sudden twist to plunge into the water, for it seemed more desirable to drown alone in that scummy dishwater than to be strangled by the sergeants in a backyard or to be locked up again. But the policeman suddenly jerked me so close to him that all hope of wrenching myself free was gone.

'Why?' I asked again.

'There's a law that you have to be happy.'

'I am happy!' I cried.

'Your sad face . . .' He shook his head.

'But this law is new,' I told him.

'It's thirty-six hours old, and I'm sure you know that every law comes into force twenty-four hours after it has been proclaimed.'

'But I've never heard of it!'

'That won't save you. It was proclaimed yesterday, over all the loudspeakers, in all the papers, and anyone'—here he looked at me scornfully—'anyone who doesn't share in the blessings of press or radio was informed by leaflets scattered from the air over every street in the country. So we'll soon find out where you've been spending the last thirty-six hours, comrade.'

He dragged me away. For the first time I noticed that it was cold and I had no coat; for the first time I became really aware of my hunger growling at the entrance to my stomach; for the first time I realized that I was also dirty, unshaved, and in rags, and that there were laws demanding that every comrade be clean, shaved, happy, and well fed. He pushed me in front of him like a scarecrow that has been found guilty of stealing and is compelled to abandon the place of its dreams at the edge of the field. The streets were empty, the police station was not far off, and, although I had known they would soon find a reason for arresting me, my heart was heavy, for he took me through the places of my childhood which I had intended to visit after looking at the harbor: public gardens that had been full of bushes, in glorious confusion, overgrown paths—all this was now leveled, orderly, neat, arranged in squares for the patriotic groups obliged to drill and march here on Mondays, Wednesdays, and Saturdays. Only the sky was as it used to be, the air same as in the old days, when my heart had been full of dreams.

Here and there as we walked along I saw the government sign displayed on the walls of a number of love-barracks, indicating whose turn it was to participate in these hygienic pleasures on Wednesdays; certain taverns also were evidently authorized to hang out the drinking sign, a beer glass cut out of tin and striped diagonally with the national colors: light brown, dark brown, light brown. Joy was doubtless already filling the hearts of those whose names appeared in the official list of Wednesday drinkers and who would thus partake of the Wednesday beer.

All the people we passed were stamped with the unmistakable mark of earnest zeal, encased in an aura of tireless activity probably intensified by the sight of the policeman. They all quickened their pace, assumed expressions of perfect devotion to duty, and the women coming out of the goods depots did their best to register that joy which was expected of them, for they were required to show joy and cheerful gaiety over the duties of the housewife, whose task it was to refresh the state worker every evening with a wholesome meal.

But all these people skillfully avoided us in such a way that no one was forced to cross our path directly. Where there were signs of life on the street, they disappeared twenty paces ahead of us, each trying to dash into a goods depot or vanish round a corner, and quite a few may have slipped into a strange house and waited nervously behind the door until the sound of our footsteps had died away.

Only once, just as we were crossing an intersection, we came face to face with an elderly man, I just caught a glimpse of his schoolteacher's badge. There was no time for him to avoid us, and he strove, after first saluting the policeman in the prescribed manner (by slapping his own head three times with the flat of his hand as a sign of total abasement)—he strove, as I say, to do his duty by spitting three times into my face and bestowing upon me the compulsory epithet of 'filthy traitor.' His aim was good, but the day had been hot, his throat must have been dry, for I received only a few tiny, rather ineffectual flecks, which—contrary to regulations—I tried involuntarily to wipe away with my sleeve, whereupon the policeman kicked me in the backside and struck me with his fist in the small of my back, adding in a flat voice, 'Phase One,' meaning: first and mildest form of punishment administrable by every policeman.

The schoolteacher had hurriedly gone on his way. Everyone else managed to avoid us; except for just one woman, who happened to be taking the prescribed stroll in the fresh air in front of a love-barracks prior to the evening's pleasures, a pale, puffy blonde who blew me a furtive kiss, and I smiled gratefully while the policeman tried to pretend he hadn't noticed. They are required to permit these women liberties that for any other comrade would unquestionably result in severe punishment; for, since they contribute substantially to the general working morale, they are tacitly considered to be outside the law, a concession whose far-reaching consequences have been branded as a sign of incipient liberalization by Professor Bleigoeth, PhD, DLitt, the political philosopher, in the obligatory (political) *Journal of Philosophy*. I had read this the previous day on my way to the capital when, in a farm outhouse, I came across a few sheets of the magazine that a student—probably the farmer's son—had embellished with some very witty comments.

Fortunately we now reached the police station, for at that moment the sirens sounded, a sign that the streets were about to be flooded with thousands of people wearing expressions of restrained joy (it being required at closing time to show restraint in one's expression of joy, otherwise it might look as though work were a burden; whereas rejoicing was to prevail when work began—rejoicing and singing), and all these thousands would have been compelled to spit at me. However, the siren indicated ten minutes before closing time, every worker being required to devote ten minutes to a thorough washing of his person, in accordance with the motto of the head of state: Joy and Soap.

The entrance to the local police station, a squat concrete box, was guarded by two sentries who, as I passed them, gave me the benefit of the customary 'physical punitive measures,' striking me hard across the temple with their rifles and cracking the muzzles of their pistols down on my collarbone, in accordance with the preamble to State Law No. I: 'Every police officer is required, when confronted by any apprehended [meaning arrested] person, to demonstrate violence *per se*, with the exception of the officer performing the arrest, the latter being privileged to participate in the pleasure of carrying out the necessary physical punitive measures during the interrogation.' The actual State Law No. I runs as follows: 'Every police officer *may* punish anyone: he *must* punish anyone who has committed a crime. For all comrades there is no such thing as exemption from punishment, only the possibility of exemption from punishment.'

We now proceeded down a long, bare corridor provided with a great many large windows. Then a door opened automatically, the sentries having already announced our arrival, and in those days, when everything was joy, obedience, and order and everyone did his best to use up the mandatory pound of soap a day—in those days the arrival of an apprehended (arrested) comrade was naturally, an event.

We entered an almost empty room containing nothing but a desk with a telephone and two chairs. I was required to remain standing in the middle of the room; the policeman took off his helmet and sat down.

At first there was silence; nothing happened. They always do it like that—that's the worst part. I could feel my face collapsing by degrees, I was tired and hungry, and by now even the last vestiges of that joy of sadness had vanished, for I knew I had had it.

After a few seconds a tall, pale-faced, silent man entered the room wearing the light-brown uniform of the preliminary interrogator. He sat down without a word and looked at me.

'Status?'

'Ordinary comrade.'

'Date of birth?'

'I/I/I,' I said.

'Last occupation?'

'Convict.'

The two men exchanged glances.

'When and where discharged?'

'Yesterday, Building 12, Cell 13.'

'Where to?'

'The capital.'

'Certificate.'

I produced the discharge certificate from my pocket and handed it to him. He clipped it to the green card on which he had begun to enter my particulars.

'Your former crime?'

'Happy face.'

The two men exchanged glances.

'Explain,' said the interrogator.

'At that time,' I said, 'my happy face attracted the attention of a police officer on a day when general mourning had been decreed. It was the anniversary of the Leader's death.'

'Length of sentence?'

'Five.'

'Conduct?'

'Bad.'

'Reason?'

'Deficient in work enthusiasm.'

'That's all.'

With that the preliminary interrogator rose, walked over to me, and neatly knocked out my three front center teeth—a sign that I was to be branded as a lapsed criminal, an intensified measure I had not counted on. The preliminary interrogator then left the room, and a fat fellow in a dark-brown uniform came in: the interrogator.

I was beaten by all of them: by the interrogator, the chief interrogator, the supreme interrogator, the examiner, and the concluding examiner. In addition, the policeman carried out all the physical punitive measures demanded by law, and on account of my sad face they sentenced me to ten years, just as five years earlier they had sentenced me to five years on account of my happy face.

I must now try to make my face register nothing at all, if I can manage to survive the next ten years of Joy and Soap . . .

1947–51   Translated by Leila Vennewitz

Sinclair Ross

Brief Biography

- Born near Prince Albert, SK, in 1908.
- Pursues career as a banker for forty-three years.
- Writes major works during the 'dirty thirties.'
- *As for Me and My House* (1941) given mixed reviews but becomes classic in 1957 reissue.
- Accomplished pianist and church organist.
- Is made a member of the Order of Canada in 1992.
- Dies in 1996 of complications from Parkinson's disease. His homosexuality, hidden during his life, is revealed by a biographer.

James Sinclair Ross was born on a homestead in Saskatchewan. Like his close friend Mavis Gallant, Ross had an unhappy childhood. After his parents separated, he and his mother moved from farm to farm. A high-school dropout, he took a job as a clerk in a variety of Prairie banks, where, except for World War II military service, he stayed until retirement in 1968. Stationed in London, England, during his service, he considered the war years happy ones due to the city's arts, opera, and culture.

After retiring from his banking career, Ross lived in Greece and Spain, returning to Canada to live in Montreal, where he was an avid filmgoer, and then to a nursing home in Vancouver. Reluctant to meet the public as an author, he always considered himself a banker 'who did a little writing on the side.' Though Ross's work was eventually embraced by the literary and scholarly community—for example, Margaret Laurence has acknowledged her debt to Ross's early work—he considered his writings failures.

Though Ross wrote three other novels, it was his first novel, *As for Me and My House* (1941), that profoundly influenced Canadian writing in general and Prairie writing in particular. The novel was first considered the perfect example of critic Northrop Frye's 'garrison mentality,' Canadians huddled together in the midst of a vast, unforgiving wilderness. In the early days of post-war Canadian nationalism, John Gray of MacMillan Publishers tried to foster a Canadian literary sensibility centred on the works of Ross, Laurence, W.O. Mitchell, and Morley Callaghan.

At first, the short stories collected in Ross's *The Lamp at Noon* (1968) were considered examples of grim Prairie realism, with blizzards, hail, and hard frost destroying the lives of Depression-era farmers. But there has been a shift towards diversity and inclusiveness in Ross scholarship, and later scholars find in his work strong poetic central images—a painted door, a dead baby, a frozen body, a woman in a well, a circus poster—which provide metaphoric possibilities for Prairie writers. One critic notes that Ross was the first Canadian writer to determine that landscape itself could be a metaphor for a character's emotional state and not just an exterior description. What was once seen as Prairie isolationism is now portrayed as a post-colonial community of migrants, minorities, and mixed households. His stories have clear thematic designs, often based on classical myths; works once read as 'naturalistic' are now seen as highly 'symbolic.' Beyond geopolitics, another generation of scholars 'rethinking Canada' finds a subtext of 'unstable identities,' 'veiled sexuality,' and 'queer gender' views embedded in Ross's fiction. Feminist critics and even psychoanalysts have revealed complex aspects to his seemingly simple prose.

'The Runaway' was written in 1949, slightly later than the Depression stories of 1938–42. In one reading, a story of disillusionment and failure emerges through the indirect narration of the protagonist's son, but some readers consider the story more of a comedy or morality tale than a tragedy, possibly inspired by Ross's reading of William Faulkner's famous story 'Barn Burning.'

The Runaway

You would have thought that old Luke Taylor was a regular and welcome visitor, the friendly, unconcerned way he rode over that afternoon, leading two of his best Black Diamond mares.

'Four-year-olds,' he said with a neighbourly smile. 'None better in my stable. But I'm running short of stall room—six more foals last spring—so I thought if you were interested we might work out a trade in steers.'

My father was interested. We were putting a load of early alfalfa in the loft, and he went on pitching a minute, aloof, indifferent, but between forkfuls he glanced down stealthily at the Diamonds, and at each glance I could see his suspicion and resistance ebb.

For more than twenty years old Luke had owned a stableful of Diamonds. They were his special pride, his passion. He bred them like a man dedicated to an ideal, culling and matching tirelessly. A horse was a credit to the Black Diamond Farm, a justification of the name, or it disappeared. There were broad-rumped, shaggy-footed work horses, slim-legged runners, serviceable in-betweens like the team he had with him now, suitable for saddle or wagon—at a pinch, even for a few days on the plough—but all, whatever their breed, possessed a flawless beauty, a radiance of pride and spirit, that quickened the pulse and brought a spark of wonder to the dullest eye. When they passed you turned from what you were doing and stood motionless, transfixed. When you met them on the road you instinctively gave them the right of way. And it didn't wear off. The hundredth time was no different from the first.

'None better in my stable,' old Luke repeated, and for once it was easy to believe him. Black coats shining in the sun like polished metal; long, rippling manes; imperious heads—the mares were superb, and they knew it. First, in a fine display of temperament, rearing rebelliously, they pretended astonishment and indignation: a barn with peeling paint and a sway-backed roof—it wasn't their due, they wouldn't submit to it! A moment later, all coy conciliation, they minced forward daintily for a nibble of our alfalfa.

I knew that since it was old Luke making the offer there must be a trick in it, that the bland voice and shifty smile must conceal some sly design, but far from trying to warn my father I held my breath, and hoped he would be weak and take them.

He was weak. A frown of annoyance at being interrupted in his work, a few critical preliminaries, looking at their teeth, feeling their knees, then a dubious, 'I've seen worse, but right now I've no real need of them. What would you be wanting in the way of trade?'

Old Luke was reasonable. He began with seven steers, and after a brief argument settled for four. 'Since we're old neighbours,' he agreed, 'and I'm running short of stall room.'

I saddled my pony Gopher and helped him home with the steers. He was talkative and friendly on the way, and when the pasture gate was safely closed he invited me into the house for a glass of lemonade. I made my excuses, of course—a barrel of lemonade, and he would still have been the man who foreclosed on a quarter-section of our land in a dry year, who up and down the countryside was as notorious for his shady deals as he was famous for his Diamonds; but cantering home I found myself relenting a little, deciding that maybe he had some good points after all.

I had wavered, it was true, before. Riding past the Taylor place it had always been a point of honour with me to keep my eyes fixed straight ahead, disdainfully, yet somehow the details of the barnyard and the aspect of the buildings had become as familiar to me as our own. My scorn had never been quite innocent of envy. The handsome grey-stone house might be the abode of guile, but I knew from one of the boys at school, whose parents sometimes visited the Taylors, that it contained a bathroom with hot and cold running water, just like the ones in town, and a mechanical piano that you played with pedals instead of your fingers. The big red hip-roofed barn might have been built with what my mother called 'his ill-gotten gains,' but in its stalls there were never fewer than twenty-four Black Diamonds. So I had my lapses. Sometimes I wished for a miracle harvest which would enable us to buy old Taylor out. Sometimes I went so far as to speculate on reconciliation and partnership.

Today, though, I wasn't just coveting the bathroom and piano. I was taking a critical look at ourselves, wondering whether our attitude towards Luke wasn't uncharitably severe, whether some of the stories told about him mightn't have been exaggerated. This time, in any case, he had been more than fair. Ten steers instead of four, and the trade would still have been in our favour.

My father had been similarly impressed. 'Luke must be getting close to seventy,' he met my mother's anger at the supper-table, 'and for all you know he's starting to repent. If he wants to turn honest and God-fearing at last it's for us to help him, not to keep raking up his past.'

'Old Luke turn God-fearing!' my mother cried bitterly.

'That's something I'll believe when I seem him trying to mend a little of the harm he's done. And you of all people to be taken in again! For a team of fancy horses!'

'But you can trust him where the Diamonds are concerned. They're his whole life. You'll find nothing in his stable but the best.'

'That's what I mean—those there's something wrong with he trades off for good fat steers.'

'Come out and look at them,' my father persisted. 'See for yourself.'

'I don't need to see. I know. If Luke got rid of them he had his reasons. They're spavined, or rouncts, or old.'

'Four-year-olds, and I checked them—teeth, feet—'

'But there are things you can't check. All the years we've known him has he once done what was right or decent? Do you know a man for twenty miles who'd trust him? Didn't he get your own land away from you for half what it was worth?' And she went on, shrill and exasperated, to pour out instance upon instance of his dishonesty and greed, everything from foreclosures on mortgages and bribes at tax and auction sales to the poker games in which, every fall for years, he had been fleecing his harvest-hands right after paying them.

Now, though, it all fell a little flat. I sat bored and restless, wondering when she would be done, and with a mild, appeasing gesture my father said, 'A lot of it's talk. For once let's give him the benefit of the doubt. We owe it to him till we're sure. It's only Christian charity.'

For a moment my mother struggled to control her anger. Then, her voice withering, she said, 'He's a sneak thief, one of the meanest, but with such fools for neighbours, just waiting to be taken in, I don't know that I can blame him.'

'We'll see,' my father answered. 'I'm going to town with them tomorrow, to see what they can do. Why don't you come along?'

My mother sat up straight and scornful. 'I'd walk first barefoot, and be less ashamed.'

The next day, however, she changed her mind. She even primped and curled a little, and found a brighter ribbon for her hat. My father, too, made his preparations. He washed the democrat, greased the axles, carefully cleaned and polished his two best sets of harness, and finally, after dinner, changed into his Sunday suit and a clean white shirt. His hands shook as he dressed. He called me in twice to crawl under the bed for a cuff button, and my mother had to help him with his tie.

At the last minute it was decided that I should stay home and hoe potatoes. For a while I sulked indignantly, but watching their departure I understood why they didn't want me with them. My father, driving up to the door with a reckless flourish of the whip, was so jaunty and important, and above the pebbly whirl of wheels as the Diamonds plunged away there was such a girlish peal of laughter from my mother! They were young again. My father had a team of

Diamonds, and my mother had something that his envious passion for them had taken from her twenty years ago. Walking over to the potato patch I realised that they couldn't possibly have taken me with them. Today's events, properly understood, were all before my time.

It was shortly after one o'clock when they set out. The round trip to town, travelling light, was about five hours with an ordinary team, and I expected, therefore, that with the Diamonds they would easily be back in good time for supper. But I had bedded down the stable, taken my own supper cold from the pantry and begun to fear there must have been a runaway or accident, when at last they arrived.

It was a return as dejected and shamefaced as the departure had been dashing and high-spirited. No whir of wheels, no peal of laughter, no snorts or capers from the Diamonds. For a minute or two, peering through the dusk, I thought that my father must have made another trade. Then I ran out to meet them, and my shout of welcome sagged to silence and bewilderment. It was a strange team of nondescript bays hitched to the democrat. The Diamonds were jogging along ignominiously behind.

'Did you think we were never coming?' my mother greeted me, the false brightness of her voice worse than the defeat of my father's rounded shoulders. 'Run along and help your father with the horses. I'll have a good supper ready in no time.'

My father's face, drawn and grey in the late twilight, restrained my curiosity as we unhitched. It wasn't till we had finished at the stable and were on our way to the house that he explained. 'They're balky—you know what that means. Not worth their keep. Trust old Luke—I might have known he'd put it over me.'

It was a bitter word. I swallowed hard and asked hopefully, 'Both of them?'

'Both of them. Right in Main Street, wouldn't take a step. Just as we were ready to start for home. Two hours—the whole town watching. I even took the whip to them, but with balky horses nothing helps. The longer they stand the worse they get. I had to unhitch at last, and hire a team from the livery stable.'

Nothing more was said, by either him or my mother, but not much imagination was needed to reconstruct the scene. His pride as he spanked up Main Street, the same pride I had witnessed earlier that day, the same youth and showmanship; and then the sudden collapse of it all, the unbearable moment of humiliation when the Diamonds, instead of springing away with flying manes and foaming mouths, striking sparks of envy and wonder from the heart of every beholder, simply stood there, chewed their bits and trembled.

For my mother, too, it had been a memorably cruel experience. Doubly cruel, for in addition to her embarrassment—and perched up on the democrat seat with the crowd around her, a town-shy woman, sensitive to her rough hands and plain clothes, she must have suffered acutely—in addition to that there was the burden of concealing it from my father, suppressing criticism and anger, pretending not to have noticed that he had made a fool of himself. For of the two she was in many ways the stronger, the more responsible, and she must have known instantly, even as they sat there in the democrat, that the Diamonds were a crisis in his life, and that to bring him safely through there was urgent need of all her skill and sympathy.

Even so, he came through badly. For it wasn't just four good steers against two balky Diamonds. It wasn't just a matter of someone getting the better of him. It was that after all these years old Taylor should still be practising fraud and trickery, still getting away with it, still prospering.

According to his lights my father was a good man, and his bewilderment was in proportion to his integrity. For years he had been weakened and confused by a conflict, on the one hand resentment at what Luke had done and got away with, on the other sincere convictions imposing patience and restraint; but through it all he had been sustained by the belief that scores were being kept, and that he would live to see a Day of Reckoning. Now, though, he wasn't sure. You could see in his glance and frown that he was beginning to wonder which he really was: the upright, God-fearing man that he had always believed himself to be, or a simple, credulous dupe. There was the encounter with the Taylors at church, for instance, just a Sunday or two after his trip to town with the Diamonds. It wasn't an accidental or inevitable encounter. After the service they deliberately came over and spoke to us. There were a few polite remarks; then old Luke, screwing up his little eyes and leering, enquired about the Diamonds. He understood we had been having trouble with them, and hoped that they were doing better now. 'They're touchy and high-strung, you know,' he said blandly. 'You can't treat them just like ordinary horses.'

My father turned without a word and walked over to the democrat. 'He's an old man,' he said quietly as we drove off. 'It's for the Lord to judge, not me.' But his expression belied the charity of his words. His mouth was hard with the suspicion that the Lord saw nothing in his behaviour to condemn.

We drove a while in silence. Then I suggested, 'He traded them off on you— why don't you try it now on someone else?'

'Two wrongs never make a right,' my mother reproved me quickly. 'Besides, they're good mares, and we'll get good colts out of them. They may even turn out all right themselves, if your father separates them, and gives them a spell of good hard work. Touchy and high-strung is right. What they need is to be brought down a peg or two.'

How could she? My father glanced at her sidewise without answering, and I saw the reproach in his eyes. Had she no feeling, then, at all? Did she not know that it was only as a team, flashing along in unison, striking sparks, taking corners on two wheels, that they were Diamonds? That separated, their identities lost among old Bill and Ned and Bessie, they would be clods, nonentities? And watching the lines around his mouth grow firm I knew that he would never consent to such a degradation. They would always be a team of Diamonds. Their foam-flecked, sun-sparked loveliness might disappoint his vanity, might elude his efforts to exploit it, but it would live on, in stall and pasture, finally in memory, resplendent and inviolate.

His vanity, though, died hard. 'Balky horses,' he remarked casually a few days later, 'are just scared horses. Nerves—a fright, maybe, when they were colts. Treat them right and they should get over it. Keep cool, I mean, and help them through their bad spells.'

Of course he was wrong. He should have known what every horseman knows, that a balky horse is never cured. If you're unscrupulous, you'll trade it off or sell it. If you're honest, you'll shoot it. Promptly, humanely, before it exasperates you to moments of rage and viciousness from which your self-respect will never quite recover. For weeks and months on end it will be a model horse, intelligent, co-operative, and then one fine day, when you're least expecting trouble, it will be a balky one again. You'll waste time and patience on it. You'll try persuasion first, then shouts and curses. You'll go back to persuasion, then degrade yourself to blows. And at last, weary and ashamed, you'll let the traces down and lead it to its stall.

But to renounce the Diamonds, now that he actually owned them, wasn't easy. He was a simple, devout man, but not by any means an other-worldly one, and all these years, struggling along in the shadow of Luke's prosperity, he had suffered, discipline himself as he would, the pangs of envy and frustration. Three hundred acres against two thousand, weather-beaten old buildings against the big stone house and hip-roofed barn, plodding work-horses against the handsome, show-off Diamonds—comparisons and a sense of failure had been inevitable.

From the beginning it was the Diamonds that had hurt him most. If Luke had indulged himself in anything else, tractors or pedigreed bulls, it would have been comparatively easy. But a horseman more passionate and discerning than my father never lived. In ordinary circumstances, being genuine, he would probably have found satisfaction in ordinary horses, like the ones he owned— humble, worthy creatures, their only fault a lack of grace and fire—but there was a splendour about the Diamonds, a poise, a dramatic loftiness, that left in its wake a blight of shabbiness and discontent. Arching their necks like emperor horses, flinging their heads up, pealing trumpet neighs—how could my father *help* wanting them? How could he turn to his own dull, patient brutes and feel anything but shame?

Yet he had never tried to acquire Black Diamonds or their equals for himself. At least one team would have been possible. He was a poor farmer, but he managed other things. In part, no doubt, it was because of his faith, his childlike sincerity. He prayed for deliverance from the vanities of the world because he wanted deliverance, and while unable to control his desire for the Diamonds, he could at least resist the temptation to possess them. But if it was in part because he struggled against the vanities of the world, it was also in part because he yielded to the vanity within himself. For one team would have been to reveal his desire, his ambition. One team would have been to set himself up for public comparison, two Black Diamonds against twenty-four.

But all that was forgotten now, lost in the excitement of actual possession. 'Nothing but nerves,' he kept saying, 'scared when they were little. I'd be balky too, if old Luke had ever had the handling of me.'

Give him his due, he worked intelligently. He took them out, for instance, when he wasn't pressed for time. He kept to quiet side-roads, where he wasn't likely to be watched or flustered. Usually he had me go along on Gopher, because it was their nature to resent another horse in front of them, and if I rode ahead they invariably responded with a competitive burst of speed. In the main things went well. So well that as the summer wore on he gradually became a little careless, and absently as it were, began to leave the unfrequented side-roads for the highway. At that, the highway was safe enough so long as they kept going. They never stopped of their own accord. There was no danger except when it came time to start them.

Mindful of this, my father always left the front gate open. His route was always a non-stop square, cross-road to cross-road, with right angle turns that could be taken at a trot. He never went so far that it was necessary to rest the Diamonds. When he met a neighbour, he resisted the temptation to discuss crops and weather, and sailed past grandly with a nod or wave.

There was one hazard, however, that he overlooked. A gust of wind took his hat one day, and impulsively, before he could think of the possible consequences, or notice old Taylor approaching from the opposite direction on horseback, he reined in the Diamonds to a standstill.

And after weeks without a single lapse, that had to be the moment for them to balk again. Was it the arrival of Taylor, I have often wondered, something about his smell or voice, that revived colthood memories? Or was it my father's anger that flared at the sight of him, and ran out through his fingers and along the reins like an electric current, communicating to them his own tensions, his conflicting impulses of hatred and forbearance? No matter—they balked, and as if to enjoy my father's mortification, old Luke too reined in and sat watching. 'Quite a man with horses,' he laughed across at me. 'One of the finest teams for miles and just look at the state he's got them in. Better see what you can do, son, before he ruins them completely.' And then, squinting over his shoulder as he rode off, he added, 'I'll tell you how to get a balky horse going. It's easy—just build a little fire under him.'

'I wouldn't put it past him at that,' my father muttered, as he climbed down and started to unhitch. 'Being what he is, the idea of fire comes natural.'

But for the time being that was all. Harvest was on us, and for the next two months the Diamonds pawed their stall. It wasn't till November, after threshing was finished and the grain hauled, that my father was free to hitch them up again. And by that time, eager as colts after their long idleness, they were in no mood for balking. Instead, they seemed ashamed of their past, and to want nothing more than to live it down, to establish themselves as dependable members of our little farmyard community. 'All they needed was the right care,' my father said complacently one day. 'They're not mean or stubborn horses by nature. It's as I've always said—something must have happened when they were colts.'

And for a week or two he was young again. Young, lighthearted, confident. Confident in the Diamonds, confident in the rightness of the world. Old Luke had traded off balky horses on him, but now, in the service of an upright man, they were already willing, loyal ones. It showed you. Plant potatoes eyes down, and up they come the right way. They were such fine, mettled horses, such a credit to creation. Watching and working with them it was impossible to doubt that at the heart of things there was wisdom, goodness, and a plan. They were an affirmation, a mighty Yea. They made the world right, and old Taylor un-important.

With it all, though, my father was a practical man, and soon he decided that the Diamonds must be put to work. There had been enough driving round the country in the democrat. It was time they got used to pulling loads and spend-ing an entire day in harness.

Care and patience were still necessary, and as a cautious beginning he hitched them up one afternoon and went for straw. (We used straw in con-siderable quantities for bedding down the stable, and not having loft room for it, brought it in, a rackful at a time, from the field, every week or ten days.) It was a short haul, and a light load. The day, moreover, was cold and windy, and it was to be expected that after standing while we built the load they would be impatient for their stall. As usual I rode Gopher, and set off for home a minute or two ahead of them.

But it was one of their bad days. I looked back after a short distance, and they hadn't moved. My father was up on the load, clicking them forward vainly.

We both tried to be nonchalant. My father climbed down and lit his pipe, threw on another forkful of straw as if he hadn't noticed anything. I led Gopher close to the Diamonds so that they could sniff at one another, then mounted him and started home a second time.

But to no avail. My father picked up the reins again; they only mouthed their bits and trembled. He tried to lead them forward; they only braced themselves, cowering against each other as if in fear of a blow.

'Let's unhitch,' I said uneasily. 'It's nearly dark, and we're only wasting time.' But ignoring me, he turned his back and lit his pipe again.

I knew there was trouble brewing. I knew from the way he was standing that the contagion had spread, that his real nature, too, was paralyzed and darkened.

'Let's unhitch,' I repeated. 'They're only getting worse. First thing they'll be as bad as when you started.'

'They're that already,' he replied, hunching his shoulders and scowling at the Diamonds. 'Unhitching's getting us nowhere. It's only giving in. I think I'll take old Luke's advice, and see what a fire will do.'

I began to protest, but he assured me that it would be a small fire. 'Not enough to burn them—just so they'll feel the heat coming up around their legs. I've heard of it before. They'll take a jump ahead, and then keep going.'

It sounded sensible enough. There was something about his voice and shoulders that forbade further protest, anyway. Without looking round again he tossed a small forkful of straw under the Diamonds, then bent cautiously to light it.

I closed my eyes a moment. When I opened them he had straightened and stepped back, and there on the ground between the Diamonds' feet, like something living that he had slipped out of his coat, was a small yellow flame, flickering up nervously against the dusk.

For a second or two, feeling its way slowly round the straw, it remained no larger than a man's outspread hand. Then, with a spurt of sparks and smoke, it shot up right to the Diamonds' bellies.

They gave a frightened snort, lunged ahead a few feet, stopped short again. The fire now, burning briskly, was directly beneath the load of straw, and even as I shouted to warn my father a tongue of flame licked up the front of the rack, and the next instant, sudden as a fan being flicked open, burst into a crackling blaze.

The Diamonds shook their heads and pawed a moment, then in terror of the flames and my father's shouts, set off across the field at a thundering, breakneck gallop. I followed on Gopher, flogging him with the ends of the reins, but straining his utmost he couldn't overtake or pass them. A trail of smoke and sparks was blowing back, and as we galloped along he kept shaking his head and coughing. Through my half-closed eyes I could see the wagon lurching dangerously over the frozen ruts of the rough wagon-trail we were following, and it flashed across my mind that if the rack upset we would ride right into it. But still I kept on lashing Gopher, pounding him with my heels. The gate was open, and there were oatstacks beside the stable. If I didn't get ahead and turn them, they would set the buildings on fire.

They turned, though, of their own accord. About a quarter of a mile from where we started the road forked, one branch turning into the barnyard, the other circling out to the highway. Riding close behind, my head lowered against the smoke and sparks, I didn't realise, till the wagon took the little ditch onto the highway at a sickening lurch, that the Diamonds were going home. Not to their new home, where they belonged now, but to old Luke Taylor's place.

I lashed and pommelled Gopher even harder, but still we couldn't gain. The highway stretched out straight and smooth, and the Diamonds were going home. Terror in their hearts, hitched to a load of fire. Through the clatter of wheels their hoof-beats sounded sharp and rhythmic like an urgent drum. Telephone poles leaped up startled and pale as we tore along, and an instant later flicked out again into the dark. Once I caught a glimpse of a horse and buggy down in the ditch, the horse rearing and white-eyed, the man leaning back on the reins with all his strength. Once it was a frantic cow, struggling to escape through the barbed-wire fence that ran alongside the road. Gopher, meanwhile, was gaining, and presently the hot smoke in our faces was a cold blast of wind. Then I could see the Diamonds, the flying manes, the sheen of the flames on their glossy hides. Then we were riding neck and neck with them.

It was a good ride. The sparks flew and the hooves thundered, and all the way I knew that for months to come the telling of it would be listened to. A good ride, but a fatal finish. The Taylor gate was open, and still galloping hard the Diamonds made a sharp swerve off the road and through it. There was a faint, splintering sound as the hind hub caught one of the posts; the next instant, only twenty or thirty feet in front of the big hip-roofed barn, wagon and rack turned over.

It was a well-built, solid load of straw, scarcely half burned away, and what was left spilled out across the yard in loose, tumbling masses that blazed up fiercely as if drenched with gasoline. I was sick with fright by this time, scarcely able to control Gopher, but even as I turned him through the gate, jerking and sawing at his bit, yelling at the top of my voice for old Taylor, I realised the danger. The loft door, where they had been putting in feed, was standing wide open. Sparks and bits of burning straw were already shooting up towards it in a steady stream.

I knew the door had to be closed, that there wasn't a second to lose, but as I jumped down from Gopher Mrs Taylor ran out of the house and began shouting at me to get back on my horse and go for Luke. He and his man had been away all afternoon to town. By this time, though, they should be nearly home again, and while I went to meet them she would telephone the neighbours.

There wasn't time to go for Luke, and I had sense enough to turn my back on her, but the Diamonds now, still hitched to the overturned wagon, were kicking and snorting wildly about the barnyard, and for two or three minutes, until the whiffle-tree snapped and they plunged off free into the darkness, I could only stand petrified and watch them. Gopher too was excited. Getting him quietened and tied meant another delay. Then I had to make my way into the barn, completely strange to me, and grope along through the darkness in search of a stairway leading to the loft.

The flames were ahead of me. Already they were licking across the littered, clear space round the door, and up the hay that was stacked and mounded to within a few feet of the roof. I watched helplessly for a minute, then sprang down the stairs again. Mrs Taylor had come as far as the door, and was still shouting at me to go for Luke. I knew that the barn was lost, but, responding to the urgency in her voice, I ran across the yard and untied Gopher. I had mounted, and was two or three hundred yards down the road to meet Luke, before I came abruptly to my senses and realized that there were horses in the barn.

By the time I had Gopher tied again the loft door was a bright rectangle of flame, and when I reached the barn the air was already dense with smoke. Shrill neighs greeted me, but for a moment I could see nothing. Then there was a sudden blaze at the far end of the feed-ally, and an instant later the out-thrust nose and flattened ears of one of the Diamonds were silhouetted against the glow.

I ran forward and squeezed in past its heels, then untied the halter-shank, but when I tried to lead it out it trembled and crushed its body tight against the side of the stall. I climbed into the manger, struck it hard across the nose; it only stamped and tossed its head. Then I tried the next stall, then the next and the next. Each time I met the same fear-crazed resistance. One of the Diamonds lashed out with its heels. Another caught me such a blow with a swing of its head that I leaned half-stunned for a minute against the manger. Another, its eyes rolling white and glassy, slashed with its teeth as I turned, and ripped my smock from shoulder to shoulder.

Meanwhile the smoke was thickening, biting at my throat and eyes like acid, and, suddenly panic-stricken, racked by a violent fit of coughing, I stumbled out dizzily to safety.

The cold wind revived me. The sight of the leaping flames cleared my eyes of smoke and sting.

I stood rooted a minute, staring. The roof by this time had burned through in several places, and huge spouts of flame and smoke were shooting up high against the darkness, spark-streaked and swift, as if blown out by a giant forge. Then I was roused by the sound of galloping hooves and the rattle of wheels, and a minute or two later the neighbours began to arrive: They came in buggies and wagons and on horseback. All at once the yard was alive with them, shouting advice and warnings to one another, running about aimlessly. A few entered the barn, only to stagger out again retching and coughing. My father was among them, and in his relief at finding me unhurt he clutched the collar of my smock and shook me till fire and men and horses were all spinning. Then old Luke arrived, and agile as a boy he leapt down from his wagon and started across the yard towards the barn. Three or four of the neighbours closed in to intercept him, but swerving sharply, then doubling back, he sprang away from them and through the door.

The same moment that he disappeared the floor of the loft collapsed. It was as if when running through the door he had sprung a trap, the way the great, billowy masses of burning hay plunged down behind him. There were tons and tons of it. The air caught it as it fell, and it blazed up throbbing like a furnace. We put our hands to our faces before the heat, and fell back across the yard.

A cry came from Mrs Taylor that was sucked up quickly into the soft, roaring silence of the flames. One of the neighbours helped her into the house. The rest of us stood, watching. It was terrible and long because we didn't know whether it had already happened, whether it was happening now, or whether it was still to happen. At last my father slipped away, and presently returned leading our own team of Diamonds. They stood quiet and spent, their heads nearly to the ground, while we righted the wagon and tied up the broken whiffle-tree. Afraid they might balk again, I mounted Gopher as usual and rode through the gate ahead of them, but at the first click of the reins they trotted off obediently. Obediently and dully, like a team of reliable old ploughhorses. Riding along beside them, listening to the soft creak and jingle of the harness, I had the feeling that we, too, had lost our Diamonds.

It was nearly nine o'clock when we reached home, but my mother was still waiting supper. 'It's as I've always said,' she kept repeating, filling our plates and taking them away untouched. '*Though the mills of God grind slowly, yet they grind exceeding small.* His own balky Diamonds, and look what they carried home to him.' She hadn't been there to see it—that was why she could say such things. 'You sow the wind and you reap the whirlwind. Better for him today if he had debts and half-a-section like the rest of us.'

But my father sat staring before him as though he hadn't heard her. There was a troubled, old look in his eyes, and I knew that for him it was not so simple as that to rule off a man's account and show it balanced. Leave Luke out of it now—say that so far as he was concerned the scores were settled but what about the Diamonds? What kind of reckoning was it that exacted life and innocence for an old man's petty greed? Why, if it was retribution, had it struck so clumsily?

'All of them,' he said at last, 'all of them but the team he was driving and my own two no-good balky ones. Prettiest horses a man ever set eyes on. It wasn't coming to them.'

'But you'll raise colts,' my mother said quickly, pouring him a fresh cup of coffee, 'and there'll be nothing wrong with them. Five or six years—why, you'll have a stableful.'

He sipped his coffee in silence a moment and then repeated softly, 'Prettiest horses a man ever set eyes on. No matter what you say, it wasn't coming to them.' But my mother's words had caught. Even as he spoke his face was brightening, and it was plain that he too, now, was thinking of the colts.

1949

Ethel Wilson

Brief Biography

- Born in 1888 in South Africa to Methodist missionaries.
- Eighteen months old when mother dies, nine when father dies of pneumonia in England; moves to British Columbia and is raised by stern religious grandmother whom she lives with until age thirty-one.
- Marries prominent physician in 1921.
- Writes major works between the end of World War II and husband's death in 1966.
- Novels include *Hetty Dorval* (1947), *The Innocent Traveller* (1949), and *Swamp Angel* (1954).
- Dies of a stroke in a Vancouver nursing home in 1980.

More than fifty years old before publishing fiction, Ethel Wilson eventually produced six volumes as well as many uncollected essays and stories. Although her public persona suggested that she considered her writing a casual, almost incidental occupation, biographer David Stouck shows that she took her craft seriously, 'serv[ing] a particularly long and earnest apprenticeship.' Called British Columbia's Jane Austen, and 'one of the foremothers of Canadian writing,' she was a cultivated and graceful stylist intrigued by the complexity of human motivations and the destinies her (often female) characters pursue in the interests of self-knowledge and social responsibility.

Like her favourite English metaphysical poet, John Donne, Wilson felt that 'no man is an island'; she believed that isolation was tempered by love and the power of friendship, family, and marriage. Although her close friend Margaret Laurence often wrote of orphans, Wilson remained silent about her feelings of parental loss, yet her characters are often grieving, motherless women. Separation and depression, shaping forces in Wilson's life, became common themes in her works. Through accidents or mistakes, many of her characters become aware of the precariousness of existence and confront their illusory pasts in order to pave the way for more authentic futures.

Although Wilson published little about her art and was not widely studied until the 1980s, she found early appreciators of her work in Laurence, whose writing Wilson encouraged, and Alice Munro, who wrote an afterword to *The Equations of Love* (1952; rpt 1990). Canadian critic George Woodcock referred to her 'Edwardian sensibility' over which a thoroughly modernist sense of irony is superimposed. More recently, feminist critics note the capacities of self-empowerment in her female characters, the role of mother and daughter relationships, and the theme of mourning. Scholars in India, China, and Austria note her disdain for nationalism—even as she stresses the importance of place in a post-colonial context, she is dubious of such concepts as 'home' in a migrant world.

From her collection *Mrs. Golightly and Other Stories* (1961), 'The Window' (like

Joyce's stories in *Dubliners*) is set in a real place presented by a series of associations. The vitality of the outside landscape of downtown Vancouver is described down to each passing duck, yet from the perspective of an outsider. Mr Willy is placed in the setting of lights, sea, mountains, and glass; his background is quickly sketched, and then the challenges to his self-imposed isolation appear. The dividing line is the large, plate glass window— as a symbol, it resonates on many levels from observation viewpoint to isolating barrier and mirror of illusions.

The Window

The great big window must have been at least twenty-five feet wide and ten feet high. It was constructed in sections divided by segments of something that did not interfere with the view; in fact the eye by-passed these divisions and looked only at the entrancing scenes beyond. The window, together with a glass door at the western end, composed a bland shallow curve and formed the entire transparent north-west (but chiefly north) wall of Mr Willy's living-room.

Upon his arrival from England Mr Willy had surveyed the various prospects of living in the quickly growing city of Vancouver with the selective and discarding characteristics which had enabled him to make a fortune and retire all of a sudden from business and his country in his advanced middle age. He settled immediately upon the very house. It was a small old house overlooking the sea between Spanish Banks and English Bay. He knocked out the north wall and made the window. There was nothing particular to commend the house except that it faced immediately on the sea-shore and the view. Mr Willy had left his wife and her three sisters to play bridge together until death should overtake them in England. He now paced from end to end of his living-room, that is to say from east to west, with his hands in his pockets, admiring the northern view. Sometimes he stood with his hands behind him looking through the great glass window, seeing the wrinkled or placid sea and the ships almost at his feet and beyond the sea the mountains, and seeing sometimes his emancipation. His emancipation drove him into a dream, and sea sky mountains swam before him, vanished, and he saw with immense release his wife in still another more repulsive hat. He did not know, nor would he have cared, that much discussion went on in her world, chiefly in the afternoons, and that he was there alleged to have deserted her. So he had, after providing well for her physical needs which were all the needs of which she was capable. Mrs Willy went on saying '. . . and he would come home my dear and never speak a word I can't tell you my dear how *frightful* it was night after night I might say for *years* I simply can't tell you . . .' No, she could not tell but she did, by day and night. Here he was at peace, seeing out of the window the crimped and wrinkled sea and the ships which passed and passed each other, the seabirds and the dream-inducing sky.

At the extreme left curve of the window an island appeared to slope into the sea. Behind this island and to the north, the mountains rose very high. In the summer time the mountains were soft, deceptive in their innocency, full of crags and crevasses and arêtes and danger. In the winter they lay magnificent, white and much higher, it seemed, than in the summer time. They tossed, static, in almost visible motion against the sky, inhabited only by eagles and—so a man had told Mr Willy, but he didn't believe the man—by mountain sheep and some cougars, bears, wild cats and, certainly, on the lower slopes, deer, and now a ski camp far out of sight. Mr Willy looked at the mountains and regretted his past youth and his present wealth. How could he endure to be old and rich and able only to look at these mountains which in his youth he had not known and did not climb. Nothing, now, no remnant of his youth would come and enable him to climb these mountains. This he found hard to believe, as old people do. He was shocked at the newly realized decline of his physical powers which had proved good enough on the whole for his years of success, and by the fact that now he had, at last, time and could not swim (heart), climb mountains (heart and legs), row a boat in a rough enticing sea (call that old age). These things have happened to other people, thought Mr Willy, but not to us, now, who have been so young, and yet it will happen to those who now are young.

Immediately across the water were less spectacular mountains, pleasant slopes which in winter time were covered with invisible skiers. Up the dark mountain at night sprang the lights of the ski-lift, and ceased. The shores of these mountains were strung with lights, littered with lights, spangled with lights, necklaces, bracelets, constellations, far more beautiful as seen through this window across the dark water than if Mr Willy had driven his car across the Lions' Gate Bridge and westwards among those constellations which would have disclosed only a shopping centre, people walking in the streets, street lights, innumerable cars and car lights like anywhere else and, up the slopes, people's houses. Then, looking back to the south across the dark water towards his own home and the great lighted window which he would not have been able to distinguish so far away, Mr Willy would have seen lights again, a carpet of glitter thrown over the slopes of the city.

Fly from one shore to the other, fly and fly back again, fly to a continent or to an island, but you are no better off than if you stayed all day at your own window (and such a window), thought Mr Willy pacing back and forth, then into the kitchen to put the kettle on for a cup of tea which he will drink beside the window, back for a glass of whisky, returning in time to see a cormorant flying level with the water, not an inch too high not an inch too low, flying out of sight. See the small ducks lying on the water, one behind the other, like beads on a string. In the mornings Mr Willy drove into town to see his investment broker and perhaps to the bank or round the park. He lunched, but not at a club. He then drove home. On certain days a woman called Mrs Ogden came in to 'do' for him. This was his daily life, very simple, and a routine was formed whose pattern could at last be discerned by an interested observer outside the window.

One night Mr Willy beheld a vast glow arise behind the mountains. The Arctic world was obviously on fire—but no, the glow was not fire glow, flame glow. The great invasion of colour that spread up and up the sky was not red, was not rose, but of a synthetic cyclamen colour. This cyclamen glow remained steady from mountain to zenith and caused Mr Willy, who had never seen the Northern Lights, to believe that these were not Northern Lights but that something had occurred for which one must be prepared. After about an hour, flanges of green as of putrefaction, and a melodious yellow arose and spread. An hour later the Northern Lights faded, leaving Mr Willy small and alone.

Sometimes as, sitting beside the window, he drank his tea, Mr Willy thought that nevertheless it is given to few people to be as happy (or contented, he would say), as he was, at his age, too. In his life of decisions, men, pressures, more men, antagonisms, fusions, fissions and Mrs Willy, in his life of hard success, that is, he had sometimes looked forward but so vaguely and rarely to a time when he would not only put this life down; he would leave it. Now he had left it and here he was by his window. As time went on, though, he had to make an effort to summon this happiness, for it seemed to elude him. Sometimes a thought or a shape (was it?), gray, like wood ash that falls in pieces when it is touched, seemed to be behind his chair, and this shape teased him and communicated to him that he had left humanity behind, that a man needs humanity and that if he ceases to be in touch with man and is not in touch with God, he does not matter. 'You do not matter any more,' said the spectre like wood ash before it fell to pieces, 'because you are no longer in touch with anyone and so you do not exist. You are in a vacuum and so you are nothing.' Then Mr Willy, at first uneasy, became satisfied again for a time after being made uneasy by the spectre. A storm would get up and the wind, howling well, would lash the window sometimes carrying the salt spray from a very high tide which it flung against the great panes of glass. That was a satisfaction to Mr Willy and within him something stirred and rose and met the storm and effaced the spectre and other phantoms which were really vague regrets. But the worst that happened against the window was that from time to time a little bird, sometimes but not often a seabird, flung itself like a stone against the strong glass of the window and fell, killed by the passion of its flight. This grieved Mr Willy, and he could not sit unmoved when the bird flew at the clear glass and was met by death. When this happened, he arose from his chair, opened the glass door at the far end of the window, descended three or four steps and sought in the grasses for the body of the bird. But the bird was dead, or it was dying, its small bones were smashed, its head was broken, its beak split, it was killed by the rapture of its flight. Only once Mr Willy found the bird a little stunned and picked it up. He cupped the bird's body in his hands and carried it into the house.

Looking up through the grasses at the edge of the rough terrace that de-scended to the beach, a man watched him return into the house, carrying the bird. Still looking obliquely through the grasses the man watched Mr Willy en-ter the room and vanish from view. Then Mr Willy came again to the door, pushed it open, and released the bird which flew away, who knows where. He closed the door, locked it, and sat down on the chair facing east beside the win-dow and began to read his newspaper. Looking over his paper he saw, to the east, the city of Vancouver deployed over rising ground with low roofs and high buildings and at the apex the tall Electric Building which at night shone like a broad shaft of golden light.

This time, as evening drew on, the man outside went away because he had other business.

Mr Willy's investment broker was named Gerald Wardho. After a time he said to Mr Willy in a friendly but respectful way, 'Will you have lunch with me at the Club tomorrow?' and Mr Willy said he would. Some time later Gerald Wardho said, 'Would you like me to put you up at the Club?'

Mr Willy considered a little the life which he had left and did not want to re-enter and also the fact that he had only last year resigned his membership in three clubs, so he said, 'That's very good of you, Wardho, but I think not. I'm enjoying things as they are. It's a novelty, living in a vacuum . . . I like it, for a time anyway.'

'Yes, but,' said Gerald Wardho, 'you'd be some time on the waiting list. It wouldn't hurt—'

'No,' said Mr Willy, 'no.'

Mr Willy had, Wardho thought, a distinguished appearance or perhaps it was an affable accustomed air, and so he had. When Mrs Wardho said to her husband, 'Gerry, there's not an extra man in this town and I need a man for Saturday,' Gerald Wardho said, 'I know a man. There's Willy.'

Mrs Wardho said doubtfully, 'Willy? Willy who? Who's Willy?'

Her husband said, 'He's fine, he's okay, I'll ask Willy.'

'How old is he?'

'About a hundred . . . but he's okay.'

'Oh-h-h,' said Mrs Wardho, 'isn't there anyone anywhere unattached young any more? Does he play bridge?'

'I'll invite him, I'll find out,' said her husband, and Mr Willy said he'd like to come to dinner.

'Do you care for a game of bridge, Mr Willy?' asked Gerald Wardho.

'I'm afraid not,' said Mr Willy kindly but firmly. He played a good game of bridge but had no intention of entering servitude again just yet, losing his freedom, and being enrolled as what is called a fourth. Perhaps later; not yet. 'If you're having bridge I'll come another time. Very kind of you, Wardho.'

'No no no,' said Gerald Wardho, 'there'll only be maybe a table of bridge for anyone who wants to play. My wife would be disappointed.'

'Well thank you very much. Black tie?'

'Yes. Black tie,' said Gerald Wardho.

And so, whether he would or no, Mr Willy found himself invited to the kind of evening parties to which he had been accustomed and which he had left behind, given by people younger and more animated than himself, and he realized that he was on his way to becoming old odd man out. There was a good deal of wood ash at these parties—that is, behind him the spectre arose, falling to pieces when he looked at it, and said 'So this is what you came to find out on this coast, so far from home, is it, or is there something else. What else is there?' The spectre was not always present at these parties but sometimes awaited him at home and said these things.

One night Mr Willy came home from an evening spent at Gerald Wardho's brother-in-law's house, a very fine house indeed. He had left lights burning and began to turn out the lights before he went upstairs. He went into the living-room and before turning out the last light gave a glance at the window which had in the course of the evening behaved in its accustomed manner. During the day the view through the window was clear or cloudy, according to the weather or the light or absence of light in the sky; but there it was—the view—never quite the same though, and that is owing to the character of oceans or of any water, great or small, and of light. Both water and light have so great an effect on land observed on any scene, rural urban or wilderness, that one begins to think that life, that a scene, is an illusion produced by influences such as water and light. At all events, by day the window held this fine view as in a frame, and the view was enhanced by ships at sea of all kinds, but never was the sea crowded, and by birds, clouds, and even aeroplanes in the sky—no people to spoil this fine view. But as evening approached, and moonless night, all the view (illusion again) vanished slowly. The window, which was not illusion, only the purveyor of illusion, did not vanish, but became a mirror which reflected against the blackness every detail of the shallow living-room. Through this clear reflection of the whole room, distant lights from across the water intruded, and so chains of light were thrown across the reflected mantelpiece, or a picture, or a human face, enhancing it. When Mr Willy had left his house to dine at Gerald Wardho's brother-in-law's house the view through the window was placidly clear, but when he returned at 11:30 the window was dark and the room was reflected from floor to ceiling against the blackness. Mr Willy saw himself entering the room like a stranger, looking at first debonair with such a gleaming shirt front and then—as he approached himself—a little shabby, his hair perhaps. He advanced to the window and stood looking at himself with the room in all its detail behind him.

Mr Willy was too often alone, and spent far too much time in that space which lies between the last page of the paper or the turning-off of the radio in surfeit, and sleep. Now as he stood at the end of the evening and the beginning of the night, looking at himself and the room behind him, he admitted that the arid feeling which he had so often experienced lately was probably what is called loneliness. And yet he did not want another woman in his life. It was a long time since he had seen a woman whom he wanted to take home or even to see again. Too much smiling. Men were all right, you talked to them about the market, the emergence of the Liberal Party, the impossibility of arriving anywhere with those people while that fellow was in office, nuclear war (instant hells opened deep in everyone's mind and closed again), South Africa where Mr Willy was born, the Argentine where Mr Wardho's brother-in-law had spent many years—and then everyone went home.

Mr Willy, as the months passed by, was dismayed to find that he had entered an area of depression unknown before, like a tundra, and he was a little frightened of this tundra. Returning from the dinner party he did not at once turn out the single last light and go upstairs. He sat down on a chair beside the window and at last bowed his head upon his hands. As he sat there, bowed, his thoughts went very stiffly (for they had not had much exercise in that direction throughout his life), to some area that was not tundra but that area where there might be some meaning in creation which Mr Willy supposed must be the place where some people seemed to find a God, and perhaps a personal God at that. Such theories, or ideas, or passions had never been of interest to him, and if he had thought of such theories, or ideas, or passions he would have dismissed them as invalid and having no bearing on life as it is lived, especially when one is too busy. He had formed the general opinion that people who hold such beliefs were either slaves to an inherited convention, hypocrites, or nit-wits. He regarded such people without interest, or at least he thought them negligible as he returned to the exacting life in hand. On the whole, though, he did not like them. It is not easy to say why Mr Willy thought these people were hypocrites or nit-wits because some of them, not all, had a strong religious faith, and why he was not a hypocrite or nit-wit because he had not a strong religious faith; but there it was.

As he sat on and on looking down at the carpet with his head in his hands he did not think of these people, but he underwent a strong shock of recognition. He found himself looking this way and that way out of his aridity for some explanation or belief beyond the non-explanation and non-belief that had always been sufficient and had always been his, but in doing this he came up against a high and solid almost visible wall of concrete or granite, set up between him and a religious belief. This wall had, he thought, been built by him through the period of his long life, or perhaps he was congenitally unable to have a belief; in that case it was no fault of his and there was no religious belief possible to him. As he sat there he came to have the conviction that the absence of a belief which extended beyond the visible world had something to do with his malaise; yet the malaise might possibly be cirrhosis of the liver or a sort of delayed male menopause. He recognized calmly that death was as inevitable as tomorrow morning or even tonight and he had a rational absence of fear of death. Nevertheless his death (he knew) had begun, and had begun—what with his awareness of age and this malaise of his—to assume a certainty that it had not had before. His death did not trouble him as much as the increasing tastelessness of living in this tundra of mind into which a belief did not enter.

The man outside the window had crept up through the grasses and was now watching Mr Willy from a point rather behind him. He was a morose man and strong. He had served two terms for robbery with violence. When he worked, he worked up the coast. Then he came to town and if he did not get into trouble it was through no fault of his own. Last summer he had lain there and, rolling over, had looked up through the grasses and into—only just into—the room where this guy was who seemed to live alone. He seemed to be a rich guy because he wore good clothes and hadn't he got this great big window and—later, he discovered—a high-price car. He had lain in the grasses and because his thoughts always turned that way, he tried to figger out how he could get in there. Money was the only thing that was any good to him and maybe the old guy didn't keep money or even carry it but he likely did. The man thought quite a bit about Mr Willy and then went up the coast and when he came down again he remembered the great big window and one or two nights he went around and about the place and figgered how he'd work it. The doors was all locked, even that glass door. That was easy enough to break but he guessed he'd go in without warning when the old guy was there so's he'd have a better chance of getting something off of him as well. Anyways he wouldn't break in, not that night, but if nothing else offered he'd do it some time soon.

Suddenly Mr Willy got up, turned the light out, and went upstairs to bed. That was Wednesday.

On Sunday he had his first small party. It seemed inevitable if only for politeness. Later he would have a dinner party if he still felt sociable and inclined. He invited the Wardhos and their in-laws and some other couples. A Mrs Lessways asked if she might bring her aunt and he said yes. Mrs Wardho said might she bring her niece who was arriving on Saturday to meet her fiancé who was due next week from Hong Kong, and the Wardhos were going to give the two young people a quiet wedding, and Mr Willy said 'Please do.' Another couple asked if they could bring another couple.

Mr Willy, surveying his table, thought that Mrs Ogden had done well. 'Oh I'm so glad you think so,' said Mrs Ogden, pleased. People began to arrive. 'Oh!' they exclaimed without fail, as they arrived, 'what a beautiful view!' Mrs Lessways' aunt who had blue hair fell delightedly into the room, turning this way and that way, acknowledging smiles and tripping to the window. 'Oh,' she cried turning to Mr Willy in a fascinating manner, 'isn't that just lovely! Edna says you're quite a recluse! I'm sure I don't blame you! Don't you think that's the loveliest view Edna . . . oh how d'you do how d'you do, isn't that the loveliest view? . . .' Having paid her tribute to the view she turned away from the window and did not see it again. The Aunt twirled a little bag covered with iridescent beads on her wrist. 'Oh!' and 'Oh!' she exclaimed, turning, 'My dear how *lovely* to see you! I didn't even know you were back! Did you have a good time?' She reminded Mr Willy uneasily of his wife. Mr and Mrs Wardho arrived accompanied by their niece Sylvia.

A golden girl, thought Mr Willy taking her hand, but her young face surrounded by sunny curls was stern. She stood, looking from one to another, not speaking, for people spoke busily to each other and the young girl stood apart, smiling only when need be and wishing that she had not had to come to the party. She drifted to the window and seemed (and was) forgotten. She looked at the view as at something seen for the first and last time. She inscribed those notable hills on her mind because had she not arrived only yesterday? And in two days Ian would be here and she would not see them again.

A freighter very low laden emerged from behind a forest and moved slowly into the scene. So low it was that it lay like an elegant black line upon the water with great bulkheads below. Like an iceberg, thought Sylvia, and her mind moved along with the freighter bound for foreign parts. Someone spoke to her and she turned. 'Oh thank you' she said for her cup of tea.

Mr Willy opened the glass door and took with him some of the men who had expressed a desire to see how far his property ran. 'You see, just a few feet, no distance,' he said.

After a while day receded and night came imperceptibly on. There was not any violence of reflected sunset tonight and mist settled down on the view with only distant dim lights aligning the north shore. Sylvia, stopping to respond to ones and twos, went to the back of the shallow room and sat down behind the out-jut of the fireplace where a wood fire was burning. Her mind was on two levels. One was all Ian and the week coming, and one—no thicker than a crust on the surface was this party and all these people talking, the Aunt talking so busily that one might think there was a race on, or news to tell. Sylvia, sitting in the shadow of the corner and thinking about her approaching lover, lost herself in this reverie, and her lips, which had been so stern, opened slightly in a tender smile. Mr Willy who was serving drinks from the dining-room where Mrs Ogden had left things ready, came upon her and, struck by her beauty, saw a different sunny girl. She looked up at him. She took her drink from him with a soft and tender smile that was grateful and happy and was only partly for him. He left her, with a feeling of beauty seen.

Sylvia held her glass and looked towards the window. She saw, to her surprise, so quickly had black night come, that the end of the room which had been a view was now a large black mirror which reflected the glowing fire, the few lights, and the people unaware of the view, its departure, and its replacement by their own reflections behaving to each other like people at a party. Sylvia watched Mr Willy who moved amongst them, taking a glass and bringing a glass. He was removed from the necessities, now, of conversation, and looked very sad. Why does he look sad, she wondered and was young enough to think, he shouldn't look sad, he is well off. She took time off to like Mr Willy and to feel sorry that he seemed melancholy.

People began to look at their watches and say good-bye. The Aunt redoubled her vivacity. The women all thanked Mr Willy for his tea party and for the beautiful beautiful view. They gave glances at the window but there was no view.

When all his guests had gone, Mr Willy, who was an orderly man, began to collect glasses and take them into the kitchen. In an armchair lay the bag covered with iridescent beads belonging to the Aunt. Mr Willy picked it up and put it on a table, seeing the blue hair of the Aunt. He would sit down and smoke for a while. But he found that when, lately, he sat down in the evening beside the window and fixed his eyes upon the golden shaft of the Electric Building, in spite of his intention of reading or smoking, his thoughts turned towards this subject of belief which now teased him, eluded, yet compelled him. He was brought up, every time, against the great stone wall, how high, how wide he knew, but not how thick. If he could, in some way, break through the wall which bounded the area of his aridity and his comprehension, he knew without question that there was a light (not darkness) beyond, and that this light could in some way come through to him and alleviate the sterility and lead him, lead him. If there were some way, even some conventional way although he did not care for convention—he would take it in order to break the wall down and reach the light so that it would enter his life; but he did not know the way. So fixed did Mr Willy become in contemplation that he looked as though he were graven in stone.

Throughout the darkened latter part of the tea party, the man outside had lain or crouched near the window. From the sands, earlier, he had seen Mr Willy open the glass door and go outside, followed by two or three men. They looked down talking, and soon went inside again together. The door was closed. From anything the watcher knew, it was not likely that the old guy would turn and lock the door when he took the other guys in. He'd just close it, see.

As night came on the man watched the increased animation of the guests preparing for departure. Like departing birds they moved here and there in the room before taking flight. The man was impatient but patient because when five were left, then three, then no one but the old guy who lived in the house, he knew his time was near. (How gay and how meaningless the scene had been, of these well-dressed persons talking and talking, like some kind of a show where nothing happened—or so it might seem, on the stage of the lighted room from the pit of the dark shore.)

The watcher saw the old guy pick up glasses and take them away. Then he came back into the room and looked around. He took something out of a chair and put it on a table. He stood still for a bit, and then he found some kind of a paper and sat down in the chair facing eastward. But the paper drooped in his hand and then it dropped to the floor as the old guy bent his head and then he put his elbows on his knees and rested his head in his hands as if he was thinking, or had some kind of a headache.

The watcher, with a sort of joy and a feeling of confidence that the moment had come, moved strongly and quietly to the glass door. He turned the handle expertly, slid inside, and slowly closed the door so that no draught should warn his victim. He moved cat-like to the back of Mr Willy's chair and quickly raised his arm. At the selfsame moment that he raised his arm with a short blunt weapon in his hand, he was aware of the swift movement of another person in the room. The man stopped still, his arm remained high, every fear was aroused. He turned instantly and saw a scene clearly enacted beside him in the dark mirror of the window. At the moment and shock of turning, he drew a sharp intake of breath and it was this that Mr Willy heard and that caused him to look up and around and see in the dark mirror the intruder, the danger, and the victim who was himself. At that still moment, the telephone rang shrilly, twice as loud in that still moment, on a small table near him.

It was not the movement of that figure in the dark mirror, it was not the bell ringing close at hand and insistently. It was an irrational and stupid fear lest his action, reproduced visibly beside him in the mirror, was being faithfully registered in some impossible way that filled the intruder with fright. The telephone ringing shrilly, Mr Willy now facing him, the play enacted beside him, and this irrational momentary fear caused him to turn and bound towards the door, to escape into the dark, banging the glass door with a clash behind him. When he got well away from the place he was angry—everything was always against him, he never had no luck, and if he hadn'ta lost his head it was a cinch he coulda done it easy.

'Damn you!' shouted Mr Willy in a rage, with his hand on the telephone, 'you might have broken it! Yes?' he said into the telephone, moderating the anger that possessed him and continuing within himself a conversation that said It was eighteen inches away, I was within a minute of it and I didn't know, it's no use telephoning the police but I'd better do that, it was just above me and I'd have died not knowing. 'Yes? Yes?' he said impatiently, trembling a little.

'Oh,' said a surprised voice, 'it *is* Mr Willy, isn't it? Just for a minute it didn't sound like you Mr Willy that was the *loveliest* party and what a lovely view and I'm sorry to be such a nuisance I kept on ringing and ringing because I thought you couldn't have gone out so soon' (tinkle tinkle) 'and you couldn't have gone to bed so soon but I do believe I must have left my little bead bag it's not the *value* but . . .' Mr Willy found himself shaking more violently now, not only with death averted and the rage of the slammed glass door but with the powerful thoughts that had usurped him and were interrupted by the dangerous moment which was now receding, and the tinkling voice on the telephone.

'I have it here. I'll bring it tomorrow,' he said shortly. He hung up the telephone and at the other end the Aunt turned and exclaimed 'Well if he isn't the rudest man I never was treated like that in my whole life d'you know what he . . .'

Mr Willy was in a state of abstraction.

He went to the glass door and examined it. It was intact. He turned the key and drew the shutter down. Then he went back to the telephone in this state of abstraction. Death or near-death was still very close, though receding. It seemed to him at that moment that a crack had been coming in the great wall that shut him off from the light but perhaps he was wrong. He dialled the police, perfunctorily not urgently. He knew that before him lay the hardest work of his life—in his life but out of his country. He must in some way and very soon break the great wall that shut him off from whatever light there might be. Not for fear of death oh God not for fear of death but for fear of something else.

1961

Margaret Laurence

Brief Biography

- Born in 1926 in Neepawa, MB, the real-life 'Manawaka.'
- Great grandfather was Premier of Manitoba.
- Terrified of public speaking.
- Her 'Manawaka' novel cycle is inspired by John Milton's *Paradise Lost*.
- Wins two Governor General's awards for *A Jest of God* and *The Diviners*.
- Receives twelve honorary degrees; Chancellor of Trent University (1981–3).
- Considered founding mother of modern Canadian literature; called 'Canada's most successful novelist' in *The Oxford Companion to Canadian Literature* (1983).
- Diagnosed with terminal cancer, commits suicide in 1987; her home is now a writer's retreat.
- *The Diviners* is repeatedly banned from the Canadian high-school curriculum until 1994.

Margaret Laurence experienced parental loss during her childhood: her mother died when she was four, her father when she was nine. As described in her coming-of-age story cycle, *A Bird in the House* (1970), she was raised by a supportive stepmother, a librarian and teacher, in her grandfather's house (now a museum). Encouraged by her stepmother and a sympathetic teacher, she wrote her first pieces for the *Winnipeg Free Press*. Biographers suggest writing

'Couldn't you explain to her mother that she has to rest a lot?' my mother said.

'The mother's not there,' my father replied. 'She took off a few years back. Can't say I blame her. Piquette cooks for them, and she says Lazarus would never do anything for himself as long as she's there. Anyway, I don't think she'd take much care of herself, once she got back. She's only thirteen, after all. Beth, I was thinking—what about taking her up to Diamond Lake with us this summer? A couple of months rest would give that bone a much better chance.'

My mother looked stunned.

'But Ewen—what about Roddie and Vanessa?'

'She's not contagious,' my father said. 'And it would be company for Vanessa.'

'Oh dear,' my mother said in distress, 'I'll bet anything she has nits in her hair.'

'For Pete's sake,' my father said crossly, 'do you think Matron would let her stay in the hospital for all this time like that? Don't be silly, Beth.'

Grandmother MacLeod, her delicately featured face as rigid as a cameo, now brought her mauve-veined hands together as though she were about to begin a prayer.

'Ewen, if that half-breed youngster comes along to Diamond Lake, I'm not going,' she announced. 'I'll go to Morag's for the summer.'

I had trouble in stifling my urge to laugh, for my mother brightened visibly and quickly tried to hide it. If it came to a choice between Grandmother MacLeod and Piquette, Piquette would win hands down, nits or not.

'It might be quite nice for you, at that,' she mused. 'You haven't seen Morag for over a year, and you might enjoy being in the city for a while. Well, Ewen dear, you do what you think best. If you think it would do Piquette some good, then we'll be glad to have her, as long as she behaves herself.'

So it happened that several weeks later, when we all piled into my father's old Nash, surrounded by suitcases and boxes of provisions and toys for my ten-month-old brother, Piquette was with us and Grandmother MacLeod, miraculously, was not. My father would only be staying at the cottage for a couple of weeks, for he had to get back to his practice, but the rest of us would stay at Diamond Lake until the end of August.

Our cottage was not named, as many were, 'Dew Drop Inn' or 'Bide-a-Wee,' or 'Bonnie Doon.' The sign on the roadway bore in austere letters only our name, MacLeod. It was not a large cottage, but it was on the lakefront. You could look out the windows and see, through the filigree of the spruce trees, the water glistening greenly as the sun caught it. All around the cottage were ferns, and sharp-branched raspberry bushes, and moss that had grown over fallen tree trunks. If you looked carefully among the weeds and grass, you could find wild strawberry plants which were in white flower now and in another month would bear fruit, the fragrant globes hanging like miniature scarlet lanterns on the thin hairy stems. The two grey squirrels were still there, gossiping at us from the tall spruce beside the cottage, and by the end of the summer they would again be tame enough to take pieces of crust from my hands. The broad moose antlers that hung above the back door were a little more bleached and fissured after the winter, but otherwise everything was the same. I raced joyfully around my kingdom, greeting all the places I had not seen for a year. My brother, Roderick, who had not been born when we were here last summer, sat on the car rug in the sunshine and examined a brown spruce cone, meticulously turning it round and round in his small and curious hands. My mother and father toted the luggage from car to cottage, exclaiming over how well the place had wintered, no broken windows, thank goodness, no apparent damage from storm-felled branches or snow.

Only after I had finished looking around did I notice Piquette. She was sitting on the swing, her lame leg held stiffly out, and her other foot scuffing the ground as she swung slowly back and forth. Her long hair hung black and straight around her shoulders, and her broad coarse-featured face bore no expression—it was blank, as though she no longer dwelt within her own skull, as though she had gone elsewhere. I approached her very hesitantly.

'Want to come and play?'

Piquette looked at me with a sudden flash of scorn.

'I ain't a kid,' she said.

Wounded, I stamped angrily away, swearing I would not speak to her for the rest of the summer. In the days that followed, however, Piquette began to interest me, and I began to want to interest her. My reasons did not appear bizarre to me. Unlikely as it may seem, I had only just realised that the Tonnerre family, whom I had always heard called half-breeds, were actually Indians, or as near as made no difference. My acquaintance with Indians was not extensive. I did not remember ever having seen a real Indian, and my new awareness that Piquette sprang from the people of Big Bear and Poundmaker, of Tecumseh, of the Iroquois who had eaten Father Brebeuf's heart—all this gave her an instant attraction in my eyes. I was a devoted reader of Pauline Johnson at this age, and sometimes would orate aloud and in an exalted voice, *West Wind, blow from your prairie nest; Blow from the mountains, blow from the west*—and so on. It seemed to me that Piquette must be in some way a daughter of the forest, a kind of junior prophetess of the wilds, who might impart to me, if I took the right approach, some of the secrets which she undoubtedly knew—where the whippoorwill made her nest, how the coyote reared her young, or whatever it was that it said in Hiawatha.

I set about gaining Piquette's trust. She was not allowed to go swimming, with her bad leg, but I managed to lure her down to the beach—or rather, she came because there was nothing else to do. The water was always icy, for the lake was fed by springs, but I swam like a dog, thrashing my arms and legs around at such speed and with such an output of energy that I never grew cold. Finally, when I had had enough, I came out and sat beside Piquette on the sand. When she saw me approaching, her hand squashed flat the sand castle she had been building, and she looked at me sullenly, without speaking.

'Do you like this place?' I asked, after a while, intending to lead on from there into the question of forest lore.

Piquette shrugged. 'It's okay. Good as anywhere.'

'I love it,' I said. 'We come here every summer.'

'So what?' Her voice was distant, and I glanced at her uncertainly, wondering what I could have said wrong.

'Do you want to come for a walk?' I asked her. 'We wouldn't need to go far. If you walk just around the point there, you come to a bay where great big reeds grow in the water, and all kinds of fish hang around there. Want to? Come on.'

She shook her head.

'Your dad said I ain't supposed to do no more walking than I got to.'

I tried another line.

'I bet you know a lot about the woods and all that, eh?' I began respectfully.

Piquette looked at me from her large dark unsmiling eyes.

'I don't know what in hell you're talkin' about,' she replied. 'You nuts or somethin'? If you mean where my old man, and me, and all them live, you better shut up, by Jesus, you hear?'

I was startled and my feelings were hurt, but I had a kind of dogged perseverance. I ignored her rebuff.

'You know something, Piquette? There's loons here, on this lake. You can see their nests just up the shore there, behind those logs. At night, you can hear them even from the cottage, but it's better to listen from the beach. My dad says we should listen and try to remember how they sound, because in a few years when more cottages are built at Diamond Lake and more people come in, the loons will go away.'

Piquette was picking up stones and snail shells and then dropping them again.

'Who gives a good goddamn?' she said.

It became increasingly obvious that, as an Indian, Piquette was a dead loss. That evening I went out by myself, scrambling through the bushes that overhung the steep path, my feet slipping on the fallen spruce needles that covered the ground. When I reached the shore, I walked along the firm damp sand to the small pier that my father had built, and sat down there. I heard someone else crashing through the undergrowth and the bracken, and for a moment I thought Piquette had changed her mind, but it turned out to be my father. He sat beside me on the pier and we waited, without speaking.

At night the lake was like black glass with a streak of amber which was the path of the moon. All around, the spruce trees grew tall and close-set, branches blackly sharp against the sky, which was lightened by a cold flickering of stars. Then the loons began their calling. They rose like phantom birds from the nests on the shore, and flew out onto the dark still surface of the water.

No one can ever describe that ululating sound, the crying of the loons, and no one who has heard it can ever forget it. Plaintive, and yet with a quality of chilling mockery, those voices belonged to a world separated by aeons from our neat world of summer cottages and the lighted lamps of home.

'They must have sounded just like that,' my father remarked, 'before any person ever set foot here.'

Then he laughed. 'You could say the same, of course, about sparrows, or chipmunks, but somehow it only strikes you that way with the loons.'

'I know,' I said.

Neither of us suspected that this would be the last time we would ever sit here together on the shore, listening. We stayed for perhaps half an hour, and then we went back to the cottage. My mother was reading beside the fireplace. Piquette was looking at the burning birch log, and not doing anything.

'You should have come along,' I said, although in fact I was glad she had not.

'Not me,' Piquette said. 'You wouldn' catch me walkin' way down there jus' for a bunch of squawkin' birds.'

Piquette and I remained ill at ease with one another. I felt I had somehow failed my father, but I did not know what was the matter, nor why she would not or could not respond when I suggested exploring the woods or playing house. I thought it was probably her slow and difficult walking that held her back. She stayed most of the time in the cottage with my mother, helping her with the dishes or with Roddie, but hardly ever talking. Then the Duncans arrived at their cottage, and I spent my days with Mavis, who was my best friend. I could not reach Piquette at all, and I soon lost interest in trying. But all that summer she remained as both a reproach and a mystery to me.

That winter my father died of pneumonia, after less than a week's illness. For some time I saw nothing around me, being completely immersed in my own pain and my mother's. When I looked outward once more, I scarcely noticed that Piquette Tonnerre was no longer at school. I do not remember seeing her at all until four years later, one Saturday night when Mavis and I were having Cokes in the Regal Café. The jukebox was booming like tuneful thunder, and beside it, leaning lightly on its chrome and its rainbow glass, was a girl.

Piquette must have been seventeen then, although she looked about twenty. I stared at her, astounded that anyone could have changed so much. Her face, so stolid and expressionless before, was animated now with a gaiety that was almost violent. She laughed and talked very loudly with the boys around her. Her lipstick was bright carmine, and her hair was cut short and frizzily permed. She had not been pretty as a child, and she was not pretty now, for her features were still heavy and blunt. But her dark and slightly slanted eyes were beautiful, and her skin-tight skirt and orange sweater displayed to enviable advantage a soft and slender body.

She saw me, and walked over. She teetered a little, but it was not due to her once-tubercular leg, for her limp was almost gone.

'Hi, Vanessa.' Her voice still had the same hoarseness. 'Long time no see, eh?'

'Hi,' I said. 'Where've you been keeping yourself, Piquette?'

'Oh, I been around,' she said. 'I been away almost two years now. Been all over the place—Winnipeg, Regina, Saskatoon. Jesus, what I could tell you! I come back this summer, but I ain't stayin.' You kids goin' to the dance?'

'No,' I said abruptly, for this was a sore point with me. I was fifteen, and thought I was old enough to go to the Saturday-night dances at the Flamingo. My mother, however, thought otherwise.

'Y'oughta come,' Piquette said. 'I never miss one. It's just about the on'y thing in this jerkwater town that's any fun. Boy, you couldn' catch me stayin' here. I don' give a shit about this place. It stinks.'

She sat down beside me, and I caught the harsh over-sweetness of her perfume.

'Listen, you wanna know something, Vanessa?' she confided, her voice only slightly blurred. 'Your dad was the only person in Manawaka that ever done anything good to me.'

I nodded speechlessly. I was certain she was speaking the truth. I knew a little more than I had that summer at Diamond Lake, but I could not reach her now any more than I had then. I was ashamed, ashamed of my own timidity, the frightened tendency to look the other way. Yet I felt no real warmth towards her— I only felt that I ought to, because of that distant summer and because my father had hoped she would be company for me, or perhaps that I would be for her, but it had not happened that way. At this moment, meeting her again, I had to admit that she repelled and embarrassed me, and I could not help despising the self-pity in her voice. I wished she would go away. I did not want to see her. I did not know what to say to her. It seemed that we had nothing to say to one another.

'I'll tell you something else,' Piquette went on. 'All the old bitches an' biddies in this town will sure be surprised. I'm gettin' married this fall—my boyfriend, he's an English fella, works in the stockyards in the city there, a very tall guy, got blond wavy hair. Gee, is he ever handsome. Got this real classy name. Alvin Gerald Cummings—some handle, eh? They call him Al.'

For the merest instant, then, I saw her. I really did see her, for the first and only time in all the years we had both lived in the same town. Her defiant face, momentarily, became unguarded and unmasked, and in her eyes there was a terrifying hope.

'Gee, Piquette—' I burst out awkwardly, 'that's swell. That's really wonderful. Congratulations—good luck—I hope you'll be happy—'

As I mouthed the conventional phrases, I could only guess how great her need must have been, that she had been forced to seek the very things she so bitterly rejected.

When I was eighteen, I left Manawaka and went away to college. At the end of my first year, I came back home for the summer. I spent the first few days in talking non-stop with my mother, as we exchanged all the news that somehow had not found its way into letters—what had happened in my life and what had happened here in Manawaka while I was away. My mother searched her memory for events that concerned people I knew.

'Did I ever write you about Piquette Tonnerre, Vanessa?' she asked one morning.

'No, I don't think so,' I replied. 'Last I heard of her, she was going to marry some guy in the city. Is she still there?'

My mother looked perturbed, and it was a moment before she spoke, as though she did not know how to express what she had to tell and wished she did not need to try.

'She's dead,' she said at last. Then, as I stared at her, 'Oh, Vanessa, when it happened, I couldn't help thinking of her as she was that summer—so sullen and gauche and badly dressed. I couldn't help wondering if we could have done something more at that time—but what could we do? She used to be around in the cottage there with me all day, and honestly, it was all I could do to get a word out of her. She didn't even talk to your father very much, although I think she liked him, in her way.'

'What happened?' I asked.

'Either her husband left her, or she left him,' my mother said. 'I don't know which. Anyway, she came back here with two youngsters, both only babies—they must have been born very close together. She kept house, I guess, for Lazarus and her brothers, down in the valley there, in the old Tonnerre place. I used to see her on the street sometimes, but she never spoke to me. She'd put on an awful lot of weight, and she looked a mess, to tell you the truth, a real slattern, dressed any old how. She was up in court a couple of times—drunk and disorderly, of course. One Saturday night last winter, during the coldest weather, Piquette was alone in the shack with the children. The Tonnerres made home brew all the time, so I've heard, and Lazarus said later she'd been drinking most of the day when he and the boys went out that evening. They had an old woodstove there—you know the kind, with exposed pipes. The shack caught fire. Piquette didn't get out, and neither did the children.'

I did not say anything. As so often with Piquette, there did not seem to be anything to say. There was a kind of silence around the image in my mind of the fire and the snow, and I wished I could put from my memory the look that I had seen once in Piquette's eyes.

I went up to Diamond Lake for a few days that summer, with Mavis and her family. The MacLeod cottage had been sold after my father's death, and I did not even go to look at it, not wanting to witness my long-ago kingdom possessed now by strangers. But one evening I went down to the shore by myself.

The small pier which my father had built was gone, and in its place there was a large and solid pier built by the government, for Galloping Mountain was now a national park, and Diamond Lake had been re-named Lake Wapakata, for it was felt that an Indian name would have a greater appeal to tourists. The one store had become several dozen, and the settlement had all the attributes of a flourishing resort—hotels, a dance-hall, cafés with neon signs, the penetrating odours of potato chips and hot dogs.

I sat on the government pier and looked out across the water. At night the lake at least was the same as it had always been, darkly shining and bearing within its black glass the streak of amber that was the path of the moon. There was no wind that evening, and everything was quiet all around me. It seemed too quiet, and then I realized that the loons were no longer here. I listened for some time, to make sure, but never once did I hear that long-drawn call, half mocking and half plaintive, spearing through the stillness across the lake.

I did not know what had happened to the birds. Perhaps they had gone away to some far place of belonging. Perhaps they had been unable to find such a place, and had simply died out, having ceased to care any longer whether they lived or not.

I remembered how Piquette had scorned to come along, when my father and I sat there and listened to the lake birds. It seemed to me now that in some unconscious and totally unrecognised way, Piquette might have been the only one, after all, who had heard the crying of the loons.

1966

Italo Calvino

Brief Biography

- Born in 1923 in Cuba, but family moves back to Italy in 1925.
- In 1964 marries his Argentinian translator in Cuba; meets revolutionary Che Guevara; moves to Paris.
- Inspired by animated cartoons and comic strips, especially *Popeye*; his favourite authors are Kafka and Borges.
- Unique, daring, and unclassifiable, he writes in many styles throughout his career: realist, neo-realist, magic realist, and fabulist.
- Most translated contemporary Italian writer.
- Candidate for Nobel Prize for Literature in 1985.
- Dies of a stroke in 1985.

Born in Cuba, where his parents were botanists, Italo Calvino returned with his family to Italy in 1925 and settled in San Remo, in the foothills of the Alps. He lived 'in a garden full of rare plants' and had a lifelong commitment to nature. Though his parents wanted him to be a scientist, he preferred to write. Refusing military service in World War II, he joined the resistance Italian Communist party. After the war, he worked on a newspaper while at the University of Turin and wrote a master's thesis on the English writer Joseph Conrad.

In 1947 Calvino joined the board of a publishing house as publicist. Influenced by fellow writers, he wrote his first stories. Like Heinrich Böll in Germany, he debated post-war Italian culture and politics while writing for communist magazines.

Disenchanted with communism (and the realistic prose of socialism) after the Russian invasion of Hungary in 1956, he made an important self-discovery: 'I conjured up the book I myself would have liked to read, the sort by an unknown writer, from another age and another country, discovered in an attic.' At first considered frivolous, like the works of Marcel Aymé,

these ingenious post-war fantasies were allegories of Italy's divisive politics and commentaries on class struggles, failed ideals, or intellectual uncertainties. Looking for a national literature, an Italian Brothers Grimm, he collected an anthology of *Italian Folktales* (1956), and, like Angela Carter, found such tales offered new perspectives on contemporary issues.

In his 'late French phase,' Calvino met leading scholars and the controversial experimental writers of Oulipo (*Ouvroir de littérature potentielle* or Workshop of Potential Literature), a group he joined in 1973. Interests in sciences, especially computer possibilities, and astronomy merged with fantastic parables in his *Cosmicomics* (1965) and *t zero* (1968). Calvino is a writer of contradictions, and these innovative stories have his typical tone of cosmic anguish and pessimism as well as his enthusiasm for postmodern experimentation. 'The Origin of the Birds' is imagined as frames in a comic strip narrated by a math equation. The boastful, ageless, and shape-changing Qfwfq—in other stories an amoeba, a dinosaur, or a racecar driver—is less a character than characteristics, brooding on alienation, loneliness, and the impossibility of correct choices.

French literary theory inspired Calvino to write *Invisible Cities* (1974), surreal descriptions of Venice as told by Marco Polo, and *Castle of Crossed Destinies* (1979), inspired by tarot cards. His tour-de-force ten-novels-in-one, *If on a winter's night a traveler . . .* (1981), was a worldwide bestseller, and by the time of its publication Calvino's style and form were often being compared to those of Jorge Luis Borges. In 1985 Calvino was invited by Harvard University to lecture on fiction. Before his death, he completed five of the lectures, published posthumously as *Six Memos for the Next Millennium* (1988), which focus on what he considered the central qualities of literature: lightness, quickness, exactitude, visibility, and multiplicity (the unwritten sixth was consistency). These descriptions are as innovative as Poe's, Borges's, or Cortázar's essays evaluating short stories and other art forms.

See Italo Calvino, from 'Why Read the Classics?' p. 389; see also Linda Hutcheon, from 'Actualizing Narrative Structures: Detective Plot, Fantasy, Games, and the Erotic,' p. 428.

The Origin of the Birds

The appearance of Birds comes relatively late, in the history of evolution, following the emergence of all the other classes of the animal kingdom. The progenitor of the Birds—or at least the first whose traces have been found by paleontologists—is the Archeopteryx (still endowed with certain characteristics of the Reptiles from which he descends), who dates from the Jurassic period, tens of millions of years after the first Mammals. This is the only exception to the successive appearance of animal groups progressively more developed in the zoological scale.

In those days we weren't expecting any more surprises,—*Qfwfq narrated,*—by then it was clear how things were going to proceed. Those who existed, existed; we had to work things out for ourselves: some would go farther, some would remain where they were, and some wouldn't manage to survive. The choice had to be made from a limited number of possibilities.

But instead, one morning I hear some singing, outside, that I have never heard before. Or rather (since we didn't yet know what singing was), I hear something making a sound that nobody has ever made before. I look out. I see an unknown animal singing on a branch. He had wings feet tail claws spurs feathers plumes fins quills beak teeth crop horns crest wattles and a star on his forehead. It was a bird; you've realized that already, but I didn't; they had never been seen before. He sang: 'Koaxpf . . . Koaxpf . . . Koaaacch . . .,' he beat his wings, striped with iridescent colors, he rose in flight, he came to rest a bit farther on, resumed his singing.

Now these stories can be told better with strip drawings than with a story composed of sentences one after the other. But to make a cartoon with the bird on the branch and me looking out and all the others with their noses in the air, I would have to remember better how a number of things were made, things I've long since forgotten; first the thing I now call bird, second what I now call I, third the branch, fourth the place where I was looking out, fifth all the others. Of these elements I remember only that they were very different from the way we would draw them now. It's best for you to try on your own to imagine the series of cartoons with all the little figures of the characters in their places, against an effectively outlined background, but you must try at the same time not to imagine the figures, or the background either. Each figure will have its little balloon with the words it says, or with the noises it makes, but there's no need for you to read everything written there letter for letter, you only need a general idea, according to what I'm going to tell you.

To begin with, you can read a lot of exclamation marks and question marks spurting from our heads, and these mean we were looking at the bird full of amazement—festive amazement, with desire on our part also to sing, to imitate that first warbling, and to jump, to see the bird rise in flight—but also full of consternation, because the existence of birds knocked our traditional way of thinking into a cocked hat.

In the strip that follows, you see the wisest of us all, old U(h), who moves from the group of the others and says: 'Don't look at him! He's a mistake!' and he holds out his hands as if he wanted to cover the eyes of those present. 'Now I'll erase him!' he says, or thinks, and to depict this desire of his we could have him draw a diagonal line across the frame. The bird flaps his wings, eludes the diagonal, and flies to safety in the opposite corner. U(h) is happy because, with that diagonal line between them, he can't see the bird any more. The bird pecks at the line, breaks it, and flies at old U(h). Old U(h), to erase him, tries to draw a couple of crossed lines over him. At the point where the two lines meet, the bird lights and lays an egg. Old U(h) pulls the lines from under him, the egg falls, the bird darts off. There is one frame all stained with egg yolk.

I like telling things in cartoon form, but I would have to alternate the action frames with idea frames, and explain for example this stubbornness of U(h)'s in not wanting to admit the existence of the bird. So imagine one of those little frames all filled with writing, which are used to bring you up to date on what went before: *After the failure of the Pterosauria, for millions and millions of years all trace of animals with wings had been lost.* ('Except for Insects,' a footnote can clarify.)

The question of winged creatures was considered closed by now. Hadn't we been told over and over that everything capable of being born from the Reptiles had been born? In the course of millions of years there was no form of living creature that hadn't had its opportunity to come forth, populate the earth, and then—in ninety-nine cases out of a hundred—decline and vanish. On this point we were all agreed: the remaining species were the only deserving ones, destined to give life to more and more highly selected progeny, better suited to their surroundings. For some time we had been tormented by doubts as to who was a monster and who wasn't, but that too could be considered long settled: all of us who existed were nonmonsters, while the monsters were all those who could exist and didn't, because the succession of causes and effects had clearly favored us, the nonmonsters, rather than them.

But if we were going to begin again with strange animals, if the Reptiles, antiquated as they were, started to pull out limbs and teguments they had never felt any need for previously, in other words if a creature impossible by definition such as a bird was instead possible (and what's more if it could be a handsome bird like this one, pleasing to the sight when he poised on the fern leaves, and to the hearing when he released his warbling), then the barrier between monsters and nonmonsters was exploded and everything was possible again.

The bird flew far off. (In the drawing you see a black shadow against the clouds in the sky: not because the bird is black but because that's the way distant birds are drawn.) And I ran after him. (You see me from behind, as I enter a vast landscape of mountains and forests.) Old U(h) is shouting at me: 'Come back, Qfwfq!'

I crossed unfamiliar zones. More than once I thought I was lost (in the drawing it only has to be depicted once), but then I would hear a 'Koaxpf . . .' and, raising my eyes, I would see the bird perched on a plant, as if he were waiting for me.

Following him like that, I reached a spot where the bushes blocked my view. I opened a path for myself: beneath my feet I saw the void. The earth ended there; I was balanced on the brink. (The spiral line rising from my head represents my dizziness.) Below, nothing could be seen: a few clouds. And the bird, in that void, went flying off, and every now and then he twisted his neck toward me as if inviting me to follow him. Follow him where, when there was nothing farther on?

And then from the white distance a shadow rose, like a horizon of mist, which gradually became clearer, with more distinct outlines. It was a continent, coming forward in the void: you could see its shores, its valleys, its heights, and already the bird was flying above them. But what bird? He was no longer alone, the whole sky over there was a flapping of wings of every color and every form.

Leaning out from the brink of our earth, I watched the continent drift toward me. 'It's crashing into us!' I shouted, and at that moment the ground trembled. (A 'bang!' written in big letters.) The two worlds, having touched, bounced apart again, then were rejoined, then separated once more. In one of these clashes I found myself flung to the other side, while the empty abyss yawned again and separated me from my world.

I looked around: I didn't recognize anything. Trees, crystals, animals, grasses—everything was different. Not only did birds inhabit the branches, but so did fish (after a manner of speaking) with spiders' legs or (you might say)

and regular way in which things were as they were, was no longer valid; in other words: this was nothing but one of the countless possibilities; nobody excluded the possibility that things could proceed in other, entirely different ways. You would have said that now each individual was ashamed of being the way he was expected to be, and was making an effort to show some irregular, unforeseen aspect: a slightly more birdlike aspect, or if not exactly birdlike, at least sufficiently so to keep him from looking out of place alongside the strangeness of the birds. I no longer recognized my neighbors. Not that they were much changed: but those who had some inexplicable characteristic which they had formerly tried to conceal now put it on display. And they all looked as if they were expecting something any moment: not the punctual succession of causes and effects as in the past, but the unexpected.

I couldn't get my bearings. The others thought I had stuck to the old ideas, to the time before the birds; they didn't understand that to me their birdish whims were only laughable: I had seen much more than that, I had visited the world of the things that could have been, and I couldn't drive it from my mind. And I had known the beauty kept prisoner in the heart of that world, the beauty lost for me and for all of us, and I had fallen in love with it.

I spent my days on the top of a mountain, gazing at the sky in case a bird flew across it. And on the peak of another mountain nearby there was old U(h), also looking at the sky. Old U(h) was still considered the wisest of us all, but his attitude toward the birds had changed.

He believed the birds were no longer a mistake, but the truth, the only truth of the world. He had taken to interpreting the birds' flight, trying to read the future in it.

'Seen anything?' he shouted to me, from his mountain.

'Nothing in sight,' I said.

'There's one!' we would shout at times, he or I.

'Where was it coming from? I didn't have time to see from what part of the sky it appeared. Tell me: where from?' he asked, all breathless. U(h) drew his auguries from the source of the flight.

Or else it was I who asked: 'What direction was it flying in? I didn't see it! Did it vanish over here or over there?' because I hoped the birds would show me the way to reach Or.

There's no use my telling you in detail the cunning I used to succeed in returning to the Continent of the Birds. In the strips it would be told with one of those tricks that work well only in drawings. (The frame is empty. I arrive. I spread paste on the upper right hand corner. I sit down in the lower left-hand corner. A bird enters, flying, from the left, at the top. As he leaves the frame, his tail becomes stuck. He keeps flying and pulls after him the whole frame stuck to his tail, with me sitting at the bottom, allowing myself to be carried along. Thus I arrive at the Land of the Birds. If you don't like this story you can think up another one: the important thing is to have me arrive there.)

I arrived and I felt my arms and legs clutched. I was surrounded by birds; one had perched on my head, one was pecking at my neck. 'Qfwfq, you're under arrest! We've caught you, at last!' I was shut up in a cell.

'Will they kill me?' I asked the jailer bird.

'Tomorrow you'll be tried and then you'll know,' he said, perched on the bars.

'Who's going to judge me?'

'The Queen of the Birds.'

The next day I was led into the throne room. But I had seen before that enormous shell-egg that was opening. I started.

'Then you're not a prisoner of the birds!' I exclaimed.

A beak dug into my neck. 'Bow down before Queen Org-Onir-Ornit-Or!'

Or made a sign. All the birds stopped. (In the drawing you see a slender, beringed hand which rises from an arrangement of feathers.)

'Marry me and you'll be safe,' Or said.

Our wedding was celebrated. I can't tell you anything about this either: the only thing that's remained in my memory is a feathery flutter of iridescent images. Perhaps I was paying for my happiness by renouncing any understanding of what I was living through.

I asked Or.

'I would like to understand.'

'What?'

'Everything, all this.' I gestured toward my surroundings.

'You'll understand when you've forgotten what you understood before.'

Night fell. The shell-egg served both as throne and as nuptial bed.

'Have you forgotten?'

'Yes. What? I don't know what, I don't remember anything.'

(Frame of Qfwfq's thoughts: *No, I still remember, I'm about to forget everything, but I'm forcing myself to remember!*)

'Come.'

We lay down together.

(Frame of Qfwfq's thoughts: *I'm forgetting ... It's beautiful to forget ... No, I want to remember ... I want to forget and remember at the same time ... Just another second and I feel I'll have forgotten ... Wait ... Oh!* An explosion marked with the word 'Flash!' or else 'Eureka!' in capital letters.)

For a fraction of a second between the loss of everything I knew before and the gain of everything I would know afterward, I managed to embrace in a single thought the world of things as they were and of things as they could have been, and I realized that a single system included all. The world of birds, of monsters, of Or's beauty was the same as the one where I had always lived, which none of us had understood wholly.

'Or! I understand! You! How beautiful! Hurrah!' I exclaimed and I sat up in the bed.

My bride let out a cry.

'Now I'll explain it to you!' I said, exultant. 'Now I'll explain everything to everyone!'

'Be quiet!' Or shouted. 'You must be quiet!'

'The world is single and what exists can't be explained without ...' I proclaimed. Now she was over me, she was trying to suffocate me (in the drawing: a breast crushing me): 'Be quiet! Be quiet!'

Hundreds of beaks and claws were tearing the canopy of the nuptial bed. The birds fell upon me, but beyond their wings I could recognize my native landscape, which was becoming fused with the alien continent.

'There's no difference. Monsters and nonmonsters have always been close to one another! What hasn't been continues to be ...'—I was speaking not only to the birds and the monsters but also to those I had always known, who were rushing in on every side.

'Qfwfq! You've lost me! Birds! He's yours!' and the Queen pushed me away.

Too late, I realized how the birds' beaks were intent on separating the two worlds that my revelation had united. 'No, wait, don't move away, the two of us together, Or ... where are you?' I was rolling in the void among scraps of paper and feathers.

(The birds, with beaks and claws, tear up the page of strips. Each flies off with a scrap of printed paper in his beak. The page below is also covered with strip drawings; it depicts the world as it was before the birds' appearance and its successive, predictable developments. I'm among the others, with a bewildered look. In the sky there are still birds, but nobody pays attention to them any more.)

Of what I understood then, I've now forgotten everything. What I've told you is all I can reconstruct, with the help of conjectures in the episodes with the most gaps. I have never stopped hoping that the birds might one day take me back to Queen Or. But are they real birds, these ones that have remained in our midst? The more I observe them, the less they suggest what I would like to remember. (The last strip is all photographs: a bird, the same bird in close-up, the head of the bird enlarged, a detail of the head, the eye ...)

1968

Clark Blaise

Brief Biography

- Born in 1940 in Fargo, ND, son of an English-Canadian mother and five-times married French-Canadian father with whom he has a troubled relationship.
- Plays competitive chess in high school.
- Graduate of the Writers' Workshop at the University of Iowa where he meets and marries Bharati Mukherjee.
- Founds the Creative Writing Program at Sir George Williams University (now Concordia), Montreal.
- His biography of Sir Sanford Fleming, who invented time zones, *Time Lord* (2001), is first best-seller.
- As dual citizen, or 'resident alien,' lives for long periods in Montreal, San Francisco, Iowa City (where he was director of the International Writing Program at the University of Iowa), and New York while raising a family in a complex, long-distance relationship of more than forty years.

As an American-born Canadian married to a woman from India, Clark Blaise considers himself both an outsider in the United States and an exile from Canada. Like his spouse, writer Bharati Mukherjee, his writing explores cultural tensions and the importance of family, place, and shifting identities, including the construction of the literary 'self.' Blaise has said, 'I think the simple act of seeing Canada as a romance and as a place "lost" to me generates sufficient energy for a lifetime of writing.'

The only Canadian ever born in Fargo, ND, Blaise is—depending on where he lives—considered Québécois, French-Canadian, or Franco-American. An unhappy, overweight child, he travelled throughout the United States and spent time with his mother and her family in Winnipeg, attending at least twenty-five schools in Alabama, Georgia, Florida, and Ohio before graduating from high school in Pittsburgh. His troubled relationship

with his 'mismatched parents in their desperate marriage' is explored in his fiction. His father, a petty criminal and failed furniture salesman, is sympathetically explored in *I Had a Father: A Post-Modern Autobiography* (1993).

Whether set in Florida, Pittsburgh, or Montreal, his stories of isolation, alienation, and displacement are 'personal fictions.' Blaise is inspired by writers of the American South; his characters are often 'poor people haunted by history, suspicious of outsiders, and suspicious of progress.' Like Alice Munro, he is sometimes called a Gothic writer. His story collections might comprise a single story cycle, and his male narrators are outsiders constantly reinventing or reinterpreting their life experiences. His main theme, writes critic Catherine Sheldrick Ross, is 'the Canadian dilemma of identity.'

In the early 1970s Blaise joined authors Raymond Fraser, Hugh Hood, Ray Smith, and John Metcalf to form the Montreal

Story Tellers Fiction Performance Group. The group brought modernist perspectives to short fiction and for five years read in school auditoriums and university campuses throughout the city. Critic Linda Leith notes that because Montreal had no English-language publisher at the time, the group emphasized the marginalized status of English-language fiction writers during a period of intense Quebec nationalism, enforced French language laws, and dominant Francophone culture.

Challenging the idea that identity is solid, stable, and fixed, Blaise's work features immigrants struggling among immigrants. Not only national identity but even a regional identity is suspect. He includes French slang and explores Francophone communities in North America in search of what he calls 'lost or imagined homelands.' His writing coincides with the postmodern idea that there can no longer be a singular or unified literary voice.

It is not surprising, then, that a story entitled 'Eyes' is about careful and precise observation of the eccentric, shocking, or suspicious. 'This business of a new country' is alarmingly voyeuristic. Withdrawing from the idea of a national identity, Blaise embraces, as critic Linda Hutcheon suggests, otherness, paradox, and ambiguity. As a narrative strategy, the unusual use of the second-person 'you' voice is ambiguous. Does it refer to the protagonist, the reader as an eavesdropper (like the peeping Tom), or do both share the experience and possible revelations?

Eyes

You jump into this business of a new country cautiously. First you choose a place where English is spoken, with doctors and bus lines at hand, and a supermarket in a *centre d'achats* not too far away. You ease yourself into the city, approaching by car or bus down a single artery, aiming yourself along the boulevard that begins small and tree-lined in your suburb but broadens into the canyoned aorta of the city five miles beyond. And by that first winter when you know the routes and bridges, the standard congestions reported from the helicopter on your favorite radio station, you start to think of moving. What's the good of a place like this when two of your neighbors have come from Texas and the French paper you've dutifully subscribed to arrives by mail two days late? These French are all around you, behind the counters at the shopping center, in a house or two on your block; why isn't your little boy learning French at least? Where's the nearest *maternelle*? Four miles away.

In the spring you move. You find an apartment on a small side street where dogs outnumber children and the row houses resemble London's, divided equally between the rundown and remodeled. Your neighbors are the young personalities of French television who live on delivered chicken, or the old pensioners who shuffle down the summer sidewalks in pajamas and slippers in a state of endless recuperation. Your neighbors pay sixty a month for rent, or three hundred; you pay two-fifty for a two-bedroom flat where the walls have been replastered and new fixtures hung. The bugs *d'antan* remain, as well as the hulks of cars abandoned in the fire alley behind, where downtown drunks sleep in the summer night.

Then comes the night in early October when your child is coughing badly, and you sit with him in the darkened nursery, calm in the bubbling of a cold-steam vaporizer while your wife mends a dress in the room next door. And from the dark, silently, as you peer into the ill-lit fire alley, he comes. You cannot believe it at first, that a rheumy, pasty-faced Irishman in slate-gray jacket and rubber-soled shoes has come purposely to your small parking space, that he has been here before and he is not drunk (not now, at least, but you know him as a panhandler on the main boulevard a block away), that he brings with him a crate that he sets on end under your bedroom window and raises himself to your window ledge and hangs there nose-high at a pencil of light from the ill-fitting blinds. And there you are, straining with him from the uncurtained nursery, watching the man watching your wife, praying silently that she is sleeping under the blanket. The man is almost smiling, a leprechaun's face that sees what you cannot. You are about to lift the window and shout, but your wheezing child lies just under you; and what of your wife in the room next door? You could, perhaps, throw open the window and leap to the ground, tackle the man before he runs and smash his face into the bricks, beat him senseless then call the cops . . . Or better, find the camera, afix the flash, rap once at the window and shoot when he turns. Do nothing and let him suffer. *He is at your mercy*, no one will ever again be so helpless—but what can you do? You know, somehow, he'll escape. If you hurt him, he can hurt you worse, later, viciously. He's been a regular at your window, he's watched the two of you when you prided yourself on being young and alone and masters of the city. He knows your child and the park he plays in, your wife and where she shops. He's a native of the place, a man who knows the city and maybe a dozen such windows, who knows the fire escapes and alleys and roofs, knows the habits of the city's heedless young.

And briefly you remember yourself, an adolescent in another country slithering through the mosquito-ridden grassy fields behind a housing development, peering into those houses where newlyweds had not yet put up drapes, how you could spend five hours in a motionless crouch for a myopic glimpse of a slender arm reaching from the dark to douse a light. Then you hear what the man cannot; the creaking of your bed in the far bedroom, the steps of your wife on her way to the bathroom, and you see her as you never have before: blond and tall and rangily built, a north-Europe princess from a constitutional monarchy, sensuous mouth and prominent teeth, pale, tennis-ball breasts cupped in her hands as she stands in the bathroom's light.

'How's Kit?' she asks. 'I'd give him a kiss except that there's no blind in there,' and she dashes back to bed, nude, and the man bounces twice on the window ledge.

'You coming?'

You find yourself creeping from the nursery, turning left at the hall and then running to the kitchen telephone; you dial the police, then hang up. How will you prepare your wife, not for what is happening, but for what has already taken place?

'It's stuffy in here,' you shout back, 'I think I'll open the window a bit.' You take your time, you stand before the blind blocking his view if he's still looking, then bravely you part the curtains. He is gone, the crate remains upright. 'Do we have any masking tape?' you ask, lifting the window a crack.

And now you know the city a little better. A place where millions come each summer to take pictures and walk around must have its voyeurs too. And that place in all great cities where rich and poor co-exist is especially hard on the people in-between. It's health you've been seeking, not just beauty; a tough urban health that will save you money in the bargain, and when you hear of a place twice as large at half the rent, in a part of town free of Texans, English, and French, free of young actors and stewardesses who deposit their garbage in pizza boxes, you move again.

It is, for you, a city of Greeks. In the summer you move you attend a movie at the corner cinema. The posters advertise a war movie, in Greek, but the uniforms are unfamiliar. Both sides wear mustaches, both sides handle machine guns, both leave older women behind dressed in black. From the posters outside there is a promise of sex; blond women in slips, dark-eyed peasant girls. There will be rubble, executions against a wall. You can follow the story from the stills alone: mustached boy goes to war, embraces dark-eyed village girl. Black-draped mother and admiring young brother stand behind. Young soldier, mustache fuller, embraces blond prostitute on a tangled bed. Enter soldiers, boy hides under sheets. Final shot, back in village. Mother in black; dark-eyed village girl in black. Young brother marching to the front.

You go in, pay your ninety cents, pay a nickel in the lobby for a wedge of *halvah*-like sweets. You understand nothing, you resent their laughter and you even resent the picture they're running. Now you know the Greek for 'Coming Attractions,' for this is a gangster movie at least thirty years old. The eternal Mediterranean gangster movie set in Athens instead of Naples or Marseilles, with smaller cars and narrower roads, uglier women and more sinister killers. After an hour the movie flatters you. No one knows you're not a Greek, that you don't belong in this theater, or even this city. That, like the Greeks, you're hanging on.

Outside the theater the evening is warm and the wide sidewalks are clogged with Greeks who nod as you come out. Like the Ramblas in Barcelona, with children out past midnight and families walking back and forth for a long city block, the men filling the coffeehouses, the women left outside, chatting. Not a blond head on the sidewalk, not a blond head for miles. Greek music pours from the coffeehouses, flies stumble on the pastry, whole families munch their *torsades molles* as they walk. Dry goods are sold at midnight from the sidewalk, like New York fifty years ago. You're wandering happily, glad that you moved, you've rediscovered the innocence of starting over.

Then you come upon a scene directly from Spain. A slim blond girl in a floral top and white pleated skirt, tinted glasses, smoking, with bad skin, ignores a persistent young Greek in a shiny Salonika suit. 'Whatsamatta?' he demands, slapping a ten-dollar bill on his open palm. And without looking back at him she drifts closer to the curb and a car makes a sudden squealing turn and lurches to a stop on the cross street. Three men are inside, the back door opens and not a word is exchanged as she steps inside. How? What refinement of gesture did we immigrants miss? You turn to the Greek boy in sympathy, you know just how he feels, but he's already heading across the street, shouting something to his friends outside a barbecue stand. You have a pocketful of bills and a Mediterranean soul, and money this evening means a woman, and blond means whore and you would spend it all on another blond with open pores; all this a block from your wife and tenement. And you hurry home.

Months later you know the place. You trust the Greeks in their stores, you fear their tempers at home. Eight bathrooms adjoin a central shaft, you hear the beatings of your son's friends, the thud of fist on bone after the slaps. Your child knows no French, but he plays cricket with Greeks and Jamaicans out in the alley behind Pascal's hardware. He brings home the oily tires from the Esso station, plays in the boxes behind the appliance store. You watch from a greasy back window, at last satisfied. None of his friends is like him, like you. He is becoming Greek, becoming Jamaican, becoming a part of this strange new land. His hair is nearly white; you can spot him a block away.

On Wednesdays the butcher quarters his meat. Calves arrive by refrigerator truck, still intact but for their split-open bellies and sawed-off hooves. The older of the three brothers skins the carcass with a small thin knife that seems all blade. A knife he could shave with. The hide rolls back in a continuous flap, the knife never pops the membrane over the fat.

Another brother serves. Like yours, his French is adequate. '*Twa lif d'hamburger*,' you request, still watching the operation on the rickety sawhorse. Who could resist? It's a Levantine treat, the calf's stumpy legs high in the air, the hide draped over the edge and now in the sawdust, growing longer by the second.

The store is filling. The ladies shop on Wednesday, especially the old widows in black overcoats and scarves, shoes, and stockings. Yellow, mangled fingernails. Wednesdays attract them with boxes in the window, and they call to the butcher as they enter, the brother answers, and the women dip their fingers in the boxes. The radio is loud overhead, music from the Greek station.

'*Une et soixante, m'sieur. Du bacon, jambon?*'

And you think, taking a few lamb chops but not their saltless bacon, how pleased you are to manage so well. It is a Byzantine moment with blood and widows and sides of dripping beef, contentment in a snowy slum at five below.

The older brother, having finished the skinning, straightens, curses, and puts away the tiny knife. A brother comes forward to pull the hide away, a perfect beginning for a gameroom rug. Then, bending low at the rear of the glistening carcass, the legs spread high and stubby, the butcher digs in his hands, ripping hard where the scrotum is, and pulls on what seems to be a strand of rubber, until it snaps. He puts a single glistening prize in his mouth, pulls again and offers the other to his brother, and they suck.

The butcher is singing now, drying his lips and wiping his chin, and still he's chewing. The old black-draped widows with the parchment faces are also chewing. On leaving, you check the boxes in the window. Staring out are the heads of pigs and lambs, some with the eyes lifted out and a red socket exposed. A few are loose and the box is slowly dissolving from the blood, and the ice beneath.

The women have gathered around the body; little pieces are offered to them from the head and entrails. The pigs' heads are pink, perhaps they've been boiled, and hairless. The eyes are strangely blue. You remove your gloves and touch the skin, you brush against the grainy ear. How the eye attracts you! How you would like to lift one out, press its smoothness against your tongue, then crush it in your mouth. And you cannot. Already your finger is numb and the head, it seems, has shifted under you. And the eye, in panic, grows white as your finger approaches. You would take that last half inch but for the certainty, in this world you have made for yourself, that the eye would blink and your neighbors would turn upon you.

1973

Angela Carter

Brief Biography

- Born in 1940.
- Struggles with anorexia as a child.
- Fluent in French and German, translates Perrault's fairy tales.
- In 1969 uses literary award money of £500 to leave husband and to move to Japan.
- *The Bloody Chamber* (1979) is inspired by Danish author Isak Dinesen and French author Colette.
- One of two films based on her short fiction, *The Company of Wolves* (1984), is directed by Neil Jordan with script by Carter.
- Dramatic public performances strengthen her written prose.
- Dies of cancer in 1992.

Though criticized during her lifetime, Angela Carter became both a cult writer and among the most studied British authors within a decade of her death from cancer. Considered a postmodern feminist, she was born in Eastbourne, near London, in the midst of the Blitz. Raised in the country by her suffragette grandmother, she always considered London 'foreign.' Her first writings, innovative cultural criticisms with a special interest in movies, cuisine, fantasy, fetishism, and contemporary writers, were inspired by her Scots journalist father.

After a divorce, she moved to Japan for two years, which 'radicalized' her and led her to question literary conventions, styles, forms, and contents. Like Poe, she explored Gothic and profane squalor, darkness, opulence, and violent fantasies. She delighted or offended readers with satirical and erotic, but always optimistic, prose.

As with some authors in Canada and the United States, Carter reacted against the traditional realism of 1970s fiction by discovering a neglected current of visionary writing. Her 'intertextual' work is based on or refers to other books and writers in a 'dialogue.' 'We live in Gothic times,' she announced, updating older forms, such as seventeenth- and eighteenth-century picaresque novels, and archaic theatre forms, such as circuses, musicals, and British pantomimes. Drawn to fairy stories, folk tales, and myths, she called herself a 'demythologizer,' breaking apart patriarchal structures by parodies and inversions. Why should women be passive and wait for Prince Charming, she complained.

Instead of 'those fragments of epiphanic experience' featured in many twentieth-century stories, she preferred the 'ornate, unnatural' style and symbolism of her favoured form, the tale. In an afterword to her first collection, *Fireworks: Nine Stories in Various Disguises* (1974), she argued that the tale, unlike the short story, 'interprets everyday experience through a system of imagery derived from subterranean areas behind everyday experience.' In 1980 Carter said of her luxuriant style, 'The short story is not minimalist, it is rococo.... It is like writing chamber music rather than symphonies.'

and she lay there. And she waited and she waited and then she waited again—surely he's been gone a long time? Until she jumps up in bed and shrieks to hear a howling, coming on the wind from the forest.

That long-drawn, wavering howl has, for all its fearful resonance, some inherent sadness in it, as if the beasts would love to be less beastly if only they knew how and never cease to mourn their own condition. There is a vast melancholy in the canticles of the wolves, melancholy infinite as the forest, endless as these long nights of winter and yet that ghastly sadness, that mourning for their own, irremediable appetites, can never move the heart for not one phrase in it hints at the possibility of redemption; grace could not come to the wolf from its own despair, only through some external mediator, so that, sometimes, the beast will look as if he half welcomes the knife that despatches him.

The young woman's brothers searched the outhouses and the haystacks but never found any remains so the sensible girl dried her eyes and found herself another husband not too shy to piss into a pot who spent the nights indoors. She gave him a pair of bonny babies and all went right as a trivet until, one freezing night, the night of the solstice, the hinge of the year when things do not fit together as well as they should, the longest night, her first good man came home again.

A great thump on the door announced him as she was stirring the soup for the father of her children and she knew him the moment she lifted the latch to him although it was years since she'd worn black for him and now he was in rags and his hair hung down his back and never saw a comb, alive with lice.

'Here I am again, missus,' he said. 'Get me my bowl of cabbage and be quick about it.'

Then her second husband came in with wood for the fire and when the first one saw she'd slept with another man and, worse, clapped his red eyes on her little children who'd crept into the kitchen to see what all the din was about, he shouted: 'I wish I were a wolf again, to teach this whore a lesson!' So a wolf he instantly became and tore off the eldest boy's left foot before he was chopped up with the hatchet they used for chopping logs. But when the wolf lay bleeding and gasping its last, the pelt peeled off again and he was just as he had been, years ago, when he ran away from his marriage bed, so that she wept and her second husband beat her.

They say there's an ointment the Devil gives you that turns you into a wolf the minute you rub it on. Or, that he was born feet first and had a wolf for his father and his torso is a man's but his legs and genitals are a wolf's. And he has a wolf's heart.

Seven years is a werewolf's natural span but if you burn his human clothing you condemn him to wolfishness for the rest of his life, so old wives hereabouts think it some protection to throw a hat or an apron at the werewolf, as if clothes made the man. Yet by the eyes, those phosphorescent eyes, you know him in all his shapes; the eyes alone unchanged by metamorphosis.

Before he can become a wolf, the lycanthrope strips stark naked. If you spy a naked man among the pines, you must run as if the Devil were after you.

It is midwinter and the robin, the friend of man, sits on the handle of the gardener's spade and sings. It is the worst time in all the year for wolves but this strong-minded child insists she will go off through the wood. She is quite sure the wild beasts cannot harm her although, well-warned, she lays a carving knife in the basket her mother has packed with cheeses. There is a bottle of harsh liquor distilled from brambles; a batch of flat oatcakes baked on the hearthstone; a pot or two of jam. The flaxen-haired girl will take these delicious gifts to a reclusive grandmother so old the burden of her years is crushing her to death. Granny lives two hours' trudge through the winter woods; the child wraps herself up in her thick shawl, draws it over her head. She steps into her stout wooden shoes; she is dressed and ready and it is Christmas Eve. The malign door of the solstice still swings upon its hinges but she has been too much loved ever to feel scared.

Children do not stay young for long in this savage country. There are no toys for them to play with so they work hard and grow wise but this one, so pretty and the youngest of her family, a little late-comer, had been indulged by her mother and the grandmother who'd knitted her the red shawl that, today, has the ominous if brilliant look of blood on snow. Her breasts have just begun to swell; her hair is like lint, so fair it hardly makes a shadow on her pale forehead; her cheeks are an emblematic scarlet and white and she has just started her woman's bleeding, the clock inside her that will strike, henceforward, once a month.

She stands and moves within the invisible pentacle of her own virginity. She is an unbroken egg; she is a sealed vessel; she has inside her a magic space the entrance to which is shut tight with a plug of membrane; she is a closed system; she does not know how to shiver. She has her knife and she is afraid of nothing.

Her father might forbid her, if he were home, but he is away in the forest, gathering wood, and her mother cannot deny her.

The forest closed upon her like a pair of jaws.

There is always something to look at in the forest, even in the middle of winter—the huddled mounds of birds, succumbed to the lethargy of the season, heaped on the creaking boughs and too forlorn to sing; the bright frills of the winter fungi on the blotched trunks of the trees; the cuneiform slots of rabbits and deer, the herringbone tracks of the birds, a hare as lean as a rasher of bacon streaking across the path where the thin sunlight dapples the russet brakes of last year's bracken.

When she heard the freezing howl of a distant wolf, her practised hand sprang to the handle of her knife, but she saw no sign of a wolf at all, nor of a naked man, neither, but then she heard a clattering among the brushwood and was gone. The sticks twitched in the grate, the clock ticked and the young man sat patiently, deceitfully beside the bed in granny's nightcap.

Rat-a-tap-tap.

Who's there, he quavers in granny's antique falsetto.

Only your granddaughter.

So she came in, bringing with her a flurry of snow that melted in tears on the tiles, and perhaps she was a little disappointed to see only her grandmother sitting beside the fire. But then he flung off the blanket and sprang to the door, pressing his back against it so that she could not get out again.

The girl looked round the room and saw there was not even the indentation of a head on the smooth cheek of the pillow and how, for the first time she'd seen it so, the Bible lay closed on the table. The tick of the clock cracked like a whip. She wanted her knife from her basket but she did not dare reach for it because his eyes were fixed upon her—huge eyes that now seemed to shine with a unique, interior light, eyes the size of saucers, saucers full of Greek fire, diabolic phosphorescence.

What big eyes you have.

All the better to see you with.

No trace at all of the old woman except for a tuft of white hair that had caught in the bark of an unburned log. When the girl saw that, she knew she was in danger of death.

Where is my grandmother?

There's nobody here but we two, my darling.

Now a great howling rose up all around them, near, very near, as close as the kitchen garden, the howling of a multitude of wolves; she knew the worst wolves are hairy on the inside and she shivered, in spite of the scarlet shawl she pulled more closely round herself as if it could protect her although it was as red as the blood she must spill.

Who has come to sing us carols, she said.

Those are the voices of my brothers, darling; I love the company of wolves. Look out of the window and you'll see them.

Snow half-caked the lattice and she opened it to look into the garden. It was a white night of moon and snow; the blizzard whirled round the gaunt, grey beasts who squatted on their haunches among the rows of winter cabbage, pointing their sharp snouts to the moon and howling as if their hearts would break. Ten wolves; twenty wolves—so many wolves she could not count them, howling in concert as if demented or deranged. Their eyes reflected the light from the kitchen and shone like a hundred candles.

It is very cold, poor things, she said; no wonder they howl so.

She closed the window on the wolves' threnody and took off her scarlet shawl, the colour of poppies, the colour of sacrifices, the colour of her menses, and, since her fear did her no good, she ceased to be afraid.

What shall I do with my shawl?

Throw it on the fire, dear one. You won't need it again.

She bundled up her shawl and threw it on the blaze, which instantly consumed it. Then she drew her blouse over her head; her small breasts gleamed as if the snow had invaded the room.

What shall I do with my blouse?

Into the fire with it, too, my pet.

The thin muslin went flaring up the chimney like a magic bird and now off came her skirt, her woollen stockings, her shoes, and on to the fire they went, too, and were gone for good. The firelight shone through the edges of her skin; now she was clothed only in her untouched integument of flesh. This dazzling, naked she combed out her hair with her fingers; her hair looked white as the snow outside. Then went directly to the man with red eyes in whose unkempt mane the lice moved; she stood up on tiptoe and unbuttoned the collar of his shirt.

What big arms you have.

All the better to hug you with.

Every wolf in the world now howled a prothalamion outside the window as she freely gave the kiss she owed him.

What big teeth you have!

She saw how his jaw began to slaver and the room was full of the clamour of the forest's Liebestod but the wise child never flinched, even when he answered:

All the better to eat you with.

The girl burst out laughing; she knew she was nobody's meat. She laughed at him full in the face, she ripped off his shirt for him and flung it into the fire, in the fiery wake of her own discarded clothing. The flames danced like dead souls on Walpurgisnacht and the old bones under the bed set up a terrible clattering but she did not pay them any heed.

Carnivore incarnate, only immaculate flesh appeases him.

She will lay his fearful head on her lap and she will pick out the lice from his pelt and perhaps she will put the lice into her mouth and eat them, as he will bid her, as she would do in a savage marriage ceremony.

The blizzard will die down.

The blizzard died down, leaving the mountains as randomly covered with snow as if a blind woman had thrown a sheet over them, the upper branches of the forest pines limed, creaking, swollen with the fall.

Snowlight, moonlight, a confusion of paw-prints.

All silent, all still.

Midnight; and the clock strikes. It is Christmas Day, the werewolves' birthday, the door of the solstice stands wide open; let them all sink through.

See! sweet and sound she sleeps in granny's bed, between the paws of the tender wolf.

1979

Mavis Gallant

Brief Biography

- Born in 1922; is raised in foster homes.
- Goes to seventeen private schools.
- Married to a Winnipeg musician for five years.
- Fluently bilingual, has lived in Paris since 1950.
- Has published more than one hundred stories in *The New Yorker*.
- Though known mostly as a short story writer, has written two novels.
- *Home Truths: Selected Canadian Stories* (1981) wins the Governor General's Award; includes 'Between Zero and One.'
- Believes that 'curiosity about the writer's life kills interest in the work itself.'

Born in Montreal to English-speaking Protestant parents, Mavis Gallant had an unhappy childhood. Her father died when she was young, and her mother abandoned her to a strict French-language boarding school when she was four. These events shaped her writing; her work reflects concern and sympathy for troubled children and adolescents constantly alert for abandonment and betrayal.

Gallant worked briefly for the National Film Board of Canada and for the *Montreal Standard*, two experiences which profoundly influenced her career. She said 'cinematic technique freed fiction from unnecessary connective tissue.' Her shape-breaking prose often shifts perspective between paragraphs. While at the *Standard*, an assignment to write photo captions for the weekend supplements exposed her to the sight of concentration camps and prompted a lifelong inquiry into the dangers of fascism (especially 'the possibilities of little fascisms in people'), expatriation, and anti-Semitism.

Gallant left journalism and Canada for fiction writing and Europe in 1950, with five hundred dollars from her newspaper and a plane ticket from an airline executive. Harsh language restrictions, religious barriers, and class structures in 1940s Quebec created a Canadian apartheid, she said. Serious authors moved to New York, London, or Paris. Although she maintained her Canadian citizenship, she lived in both southern France and Germany, establishing a permanent residence in Paris. Her post-war Paris is not glamorous but gloomy. As a Canadian in post-war Europe, she brought her own perspectives to European history. In her most characteristic stories she questions why the Holocaust happened. Why does private memory differ from public history? How do we remember or find reasonable perspectives? Like Heinrich Böll, she asks what happened to those in forced military service, survivors of bombings, and survivors of the camps. What caused the psychic immobility and denial of post-war Germany? Why were Germans unable to shed past behaviours and false ideals? Her stories portray characters in exile, dislocated, unhappy, and always homeless amid the breakdown of nation-states.

Long neglected in Canada (in part because her books were not available), Gallant established her Canadian career with the publication of *From the Fifteenth District* (1979) and *Home Truths* (1981) and is now regarded as one of the country's greatest short fiction writers. In an unusual departure, she has also written four interlinked story cycles, including the semi-autobiographical and plotless six-part Linnet Muir story cycle, of which 'Between Zero and One' is one part (a 'linnet,' like a 'mavis,' is an archaic Scottish word for song thrush). Similar to Alice Munro's evocation of southern Ontario provincialism, Gallant's elegiac evocation of a stifling 1940s Montreal and her precise depiction of working for a male-dominated wartime newspaper reveal three layers of memory and anxieties as well as three characters: the narrator recalls the adult recalling the child. Critics have variously called Gallant's technique 'broken consciousness,' 'modular fiction,' and 'subversive in its disrupted sequence.' For Gallant, time and memory are as flexible as the borders she crosses.

See Mavis Gallant, from 'What Is Style?', p. 435.

Between Zero and One

When I was young I thought that men had small lives of their own creation. I could not see why, born enfranchised, without the obstacles and constraints attendant on women, they set such close limits for themselves and why, once the limits had been reached, they seemed so taken aback. I could not tell much difference between a man aged thirty-six, about, and one forty or fifty; it was impossible to fix the borderline of this apparent disappointment. There was a space of life I used to call 'between Zero and One' and then came a long mystery. I supposed that men came up to their wall, their terminal point, quite a long way after One. At that time I was nineteen and we were losing the war. The news broadcast in Canada was flatly optimistic, read out in the detached nasal voices de rigueur for the CBC. They were voices that seemed to be saying, 'Good or bad, it can't affect *us*.' I worked in a building belonging to the federal government—it was a heavy Victorian structure of the sort that exists on every continent, wherever the British thought they'd come to stay. This one had been made out of the reddish-brown Montreal stone that colors, in memory, the streets of my childhood and that architects have no use for now. The office was full of old soldiers from one war before: Ypres (pronounced 'Wipers') and Vimy Ridge were real, as real as this minute, while Singapore, Pearl Harbor, Voronezh were the stuff of fiction. It seemed as if anything that befell the young, even dying, was bound to be trivial.

'Half of 'em'll never see any fighting,' I often heard. 'Anyway not like in the trenches.' We did have one veteran from the current war—Mac Kirkconnell, who'd had a knock on the head during his training and was now good for nothing except civilian life. He and two others were the only men under thirty left

of it. 'It looks good,' he said. 'It sounds good. What is its meaning? Sweet bugger all.' A few girls equipped with rackety typewriters and adding machines sat grouped at the far end of the room, separated from the men by a balustrade. I was the first woman ever permitted to work on the men's side of this fence. A pigeon among the cats was how it sometimes felt. My title was 'aide.' Today it would be something like 'trainee.' I was totally unqualified for this or any other kind of work and had been taken on almost at my own insistence that they could not do without me.

'Yes, I know all about that,' I had replied, to everything.

'Well, I *suppose* it's all right,' said Chief Engineer. The hiring of girls usually fell to a stout grim woman called 'Supervisor,' but I was not coming in as a typist. He had never interviewed a girl before and he was plainly uncomfortable, asking me questions with all the men straining to hear. There were no young men left on account of the war, and the office did need someone. But what if they trained me, he said, at great cost and expense to the government, and what if I then did the dreadful thing girls were reputed to do, which was to go off and get married? It would mean a great waste of time and money just when there was a war on.

I was engaged, but not nearly ready for the next step. In any case, I told him, even if I did marry I would need to go on working, for my husband would more than likely be sent overseas. What Chief Engineer did not know was that I was a minor with almost no possibility of obtaining parental consent. Barring some bright idea, I could not do much of anything until I was twenty-one. For this interview I had pinned back my long hair; I wore a hat, gloves, earrings, and I folded my hands on my purse in a conscious imitation of older women. I did not mind the interview, or the furtively staring men. I was shy, but not self-conscious. Efforts made not to turn a young girl's head—part of an education I had encountered at every stage and in every sort of school—had succeeded in making me invisible to myself. My only commercial asset was that I knew French, but French was of no professional use to anyone in Canada then—not even to French Canadians; one might as well have been fluent in Pushtu. Nevertheless I listed it on my application form, along with a very dodgy 'German' (private lessons between the ages of eight and ten) and an entirely impudent 'Russian': I was attending Russian evening classes at McGill, for reasons having mainly to do with what I believed to be the world's political future. I recorded my age as twenty-two, hoping to be given a grade and a salary that would correspond. There were no psychological or aptitude tests; you were taken at your word and lasted according to performance. There was no social security and only the loosest sort of pension plan; hiring and firing involved no more paperwork than a typed letter—sometimes not even that. I had an unmistakably Montreal accent of a kind now almost extinct, but my having attended school in the United States gave me a useful vagueness of background.

And so, in an ambience of doubt, apprehension, foreboding, incipient danger, and plain hostility, for the first time in the history of the office a girl was allowed to sit with the men. And it was here, at the desk facing Bertie Knox's, on the only uncomfortable chair in the room, that I felt for the first time that almost palpable atmosphere of sexual curiosity, sexual resentment, and sexual fear that the presence of a woman can create where she is not wanted. If part of the resentment vanished when it became clear that I did not know what I was doing, the feeling that women were 'trouble' never disappeared. However, some of the men were fathers of daughters, and they quickly saw that I was nothing like twenty-two. Some of them helped me then, and one man, Hughie Pryor, an engineer, actually stayed late to do some of my work when I fell behind.

Had I known exactly what I was about, I might not have remained for more than a day. Older, more experienced, I'd have called it a dull place. The men were rotting quietly until pension time. They kept to a slow English-rooted civil-service pace; no one wasted office time openly, but no one produced much, either. Although they could squabble like hens over mislaid pencils, windows open or shut, borrowed triangles, special and sacred pen nibs used for tracing maps, there was a truce about zeal. The fact is that I did not know the office was dull. It was so new to me, so strange, such another climate, that even to flow with the sluggish tide training men and women into the heart of the city each day was a repeated experiment I sensed, noted, recorded, as if I were being allowed to be part of something that was not really mine. The smell of the building was of school—of chalk, dust, plaster, varnish, beeswax. Victorian, Edwardian, and early Georgian oil portraits of Canadian captains of industry, fleshed-out pirate faces, adorned the staircase and halls—a daily reminder that there are two races, those who tread on people's lives, and the others. The latest date on any of the portraits was about 1925: I suppose photography had taken over. Also by then the great fortunes had been established and the surviving pirates were retired, replete and titled, usually to England. Having had both French and English schooling in Quebec, I knew that these pink-cheeked marauders were what English-speaking children were led to admire (without much hope of emulation, for the feast was over). They were men of patriotism and of action; we owed them everything. They were in a positive, constructive way a part of the Empire and of the Crown; this was a good thing. In a French education veneration was withheld from anyone except the dead and defeated, ranging from General Montcalm expiring at his last battle to a large galaxy of maimed and crippled saints. Deprivation of the senses, mortification of mind and body were imposed, encouraged, for phantom reasons—something to do with a tragic past and a deep fear of life itself. Montreal was a city where the greater part of the population were wrapped in myths and sustained by belief in magic. I had been to school with little girls who walked in their sleep and had visions; the nuns who had taught me seemed at ease with the dead. I think of them even now as strange, dead, punishing creatures who neither ate nor breathed nor slept. The one who broke one of my fingers with a ruler was surely a spirit without a mind, tormented, acting in the vengeful driven way of homeless ghosts. In an English school visions would have been smartly dealt with—cold showers, the parents summoned, at the least a good stiff talking-to. These two populations, these two tribes, knew nothing whatever about each other. In the very poorest part of the east end of the city, apparitions were commonplace; one lived among a mixture of men and women and their imaginings. I would never have believed then that anything could ever stir them from their dark dreams. The men in the portraits were ghosts of a kind, too; they also seemed to be saying, 'Too late, too late for you,' and of course in a sense so it was: It was too late for anyone else to import Chinese and Irish coolie labor and wring a railway out of them. That had already been done. Once I said to half-blind Mr Tracy, 'Things can't just stay this way.'

'Change is always for the worse' was his reply. His own father had lost all his money in the Depression, ten years before; perhaps he meant that.

I climbed to the office in a slow reassuring elevator with iron grille doors, sharing it with inexpressive women and men—clearly, the trodden-on. No matter how familiar our faces became, we never spoke. The only sound, apart from the creaking cable, was the gasping and choking of a poor man who had been gassed at the Somme and whose lungs were said to be in shreds. He had an old man's pale eyes and wore a high stiff collar and stared straight before him, like everyone else. Some of the men in my office had been wounded, too, but they made it sound pleasant. Bertie Knox said he had hobbled on one leg and crutches in the 1918 Allied victory parade in Paris. According to him, when his decimated regiment followed their Highland music up the Champs-Élysées, every pretty girl in Paris had been along the curb, fighting the police and screaming and trying to get at Bertie Knox and take him home.

'It was the kilts set 'em off,' said Bertie Knox. 'That and the wounds. And the Jocks played it up for all they was worth, bashing the very buggery out of the drums.' 'Jocks' were Scots in those days—nothing more.

Any mention of that older war could bring the men to life, but it had been done with for more than twenty years now. Why didn't they move, walk, stretch, run? Each of them seemed to inhabit an invisible square; the square was shared with *my* desk, *my* graph paper, *my* elastic bands. The contents of the square were tested each morning: The drawers of my own desk—do they still open and shut? My desk lamp—does it still turn on and off? Have my special coat hanger, my favorite nibs, my drinking glass, my calendar, my children's pictures, my ashtray, the one I brought from home, been tampered with during the night? Sometimes one glimpsed another world, like an extra room ('It was my young daughter made my lunch today'—said with a dismissive shrug, lest it be taken for boasting) or a wish outdistanced, reduced, shrunken, trailing somewhere in the mind: 'I often thought I wanted ...' 'Something I wouldn't have minded having . . .' Easily angry, easily offended, underpaid, at the mercy of accidents—an illness in the family could wipe out a life's savings—still they'd have resisted change for the better. Change was double-edged; it might mean improving people with funny names, letting them get uppity. What they had instead were marks of privilege—a blind sureness that they were superior in every way to French Canadians, whom in some strange fashion they neither heard nor saw (a lack of interest that was doubly and triply returned); they had the certainty they'd never be called on to share a washroom or a drawing board or to exchange the time of day with anyone 'funny' (applications from such people, in those days, would have been quietly set aside); most important of all, perhaps, they had the distinction of the individual hand towel. These towels, as stiff as boards, reeking of chloride bleach, were distributed once a week by a boy pushing a trolley. They were distributed to men, but not even to *all* men. The sanctioned carried them to the washroom, aired and dried them on the backs of chairs, kept them folded in a special drawer. Assimilated into a male world, I had one too. The stenographers and typists had to make do with paper towels that scratched when new and dissolved when damp. Any mistake or oversight on towel day was a source of outrage: 'Why the bejesus do I get a torn one three times running? You'd think I didn't count for anything round here.' It seemed a true distress; someday some simple carelessness might turn out to be the final curse: They were like that prisoner of Mussolini, shut up for life, who burst into tears because the soup was cold. When I received presents of candy I used to bring them in for the staff; these wartime chocolates tasted of candle wax but were much appreciated nonetheless. I had to be careful to whom I handed the box first: I could not begin with girls, which I'd have thought natural, because Supervisor did not brook interruptions. I would transfer the top layer to the lid of the box for the girls, for later on, and then consider the men. A trinity of them occupied glass cubicles. One was diabetic; another was Mr Tracy, who, a gentle alcoholic, did not care for sweets; and the third was Mr Curran. Skipping all three I would start with Chief Engineer McCreery and descend by way of Assistant Chief Engineers Grade I and then II; I approached them by educational standards, those with degrees from McGill and Queen's—Queen's first—to, finally, the technicians. By that time the caramels and nougats had all been eaten and nothing left but squashy orange and vanilla creams nobody liked. Then, then, oh God, who was to receive the affront of the last chocolate, the one reposing among crumbs and fluted paper casings? Sometimes I was cowardly and left the box adrift on a drawing board with a murmured 'Pass it along, would you?'

I was deeply happy. It was one of the periods of inexplicable grace when every day is a new parcel one unwraps, layer on layer of tissue paper covering bits of crystal, scraps of words in a foreign language, pure white stones. I spent my lunch hours writing in notebooks, which I kept locked in my desk. The men never bothered me, apart from trying to feed me little pieces of cake. They were all sad when I began to smoke—I remember that. I could write without hearing anyone, but poetry was leaving me. It was not an abrupt removal but like a recurring tide whose high-water mark recedes inch by inch. Presently I was deep inland and the sea was gone. I would mourn it much later: It was such a gentle separation at the time that I scarcely noticed. I had notebooks stuffed with streets and people: My journals were full of 'but what he *really* must have meant was . . .' There were endless political puzzles I tried to solve by comparing one thing with another, but of course nothing matched; I had not lost my adolescent habit of private, passionate manifestos. If politics was nothing but chess—Mr Tracy's ways of sliding out of conviction—K was surely Social Justice and Q Extreme Morality. I was certain of this, and that after the war—unless we were completely swallowed up, like those Canadian battalions at Hong Kong—K and Q would envelop the world. Having no one to listen to, I could not have a thought without writing it down. There were pages and pages of dead butterflies, wings without motion or lift. I began to ration my writing, for fear I would dream through life as my father had done. I was afraid I had inherited a poisoned gene from him, a vocation without a gift. He had spent his own short time like a priest in charge of a relic, forever expecting the blessed blood to liquefy. I had no assurance I was not the same. I was so like him in some ways that a man once stopped me in front of the Bell Telephone building on Beaver Hall Hill and said, 'Could you possibly be Angus Muir's sister?' That is how years telescope in men's minds. That particular place must be the windiest in Montreal, for I remember dust and ragged papers blowing in whirlpools and that I had to hold my hair. I said, 'No, I'm not,' without explaining that I was not his sister but his daughter. I had heard people say, referring to me but not knowing who I was, 'He had a daughter, but apparently she died.' We couldn't *both* be dead. Having come down on the side of life, I kept my distance. Writing now had to occupy an enormous space. I had lived in New York until a year before and there were things I was sick with missing. There was no theater, no music; there was one museum of art with not much in it. There was not even a free public lending library in the sense of the meaning that would have been given the words 'free public lending library' in Toronto or New York. The municipal library was considered a sinister joke. There was a persistent, apocryphal story among English Canadians that an American philanthropic foundation (the Carnegie was usually mentioned) had offered to establish a free public lending library on condition that its contents were not to be censored by the provincial government of Quebec or by the Catholic Church, and that the offer had been turned down. The story may not have been true but its persistence shows the political and cultural climate of Montreal then. Educated French Canadians summed it up in shorter form: Their story was that when you looked up 'Darwin' in the card index of the Bibliothèque de Montreal you found 'See anti-Darwin.' A Canadian actress I knew in New York sent me the first published text of *The Skin of Our Teeth*. I wrote imploring her to tell me everything about the production—the costumes, the staging, the voices. I've never seen it performed—not read it since the end of the war. I've been told that it doesn't hold, that it is not rooted in anything specific. It was then; its Ice Age was Fascism. I read it the year of Dieppe, in a year when 'Russia' meant 'Leningrad,' when Malta could be neither fed nor defended. The Japanese were anywhere they wanted to be. Vast areas of the world were covered with silence and ice. One morning I read a little notice in the *Gazette* that Miss Margaret Urn would be taking auditions for the Canadian Broadcasting Corporation. I presented myself during my lunch hour with *The Skin of Our Teeth* and a manuscript one-act play of my own, in case. I had expected to find queues of applicants but I was the only one. Miss Urn received me in a small room of a dingy office suite on St. Catherine Street. We sat down on opposite sides of a table. I was rendered shy by her bearing, which had a headmistress quality, and perplexed by her accent—it was the voice any North American actor will pick up after six months of looking for work in the West End, but I did not know that. I opened *The Skin of Our Teeth* and began to read. It was floating rather than reading, for I had much of it by heart. When I read 'Have you milked the mammoth?' Miss Urn stopped me. She reached over the table and placed her hand on the page.

'My dear child, what is this rubbish?' she said.

I stammered, 'It is a . . . a play in New York.'

Oh, fool. The worst thing to say. If only I had said, 'Tallulah Bankhead,' adding swiftly, 'London, before the war.' Or, better, 'An Edwardian farce. Queen Alexandra, deaf though she was, much appreciated the joke about the separation of m and n.' 'A play in New York' evoked a look Canada was making me familiar with: amusement, fastidious withdrawal, gentle disdain. What a strange city to have a play in, she might have been thinking.

'Try reading this,' she said.

I shall forget everything about the war except that at the worst point of it I was asked to read *Dear Octopus*. If Miss Urn had never heard of Thornton Wilder I had never heard of Dodie Smith. I read what I took to be parody. Presently it dawned on me these were meant to be real people. I broke up laughing because of Sabina, Fascism, the Ice Age that was perhaps upon us, because of the one-act play still in my purse. She took the book away from me and closed it and said I would, or would not, be hearing from her.

Now there was excitement in the office: A second woman had been brought in. Mrs Ireland was her name. She had an advanced degree in accountancy and she was preparing a doctorate in some branch of mathematics none of the men were familiar with. She was about thirty-two. Her hair was glossy and dark; she wore it in braids that became a rich mahogany color when they caught the light. I admired her hair, but the rest of her was angry-looking—flushed cheeks, red hands and arms. The scarf around her throat looked as though it had been wound and tied in a fury. She tossed a paper on my desk and said, 'Check this. I'm in a hurry.' Chief Engineer looked up, looked at her, looked down. A play within the play, a subplot, came to life; I felt it exactly as children can sense a situation they have no name for. In the afternoon she said, 'Haven't you done that yet?' She had a positive, hammering sort of voice. It must have carried as far as the portraits in the hall. Chief Engineer unrolled a large map showing the mineral resources of eastern Canada and got behind it. Mrs Ireland called, to the room in general, 'Well, is she supposed to be working for me or isn't she?' Oh? I opened the bottom drawer of my desk, unlocked the middle drawer, began to pack up my personal affairs. I saw that I'd need a taxi: I had about three pounds of manuscripts and notes, and what seemed to amount to a wardrobe. In those days girls wore white gloves to work; I had two extra pairs of these, and a makeup kit, and extra shoes. I began filling my wastebasket with superfluous cargo. The room had gone silent: I can still see Bertie Knox's ratty little eyes judging, summing up, taking the measure of this new force. Mr Tracy, in his mauve glasses, hands in his pockets, came strolling out of his office; it was a sort of booth, with frosted-glass panels that did not go up to the ceiling. He must have heard the shouting and then the quiet. He and Mr Curran and Mr Elwitt, the diabetic one, were higher in rank than Chief Engineer, higher than Office Manager; they could have eaten Supervisor for tea and no one would dare complain. He came along easily—I never knew him to rush. I remember now that Chief Engineer called him 'Young Tracy,' because of his father; 'Old Tracy'—the real Tracy, so to speak—was the one who'd gone bust in the Depression. That was why Young Tracy had this job. He wasn't all that qualified, really; not so different from me. He sat down on Bertie Knox's desk with his back to him.

'Well, bolshie,' he said to me. This was a long joke: it had to do with my political views, as he saw them, and it was also a reference to a character in an English comic called 'Pip and Squeak' that he and I had both read as children—we'd discussed it once. Pip and Squeak were a dog and a penguin. They had a son called Wilfred, who was a rabbit. Bolshie seemed to be a sort of acquaintance. He went around carrying one of those round black bombs with a sputtering fuse. He had a dog, I think—a dog with whiskers. I had told Mr Tracy how modern educators were opposed to 'Pip and Squeak.' They thought that more than one generation of us had been badly misled by the unusual family unit of dog, penguin, and rabbit. It was argued that millions of children had grown up believing that if a dog made advances to a female penguin she would produce a rabbit. 'Not a *rabbit*,' said Mr Tracy reasonably. '*Wilfred*.'

I truly liked him. He must have thought I was going to say something now, if only to rise to the tease about 'bolshie,' but I was in the grip of that dazzling anger that is a form of snow blindness, too. I could not speak, and anyway didn't want to. I could only go on examining a pencil to see if it was company property or mine—as if that mattered. 'Are you taking the day off or trying to leave me?' he said. I can feel that tense listening of men pretending to work. 'I was looking over your application form,' he said. 'D'you know that your father knew my father? Yep. A long time ago. My father took it into his head to commission a mural for a plant in Sorel. Brave thing to do. Nobody did anything like that. Your father said it wasn't up his street. Suggested some other guy. My old man took the *two* of them down to Sorel. Did a lot of clowning around, but the Depression was just starting, so the idea fell through. My old man enjoyed it, though.'

'Clowning around' could not possibly have been my father, but then the whole thing was so astonishing. 'I should have mentioned it to you when you first came in,' he said, 'but I didn't realize it myself. There must be a million people called Muir; I happened to be looking at your form because apparently you're due for a raise.' He whistled something for a second or two, then laughed and said, 'Nobody ever quits around here. It can't be done. It upsets the delicate balance between labor and government. You don't want to do that. What do you want to do that for?'

'Mr Curran doesn't like me.'

'Mr Curran is a brilliant man,' he said. 'Why, if you knew Curran's whole story you'd'—he paused—'you'd stretch out the hand of friendship.'

'I've been asking and asking for a chair that doesn't wobble.'

'Take the day off,' he said. 'Go to a movie or something. Tomorrow we'll start over.' His life must have been like that. 'You know, there's a war on. We're all needed. Mrs Ireland has been brought here from . . .'

'From Trahnah,' said Mrs Ireland.

'Yes, from Toronto, to do important work. I'll see something gets done about that chair.'

He stood up, hands in his pockets, slouching, really; gave an affable nod all round. The men didn't see; their noses were almost touching their work. He strolled back to his glass cubicle, whistling softly. The feeling in the room was like the sight of a curtain raised by the wind now sinking softly.

'Oh, Holy Hannah!' Mrs Ireland burst out. 'I thought this was supposed to be a wartime agency!'

No one replied. *My father knew your father. I'll see something gets done about that chair.* So that is how it works among men. To be noted, examined, compared.

Meanwhile I picked up the paper she'd tossed on my desk hours before and saw that it was an actuarial equation. I waited until the men had stopped being aware of us and took it over and told her I could not read it, let alone check it. It had obviously been some kind of test.

She said, 'Well, it was too much to hope for. I have to single-handedly work out some wartime overtime pensions plan taking into account the cost of living and the earnest hope that the Canadian dollar won't sink.' And I was to have been her assistant. I began to admire the genius someone—Assistant Chief Engineer Macaulay, perhaps—had obviously seen in me. Mrs Ireland went on, 'I gather after this little comic opera we've just witnessed that you're the blue-eyed girl around here.' (Need I say that I'd hear this often? That the rumor I was Mr Tracy's mistress now had firm hold on the feminine element in the room—though it never gained all the men—particularly on the biddies, the two or three old girls loafing along to retirement, in comfortable corsets that gave them a sort of picket fence around the middle? That the obscene anonymous notes I sometimes found on my desk—and at once unfairly blamed on Bertie Knox—were the first proof I had that prolonged virginity can be the mother of invention?) 'You can have your desk put next to mine,' said Mrs Ireland. "I'll try to dig some good out of you.'

But I had no intention of being mined by Mrs Ireland. Remembering what Mr Tracy had said about the hand of friendship I told her, truthfully, that it would be a waste for her and for me. My name was down to do documentary-film work, for which I thought I'd be better suited; I was to be told as soon as a vacancy occurred.

'Then you'll have a new girl' I said. 'You can teach her whatever you like.'

'*Girl?*' She could not keep her voice down, ever. 'There'll not be a girl in this office again, if I have a say. Girls make me sick, sore, and weary.'

I thought about that for a long time. I had believed it was only because of the men that girls were parked like third-class immigrants at the far end of the room—the darkest part, away from the windows—with the indignity of being watched by Supervisor, whose whole function was just that. But there, up on the life raft, stepping on girls' fingers, was Mrs Ireland, too. If that was so, why didn't Mrs Ireland get along with the men, and why did they positively and openly hate her—openly especially after Mr Tracy's extraordinary and instructive sorting out of power?

'What blinking idiot would ever marry *her*?' said Bertie Knox. 'Ten to one she's not married at all. Ireland must be her maiden name. She thinks the 'Mrs' sounds good.' I began to wonder if she was not a little daft sometimes: She used to talk to herself; quite a lot of it was about me.

'You can't run a wartime agency with *that* going on,' she'd say loudly. 'That' meant poor Mr Tracy and me. Or else she would declare that it was unpatriotic of me to be drawing a man's salary. Here I think the men agreed. The salary was seventy-five dollars a month, which was less than a man's if he was doing the same work. The men had often hinted it was a lot for a girl. Girls had no expenses; they lived at home. Money paid them was a sort of handout. When I protested that I had the same expenses as any bachelor and did not live at home, it was countered by a reasonable 'Where you live is up to you.' They looked on girls as parasites of a kind, always being taken to restaurants and fed by men. They calculated the cost of probable outings, even to the Laura Secord chocolates I might be given, and rang the total as a casual profit to me. Bertie Knox used to sing, 'I think that I shall never see a dame refuse a meal that's free.' Mrs Ireland said that all this money would be better spent on soldiers who were dying, on buying war bonds and plasma, on the purchase of tanks and Spitfires. 'When I think of parents scrimping to send their sons to college!' she would conclude. All this was floods of clear water; I could not give it a shape. I kept wondering what she expected me to *do*, for that at least would throw a shadow on the water, but then she dropped me for a time in favor of another crusade, this one against Bertie Knox's singing. He had always sung. His voice conveyed rakish parodies of hymns and marches to every corner of the room. Most of the songs were well known; they came back to us from the troops, were either simple and rowdy or expressed a deep skepticism about the war, its aims and purposes, the way it was being conducted, and about the girls they had left at home. It was hard to shut Bertie Knox up: He had been around for a long time. Mrs Ireland said she had not had the education she'd had to come here and listen to foul language. Now absolutely and flatly forbidden by Chief Engineer to sing any ribald song *plainly*, Bertie Knox managed with umptee-um syllables as best he could. He became Mrs Ireland's counterpoint.

'I know there's a shortage of men,' Mrs Ireland would suddenly burst out.

'Oh umptee turn titty,' sang Bertie Knox.

'And that after this war it will be still worse . . .'

'Ti umpty dum diddy.'

'There'll hardly be a man left in the world worth his salt . . .'

'Tee umpty turn tumpty.'

'But what I do not see . . .'

'Tee diddle dee dum.'

'Is why a totally unqualified girl . . .'

'Turn tittle umpty tumpty.'

'Should be subsidized by the taxpayers of this country . . .'

'Pum pum tee umpty pumpee.'

'Just because her father failed to paint . . .'

'Oh umpty tumpty tumpty.'

'A mural down in . . .'

'Tee umpty dum dum.'

'Sorel.'

'Turn turn, oh, dum dum, oh, pum pum, oh, oh, uuuum.'

'Subsidized' stung, for I worked hard. Having no training I had no short-cuts. There were few mechanical shortcuts of any kind. The engineers used slide rules, and the machines might baffle today because of their simplicity. As for a computer, I would not have guessed what it might do or even look like. Facts were recorded on paper and stored in files and summarized by doing sums and displayed in some orderly fashion on graphs. I sat with one elbow on my desk, my left hand concealed in my hair. No one could see that I was counting on my fingers, in units of five and ten. The system by twelves would have finished me; luckily no one mentioned it. Numbers were a sunken world; they were a sea-scape from which perfect continents might emerge at any minute. I never saw more than their outline. I was caught on Zero. If zero meant Zero, how could you begin a graph on nothing? How could anything under zero be anything but Zero too? I spoke to Mr Tracy: What occupied the space between Zero and One? It must be something arbitrary, not in the natural order of numbers. If One was solid ground, why not begin with One? Before One there was what? Thin air? Thin air must be Something. He said kindly, 'Don't worry your head,' and if I had continued would certainly have added, 'Take the day off.' Chief Engineer McCreery often had to remind me, 'But we're not *paying* you to think!' If that was so, were we all being paid not to think? At the next place I worked things were even worse. It was another government agency, called Dominion Film Center—my first brush with the creative life. Here one was handed a folded thought like a shapeless school uniform and told, 'There, wear that.' Everyone had it on, regardless of fit. It was one step on: 'We're not paying you to think about whatever you are thinking.' I often considered approaching Mrs Ireland, but she would not accept even a candy from me, let alone a question. 'There's a war on' had been her discouraging refusal of a Life Saver once.

The men by now had found out about her husband. He had left school at Junior Fourth (Grade Seven) and 'done nothing to improve himself.' He was a Pole. She was ashamed of having a name that ended in 'ski' and used her maiden name; Bertie Knox hadn't been far off. Thinking of it now, I realize she might not have been ashamed but only aware that the 'ski' name on her application could have relegated it to a bottom drawer. Where did the men get their information, I wonder. Old 'ski' was a lush who drank her paycheck and sometimes beat her up; the scarves she wound around her neck were meant to cover bruises.

That she was unhappily married I think did not surprise me. What impressed me was that so many of the men were too. I had become engaged to be married, for the third time. There was a slight overlapping of two, by which I mean that the one in Halifax did not know I was also going to marry the one from the West. To the men, who could not follow my life as closely as they'd have wanted—I gave out next to nothing—it seemed like a long betrothal to some puppy in uniform, whom they had never seen, and whose Christian name kept changing. One of my reasons for discretion was that I was still underage. Until now I had been using my minority as an escape hatch, the way a married man will use his wife—for 'Ursula will never divorce' I substituted 'My mother will never consent.' Once I had made up my mind I simply began looking for roads around the obstacle; it was this search, in fact, that made me realize I must be serious. No one, no one at all, knew what I was up to, or what my entirely apocryphal emancipation would consist of; all that the men knew was that this time it did look as if I was going through with it. They took me aside, one after the other, and said, 'Don't do it, Linnet. Don't do it.' Bertie Knox said, 'Once you're in it, you're in it, kiddo.' I can't remember any man ever criticizing his own wife—it is something men don't often do, anywhere—but the warning I had was this: Marriage was a watershed that transformed sweet, cheerful, affectionate girls into, well, their own mothers. Once a girl had caught (their word) a husband she became a whiner, a snooper, a killjoy, a wet blanket, a grouch, and a bully. What I gleaned out of this was that it seemed hard on the men. But then even Mrs Ireland, who never said a word to me, declared, 'I think it's terrible.' She said it was insane for me to marry someone on his way overseas, to tie up my youth, to live like a widow without a widow's moral status. Why were she and I standing together, side by side, looking out the window at a gray sky, at pigeons, at a streetcar grinding up the steep street? We could never possibly have stood close, talking in low voices. And yet there she is; there I am with Mrs Ireland. For once she kept her voice down. She looked out—not at me. She said the worst thing of all. Remembering it, I see the unwashed windowpane. She said, 'Don't you girls ever know when you're well off? Now you've got no one to lie to you, to belittle you, to make a fool of you, to stab you in the back.' But we were different—different ages, different women, two lines of a graph that could never cross.

Mostly when people say 'I know exactly how I felt' it can't be true, but here I am sure—sure of Mrs Ireland and the window and of what she said. The recollection has something to do with the blackest kind of terror, as stunning as the bolts of happiness that strike for no reason. This blackness, this darkening, was not wholly Mrs Ireland, no; I think it had to do with the men, with squares and walls and limits and numbers. How do you stand if you stand upon Zero? What will the passage be like between Zero and One? And what will happen at One? Yes, what will happen?

1981

Elizabeth Spencer

Brief Biography

- Born in 1921 in Mississippi into a prosperous merchant family with strict Presbyterian parents.
- Though known as a Southern writer, lives much of her life in Italy and Montreal.
- Writer-in-residence and adjunct professor of creative writing at Concordia University, 1976–86.
- *The Light in the Piazza*, a musical based on her novel, opens in 2005 and wins six Tony awards.
- Has published nine novels and seven short story collections.
- Her manuscripts are in Ottawa's National Library.

Elizabeth Spencer was born in Carollton, Mississippi; her large and privileged family was one generation removed from the Civil War. Describing the 1940s South as 'a crippled land' and 'as rigidly bounded as a high-security prison,' she lived abroad and considers her writing 'an art shaped by exile.'

Although her family viewed living outside Mississippi as an outrage and a defiance of their wishes, Spencer once said 'there's a second country for everybody.' In 1953 she won a Guggenheim Fellowship to live in Italy; she married an Englishman and stayed in the country until 1961. It was here where she wrote her best-known book, *The Light in the Piazza* (1960), which became a successful film (1962) and Broadway musical (2005). She and her husband also lived in Montreal from 1961 to 1986. For ten years, she was a professor of creative writing at Concordia University. She considered Quebec similar to 'Ole Miss' with a parallel sense of conquest and loss of the Confederacy.

When Spencer began writing, the dominant Mississippi writer (and literary industry) was William Faulkner. Men ruled the universities, clubs, and asso-

ciations. Women writers were considered 'sentimental' or 'Southern belles.' Yet a 'Southern Renaissance' of women writers slowly gained momentum. With her writer friends Eudora Welty and Katherine Anne Porter as mentors in the 1940s, Spencer and other writers found a lifetime of friendship and support from a literary community of women, who met through writing circles, correspondence, and festivals.

In the supposedly 'illiterate' South, three clear strands of women ask 'What is Southern writing?' African-American writers (1993 Nobel laureate Toni Morrison, Alice Walker), post-Faulkner writers (Eudora Welty, Flannery O'Connor), and a new generation of women writers (Bobbi Ann Mason, Gail Godwin) reconnect to prior generations of women from new perspectives of American multiculturalism and identity politics. Is 'the South' a real place, perhaps in opposition to someplace else, or a 'remembered place'? Spencer's South is neither the Faulknerian 'monumental moment' nor the nostalgic and sentimental tradition of *Gone with the Wind*. Like Alice Munro's or Mavis Gallant's stories, her fiction makes a visceral connection to the past and childhood, perhaps as a way to preserve memories of a culture forever lost with the construction of an interstate highway. Spanning a six-decade career, Spencer's storytelling derives from a distinctly Southern female tradition; the South is always described as a feminine place, 'Old Dixie.' Critics colourfully define this feminist mythmaking in various terms: 'liminal tradition,' 'privileged space,' 'resetting the table,' and 'a verbal quilt.' Distanced from the street, the kitchen, and men, uniquely women's stories are told on porches, on balconies, or in beauty parlours in genres variously described as counter-pastoral, problem literature, or Southern grotesque or Gothic.

Scholars suggest that many 'Southern Gothic' stories have a sense of mystery and themes of enclosure, repressed fears and angers, or entrapment and escape. The unique blend of nostalgia, dialects, and distinct regional topics are now both celebrated and criticized in Southern fiction. Challenging traditional images of Southern women as frail and dependent on men, Elizabeth Spencer is neither domestic nor delicate. Regarding her controlled style, she told an interviewer that she avoids 'sensitive poetic prose like Katherine Mansfield's.' In one story, the narrator remarks, 'I like Jell-O pudding because it has a tough satin finish.' In 'The Girl Who Loved Horses,' tradition confronts change. Beneath the story's well-articulated surface are troubling depths: cars and guns, an absent father, and a stalker and potential rapist.

The Girl Who Loved Horses

She had drawn back from throwing a pan of bird scraps out the door because she heard what was coming, the two-part pounding of a full gallop, not the graceful triple notes of a canter. They were mounting the drive now, turning into the stretch along the side of the house; once before, someone appearing at the screen door had made the horse shy, so that, barely held beneath the rider, barely restrained, he had plunged off into the flower beds. So she stepped back from the door and saw the two of them shoot past, rounding a final corner, heading for the straight run of drive into the cattle gate and the barn lot back of it.

She flung out the scraps, then walked to the other side of the kitchen and peered through the window, raised for spring, toward the barn lot. The horse had slowed, out of habit, knowing what came next. And the white shirt that had passed hugged so low as to seem some strange part of the animal's trappings, or as though he had run under a low line of drying laundry and caught something to an otherwise empty saddle and bare withers, now rose up, angling to an upright posture. A gloved hand extended to pat the lathered neck.

'Lord have mercy,' the woman said. The young woman riding the horse was her daughter, but she was speaking also for her son-in-law, who went in for even more reckless behavior in the jumping ring the two of them had set up. What she meant by it was that they were going to kill themselves before they ever had any children, or if they did have children safely they'd bring up the children to be just as foolish about horses and careless of life and limb as they were themselves.

The young woman's booted heel struck the back steps. The screen door banged.

'You ought not to bring him in hot like that,' the mother said. 'I do know that much.'

'Cottrell is out there,' she said.

'It's still March, even if it has got warm.'

'Cottrell knows what to do.'

She ran water at the sink, and cupping her hand, drank primitive fashion out of it, bending to the tap, then wet her hands in the running water and thrust her fingers into the dusty, sweat-damp roots of her sand-colored hair. It had been a good ride.

'I hope he doesn't take up too much time,' the mother said. 'My beds need working.'

She spoke mildly but it was always part of the same quarrel they were in like a stream that was now a trickle, now a still pool, but sometimes after a freshet could turn into a torrent. Such as: 'Y'all are just crazy. Y'all are wasting everything on those things. And what are they? I know they're pretty and all that, but they're not a thing in the world but animals. Cows are animals. You can make a lot more money in cattle, than carting those things around over two states and three counties.'

She could work herself up too much to eat, leaving the two of them at the table, but would see them just the same in her mind's eye, just as if she'd stayed. There were the sandy-haired young woman, already thirty—married four years and still apparently with no intention of producing a family (she was an only child and the estate, though small, was a fine piece of land)—and across from her the dark spare still young man she had married.

She knew how they would sit there alone and not even look at one another or discuss what she'd said or talk against her; they would just sit there and maybe pass each other some food or one of them would get up for the coffeepot. The fanatics of a strange cult would do the same, she often thought, loosening her long hair upstairs, brushing the gray and brown together to a colorless patina, putting on one of her long cotton gowns with the ruched neck, crawling in between white cotton sheets. She was a widow and if she didn't want to sit up and try to talk to the family after a hard day, she didn't have to. Reading was a joy, lifelong. She found her place in *Middlemarch*, one of her favorites.

But during the day not even reading (if she'd had the time) could shut out the sounds from back of the privet hedge, plainly to be heard from the house. The trudging of the trot, the pause, the low directive, the thud of hoofs, the heave and shout, and sometimes the ring of struck wood as a bar came down. And every jump a risk of life and limb. One dislocated shoulder—Clyde's, thank heaven, not Deedee's—a taping, a sling, a contraption of boards, and pain 'like a hot knife,' he had said. A hot knife. Wouldn't that hurt anybody enough to make him quit risking life and limb with those two blood horses, quit at least talking about getting still another one while swallowing down pain-killer he said he hated to be sissy enough to take?

'Uh-huh,' the mother said. 'But it'll be Deborah next. You thought about that?'

'Aw, now, Miss Emma,' he'd lean back to say, charming her through his warrior's haze of pain. 'Deedee and me—that's what we're hooked on. Think of us without it, Mama. You really want to kill us. We couldn't live.'

He was speaking to his mother-in-law but smiling at his wife. And she, Deborah, was smiling back.

Her name was Deborah Dale, but they'd always, of course, being from LaGrange, Tennessee, right over the Mississippi border, that is to say, real South, had had a hundred nicknames for her. Deedee, her father had named her, and 'Deeds' her funny cousins said—'Hey, Deeds, how ya' doin'?' Being on this property in a town of pretty properties, though theirs was a little way out, a little bit larger than most, she was always out romping, swimming in forbidden creeks, climbing forbidden fences, going barefoot too soon in the spring, the last one in at recess, the first one to turn in an exam paper. ('Are you quite sure that you have finished, Deborah?' 'Yes, ma'am.')

When she graduated from ponies to that sturdy calico her uncle gave her, bringing it in from his farm because he had an eye for a good match, there was almost no finding her. 'I always know she's somewhere on the place,' her mother said. 'We just can't see it all at once,' said her father. He was ailing even back then but he undertook walks. Once when the leaves had all but gone from the trees, on a warm November afternoon, from a slight rise, he saw her down in a little-used pasture with a straight open stretch among some oaks. The ground was spongy and clotted with damp and even a child ought not to have tried to run there, on foot. But there went the calico with Deedee clinging low, going like the wind, and knowing furthermore out of what couldn't be anything but long practice, where to turn, where to veer, where to stop.

'One fine afternoon,' he said to himself, suspecting even then (they hadn't told him yet) what his illness was, 'and Emma's going to be left with nobody.' He remarked on this privately, not without anguish and not without humor.

They stopped her riding, at least like that, by sending her off to boarding school, where a watchful ringmaster took 'those girls interested in equitation' out on leafy trails, 'at the walk, at the trot, and at the canter.' They also, with that depth of consideration which must flourish even among those Southerners unlucky enough to wind up in the lower reaches of hell, kept her young spirit out of the worst of the dying. She just got a call from the housemother one night. Her father had 'passed away.'

After college she forgot it, she gave it up. It was too expensive, it took a lot of time and devotion, she was interested in boys. Some boys were interested in her. She worked in Memphis, drove home to her mother every night. In winter she had to eat breakfast in the dark. On some evenings the phone rang; on some it was silent. Her mother treated both kinds of evenings just the same.

To Emma Tyler it always seemed that Clyde Mecklin materialized out of nowhere. She ran straight into him when opening the front door one evening to get the paper off the porch, he being just about to turn the bell or knock. There he stood, dark and straight in the late light that comes after first dark and is so clear. He was clear as anything in it, clear as the first stamp of a young man ever cast.

'Is Deb'rah here?' At least no Yankee. But not Miss Tyler or Miss Deborah Tyler, or Miss Deborah. No, he was city all right.

She did not answer at first.

'What's the matter, scare you? I was just about to knock.' She still said nothing.

'Maybe this is the wrong place,' he said.

'No, it's the right place,' Emma Tyler finally said. She stepped back and held the door wider. 'Come on in.'

'Scared the life out of me,' she told Deborah when she finally came down to breakfast the next day, Clyde's car having been heard to depart by Emma Tyler in her upstairs bedroom at an hour she did not care to verify. 'Why didn't you tell me you were expecting him? I just opened the door and there he was.'

'I liked him so much,' said Deborah with grave honesty. 'I guess I was scared he wouldn't come. That would have hurt.'

'Do you still like him?' her mother ventured, after this confidence.

'He's all for outdoors,' said Deborah, as dreamy over coffee as any mother had ever beheld. 'Everybody is so indoors. He likes hunting, going fishing, farms.'

'Has he got one?'

'He'd like to have. All he's got's this job. He's coming back next weekend. You can talk to him. He's interested in horses.'

'But does he know we don't keep horses anymore?'

'That was just my thumbnail sketch,' said Deborah. 'We don't have to run out and buy any.'

'No, I don't imagine so,' said her mother, but Deborah hardly remarked the peculiar turn of tone, the dryness. She was letting coast through her head the scene: her mother (whom she now loved better than she ever had in her life) opening the door just before Clyde knocked, so seeing unexpectedly for the first time, that face, that head, that being. . . . When he had kissed her her ears drummed, and it came back to her once more, not thought of in years, the drumming hoofs of the calico, and the ghosting father, behind, invisible, observant, off on the bare distant November rise.

It was after she married that Deborah got beautiful. All LaGrange noticed it. 'I declare,' they said to her mother or sometimes right out to her face, 'I always said she was nice-looking but I never thought anything like that.'

Emma first saw the boy in the parking lot. He was new. In former days she'd parked in front of nearly any place she wanted to go—hardware, or drugstore, or courthouse: change for the meter was her biggest problem. But so many streets were one-way now and what with the increased numbers of cars, the growth of the town, those days were gone; she used a parking lot back of a café, near the newspaper office. The entrance to the lot was a bottleneck of a narrow drive between the two brick buildings; once in, it was hard sometimes to park.

That day the boy offered to help. He was an expert driver, she noted, whereas Emma was inclined to perspire, crane, and fret, fearful of scraping a fender or grazing a door. He spun the wheel with one hand; a glance told him all he had to know; he as good as sat the car in place, as skillful (she reluctantly thought) as her children on their horses. When she returned an hour later, the cars were denser still; he helped her again. She wondered whether to tip him. This happened twice more.

'You've been so nice to me,' she said, the last time. 'They're lucky to have you.'

'It's not much of a job,' he said. 'Just all I can get for the moment. Being new and all.'

'I might need some help,' she said. 'You can call up at the Tyler place if you want to work. It's in the book. Right now I'm in a hurry.'

On the warm June day, Deborah sat the horse comfortably in the side yard and watched her mother and the young man (whose name was Willett? Williams?), who, having worked the beds and straightened a fence post, was now replacing warped fence boards with new ones.

'Who is he?' she asked her mother, not quite low enough, and meaning what a Southern woman invariably means by that question, not what is his name but where did he come from, is he anybody we know? What excuse, in other words, does he have for even being born?

'One thing, he's a good worker,' her mother said, preening a little. Did they think she couldn't manage if she had to? 'Now don't you make him feel bad.'

'Feel bad!' But once again, if only to spite her mother, who was in a way criticizing her and Clyde by hiring anybody at all to do work that Clyde or the Negro help would have been able to do if only it weren't for those horses—once again Deborah had spoken too loudly.

If she ever had freely to admit things, even to herself, Deborah would have to say she knew she not only looked good that June day, she looked sexy as hell. Her light hair, tousled from a ride in the fields, had grown longer in the last year; it had slipped its pins on one side and lay in a sensuous lock along her cheek. A breeze stirred it, then passed by. Her soft poplin shirt was loose at the throat, the two top buttons open, the cuffs turned back to her elbows. The new horse, the third, was gentle, too much so (this worried them); she sat it easily, one leg up, crossed lazily over the flat English pommel, while the horse, head stretched down, cropped at the tender grass. In the silence between their voices, the tearing of the grass was the only sound except for a shrill jay's cry.

'Make him feel bad!' she repeated.

The boy looked up. The horse, seeking grass, had moved forward; she was closer than before, eyes looking down on him above the rise of her breasts and throat; she saw the closeness go through him, saw her presence register as strongly as if the earth's accidental shifting had slammed them physically together. For a minute there was nothing but the two of them. The jay was silent; even the horse, sensing something, had raised his head.

Stepping back, the boy stumbled over the pile of lumber, then fell in it. Deborah laughed. Nothing, that day, could have stopped her laughter. She was beautifully, languidly, atop a fine horse on the year's choice day at the peak of her life.

'You know what?' Deborah said at supper, when they were discussing her mother's helper. 'I thought who he looks like. He looks like Clyde.'

'The poor guy,' Clyde said. 'Was that the best you could do?'

Emma sat still. Now that she thought of it, he did look like Clyde. She stopped eating, to think it over. What difference did it make if he did? She returned to her plate.

Deborah ate lustily, her table manners unrestrained. She swabbed bread into the empty salad bowl, drenched it with dressing, bit it in hunks.

'The poor woman's Clyde, that's what you hired,' she said. She looked up.

The screen door had just softly closed in the kitchen behind them. Emma's hired man had come in for his money.

It was the next day that the boy, whose name was Willett or Williams, broke the riding mower by running it full speed into a rock pile overgrown with weeds but clearly visible, and left without asking for pay but evidently taking with him in his car a number of selected items from barn, garage, and tack room, along with a transistor radio that Clyde kept in the kitchen for getting news with his early coffee.

Emma Tyler, vexed for a number of reasons she did not care to sort out (prime among them was the very peaceful and good time she had been having with the boy the day before in the yard when Deborah had chosen to ride over and join them), telephoned the police and reported the whole matter. But boy, car, and stolen articles vanished into the nowhere. That was all, for what they took to be forever.

Three years later, aged thirty-three, Deborah Mecklin was carrying her fine head higher than ever uptown in LaGrange. She drove herself on errands back and forth in car or station wagon, not looking to left or right, not speaking so much as before. She was trying not to hear from the outside what they were now saying about Clyde, how well he'd done with the horses, that place was as good as a stud farm now, that he kept ten or a dozen, advertised and traded, as well as showed. And the money was coming in hard and fast. But, they would add, he moved with a fast set, and there was also the occasional gossip item, too often, in Clyde's case, with someone ready to report first hand; look how quick, now you thought of it, he'd taken up with Deborah, and how she'd snapped him up too soon to hear what his reputation was, even back then. It would be a cold day in August before any one woman would be enough for him. And his father before him? And his father before him. So the voices said.

Deborah, too, was trying not to hear what was still sounding from inside her head after her fall in the last big horse show:

The doctor: You barely escaped concussion, young lady.

Clyde: I just never saw your timing go off like that. I can't get over it.

Emma: You'd better let it go for a while, honey. There're other things, so many other things.

Back home, she later said to Emma: 'Oh, Mama, I know you're right sometimes, and sometimes I'm sick of it all, but Clyde depends on me, he always has, and now look—'

'Yes, and 'Now look' is right, he has to be out with it to keep it all running. You got your wish, is all I can say.'

Emma was frequently over at her sister-in-law Marian's farm these days. The ladies were aging, Marian especially down in the back, and those twilights in the house alone were more and more all that Deedee had to keep herself company with. Sometimes the phone rang and there'd be Clyde on it, to say he'd be late again. Or there'd be no call at all. And once she (of all people) pressed some curtains and hung them, and once hunted for old photographs, and once, standing in the middle of the little-used parlor among the walnut Victorian furniture upholstered in gold and blue and rose, she had said 'Daddy?' right out loud, like he might have been there to answer, really been there. It had surprised her, the word falling out like that as though a thought took reality all by itself and made a word on its own.

And once there came a knock at the door.

All she thought, though she hadn't heard the car, was that it was Clyde and that he'd forgotten his key, or seeing her there, his arms loaded maybe, was asking her to let him in. It was past dark. Though times were a little more chancy now, LaGrange was a safe place. People nearer to town used to brag that if they went off for any length of time less than a weekend and locked the doors, the neighbors would get their feelings hurt; and if the Tylers lived further out and 'locked up,' the feeling for it was ritual mainly, a precaution.

She glanced through the sidelight, saw what she took for Clyde, and opened the door. There were cedars in the front yard, not too near the house, but dense enough to block out whatever gathering of light there might have been from the long slope of property beyond the front gate. There was no moon.

The man she took for Clyde, instead of stepping through the door or up to the threshold to greet her, withdrew a step and leaned down and to one side, turning outward as though to pick up something. It was she who stepped forward, to greet, help, inquire; for deep within was the idea her mother had seen to it was firmly and forever planted: that one day one of them was going to get too badly hurt by 'those things' ever to be patched up.

So it was in outer dark, three paces from the safe threshold and to the left of the area where the light was falling outward, a dim single sidelight near the mantelpiece having been all she had switched on, too faint to penetrate the sheer gathered curtains of the sidelight, that the man at the door rose up, that he tried to take her. The first she knew of it, his face was in hers, not Clyde's but something like it and at Clyde's exact height, so that for the moment she thought that some joke was on, and then the strange hand caught the parting of her blouse, a new mouth fell hard on her own, one knee thrust her legs apart, the free hand diving in to clutch and press against the thin nylon between her thighs. She recoiled at the same time that she felt, touched in the quick, the painful glory of desire brought on too fast—looking back on that instant's two-edged meaning, she would never hear about rape without the lightning quiver of ambivalence within the word. However, at the time no meditation stopped her knee from coming up into the nameless groin and nothing stopped her from tearing back her mouth slathered with spit so suddenly smeared into it as to drag it into the shape of a scream she was unable yet to find a voice for. Her good right arm struck like a hard backhand against a line-smoking tennis serve. Then from the driveway came the stream of twin headlights thrusting through the cedars.

'Bitch!' The word, distorted and low, was like a groan; she had hurt him, freed herself for a moment, but the struggle would have just begun except for the lights, and the screams that were just trying to get out of her. 'You fucking bitch.' He saw the car lights, wavered, then turned. His leap into the shrubbery was bent, like a hunchback's. She stopped screaming suddenly. Hurt where he lived, she thought. The animal motion, wounded, drew her curiosity for a second. Saved, she saw the car sweep round the drive, but watched the bushes shake, put up her hand to touch but not to close the torn halves of the blouse, which was ripped open to her waist.

Inside, she stood looking down at herself in the dim light. There was a nail scratch near the left nipple, two teeth marks between elbow and wrist where she'd smashed into his mouth. She wiped her own mouth on the back of her hand, gagging at the taste of cigarette smoke, bitterly staled. Animals! She'd always had a special feeling for them, a helpless tenderness. In her memory the bushes, shaking to a crippled flight, shook forever.

She went upstairs, stood trembling in her mother's room (Emma was away), combed her hair with her mother's comb. Then, hearing Clyde's voice calling her below, she stripped off her ravaged blouse and hastened across to their own rooms to hide it in a drawer, change into a fresh one, come downstairs. She had made her decision already. Who was this man? A nothing . . . an unknown. She hated women who shouted Rape! Rape! It was an incident, but once she told it everyone would know, along with the police, and would add to it: they'd say she'd been violated. It was an incident, but Clyde, once he knew, would trace him down. Clyde would kill him.

'Did you know the door was wide open?' He was standing in the living room.

'I know. I must have opened it when I heard the car. I thought you were stopping in the front.'

'Well, I hardly ever do.' 'Sometimes you do.'

'Deedee, have you been drinking?'

'Drinking . . .? Me?' She squinted at him, joking in her own way; it was a standing quarrel now that alone she sometimes poured one or two.

He would check her breath but not her marked body. Lust with him was mole-dark now, not desire in the soft increase of morning light, or on slowly westering afternoons, or by the night light's glow. He would kill for her because she was his wife. . . .

'Who was that man?'

Uptown one winter afternoon late, she had seen him again. He had been coming out of the hamburger place and looking back, seeing her through the street lights, he had turned quickly into an alley. She had hurried to catch up, to see. But only a form was hastening there, deeper into the unlit slit between brick walls, down toward a street and a section nobody went into without good reason.

'That man,' she repeated to the owner (also the proprietor and cook) in the hamburger place. 'He was in here just now.'

'I don't know him. He hangs around. Wondered myself. You know him?'

'I think he used to work for us once, two or three years ago. I just wondered.'

'I thought I seen him somewhere myself.'

'He looks a little bit like Clyde.'

'Maybe so. Now you mention it.' He wiped the counter with a wet rag. 'Get you anything, Miss Deb'rah?'

'I've got to get home.'

'Y'all got yourselves some prizes, huh?' 'Aw, just some good luck.' She was gone.

Prizes, yes. Two trophies at the Shelby County Fair, one in Brownsville where she'd almost lost control again, and Clyde not worrying about her so much as scolding her. His recent theory was that she was out to spite him. He would think it if he was guilty about the women, and she didn't doubt any more that he was. But worse than spite was what had got to her, hating as she did to admit it.

It was fear.

She'd never known it before. When it first started she hadn't even known what the name of it was.

Over two years ago, Clyde had started buying colts not broken yet from a stud farm south of Nashville, bringing them home for him and Deborah to get in shape together. It saved a pile of money to do it that way. She'd been thrown in consequence three times, trampled once, a terrifying moment as the double reins had caught up her outstretched arm so she couldn't fall free. Now when she closed her eyes at night, steel hoofs sometimes hung through the dark above them, and she felt hard ground beneath her head, smelled smeared grass on cheek and elbow. To Clyde she murmured in the dark: 'I'm not good at it any more.' 'Why, Deeds, you were always good. It's temporary, honey. That was a bad day.'

A great couple. That's what Clyde thought of them. But more than half their name had been made by her, by the sight of her, Deborah Mecklin, out in full dress, black broadcloth and white satin stock with hair drawn trimly back beneath the smooth rise of the hat, entering the show ring. She looked damned good back of the glossy neck's steep arch, the pointed ears and lacquered hoofs which hardly touched earth before springing upward, as though in the instant before actual flight. There was always the stillness, then the murmur, the rustle of the crowd. At top form she could even get applause. A fame for a time spread round them. The Mecklins. Great riders. 'Ridgewood Stable. Blood horses trained. Saddle and Show.' He'd had it put up in wrought iron, with a sign as well, Old English style, of a horseman spurring.

('Well, you got to make money,' said Miss Emma to her son-in law. 'And don't I know it,' she said. 'But I just hate to think how many times I kept those historical people from putting up a marker on this place. And now all I do is worry one of y'all's going to break your neck. If it wasn't for Marian needing me and all . . . I just can't sleep a wink over here.'

('You like to be over there anyway, Mama,' Deborah said. 'You know we want you here.'

('Sure, we want you here,' said Clyde. 'As for the property, we talked it all out beforehand. I don't think I've damaged it any way.'

('I just never saw it as a horse farm. But it's you all I worry about. It's the danger.')

Deborah drove home.

When the workingman her mother had hired three years before had stolen things and left, he had left too on the garage wall inside, a long pair of crossing diagonal lines, brown, in mud, Deborah thought, until she smelled what it was, and there were the blood-stained menstrual pads she later came across in the driveway, dug up out of the garbage, strewed out into the yard.

She told Clyde about the first but not the second discovery. 'Some critters are mean,' he'd shrugged it off. 'Some critters are just mean.'

They'd been dancing, out at the club. And so in love back then, he'd turned and turned her, far apart, then close, talking into her ear, making her laugh and answer, but finally he said: 'Are you a mean critter, Deedee? Some critters are mean.' And she'd remembered what she didn't tell

But in those days Clyde was passionate and fun, both marvelously together, and the devil appearing at midnight in the bend of a country road would not have scared her. Nothing would have. It was the day of her life when they bought the first two horses.

'I thought I seen him somewhere myself.'

'He looks a little bit like Clyde.'

And dusk again, a third and final time.

The parking lot where she'd come after a movie was empty except for a few cars. The small office was unlighted, but a man she took for the attendant was bending to the door on the far side of a long cream-colored sedan near the back fence. 'Want my ticket?' she called. The man straightened, head rising above the body frame, and she knew him. Had he been about to steal a car, or was he breaking in for whatever he could find, or was it her coming all along that he was waiting for? However it was, he knew her as instantly as she knew him. Each other was what they had, by whatever design or absence of it, found. Deborah did not cry out or stir.

Who knew how many lines life had cut away from him down through the years till the moment when an arrogant woman on a horse had ridden him down with lust and laughter? He wasn't bad-looking; his eyes were beautiful; he was the kind to whom nothing good could happen. From that bright day to this chilly dusk, it had probably just been the same old story.

Deborah waited. Someway or other, what was coming, threading through the cars like an animal lost for years catching the scent of a former owner, was her own.

('You're losing nerve, Deedee,' Clyde had told her recently. 'That's what's really bothering me. You're scared, aren't you?')

The bitter-stale smell of cigarette breath, though not so near as before, not forced against her mouth, was still unmistakably familiar. But the prod of a gun's muzzle just under the rise of her breast was not. It had never happened to her before. She shuddered at the touch with a chill spring-like start of something like life, which was also something like death.

'Get inside,' he said.

'Are you the same one?' she asked. 'Just tell me that. Three years ago, Mama hired somebody. Was that you?'

'Get in the car.'

She opened the door, slid over to the driver's seat, found him beside her. The gun, thrust under his crossed arm, resumed its place against her.

'Drive.'

'Was it you the other night at the door?' Her voice trembled as the motor started, the gear caught.

'He left me with the lot; ain't nobody coming.' The car eased into an empty street.

'Go out of town. The Memphis road.'

She was driving past familiar, cared-for lawns and houses, trees and intersections. Someone waved from a car at a stoplight, taking them for her and Clyde. She was frightened and accepting fear, which come to think of it was all she'd been doing for months, working with those horses. ('Don't let him bluff you, Deedee. It's you or him. He'll do it if he can.')

'What do you want with me? What is it you want?'

He spoke straight outward, only his mouth moving, watching the road, never turning his head to her. 'You're going out on that Memphis road and you're going up a side road with me. There's some woods I know. When I'm through with you you ain't never going to have nothing to ask nobody about me because you're going to know it all and it ain't going to make you laugh none, I guarantee.'

Deborah cleared the town and swinging into the highway wondered at herself. Did she want him? She had waited when she might have run. Did she want, trembling, pleading, degraded, finally to let him have every single thing his own way?

(Do you see steel hoofs above you over and over because you want them one day to smash into your brain?

('Daddy, Daddy,' she had murmured long ago when the old unshaven tramp had come up into the lawn, bleary-eyed, face blood-burst with years of drink and weather, frightening as the boogeyman, 'raw head and bloody bones,' like the Negro women scared her with. That day the sky streamed with end-of-the-world fire. But she hadn't called so loudly as she might have, she'd let him come closer, to look at him better, until the threatening voice of her father behind her, just on the door's slamming, had cried: 'What do you want in this yard? What you think you want here? Deborah! You come in this house this minute!' But the mystery still lay dark within her, forgotten for years, then stirring to life again: When I said 'Daddy, Daddy?' was I calling to the tramp or to the house? Did I think the tramp was him in some sort of joke or dream or trick? If not, why did I say it? Why?

('Why do you ride a horse so fast, Deedee? Why do you like to do that?' *I'm going where the sky breaks open.* 'I just like to.' 'Why do you like to drive so fast?' 'I don't know.')

Suppose he kills me, too, thought Deborah, striking the straight stretch on the Memphis road, the beginning of the long rolling run through farms and woods. She stole a glance to her right. He looked like Clyde, all right. What right did he have to look like Clyde?

('It's you or him, Deedee.' All her life they'd said that to her from the time her first pony, scared at something, didn't want to cross a bridge. 'Don't let him get away with it. It's you or him.')

Righting the big car into the road ahead, she understood what was demanded of her. She pressed the accelerator gradually downward toward the floor.

'And by the time he realized it,' she said, sitting straight in her chair at supper between Clyde and Emma, who by chance were there that night together; '—by the time he knew, we were hitting above seventy-five, and he said, "What you speeding for?" and I said, "I want to get it over with." And he said, "Okay, but that's too fast." By that time we were touching eighty and he said, "What the fucking hell"—excuse me, Mama—"you think you're doing? You slow this thing down." So I said, "I tell you what I'm doing. This is a rolling road with high banks and trees and lots of curves. If you try to take the wheel away from me, I'm going to wreck us both. If you try to sit there with that gun in my side I'm going to go faster and faster and sooner or later something will happen, like a curve too sharp to take or a car too many to pass with a big truck coming and we're both going to get smashed up at the very least. It won't do any good to shoot me when it's more than likely both of us would die. You want that?"

'He grabbed at the wheel but I put on another spurt of speed and when he pulled at the wheel we side-rolled, skidded back, and another car coming almost didn't get out of the way. I said, "You see what you're doing, I guess." And he said, "Jesus God." Then I knew I had him, had whipped him down.

'But it was another two or three miles like that before he said, "Okay, okay, so I quit. Just slow down and let's forget it." And I said, "You give me that gun. The mood I'm in, I can drive with one hand or no hands at all, and don't think I won't do it." But he wanted his gun at least, I could tell. He didn't give in till a truck was ahead and we passed but barely missed a car that was coming (it had to run off the concrete), and he put it down, in my lap.'

(Like a dog, she could have said, but didn't. And I felt sorry for him, she could have added, because it was his glory's end.)

'So I said, "Get over, way over," and he did, and I coasted from fast to slow. I turned the gun around on him and let him out on an empty stretch of road, by a rise with a wood and a country side road rambling off, real pretty, and I thought, Maybe that's where he was talking about, where he meant to screw hell—excuse me, Mama—out of me. I held the gun till he closed the door and went down in the ditch a little way, then I put the safety catch on and threw it at him. It hit his shoulder, then fell in the weeds. I saw it fall, driving off.'

'Oh, my poor baby,' said Emma. 'Oh, my precious child.'

It was Clyde who rose, came round the table to her, drew her to her feet, held her close. 'That's nerve,' he said. 'That's class.' He let her go and she sat down again. 'Why didn't you shoot him?'

'I don't know.'

'He was the one we hired that time,' Emma said. 'I'd be willing to bet you anything.'

'No, it wasn't,' said Deborah quickly. 'This one was blond and short, red-nosed from too much drinking, I guess. Awful like Mickey Rooney, gone and gotten old. Like the boogeyman, I guess.'

'The poor woman's Mickey Rooney. You women find yourselves the damned-est men.'

'She's not right about that,' said Emma. 'What do you want to tell that for? I know it was him. I feel like it was.'

'Why'd you throw the gun away?' Clyde asked. 'We could trace that.'

'It's what I felt like doing,' she said. She had seen it strike, how his shoulder, struck, went back a little.

Clyde Mecklin sat watching his wife. She had scarcely touched her food, and now, pale, distracted, she had risen to wander toward the windows, look out at the empty lawn, the shrubs and flowers, the stretch of white-painted fence, ghostly by moonlight.

'It's the last horse I'll ever break,' she said, more to herself than not, but Clyde heard and stood up and was coming to her.

'Now, Deedee—'

'When you know you know,' she said, and turned, her face set against him: her anger, her victory, held up like a blade against his stubborn willfulness. 'I want my children now,' she said.

At the mention of children, Emma's presence with them became multiple and vague; it trembled with thanksgiving, it spiraled on wings of joy.

Deborah turned again, back to the window. Whenever she looked away, the eyes by the road were there below her: they were worthless, nothing, but infinite, never finishing—the surface there was no touching bottom for—taking to them, into themselves, the self that was hers no longer.

1981

Margaret Atwood

Brief Biography

- Born in 1939 in Ottawa; her well-read father was a forest entomologist.
- Holds sixteen honorary degrees.
- Wins Man Booker Prize for *The Blind Assassin* (2000).
- Invents the LongPen, a computer-aided gadget that allows her to autograph books remotely.
- Draws cartoon strip, *Kanadian Kulture Komic*, under pseudonym Bart Gerrard, in Toronto magazine, poking fun at herself, fame, and interviewers.
- Feminist critic, defender of human rights and advocate for women's rights.
- Occasionally designs her book covers.
- Has served as writer-in-residence in Canada, the United States, and Australia; has lectured around the world.
- With husband, novelist Graeme Gibson, is an avid birdwatcher.

Canada's best-known writer both at home and abroad, Margaret Atwood is also a prolific writer of more than fifty books, including a dozen novels and more than fifteen poetry collections. Born in Ottawa, the second of three children, she spent much of her childhood in northern Quebec and Ontario, where her zoologist father studied insects at research stations. As a result, metaphors of wilderness, ecological awareness, and animals appear in her works.

Her mother, a dietician, was an important role model. Atwood was home-schooled until grade eight, and her early reading of popular fiction, gothic romances, comics, fairy tales, and mythology informs much of her fiction. A student of critic Northrop Frye, she graduated from the University of Toronto and earned an MA at Radcliffe—now merged with Harvard—intending to complete a PhD on 'meta-physical romance' and popular Victorian novelist H. Rider Haggard. Instead, she began 'thinking seriously about Canada having a shape and culture of its own.'

Professor David Staines of the University of Ottawa sees Atwood's career in three stages: award-winning poet 'mapping her country'; advocate for social change through fiction; and, finally, passionate enthusiast for Canada's past and 'Canada in the world.' As an observer of popular culture, Atwood considers the social implications of politics and consequences of technology in her science fiction novels. However, she prefers the term 'speculative' fiction. Such novels explore social changes both positive (utopia) or, more often, negative (dystopia). Most importantly, she defends the writer's imagination for portraying 'who we are and what we want.' *The Handmaid's Tale* (1985) and *Oryx and Crake* (2003) were worldwide best-sellers; the former became a popular movie (1990). Atwood is also both a social critic and defender of Canadian cultural autonomy and freedom of speech. Her entertaining critical books include *Survival: A Thematic Guide to Canadian Literature* (1972), *Strange Things: The Malevolent North in Canadian Literature* (1995), *Negotiating with the Dead: A Writer on Writing* (2002), and *Payback: Debt and the Shadow Side of Wealth* (Massey Lectures, 2008). As an icon and media star, feminist and social activist, her provocative opinions on such issues as PEN, Amnesty International, nuclear disarmament, and environmental issues are eagerly sought.

Central to Atwood's writing are criticisms of those who either ignore or silence women, or place them in passive or secondary roles. To compare and contrast women's roles, she often evokes nineteenth-century Canadian women, such as Susanna Moodie in her poems and the murderess Grace Marks in her novel *Alias Grace* (1996); she has also written the libretto for an opera on Pauline Johnson. To give women voice and power, Atwood revisions male stories from the perspectives of female characters. She has reworked Homer's *The Odyssey* from the viewpoints of Circe and Penelope and Shakespeare's *Hamlet* from Gertrude's side.

Her dark humour is in the tradition of satirists. 'Happy Endings' explores relationships from six angles. Drawing on the convention of fairy tales, the story is also a commentary on writing, especially plots. Atwood challenges writers who rely on simplistic literary conventions; she also criticizes stereotypes and gender roles. Yet her deceptively simple story has a deeper purpose: love draws characters together, though always with consequences. For characters, authors, and readers, the outcome is always death. What matters is the quality of life between beginnings and endings.

See Margaret Atwood, from 'Communion: Nobody to Nobody: The Eternal Triangle,' p. 470.

Happy Endings

John and Mary meet.
What happens next?
If you want a happy ending, try A.

A

John and Mary fall in love and get married. They both have worthwhile and remunerative jobs which they find stimulating and challenging. They buy a charming house. Real estate values go up. Eventually, when they can afford live-in help, they have two children, to whom they are devoted. The children turn out well. John and Mary have a stimulating and challenging sex life and worthwhile friends. They go on fun vacations together. They retire. They both have hobbies which they find stimulating and challenging. Eventually they die. This is the end of the story.

B

Mary falls in love with John but John doesn't fall in love with Mary. He merely uses her body for selfish pleasure and ego gratification of a tepid kind. He comes to her apartment twice a week and she cooks him dinner, you'll notice that he doesn't even consider her worth the price of a dinner out, and after he's eaten dinner he fucks her and after that he falls asleep, while she does the dishes so he won't think she's untidy, having all those dirty dishes lying around, and puts on fresh lipstick so she'll look good when he wakes up, but when he wakes up he doesn't even notice, he puts on his socks and his shorts and his pants and his shirt and his tie and his shoes, the reverse order from the one in which he took them off. He doesn't take off Mary's clothes, she takes them off herself, she acts as if she's dying for it every time, not because she likes sex exactly, she doesn't, but she wants John to think she does because if they do it often enough surely he'll get used to her, he'll come to depend on her and they will get married, but John goes out the door with hardly so much as a good-night and three days later he turns up at six o'clock and they do the whole thing over again.

Mary gets run-down. Crying is bad for your face, everyone knows that and so does Mary but she can't stop. People at work notice. Her friends tell her John is a rat, a pig, a dog, he isn't good enough for her, but she can't believe it. Inside John, she thinks, is another John, who is much nicer. This other John will emerge like a butterfly from a cocoon, a Jack from a box, a pit from a prune, if the first John is only squeezed enough.

One evening John complains about the food. He has never complained about the food before. Mary is hurt.

Her friends tell her they've seen him in a restaurant with another woman, whose name is Madge. It's not even Madge that finally gets to Mary: it's the restaurant. John has never taken Mary to a restaurant. Mary collects all the sleeping pills and aspirins she can find, and takes them and a half a bottle of sherry. You can see what kind of a woman she is by the fact that it's not even whiskey. She leaves a note for John. She hopes he'll discover her and get her to the hospital in time and repent and then they can get married, but this fails to happen and she dies.

John marries Madge and everything continues as in A.

C

John, who is an older man, falls in love with Mary, and Mary, who is only twenty-two, feels sorry for him because he's worried about his hair falling out.

She sleeps with him even though she's not in love with him. She met him at work. She's in love with someone called James, who is twenty-two also and not yet ready to settle down.

John on the contrary settled down long ago: this is what is bothering him. John has a steady, respectable job and is getting ahead in his field, but Mary isn't impressed by him, she's impressed by James, who has a motorcycle and a fabulous record collection. But James is often away on his motorcycle, being free. Freedom isn't the same for girls, so in the meantime Mary spends Thursday evenings with John. Thursdays are the only days John can get away.

John is married to a woman called Madge and they have two children, a charming house which they bought just before the real estate values went up, and hobbies which they find stimulating and challenging, when they have the time. John tells Mary how important she is to him, but of course he can't leave his wife because a commitment is a commitment. He goes on about this more than is necessary and Mary finds it boring, but older men can keep it up longer so on the whole she has a fairly good time.

One day James breezes in on his motorcycle with some top-grade California hybrid and James and Mary get higher than you'd believe possible and they climb into bed. Everything becomes very underwater, but along comes John, who has a key to Mary's apartment. He finds them stoned and entwined. He's hardly in any position to be jealous, considering Madge, but nevertheless he's overcome with despair. Finally he's middle-aged, in two years he'll be as bald as an egg and he can't stand it. He purchases a handgun, saying he needs it for target practice—this is the thin part of the plot, but it can be dealt with later—and shoots the two of them and himself.

Madge, after a suitable period of mourning, marries an understanding man called Fred and everything continues as in A, but under different names.

D

Fred and Madge have no problems. They get along exceptionally well and are good at working out any little difficulties that may arise. But their charming house is by the seashore and one day a giant tidal wave approaches. Real estate values go down. The rest of the story is about what caused the tidal wave and how they escape from it. They do, though thousands drown, but Fred and Madge are virtuous and lucky. Finally on high ground they clasp each other, wet and dripping and grateful, and continue as in A.

E

Yes, but Fred has a bad heart. The rest of the story is about how kind and understanding they both are until Fred dies. Then Madge devotes herself to charity

work until the end of A. If you like, it can be 'Madge,' 'cancer,' 'guilty and confused,' and 'bird watching.'

F

If you think this is all too bourgeois, make John a revolutionary and Mary
a counterespionage agent and see how far that gets you. Remember, this is
Canada. You'll still end up with A, though in between you may get a lustful
brawling saga of passionate involvement, a chronicle of our times, sort of.

You'll have to face it, the endings are the same however you slice it. Don't be
deluded by any other endings, they're all fake, either deliberately fake, with
malicious intent to deceive, or just motivated by excessive optimism if not by
downright sentimentality.
    The only authentic ending is the one provided here:
    John and Mary die. John and Mary die. John and Mary die.

So much for endings. Beginnings are always more fun. True connoisseurs, however, are known to favor the stretch in between, since it's the hardest to do anything with.
    That's about all that can be said for plots, which anyway are just one thing
after another, a what and a what and a what.
    Now try How and Why.

1983

Jorge Luis Borges

Brief Biography

- Born in Buenos Aires in 1899; mother is descended from Argentinian military heroes.
- Inherits eye disease; says as an adult he could see only 'the yellow colour of a tiger.'
- Is fired from library job in 1946; appointed poultry inspector but declines position.
- Head of Argentina's National Library 1955–73; resigns after Peron government is reinstated.
- In 1961 international publishers' jury awards the Formentor Prize to Borges and Samuel Beckett as the writers most likely to change literary history.
- Briefly married and divorced, he lives with his sister and mother most of his life.
- At age eighty-six, a few weeks before his death, marries his secretary, a PhD student.
- Dies of liver cancer in Geneva in 1986.

When Jorge Luis Borges was seventy years old and almost totally blind from hereditary eye disease, he became a literary superstar who began winning dozens of awards, inspiring dissertations and biographies. Yet he was so shy that he required psychoanalysis before a lecture tour. He claimed someone else named 'Borges' wrote his books. Defining himself simply as a reader and writer, he was influenced by his father's large library of British books, especially those by Rudyard Kipling, Robert Louis Stevenson, and William Shakespeare.

Borges's family moved from Buenos Aires to Geneva just prior to World War I. Graduating with a BA from the College of Geneva, Borges moved briefly to Spain and joined the literary group 'Ultraist.' He began to amass a deep knowledge of Western literature and philosophy with a special interest in ancient, obscure, or even non-existent books. Inspired by James Joyce's *Dubliners*—he translated Joyce into Spanish—on his return to Buenos Aires in 1921, he joined 'Ultraismo,' an avant-garde literary group of writers and artists who wanted to create a style apart from the colonizing Spanish or English.

Hallucinations from blood poisoning and a subsequent fear that he had lost his ability to write led to his innovative style. Borges's new stories were parodies of detective fiction, meditations on literature or philosophies, and intellectual puzzles. His main characters were often sketchily portrayed detectives, scholars, or writers. In originality, he belongs to a unique group of writers of the fantastic: Edgar Allan Poe, Franz Kafka, Italo Calvino, Angela Carter, and Julio Cortázar. But he replaced nineteenth-century horror and fear with twentieth-century metaphysical thought. Biographer E.R. Monegal notes that Borges created a new genre, 'the essayistic short story that postulates the existence of non-existent books and authors and proceeds to explain and discuss them.' Noting little difference between fiction's dramatic conflict and literary debate within an essay, Borges altered the boundaries between essays, poetry, and philosophy. He also suggested that reading was as creative as writing, which revolutionized experimental fiction writing and literary criticism.

As a librarian, Borges became fascinated with catalogues and encyclopedias. The tedious work of cataloguing library books at a Buenos Aires branch library inspired his most characteristic writings. Calling them 'ficciones' (fictions), instead of stories, he redefined the genre as definitively as Poe with his descriptions of labyrinths, mazes, mirrors, or dreams. A skeptical philosopher, he argued that since

nothing is knowable, nothing is impossible. Time could be reversed, individuals could switch identities, and stories could be dreams that end when the dreamer awakens.

Borges's short story collections, *Universal History of Infamy* (1932), *Ficciones* (1944), and *The Aleph* (1949), deal with the problems of identity, memory, and guilt. His final published story, 'Shakespeare's Memory,' is a first-person narrative by Hermann Sörgel, an aging, lonely, partially blind scholar with guilty secrets in his past. It can be read as a modern-day horror story, a subtle exploration of memory and its interconnections with identity, a brooding tribute to the works of genius, or even, like Kafka's 'A Report to an Academy,' a satire on academia.

Shakespeare's Memory

There are devotees of Goethe, of the Eddas, of the late song of the Nibelungen; my fate has been Shakespeare. As it still is, though in a way that no one could have foreseen—no one save one man. Daniel Thorpe, who has just recently died in Pretoria. There is another man, too, whose face I have never seen.

My name is Hermann Sörgel. The curious reader may have chanced to leaf through my *Shakespeare Chronology*, which I once considered essential to a proper understanding of the text: it was translated into several languages, including Spanish. Nor is it beyond the realm of possibility that the reader will recall a protracted diatribe against an emendation inserted by Theobald into his critical edition of 1734—an emendation which became from that moment on an unquestioned part of the canon. Today I am taken a bit aback by the uncivil tone of those pages, which I might almost say were written by another man. In 1914 I drafted, but did not publish, an article on the compound words that the Hellenist and dramatist George Chapman coined for his versions of Homer; in forging these terms, Chapman did not realize that he had carried English back to its Anglo-Saxon origins, the *Ursprung* of the language. It never occurred to me that Chapman's voice, which I have now forgotten, might one day be so familiar to me ... A scattering of critical and philological 'notes,' as they are called, signed with my initials, complete, I believe, my literary biography. Although perhaps I might also be permitted to include an unpublished translation of *Macbeth*, which I began in order to distract my mind from the thought of the death of my brother, Otto Julius, who fell on the western front in 1917. I never finished translating the play; I came to realize that English has (to its credit) two registers—the Germanic and the Latinate—while our own German, in spite of its greater musicality, must content itself with one.

I mentioned Daniel Thorpe. I was introduced to Thorpe by Major Barclay at a Shakespeare conference. I will not say where or when; I know all too well that such specifics are in fact vaguenesses.

More important than Daniel Thorpe's face, which my partial blindness helps me to forget, was his notorious lucklessness. When a man reaches a certain age, there are many things he can feign; happiness is not one of them. Daniel Thorpe gave off an almost physical air of melancholy.

After a long session, night found us in a pub—an undistinguished place that might have been any pub in London. To make ourselves feel that we were in England (which of course we were), we drained many a ritual pewter mug of dark warm beer.

'In Punjab,' said the major in the course of our conversation, 'a fellow once pointed out a beggar to me. Islamic legend apparently has it, you know, that King Solomon owned a ring that allowed him to understand the language of the birds. And this beggar, so everyone believed, had somehow come into possession of that ring. The value of the thing was so beyond all reckoning that the poor bugger could never sell it, and he died in one of the courtyards of the mosque of Wazil Khan, in Lahore.'

It occurred to me that Chaucer must have been familiar with the tale of that miraculous ring, but mentioning it would have spoiled Barclay's anecdote.

'And what became of the ring?' I asked.

'Lost now, of course, as that sort of magical thingamajig always is. Probably in some secret hiding place in the mosque, or on the finger of some chap who's off living somewhere where there're no birds.'

'Or where there are so many,' I noted, 'that one can't make out what they're saying for the racket. Your story has something of the parable about it, Barclay.'

It was at that point that Daniel Thorpe spoke up. He spoke, somehow, impersonally, without looking at us. His English had a peculiar accent, which I attributed to a long stay in the East.

'It is not a parable,' he said. 'Or if it is, it is nonetheless a true story. There are things that have a price so high they can never be sold.'

The words I am attempting to reconstruct impressed me less than the conviction with which Daniel Thorpe spoke them. We thought he was going to say something further, but suddenly he fell mute, as though he regretted having spoken at all. Barclay said good night. Thorpe and I returned together to the hotel. It was quite late by now, but Thorpe suggested we continue our conversation in his room. After a short exchange of trivialities, he said to me:

'Would you like to own King Solomon's ring? I offer it to you. That's a metaphor, of course, but the thing the metaphor stands for is every bit as wondrous as that ring. Shakespeare's memory, from his youngest boyhood days to early April, 1616—I offer it to you.'

I could not get a single word out. It was as though I had been offered the ocean.

Thorpe went on:

'I am not an impostor. I am not insane. I beg you to suspend judgment until you hear me out. Major Barclay no doubt told you that I am, or was, a military physician. The story can be told very briefly. It begins in the East, in a field hospital, at dawn. The exact date is not important. An enlisted man named Adam Clay, who had been shot twice, offered me the precious memory almost literally with his last breath. Pain and fever, as you know, make us creative; I accepted his offer without crediting it—and besides, after a battle, nothing seems so very strange. He barely had time to explain the singular conditions of the gift: The one who possesses it must offer it aloud, and the one who is to receive it must accept it the same way. The man who gives it loses it forever.'

The name of the soldier and the pathetic scene of the bestowal struck me as 'literary' in the worst sense of the word. It all made me a bit leery.

'And you, now, possess Shakespeare's memory?'

'What I possess,' Thorpe answered, 'are still *two* memories—my own personal memory and the memory of that Shakespeare that I partially am. Or rather, two memories possess *me*. There is a place where they merge, somehow. There is a woman's face . . . I am not sure what century it belongs to.'

'And the one that was Shakespeare's—' I asked. 'What have you done with it?'

There was silence.

'I have written a fictionalized biography,' he then said at last, 'which garnered the contempt of critics but won some small commercial success in the United States and the colonies. I believe that's all . . . I have warned you that my gift is not a sinecure. I am still waiting for your answer.'

I sat thinking. Had I not spent a lifetime, colorless yet strange, in pursuit of Shakespeare? Was it not fair that at the end of my labors I find him?

I said, carefully pronouncing each word:

'I accept Shakespeare's memory.'

Something happened; there is no doubt of that. But I did not feel it happen. Perhaps just a slight sense of fatigue, perhaps imaginary.

I clearly recall that Thorpe did tell me:

'The memory has entered your mind, but it must be "discovered." It will emerge in dreams or when you are awake, when you turn the pages of a book or turn a corner. Don't be impatient; don't *invent* recollections. Chance in its mysterious workings may help it along, or it may hold it back. As I gradually forget, you will remember. I can't tell you how long the process will take.'

We dedicated what remained of the night to a discussion of the character of Shylock. I refrained from trying to discover whether Shakespeare had had personal dealings with Jews. I did not want Thorpe to imagine that I was putting him to some sort of test. I did discover (whether with relief or uneasiness, I cannot say) that his opinions were as academic and conventional as my own.

In spite of that long night without sleep, I hardly slept at all the following night. I found, as I had so many times before, that I was a coward. Out of fear of disappointment, I could not deliver myself up to openhanded hope. I preferred to think that Thorpe's gift was illusory. But hope did, irresistibly, come to prevail. I would possess Shakespeare, and possess him as no one had ever possessed anyone before—not in love, or friendship, or even hatred. I, in some way, would *be* Shakespeare. Not that I would write the tragedies or the intricate sonnets— but I would recall the instant at which the witches (who are also the Fates) had been revealed to me, the other instant at which I had been given the vast lines:

> And shake the yoke of inauspicious stars
> From this world-weary flesh.

I would remember Anne Hathaway as I remembered that mature woman who taught me the ways of love in an apartment in Lübeck so many years ago. (I tried to recall that woman, but I could only recover the wallpaper, which was yellow, and the light that streamed in through the window. This first failure might have foreshadowed those to come.)

I had hypothesized that the images of that wondrous memory would be primarily visual. Such was not the case. Days later, as I was shaving, I spoke into the mirror a string of words that puzzled me; a colleague informed me that they were from Chaucer's 'A.B.C.' One afternoon, as I was leaving the British Museum, I began whistling a very simple melody that I had never heard before.

The reader will surely have noted the common thread that links these first revelations of the memory: it was, in spite of the splendor of some metaphors, a good deal more auditory than visual.

De Quincey says that man's brain is a palimpsest. Every new text covers the previous one, and is in turn covered by the text that follows—but all-powerful Memory is able to exhume any impression, no matter how momentary it might have been, if given sufficient stimulus. To judge by the will he left, there had been not a single book in Shakespeare's house, not even the Bible, and yet everyone is familiar with the books he so often repaired to: Chaucer, Gower, Spenser, Christopher Marlowe, Holinshed's *Chronicle*, Florio's Montaigne, North's Plutarch. I possessed, at least potentially, the memory that had been Shakespeare's; the reading (which is to say the rereading) of those old volumes would, then, be the stimulus I sought. I also reread the sonnets, which are his work of greatest immediacy. Once in a while I came up with the explication, or with many explications. Good lines demand to be read aloud; after a few days I effortlessly recovered the harsh *r*'s and open vowels of the sixteenth century.

In an article I published in the *Zeitschrift für germanische Philologie*, I wrote that Sonnet 127 referred to the memorable defeat of the Spanish Armada. I had forgotten that Samuel Butler had advanced that same thesis in 1899.

A visit to Stratford-on-Avon was, predictably enough, sterile.

Then came the gradual transformation of my dreams. I was to be granted neither splendid nightmares *à la* de Quincey nor pious allegorical visions in the manner of his master Jean Paul*; it was unknown rooms and faces that entered my nights. The first face I identified was Chapman's; later there was Ben Jonson's, and the face of one of the poet's neighbors, a person who does not figure in the biographies but whom Shakespeare often saw.

The man who acquires an encyclopedia does not thereby acquire every line, every paragraph, every page, and every illustration; he acquires the *possibility* of becoming familiar with one and another of those things. If that is the case with a concrete, and relatively simple, entity (given, I mean, the alphabetical order of its parts, etc.), then what must happen with a thing which is abstract and variable—*ondoyant et divers*? A dead man's magical memory, for example?

No one may capture in a single instant the fullness of his entire past. That gift was never granted even to Shakespeare, so far as I know, much less to me, who was but his partial heir. A man's memory is not a summation; it is a chaos of vague possibilities. St. Augustine speaks, if I am not mistaken, of the palaces and the caverns of memory. That second metaphor is the more fitting one. It was into those caverns that I descended.

Like our own, Shakespeare's memory included regions, broad regions, of shadow—regions that he willfully rejected. It was not without shock that I remembered how Ben Jonson had made him recite Latin and Greek hexameters, and how his ear—the incomparable ear of Shakespeare—would go astray in many of them, to the hilarity of his fellows.

I knew states of happiness and darkness that transcend common human experience.

Without my realizing it, long and studious solitude had prepared me for the docile reception of the miracle. After some thirty days, the dead man's memory had come to animate me fully. For one curiously happy week, I almost believed myself Shakespeare. His work renewed itself for me. I know that for Shakespeare the moon was less the moon than it was Diana, and less Diana than that dark drawn-out word *moon*. I noted another discovery: Shakespeare's apparent instances of inadvertence—those *absences dans l'infini* of which Hugo apologetically speaks—were deliberate. Shakespeare tolerated them—or actually interpolated them—so that his discourse, destined for the stage, might appear to be spontaneous, and not overly polished and artificial (*nicht allzu glatt und gekünstelt*). That same goal inspired him to mix his metaphors:

my way of life
Is fall'n into the sear, the yellow leaf.

One morning I perceived a sense of guilt deep within his memory. I did not try to define it; Shakespeare himself has done so for all time. Suffice it to say that the offense had nothing in common with perversion.

I realized that the three faculties of the human soul—memory, understanding, and will—are not some mere Scholastic fiction. Shakespeare's memory was able to reveal to me only the circumstances of *the man* Shakespeare. Clearly, these circumstances do not constitute the uniqueness of *the poet*; what matters is the literature the poet produced with that frail material.

I was naive enough to have contemplated a biography, just as Thorpe had. I soon discovered, however, that that literary genre requires a talent for writing that I do not possess. I do not know how to tell a story. I do not know how to tell *my own* story, which is a great deal more extraordinary than Shakespeare's. Besides, such a book would be pointless. Chance, or fate, dealt Shakespeare those trivial terrible things that all men know; it was his gift to be able to transmute them into fables, into characters that were much more alive than the gray man who dreamed them, into verses which will never be abandoned, into verbal music. What purpose would it serve to unravel that wondrous fabric, besiege and mine the tower, reduce to the modest proportions of a documentary biography or a realistic novel the sound and fury of *Macbeth*?

Goethe, as we all know, is Germany's official religion; the worship of Shakespeare, which we profess not without nostalgia, is more private. (In England, the official religion is Shakespeare, who is so unlike the English; England's sacred book, however, is the Bible.)

Throughout the first stage of this adventure I felt the joy of being Shakespeare; throughout the last, terror and oppression. At first the waters of the two memories did not mix; in time, the great torrent of Shakespeare threatened to flood my own modest stream—and very nearly did so. I noted with some nervousness that I was gradually forgetting the language of my parents. Since personal identity is based on memory, I feared for my sanity.

My friends would visit me; I was astonished that they could not see that I was in hell.

I began not to understand the everyday world around me (*die alltägliche Umwelt*). One morning I became lost in a welter of great shapes forged in iron, wood, and glass. Shrieks and deafening noises assailed and confused me. It took me some time (it seemed an infinity) to recognize the engines and cars of the Bremen railway station.

As the years pass, every man is forced to bear the growing burden of his memory. I staggered beneath two (which sometimes mingled)—my own and the incommunicable other's.

The wish of all things, Spinoza says, is to continue to be what they are. The stone wishes to be stone, the tiger, tiger—and I wanted to be Hermann Sörgel again.

I have forgotten the date on which I decided to free myself. I hit upon the easiest way: I dialed telephone numbers at random. The voice of a child or a woman would answer; I believed it was my duty to respect their vulnerable estates. At last a man's refined voice answered.

'Do you,' I asked, 'want Shakespeare's memory? Consider well: it is a solemn thing I offer, as I can attest.'

An incredulous voice replied:

'I will take that risk. I accept Shakespeare's memory.'

I explained the conditions of the gift. Paradoxically, I felt both a *nostalgie* for the book I should have written, and now never would, and a fear that the guest, the specter, would never abandon me.

I hung up the receiver and repeated, like a wish, these resigned words:

Simply the thing I am shall make me live.

I had invented exercises to awaken the antique memory; I had now to seek others to erase it. One of many was the study of the mythology of William Blake, that rebellious disciple of Swedenborg. I found it to be less complex than merely complicated.

That and other paths were futile; all led me to Shakespeare.

I hit at last upon the only solution that gave hope courage: strict, vast music—Bach.

P.S. (1924)—I am now a man among men. In my waking hours I am Professor Emeritus Hermann Sörgel; I putter about the card catalog and compose erudite trivialities, but at dawn I sometimes know that the person dreaming is that other man. Every so often in the evening I am unsettled by small, fleeting memories that are perhaps authentic.

1983

Jose Dalisay, Jr

Brief Biography

- Born in Romblon, Philippines, in 1954.
- Imprisoned under martial law in 1973; many friends are tortured.
- 1984–91 educated in the Philippines and Wisconsin and begins teaching career.
- Has published fifteen books—novels, stories, plays, and essays— and won five National Book Awards from Manila Critics Circle.
- Considered among top 100 Filipino artists of the century.
- Is a popular teacher; *The Knowing Is in the Writing: Notes on the Practice of Fiction* (2006) quickly becomes standard text in the Philippines.
- Weekly column, *Pinoy Penman*, reports on travels, authors, books, and Filipino literacy and culture.
- Writes fiction in English, but drama in Tagalog, one of more than 100 Philippine languages.
- Obsessed by Mac computers and Volkswagen Beetles; avidly collects old fountain pens and 1950s Bulova watches.

A prominent Filipino fiction writer, dramatist, journalist, editor, and professor at the University of the Philippines, Jose Dalisay, Jr, has helped bring Filipino literature and culture to Westerners. Scholars assert that the Filipino experience with colonial oppression, US imperialism, and globalization has created 'negotiated identities.' But literary modernism also suggested new models for expression. After the country's Martial Law years (1972–86) came a resurgence of nationalistic pride among writers and artists. Many, including Dalisay, were former political prisoners concerned with a Filipino identity.

Dalisay studied English and American writers, citing realists like W. Somerset Maugham, Graham Greene, and John Updike as early influences. He argues for a simple, direct style: 'The mastery of the sentence is the writer's truest hallmark,' he wrote in one of his weekly columns, while acknowledging the challenges that slang, dialect, and dozens of languages present. He considers electronic communication a new form of protest literature, noting that hundreds of millions of e-mails and text messages were used to depose his country's president in 2001. Because of a century of American military presence, English is the Philippines' prevalent language, yet 'Filipino is a language of resistance,' Dalisay believes. Like Edwidge Danticat, he also notes the 'troubled, thorny, and challenging relationship' between literature and politics. In his politics, Dalisay is associated with a group of writers called 'the Second Propaganda Movement,' who emulate a revolutionary nineteenth-century poet-hero.

In a literary magazine, Dalisay said, 'We write about the loneliness and hardship of the Filipino worker and migrant abroad, about our love–hate relationship with America, about sexuality and gender, about marginalized communities, about holding on to one's identity in an increasingly homogenized universe.' Dalisay's most recent novel, *Soledad's Sister* (2006), shortlisted for the first Man Asian Literary Prize, begins with a misidentified corpse of a migrant worker and explores the interconnections among identity, foreign oppression, and Philippine bureaucracy.

The realist story 'Heartland' looks back to the repressive regime of Philippine President Ferdinand Marcos. However, because Marcos was still in power when the story was written, Dalisay set it in the distant past, specifically during the 1890s conflict between Filipino revolutionaries and the Spanish colonizers. Its graphic portrayal of violence starkly contrasts with Stephen Crane's impressionistic war story 'A Mystery of Heroism.' The protagonists of each story are very different, as well: while Crane's Collins is naively reckless, Dr Ferrariz is educated and cynical. Yet, surprisingly, during the course of their brutal experiences, both men discover untapped resources within themselves.

Heartland

The dawn broke weakly, like a soldier of a defeated army rising at reveille, for nothing. The sun was a yellow smudge in the kettle-gray sky. It shimmered, shivered, and dissolved quickly in the wetness that crept over the encampment and everything in it; and the air, rich with vapor, carried the morning crisply into every tent—horses' dung; the grass, crushed where the caissons had rolled over it; alcohol and ether, festering sores, cordite, and burnt greenwood.

Ferrariz was seized in the middle of a dream by the sensation of a large ball of iron lodging in his groin, settling there, growing and pushing against the skin to break free. The pressure rose to his temples and raised a cold sweat on his head and thighs. He came to and recalled briefly what his dream had been about: Carmela, at the *baile*, teasing him to take her sister; he felt confused, distressed, and intensely alive. He got up from the cot and relieved himself in an enameled chamberpot in the far corner of the tent. It was a silly thing to drag along in a battlefield full of holes and craters of every sort, and where an incoming round could, in a flash, rip canvas and wood, flesh and bone, mind and memory apart so that nothing much really mattered upon the instant. But Ferrariz treasured the little comfort it afforded him, he was a discreet and well-mannered man, despite the raggedness of the war. The chamber pot reminded him of soft beds and spotless linen. He thought of his dream again, had difficulty remembering the scenes, missing a detail here and there, and then suddenly he lost everything, as if a rag had been wiped across his brow.

It happened most mornings, grieving him more than the shattered legs and nerves he saw to daily and tried to mend, often with little more than morphine. Blood came with the business; it meant nothing now, the corpses piled in the wagon behind the camp, bloated and dripping; the physical fact of death was the first lesson any surgeon learned. Army doctors saw the worst of it; masses of men threw themselves at each other and when their work was done were brought back in the beast-drawn wagons, the crippled standing over their fallen comrades, clutching at the sides for balance as the bodies shifted beneath them when the wheels slipped into a rut or struck a rock. The rest of the infantry straggled in a file behind the wagons. He met them calmly, the burial detail beside him; it was the easiest of his tasks to certify the dead. It was only a trifle more difficult to decide who among the wounded would be sent back to the fighting.

He saw through malingerers with a practiced eye. Their faces demanded pity and it was simple to refuse them. He did not have space enough in the extended tent they called a field hospital—when they had gathered enough men in to justify the status—for the genuinely injured. Only those who could not walk on their own two feet were temporarily excused. At least three men already lost their feet willingly; the nature of their wounds was suspect, but Ferrariz did not care to assist the work of the courts-martial.

He cared very little, indeed, for the War and the army he nominally belonged to. That the war itself was pointless had long been evident to him. The natives had staged a revolution, and their task was to put it down by sheer force and attrition, because nothing else seemed manageable. The battalion marched into the interior through towns and villages named after a brace of saints. Each little huddle in the wilderness looked more miserable than that before it. The stench of the wretched clung to the walls of the mud-floored shacks they entered, seeping from dark patches in the straw. With few exceptions they found the villages deserted and stripped of all things useful. Ferrariz remembered the old man in San Victorino, betel juice streaming from the sides of his mouth, blind to the world and reason; and the headman of Santa Fe, rushing to greet them with a crude copy of their own flag. After they had been shot, their villages were burned and the army moved on. Behind them, the natives reemerged from shadow and tropic foliage with fresh bamboo and palm from the mangrove swamps. In less than a day, villages were remade and pigs were slaughtered, to go with coconut liquor. The people feasted, danced, and slept fitfully when they had had their fill.

That, to a large extent, was the revolutionary war as the company of Dr. Ferrariz knew it. It was as fruitless as hacking through the undergrowth—the infernal tangle of thorns and weeds that turned a man mad over nothing—and hoping that it would grow no more, that the rest of it would wither from sheer shock.

There was a rebels' army in the mountains, with generals, colonels, and captains of their own. These officers wore uniforms for their men to respond to; the men wore what the women had packed into their bundles. They even wore, Ferrariz heard with amusement, banana leaves and *buri* fronds, and stole into camps disguised as such, ever keen to slit the throats of the unsuspecting. The rebels trained monkeys at this task; they turned snakes and leeches loose upon the sleeping; they colored streams and wells with the blood of the kidnapped, so the rumors said. The truth mattered little, the doctor knew; confusion, at least, kept the men alert. The dead kept coming, with lead in their kidneys, brains, and kneecaps. Ferrariz imagined the instant of clarity—no monkeys there, nor razor-edged palms, only guns spitting bullets of familiar, fateful caliber. The enemy was made up of regular men, no need to count their ribs.

Ferrariz himself felt no unusual passion for anyone or anything. He felt colder than those horse-brained officers all wrapped up in their war. But then he understood that it was in the natural order of things for men to quarrel violently and do murder within the species. The brain was imperfect; scars and strange secretions turned children against their own mother.

The doctor liked to think that he faced his duties with the proper detachment and consistency. Before the war he had served briefly with the poorman's hospital in the capital. He saw infants born with open skulls and bellies; he saw and memorized the progressive ravages of ulcers, consumption, and diseases of the flesh. He developed what people took to be judgment and efficiency. When a patient seemed more likely to survive, he slapped a compress to the man's head or prescribed him a placebo and sent him home happy. When he slipped beyond a certain point, Ferrariz drove a vialful of morphine into his arm and wished him good night. It was, he reasoned, the only sane and moral policy to apply. It kept his mind clear and his soul pure on the battlefield as far as he was concerned. The morphine killed no one; it simply eased what was left of life. His hands rarely shook and his sutures were neat, a surgeon's pride; but when he shaved and saw the tiredness in his eyes he knew that he was bored with and hated disease and injury and the consistency of it.

They were five days deep into the heartland, in pursuit of a rebel band no more than a fourth of their size. The men rushed into the forests eager for contact, the heat of the crackling, choleric air in the soulless huts now far behind them. The first patrols found no one; those, more timid, who came after them met savage fire from anthills, aeries, mud pools, and the hollows of fallen trees, or so it seemed to their unfocused eyes. The first group turned and again met nothing but the sight of carnage and the terror of laughter and battle cries in some strange and native pitch threatening to return, to mock them as they moved their dead. With all these gaping wounds and little deaths Ferrariz had begun forgetting his dreams within a minute of his rising. It was extremely annoying to the calm and collected man, whose chamberpot tinkled with what he thought was a ball of iron.

They brought him back to camp shortly before noon, trussed up in the wagon beside the headless body of a soldier named Venegas. A bloody flour sack at Venegas's feet gathered fat bottle-green flies.

Quirino Venegas, twenty-four and husband to a cobbler's daughter in Cadiz, had stood sentry in the forward outpost the night before and, like a privileged few before him, had fallen to the spell of the fireflies. It was neither rumor nor the devil's work. On certain nights, given the rare agreement of weather, instinct, and the indulgence of predators, fireflies of a family gathered themselves into balls beneath the canopy, these luminescent hives throbbing in the night like low-hung moons in a mahogany-leaf sky. At times such a ball would move abruptly, or explode in a thousand curving, deathless sparks, as when Venegas approached. The ball recomposed itself at a safer distance, a beacon in the mists; and Venegas, giggling at his luck and thinking of the words he would be using in his letter to Cadiz, ran after the fireflies, rifle thumping wildly against his side, and saw the other.

Venegas froze, unslung his weapon, and tried desperately to peel back the fingers that seemed to be digging into his guts. A dry scream rose in his throat, stopping short of his teeth. The bush crackled nearby with the other's movement; the fireflies fled, faithless and fugitive. The soldier pressed his back to a tree and hugged his rifle as though it were the blessed cross. *Ave Maria, Madre de Dios.* The other was the enemy, because the only man with him on the detail was his good friend Simeon, who was sleeping at the post just then. Simeon had never seen the lights and would have enjoyed his story. But Simeon had already shot a rebel dead while Venegas had never seen them face-to-face, until that moment. A feeling welled in his breast, a kind of courage; he would get his own man, with a little pluck. He eased his breathing and his grip and waited for the enemy.

The shot took him in the guts below his heart, tearing tissue but no bone. He felt astonishment more than pain; that would come, but at the moment he groped for answers, and fell on his nose and mouth in the mud.

Boots sloshed his way, they stopped at his feet, moved to his side. Whoever he was took time to catch his breath.

The first jab of pain hit him when he moved; the booted one tried to roll him over with the rifle as a prod. Instead of provoking the man to use the thing again, the rebel helped his weight along and felt a fiery liquid shoot into his veins from somewhere in the middle of him; it did nothing against the chill creeping up from his feet. He tasted salt and oil at the mouth. His head dropped to a side, the man on the other. Opening his eyes by the barest fraction, he saw the bolo lying within reach. He moved and the soldier stiffened instantly, pressing the rifle to his jaw.

He lay still and closed his eyes. The soldier knew he was alive, but had not decided what to do with him, Venegas who had so recently bargained with his God and Virgin and who now commanded a captive's breath. The muzzle trembled against the skin of the rebel's jaw, then lifted; a boot creaked; the man was kneeling over him. The rebel marked by his captor's breathing the distance to his face. A hand searched his pocket and his neck for treasure, and paused, as though the soldier had only then realized that his enemy was in uniform, though barely a boy, whose eyes were those of a man, eyes which opened and stared at him suddenly as the boy reached for the bolo and with a cry of pain and fury lopped the head of Quirino Venegas off his shoulders.

It was the good soldier Simeon who discovered them that morning, the rebel and his headless friend. Simeon gaped and puked, and, these protests of the gut done with, Simeon turned loose his fury upon the body of the boy, who lay sprawled on his back, a dull brown stain on his chest, his cream cotton shirt wet with dew.

Simeon grabbed Venegas's rifle and shot the boy in the face with a click; its chamber was empty. Simeon raised the rifle high in the air and brought it crashing down on the rebel's mouth, drawing the crack of broken teeth and a barely audible moan.

Simeon screamed, throwing the rifle in fear as though it were the devil's staff. The boy was alive.

And Venegas's head, lying in the mud with its eyes on the river, carried the same look of terror and astonishment.

The Major joined Ferrariz and the burial detail at the gate, gathering his great-coat about his shoulders. It was bound to rain. The clouds sat low and ragged on the mountains' backs, the angry riders of solidly unmoving steeds.

The Major was a small man even in his boots, although he seemed to have once been fuller of body, here and there. But he was no weakling; he absorbed energy and kept it quietly like a shrunken fig. A year in the tropics had stripped his body of all but the most essential things, excepting the large blue veins that snaked across his temples like a hero's wreath.

He was a spare and practical man all told. His one folly was his hair, the color of well-burnt ash, which was swept back, neatly on either side of a perfect furrow, plastered to his skull with a perfumed kind of gelatin. He kept this in a special tin, which served him as the chamberpot did the surgeon. Most of his men tucked crumbling letters into their knapsacks or taught their favorite song to others, until they cried. He preferred vanity to sentiment or even comfort on that score; it declared more, lifted his foot smartly forward. Ferrariz looked like a shabby bear beside him, rubbing his palms as if he had never seen winter in the old country. It was impatience rather than the cold, or troubled nerves. A thick beef stew was steaming in the officers' mess and the wagon was late. Ferrariz wondered if the Major had had his lunch; it was possible, for a few quick minutes, after chatting up the man Simeon. Ferrariz had stayed with the soldier without saying much, letting him babble on about the bodies in the mud, already convinced that Simeon had suffered no lasting damage and would be his own story's hero in a day or so of more fanciful retelling. The Major came in time to hear the simplest of it and had sent men to fetch Venegas and the body.

A drizzle fell and Ferrariz put a felt cap to his head. The Major, who always wore a cap in the open over his well-tended hair, glanced briefly at him and returned his gaze to the road.

Figures, schemes, and all sorts of mean and evil dreams were running through the Major's mind. In less than five days in the interior, he had lost nearly two dozen men against six bodies of the enemy left in the bush. He had inspected each of these six bodies, vexed to find all of them irretrievably and uselessly dead. He had poked the tip of his saber into the eyeball of one of them, just to be certain; something like the white of an egg oozed out. He flicked the dead man's collar aside and saw the scratch on the side of the neck. The killer had claimed the prize that went with such sweetly personal victories—a brass bauble of some sort, inscribed in a language he vaguely recognized as holy. The six were peasants; their feet were large, their cracked toes splayed wide apart.

The bodies of his own men also often returned shoeless, and even, when they had been left out for a time, disgustingly naked. But that was hardly the worst of things. Many of those two dozen lost their ears and noses as well, or else were cut up badly in the most unnecessary places. As the men had all been shot, it was to be assumed that the enemy was playing, on the side, a gruesome kind of sport. There was a man who returned—alive—without his hands, which had been severed neatly at the wrists, whose screams filled the night until the doctor's ministrations took effect. And now Venegas lost his head. The Major thought of the headless soldier running back to camp with nothing to scream through.

The Major stared at the wagon coming down the road, drawn by a native bull whose head swayed from side to side. The stupid man must have stuck his neck out like that.

Ferrariz dipped into his pocket for a handkerchief and blew his nose. The burial detail, two men leaning on their shovels, looked tiredly at the scene. Ferrariz shifted and folded the handkerchief absently. The taller of the two gravediggers pulled his shovel from the wet earth; it came off with a soft sucking sound.

The light rain slid off the polished brim of the Major's cap. He pulled it down slightly over his eyes, so that he faced a curved horizon. Before this posting, at the Academy, they said he possessed a certain charm, a light and even comic wit for the ladies, and a crushing knowledge of affairs for manly debate over brandy in the study. This was when he had taken on the habit of parting his hair straight down the middle so that, with the veins and his ample brow, full accent was laid upon his being a man of deliberate thought.

But in those monkey-infested islands the Major had few occasions for charm or repartee. Not until this morning, in the brief course of their campaign, had he felt the tingle in his body that he remembered went with the first day of any war and with moving smartly down the reception line of a grand ball.

He wished to meet the rebel and confirm the existence of their first live prisoner personally. If his man was right, they had an officer at that. Not that the Major cared for the native ranks; the poor coconut Napoleons and banana Wellingtons would never have heard of Clausewitz to begin with. But they quite possibly knew a few useful things that the dead took with them.

The wagon stopped before the party and the Major saw the enemy who had passed out on top of Venegas's body. It was a young face, as dark as they come, with high cheekbones, a squat nose, and a large jaw, a plain kind of face that told him nothing, yet. Ferrariz looked at the broken figure on the wagon floor and saw another face, one that had been terribly bashed in; its lips were cut and swollen; the jagged edge of a cracked tooth stared out of the open mouth; a cheek was turning black. It was a mess of gristle, dirt, and fluid—blood, saliva, mud, and rain—as if the boy had wandered coverless into a storm of rifle butts and leather heels. The surgeon glanced at the men who went with the wagon. They were looking elsewhere, one of them murmuring something strained, an enraged lament, to the tall gravedigger. The murmurer dealt a chop to the air and the gravedigger winced. No one was moving to get Venegas's body or his head in the sack.

The Major studied the boy's uniform. It was such a hopeless army. No name, no signs of rank but the rough cotton thing itself to distinguish the boy from his—the man sought and found the word—playmates. He was probably a corporal, the Major guessed, probably sixteen, they were that desperate. The boy had no firearms. He was such a poor rebel, but the Major was not going to be fooled. Tell that to Venegas, he thought.

Ferrariz coughed and the Major nodded. The doctor opened the boy's shirt and checked the wound, blue-black around the point of entry, deep red at the mouth. Ferrariz asked a question of the sergeant in charge of the wagon detail. The sergeant shrugged; the other soldier who had been murmuring tapped his arm quickly with a small and eager smile. Ferrariz leaned over the boy's body and pressed gently down the length of the other arm, suddenly encountering nothing, and for a second he thought that someone, probably that soldier, had cut the arm off in half-hearted revenge. But there was little blood on the outside of the sleeve. Ferrariz pulled and eased the lower arm out from under the body. The arm flopped whichever way.

Shot, bashed, and broken. Ferrariz mentally ticked off the likely complications, the degrees of spoilage a body like this underwent. Attacks of delirium, the rot of gangrene. Worst of all—and remarking upon this, Ferrariz felt something close to sadness—the boy had nothing to live for.

'He's going to die,' he said to the Major, turning aside politely and sniffing again into his handkerchief. The weather was awful; he was steaming inside his brown wool jacket. Give him an hour, he thought of the boy, who hardly seemed worth the wagon ride.

The Major looked intently at the body, saying nothing. Ferrariz crooked a finger at the two gravediggers, who dropped their tools and hurried over. They hauled the boy off the wagon feet first; they tried to hold him by the broken arm and the body sagged to the ground. The soldiers laughed. Venegas's raw neck stared at them, as if wanting badly to join in. Nobody was scared of Venegas anymore; they had taken their horror out on the boy. The doctor reached over for the sack and peered inside. The smiles vanished, and each man in his mind implored the doctor to keep the head where it was. Ferrariz was simply being curious, professionally. He had practiced all sorts of cuts and slices on cadavers before, but never quite so decisively. It seemed easier vein by vein.

'Make him live,' the Major said.

Ferrariz realized with a start that it was not Venegas, of course, whom the Major wished to revive. Ferrariz toyed with the thought of stitching the soldier's head back on as a joke. It was insane but so was this other notion and he felt like telling the Major so.

But the Major was already snapping out orders to his men, now scurrying about like harried ants to produce the stretcher nobody thought would be needed.

A flush rose to the Major's cheeks, a flush that felt good. It was a day for men of deliberate thought.

Ferrariz was holding on to the wagon, his mouth half-open, the boy at his feet.

'It won't do,' he said. 'I can't save him.'

'Bosh. Try, Ferrariz. It'll do you good.'

'I'm telling you, this boy's . . .'

'Do it, you quack!' the Major shrieked and stalked away. Goddamned good-for-nothing chamberpot fancier. Two dozen men all goddamned certified dead with his goddamned flowery signature, the bloody incompetent quack.

Ferrariz trembled with his own anger, wishing at that moment to simplify things and drive a pick straight through the Major's skull. When the Major breathed his last, he swore, he was going to perform the autopsy by the book, beginning with shaving off that idiotic hairthing. Army doctors had trouble enough with diarrhea, syphilis, and footsores to have had to contend as well with the addled brains of martinets.

But the Major had turned to him again and spoke in a more even voice that was almost pleading.

'Save him. The boy could help us. Help save us all.'

It was true. The doctor sighed forcefully to expel his anger and contemplated the enormity of the task.

After three days on the sickbed the boy came awake and screamed. The doctor, who was out watching the packhorses feed, rushed back to the tent upon being told the news.

Ferrariz had insisted on having the boy moved to his own place. There were ugly plots afoot, he was certain of it. The boy was enemy, bastard killer. He deserved other fortunes than to be nursed and guarded like the King's own son when the feet of privates were rotting in their cheap rotten boots.

The Major had agreed, securing the tent all the same with sentries who chuckled every time the chamberpot tinkled.

Ferrariz reserved notice of such little things; for three days he worked like a driven man, cleaning out and dressing the boy's wounds, setting the arm, packing cold compresses upon the swellings. He felt godlike in that mission. He unpacked his books from their mildewed boxes, brushed off the fungi, and reviewed and relived the passion of the way of healing. He watched miracles work themselves upon the boy and stood back amazed at his own handiwork. When he was through, when he faced nothing more than that penance of waiting for the boy to revive, Ferrariz realized that his eyes were wet. Not since he stepped into the University, knowing nothing, had he felt as much of an honest man.

Ferrariz knew what to listen for from far off. They were cries, not really screams—cries of fear, cries of pain, cries of misery. The boy was going to open his eyes to the sight of another face intent on drawing the life out of him. The surgeon had used the morphine sparingly, anxious to return feeling to the boy, no matter pain. What the boy was going to suffer most—and Ferrariz believed in the existence of a kind of instinct that told people of it—was the loss of the sense to live. The boy was going to meet the Major.

The doctor himself knew nothing certain of the Major's plans for the boy. Surely the boy was of no great importance? But he had killed, in a terrible way. But it was sheer animal reflex, surely, by no means an act of war? Surely the boy needed to defend himself from Venegas, as he needed to defend himself again very soon from a battalion of the man's friends? Perhaps the boy was going to be a hostage, yes, perhaps the Major thought that, too. Perhaps the boy was going to be traded for one of their lost men. Perhaps the boy was a native prince, and the Major had seen the secret signs, having studied him so closely.

Ferrariz found himself pleading for the boy's life in his thoughts and he grieved for his hopes, leaves in the wind.

His name was Makaraig; he was fifteen. That was all. He was a soldier in the Army of Independence. He pointed to his uniform. Of course. What of it? It was a cousin's, a captain's or other, he wasn't sure, he was a dunce about those things. It was very cold where they were staying, up there. That night. They had sent him out to fetch wood. He had borrowed the shirt with the long loose sleeves; the fabric was thicker. He had lost his way. How?

Makaraig thought deeply, trying to remember. He found it very hard to think of anything. The first questions were easy. He tensed up and tried to breathe. Pain bored through his chest; it was tightly bandaged but a rust red spot crept through the gauze and it hurt. The left side of him, too, felt thrice its size. His words slid out of lips he could hardly part and even then only with pain. Pain, he was all pain. And the man expected him to think.

The man—he had a funny beard, but Makaraig could not laugh—had fed him soup from a bowl, spoon by spoon through his savaged mouth. He tasted nothing but salt, but the warmth of it was good inside.

'How?'

The man's voice was unlike the others he had heard through the canvas. The man's voice was firm and his accent was all wrong but his was a voice the boy had come to be used to. It spoke to him at night, lulling him to sleep. It banished evil. 'How?'

He saw them in the trees, the fireflies.

They were beautiful. They were like a dream. When you tried to touch them, they left you, laughing.

He had followed the fireflies.

And when Makaraig remembered this, he wanted to smile, but for the pain.

The tent's door flaps flew open and the boy, staring, began to wail.

The Major took no notice of it, addressing himself to Ferrariz, who still had the bowl and spoon in his hands. Drops of soup fell on the doctor's lap.

'Healthy dog, is he now?'

'Barely,' Ferrariz mumbled, cleaning up. 'He can't move.'

'He's eaten,' the Major said. He had his riding crop in his hand and he gestured at the bowl with it.

'You told me to take care of him,' the doctor said, trying to sound very annoyed, but the plea showed through the hoarseness.

'He's going to save us,' the Major said, pleasantly.

'He's already saved me!' Ferrariz shook violently.

The Major looked down at him with contempt.

'Don't be any more of a fool than you have to be.'

Tears were streaming down Makaraig's cheeks. The Major faced him suddenly and struck him across the nose with the crop. Makaraig's mouth wanted to fly open but for the pain, the pain.

'No gift for speech, hm? Can you talk? Let's help you along, shall we?'

Makaraig's eyes rolled upwards. The Major was poking his crop down the boy's throat. Makaraig vomited blood and soup.

Ferrariz was sobbing into his palms, muttering a prayer.

'You puked,' the Major accused the boy. 'You goddamned puked on me.'

'He's only a boy, for the Virgin's sake, Major! He lost his way Major please Major ...'

The Major rested the tip of his crop gently on the spot of blood in the boy's belly.

'Get out, Ferrariz.'

'He knows nothing, you ass!'

The crop whipped to the doctor's nose, barely grazing it. 'Get out,' the Major said, 'or you are going to wish you had never seen this boy.'

'You're going to kill him,' Ferrariz whined on his way out.

'Troop strength, deployment, order of battle. These, baboon, are the basic references of military intelligence estimates . . .'

The door flaps closed behind the doctor. The rain was falling and the cavalrymen were hurrying their horses to shelter. A horse and rider passed Ferrariz and splattered him with mud.

"I'm sorry," Ferrariz said.

The rider slowed his mount, puzzled.

A scream rose through the tumult and the rider spurred his horse forward, as though to escape before it reached him.

'I'm sorry,' Ferrariz said again, remembering Carmela, his chamberpot, and morphine.

1984

Amy Hempel

Brief Biography

- Born in 1951 in Chicago.
- 'In the Cemetery Where Al Jolson Is Buried' (1983), her first published story, is her most anthologized.
- Described by critics as a minimalist, a miniaturist, or a pointillist; prefers, like Raymond Carver, to be called a precisionist.
- Has published five short story collections, including *The Collected Stories* (2006).
- Obsessed with pet dogs, owns several labs; breeds and trains seeing eye dogs; and dogs appear as characters. In 1995 edits a collection of poems about writers' dogs.
- Dislikes flying and computers; revises in longhand.
- In 2006 enrols in a criminal forensics course to counteract her fear of death and explore the 'whodunit and whydunit' connections between character and story.

One of America's most anthologized and studied contemporary writers, Amy Hempel is a reluctant storyteller. Raised in Denver, CO, she completed high school in Chicago and lived in San Francisco during the late 1960s. Struggling as a journalist, she unknowingly found story material in her own early experiences. When she was nineteen, her mother committed suicide and a year later, so did her maternal aunt. In her twenties she had two serious car accidents. The personal traumas of her life appear in her stories of car crashes and suicides as recalled by survivors.

A writing workshop at Columbia

University taught by Gordon Lish (later her editor, who also edited Raymond Carver) turned personal travails into her first collection, *Reasons to Live* (1985), and Hempel subsequently found acclaim as one of a group of 'minimalists,' which included Carver, Richard Ford, and Ann Beattie. Minimalism has generated spirited debate. Was it the logical conclusion to modernism emerging from Poe and Chekhov? A postmodernist reaction to an empty world? Or something new entirely? Critics decried the form's motiveless characters in meaningless actions, calling minimalism a pretentious fad. Supporters claimed that poetic precision, to 'frame an empty space,' required sensitivity, wit, and an ear for tone, be it melancholia or dread. Scholars suggested minimalist prose was the perfect reaction to America's excessive capitalism, militarism, and hedonistic spending. Hempel's characters are not dehumanized, her defenders argued, but broken and disillusioned, often by the 'emotional focus' of undescribed events beyond the written page.

Drawn from popular culture or from reactions to other stories or magazine articles, many Hempel stories lack the traditional narrative comfort markers of setting, event, time, plot, scenes, details, transitions, or point of view; some entire stories are only one sentence. In a *Paris Review* interview she said, 'That is how I assemble stories . . . at the sentence level. Not by coming up with a sweeping story line.' Her prose has perfect rhythm and emotional depth, often with a combination of comedic observations, pathos, and loss. As for her mosaic-like constructions, she told the *Atlantic Monthly*: 'I'm not first and foremost interested in story and the what-happens, but I'm interested in who's telling it and how they're telling it and the effects of whatever happened on the characters and the people.'

'Nashville Gone to Ashes' emerged as a creative writing exercise, she told CBC's Eleanor Wachtel: the assignment was to write a story from the point of view of someone as far from yourself as you can imagine. She recalled a man she knew who kept the 'cremains' of his dog on his desk and often spoke in the voice of the dog. The subject matter of all her stories is bleak (accidents, death, bad marriages), but she manages to find dark humour in her writing, 'moments where the light shifts,' or 'the dull headache behind the story'—and a dog you can trust.

Nashville Gone to Ashes

After the dog's cremation, I lie in my husband's bed and watch the Academy Awards for animals. That is not the name of the show, but they give prizes to animals for Outstanding Performance in a movie, on television, or in a commercial. Last year the Schlitz Malt Liquor bull won. The time before that, it was Fred the Cockatoo. Fred won for draining a tinky bottle of 'liquor' and then reeling and falling over drunk. It is the best thing on television is what my husband Flea said.

With Flea gone, I watch out of habit.

On top of the warm set is big white Chuck, catching a portion of his four million winks. His tail hangs down and bisects the screen. On top of the dresser, and next to the phone, is the miniature pine crate that holds Nashville's gritty ashes.

Neil the Lion cops the year's top honors. The host says Neil is on location in Africa, but accepting for Neil is his grandson Winston. A woman approaches the stage with a ten-week cub in her arms, and the audience all goes *Awwww*. The home audience, too, I bet. After the cub, they bring the winners on stage together. I figure they must have been sedated—because none of them are biting each other.

I have my own to tend to. Chuck needs tomato juice for his urological problem. Boris and Kirby need brewer's yeast for their nits. Also, I left the vacuum out and the mynah bird is shrieking. Birds think a vacuum-cleaner hose is a snake.

Flea sold his practice after the stroke, so these are the only ones I look after now. These are the ones that always shared the house.

My husband, by the way, was F. Lee Forest, DVM.

The hospital is right next door to the house.

It was my side that originally bought him the practice. I bought it for him with the applesauce money. My father made an applesauce fortune because *his* way did not use lye to take off the skins. Enough of it was left to me that I had the things I wanted. I bought Flea the practice because I could.

Will Rogers called vets the noblest of doctors because their patients can't tell them what's wrong. The doctor has to reach, and he reaches with his heart.

I think it was that love that I loved. That kind of involvement was reassuring; I felt it would extend to me, as well. That it did not or that it did, but only as much and no more, was confusing at first. I thought, My love is so good, why isn't it calling the same thing back?

Things might have collapsed right there. But the furious care he gave the animals gave me hope and kept me waiting.

I did not take naturally to my husband's work. For instance, I am allergic to cats. For the past twenty years, I have had to receive immunotherapy. These are not pills; they are injections.

Until I was seventeen, I thought a ham was an animal. But I was not above testing a stool sample next door.

I go to the mynah first and put the vacuum cleaner away. This bird, when it isn't shrieking, says only one thing. Flea taught it what to say. He put a sign on its cage that reads *Tell me I'm stupid*. So you say to the bird, 'Okay, you're stupid,' and the bird says, real sarcastic, 'I can talk—can *you* fly?'

Flea could have opened in Vegas with that. But there is no cozying up to a bird.

It will be the first to go, the mynah. The second if you count Nashville.

I promised Flea I would take care of them, and I am. I screened the new owners myself.

Nashville was his favorite. She was a grizzle-colored saluki with lightly feathered legs and Nile-green eyes. You know those skinny dogs on Egyptian pots? Those are salukis, and people worshiped them back then.

Flea acted like he did, too.

He fed that dog dates.

I used to watch her carefully spit out the pit before eating the next one. She sat like a sphinx while he reached inside her mouth to massage her licorice gums. She let him nick tartar from her teeth with his nail.

This is the last time I will have to explain that name. The pick of the litter was named Memphis. They are supposed to have Egyptian names. Flea misunderstood and named his Nashville. A woman back East owns Boston.

At the end of every summer, Flea took Nashville to the Central Valley. They hunted some of the rabbits out of the vineyards. It's called coursing when you use a sight hound. With her keen vision, Nashville would spot a rabbit and point it for Flea to come after. One time she sighted straight up at the sky—and he said he followed her gaze to a plane, crossing the sun.

Sometimes I went along, and one time we let Boris hunt, too.

Boris is a Russian wolfhound. He is the size of a float in the Rose Bowl Parade.

He's a real teenager of a dog—if Boris didn't have whiskers, he'd have pimples. He goes through two nyla-bones a week, and once he ate a box of nails.

That's right, a box.

The day we loosed Boris on the rabbits he had drunk a cup of coffee. Flea let him have it, with Half-and-Half, because caffeine improves a dog's trailing. But Boris was so excited, he didn't distinguish his prey from anyone else. He even charged me—him, a whole hundred pounds of wolfhound, cranked up on Maxwell House. A sight like that will put a hem in your dress. Now I confine his hunting to the park, let him chase park squab and bald-tailed squirrel.

The first thing F. Lee said after his stroke, and it was three weeks after, was 'hanky panky.' I believe these words were intended for Boris. Yet Boris was the one who pushed the wheelchair for him. On a flat pave of sidewalk, he took a running start. When he jumped, his front paws pushed at the back of the chair, rolling Flea yards ahead with surprising grace.

I asked how he'd trained Boris to do that, and Flea's answer was, 'I didn't.'

I could love a dog like that, if he hadn't loved him first.

Here's a trick I found for how to finally get some sleep. I sleep in my husband's bed. That way the empty bed I look at is my own.

Cold nights I pull his socks on over my hands. I read in his bed. People still write from when Flea had the column. He did a pet Q and A for the newspaper.

The new doctor sends along letters for my amusement. Here's one I liked—a man thinks his cat is homosexual.

The letter begins, 'My cat Frank (not his real name) . . .'

In addition to Flea's socks, I also wear his watch.

A lot of us wear our late-husband's watch.

It's the way we tell each other.

At bedtime, I think how Nashville slept with Flea. She must have felt to him like a sack of antlers. I read about a marriage breaking up because the man let his Afghan sleep in the marriage bed.

I had my own bed. I slept in it alone, except for those times when we needed—not sex—but sex was how we got there.

In the mornings, I am not alone. With Nashville gone, Chuck comes around.

Chuck is a white-haired, blue-eyed cat, one of the few that aren't deaf—not that he comes when he hears you call. His fur is thick as a beaver's; it will hold the tracing of your finger.

Chuck, behaving, is the Nashville of cats. But the most fun he knows is pulling every tissue from a pop-up box of Kleenex. When he gets too rowdy, I slow him down with a comb. Flea showed me how. Scratching the teeth of a comb will make a cat yawn. Then you have him where you want him—any cat, however cool.

Animals are pure, Flea used to say. There is nothing deceptive about them. I would argue: think about cats. They stumble and fall, then quickly begin to wash—I meant to do that. Pretense is deception, and cats pretend: Who me? They move in next door where the food is better and meet you in the street and don't know your name, or *their* name.

But in the morning Chuck purrs against my throat, and it feels like prayer.

In the morning is when I pray.

The mailman changed his mind about the bird, and when Mrs Kaiser came for Kirby and Chuck, I could not find either one. I had packed their supplies in a bag by the door—Chuck's tomato juice and catnip mouse, Kirby's milk of magnesia tablets to clean her teeth.

You would expect this from Chuck. But Kirby is responsible. She's been around the longest, a delicate smallish golden retriever trained by professionals for television work. She was going to get a series, but she didn't grow to size. Still, she can do a number of useless tricks. The one that wowed them in the waiting room next door was Flea putting Kirby under arrest.

'Kirby,' he'd say, 'I'm afraid you are under arrest.' And the dog would back up flush to the wall. 'I am going to have to frisk you, Kirb,' and she'd slap her paws against the wall, standing still while Flea patted her sides.

Mrs Kaiser came to visit after her own dog died.

When Kirby laid a paw in her lap, Mrs Kaiser burst into tears.

I thought, God love a dog that hustles.

It is really just that Kirby is head-shy and offers a paw instead of her head to pat. But Mrs Kaiser remembered the gesture. She agreed to take Chuck, too, when I said he needed a childless home. He gets jealous of kids and has asthma attacks. Myself, I was thinking, with Chuck gone I could have poinsettias and mistletoe in the house at Christmas.

When they weren't out back, I told Mrs Kaiser I would bring them myself as soon as they showed. She was standing in the front hall talking to Boris. Rather, she was talking *for* Boris.

"'Oh,' he says, he says, "what a nice bone," he says, he says, "can *I* have a nice bone?"'

Boris walked away and collapsed on a braided rug.

"'Boy,' he says, he says, "boy, am I bushed."'

Mrs Kaiser has worn her husband's watch for years.

When she was good and gone, the animals wandered in. Chuck carried a half-eaten chipmunk in his mouth. He dropped it on the kitchen floor, a reminder of the cruelty of a world that lives by food.

After F. Lee's death, someone asked me how I was. I said that I finally had enough hangers in the closet. I don't think that that is what I meant to say. Or maybe it is.

Nashville *died* of *her* broken heart. She refused her food and simply called it quits.

An infection set in.

At the end, I myself injected the sodium pentobarbital.

I felt upstaged by the dog, will you just listen to me!

But the fact is, I think all of us were loved just the same. The love Flea gave to me was the same love he gave them. He did not say to the dogs, I will love you if you keep off the rug. He would love them no matter what they did.

It's what I got, too.

I wanted conditions.

God, how's that for an admission!

My husband said an animal can't disappoint you. I argued this, too. I said, Of course it can. What about the dog who goes on the rug? How does it feel when your efforts to alter behavior come to nothing?

I *know* how it feels.

I would like to think bigger thoughts. But it looks like I don't have a memory of our life that does not include one of the animals.

Kirby still carries in his paper Sunday mornings.

She used to watch while Flea did the crossword puzzle. He pretended to consult her: 'I can see why you'd say *dog*, but don't you see—*cat* fits just as well?'

Boris and Kirby still scrap over his slippers. But as Flea used to say, the trouble seldom exceeds their lifespan.

Here we all still are. Boris, Kirby, Chuck—Nashville gone to ashes. Before going to bed I tell the mynah bird she may not be dumb but she's stupid.

Flowers were delivered on our anniversary. The card said the roses were sent by F. Lee. When I called the florist, he said Flea had 'love insurance.' It's a service they provide for people who forget. You tell the florist the date, and automatically he sends flowers.

Getting the flowers that way had me spooked. I thought I would walk it off, the long way, into town.

Before I left the house, I gave Laxatone to Chuck. With the weather warming up, he needs to get the jump on furballs. Then I set his bowl of Kibbles in a shallow dish of water. I added to the water a spoonful of liquid dish soap. Chuck eats throughout the day; the soapy moat keeps bugs off his plate.

On the walk into town I snapped back into myself. Two things happened that I give the credit to.

The first thing was the beggar. He squatted on the walk with a dog at his side. He had with him an aged sleeping collie with granular runny eyes. Under its nose was a red plastic dish with a sign that said *Food for dog—donation please.*

The dog was as quiet as any Flea had healed and then rocked in his arms while the anesthesia wore off.

Blocks later, I bought a pound of ground beef.

I nearly ran the distance back.

The two were still there, and a couple of quarters were in the dish. I felt pretty good about handing over the food. I felt good until I turned around and saw the man who was watching me. He leaned against the grate of a closed shoe-repair with an empty tin cup at his feet. He had seen. And I was giving *him—nothing.*

How far do you take a thing like this? I think you take it all the way to heart. We give what we can—that's as far as the heart can go.

This was the first thing that turned me back around to home. The second was just plain rain.

1985

Bharati Mukherjee

Brief Biography

- Born in Calcutta in 1940 into a large, wealthy, Bengali-speaking, Hindu Brahmin family of over forty people, including servants and bodyguards.
- Begins writing at age five.
- In 1961 immigrates to the United States as a student; moves to Canada in 1968 and becomes a Canadian citizen in 1972.
- Her 1981 essay on racism changed Canadian public policy.
- In 1980 returns to the United States and becomes a US citizen in 1988.
- Wins National Book Critics Circle Award for *The Middleman and Other Stories* (1989).
- Writes in many styles, from realist to magic realism.
- Studies horoscopes; constantly watches news; has a TV in every room.

In her controversial redefinition of immigration, Bharati Mukherjee has moved to the forefront of revisionist cultural politics. While some critics complain that she portrays Indian culture negatively and embraces American lifestyles too enthusiastically, she counters that she is fully aware of American social problems but is involved in a more complex 're-rooting [of] herself in a new culture.' In her writing, she debates whether or not there can be an 'American identity' given the changing nature of society through immigration and the constant movement of populations.

Because of childhood years spent in a boarding school, England represented 'colonialism' to her and because her father suggested she get a degree in America, Mukherjee immigrated to the United States when she was twenty-one. In 1963 she graduated from the Iowa Writers' Workshop, where she was mentored by Bernard Malamud and opposed 'minimalism,' believing it excluded writers with

'large stories to tell.' At the workshop she met short story writer Clark Blaise, whom she married (breaking from her family's tradition of arranged marriage). The couple immigrated to Canada in 1968.

Critics divide Mukherjee's career into three phases: the exile from India, the expatriate in Canada, and the immigrant to the United States. Although as a teenager she found her own culture 'vaguely shameful' and not a 'fit subject,' Mukherjee was later inspired to write about 'hypocrisy and suppression' in Calcutta as James Joyce did about Dublin in *Dubliners*. Co-written with Blaise, *Days and Nights in Calcutta* (1977) is an ambivalent exploration of her Indian heritage. Their book *The Sorrow and the Terror: The Haunting Legacy of the Air India Tragedy* (1987) details Canada's bloodiest terrorist act—the bombing of a passenger jet that killed over 300 Canadians of Indian descent and Indian nationals. In a provocative article, 'An Invisible Woman' (*Saturday Night*, 1981), she claimed that Canada was inhospitable and racist. She described herself in the article as an 'unforgiving queen of bitterness.'

After she and Blaise left Canada to teach in American universities, Mukherjee became a US citizen. Despite her experiences of British colonialism and Gandhian nationalism in India and post-colonialism in Canada, she does not accept labels and emphasizes that she is now an 'American writer of Indian origin.' She optimistically argues that identity transformation is not a loss of one's history and original culture, but a gain, part of the 'cultural narrative' of America. In a world where stability is doubtful, she argues against competing concepts of multiculturalism, 'bi-culturalism,' 'cultural mosaic,' and 'melting pot' as restrictive, separating, or excluding. Instead of a dominant culture, she endorses 'communities of equals' that are not confronting or compartmentalized, but flowing, overlapping, criss-crossing, and exchanging mutually influential ideas. She dramatizes this concept in her best-known work, *Jasmine* (1989), in which her main character changes careers and identities to survive in America. Her novel *Desirable Daughters* (2003) challenges restrictive Indian traditions of class, caste, language, and birthplace, and uses images of California's fault lines to express tensions between cultures.

Mukherjee sets a tone of pessimism and homelessness with the bored Indian wife of an academic in 'The Lady from Lucknow,' written just after she moved from Canada to the United States. Her main character is 'between cultures' and has 'not-quite' adapted to the American way of life and its sophisticated technologies. Her adultery with a dull, middle-aged American is an isolating fantasy, a misreading of a situation, not community integration.

See Geoff Hancock, from 'Interview with Bharati Mukherjee,' p. 456.

The Lady from Lucknow

When I was four, one of the girls next door fell in love with a Hindu. Her father intercepted a love note from the boy, and beat her with his leather sandals. She died soon after. I was in the room when my mother said to our neighbour, 'The Nawab-*sahib* had no choice, but Husseina's heart just broke, poor dear.' I was an army doctor's daughter, and I pictured the dead girl's heart—a rubbery squeezable organ with auricles and ventricles—first swelling, then bursting and coating the floor with thick, slippery blood.

We lived in Lucknow at the time, where the Muslim community was large. This was just before the British took the fat, diamond-shaped subcontinent and created two nations, a big one for the Hindus and a littler one for us. My father moved us to Rawalpindi in Pakistan two months after Husseina died. We were a family of soft, voluptuous children, and my father wanted to protect us from the Hindus' shameful lust.

I have fancied myself in love many times since, but never enough for the emotions to break through tissue and muscle. Husseina's torn heart remains the standard of perfect love.

At seventeen I married a good man, the fourth son of a famous poet-cum-lawyer in Islamabad. We have a daughter, seven, and a son, four. In the Muslim communities we have lived in, we are admired. Iqbal works for IBM, and because of his work we have made homes in Lebanon, Brazil, Zambia, and France. Now we live in Atlanta, Georgia, in a wide, new house with a deck and a backyard that runs into a golf course. IBM has been generous to us. We expect to pass on this good, decent life to our children. Our children are ashamed of the dingy cities where we got our start.

Some Sunday afternoons when Iqbal isn't at a conference halfway across the world, we sit together on the deck and drink gin and tonics as we have done on Sunday afternoons in a dozen exotic cities. But here, the light is different somehow. A gold haze comes off the golf course and settles on our bodies, our new house. When the light shines right in my eyes, I pull myself out of the canvas deck chair and lean against the railing that still smells of forests. Everything in Atlanta is so new!

'Sit,' Iqbal tells me. 'You'll distract the golfers. Americans are crazy for sex, you know that.'

He half rises out of his deck chair. He lunges for my breasts in mock passion. I slip out of his reach.

At the bottom of the backyard, the golfers, caddies, and carts are too minute to be bloated with lust.

But, who knows? One false thwock! of their golfing irons, and my little heart, like a golf ball, could slice through the warm air and vanish into the jonquil-yellow beyond.

It isn't trouble that I want, though I do have a lover. He's an older man, an immunologist with the Center of Disease Control right here in town. He comes to see me when Iqbal is away at high-tech conferences in sunny, remote resorts. Just think, Beirut was once such a resort! Lately my lover comes to me on Wednesdays even if Iqbal's in town.

'I don't expect to live till ninety-five,' James teases on the phone. His father died at ninety-three in Savannah. 'But I don't want a bullet in the brain from a jealous husband right now.'

Iqbal owns no firearms. Jealousy would inflame him.

Besides, Iqbal would never come home in the middle of the day. Not even for his blood pressure pills. The two times he forgot them last month, I had to take the bottle downtown. One does not rise through the multinational hierarchy coming home in midday, arriving late, or leaving early. Especially, he says, if you're a 'not-quite' as we are. It is up to us to set the standards.

Wives who want to be found out will be found out. Indiscretions are deliberate. The woman caught in mid-shame is a woman who wants to get out. The rest of us carry on.

James flatters me indefatigably; he makes me feel beautiful, exotic, responsive. I am a creature he has immunized of contamination. When he is with me, the world seems a happy enough place.

Then he leaves. He slips back into his tweed suit and backs out of my driveway.

I met James Beamish at a reception for foreign students on the Emory University campus. Iqbal avoids these international receptions because he thinks of them as excuses for looking back when we should be looking forward. These evenings are almost always tedious, but I like to go; just in case there's someone new and fascinating. The last two years, I've volunteered as host in the 'hospitality program.' At Thanksgiving and Christmas, two lonely foreign students are sent to our table.

That first evening at Emory we stood with name tags on lapels, white ones for students and blue ones for hosts. James was by a long table, pouring Chablis into a plastic glass. I noticed him right off. He was dressed much like the other resolute, decent men in the room. But whereas the other men wore white or blue shirts under their dark wool suits, James's shirt was bright red.

His wife was with him that evening, a stoutish woman with slender ankles and expensive shoes.

'Darling,' she said to James. 'See if you can locate our Palestinian.' Then she turned to me, and smiling, peered into my name tag. 'I'm Nafeesa Hafeez,' I helped out.

'Na-fee-sa,' she read out. 'Did I get that right?'

'Yes, perfect,' I said.

'What a musical name,' she said. 'I hope you'll be very happy here. Is this your first time abroad?'

James came over with a glass of Chablis in each hand. 'Did we draw this lovely lady? Oops, I'm sorry, you're a *host*, of course.' A mocking blue light was in his eyes. 'Just when I thought we were getting lucky, dear.'

'Darling, ours is a Palestinian. I told you that in the car. This one is obviously not Palestinian, are you, dear?' She took a bright orange notebook out of her purse and showed me a name.

I had to read it upside-down. Something Waheed. School of Dentistry. 'What are you drinking?' James asked. He kept a glass for himself and gave me the other one.

Maybe James Beamish said nothing fascinating that night, but he was attentive, even after the Beamishes' Palestinian joined us. Mrs Beamish was brave, she asked the dentist about his family and hometown. The dentist described West Beirut in detail. The shortage of bread and vegetables, the mortar poundings, the babies bleeding. I wonder when aphasia sets in. When does a dentist, even a Palestinian dentist, decide it's time to cut losses.

Then my own foreign student arrived. She was an Indian Muslim from Lucknow, a large, bold woman who this far from our common hometown claimed me as a country-woman. India, Pakistan, she said, not letting go of my hand, what does it matter?

I'd rather have listened to James Beamish but I couldn't shut out the woman's voice. She gave us her opinions on Thanksgiving rituals. She said, 'It is very odd that the pumpkin vegetable should be used for dessert, no? We are using it as vegetable only. Chhi! Pumpkin as a sweet. The very idea is horrid.'

I promised that when she came to our house for Thanksgiving, I'd make sweetmeats out of ricotta cheese and syrup. When you live in as many countries as Iqbal has made me, you can't tell if you pity, or if you envy, the women who stayed back.

I didn't hear from James Beamish for two weeks. I thought about him. In fact I couldn't get him out of my mind. I went over the phrases and gestures, the mocking light in the eyes, but they didn't add up to much. After the first week, I called Amina and asked her to lunch. I didn't know her well but her husband worked at the Center for Disease Control. Just talking to someone connected with the Center made me feel good. I slipped his name into the small talk with Amina and her eyes popped open, 'Oh, he's famous!' she exclaimed, and I shrugged modestly. I stayed home in case he should call. I sat on the deck and in spite of the cold, pretended to read Barbara Pym novels. Lines from Donne and Urdu verses about love floated in my skull.

I wasn't sure Dr Beamish would call me. Not directly, that is. Perhaps he would play a subtler game, get his wife to invite Iqbal and me for drinks. Maybe she'd even include their Palestinian and my Indian and make an international evening out of it. It sounded plausible.

Finally James Beamish called me on a Tuesday afternoon, around four. The children were in the kitchen, and a batch of my special chocolate sludge cookies was in the oven.

'Hi,' he said, then nothing for a bit. Then he said, 'This is James Beamish from the CDC. I've been thinking of you.'

He was between meetings, he explained. Wednesday was the only flexible day in his week, his day for paperwork. Could we have lunch on Wednesday?

The cookies smelled gooey hot, not burned. My daughter had taken the cookie sheet out and put in a new one. She'd turned the cold water faucet on so she could let the water drip on a tiny rosebud burn on her arm.

I felt all the warm, familiar signs of lust and remorse. I dabbed the burn with an ice cube wrapped in paper towel and wondered if I'd have time to buy a new front-closing bra after Iqbal got home.

James and I had lunch in a Dekalb County motel lounge.

He would be sixty-five in July, but not retire till sixty-eight. Then he would live in Tonga, in Fiji, see the world, travel across Europe and North America in a Winnebago. He wouldn't be tied down. He had five daughters and two grandsons, the younger one aged four, a month older than my son. He had been in the navy during the war (*his* war), and he had liked that.

I said, 'Goodbye, Mama, I'm off to Yokohama.' It was silly, but it was the only war footage I could come up with, and it made him laugh.

'You're special,' he said. He touched my knee under the table. 'You've already been everywhere.'

'Not because I've wanted to.'

He squeezed my knee again, then paid with his Master-Card card.

As we were walking through the parking lot to his car (it was a Cougar or a Buick, and not German or British as I'd expected), James put his arm around my shoulders. I may have seen the world but I haven't gone through the American teenage rites of making out in parked cars and picnic grounds, so I walked briskly out of his embrace. He let his hand slide off my shoulder. The hand slid down my back. I counted three deft little pats to my bottom before he let his hand fall away.

Iqbal and I are sensual people, but secretive. The openness of James Beamish's advance surprised me.

I got in his car, wary, expectant. 'Do up the seatbelt,' he said.

He leaned into his seatbelt and kissed me lightly on the lips. I kissed him back, hard. 'You don't panic easily, do you?' he said. The mocking blue light was in his eyes again. His tongue made darting little thrusts and probes past my lips.

Yes, I do, I would have said if he'd let me.

We held hands on the drive to my house. In the driveway he parked behind my Honda. 'Shall I come in?'

I said nothing. Love and freedom drop into our lives. When we have to beg or even agree, it's already too late.

'Let's go in.' He said it very softly.

I didn't worry about the neighbours. In his grey wool slacks and tweed jacket, he looked too old, too respectable, for any sordid dalliance with a not-quite's wife.

Our house is not that different in size and shape from the ones on either side. Only the inside smells of heavy incense, and the walls are hung with rows of miniature paintings from the reign of Emperor Akbar. I took James's big wrinkled hand in mine. Adultery in my house is probably no different, no quieter, than in other houses in this neighbourhood.

Afterwards it wasn't guilt I felt (guilt comes with desire not acted), but wonder that while I'd dashed out Tuesday night and bought myself silky new underwear, James Beamish had worn an old T-shirt and lemon-pale boxer shorts.

Perhaps he hadn't planned on seducing a Lucknow lady that afternoon. Adventure and freedom had come to him out of the blue, too. Or perhaps only younger men like Iqbal make a fetish of doing sit-ups and dieting and renewing their membership at the racquet club when they're on the prowl.

October through February our passion held. When we were together, I felt cherished. I only played at being helpless, hysterical, cruel. When James left, I'd spend the rest of the afternoon with a Barbara Pym novel. I kept the novels open at pages in which excellent British women recite lines from Marvell to themselves. I didn't read. I watched the golfers trudging over brown fairways instead. I let the tiny golfers—clumsy mummers—tell me stories of ambitions unfulfilled. Golf carts lurched into the golden vista. I felt safe.

In the first week of March we met in James's house for a change. His wife was in Madison to babysit a grandson while his parents flew to China for a three-week tour. It was a thrill to be in his house. I fingered the book spines, checked the colour of sheets and towels, the brand names of cereals and detergents. Jane Fonda's Workout record was on the VCR. He was a man who took exceptional care of himself, this immunologist. Real intimacy, at last. The lust of the winter months had been merely foreplay. I felt at home in his house, in spite of the albums of family photographs on the coffee table and the brutish metal vulvas sculpted by a daughter in art school and stashed in the den. James was more talkative in his own house. He showed me the photos he wanted me to see, named real lakes and mountains. His family was real, and not quite real. The daughters were hardy, outdoor types. I saw them hiking in Zermatt and bicycling through Europe. They had red cheeks and backpacks. Their faces were honest and marvellously ordinary. What would they say if they knew their father, at sixty-five, was in bed with a married woman from Lucknow? I feared and envied their jealousy more than any violence in my husband's heart.

Love on the decline is hard to tell from love on the rise. I have lived a life perched on the edge of ripeness and decay. The traveller feels at home everywhere, because she is never at home anywhere. I felt the hot red glow of blood rushing through capillaries.

His wife came back early, didn't call, caught a ride from Hartsfield International with a friend. She had been raised in Saskatchewan, and she'd remained thrifty.

We heard the car pull into the driveway, the loud 'thank yous' and 'no, I couldn'ts' and then her surprised shout, 'James? Are you ill? What're you doing home?' as she shut the front door.

We were in bed, sluggish cozy and still moist under the goosedown quilt that the daughter in Madison had sent them as a fortieth anniversary gift some years before. His clothes were on top of a long dresser; mine were on the floor, the stockings wrinkled and looking legless.

James didn't go to pieces. I had to admire that. He said, 'Get in the bathroom. Get dressed. I'll take care of this.'

I am submissive by training. To survive, the Asian wife will usually do as she is told. But this time I stayed in bed.

'How are you going to explain me away, James? Tell her I'm the new cleaning woman?' I laughed, and my laugh tinkled flirtatiously, at least to me.

'Get in the bathroom.' This was the fiercest I'd ever heard him.

'I don't think so,' I said. I jerked the quilt off my body but didn't move my legs.

So I was in bed with the quilt at my feet, and James was by the dresser buttoning his shirt when Kate Beamish stood at the door.

She didn't scream. She didn't leap for James's throat—or mine. I'd wanted passion, but Kate didn't come through. I pulled the quilt over me.

I tried insolence. 'Is your wife not the jealous kind?' I asked.

'Let's just get over this as quietly and quickly as we can, shall we?' she said. She walked to the window in her brown Wallabies. 'I don't see any unfamiliar cars, so I suppose you'll expect James to drive you home.'

'She's the jealous type,' James said. He moved toward his wife and tried to guide her out of the bedroom.

'I'm definitely the jealous kind,' Kate Beamish said. 'I might have stabbed you if I could take you seriously. But you are quite ludicrous lounging like a Goya nude on my bed.' She gave a funny little snort. I noticed straggly hairs in her nostrils and looked away.

James was running water in the bathroom sink. Only the panicky ones fall apart and call their lawyers from the bedroom.

She sat on my side of the bed. She stared at me. If that stare had made me feel secretive and loathsome, I might not have wept, later. She plucked the quilt from my breasts as an internist might, and snorted again. 'Yes,' she said, 'I don't deny a certain interest he might have had,' but she looked through my face to the pillow behind, and dropped the quilt as she stood. I was a shadow without depth or colour, a shadow-temptress who would float back to a city of teeming millions when the affair with James had ended.

I had thought myself provocative and fascinating. What had begun as an adventure had become shabby and complex. I was just another involvement of a white man in a pokey little outpost, something that 'men do' and then come to their senses while the *memsahibs* drink gin and tonic and fan their faces. I didn't merit a stab wound through the heart.

It wasn't the end of the world. It was humorous, really. Still. I let James call me a cab. That half hour wait for the cab, as Kate related tales of the grandson to her distracted husband was the most painful. It came closest to what Husseina must have felt. At least her father, the Nawab-*sahib*, had beaten her.

I have known all along that perfect love has to be fatal. I have survived on four of the five continents. I get by because I am at least moderately charming and open-minded. From time to time, James Beamish calls me. 'She's promised to file for divorce.' Or 'Let's go away for a weekend. Let's go to Bermuda. Have lunch with me this Wednesday.' Why do I hear a second voice? She has laughed at me. She has mocked my passion.

I want to say yes. I want to beg him to take me away to Hilton Head in his new, retirement Winnebago. The golden light from the vista is too yellow. Yes, *please*, let's run away, keep this new and simple.

I can hear the golf balls being thwocked home by clumsy mummers far away where my land dips. My arms are numb, my breathing loud and ugly from pressing hard against the cedar railing. The pain in my chest will not go away. I should be tasting blood in my throat by now.

1985

Raymond Carver

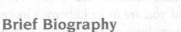

Brief Biography

- Born in 1938 in Clatskanie, OR.
- First collection is *Will You Please Be Quiet, Please?* (1976).
- Nominated for National Book Award in 1976; in 1979 wins Guggenheim Fellowship, professorship at Syracuse University.
- Style and characters called 'dirty realism'; his works reinvigorate interest in short fiction.
- In 1977 gives up drinking after four bouts of acute alcoholism, meets poet Tess Gallagher.
- In 1983, wins a prize, $35,000 tax-free annually for five years.
- Hobby is salmon fishing.
- Buys a Mercedes-Benz with advance for unproduced screenplay on Dostoevsky.
- Dies of lung cancer in 1988.
- Robert Altman movie *Short Cuts* (1993) is based on several Carver stories.

Born in a sawmill town in Oregon, Raymond Carver grew up in Yakima, WA, where his alcoholic father worked on the Grand Coulee Dam. Married as a teenager, Carver was a father of two by age twenty. After a succession of low-paying jobs, he moved his young family to his mother-in-law's house in California where he felt 'displaced.' He enrolled at a California college and took a class from the then-unknown writer John Gardner. Though he lacked the tuition to complete the two-year program, Carver also attended one year of the Iowa Writers' Workshop. Unlike postmodern writers of the day, he preferred traditional modernist authors, especially Ernest Hemingway, Franz Kafka, William Faulkner, and, above all, Anton Chekhov. Hemingway's 'cadence' and 'iceberg theory' (emotions, feelings, and motivations are beneath the textual surface) influenced Carver's prose about dead-end jobs. Vulnerable men, bad behaviour, and confused longing for a better life were 'an emotional reservoir' for his fiction.

After working as a textbook editor, Carver taught writing. His early stories were heavily edited by controversial editor Gordon Lish, who also edited Amy Hempel. This editing, combined with Carver's extensive revisions and his influence on writers, led him to become known (in spite of his protests) as a 'minimalist' writer. He wrote in many styles, but always strove for 'economy of words,' which he eventually called 'precisionist.' His seemingly easy style was much imitated but hard won. Feeling and 'emotional punches' were his criteria for a story's success, and Carver revised constantly to achieve these effects. His final collections, *Cathedral* (1984) and *Where I'm Calling From* (1988), representing twenty-five years of writing, were more expansive, with edits removed.

An alcoholic for many years, Carver began his 'second life' in 1977 when he stopped drinking and met West coast poet Tess Gallagher. The pair moved to New York state, where she worked as head of a writing program, he as a professor. Carver became a successful (and, with the help of Alcoholics Anonymous, sober) author with critical acclaim for his five story collections and five volumes of poetry. They moved to Port Angeles, WA (Carver always considered himself 'a writer from the west'). Having divorced his wife, he married Gallagher in 1988, but died six weeks later of lung cancer at age fifty.

Like many of Carver's stories, 'Feathers' is told by a working-class male narrator and begins with a typical situation that quickly escalates into the extraordinary, even the grotesque. Motives and explanations are elusive, glimpsed partly through dialogue, but mostly through gaps in the narrative where possibilities multiply. Laurie Champion has noted that 'Feathers' contains seventeen direct references to silence. The story's ending has sparked much debate. Is it open-ended, perhaps a reflection of the narrator's lack of self-examination? Or is it inevitable, arising out of the story's mood, imagery, and the many nuanced silences?

See Raymond Carver, from 'On Writing,' p. 432; see also Cynthia J. Hallett, from 'Minimalism and the Short Story,' p. 420.

Feathers

This friend of mine from work, Bud, he asked Fran and me to supper. I didn't know his wife and he didn't know Fran. That made us even. But Bud and I were friends. And I knew there was a little baby at Bud's house. That baby must have been eight months old when Bud asked us to supper. Where'd those eight months go? Hell, where's the time gone since? I remember the day Bud came to work with a box of cigars. He handed them out in the lunchroom. They were drugstore cigars. Dutch Masters. But each cigar had a red sticker on it and a wrapper that said IT'S A BOY! I didn't smoke cigars, but I took one anyway. 'Take a couple,' Bud said. He shook the box. 'I don't like cigars either. This is her idea.' He was talking about his wife. Olla.

I'd never met Bud's wife, but once I'd heard her voice over the telephone. It was a Saturday afternoon, and I didn't have anything I wanted to do. So I called Bud to see if he wanted to do anything. This woman picked up the phone and said, 'Hello.' I blanked and couldn't remember her name. Bud's wife. Bud had said her name to me any number of times. But it went in one ear and out the other. 'Hello!' the woman said again. I could hear a TV going. Then the woman said, 'Who is this?' I heard a baby start up. 'Bud!' the woman called. 'What?' I heard Bud say. I still couldn't remember her name. So I hung up. The next time I saw Bud at work I sure as hell didn't tell him I'd called. But I made a point of getting him to mention his wife's name. 'Olla,' he said. Olla, I said to myself. *Olla.*

'No big deal,' Bud said. We were in the lunchroom drinking coffee. 'Just the four of us. You and your missus, and me and Olla. Nothing fancy. Come around seven. She feeds the baby at six. She'll put him down after that, and then we'll eat. Our place isn't hard to find. But here's a map.' He gave me a sheet of paper with all kinds of lines indicating major and minor roads, lanes and such, with arrows pointing to the four poles of the compass. A large X marked the location of his house. I said, 'We're looking forward to it.' But Fran wasn't too thrilled.

That evening, watching TV, I asked her if we should take anything to Bud's.

'Like what?' Fran said. 'Did he say to bring something? How should I know? I don't have any idea.' She shrugged and gave me this look. She'd heard me before on the subject of Bud. But she didn't know him and she wasn't interested in knowing him. 'We could take a bottle of wine,' she said. 'But I don't care. Why don't you take some wine?' She shook her head. Her long hair swung back and forth over her shoulders. Why do we need other people? she seemed to be saying. We have each other. 'Come here,' I said. She moved a little closer so I could hug her. Fran's a big tall drink of water. She has this blond hair that hangs down her back. I picked up some of her hair and sniffed it. I wound my hand in her hair. She let me hug her. I put my face right up in her hair and hugged her some more.

Sometimes when her hair gets in her way she has to pick it up and push it over her shoulder. She gets mad at it. 'This hair,' she says. 'Nothing but trouble.' Fran works in a creamery and has to wear her hair up when she goes to work. She has to wash it every night and take a brush to it when we're sitting in front of the TV. Now and then she threatens to cut it off. But I don't think she'd do that. She knows I like it too much. She knows I'm crazy about it. I tell her I fell in love with her because of her hair. I tell her I might stop loving her if she cut it. Sometimes I call her 'Swede.' She could pass for a Swede. Those times together in the evening she'd brush her hair and we'd wish out loud for things we didn't have. We wished for a new car, that's one of the things we wished for. And we wished we could spend a couple of weeks in Canada. But one thing we didn't wish for was kids. The reason we didn't have kids was that we didn't want kids. Maybe sometime, we said to each other. But right then, we were waiting. We thought we might keep on waiting. Some nights we went to a movie. Other nights we just stayed in and watched TV. Sometimes Fran baked things for me and we'd eat whatever it was all in a sitting.

'Maybe they don't drink wine,' I said.

'Take some wine anyway,' Fran said. 'If they don't drink it, we'll drink it.'

'White or red?' I said.

'We'll take something sweet,' she said, not paying me any attention. 'But I don't care if we take anything. This is your show. Let's not make a production out of it, or else I don't want to go. I can make a raspberry coffee ring. Or else some cupcakes.'

'They'll have dessert,' I said. 'You don't invite people to supper without fixing a dessert.'

'They might have rice pudding. Or Jell-O! Something we don't like,' she said. 'I don't know anything about the woman. How do we know what she'll have? What if she gives us Jell-O?' Fran shook her head. I shrugged. But she was right. 'Those old cigars he gave you,' she said. 'Take them. Then you and him can go off to the parlor after supper and smoke cigars and drink port wine, or whatever those people in movies drink.'

'Okay, we'll just take ourselves,' I said.

Fran said, 'We'll take a loaf of my bread.'

Bud and Olla lived twenty miles or so from town. We'd lived in that town for three years, but, damn it, Fran and I hadn't so much as taken a spin in the country. It felt good driving those winding little roads. It was early evening, nice and warm, and we saw pastures, rail fences, milk cows moving slowly toward old barns. We saw red-winged blackbirds on the fences, and pigeons circling around haylofts. There were gardens and such, wildflowers in bloom, and little houses set back from the road. I said, 'I wish we had us a place out here.' It was just an idle thought, another wish that wouldn't amount to anything. Fran didn't answer. She was busy looking at Bud's map. We came to the four-way stop he'd marked. We turned right like the map said and drove exactly three and three-tenths miles. On the left side of the road, I saw a field of corn, a mailbox, and a long, graveled driveway. At the end of the driveway, back in some trees, stood a house with a front porch. There was a chimney on the house. But it was summer, so, of course, no smoke rose from the chimney. But I thought it was a pretty picture, and I said so to Fran.

'It's the sticks out here,' she said.

I turned into the drive. Corn rose up on both sides of the drive. Corn stood higher than the car. I could hear gravel crunching under the tires. As we got up close to the house, we could see a garden with green things the size of baseballs hanging from the vines.

'What's that?' I said.

'How should I know?' she said. 'Squash, maybe. I don't have a clue.'

'Hey, Fran,' I said. 'Take it easy.'

She didn't say anything. She drew in her lower lip and let it go. She turned off the radio as we got close to the house.

A baby's swing-set stood in the front yard and some toys lay on the porch. I pulled up in front and stopped the car. It was then that we heard this awful squall. There was a baby in the house, right, but this cry was too loud for a baby.

'What's that sound?' Fran said.

Then something as big as a vulture flapped heavily down from one of the trees and landed just in front of the car. It shook itself. It turned its long neck toward the car, raised its head, and regarded us.

'Goddamn it,' I said. I sat there with my hands on the wheel and stared at the thing.

'Can you believe it?' Fran said. 'I never saw a real one before.'

We both knew it was a peacock, sure, but we didn't say the word out loud. We just watched it. The bird turned its head up in the air and made this harsh cry again. It had fluffed itself out and looked about twice the size it'd been when it landed.

'Goddamn,' I said again. We stayed where we were in the front seat.

The bird moved forward a little. Then it turned its head to the side and braced itself. It kept its bright, wild eye right on us. Its tail was raised, and it was like a big fan folding in and out. There was every color in the rainbow shining from that tail.

'My God,' Fran said quietly. She moved her hand over to my knee.

'Goddamn,' I said. There was nothing else to say.

The bird made this strange wailing sound once more. '*May-awe, may-awe!*' it went. If it'd been something I was hearing late at night and for the first time, I'd have thought it was somebody dying, or else something wild and dangerous.

The front door opened and Bud came out on the porch. He was buttoning his shirt. His hair was wet. It looked like he'd just come from the shower.

'Shut yourself up, Joey!' he said to the peacock. He clapped his hands at the bird, and the thing moved back a little. 'That's enough now. That's right, shut up! You shut up, you old devil!' Bud came down the steps. He tucked in his shirt as he came over to the car. He was wearing what he always wore to work—blue jeans and a denim shirt. I had on my slacks and a short-sleeved sport shirt. My good loafers. When I saw what Bud was wearing, I didn't like it that I was dressed up.

'Glad you could make it,' Bud said as he came over beside the car. 'Come on inside.'

'Hey, Bud,' I said.

Fran and I got out of the car. The peacock stood off a little to one side, dodging its mean-looking head this way and that. We were careful to keep some distance between it and us.

'Any trouble finding the place?' Bud said to me. He hadn't looked at Fran. He was waiting to be introduced.

'Good directions,' I said. 'Hey, Bud, this is Fran. Fran, Bud. She's got the word on you, Bud.'

He laughed and they shook hands. Fran was taller than Bud. Bud had to look up.

'He talks about you,' Fran said. She took her hand back. 'Bud this, Bud that. You're about the only person down there he talks about. I feel like I know you.' She was keeping an eye on the peacock. It had moved over near the porch.

'This here's my friend,' Bud said. 'He *ought* to talk about me.' Bud said this and then he grinned and gave me a little punch on the arm.

Fran went on holding her loaf of bread. She didn't know what to do with it. She gave it to Bud. 'We brought you something.'

Bud took the loaf. He turned it over and looked at it as if it was the first loaf of bread he'd ever seen. 'This is real nice of you.' He brought the loaf up to his face and sniffed it.

'Fran baked that bread,' I told Bud.

Bud nodded. Then he said, 'Let's go inside and meet the wife and mother.'

He was talking about Olla, sure. Olla was the only mother around. Bud had told me his own mother was dead and that his dad had pulled out when Bud was a kid.

The peacock scuttled ahead of us, then hopped onto the porch when Bud opened the door. It was trying to get inside the house.

'Oh,' said Fran as the peacock pressed itself against her leg.

'Joey, goddamn it,' Bud said. He thumped the bird on the top of its head. The peacock backed up on the porch and shook itself. The quills in its train rattled as it shook. Bud made as if to kick it, and the peacock backed up some more. Then Bud held the door for us. 'She lets the goddamn thing in the house. Before long, it'll be wanting to eat at the goddamn table and sleep in the goddamn bed.'

Fran stopped just inside the door. She looked back at the cornfield. 'You have a nice place,' she said. Bud was still holding the door. 'Don't they, Jack?'

'You bet,' I said. I was surprised to hear her say it.

'A place like this is not all it's cracked up to be,' Bud said, still holding the door. He made a threatening move toward the peacock. 'Keeps you going. Never a dull moment.' Then he said, 'Step on inside, folks.'

I said, 'Hey, Bud, what's that growing there?'

'Them's tomatoes,' Bud said.

'Some farmer I got,' Fran said, and shook her head.

Bud laughed. We went inside. This plump little woman with her hair done up in a bun was waiting for us in the living room. She had her hands rolled up in her apron. The cheeks of her face were bright red. I thought at first she might be out of breath, or else mad at something. She gave me the once-over, and then her eyes went to Fran. Not unfriendly, just looking. She stared at Fran and continued to blush.

Bud said, 'Olla, this is Fran. And this is my friend Jack. You know all about Jack. Folks, this is Olla.' He handed Olla the bread.

'What's this?' she said. 'Oh, it's homemade bread. Well, thanks. Sit down anywhere. Make yourselves at home. Bud, why don't you ask them what they'd like to drink. I've got something on the stove.' Olla said that and went back into the kitchen with the bread.

'Have a seat,' Bud said. Fran and I plunked ourselves down on the sofa. I reached for my cigarettes. Bud said, 'Here's an ashtray.' He picked up something heavy from the top of the TV. 'Use this,' he said, and he put the thing down on the coffee table in front of me. It was one of those glass ashtrays made to look like a swan. I lit up and dropped the match into the opening in the swan's back. I watched a little wisp of smoke drift out of the swan.

The color TV was going, so we looked at that for a minute. On the screen, stock cars were tearing around a track. The announcer talked in a grave voice. But it was like he was holding back some excitement, too. 'We're still waiting to have official confirmation,' the announcer said.

'You want to watch this?' Bud said. He was still standing.

I said I didn't care. And I didn't. Fran shrugged. What difference could it make to her? she seemed to say. The day was shot anyway.

'There's only about twenty laps left,' Bud said. 'It's close now. There was a big pile-up earlier. Knocked out half-a-dozen cars. Some drivers got hurt. They haven't said yet how bad.'

'Leave it on,' I said. 'Let's watch it.'

'Maybe one of those damn cars will explode right in front of us,' Fran said. 'Or else maybe one'll run up into the grandstand and smash the guy selling the crummy hot dogs.' She took a strand of hair between her fingers and kept her eyes fixed on the TV.

Bud looked at Fran to see if she was kidding. 'That other business, that pile-up, was something. One thing led to another. Cars, parts of cars, people all over the place. Well, what can I get you? We have ale, and there's a bottle of Old Crow.'

'What are you drinking?' I said to Bud.

'Ale,' Bud said. 'It's good and cold.'

'I'll have ale,' I said.

'I'll have some of that Old Crow and a little water,' Fran said. 'In a tall glass, please. With some ice. Thank you, Bud.'

'Can do,' Bud said. He threw another look at the TV and moved off to the kitchen.

Fran nudged me and nodded in the direction of the TV. 'Look up on top,' she whispered. 'Do you see what I see?' I looked at where she was looking. There was a slender red vase into which somebody had stuck a few garden daisies. Next to the vase, on the doily, sat an old plaster-of-Paris cast of the most crooked, jaggedy teeth in the world. There were no lips to the awful-looking thing, and no jaw either, just these old plaster teeth packed into something that resembled thick yellow gums.

Just then Olla came back with a can of mixed nuts and a bottle of root beer. She had her apron off now. She put the can of nuts onto the coffee table next to the swan. She said, 'Help yourselves. Bud's getting your drinks.' Olla's face came on red again as she said this. She sat down in an old cane rocking chair and set it in motion. She drank from her root beer and looked at the TV. Bud came back carrying a little wooden tray with Fran's glass of whiskey and water and my bottle of ale. He had a bottle of ale on the tray for himself.

'You want a glass?' he asked me.

I shook my head. He tapped me on the knee and turned to Fran.

She took her glass from Bud and said, 'Thanks.' Her eyes went to the teeth again. Bud saw where she was looking. The cars screamed around the track. I took the ale and gave my attention to the screen. The teeth were none of my business. 'Them's what Olla's teeth looked like before she had her braces put on,' Bud said to Fran. 'I've got used to them. But I guess they look funny up there. For the life of me, I don't know why she keeps them around.' He looked over at Olla. Then he looked at me and winked. He sat down in his La-Z-Boy and crossed one leg over the other. He drank from his ale and gazed at Olla.

Olla turned red once more. She was holding her bottle of root beer. She took a drink of it. Then she said, 'They're to remind me how much I owe Bud.'

'What was that?' Fran said. She was picking through the can of nuts, helping herself to the cashews. Fran stopped what she was doing and looked at Olla. 'Sorry, but I missed that.' Fran stared at the woman and waited for whatever thing it was she'd say next.

Olla's face turned red again. 'I've got lots of things to be thankful for,' she said. 'That's one of the things I'm thankful for. I keep them around to remind me how much I owe Bud.' She drank from her root beer. Then she lowered the bottle and said, 'You've got pretty teeth, Fran. I noticed right away. But these teeth of mine, they came in crooked when I was a kid.' With her fingernail, she tapped a couple of her front teeth. She said, 'My folks couldn't afford to fix teeth. These teeth of mine came in just any which way. My first husband didn't care what I looked like. No, he didn't! He didn't care about anything except where his next drink was coming from. He had one friend only in this world, and that was his bottle.' She shook her head. 'Then Bud come along and got me out of that mess. After we were together, the first thing Bud said was, "We're going to have them teeth fixed." That mold was made right after Bud and I met, on the occasion of my second visit to the orthodontist. Right before the braces went on.'

Olla's face stayed red. She looked at the picture on the screen. She drank from her root beer and didn't seem to have any more to say.

'That orthodontist must have been a whiz,' Fran said. She looked back at the horror-show teeth on top of the TV.

'He was great,' Olla said. She turned in her chair and said, 'See?' She opened her mouth and showed us her teeth once more, not a bit shy now.

Bud had gone to the TV and picked up the teeth. He walked over to Olla and held them up against Olla's cheek. 'Before and after,' Bud said.

Olla reached up and took the mold from Bud. 'You know something? That orthodontist wanted to keep this.' She was holding it in her lap while she talked. 'I said nothing doing. I pointed out to him they were *my* teeth. So he took pictures of the mold instead. He told me he was going to put the pictures in a magazine.'

Bud said, 'Imagine what kind of magazine that'd be. Not much call for that kind of publication, I don't think,' he said, and we all laughed.

'After I got the braces off, I kept putting my hand up to my mouth when I laughed. Like this,' she said. 'Sometimes I still do it. Habit. One day Bud said, "You can stop doing that anytime, Olla. You don't have to hide teeth as pretty as that. You have nice teeth now."' Olla looked over at Bud. Bud winked at her. She grinned and lowered her eyes.

Fran drank from her glass. I took some of my ale. I didn't know what to say to this. Neither did Fran. But I knew Fran would have plenty to say about it later.

I said, 'Olla, I called here once. You answered the phone. But I hung up. I don't know why I hung up.' I said that and then sipped my ale. I didn't know why I'd brought it up now.

'I don't remember,' Olla said. 'When was that?'

'A while back.'

'I don't remember,' she said and shook her head. She fingered the plaster teeth in her lap. She looked at the race and went back to rocking.

Fran turned her eyes to me. She drew her lip under. But she didn't say anything.

Bud said, 'Well, what else is new?'

'Have some more nuts,' Olla said. "Supper'll be ready in a little while."

There was a cry from a room in the back of the house.

'Not him,' Olla said to Bud, and made a face.

'Old Junior boy,' Bud said. He leaned back in his chair, and we watched the rest of the race, three or four laps, no sound.

Once or twice we heard the baby again, little fretful cries coming from the room in the back of the house.

'I don't know,' Olla said. She got up from her chair. 'Everything's about ready for us to sit down. I just have to take up the gravy. But I'd better look in on him first. Why don't you folks go out and sit down at the table? I'll just be a minute.'

'I'd like to see the baby,' Fran said.

Olla was still holding the teeth. She went over and put them back on top of the TV. 'It might upset him just now,' she said. 'He's not used to strangers. Wait and see if I can get him back to sleep. Then you can peek in. While he's asleep.' She said this and then she went down the hall to a room, where she opened a door. She eased in and shut the door behind her. The baby stopped crying.

Bud killed the picture and we went in to sit at the table. Bud and I talked about things at work. Fran listened. Now and then she even asked a question. But I could tell she was bored, and maybe feeling put out with Olla for not letting her see the baby. She looked around Olla's kitchen. She wrapped a strand of hair around her fingers and checked out Olla's things.

Olla came back into the kitchen and said, 'I changed him and gave him his rubber duck. Maybe he'll let us eat now. But don't bet on it.' She raised a lid and took a pan off the stove. She poured red gravy into a bowl and put the bowl on the table. She took lids off some other pots and looked to see that everything was ready. On the table were baked ham, sweet potatoes, mashed potatoes, lima beans, corn on the cob, salad greens. Fran's loaf of bread was in a prominent place next to the ham.

'I forgot the napkins,' Olla said. 'You all get started. Who wants what to drink? Bud drinks milk with all of his meals.'

'Milk's fine,' I said.

'Water for me,' Fran said. 'But I can get it. I don't want you waiting on me. You have enough to do.' She made as if to get up from her chair.

Olla said, 'Please. You're company. Sit still. Let me get it.' She was blushing again.

We sat with our hands in our laps and waited. I thought about those plaster teeth. Olla came back with napkins, big glasses of milk for Bud and me, and a glass of ice water for Fran. Fran said, 'Thanks.'

'You're welcome,' Olla said. Then she seated herself. Bud cleared his throat. He bowed his head and said a few words of grace. He talked in a voice so low I could hardly make out the words. But I got the drift of things—he was thanking the Higher Power for the food we were about to put away.

'Amen,' Olla said when he'd finished.

Bud passed me the platter of ham and helped himself to some mashed potatoes. We got down to it then. We didn't say much except now and then Bud or

I would say, 'This is real good ham.' Or, 'This sweet corn is the best sweet corn I ever ate.'

'This bread is what's special,' Olla said.

'I'll have some more salad, please, Olla,' Fran said, softening up maybe a little.

'Have more of this,' Bud would say as he passed me the platter of ham, or else the bowl of red gravy.

From time to time, we heard the baby make its noise. Olla would turn her head to listen, then, satisfied it was just fussing, she would give her attention back to her food.

'The baby's out of sorts tonight,' Olla said to Bud.

'I'd still like to see him,' Fran said. 'My sister has a little baby. But she and the baby live in Denver. When will I ever get to Denver? I have a niece I haven't even seen.' Fran thought about this for a minute, and then she went back to eating.

Olla forked some ham into her mouth. 'Let's hope he'll drop off to sleep,' she said.

Bud said, 'There's a lot more of everything. Have some more ham and sweet potatoes, everybody.'

'I can't eat another bite,' Fran said. She laid her fork on her plate. 'It's great, but I can't eat any more.'

'Save room,' Bud said. 'Olla's made rhubarb pie.' Fran said, 'I guess I could eat a little piece of that. When everybody else is ready.'

'Me, too,' I said. But I said it to be polite. I'd hated rhubarb pie since I was thirteen years old and had got sick on it, eating it with strawberry ice cream.

We finished what was on our plates. Then we heard that damn peacock again. The thing was on the roof this time. We could hear it over our heads. It made a ticking sound as it walked back and forth on the shingles.

Bud shook his head. 'Joey will knock it off in a minute. He'll get tired and turn in pretty soon,' Bud said. 'He sleeps in one of them trees.'

The bird let go with its cry once more. '*May-awe!*' it went. Nobody said anything. What was there to say?

Then Olla said, 'He wants in, Bud.'

'Well, he can't come in,' Bud said. 'We got company, in case you hadn't noticed. These people don't want a goddamn old bird in the house. That dirty bird and your old pair of teeth! What're people going to think?' He shook his head. He laughed. We all laughed. Fran laughed along with the rest of us.

'He's not *dirty*, Bud,' Olla said. 'What's gotten into you? You like Joey. Since when did you start calling him dirty?'

'Since he shit on the rug that time,' Bud said. 'Pardon the French,' he said to Fran. 'But, I'll tell you, sometimes I could wring that old bird's neck for him. He's not even worth killing, is he, Olla? Sometimes, in the middle of the night, he'll bring me up out of bed with that cry of his. He's not worth a nickel—right, Olla?'

Olla shook her head at Bud's nonsense. She moved a few lima beans around on her plate.

'How'd you get a peacock in the first place?' Fran wanted to know.

Olla looked up from her plate. She said, 'I always dreamed of having me a peacock. Since I was a girl and found a picture of one in a magazine. I thought it was the most beautiful thing I ever saw. I cut the picture out and put it over my bed. I kept that picture for the longest time. Then when Bud and I got this place, I saw my chance. I said, "Bud, I want a peacock." Bud laughed at the idea.'

'I finally asked around,' Bud said. 'I heard tell of an old boy who raised them over in the next county. Birds of paradise, he called them. We paid a hundred bucks for that bird of paradise,' he said. He smacked his forehead. 'God Almighty, I got me a woman with expensive tastes.' He grinned at Olla.

'Bud,' Olla said, 'you know that isn't true. Besides everything else, Joey's a good watchdog,' she said to Fran. 'We don't need a watchdog with Joey. He can hear just about anything.'

'If times get tough, as they might, I'll put Joey in a pot,' Bud said. 'Feathers and all.'

'Bud! That's not funny,' Olla said. But she laughed and we got a good look at her teeth again.

The baby started up once more. It was serious crying this time. Olla put down her napkin and got up from the table.

Bud said, 'If it's not one thing, it's another. Bring him on out here, Olla.'

'I'm going to,' Olla said, and went to get the baby.

The peacock wailed again, and I could feel the hair on the back of my neck. I looked at Fran. She picked up her napkin and then put it down. I looked toward the kitchen window. It was dark outside. The window was raised, and there was a screen in the frame. I thought I heard the bird on the front porch.

Fran turned her eyes to look down the hall. She was watching for Olla and the baby.

After a time, Olla came back with it. I looked at the baby and drew a breath. Olla sat down at the table with the baby. She held it up under its arms so it could stand on her lap and face us. She looked at Fran and then at me. She wasn't blushing now. She waited for one of us to comment.

'Ah!' said Fran.

'What is it?' Olla said quickly.

'Nothing,' Fran said. 'I thought I saw something at the window. I thought I saw a bat.'

'We don't have any bats around here,' Olla said.

'Maybe it was a moth,' Fran said. 'It was something. Well,' she said, 'isn't that some baby.'

Bud was looking at the baby. Then he looked over at Fran. He tipped his chair onto its back legs and nodded. He nodded again, and said, 'That's all right, don't worry any. We know he wouldn't win no beauty contests right now. He's no Clark Gable. But give him time. With any luck, you know, he'll grow up to look like his old man.'

The baby stood in Olla's lap, looking around the table at us. Olla had moved her hands down to its middle so that the baby could rock back and forth on its fat legs. Bar none, it was the ugliest baby I'd ever seen. It was so ugly I couldn't say anything. No words would come out of my mouth. I don't mean it was diseased or disfigured. Nothing like that. It was just ugly. It had a big red face, pop eyes, a broad forehead, and these big fat lips. It had no neck to speak of, and it had three or four fat chins. Its chins rolled right up under its ears, and its ears stuck out from its bald head. Fat hung over its wrists. Its arms and fingers were fat. Even calling it ugly does it credit.

The ugly baby made its noise and jumped up and down on its mother's lap. Then it stopped jumping. It leaned forward and tried to reach its fat hand into Olla's plate.

I've seen babies. When I was growing up, my two sisters had a total of six babies. I was around babies a lot when I was a kid. I've seen babies in stores and so on. But this baby beat anything. Fran stared at it, too. I guess she didn't know what to say either.

'He's a big fellow, isn't he?' I said.

Bud said, 'He'll by God be turning out for football before long. He sure as hell won't go without meals around this house.'

As if to make sure of this, Olla plunged her fork into some sweet potatoes and brought the fork up to the baby's mouth. 'He's my baby, isn't he?' she said to the fat thing, ignoring us.

The baby leaned forward and opened up for the sweet potatoes. It reached for Olla's fork as she guided the sweet potatoes into its mouth, then clamped down. The baby chewed the stuff and rocked some more on Olla's lap. It was so pop-eyed, it was like it was plugged into something.

Fran said, 'He's some baby, Olla.'

The baby's face screwed up. It began to fuss all over again.

'Let Joey in,' Olla said to Bud.

Bud let the legs of his chair come down on the floor. 'I think we should at least ask these people if they mind,' Bud said.

Olla looked at Fran and then she looked at me. Her face had gone red again. The baby kept prancing in her lap, squirming to get down.

'We're friends here,' I said. 'Do whatever you want.'

Bud said, 'Maybe they don't want a big old bird like Joey in the house. Did you ever think of that, Olla?'

'Do you folks mind?' Olla said to us. 'If Joey comes inside? Things got headed in the wrong direction with that bird tonight. The baby, too, I think. He's used to having Joey come in and fool around with him a little before his bedtime. Neither of them can settle down tonight.'

'Don't ask us,' Fran said. 'I don't mind if he comes in. I've never been up close to one before. But I don't mind.' She looked at me. I suppose I could tell she wanted me to say something.

'Hell, no,' I said. 'Let him in.' I picked up my glass and finished the milk.

Bud got up from his chair. He went to the front door and opened it. He flicked on the yard lights.

'What's your baby's name?' Fran wanted to know.

'Harold,' Olla said. She gave Harold some more sweet potatoes from her plate. 'He's real smart. Sharp as a tack. Always knows what you're saying to him. Don't you, Harold? You wait until you get your own baby, Fran. You'll see.'

Fran just looked at her. I heard the front door open and then close.

'He's smart, all right,' Bud said as he came back into the kitchen. 'He takes after Olla's dad. Now there was one smart old boy for you.'

I looked around behind Bud and could see that peacock hanging back in the living room, turning its head this way and that, like you'd turn a hand mirror. It shook itself, and the sound was like a deck of cards being shuffled in the other room.

It moved forward a step. Then another step.

'Can I hold the baby?' Fran said. She said it like it would be a favor if Olla would let her.

Olla handed the baby across the table to her.

Fran tried to get the baby settled in her lap. But the baby began to squirm and make its noises.

'Harold,' Fran said.

Olla watched Fran with the baby. She said, 'When Harold's grandpa was sixteen years old, he set out to read the encyclopedia from A to Z. He did it, too. He finished when he was twenty. Just before he met my mama.'

'Where's he now?' I asked. 'What's he do?' I wanted to know what had become of a man who'd set himself a goal like that.

'He's dead,' Olla said. She was watching Fran, who by now had the baby down on its back and across her knees. Fran chucked the baby under one of its chins. She started to talk baby talk to it.

'He worked in the woods,' Bud said. 'Loggers dropped a tree on him.'

'Mama got some insurance money,' Olla said. 'But she spent that. Bud sends her something every month.'

'Not much,' Bud said. 'Don't have much ourselves. But she's Olla's mother.'

By this time, the peacock had gathered its courage and was beginning to move slowly, with little swaying and jerking motions, into the kitchen. Its head was erect but at an angle, its red eyes fixed on us. Its crest, a little sprig of feath-ers, stood a few inches over its head. Plumes rose from its tail. The bird stopped a few feet away from the table and looked us over.

'They don't call them birds of paradise for nothing,' Bud said.

Fran didn't look up. She was giving all her attention to the baby. She'd be-gun to patty-cake with it, which pleased the baby somewhat. I mean, at least the thing had stopped fussing. She brought it up to her neck and whispered something into its ear.

'Now,' she said, 'don't tell anyone what I said.'

The baby stared at her with its pop eyes. Then it reached and got itself a baby handful of Fran's blond hair. The peacock stepped closer to the table. None of us said anything. We just sat still. Baby Harold saw the bird. It let go of Fran's hair and stood up on her lap. It pointed its fat fingers at the bird. It jumped up and down and made noises.

The peacock walked quickly around the table and went for the baby. It ran its long neck across the baby's legs. It pushed its beak in under the baby's pa-jama top and shook its stiff head back and forth. The baby laughed and kicked its feet. Scooting onto its back, the baby worked its way over Fran's knees and down onto the floor. The peacock kept pushing against the baby, as if it was a game they were playing. Fran held the baby against her legs while the baby strained forward.

'I just don't believe this,' she said.

'That peacock is crazy, that's what,' Bud said. 'Damn bird doesn't know it's a bird, that's its major trouble.'

Olla grinned and showed her teeth again. She looked over at Bud. Bud pushed his chair away from the table and nodded.

It *was* an ugly baby. But, for all I know, I guess it didn't matter that much to Bud and Olla. Or if it did, maybe they simply thought, So okay if it's ugly. It's our baby. And this is just a stage. Pretty soon there'll be another stage. There is this stage and then there is the next stage. Things will be okay in the long run, once all the stages have been gone through. They might have thought some-thing like that.

Bud picked up the baby and swung him over his head until Harold shrieked. The peacock ruffled its feathers and watched.

Fran shook her head again. She smoothed out her dress where the baby had been. Olla picked up her fork and was working at some lima beans on her plate.

Bud shifted the baby onto his hip and said, 'There's pie and coffee yet.'

That evening at Bud and Olla's was special. I knew it was special. That eve-ning I felt good about almost everything in my life. I couldn't wait to be alone with Fran to talk to her about what I was feeling. I made a wish that evening. Sitting there at the table, I closed my eyes for a minute and thought hard. What I wished for was that I'd never forget or otherwise let go of that evening. That's one wish of mine that came true. And it was bad luck for me that it did. But, of course, I couldn't know that then.

'What are you thinking about, Jack?' Bud said to me.

'I'm just thinking,' I said. I grinned at him.

'A penny,' Olla said.

I just grinned some more and shook my head.

After we got home from Bud and Olla's that night, and we were under the covers, Fran said, 'Honey, fill me up with your seed!' When she said that, I heard her all the way down to my toes, and I hollered and let go.

Later, after things had changed for us, and the kid had come along, all of that, Fran would look back on that evening at Bud's place as the beginning of the change. But she's wrong. The change came later—and when it came, it was like something that happened to other people, not something that could have happened to us.

'Goddamn those people and their ugly baby,' Fran will say, for no apparent reason, while we're watching TV late at night. 'And that smelly bird,' she'll say. 'Christ, who needs it!' Fran will say. She says this kind of stuff a lot, even though she hasn't seen Bud and Olla since that one time.

Fran doesn't work at the creamery anymore, and she cut her hair a long time ago. She's gotten fat on me, too. We don't talk about it. What's to say?

I still see Bud at the plant. We work together and we open our lunch pails together. If I ask, he tells me about Olla and Harold. Joey's out of the picture. He flew into his tree one night and that was it for him. He didn't come down. Old age, maybe, Bud says. Then the owls took over. Bud shrugs. He eats his sandwich and says Harold's going to be a linebacker someday. 'You ought to see that kid,' Bud says. I nod. We're still friends. That hasn't changed any. But I've gotten careful with what I say to him. And I know he feels that and wishes it could be different. I wish it could be, too.

Once in a blue moon, he asks about my family. When he does, I tell him everybody's fine. 'Everybody's fine,' I say. I close the lunch pail and take out my cigarettes. Bud nods and sips his coffee. The truth is, my kid has a conniving streak in him. But I don't talk about it. Not even with his mother. Especially her. She and I talk less and less as it is. Mostly it's just the TV. But I remember that night. I recall the way the peacock picked up its gray feet and inched around the table. And then my friend and his wife saying good night to us on the porch. Olla giving Fran some peacock feathers to take home. I remember all of us shaking hands, hugging each other, saying things. In the car, Fran sat close to me as we drove away. She kept her hand on my leg. We drove home like that from my friend's house.

1988

Alice Munro

Brief Biography

- Born in 1931.
- Parents struggle with a mink and silver fox farm; a turkey farm also fails.
- In 1963, moves with husband to Victoria, BC, where she helps him run a bookstore; moves back to Ontario after their divorce in 1972.
- Wins three Governor General's awards and two Giller prizes.
- In 1983 tours China with Canada's first literary delegation.
- Books translated into twenty languages; fifty stories published in *The New Yorker*.
- Adaptation of story 'Boys and Girls' wins Oscar in 1984.
- Adaptation of 'The Bear Came over the Mountain,' as *Away from Her*, is nominated for two Oscars in 2007.
- In 2009 wins £60,000 Man Booker International Prize for lifetime achievement.

Born Alice Laidlaw in Wingham, ON, Munro describes her poverty-stricken youth as the 'emotional reality' behind her stories. Though she is not an autobiographical writer, many of her stories are narrated by adult women recalling a repressive past that shaped their lives. Scholars associate Munro's use of bleak landscapes and focus on spiritual anxiety, small-town confinement, and dysfunctional families with 'southern Ontario Gothic' writers such as Margaret Atwood, Timothy Findley, Jane Urquhart, Barbara Gowdy, Matt Cohen, and Marian Engel. Sinister ambiguities, distorted realities, and dark psychologies appear in her carefully paced and detailed stories. Many depict violence against women, tense mother–daughter relationships, accidents, suicides, or drownings.

Munro had many part-time jobs, never completed university, and wrote in spare moments while raising three children. After years of being published in small magazines and having her stories broadcast on CBC Radio's literary programs, Munro won the first of three Governor General's awards for her first collection, *Dance of the Happy Shades* (1968). Her story cycle, *Lives of Girls and Women* (1971), became a classic Canadian literary text. She does not write novels, instead basing her career on 'the marginal form' of short stories set in inhibited small-town Ontario. Responding to remarks that her characters are 'marginalized women,' Munro told interviewer Judith Miller that 'there was a feeling that women could write about the freakish, the marginal. . . . I came to feel that was our territory, whereas the mainstream big novel about real life was men's territory. . . . Maybe it was because I grew up on a margin.' Though she was once considered a 'realistic' writer, her dozen collections, with their disjointed chronology and recurring characters, are now regarded as a unity, a grand story cycle of thematic and emotional motifs.

Though her early stories have epiphanies, Munro's later works flow unplotted through time and space, almost dreamlike, towards a different kind of illumination. Munro calls lapses of memory or juxtaposed moments of time the 'funny jumps' of living. She refers to these fleeting glimpses as 'clear patches,' suggestions not solutions, which might be a moment of hope or despair, regret or acceptance, outside language, or particular only to the character.

Scrupulous research and many revisions locate the exact detail in Munro's graceful prose. Despite such documentary precision, allusions, intertextual references, and uncertainty are close to the surface of her fiction. In 'Pictures of the Ice,' photographs, mirrors, and images of water and ice reveal gaps between surfaces and deeper awareness; traditional Christian symbolism suggests conflict between characters Brent and Austin. Though the story's characters seem to find a deceptive happiness, 'Pictures of the Ice' portrays poverty, dependence, and physical decline as well as guilt and deception. Austin, the 'absent' protagonist, is typically ambiguous: he might be saint or liar, hero or villain.

See Geoff Hancock, from 'Interview with Alice Munro,' p. 453.

Pictures of the Ice

Three weeks before he died—drowned in a boating accident in a lake whose name nobody had heard him mention—Austin Cobbett stood deep in the clasp of a three-way mirror in Crawford's Men's Wear, in Logan, looking at himself in a burgundy sports shirt and a pair of cream, brown, and burgundy plaid pants. Both permanent press.

'Listen to me,' Jerry Crawford said to him. 'With the darker shirt and the lighter pants you can't go wrong. It's youthful.'

Austin cackled. 'Did you ever hear that expression "mutton dressed as lamb"?'

'Referred to ladies,' Jerry said. 'Anyway, it's all changed now. There's no old men's clothes, no old ladies' clothes anymore. Style applies to everybody.'

When Austin got used to what he had on, Jerry was going to talk him into a neck scarf of complementary colors and a cream pullover. Austin needed all the cover-up he could get. Since his wife died, about a year ago, and they finally got a new minister at the United Church (Austin, who was over seventy, was officially retired but had been hanging on and filling in while they haggled over hiring a new man and what they would pay him), he had lost weight, his muscles had shrunk, he was getting the potbellied caved-in shape of an old man. His neck was corded and his nose lengthened and his cheeks drooping. He was a stringy old rooster—stringy but tough, and game enough to gear up for a second marriage.

'The pants are going to have to be taken in,' Jerry said. 'You can give us time for that, can't you? When's the happy happy day?'

Austin was going to be married in Hawaii, where his wife, his wife-to-be, lived. He named a date a couple of weeks ahead.

Phil Stadelman from the Toronto Dominion Bank came in then and did not recognize Austin from the back, though Austin was his own former minister. He'd never seen him in clothes like that.

Phil told his AIDS joke—Jerry couldn't stop him.

Why did the Newfie put condoms on his ears?

Because he didn't want to get hearing aids.

Then Austin turned around, and instead of saying, 'Well, I don't know about you fellows, but I find it hard to think of AIDS as a laughing matter,' or 'I wonder what kind of jokes they tell in Newfoundland about the folks from Huron County,' he said, 'That's rich.' He laughed.

That's rich. Then he asked Phil's opinion of his clothes. 'Do you think they're going to laugh when they see me coming in Hawaii?'

Karin heard about this when she went into the doughnut place to drink a cup of coffee after finishing her afternoon stint as a crossing guard. She sat at the counter and heard the men talking at a table behind her. She swung around on the stool and said, 'Listen, I could have told you, he's changed. I see him every day and I could have told you.'

Karin is a tall, thin woman with a rough skin and a hoarse voice and long blond hair dark for a couple of inches at the roots. She's letting it grow out dark and it's got to where she could cut it short, but she doesn't. She used to be a lanky blond girl, shy and pretty, riding around on the back of her husband's motorcycle. She has gone a little strange, not too much, and couldn't be a crossing guard, ever since Austin Cobbett's recommendation. She interrupts conversations. She wears an old navy-blue duffel coat. She has a grudge against her ex-husband and she has a public grudge against her ex-husband and she has written with her finger: *Fake Christian. Kiss* at she wrote *Lazarus Sucks,* it off with her sleeve. into trouble—the trouble with the Chief of Police—, only against Lazarus House now.

Karin lives where upstairs over the hardware store in the back and kitchen baby's) and a kitchen stin's, cleaning out his house Hawaii. The house he lives in . The church has built the and a double garage—ministers wives often work now; it's a big help if they can get jobs as nurses or teachers, and in that case you need two cars. The old parsonage is a grayish-white brick house with blue-painted trim on the veranda and the gables. It needs a lot of work. Insulating, sandblasting, new paint, new window frames, new tiles in the bathroom. Walking back to her own place at night, Karin sometimes occupies her mind thinking what she'd do to that place if it was hers and she had the money.

Austin shows her a picture of Sheila Brothers, the woman he is to marry. Actually, it's a picture of the three of them—Austin, his wife, and Sheila Brothers, in front of a log building and some pine trees. A Retreat, where he—they—first met Sheila. Austin has on his minister's black shirt and turned collar; he looks shifty, with his apologetic, ministerial smile. His wife is looking away from him, but the big bow of her flowered scarf flutters against his neck. Fluffy white hair, trim figure. Chic. Sheila Brothers—Mrs Brothers, a widow—is looking straight ahead, and she is the only one who seems really cheerful. Short fair hair combed around her face in a businesslike way, brown slacks, white sweatshirt, with the fairly large bumps of her breasts and stomach plain to see, she meets the camera head-on and doesn't seem worried about what it will make of her.

'She looks happy,' Karin says.

'Well. She didn't know she was going to marry me, at the time.'

He shows her a postcard picture of the town where Sheila lives. The town where he will live in Hawaii. Also a photograph of her house. The town's main street has a row of palm trees down the middle, it has low white or pinkish buildings, lampposts with brimming flower baskets, and over all a sky of deep turquoise in which the town's name—a Hawaiian name there is no hope of pronouncing or remembering—is written in flowing letters like silk ribbon. The name floating in the sky looked as possible as anything else about it. As for the house, you could hardly make it out at all—just a bit of balcony among the red and pink and gold flowering trees and bushes. But there was the beach in front of it, the sand pure as cream and the jewel-bright waves breaking. Where Austin Cobbett would walk with friendly Sheila. No wonder he needed all new clothes.

What Austin wants Karin to do is clear everything out. Even his books, his old typewriter, the pictures of his wife and children. His son lives in Denver, his daughter in Montreal. He has written to them, he has talked to them on the phone, he has asked them to claim anything they want. His son wants the dining room furniture, which a moving-truck will pick up next week. His daughter said she didn't want anything. (Karin thinks she's apt to reconsider; people always want *something*.) All the furniture, books, pictures, curtains, rugs, dishes, pots, and pans are to go to the Auction Barn. Austin's car will be auctioned as well, and his power mower and the snowblower his son gave him last Christmas. These will be sold after Austin leaves for Hawaii, and the money is to go to Lazarus House. Austin started Lazarus House when he was a minister. Only he didn't call it that; he called it Turnaround House. But now they have decided— Brent Duprey has decided—it would be better to have a name that is more religious, more Christian.

At first Austin was just going to give them all these things to use in or around the House. Then he thought that it would be showing more respect to give them the money, to let them spend it as they liked, buying things they liked, instead of using his wife's dishes and sitting on his wife's chintz sofa.

'What if they take the money and buy lottery tickets with it?' Karin asks him. 'Don't you think it'll be a big temptation to them?'

'You don't get anywhere in life without temptations,' Austin says, with his maddening little smile. 'What if they won the lottery?'

'Brent Duprey is a snake.'

Brent has taken over the whole control of Lazarus House, which Austin started. It was a place for people to stay who wanted to stop drinking or some other way of life they were in; now it's a born-again sort of place, with nightlong sessions of praying and singing and groaning and confessing. That's how Brent got hold of it—by becoming more religious than Austin. Austin got Brent to stop drinking; he pulled and pulled on Brent until he pulled him right out of the life he was leading and into a new life of running this House with money from the church, the government, and so on, and he made a big mistake, Austin did, in thinking he could hold Brent there. Brent once started on the holy road went shooting on past; he got past Austin's careful quiet kind of religion in no time and cut Austin out with the people in his own church who wanted a stricter, more ferocious kind of Christianity. Austin was shifted out of Lazarus House and the church at about the same time, and Brent bossed the new minister around without difficulty. And in spite of this, or because of it, Austin wants to give Lazarus House the money.

'Who's to say whether Brent's way isn't closer to God than mine is, after all?' he says.

Karin says just about anything to anybody now. She says to Austin, 'Don't make me puke.'

Austin says she must be sure to keep a record of her time, so she will be paid for all this work, and also, if there is anything here that she would particularly like, to tell him, so they can discuss it.

'Within reason,' he says. 'If you said you'd like the car or the snowblower, I guess I'd be obliged to say no, because that would be cheating the folks over at Lazarus House. How about the vacuum cleaner?'

Is that how he sees her—as somebody who's always thinking about cleaning houses? The vacuum cleaner is practically an antique, anyway.

'I bet I know what Brent said when you told him I was going to be in charge of all this,' she says. 'I bet he said, "Are you going to get a lawyer to check up on her?" He did! Didn't he?'

Instead of answering that, Austin says, 'Why would I trust a lawyer any more than I trust you?'

'Is that what you said to him?'

'I'm saying it to you. You either trust or you don't trust, in my opinion. When you decide you're going to trust, you have to start where you are.'

Austin rarely mentions God. Nevertheless you feel the mention of God hovering on the edge of sentences like these, and it makes you so uneasy—Karin gets a crumbly feeling along her spine—that you wish he'd say it and get it over with.

Four years ago Karin and Brent were still married, and they hadn't had the baby yet or moved to their place above the hardware store. They were living in the old slaughterhouse. That was a cheap apartment building belonging to Morris Fordyce, but it really had at one time been a slaughterhouse. In wet weather Karin could smell pig, and always she smelled another smell that she thought was blood. Brent sniffed around the walls and got down and sniffed the floor, but he couldn't smell what she was smelling. How could he smell anything but the clouds of boozy breath that rose from his own gut? Brent was a drunk then, but not a sodden drunk. He played hockey on the OT (over thirty, old-timers) hockey team—he was quite a bit older than Karin—and he claimed that he had never played sober. He worked for Fordyce Construction for a while, and then he worked for the town, cutting up trees. He drank on the job when he could, and after work he drank at the Fish and Game Club or at the Green Haven Motel Bar, called the Greasy Heaven. One night he got a bulldozer going, which was sitting outside the Greasy Heaven, and he drove it across town to the Fish and Game Club. Of course he was caught, and charged with impaired driving of a bulldozer, a big joke all over town. Nobody who laughed at the joke came around to pay the fine. And Brent just kept getting wilder. Another night he took down the stairs that led to their apartment. He didn't bash the steps out in a fit of temper; he removed them thoughtfully and methodically, steps and uprights one by one, backing downstairs as he did so and leaving Karin cursing at the top. First she was laughing at him—she had had a few beers herself by that time—then, when she realized he was in earnest, and she was being marooned there, she started cursing. Coward neighbors peeped out of the doors behind him.

Brent came home the next afternoon and was amazed, or pretended to be. 'What happened to the *steps*?' he yelled. He stomped around the hall, his lined, exhausted, excited face working, his blue eyes snapping, his smile innocent and conniving. 'God damn that Morris! God-damn steps caved in. I'm going to sue the shit out of him. God damn *fuck*!' Karin was upstairs with nothing to eat but half a package of Rice Krispies with no milk, and a can of yellow beans. She had thought of phoning somebody to come with a ladder, but she was too mad and stubborn. If Brent wanted to starve her, she would show him. She would starve.

That time was really the beginning of the end, the change. Brent went around to see Morris Fordyce to beat him up and tell him about how he was going to have the shit sued out of him, and Morris talked to him in a reasonable, sobering way until Brent decided not to sue or beat up Morris but to commit suicide instead. Morris called Austin Cobbett then, because Austin had a reputation for knowing how to deal with people who were in a desperate way. Austin didn't talk Brent out of drinking then, or into the church, but he talked him out of suicide. Then, a couple of years later when the baby died, Austin was the only minister they knew to call. By the time he came to see them, to talk about the funeral, Brent had drunk everything in the house and gone out looking for more. Austin went after him and spent the next five days—with a brief time out for burying the baby—just staying with him on a bender. Then he spent the next week nursing him out of it, and the next month talking to him or sitting with him until Brent decided he would not drink anymore, he had been put in touch with God. Austin said that Brent meant by that that he had been put in touch with the fullness of his own life and the power of his innermost self. Brent said it was not for one minute himself; it was God.

Karin went to Austin's church with Brent for a while; she didn't mind that. She could see, though, that it wasn't going to be enough to hold Brent. She saw him bouncing up to sing the hymns, swinging his arms and clenching his fists, his whole body primed up. It was the same as he was after three or four beers when there was no way he could stop himself going for more. He was bursting. And soon enough he burst out of Austin's hold and took a good part of the church with him. A lot of people had wanted that loosening, more noise and praying and singing and not so much quiet persuading talking; they'd been wanting it for a long while.

None of it surprised her. It didn't surprise her that Brent learned to fill out papers and make the right impression and get government money; that he took over Turnaround House, which Austin had got him into, and kicked Austin out. He'd always been full of possibilities. It didn't really surprise her that he got as mad at her now for drinking one beer and smoking one cigarette as he used to do when she wanted to stop partying and go to bed at two o'clock. He said he was giving her a week to decide. No more drinking, no more smoking, Christ as her Saviour. One week. Karin said don't bother with the week. After Brent was gone, she quit smoking, she almost quit drinking, she also quit going to Austin's church. She gave up on nearly everything but a slow, smoldering grudge against Brent, which grew and grew. One day Austin stopped her on the street and she thought he was going to say some gentle, personal, condemning thing to her, for her grudge or her quitting church, but all he did was ask her to come and help him look after his wife, who was getting home from the hospital that week.

Austin is talking on the phone to his daughter in Montreal. Her name is Megan. She is around thirty, unmarried, a television producer.

'Life has a lot of surprises up its sleeve,' Austin says. 'You know this has nothing to do with your mother. This is a new life entirely. But I regret . . . No, no.

I just mean there's more than one way to love God, and taking pleasure in the world is surely one of them. That's a revelation that's come on me rather late. Too late to be of any use to your mother. . . . No. Guilt is a sin and a seduction. I've said that to many a poor soul that liked to wallow in it. Regret's another matter. How could you get through a long life and escape it?'

I was right, Karin is thinking; Megan does want something. But after a little more talk—Austin says that he might take up golf, don't laugh, and that Sheila belongs to a play-reading club, he expects he'll be a star at that, after all his pulpit haranguing—the conversation comes to an end. Austin comes out to the kitchen—the phone is in the front hall; this is an old-fashioned house—and looks up at Karin, who is cleaning out the high cupboards.

'Parents and children, Karin,' he says, sighing, sighing, looking humorous. 'Oh, what a tangled web we weave, when first we—have children. Then they always want us to be the same, they want us to be parents—it shakes them up dreadfully if we should do anything they didn't think we'd do. Dreadfully.'

'I guess she'll get used to it,' Karin says, without much sympathy.

'Oh, she will, she will. Poor Megan.'

Then he says he's going uptown to have his hair cut. He doesn't want to leave it any longer, because he always looks and feels so foolish with a fresh haircut. His mouth turns down as he smiles—first up, then down. That downward slide is what's noticeable on him everywhere— face slipping down into neck wattles, chest emptied out and mounded into that abrupt, queer little belly. The flow has left dry channels, deep lines. Yet Austin speaks—it's his perversity to speak—as if out of a body that is light and ready and a pleasure to carry around.

In a short time the phone rings again and Karin has to climb down and answer it.

'Karin? Is that you, Karin? It's Megan!'

'Your father's just gone up to get a haircut.'

'Good. Good. I'm glad. It gives me a chance to talk to you. I've been hoping I'd get a chance to talk to you.'

'Oh,' says Karin.

'Karin. Now, listen. I know I'm behaving just the way adult children are supposed to behave in this situation. I don't like it. I don't like that in myself. But I can't help it. I'm suspicious. I wonder what's going on. Is he all right? What do you think of it? What do you think of this woman he's going to marry?'

'All I ever saw of her is her picture,' Karin says.

'I am terribly busy right now and I can't just drop everything and come home and have a real heart-to-heart with him. Anyway, he's very difficult to talk to. He makes all the right noises, he seems so open, but in reality he's very closed. He's never been at all a personal kind of person, do you know what I mean? He's never done anything before for a *personal* kind of reason. He always did things *for* somebody. He always liked to find people who *needed* things done for them, a lot. Well, you know that. Even bringing you into the house, you know, to look after Mother—it wasn't exactly for Mother's sake or his sake he did that.'

Karin can picture Megan—the long, dark, smooth hair, parted in the middle and combed over her shoulders, the heavily made-up eyes and tanned skin and pale-pink lipsticked mouth, the handsomely clothed plump body. Wouldn't her voice bring such looks to mind even if you'd never seen her? Such smoothness, such rich sincerity. A fine gloss on every word and little appreciative spaces in between. She talks as if listening to herself. A little too much that way, really. Could she be drunk?

'Let's face it, Karin. Mother was a snob.' (Yes, she is drunk.) 'Well, she had to have something. Dragged around from one dump to another, always doing good. Doing good wasn't her thing at all. So now, *now*, he gives it all up, he's off to the easy life. In Hawaii! Isn't it bizarre?'

'Bizarre.' Karin has heard that word on television and heard people, mostly teenagers, say it, and she knows it is not the church bazaar Megan's talking about. Nevertheless that's what the word makes her think of—the church bazaars that Megan's mother used to organize, always trying to give them some style and make things different. Striped umbrellas and a sidewalk café one year, Devonshire teas and a rose arbor the next. Then she thinks of Megan's mother on the chintz-covered sofa in the living room, weak and yellow after her chemotherapy, one of those padded, perky kerchiefs around her nearly bald head. Still, she could look up at Karin with a faint, formal surprise when Karin came into the room. 'Was there something you wanted, Karin?' The thing that Karin was supposed to ask her, she would ask Karin.

Bizarre. Bazaar. Snob. When Megan got in that dig, Karin should have said, at least, 'I know that.' All she can think to say is 'Megan. This is costing you money.'

'Money, Karin! We're talking about my *father*. We're talking about whether my father is sane or whether he has flipped his *wig*, Karin!'

A day later a call from Denver. Don, Austin's son, is calling to tell his father that they better forget about the dining-room furniture, the cost of shipping it is too high. Austin agrees with him. The money could be better spent, he says. What's furniture? Then Austin is called upon to explain about the Auction Barn and what Karin is doing.

'Of course, of course, no trouble,' Austin says. 'They'll list everything they get and what it sold for. They can easily send a copy. They've got a computer, I understand. No longer the Dark Ages up here. . . .'

'Yes,' Austin says. 'I hoped you'd see it that way about the money. It's a project close to my heart. And you and your sister are providing well for yourselves. I'm very fortunate in my children. . . .'

'The Old Age Pension and my minister's pension,' he says. 'Whatever more could I want? And this lady, this lady, I can tell you, Sheila—she is not short of money, if I can put it that way. . . .' He laughs rather mischievously at something his son says.

After he hangs up, he says to Karin, 'Well, my son is worried about my finances and my daughter is worried about my mental state. My mental-emotional state. The male and female way of looking at things. The male and female way of expressing their anxiety. Underneath it's the same thing. The old order changeth, yielding place to new.'

Don wouldn't remember everything that was in the house, anyway. How could he? He was here the day of the funeral and his wife wasn't with him; she was too pregnant to come. He wouldn't have her to rely on. Men don't remember that sort of thing well. He just asked for the list so that it would look as if he were keeping track of everything and nobody'd better try to hoodwink him. Or hoodwink his father.

There were things Karin was going to get, and nobody need know where she had got them. Nobody came up to her place. A willow-pattern plate. The blue-and-gray flowered curtains. A little, fat jug of ruby-colored glass with a silver lid. A white damask cloth, a tablecloth, that she had ironed till it shone like a frosted snowfield, and the enormous napkins that went with it. The tablecloth alone weighed as much as a child, and the napkins would flop out of wineglasses like lilies—if you had wineglasses. Just as a start, she has already taken home six silver spoons in her coat pocket. She knows enough not to disturb the silver tea service or the good dishes. But some pink glass dishes for dessert, with long stems, have taken her eye. She can see her place transformed, with these things in it. More than that, she can feel the quiet and content they would extend to her. Sitting in a room so furnished, she wouldn't need to go out. She would never need to think of Brent, and ways to torment him. A person sitting in such a room could turn and floor anybody trying to intrude.

Was there something you wanted?

On Monday of Austin's last week—he was supposed to fly to Hawaii on Saturday—the first big storm of the winter began. The wind came in from the west, over the lake; there was driving snow all day and night. Monday and Tuesday the schools were closed, so Karin didn't have to work as a guard. But she couldn't stand staying indoors; she put on her duffel coat and wrapped her head and half her face in a wool scarf and plowed through the snow-filled streets to the parsonage.

The house is cold, the wind is coming in around the doors and windows. In the kitchen cupboard along the west wall, the dishes feel like ice. Austin is dressed but lying down on the living-room sofa, wrapped in various quilts and blankets. He is not reading or watching television or dozing, as far as she can tell—just staring. She makes him a cup of instant coffee.

'Do you think this'll stop by Saturday?' she says. She has the feeling that if he doesn't go Saturday, he just may not go at all. The whole thing could be called off, all plans could falter.

'It'll stop in due time,' he says. 'I'm not worried.'

Karin's baby died in a snowstorm. In the afternoon, when Brent was drinking with his friend Rob and watching television, Karin said that the baby was sick and she needed money for a taxi to take him to the hospital. Brent told her to fuck off. He thought she was just trying to bother him. And partly she was— the baby had just thrown up once, and whimpered, and he didn't seem very hot. Then about suppertime, with Rob gone, Brent went to pick up the baby and play with him, forgetting that he was sick. 'This baby's like a hot coal!' he yelled at Karin, and wanted to know why she hadn't got the doctor, why she hadn't taken the baby to the hospital. 'You tell me why,' said Karin, and they started to fight. 'You said he didn't need to go,' said Karin. 'OK, so he doesn't need to go.' Brent called the taxi company, and the taxis weren't going out because of the storm, which up to then neither he nor Karin had noticed. He called the hospital and asked them what to do, and they said to get the fever down by wrapping the baby in wet towels. So they did that, and by midnight the storm had quieted down and the snowplows were out on the streets and they got the baby to the hospital. But he died. He probably would have died no matter what they'd done; he had meningitis. Even if he'd been a fussed-over precious little baby in a home where the father didn't get drunk and the mother and father didn't have fights, he might have died; he probably would have died, anyway.

Brent wanted it to be his fault, though. Sometimes he wanted it to be their fault. It was like sucking candy to him, that confession. Karin told him to shut up, she told him to *shut up*.

She said, 'He would have died anyway.'

When the storm is over, Tuesday afternoon, Karin puts on her coat and goes out and shovels the parsonage walk. The temperature seems to be dropping even lower; the sky is clear. Austin says they're going to go down to the lake to look at the ice. If there is a big storm like this fairly early in the year, the wind drives the waves up on the shore and they freeze there. Ice is everywhere, in unlikely formations. People go down and take pictures. The paper often prints the best of them. Austin wants to take some pictures, too. He says it'll be something to show people in Hawaii. So Karin shovels the car out, too, and off they go, Austin driving with great care. And nobody else is down there. It's too cold. Austin hangs on to Karin as they struggle along the boardwalk—or where the boardwalk must be, under the snow. Sheets of ice drop from the burdened branches of the willow trees to the ground, and the sun shines through them from the west; they're like walls of pearl. Ice is woven through the wire of the high fence to make it like a honeycomb. Waves have frozen as they hit the shore, making mounds and caves, a crazy landscape, out to the rim of the open water. And all the playground equipment, the children's swings and climbing bars, has been transformed by ice, hung with organ pipes or buried in what looks like half-carved statues, shapes of ice that might be people, animals, angels, monsters, left unfinished.

Karin is nervous when Austin stands alone to take pictures. He seems shaky to her—and what if he fell? He could break a leg, a hip. Old people break a hip and that's the end of them. Even taking off his gloves to work the camera seems risky. A frozen thumb might be enough to keep him here, make him miss his plane.

Back in the car, he does have to rub and blow on his hands. He lets her drive. If something dire happened to him, would Sheila Brothers come here, take over his care, settle into the parsonage, countermand his orders?

'This is strange weather,' he says. 'Up in northern Ontario it's balmy, even the little lakes are open, temperatures above freezing. And here we are in the grip of the ice and the wind straight off the Great Plains.'

'It'll be all the same to you when you get to Hawaii,' Karin says firmly. 'Northern Ontario or the Great Plains or here, you'll be glad to be out of it. Doesn't she ever call you?'

'Who?' says Austin.

'*Her.* Mrs Brothers.'

'Oh, Sheila. She calls me late at night. The time's so much earlier, in Hawaii.'

The phone rings with Karin alone in the house the morning before Austin is to leave. A man's voice, uncertain and sullen-sounding.

'He isn't here right now,' Karin says. Austin has gone to the bank. 'I could get him to call you when he comes in.'

'Well, it's long distance,' the man says. 'It's Shaft Lake.'

'Shaft Lake,' repeats Karin, feeling around on the phone shelf for a pencil.

'We were just wondering. Like we were just checking. That we got the right time that he gets in. Somebody's got to drive down and meet him. So he gets in to Thunder Bay at three o'clock, is that right?'

Karin has stopped looking for a pencil. She finally says, 'I guess that's right. As far as I know. If you called back around noon, he'd be here.'

'I don't know for sure I can get to a phone, around noon. I'm at the hotel here but then I got to go someplace else. I'd just as soon leave him the message. Somebody's going to meet him at the airport in Thunder Bay three o'clock tomorrow. OK?'

'OK,' says Karin.

'You could tell him we got him a place to live, too.'

'Oh. OK.'

'It's a trailer. He said he wouldn't mind living in a trailer. See, we haven't had any minister here in a long time.'

'Oh,' says Karin. 'OK. Yes. I'll tell him.'

As soon as she has hung up, she finds Megan's number on the list above the phone, and dials it. It rings three or four times and then Megan's voice comes on, sounding brisker than the last time Karin heard it. Brisk but teasing.

'The lady of the house regrets that she cannot take your call at the moment, but if you would leave your name, message, and phone number she will try to get back to you as soon as possible.'

Karin has already started to say she is sorry, but, this is important, when she is interrupted by a beep, and realizes it's one of those machines. She starts again, speaking quickly but distinctly after a deep breath.

'I just wanted to tell you. I just wanted you to know. Your father is fine. He is in good health, and mentally he is fine and everything. So you don't have to worry. He is off to Hawaii tomorrow. I was just thinking about—I was just thinking about our conversation on the phone. So I thought I'd tell you, not to worry. This is Karin speaking.'

And she just gets all that said in time, when she hears Austin at the door. Before he can ask or wonder what she's doing there in the hall, she fires a series of questions at him. Did he get to the bank? Did the cold make his chest hurt? When was it the Auction Barn truck was coming? When did the people from the Board want the parsonage keys? Was he going to phone Don and Megan before he left or after he got there, or what?

Yes. No. Monday for the truck. Tuesday for the keys, but no rush—if she wasn't finished, then Wednesday would be OK. No more phone calls. He and his children have said all they need to say to each other. Once he's there, he will write them a letter. Write each of them a letter.

'After you're married?'

Yes. Well. Maybe sooner than that.

He has laid his coat across the bannister railing. Then she sees him put out a hand to steady himself, holding on to the railing. He pretends to be fiddling around with his coat.

'You OK?' she says. 'You want a cup of coffee?'

For a moment he doesn't say anything. His eyes swim past her. How can anybody believe that this tottery old man, whose body looks to be shrivelling day by day, is on his way to marry a comforting widow and spend his days from now on walking on a sunny beach? It isn't in him to do such a thing, ever. He means to wear himself out, quick, quick, on people as thankless as possible, thankless as Brent. Meanwhile fooling all of them into thinking he's changed his spots. Otherwise, somebody might stop him going. Slipping out from under, fooling them, enjoying it.

But he really is after something in the coat. He brings out a pint of whiskey.

'Put a little of that in a glass for me,' he says. 'Never mind the coffee. Just a precaution. Against weakness. From the cold.'

He is sitting on the steps when she brings him the whiskey. He drinks it shakily. He wags his head back and forth, as if trying to get it clear. He stands up. 'Much better,' he says. 'Oh, very much better. Now, about those pictures of the ice, Karin. I was wondering, could you pick them up next week? If I left you the money? They're not ready yet.'

Even though he's just in from the cold, he's white. Put a candle behind his face, it'd shine through as if he were wax or thin china.

'You'll have to leave me your address,' she says. 'Where to send them.'

'Just hang on to them till I write you. That'd be best.'

So she has ended up with a whole roll of pictures of the ice, along with all those other things that she had her mind set on. The pictures show the sky bluer than it ever was, but the weaving in the fence, the shape of the organ pipes are not so plain to see. There needs to be a human figure, too, to show the size that things were. She should have taken the camera and captured Austin—who has vanished. He has vanished as completely as the ice, unless the body washes up in the spring. A thaw, a drowning, and they both disappear. Karin looks at these pictures of the pale, lumpy ice monstrosities, these pictures Austin took, so often that she gets the feeling that he is in them, after all. He's a blank in them, but bright.

She thinks now that he knew. Right at the last he knew that she'd caught on to him, she understood what he was up to. No matter how alone you are, and how tricky and determined, don't you need one person to know? She could be the one for him. Each of them knew what the other was up to, and didn't let on, and that was a link beyond the usual. Every time she thinks of it, she feels approved of—a most unexpected thing.

She puts one of the pictures in an envelope, and sends it to Megan. (She tore the list of addresses and phone numbers off the wall, just in case.) She sends another to Don. And another, stamped and addressed, across town, to Brent. She doesn't write anything on the pictures or enclose any note. She won't be bothering any of these people again. The fact is, it won't be long till she'll be leaving here.

She just wants to make them wonder.

1990

Diane Schoemperlen

Brief Biography

- Born in 1954 in Thunder Bay, ON; educated at Lakehead University.
- Studies with W.O. Mitchell and Alice Munro at Banff Centre; lives in Canmore, AB, for a decade as avalanche researcher, bank teller, reporter, and typesetter.
- Has taught Creative Writing at St Lawrence College and many workshops.
- Wins 1998 Governor General's Award for *Forms of Devotion: Stories and Pictures*.
- Many stories from out-of-print or small press editions in *Red Plaid Shirt: Stories New and Collected* (2003).
- Deeply affected by 9/11, she compiles *Names of the Dead: An Elegy for the Victims of September 11* (2004).
- Has published three novels: *In the Language of Love* (1994), based on a 100-word association test; *Our Lady of the Lost and Found* (2001); and *At a Loss for Words* (2008), a 'post-romantic' novel based on e-mails.
- Is a single mother.

A Canadian 'metafictionist,' Diane Schoemperlen challenges the conventions of fiction. Metafiction, an elusive term, questions reality, the making of fiction, and even the reading of fiction. While her stories dramatize traditional relationships, they are similar to Amy Hempel's stories in their lack of the traditional features of plot, climax, and resolution. As the narrator in Schoemperlen's story 'Five Small Rooms (A Murder Mystery)' observes, 'Do not expect that your life will follow the orderly unfolding of beginning, middle, and end.'

During the twentieth century, European and American poets, painters, musicians, and filmmakers from many art movements like Dada, Surrealism, Cubism, and Pop Art blended tragedy and anxiety, high and low cultures, with dark humour. From here emerged 'collage writing,' a postmodern technique that juxtaposes variant texts and images. The method was adapted by many feminist artists, including Schoemperlen, one of whose characters is a collage artist. A remark by her son that her stories had no pictures moved Schoemperlen closer to graphic fiction with visual elements such as photographs, wood engravings, Victorian illustrations, and her own collages. Sometimes she uses excerpts from graphs, documentary forms, or statistics. Like Jose Dalisay, Jr, she is fascinated by communication technologies; her most recent novel, *At a Loss for Words*, includes e-mails. She told an interviewer: 'The phenomenon of an e-mail romance is particular to our age. . . . But it has its limitations too, as the characters in the book soon discover. And it has its dangers.'

Schoemperlen often writes about male–female relationships, extramarital affairs, or the difficulties of parenting. In the midst of conflicting and often limited choices, her characters seek some form of coherence. In humorous or ironic tones, she suggests fragmented lives must obviously lead to fragmented fiction. But her wildly inventive forms are not literary gimmicks: they are clues to understanding her characters' confusion and vulnerability. Often disappointed, unhappy, or depressed, working-class women mull over their emotional situations from a variety of perspectives. Alice Munro describes Schoemperlen's repetitive, circling, and overlapping style as 'close to the rhythm of memory.'

Yet Schoemperlen's work also deals with contemporary spirituality. In the novel *Our Lady of the Lost and Found*, Schoemperlen ventures into social and cultural commentary when she takes the Virgin Mary to a shopping mall. Faith, she suggests, is a shield against life's challenges, and somehow in the midst of un-conventional forms and structures, her characters find solace, even healing. In the title story from *Forms of Devotion* she writes, 'nothing is mundane.' Short fiction often suggests the intuitive aspects of the world. As American story writer Flannery O'Connor explains in her essay 'The Grotesque in Southern Fiction,' stories 'make alive some experience which we are not accustomed to observe every day. . . . Their fictional qualities lean away from typical social patterns, towards mystery and the unexpected.'

Always questioning, Schoemperlen uses exaggerated dictionary-ese both to throw doubt on meanings and to dramatize the difficulties of communication in 'The Antonyms of Fiction.' Reminiscent of Edith Wharton's 'A Journey,' the story focuses on the most ordinary, yet elusive, contradictory, and, ultimately, most essential moments of an important relationship.

The Antonyms of Fiction

FACT

The facts of the matter are these:

When I was twenty-one years old, I met and fell in love with a man named Jonathan Wright. We met at a Christmas party given by a mutual friend and two months later he moved in with me. We made a lot of jokes about him being Mr Right. Two years later he moved out. After a brief but intensely unpleasant period of accusations, hysterics, and the odd suicide threat, it became what is fondly referred to as 'an amicable separation' and then we made a lot of jokes about him being Mr Not-So-Right-After-All. We remained (or should I say, we *became*) friends, suggesting that maybe someday, maybe ten years from now, who knows, maybe then we would get back together again and get it right. This led to another batch of bad jokes about him being Mr Not-Right-Now. All of this happened ten years ago.

Sometime later I moved away, two thousand miles away in fact, back to the city I'd come from in the first place. For a while Jonathan and I kept in touch with birthday cards, Christmas cards, and the occasional phone call for no good reason. Neither one of us was much good at writing real letters.

Eventually, as so often happens over distance and the passage of time, our sporadic attempts at maintaining communication petered out and we lost track of each other's lives. I can't remember now the last time I heard from Jonathan. I also can't remember the last time Jonathan and I made love. I can remember the first time very clearly but not the last because, as so often happens, I didn't know it was to be the last time at the time and so I was not paying as much poignant attention as I might have been.

Last Sunday morning at ten o'clock, I had a phone call from a woman named Madeline Kane, a woman I hadn't heard from in years and who was, in fact, the mutual friend who'd given the Christmas party at which Jonathan and I first met. Madeline was calling Sunday morning to tell me that Jonathan was dead. She said she thought I would want to know. She said she thought I would want to know the truth. But as it turned out, she knew nothing, nothing but the facts.

TRUTH

According to *The Concise Oxford Dictionary of Current English,* truth is *the quality or state of being true or accurate or honest or sincere or loyal or accurately shaped or adjusted.*

There were at least forty people at Madeline Kane's Christmas party that year. It was a small friendly town and many of the residents, like myself, had moved there from other places and so did not have family handy for such festive occasions. We tended to gather frequently for these pot-luck parties, bearing from one house to another hearty steaming casseroles, salad in wooden bowls the size of wagon wheels, and many jumbo bottles of cheap wine.

At Madeline Kane's Christmas party, there was a big Scotch pine tied to the wall so it wouldn't topple over and we all helped decorate it before dinner, stringing popcorn and cranberries, arguing amiably about the proper way to put on the tinsel: the one-strand-at-a-time advocates versus the heave-a-whole-handful-with-your-eyes-closed contingent.

After dinner, we brought out the guitars and sang for hours. Jonathan Wright sang that Kenny Rogers song, 'Don't Fall In Love With A Dreamer.' And so of course I did.

After the party, he came home with me. After we got undressed and climbed into my bed, I said, 'I just want to sleep with you, I don't want to make love,' and he said, 'That's okay, I just want to be close to you tonight.'

In the morning we made love for a long time. In fact, we stayed in bed all day which was something I had never done before.

Jonathan Wright and I loved each other suddenly and, in reality, we were very happy for a while.

REALITY

According to *The Concise Oxford Dictionary of Current English*, reality is *the property of being real*. According to *The Concise Oxford Dictionary of Current English*, real is *actually existing as a thing or occurring in fact, objective, genuine, rightly so called, natural, sincere, not merely apparent or nominal or supposed or pretended or artificial or hypocritical or affected*.

In fiction, we are accustomed to encountering people driven to extremes, people brought to their proverbial knees by love and loss and other such earth-shaking heart-stopping soul-shifting events, people who are thrashing around inside their lives instead of just living them. In reality, these extremes are merely the end points of the continuum. In reality, it is all the points in between, cumulative and connected, if not downright boring, which are the important part. In real life, it is all the points in between which comprise the real life we are really living. In real life, people driven repeatedly to the limit are very hard to take. The friends of such people (if they have any friends left) suspect they are crazy, emotionally disturbed, mentally unbalanced, manic-depressive, but mostly just plain foolish. In reality, people who go from one extreme to the other (and back again) on a regular basis are more fun to read about than to know.

Jonathan Wright and I loved each other suddenly and, in reality, we were very unhappy after a while.

NON-FICTION

On the phone last Sunday morning, Madeline Kane took down my current address and sent me the newspaper clipping and the obituary, which arrived in the mail today. It was unlikely that Jonathan's death would be noted in the newspaper here two thousand miles away. It would be considered local news.

Both these versions of the story are very short and to the point. As if there was a point. As if the truth could really be known.

The newspaper clipping said:

> Jonathan Wright, 38, was shot to death in his apartment on Saturday night. An eyewitness, unidentified for her own protection, told police that when Mr Wright answered a knock at the door at approximately 3 a.m., a lone gunman shot him twice in the head and then fled on foot. Police have neither confirmed nor denied the many rumours surrounding the case. Investigation continues.

The obituary said:

> WRIGHT, **Jonathan Lawrence**—Suddenly at his residence on Sunday, August 5, 1991, Jonathan Lawrence Wright in his 38th year, beloved son

of David and Elizabeth Wright, dear brother of Patricia and Susan, sadly missed by several aunts and uncles. Resting at Goodman Funeral Home. Friends will be received on Wednesday, 7–9 p.m. Funeral Service will be held in the Chapel, Thursday, August 9 at 2 p.m. Interment Landsmere Cemetery.

POETRY

I never expected to see you again / but I never expected you to die either. / I hadn't seen you in so many years: / it was as if you were already dead / or / it was as if you would never die / would just go on living somewhere else / two thousand miles away / while I was still here / going on about my business / never giving you a second thought. / Unless a stranger in the street happened to have / a jacket, a walk, a smile, / or a receding hairline just like yours. / Unless I happened to be cooking your favourite meal / for another lover (pork chops, green beans, mashed/you called them 'smashed' / potatoes) and it turned out he didn't like pork. / Unless I surprised myself / looking through the old photo album / and weeping. / If this were a poem / I would have had a premonition / a cold-sweat shiver down my spine / at the very moment you died. / If this were a poem / I would still be able to see your face / your real face / not your other face, shot to pieces / exploding all over the wall / like the time we were splitting up / I was crying / you were drunk and raging / threw a whole plate of spaghetti across the room / and nobody cleaned it up for a week. / If this were a poem / I would be able to remember everything / including the weight of your body on mine / and how it felt to love you. / If this were a poem / the truth would be known.

FICTION

But the truth of the matter is: this is fiction.

Pure fiction.

Pure: *mere, simple, sheer, not corrupt, morally undefiled, guiltless, sincere, chaste.*

Fiction: *feigning, invention, conventionally accepted falsehood.*

Pure fiction: a convenient literary device which allows me to say that I never knew a man named Jonathan Wright, there was no Christmas party at Madeline Kane's house ten years ago, no Scotch pine, no tinsel, no Kenny Rogers song, no dreamers falling fast into love, and no bad jokes. Which allows me to say that I never cried into your angry arms, there was no spaghetti splattered on the wall, and I never ever missed you.

If the truth were known, this is fiction, a valuable revisionist device which allows me to say there was no man at the door with a gun.

1991

Michael Dougan

Brief Biography

- Born in East Texas in 1954.
- Uses own life and stories of relatives as inspiration for his work.
- Publishes two (mostly) autobiographical collections: *East Texas: Tales from Behind the Pine Curtain* (1988) and *I Can't Tell You Anything* (1993).
- In 2006 hired as staff writer for animated MTV series *The Dangwoods*.
- *The Anthology of Graphic Fiction, Cartoons, and True Stories*, ed. Ivan Brunetti (2006), the first work of its kind, includes 'Black Cherry'; one year later, *Modern Fiction Studies* devotes a special issue to graphic narrative.
- Has special interest in Japanese pop culture; the popularity of graphic fiction is international; Japanese comics (manga) are a multimillion dollar business.

A vital new branch of contemporary literature, graphic fiction comprises not just fiction, but also memoirs, autobiography, and politics. Beneath the surface appeal are unique aesthetics of telling a story through hand drawings. Though sometimes humorous, graphic fiction often deals with mature themes, from personal issues such as isolation and depression to large-scale ones such as political corruption and futuristic visions.

Though satirical, and frequently political, drawings appeared in the sixteenth century, formal comics began in nineteenth-century newspapers. The Sunday supplements became monthly magazine inserts, often reprinted as collections of comic strips. Public demand for new material led to the creation of comic books. During World War II, patriotic superheroes ruled such publications. Youth culture as a post-war phenomenon was paralleled by the rise of cheap comics. Post-war horror, crime, and violent comics led to accusations of youthful corruption. In response, the 1954 Comics Code Authority (CCA) regulated that 'good' must always prevail over 'evil' and wrongdoers be punished. As comic code restrictions loosened, however, alternative comics, or comix—the 'x' suggesting x-rated content—found their way into 1960s counterculture.

Sixties liberalism inspired young adult publications like *Zap* and *East Village Other*, as well as the careers of famous cartoonists like Art Spiegelman (who won a Pulitzer Prize for his holocaust-themed novel *Maus* [1992]) and counterculture icon Robert Crumb. Narrative in the form of comics evolved from indie stores, conventions, 'zines, and weblogs into a subject for academic study, one so new that it still lacks a formal name—is it graphic narrative, graphic fiction, or graphic literature?

The syndicated corporate model of comic books used assembly-line production: each stage (storyboards, stories, pencils, inks) was done by various artists. Sometimes a strong personality emerged—Stan Lee, for example, who published three issues of *The Amazing Spider-Man* (1971) in defiance of the CCA's ban on portraying drug use in comics. But most cartoonists, like Donald Duck illustrator Carl Barks, remained unknown. On the other hand, 'unsuitable' comics were owned by cartoonists and evolved into graphic literature. By 2000, new developments in CGI technology, sound, and home theatres meant superhero 'brand' movies (*Batman*, *X-Men*, and *Spider-man*) competed with films adapted from graphic novels such as Frank Miller's *Sin City* and *300* and Alan Moore's *Watchmen*; likewise, *American Splendor*, *Road to Perdition*, and *A History of Violence* raised public interest.

Michael Dougan is a 'second generation' American cartoonist whose offbeat humour and depiction of outcasts and eccentrics derive from alternative comix. Inspired more by writers and journalists than cartoonists, he has been influenced by the autobiographical monologues of the performer Spalding Gray, non-fiction essayists, and the 'long, quirky monologues' of his southern relatives. Growing up in East Texas, which he describes as 'weird . . . might as well be Poland,' and now a Seattle resident, he admires the 'small-scale portrait-like short stories' of fellow Pacific Northwestener Raymond Carver. Dougan's second collection, *I Can't Tell You Anything* (1993), includes amusing recollections of a summer job as a hearse driver, shooting a car with a rifle for fun, and a threatening encounter with a rooster. Dougan told an interviewer, 'It was fashionable for my generation of cartoonists to experiment with low-key autobiographical narratives in an effort to set ourselves apart from fantasy and superhero comics.'

In 'Black Cherry,' Dougan presents a long-suffering but humane narrator whose observations of dissatisfied, lonely, or lost characters make a dead-end job manageable. Though the reader's eyes are drawn to the story's well-composed frames and gutters featuring strongly drawn caricatures, Dougan, like traditional non-graphic writers, skillfully uses tone, mood, setting, and character to suggest symptoms of malaise in a larger culture and to connect to larger areas of unhappiness or oppression.

BLACK CHERRY

BY MICHAEL DOUGAN

Several years ago I had two jobs — in the mornings I was a janitor at a movie house, cleaning up after the "Rocky Horror Picture Show" audience. I liked it because no one bothered me.

My cleaning partner was Rachel, a Yale graduate who also had two jobs.

Then I would endure my afternoon shift at the ice cream parlor. I hated it.

Hmmm...

For minimum wage I had to be nice to people who could take forever trying to choose which flavor they wanted.

I would look at their glazed expressions, secretly thinking homicidal thoughts, while they made up their minds.

Oh for goodness sake, they all look so delicious!

...and all this to the oppressive sound of elevator jazz.

Then I'd go home, sleep, get up, clean the theatre, and go to the ice cream parlor again.

It seemed to go on forever...

The one thing that made the job interesting was the parade of eccentric, crazy, lonely, and downright mentally ill people that frequented the shop. Some came to hustle free coffee, some just wanted attention, some seemed to have a routine in the neighborhood that ran like clockwork, like the "Black Cherry" man...

The "Black Cherry" man came into the ice cream parlor every day. He would walk up to the counter, look at me with empty grey eyes, and say:

BLACK CHERRY.

He looked completely gone, but here was a man who knew exactly what he wanted. He wanted a black cherry soda. He gave me exact change, sat in the same chair and looked out the same window at the same time every single day...

NOT EVERY NUTCASE WAS BONAFIDE CRAZY. SOME WERE JUST LONELY. ONE WOMAN WHOSE NAME I NEVER KNEW, CAME UP IN A LIMO AND DRANK TWO DOUBLE CAPPUCINOS ON HER WAY TO DANCE CLASS. SHE WAS YOUNG AND VERY BEAUTIFUL, MARRIED TO A WEALTHY MAN MUCH OLDER THAN SHE.

DO YOU LIKE MY HAIRCUT?

HER HUSBAND HAD SOME KIND OF ILLNESS, HE WAS AN INVALID. SHE HAD ALL THIS SEX APPEAL, WITH NO PLACE TO GO, AND SEEMED TO THRIVE ON FLATTERY. SHE'D FLIRT AND BUZZ, DRINKING THESE DOUBLES WHILE HER DRIVER WAITED. THEN SHE'D BE GONE.

THEN THE BLACK CHERRY WOULD COME IN - HIS ROUTINE WAS PERFECTLY PREDICTABLE.

BLACK CHERRY.

I'LL NEVER FORGET THE LAST TIME I SERVED THE BLACK CHERRY MAN. I WAS LATE TO WORK AND KIND OF TESTY, BUT NO MORE THAN USUAL. BLACK CHERRY CAME IN.

BLACK CHERRY

I MADE HIS BLACK CHERRY SODA.

HE NEVER SAID "A CHERRY SODA PLEASE" OR "I'D LIKE A BLACK CHERRY SODA." IT WAS ALWAYS "BLACK CHERRY." IT BUGGED ME.

YOU SURE ARE PREDICTABLE...

?

EVERY DAY YOU COME IN HERE AND ORDER THE SAME THING.

HE JUST LOOKED OUT THE WINDOW. I TURNED AROUND AND CLEANED THE MILKSHAKE MACHINE, THINKING ABOUT HOW MUCH I HATED MY JOB.

WHEN I TURNED AROUND AGAIN, HE WAS CRYING... HIS MOUTH WAS OPEN, TEARS WERE FLOWING, AND HE WASN'T MAKING A SOUND.

I NEVER SERVED THE BLACK CHERRY AGAIN. HE DIDN'T COME IN, BUT HE WALKED UP TO THE WINDOW EVERY DAY AT EXACTLY THE SAME TIME AND LOOKED AT ME WITH THOSE EMPTY GREY EYES...
I QUIT MY JOB A FEW WEEKS LATER TO START WORKING AT A COFFEE STORE DOWN THE STREET.

Shani Mootoo

Brief Biography

- Of Indian descent; born in Dublin in 1958.
- At three months is sent to live in Trinidad.
- Moves to Canada at age nineteen; earns MFA from University of Western Ontario in 1980 and begins successful career as multi-media visual artist; exhibits internationally, including at New York's Museum of Modern Art.
- In 1993 publishes short fiction collection, *Out on Main Street*.
- First novel, *Cereus Blooms at Night* (1996), is written after three visits to a prison for sex offenders; is finalist for Giller Prize.
- Cousin of Canadian writer Neil Bissoondath and distant relative of Nobel laureate Sir V.S. Naipaul.

Shani Mootoo grew up in the West Indies and was raised primarily by her grandmother, a third-generation Trinidadian of Indian descent. She moved to Canada when she was nineteen, living in London, Vancouver, and Edmonton, where she served as writer-in-residence at the University of Alberta.

Mootoo began her artistic career as a painter and videomaker. A survivor of sexual abuse, she often incorporated elements of abuse in her paintings. Mootoo says that therapy taught her to confront her repressed feelings and to express them through language, an act strongly discouraged within her family, where she was silenced for speaking the truth and told to behave like a well-brought-up Indian girl. Although Mootoo slowly gained the confidence to put her experiences into words, she was reluctant to publish her writing until a fellow artist showed Mootoo's journal to a Vancouver publisher that specialized in gay and lesbian writing. Encouraged, Mootoo wrote the stories in *Out on Main Street*. Her characters, settings, and situations often mirror those in her own life.

As noted by Angela Carter and Barbara Gowdy, women's bodies are often 'a site of protest' that inevitably raise larger questions about the nature of identity and authenticity. Contemporary critics often study Mootoo's fiction in relation to the conflux or confusion of identities—ethnic, racial, and gendered. In her novels *Cereus Blooms at Night* (1996), *He Drown She In the Sea* (2005), and *Valmiki's Daughter* (2008), Mootoo puts forward the concept of an 'imagined community,' a challenge to the reader's understanding and acceptance. In an interview in the *Journal of Lesbian Studies*, she describes this world: 'The stories I write are not agenda-driven, but I have found that I am most passionate about a story line when it is an appeal to the larger world for acceptance for me and for people like myself—as we are, not as the larger world would like us to be.'

Unlike Bharati Mukherjee, another writer of the East Asian diaspora, Mootoo has found her adopted country hospitable to the immigrant experience, a place where her identity doesn't depend on ancestry and social expectations. She considers herself a Canadian writer—not an 'Indo-Trinidadian-Irish-Canadian-lesbian writer.' British critic Donna McCormack uses the term 'queer post-colonial' to describe Mootoo's hopeful, perhaps utopian, relationships among characters. As class, race, gender, and origin interact, such 'spaces of transformation' have the political potential to empower individuals as part of a greater and more tolerant community.

'Out on Main Street' relates the experience of the narrator, an Indo-Trinidadian 'butch' lesbian, and her 'femme' girlfriend at a Punjabi restaurant on Vancouver's Main Street. The story, told in the exotic cadences of Trinidadian English, is fraught with the tensions and insecurities of the narrator who is, on the one hand, judged for not knowing the authentic Indian names of the sweets and, on the other, looked down upon for expressing her true sexuality. Yet in the 'imagined community' of Main Street, the narrator's amused detachment allows her to prevail over intolerance, while the story quietly suggests that the myth of the West is more than heterosexual and masculine.

See Maya Khankoje, from 'To Bend but not to Bow,' p. 458.

Out on Main Street

1.

Janet and me? We does go Main Street to see pretty pretty sari and bangle, and to eat we belly full a burfi and gulub jamoon, but we doh go too often because, yuh see, is dem sweets self what does give people like we a presupposition for untameable hip and thigh.

Another reason we shy to frequent dere is dat we is watered-down Indians—we ain't good grade A Indians. We skin brown, is true, but we doh even think 'bout India unless something happen over dere and it come on de news. Mih family remain Hindu ever since mih ancestors leave India behind, but nowadays dey doh believe in praying unless things real bad, because, as mih father always singing, like if is a mantra: 'Do good and good will be bestowed unto you.' So he is a veritable saint cause he always doing good by his women friends and dey chilren. I sure some a dem must be mih half sister and brother, oui!

Mostly, back home, we is kitchen Indians: some kind a Indian food every day, at least once a day, but we doh get cardamom and other fancy spice down dere so de food not spicy like Indian food I eat in restaurants up here. But it have one thing we doh make joke 'bout down dere: we like we meethai and sweetrice too much, and it remain overly authentic, like de day Naana and Naani step off de boat in Port of Spain harbour over a hundred and sixty years ago. Check out dese hips here nah, dey is pure sugar and condensed milk, pure sweetness!

But Janet family different. In de ole days when Canadian missionaries land in Trinidad dey used to make a bee-line straight for Indians from down South.

And Janet great grandparents is one a de first South families dat exchange over from Indian to Presbyterian. Dat was a long time ago.

When Janet born, she father, one Mr John Mahase, insist on asking de Reverend MacDougal from Trace Settlement Church, a leftover from de Canadian Mission, to name de baby girl. De good Reverend choose de name Constance cause dat was his mother name. But de mother a de child, Mrs Savitri Mahase, wanted to name de child sheself. Ever since Savitri was a lil girl she like de yellow hair, fair skin and pretty pretty clothes Janet and John used to wear in de primary school reader—since she lil she want to change she name from Savitri to Janet but she own father get vex and say how Savitri was his mother name and how she will insult his mother if she gone and change it. So Savitri get she own way once by marrying this fella name John, and she do a encore, by calling she daughter Janet, even doh husband John upset for days at she for insulting de good Reverend by throwing out de name a de Reverend mother.

So dat is how my girlfriend, a darkskin Indian girl with thick black hair (pretty fuh so!) get a name like Janet.

She come from a long line a Presbyterian school teacher, headmaster and headmistress. Savitri still teaching from de same Janet and John reader in a primary school in San Fernando, and John, getting more and more obtuse in his ole age, is headmaster more dan twenty years now in Princes Town Boys' Presbyterian High School. Everybody back home know dat family good good. Dat is why Janet leave in two twos. Soon as A Level finish she pack up and take off like a jet plane so she could live without people only shoo-shooing behind she back ... 'But A A! Yuh ain't hear de goods 'bout John Mahase daughter, gyul? How yuh mean yuh ain't hear? Is a big thing! Everybody talking 'bout she. Hear dis, nah! Yuh ever see she wear a dress? Yes! Doh look at mih so. Yuh reading mih right!'

Is only recentish I realize Mahase is a Hindu last name. In de ole days every Mahase in de country turn Presbyterian and now de name doh have no association with Hindu or Indian whatsoever. I used to think of it as a Presbyterian Church name until some days ago when we meet a Hindu fella fresh from India name Yogdesh Mahase who never even hear of Presbyterian.

De other day I ask Janet what she know 'bout Divali. She say, 'It's the Hindu festival of lights, isn't it?' like a line straight out a dictionary. Yuh think she know anything 'bout how lord Rama get himself exile in a forest for fourteen years, and how when it come time for him to go back home his followers light up a pathway to help him make his way out, and dat is what Divali lights is all about? All Janet know is 'bout going for drive in de country to see light, and she could remember looking forward, around Divali time, to the lil brown paper-bag packages full a burfi and parasad that she father Hindu students used to bring for him.

One time in a Indian restaurant she ask for parasad for dessert. Well! Since den I never go back in dat restaurant, I embarrass fuh so!

I used to think I was a Hindu *par excellence* until I come up here and see real flesh and blood Indian from India. Up here, I learning 'bout all kind a custom and food and music and clothes dat we never see or hear 'bout in good ole Trinidad. Is de next best thing to going to India, in truth, oui! But Indian store clerk on Main Street doh have no patience with us, specially when we talking English to dem. Yuh ask dem a question in English and dey insist on giving de answer in Hindi or Punjabi or Urdu or Gujarati. How I suppose to know de difference even! And den dey look at yuh disdainful disdainful—like yuh disloyal, like yuh is a traitor.

But yuh know, it have one other reason I real reluctant to go Main Street. Yuh see, Janet pretty fuh so! And I doh like de way men does look at she, as if because she wearing jeans and T-shirt and high-heel shoe and make-up and have long hair loose and flying about like she is a walking-talking shampoo ad, dat she easy. And de women always looking at she beady eye, like she loose and going to thief dey man. Dat kind a thing always make me want to put mih arm round she waist like, she is my woman, take yuh eyes off she! and shock de false teeth right out dey mouth. And den is a whole other story when dey see me with mih crew cut and mih blue jeans tuck inside mih jim-boots. Walking next to Janet, who so femme dat she redundant, tend to make me look like a gender dey forget to classify. Before going Main Street I does parade in front de mirror practicing a jiggly-wiggly kind a walk. But if I ain't walking like a strong-man monkey I doh exactly feel right and I always revert back to mih true colours. De men dem does look at me like if dey is exactly what I need a taste of to cure me good and proper. I could see dey eyes watching Janet and me, dey face growing dark as dey imagining all kind a situation and position. And de women dem embarrass fuh so to watch me in mih eye, like dey fraid I will jump up and try to kiss dem, or make pass at dem. Yuh know, sometimes I wonder if I ain't mad enough to do it just for a little bacchanal, nah!

Going for a outing with mih Janet on Main Street ain't easy! If only it wasn't for burfi and gulub jamoon! If only I had a learned how to cook dem kind a thing before I leave home and come up here to live!

2.

In large deep-orange Sanskrit-style letters, de sign on de saffron-colour awning above de door read 'Kush Valley Sweets.' Underneath in smaller red letters it had 'Desserts Fit For The Gods.' It was a corner building. The front and side was one big glass wall. Inside was big. Big like a gymnasium. Yuh could see in through de brown tint windows: dark brown plastic chair, and brown table, each one de length of a door, line up stiff and straight in row after row like if is a school room.

Before entering de restaurant I ask Janet to wait one minute outside with me while I rumfle up mih memory, pulling out all de sweet names I know from home, besides burfi and gulub jamoon: meethai, jilebi, sweetrice (but dey call dat kheer up here), and ladhoo. By now, of course, mih mouth watering fuh so! When I feel confident enough dat I wouldn't make a fool a mih Brown self by asking what dis one name? and what dat one name? we went in de restaurant. In two twos all de spice in de place take a flying leap in our direction and give us one big welcome hug up, tight fuh so! Since den dey take up permanent residence in de jacket I wear dat day!

Mostly it had women customers sitting at de tables, chatting and laughing, eating sweets and sipping masala tea. De only men in de place was de waiters, and all six waiters was men. I figure dat dey was brothers, not too hard to conclude, because all a dem had de same full round chin, round as if de chin stretch tight over a ping-pong ball, and dey had de same big roving eyes. I know better dan to think dey was mere waiters in de employ of a owner who chook up in a office in de back. I sure dat dat was dey own family business, dey stomach proudly preceeding dem and dey shoulders throw back in de confidence of dey ownership.

It ain't dat I paranoid, yuh understand, but from de moment we enter de fellas dem get over-animated, even armorously agitated. Janet again! All six pair a eyes land up on she, following she every move and body part. Dat in itself is something dat does madden me, oui! but also a kind a irrational envy have a tendency to manifest in me. It was like I didn't exist. Sometimes it could be a real problem going out with a good-looker, yes! While I ain't remotely interested in having a squeak of a flirtation with a man, it doh hurt a ego to have a man notice yuh once in a very long while. But with Janet at mih side, I doh have de chance of a penny shave-ice in de hot sun. I tuck mih elbows in as close to mih sides as I could so I wouldn't look like a strong man next to she, and over to de l-o-n-g glass case jam up with sweets I jiggle and wiggle in mih best imitation a some a dem gay fellas dat I see downtown Vancouver, de ones who more femme dan even Janet. I tell she not to pay de brothers no attention, because if any a dem flirt with she I could start a fight right dere and den. And I didn't feel to mess up mih crew cut in a fight.

De case had sweets in every nuance of colour in a rainbow. Sweets I never before see and doh know de names of. But dat was alright because I wasn't going to order dose ones anyway.

Since before we leave home Janet have she mind set on a nice thick syrupy curl a jilebi and a piece a plain burfi so I order dose for she and den I ask de waiter-fella, resplendent with thick thick bright-yellow gold chain and ID bracelet, for a stick a meethai for mihself. I stand up waiting by de glass case for it but de waiter/owner lean up on de back wall behind de counter watching me like he ain't hear me. So I say loud enough for him, and every body else in de room to hear, 'I would like to have one piece a meethai please,' and den he smile and lift up his hands, palms open-out motioning across de vast expanse a glass case, and he say, 'Your choice! Whichever you want, Miss.' But he still lean up against de back wall grinning. So I stick mih head out and up like a turtle and say louder, and slowly, 'One piece a meethai—dis one!' and I point sharp to de stick a flour mix with ghee, deep fry and den roll up in sugar. He say, 'That is koorma, Miss. One piece only?'

Mih voice drop low all by itself. 'Oh ho! Yes, one piece. Where I come from we does call dat meethai.' And den I add, but only loud enough for Janet to hear, 'And mih name ain't "Miss."'

He open his palms out and indicate de entire panorama a sweets and he say, 'These are all meethai, Miss. Meethai is Sweets. Where are you from?'

I ignore his question and to show him I undaunted, I point to a round pink ball and say, 'I'll have one a dese sugarcakes too please.' He start grinning broad broad like if he half-pitying, half-laughing at dis Indian-in-skin-colour-only, and den he tell me, 'That is called chum-chum, Miss.' I snap back at him, 'Yeh, well back home we does call dat sugarcake, Mr Chum-chum.'

At de table Janet say, 'You know, Pud (Pud, short for Pudding; is dat she does call me when she feeling close to me, or sorry for me), it's true that we call that "meethai" back home. Just like how we call "siu mai" "tim sam." As if "dim sum" is just one little piece a food. What did he call that sweet again?'

'Cultural bastards, Janet, cultural bastards. Dat is what we is. Yuh know, one time a fella from India who living up here call me a bastardized Indian because I didn't know Hindi. And now look at dis, nah! De thing is: all a we in Trinidad is cultural bastards, Janet, all a we. *Toutes bagailles*! Chinese people, Black people, White people. Syrian. Lebanese. I looking forward to de day I find out dat place inside me where I am nothing else but Trinidadian, whatever dat could turn out to be.'

I take a bite a de chum-chum, de texture was like grind-up coconut but it had no coconut, not even a hint a coconut taste in it. De thing was juicy with sweet rose water oozing out a it. De rose water perfume enter mih nose and get trap in mih cranium. Ah drink two cup a masala tea and a lassi and still de rose water perfume was on mih tongue like if I had a overdosed on Butchart Gardens.

Suddenly de door a de restaurant spring open wide with a strong force and two big burly fellas stumble in, almost rolling over on to de ground. Dey get up, eyes red and slow and dey skin burning pink with booze. Dey straighten up so much to overcompensate for falling forward, dat dey find deyself leaning backward. Everybody stop talking and was watching dem. De guy in front put his hand up to his forehead and take a deep Walter Raleigh bow, bringing de hand down to his waist in a rolling circular movement. Out loud he greet everybody with 'Alarm o salay koom.' A part a me wanted to bust out laughing. Another part make mih jaw drop open in disbelief. De calm in de place get rumfle up. De two fellas dem, feeling chupid now because nobody reply to dey greeting, gone up to de counter to Chum-chum trying to make a little conversation with him. De same booze-pink alarm-o-salay-koom-fella say to Chum-chum, 'Hey, howaryah?'

Chum-Chum give a lil nod and de fella carry right on, 'Are you Sikh?'

Chum-chum brothers converge near de counter, busying deyselves in de vicinity. Chum-chum look at his brothers kind a quizzical, and he touch his cheek and feel his forehead with de back a his palm. He say, 'No, I think I am fine, thank you. But I am sorry if I look sick, Sir.'

De burly fella confuse now, so he try again.

'Where are you from?'

Chum-chum say, 'Fiji, Sir.'

'Oh! Fiji, eh! Lotsa palm trees and beautiful women, eh! Is it true that you guys can have more than one wife?'

De exchange make mih blood rise up in a boiling froth. De restaurant suddenly get a gruff quietness 'bout it except for a woman I hear whispering angrily to another woman at de table behind us, 'I hate this! I just hate it! I can't stand to see our men humiliated by them, right in front of us. He should refuse to serve them, he should throw them out. Who on earth do they think they are? The awful fools!' And de friend whisper back, 'If he throws them out all of us will suffer in the long run.'

I could discern de hair on de back a de neck a Chum-chum brothers standing up, annoyed, and at de same time de brothers look like dey was shrinking in stature. Chum-chum get serious, and he politely say, 'What can I get for you?'

Pinko get de message and he point to a few items in de case and say, 'One of each, to go please.'

Holding de white take-out box in one hand he extend de other to Chum-chum and say, 'How do you say "Excuse me, I'm sorry" in Fiji?'

Chum-chum shake his head and say, 'It's okay. Have a good day.'

Pinko insist, 'No, tell me please. I think I just behaved badly, and I want to apologize. How do you say "I'm sorry" in Fiji?'

Chum-chum say, 'Your apology is accepted. Everything is okay.' And he discreetly turn away to serve a person who had just entered de restaurant. De fellas take de hint dat was broad like daylight, and back out de restaurant like two little mouse.

Everybody was feeling sorry for Chum-chum and Brothers. One a dem come up to de table across from us to take a order from a woman with a giraffe-long neck who say, 'Brother, we mustn't accept how these people think they can treat us. You men really put up with too many insults and abuse over here. I really felt for you.'

Another woman gone up to de counter to converse with Chum-chum in she language. She reach out and touch his hand, sympathy-like. Chum-chum hold the one hand in his two and make a verbose speech to her as she nod she head in agreement generously. To italicize her support, she buy a take-out box a two burfi, or rather, dat's what I think dey was.

De door a de restaurant open again, and a bevy of Indian-looking women saunter in, dress up to weaken a person's decorum. De Miss Universe pageant traipse across de room to a table. Chum-chum and Brothers start smoothing dey hair back, and pushing de front a dey shirts neatly into dey pants. One brother take out a pack a Dentyne from his shirt pocket and pop one in his mouth. One take out a comb from his back pocket and smooth down his hair. All a dem den converge on dat single table to take orders. Dey begin to behave like young pups in mating season. Only, de women dem wasn't impress by all this tra-la-la at all and ignore dem except to make dey order, straight to de point. Well, it look like Brothers' egos were having a rough day and dey start roving 'bout de room, dey egos and de crotch a dey pants leading far in front dem. One brother gone over to Giraffebai to see if she want anything more. He call she 'dear' and put his hand on she back. Giraffebai straighten she back in surprise and reply in a not-too-friendly way. When he gone to write up de bill she see me looking at she and she say to me, 'Whoever does he think he is! Calling me dear and touching me like that! Why do these men always think that they have permission to touch whatever and wherever they want! And you can't make a fuss about it in public, because it is exactly what those people out there want to hear about so that they can say how sexist and uncivilized our culture is.'

I shake mih head in understanding and say, 'Yeah. I know. Yuh right!'

De atmosphere in de room take a hairpin turn, and it was man aggressing on woman, woman warding off a herd a man who just had dey pride publicly cut up a couple a times in just a few minutes.

One brother walk over to Janet and me and he stand up facing me with his hands clasp in front a his crotch, like if he protecting it. Stiff stiff, looking at me, he say, 'Will that be all?'

Mih crew cut start to tingle, so I put on mih femmest smile and say, 'Yes, that's it, thank you. Just the bill please.' De smartass turn to face Janet and he remove his hands from in front a his crotch and slip his thumbs inside his pants like a cowboy 'bout to do a square dance. He smile, looking down at her attentive fuh so, and he say, 'Can I do anything for you?'

I didn't give Janet time fuh his intent to even register before I bulldoze in mih most un-femmest manner, 'She have everything she need, man, thank you. The bill please.' Yuh think he hear me? It was like I was talking to thin air. He remain smiling at Janet, but she, looking at me, not at him, say, 'You heard her. The bill please.'

Before he could even leave de table proper, I start mih tirade. 'But A A! Yuh see dat? Yuh could believe dat! De effing so-and-so! One minute yuh feel sorry fuh dem and next minute dey harassing de heck out a you. Janet, he crazy to mess with my woman, yes!' Janet get vex with me and say I overreacting, and is not fuh me to be vex, but fuh she to be vex. Is she he insult, and she could take good enough care a sheself.

I tell she I don't know why she don't cut off all dat long hair, and stop wearing lipstick and eyeliner. Well, who tell me to say dat! She get real vex and say dat nobody will tell she how to dress and how not to dress, not me and not any man. Well I could see de potential dat dis fight had coming, and when Janet get fighting vex, watch out! It hard to get a word in edgewise, yes! And she does bring up incidents from years back dat have no bearing on de current situation. So I draw back quick quick but she don't waste time; she was already off to a good start. It was best to leave right dere and den.

Just when I stand up to leave, de doors dem open up and in walk Sandy and Lise, coming for dey weekly hit a Indian sweets. Well, with Sandy and Lise is a dead giveaway dat dey not dressing fuh any man, it have no place in dey life fuh man-vibes, and dat in fact dey have a blatant penchant fuh women. Soon as dey enter de room yuh could see de brothers and de couple men customers dat had come in minutes before stare dem down from head to Birkenstocks, dey eyes bulging with disgust. And de women in de room start shoo-shooing, and putting dey hand in front dey mouth to stop dey surprise, and false teeth, too, from falling out. Sandy and Lise spot us instantly and dey call out to us, shameless, loud, and affectionate. Dey leap over to us, eager to hug up and kiss like if dey hadn't seen us for years, but it was really only since two nights aback when we went out to dey favourite Indian restaurant for dinner. I figure dat de display was a genuine happiness to be seen wit us in dat place. While we stand up dere chatting, Sandy insist on rubbing she hand up and down Janet back—wit friendly intent, mind you, and same time Lise have she arm round Sandy waist. Well, all cover get blown. If it was even remotely possible dat I wasn't noticeable before, now Janet and I were over-exposed. We could a easily suffer from hypothermia, specially since it suddenly get cold cold in dere. We say goodbye, not soon enough, and as we were leaving I turn to acknowledge Giraffebai, but instead a any recognition of our buddiness against de fresh brothers, I get a face dat look like it was in de presence of a very foul smell.

De good thing, doh, is dat Janet had become so incensed 'bout how we get scorned, dat she forgot I tell she to cut she hair and to ease up on de make-up, and so I get save from hearing 'bout how I too jealous, and how much I inhibit she, and how she would prefer if I would grow *my* hair, and wear lipstick and put on a dress sometimes. I so glad, oui! dat I didn't have to go through hearing how I too demanding a she, like de time, she say, I prevent she from seeing a ole boyfriend when he was in town for a couple hours *en route* to live in Australia with his new bride (because, she say, I was jealous dat ten years ago dey sleep together.) Well, look at mih crosses, nah! Like if I really so possessive and jealous!

So tell me, what yuh think 'bout dis nah, girl?

1993

Edwidge Danticat

Brief Biography

- Born in Port-au-Prince, Haiti, in 1969.
- Parents immigrate to the United States; Danticat is raised in Haiti by her aunt and uncle.
- Grows up speaking Creole and French; learns English when she reunites with her parents in New York City when she is twelve years old.
- At age twenty-five, publishes autobiographical novel *Breath, Eyes, Memory*, which becomes an Oprah Book Club best-seller.
- Follows with *Krik? Krak!* (1995) and two novels, *Farming of Bones* (1998) and *Dew Breaker* (2004).
- Associate producer of Jonathan Demme documentary about Haitian torture survivors, *Courage and Pain* (1996).
- Memoir, *Brother, I'm Dying* (2007), which won the National Book Critics Circle Award, describes her eighty-one-year-old uncle's death in the custody of the US Department of Homeland Security.

The fiction of Edwidge Danticat evokes the struggle for personal and collective autonomy amid political oppression. Between the 1970s and 1990s, tens of thousands of Haitians left their homeland for political reasons, fleeing to the United States and Canada (many settled in Quebec, site of the third-largest Haitian diaspora). Danticat's father left Haiti in 1971 during the dictatorship of François Duvalier ('Papa-Doc'); her mother followed two years later. Danticat remained in Haiti and was raised by her aunt and uncle. When she was twelve, she joined her parents in New York City.

Isolated in an alien culture and embarrassed by her heavily accented English, Danticat sought solace in books and writing. After earning a BA in French literature, she felt pressured to secure a well-paying job. Accepted to New York University's Wagner Graduate School of Public Service, she planned to specialize in international affairs; however, she enrolled instead in Brown University's Creative Writing program. Her MFA thesis became her first novel, *Breath, Eyes, Memory* (1994), a semi-autobiographical account of a girl raised in Haiti who reunites with her parents in the United States.

Danticat typifies the ambivalence of the immigrant experience: the dual need to redefine oneself in light of mainstream values yet remain connected to the memory of the homeland, what she calls the 'bridge' enabling immigrants to rebuild their lives: 'So the writing comes out of that experience. Of having plantains with my thanksgiving turkey and dancing konpa in Manhattan,' she said in an interview in *Transition*. Despite devastation and loss, her characters are testaments to human perseverance: love is forged or reaffirmed from seemingly unbreakable bonds of suffering. Relationships between mothers and their daughters figure prominently in several stories from *Krik? Krak!*, her short story collection. In one story, a mother dies after a prison beating, and her daughter recalls their visits to Massacre River where thousands of Haitian sugar cane workers were slaughtered in 1937. Another features an Americanized daughter who discovers her immigrant mother's secret life after following her in New York City. In the epilogue to the nine stories, 'Women Like Us,' the narrator ponders, while braiding her hair, the long lineage of mothers and daughters, linking it to the act of writing: '[a] thousand women urging you to speak through the blunt tip of your pencil.'

Danticat's oral storytelling roots are evident in the title of *Krik? Krak!*. In the ritualistic Haitian formula, 'Krik?' is the question the storyteller asks of an audience; the reply 'Krak!' shows the listener's eagerness to hear an anecdote or humorous tale. However, the stories in *Krik? Krak!* are neither anecdotal nor humorous. Interviewed by *The Journal of Caribbean Literatures*, Danticat said she is drawn to 'stories that haunt me, want to make me cry … to painful situations, things that make me sad. I write them until I feel a little better about them.' 'Children of the Sea', one of the stories from this collection, is both haunting and painful. It depicts, in epistolary form, star-crossed lovers in their attempt to escape the brutalities of the *Tonton Macoutes*, Haiti's notorious secret police.

Children of the Sea

They say behind the mountains are more mountains. Now I know it's true. I also know there are timeless waters, endless seas, and lots of people in this world whose names don't matter to anyone but themselves. I look up at the sky and I see you there. I see you crying like a crushed snail, the way you cried when I helped you pull out your first loose tooth. Yes, I did love you then. Somehow when I looked at you, I thought of fiery red ants. I wanted you to dig your fingernails into my skin and drain out all my blood.

I don't know how long we'll be at sea. There are thirty-six other deserting souls on this little boat with me. White sheets with bright red spots float as our sail.

When I got on board I thought I could still smell the semen and the innocence lost to those sheets. I look up there and I think of you and all those times you resisted. Sometimes I felt like you wanted to, but I knew you wanted me to respect you. You thought I was testing your will, but all I wanted was to be near you. Maybe it's like you've always said. I imagine too much. I am afraid I am going to start having nightmares once we get deep at sea. I really hate having the sun in my face all day long. If you see me again, I'll be so dark.

Your father will probably marry you off now, since I am gone. Whatever you do, please don't marry a soldier. They're almost not human.

haiti est comme tu l'as laissé. yes, just the way you left it. bullets day and night. same hole. same everything. i'm tired of the whole mess. i get so cross and

irritable. i pass the time by chasing roaches around the house. i pound my heel on their heads. they make me so mad. everything makes me mad. i am cramped inside all day. they've closed the schools since the army took over. no one is mentioning the old president's name. papa burnt all his campaign posters and old buttons. manman buried her buttons in a hole behind the house. she thinks he might come back. she says she will unearth them when he does. no one comes out of their house. not a single person. papa wants me to throw out those tapes of your radio shows. i destroyed some music tapes, but i still have your voice. i thank god you got out when you did. all the other youth federation members have disappeared. no one has heard from them. i think they might all be in prison. maybe they're all dead. papa worries a little about you. he doesn't hate you as much as you think. the other day i heard him asking manman, do you think the boy is dead? manman said she didn't know. i think he regrets being so mean to you. i don't sketch my butterflies anymore because i don't even like seeing the sun. besides, manman says that butterflies can bring news. the bright ones bring happy news and the black ones warn us of deaths. we have our whole lives ahead of us. you used to say that, remember? but then again things were so very different then.

There is a pregnant girl on board. She looks like she might be our age. Nineteen or twenty. Her face is covered with scars that look like razor marks. She is short and speaks in a singsong that reminds me of the villagers in the north. Most of the other people on the boat are much older than I am. I have heard that a lot of these boats have young children on board. I am glad this one does not. I think it would break my heart watching some little boy or girl every single day on this sea, looking into their empty faces to remind me of the hopelessness of the future in our country. It's hard enough with the adults. It's hard enough with me.

I used to read a lot about America before I had to study so much for the university exams. I am trying to think, to see if I read anything more about Miami. It is sunny. It doesn't snow there like it does in other parts of America. I can't tell exactly how far we are from there. We might be barely out of our own shores. There are no borderlines on the sea. The whole thing looks like one. I cannot even tell if we are about to drop off the face of the earth. Maybe the world is flat and we are going to find out, like the navigators of old. As you know, I am not very religious. Still I pray every night that we won't hit a storm. When I do manage to sleep, I dream that we are caught in one hurricane after another. I dream that the winds come of the sky and claim us for the sea. We go under and no one hears from us again.

I am more comfortable now with the idea of dying. Not that I have completely accepted it, but I know that it might happen. Don't be mistaken. I really do not want to be a martyr. I know I am no good to anybody dead, but if that is what's coming, I know I cannot just scream at it and tell it to go away.

I hope another group of young people can do the radio show. For a long time that radio show was my whole life. It was nice to have radio like that for a while, where we could talk about what we wanted from government, what we wanted for the future of our country.

There are a lot of Protestants on this boat. A lot of them see themselves as Job or the Children of Israel. I think some of them are hoping something will plunge down from the sky and part the sea for us. They say the Lord gives and the Lord takes away. I have never been given very much. What was there to take away?

if only i could kill. if i knew some good wanga magic, i would wipe them off the face of the earth. a group of students got shot in front of fort dimanche prison today. they were demonstrating for the bodies of the radio six. that is what they are calling you all. the radio six. you have a name. you have a reputation. a lot of people think you are dead like the others. they want the bodies turned over to the families. this afternoon, the army finally did give some bodies back. they told the families to go collect them at the rooms for indigents at the morgue. our neighbor madan roger came home with her son's head and not much else. honest to god, it was just his head. at the morgue, they say a car ran over him and took the head off his body. when madan roger went to the morgue, they gave her the head. by the time we saw her, she had been carrying the head all over port-au-prince. just to show what's been done to her son. the macoutes by the house were laughing at her. they asked her if that was her dinner. it took ten people to hold her back from jumping on them. they would have killed her, the dogs. i will never go outside again. not even in the yard to breathe the air. they are always watching you, like vultures. at night i can't sleep. i count the bullets in the dark. i keep wondering if it is true. did you really get out? i wish there was some way i could be sure that you really went away. yes, i will. i will keep writing like we promised to do. i hate it, but i will keep writing. you keep writing too, okay? and when we see each other again, it will seem like we lost no time.

Today was our first real day at sea. Everyone was vomiting with each small rocking of the boat. The faces around me are showing their first charcoal layer of sunburn. 'Now we will never be mistaken for Cubans,' one man said. Even though some of the Cubans are black too. The man said he was once on a boat with a group of Cubans. His boat had stopped to pick up the Cubans on an island off the Bahamas. When the Coast Guard came for them, they took the Cubans to Miami and sent him back to Haiti. Now he was back on the boat with some papers and documents to show that the police in Haiti were after him. He had a broken leg too, in case there was any doubt.

One old lady fainted from sunstroke. I helped revive her by rubbing some of the salt water on her lips. During the day it can be so hot. At night, it is so cold.

Since there are no mirrors, we look at each others faces to see just how frail and sick we are starting to look.

Some of the women sing and tell stories to each other to appease the vomiting. Still, I watch the sea. At night, the sky and the sea are one. The stars look so huge and so close. They make for very bright reflections in the sea. At times I feel like I can just reach out and pull a star down from the sky as though it is a breadfruit or a calabash or something that could be of use to us on this journey.

When we sing, *Beloved Haiti, there is no place like you. I had to leave you before I could understand you,* some of the women start crying. At times, I just want to stop in the middle of the song and cry myself. To hide my tears, I pretend like I am getting another attack of nausea, from the sea smell. I no longer join in the singing.

You probably do not know much about this, because you have always been so closely watched by your father in that well-guarded house with your genteel mother. No, I am not making fun of you for this. If anything, I am jealous. If I was a girl, maybe I would have been at home and not out politicking and getting myself into something like this. Once you have been at sea for a couple of days, it smells like every fish you have ever eaten, every crab you have ever caught, every jellyfish that has ever bitten your leg. I am so tired of the smell. I am also tired of the way the people on this boat are starting to stink. The pregnant girl, Célianne, I don't know how she takes it. She stares into space all the time and rubs her stomach.

I have never seen her eat. Sometimes the other women offer her a piece of bread and she takes it, but she has no food of her own. I cannot help feeling like she will have this child as soon as she gets hungry enough.

She woke up screaming the other night. I thought she had a stomach ache. Some water started coming into the boat in the spot where she was sleeping. There is a crack at the bottom of the boat that looks as though, if it gets any bigger, it will split the boat in two. The captain cleared us aside and used some tar to clog up the hole. Everyone started asking him if it was okay, if they were going to be okay. He said he hoped the Coast Guard would find us soon.

You can't really go to sleep after that. So we all stared at the tar by the moonlight. We did this until dawn. I cannot help but wonder how long this tar will hold out.

papa found your tapes. he started yelling at me, asking if I was crazy keeping them. he is just waiting for the gasoline ban to be lifted so we can get out of the city. he is always pestering me these days because he cannot go out driving his van. all the american factories are closed. he kept yelling at me about the tapes. he called me selfish, and he asked if i hadn't seen or heard what was happening to man-crazy whores like me. i shouted that i wasn't a whore. he had no business calling me that. he pushed me against the wall for

disrespecting him. he spat in my face. i wish those macoutes would kill him. i wish he would catch a bullet so we could see how scared he really is. he said to me, i didn't send your stupid trouble maker away. i started yelling at him. yes, you did. yes, you did. yes, you did, you pig peasant. i don't know why i said that. he slapped me and kept slapping me really hard until manman came and grabbed me away from him. i wish one of those bullets would hit me.

The tar is holding up so far. Two days and no more leaks. Yes, I am finally an African. I am even darker than your father. I wanted to buy a straw hat from one of the ladies, but she would not sell it to me for the last two gourdes I have left in change. Do you think your money is worth anything to me here? she asked me. Sometimes, I forget where I am. If I keep daydreaming like I have been doing, I will walk off the boat to go for a stroll.

The other night I dreamt that I died and went to heaven. This heaven was nothing like I expected. It was at the bottom of the sea. There were starfishes and mermaids all around me. The mermaids were dancing and singing in Latin like the priests do at the cathedral during Mass. You were there with me too, at the bottom of the sea. You were with your family, off to the side. Your father was acting like he was better than everyone else and he was standing in front of a sea cave blocking you from my view. I tried to talk to you, but every time I opened my mouth, water bubbles came out. No sounds.

they have this thing now that they do. if they come into a house and there is a son and mother there, they hold a gun to their heads. they make the son sleep with his mother. if it is a daughter and father, they do the same thing. some nights papa sleeps at his brother's, uncle pressoir's house. uncle pressoir sleeps at our house, just in case they come. that way papa will never be forced to lie down in bed with me. instead, uncle pressoir would be forced to, but that would not be so bad. we know a girl who had a child by her father that way. that is what papa does not want to happen, even if he is killed. there is still no gasoline to buy. otherwise we would be in ville rose already. papa has a friend who is going to get him some gasoline from a soldier. as soon as we get the gasoline, we are going to drive quick and fast until we find civilization. that's how papa puts it, civilization. he says things are not as bad in the provinces. i am still not talking to him. i don't think i ever will. manman says it is not his fault. he is trying to protect us. he cannot protect us. only god can protect us. the soldiers can come and do with us what they want. that makes papa feel weak, she says. he gets angry when he feels weak. why should he be angry with me? i am not one of the pigs with the machine guns. she asked me what really happened to you. she said she saw your parents before they left for the provinces. they did not want to tell her anything. i told her you took a boat after they raided the radio station. you escaped and took a boat to heaven knows where. she said, he was going to make a good man, that boy.

sharp, like a needle point, that boy, he took the university exams a year before everyone else in this area. manman has respect for people with ambitions. she said papa did not want you for me because it did not seem as though you were going to do any better for me than he and manman could. he wants me to find a man who will do me some good. someone who will make sure that i have more than i have now. it is not enough for a girl to be just pretty anymore. we are not that well connected in society. the kind of man that papa wants for me would never have anything to do with me. all anyone can hope for is just a tiny bit of love, manman says, like a drop in a cup if you can get it, or a waterfall, a flood, if you can get that too. we do not have all that many high-up connections, she says, but you are an educated girl. what she counts for educated is not much to anyone but us anyway. they should be announcing the university exams on the radio next week. then i will know if you passed. i will listen for your name.

We spent most of yesterday telling stories. Someone says, Krik? You answer, Krak! And they say, I have many stories I could tell you, and then they go on and tell these stories to you, but mostly to themselves. Sometimes it feels like we have been at sea longer than the many years that I have been on this earth. The sun comes up and goes down. That is how you know it has been a whole day. I feel like we are sailing for Africa. Maybe we will go to Guinin, to live with the spirits, to be with everyone who has come and has died before us. They would probably turn us away from there too. Someone has a transistor and sometimes we listen to radio from the Bahamas. They treat Haitians like dogs in the Bahamas, a woman says. To them, we are not human. Even though their music sounds like ours. Their people look like ours. Even though we had the same African fathers who probably crossed these same seas together.

Do you want to know how people go to the bathroom on the boat? Probably the same way they did on those slaves ships years ago. They set aside a little corner for that. When I have to pee, I just pull it, lean over the rail, and do it very quickly. When I have to do the other thing, I rip a piece of something, squat down and do it, and throw the waste in the sea. I am always embarrassed by the smell. It is so demeaning having to squat in front of so many people. People turn away, but not always. At times I wonder if there is really land on the other side of the sea. Maybe the sea is endless. Like my love for you.

last night they came to madan roger's house. papa hurried inside as soon as madan roger's screaming started. the soldiers were looking for her son. madan roger was screaming, you killed him already. we buried his head. you can't kill him twice. they were shouting at her, do you belong to the youth federation with those vagabonds who were on the radio? she was yelling, do i look like a youth to you? can you identify your son's other associates? they asked her. papa had us tiptoe from the house into the latrine out back. we could hear it all from there. i thought i was going to choke on the smell of rotting poupou. they kept shouting at madan roger, did your son belong to the youth federation? wasn't he on the radio talking about the police? did he say, down with tonton macoutes? did he say, down with the army? he said that the military had to go; didn't he write slogans? he had meetings, didn't he? he demonstrated on the streets. you should have advised him better. she cursed on their mothers' graves. she just came out and shouted it, i hope your mothers will never rest in their cursed graves! she was just shouting it out, you killed him once already! you want to kill me too? go ahead. i don't care anymore. i'm dead already. you have already done the worst to me that you can do. you have killed my soul. they kept at it, asking her questions at the top of their voices: was your son a traitor? tell me all the names of his friends who were traitors just like him. madan roger finally shouts, yes, he was one! he belonged to that group. he was on the radio. he was on the streets at these demonstrations. he hated you like i hate you criminals. you killed him. they start to pound at her. you can hear it. you can hear the guns coming down on her head. it sounds like they are cracking all the bones in her body. manman whispers to papa, you can't just let them kill her. go and give them some money like you gave them for your daughter. papa says, the only money i have left is to get us out of here tomorrow. manman whispers, we cannot just stay here and let them kill her. manman starts moving like she is going out the door. papa grabs her neck and pins her to the latrine wall. tomorrow we are going to ville rose, he says. you will not spoil that for the family. you will not put us in that situation. you will not get us killed. going out there will be like trying to raise the dead. she is not dead yet, manman says, maybe we can help her. i will make you stay if i have to, he says to her. my mother buries her face in the latrine wall. she starts to cry. you can hear madan roger screaming. they are beating her, pounding on her until you don't hear anything else. manman tells papa, you cannot let them kill somebody just because you are afraid. papa says, oh yes, you *can* let them kill somebody because you are afraid. they are the law. it is their right. we are just being good citizens, following the law of the land. it has happened before all over this country and tonight it will happen again and there is nothing we can do.

Célianne spent the night groaning. She looks like she has been ready for a while, but maybe the child is being stubborn. She just screamed that she is bleeding. There is an older woman here who looks like she has had a lot of children herself. She says Célianne is not bleeding at all. Her water sack has broken.

The only babies I have ever seen right after birth are baby mice. Their skin looks veil thin. You can see all the blood vessels and all their organs. I have always wanted to poke them to see if my finger would go all the way through the skin.

I have moved to the other side of the boat so I will not have to look *inside* Célianne. People are just watching. The captain asks the midwife to keep Célianne steady so she will not rock any more holes into the boat. Now we have three cracks covered with tar. I am scared to think of what would happen if we had to choose among ourselves who would stay on the boat and who should die. Given the choice to make a decision like that, we would all act like vultures, including me.

The sun will set soon. Someone says that this child will be just another pair of hungry lips. At least it will have its mother's breasts, says an old man. Everyone will eat their last scraps of food today.

there is a rumor that the old president is coming back. there is a whole bunch of people going to the airport to meet him. papa says we are not going to stay in port-au-prince to find out if this is true or if it is a lie. they are selling gasoline at the market again. the carnival groups have taken to the streets. we are heading the other way, to ville rose. maybe there i will be able to sleep at night. it is not going to turn out well with the old president coming back, manman now says. people are just too hopeful, and sometimes hope is the biggest weapon of all to use against us. people will believe anything. they will claim to see the christ return and march on the cross backwards if there is enough hope. manman told papa that you took the boat. papa told me before we left this morning that he thought himself a bad father for everything that happened. he says a father should be able to speak to his children like a civilized man. all the craziness here has made him feel like he cannot do that anymore. all he wants to do is live. he and manman have not said a word to one another since we left the latrine. i know that papa does not hate us, not in the way that i hate those soldiers, those macoutes, and all those people here who shoot guns. on our way to ville rose, we saw dogs licking two dead faces. one of them was a little boy who was lying on the side of the road with the sun in his dead open eyes. we saw a soldier shoving a woman out of a hut, calling her a witch. he was shaving the woman's head, but of course we never stopped. papa didn't want to go in madan roger's house and check on her before we left. he thought the soldiers might still be there. papa was driving the van real fast. i thought he was going to kill us. we stopped at an open market on the way. manman got some black cloth for herself and for me. she cut the cloth in two pieces and we wrapped them around our heads to mourn madan roger. when i am used to ville rose, maybe i will sketch you some butterflies, depending on the news that they bring me.

Célianne had a girl baby. The woman acting as a midwife is holding the baby to the moon and whispering prayers. . . . *God, this child You bring into the world, please guide her as You please through all her days on this earth.* The baby has not cried.

We had to throw our extra things in the sea because the water is beginning to creep in slowly. The boat needs to be lighter. My two gourdes in change had to be thrown overboard as an offering to Agwé, the spirit of the water. I heard the captain whisper to someone yesterday that they might have to *do something* with some of the people who never recovered from seasickness. I am afraid that soon they may ask me to throw out this notebook. We might all have to strip down to the way we were born, to keep ourselves from drowning.

Célianne's child is a beautiful child. They are calling her Swiss, because the word *Swiss* was written on the small knife they used to cut her umbilical cord. If she was my daughter, I would call her soleil, sun, moon, or star, after the elements. She still hasn't cried. There is gossip circulating about how Célianne became pregnant. Some people are saying that she had an affair with a married man and her parents threw her out. Gossip spreads here like everywhere else.

Do you remember our silly dreams? Passing the university exams and then studying hard to go until the end, the farthest of all that we can go in school. I know your father might never approve of me. I was going to try to win him over. He would have to cut out my heart to keep me from loving you. I hope you are writing like you promised. Jésus, Marie, Joseph! Everyone smells so bad. They get into arguments and they say to one another, 'It is only my misfortune that would lump me together with an indigent like you.' Think of it. They are fighting about being superior when we all might drown like straw.

There is an old toothless man leaning over to see what I am writing. He is sucking on the end of an old wooden pipe that has not seen any fire for a very long time now. He looks like a painting. Seeing things simply, you could fill a museum with the sights you have here. I still feel like such a coward for running away. Have you heard anything about my parents? Last time I saw them on the beach, my mother had a *kriz*. She just fainted on the sand. I saw her coming to as we started sailing away. But of course I don't know if she is doing all right.

The water is really piling into the boat. We take turns pouring bowls of it out. I don't know what is keeping the boat from splitting in two. Swiss isn't crying. They keep slapping her behind, but she is not crying.

of course the old president didn't come. they arrested a lot of people at the airport, shot a whole bunch of them down. i heard it on the radio. while we were eating tonight, i told papa that i love you. i don't know if it will make a difference. i just want him to know that i have loved somebody in my life. in case something happens to one of us, i think he should know this about me, that i have loved someone besides only my mother and father in my life. i know you would understand. you are the one for large noble gestures. i just wanted him to know that i was capable of loving somebody. he looked me straight in the eye and said nothing to me. i love you until my hair shivers at the thought of anything happening to you. papa just turned his face away

like he was rejecting my very birth. i am writing you from under the banyan tree in the yard in our new house. there are only two rooms and a tin roof that makes music when it rains, especially when there is hail, which falls like angry tears from heaven. there is a stream down the hill from the house, a stream that is too shallow for me to drown myself. manman and i spend a lot of time talking under the banyan tree. she told me today that sometimes you have to choose between your father and the man you love. her whole family did not want her to marry papa because he was a gardener from ville rose and her family was from the city and some of them had even gone to university. she whispered everything under the banyan tree in the yard so as not to hurt his feelings. i saw him looking at us hard from the house. i heard him clearing his throat like he heard us anyway, like we hurt him very deeply somehow just by being together.

Célianne is lying with her head against the side of the boat. The baby still will not cry. They both look very peaceful in all this chaos. Célianne is holding her baby tight against her chest. She just cannot seem to let herself throw it in the ocean. I asked her about the baby's father. She keeps repeating the story now with her eyes closed, her lips barely moving.

She was home one night with her mother and brother Lionel when some ten or twelve soldiers burst into the house. The soldiers held a gun to Lionel's head and ordered him to lie down and become intimate with his mother. Lionel refused. Their mother told him to go ahead and obey the soldiers because she was afraid that they would kill Lionel on the spot if he put up more of a fight. Lionel did as his mother told him, crying as the soldiers laughed at him, pressing the gun barrels farther and farther into his neck.

Afterwards, the soldiers tied up Lionel and their mother, then they each took turns raping Célianne. When they were done, they arrested Lionel, accusing him of moral crimes. After that night, Célianne never heard from Lionel again.

The same night, Célianne cut her face with a razor so that no one would know who she was. Then as facial scars were healing, she started throwing up and getting rashes. Next thing she knew, she was getting big. She found out about the boat and got on. She is fifteen.

manman told me the whole story today under the banyan tree. the bastards were coming to get me. they were going to arrest me. they were going to peg me as a member of the youth federation and then take me away. papa heard about it. he went to the post and paid them money, all the money he had. our house in port-au-prince and all the land his father had left him, he gave it all away to save my life. this is why he was so mad. tonight manman told me this under the banyan tree. i have no words to thank him for this. i don't know how. you must love him for this, manman says, you must. it is something you

can never forget, the sacrifice he has made. i cannot bring myself to say thank you. now he is more than my father. he is a man who gave everything he had to save my life. on the radio tonight, they read the list of names of people who passed the university exams. you passed.

We got some relief from the seawater coming in. The captain used the last of his tar, and most of the water is staying out for a while. Many people have volunteered to throw Célianne's baby overboard for her. She will not let them. They are waiting for her to go to sleep so they can do it, but she will not sleep. I never knew before that dead children looked purple. The lips are the most purple because the baby is so dark. Purple like the sea after the sun has set.

Célianne is slowly drifting off to sleep. She is very tired from the labor. I do not want to touch the child. If anybody is going to throw it in the ocean, I think it should be her. I keep thinking, they have thrown every piece of flesh that followed the child out of her body into the water. They are going to throw the dead baby in the water. Won't these things attract sharks?

Célianne's fingernails are buried deep in the child's naked back. The old man with the pipe just asked, 'Kompè, what are you writing?' I told him, 'My will.'

i am getting used to ville rose. there are butterflies here, tons of butterflies. so far none has landed on my hand, which means they have no news for me. i cannot always bathe in the stream near the house because the water is freezing cold. the only time it feels just right is at noon, and then there are a dozen eyes who might see me bathing. i solved that by getting a bucket of water in the morning and leaving it in the sun and then bathing myself once it is night under the banyan tree. the banyan now is my most trusted friend. they say banyans can last hundreds of years. even the branches that lean down from them become like trees themselves. a banyan could become a forest, manman says, if it were given a chance. from the spot where i stand under the banyan, i see the mountains, and behind those are more mountains still. so many mountains that are bare like rocks. i feel like all those mountains are pushing me farther and farther away from you.

She threw it overboard. I watched her face knot up like a thread, and then she let go. It fell in a splash, floated for a while, and then sank. And quickly after that she jumped in too. And just as the baby's head sank, so did hers. They went together like two bottles beneath a waterfall. The shock lasts only so long. There was no time to even try and save her. There was no question of it. The sea in that spot is like the sharks that live there. It has no mercy.

They say I have to throw my notebook out. The old man has to throw out his hat and his pipe. The water is rising again and they are scooping it out. I asked for a few seconds to write this last page and then promised that I would let it go. I know you will probably never see this, but it was nice imagining that I had you here to talk to.

I hope my parents are alive. I asked the old man to tell them what happened to me, if he makes it anywhere. He asked me to write his name in 'my book.' I asked him for his full name. It is Justin Moïse André Nozius Joseph Frank Osnac Maximilien. He says it all with such an air that you would think him a king. The old man says, 'I know a Coast Guard ship is coming. It came to me in my dream.' He points to a spot far into the distance. I look where he is pointing. I see nothing. From here, ships must be like a mirage in the desert.

I must throw my book out now. It goes down to them, Célianne and her daughter and all those children of the sea who might soon be claiming me.

I go to them now as though it was always meant to be, as though the very day that my mother birthed me, she had chosen me to live life eternal, among the children of the deep blue sea, those who have escaped the chains of slavery to form a world beneath the heavens and the blood-drenched earth where you live.

Perhaps I was chosen from the beginning of time to live there with Agwé at the bottom of the sea. Maybe this is why I dreamed of the starfish and the mermaids having the Catholic Mass under the sea. Maybe this was my invitation to go. In any case, I know that my memory of you will live even there as I too become a child of the sea.

today i said thank you. i said thank you, papa, because you saved my life. he groaned and just touched my shoulder, moving his hand quickly away like a butterfly. and then there it was, the black butterfly floating around us. i began to run and run so it wouldn't land on me, but it had already carried its news. i know what must have happened. tonight i listened to manman's transistor under the banyan tree. all i hear from the radio is more killing in port-au-prince. the pigs are refusing to let up. i don't know what's going to happen, but i cannot see staying here forever. i am writing to you from the bottom of the banyan tree. manman says that banyan trees are holy and sometimes if we call the gods from beneath them, they will hear our voices clearer. now there are always butterflies around me, black ones that i refuse to let find my hand. i throw big rocks at them, but they are always too fast. last night on the radio, i heard that another boat sank off the coast of the bahamas. i can't think about you being in there in the waves. my hair shivers. from here, i cannot even see the sea. behind these mountains are more mountains and more black butterflies still and a sea that is endless like my love for you.

1995

Greg Hollingshead

Brief Biography

- Born in 1947 near Toronto; travels in Europe and North Africa and lives in England for five years.
- In a cave in Crete begins an unpublished novel about global warming.
- Returns to Canada in 1975, starts a university teaching career.
- Wins the Governor General's Award for Fiction for *The Roaring Girl* (1995), which becomes a best-seller.
- A tireless reviser, has published three short fiction collections and three novels.
- Currently professor emeritus at the University of Alberta and director of writing programs at Banff Centre.

Greg Hollingshead, who grew up in the suburban community of Woodbridge, ON, was a poet before he became a fiction writer. He was twenty when editor Dennis Lee included his poems in an anthology of young Toronto poets. Though neither of his parents completed high school, Hollingshead received his MA from the University of Toronto and completed his PhD at the University of London, England. He returned to Canada to teach at the University of Alberta, where he specialized in eighteenth-century literature and creative writing.

Influenced by the experimental writings of Samuel Beckett, Thomas Pynchon, and William S. Burroughs and encouraged by his friend and novelist Matt Cohen (Governor General's Award winner, 1999), Hollingshead published his first short story collection, *Famous Players*, in 1982, following it with *White Buick* and his first novel, *Spin Dry*, in 1992. His friend Barbara Gowdy suggested he submit a manuscript to her publisher; with his third story collection, *The Roaring Girl* (1995), Hollingshead established himself as a unique voice in Canadian writing.

Hollingshead considers his voice and sensibility distinctly Canadian: 'The sensibility that informed me growing up I think of as a national one, with some regional variation. It's the sense of humour, a loser's, really, chipping away at pretension. It's the spaces left for mystery.'

While Hollingshead's fictional works exhibit a wide variety of forms, styles, and techniques (including eighteenth-century forms), they are unified in their depiction of seemingly ordinary characters who are quietly deluded. Specific details, realistic dialogue, and an epigrammatic style often blend with elements of the absurd to create commentaries on modern life. Like Thomas King, Hollingshead uses humour to reveal underlying pathos and intolerance. However, whether using the first-person or third-person point of view, Hollingshead lets his characters speak for themselves as they negotiate the conflux of inner needs and outer betrayals; he illuminates the limited perspectives of his characters but does not pass judgment on them. The main characters in his most recent novels, *The Healer* (1998) and *Bedlam* (2004), may be delusional or insane, but

Hollingshead is more interested in their inner 'reality' and in the 'politics of [their] treatment.'

The concerns of the first-person narrator of 'The People of the Sudan,' from *The Roaring Girl*, reflect those of a beleaguered suburban housewife burdened with three children and the daily stresses of a 'working marriage.' From the beginning, Hollingshead reveals the many tiny deceptions that make up the fabric of her everyday life. 'My fiction is about not seeing what's there,' Hollingshead has said. 'Children live with a certain degree of mystery about life. Adults devise structures of blindness to keep them from seeing and understanding.' Irony arises in part from the need to insinuate the deeper truths of the story that his characters fail to see: 'All literary technique is finally about letting the reader into the text. Nuance opens the door; explicitness slams it. Reading is a game we play with the author; he lets us know the rules, but he doesn't play for us.'

See Greg Hollingshead, from 'Short Story vs Novel,' p. 412.

The People of the Sudan

The first we ever heard about the box, Dave had his arm over the back of the seat ready to reverse down the Gunns' driveway. We'd been standing around on their lawn trying to say goodbye for almost an hour, me shifting Jessica from one arm to the other and Dave staring miserably at Troy and Becky, our other two, who kept going limp and rigid at the same time, the way they do when they're bored nutso. The Gunns don't have kids. Rolf Gunn was going on to Dave about his and Big Elspeth's new Baskin-Robbins franchise, and Big Elspeth was going on to me about her work on behalf of the whales and how it's never too late to get draped.

'I mean, your colours are your colours.'

'So what happens when you go grey?'

These words were mine, they had come from my mouth.

'Your colours don't change,' Big Elspeth said briskly. 'That's the whole point. They *are* you.'

At that moment Dave caught my eye, and suddenly I couldn't stand this. 'Okay kids,' I said. 'Time to go.'

As if it had been us waiting for them.

By that time the sun was practically down, we'd have to stop at a highway place for dinner, we wouldn't get home until after ten, the kids would be wired and sleep badly, and Troy had soccer practice at seven a.m.

Anyways, Dave's arm was over the back of the seat, and this was it—when Troy tapped him on the shoulder. I half-turned to tell Troy not to annoy his father when he was trying to back out, and there at Dave's window was Rolf Gunn's face. I pointed at it. Slowly Dave lifted his arm off the back of the seat.

His eyes came around, and I could see them preparing for what more Rolf had to say while his left hand rolled down the window.

Like a hound, Rolf tipped his face, indicating the rear of our station wagon. 'I thought you'd have more stuff.' From the way he said this, you would think we had let him down.

'We didn't bring Ralph,' Dave reminded him. Ralph's our dog. Ralph-Rolf, it's too confusing for Ralph at the Gunns.'

'Ralphus,' Becky whimpered.

'You'll see Ralph soon enough,' I told her sharply.

I could hear the faint brush of fabric like a little gasp.

'Listen,' Rolf said. 'You people have plenty of room to take something back with you.'

Dave swung his head as if to consult with me, but he wasn't looking out his eyes. He swung it back. 'Sure,' he said. 'If it fits.'

'It'll fit.' Already Rolf was walking towards the garage.

Dave watched him for a moment, and then he did look at me. The look said we weren't in our twenties any more, it said it was time to stop hoofing and mugging to this particular tune.

I didn't confirm or deny, I just returned Dave eyeball for eyeball, and the feeling for me was the one when you know that everything is about to blow wide open, that you are very close to doing the one small thing that will break the yolk with these people.

And then Big Elspeth was at my window, which I rolled down.

'Hi again,' I said.

'This is really great of you.'

'What do we do with it?'

I was watching Rolf come out of the garage pushing a dolly. Tipped on the dolly was a large-appliance sort of box, strapped with steel bands.

'Just call the number for the return address that's written on it,' Big Elspeth said. 'They'll be literally waiting by the phone. I can't believe how convenient this is.'

Dave was getting out to reorganize the back.

'What's in it?' I asked.

'Relief,' Big Elspeth said. 'From people we know. Wonderful people. People they know are going to the Sudan, and they need to have it right away.'

The box was coming closer, and it wasn't getting any smaller.

'Why do you have it?' I asked.

'I remembered you guys were coming down, so I said we'd take care of it. I knew you wouldn't mind.'

'What's a phone call?' I said.

Behind me I could hear Dave doing the lifting. Rolf of course has a bad back. It wasn't going well, and then I heard Dave say, 'It won't fit.'

'There's always the roof,' Rolf told him.

It took them another forty minutes to get the box tied to the roof rack secure enough to satisfy Dave. While this was going on, I talked the kids back into the house for another bathroom visit so we wouldn't have to stop right away, but also so I wouldn't have to sit in the car and wait for a bungee cord to whap out somebody's eye.

Big Elspeth followed us inside and stood around filling the bathroom doorway. After a few minutes she said, 'Aileen, I just don't know how you do it.'

'Do what?' I was wiping Becky.

'Sacrifice your life this way.'

I shrugged. 'It's my life, there's no sacrifice.'

'No, I mean I really admire it.'

When we were back in the car, she leaned in the window, confidential. 'Aileen, you're a Winter, I know it. These pastels you wear only bring out the pastiness. Promise me you'll think black.'

'I think black all the time, Elspeth.'

'I hate carrying things on the roof,' Dave said as we pulled away.

I nodded. We were both remembering a couple of years ago driving down the highway, the car slowing down, speeding up, slowing down, and Dave saying the gas line must be blocked, but what it was was the wind resistance as it lifted Troy's crib, which was folded flat and strapped to the roof rack, and then, when the car slowed down, lowered the crib, so the car would speed up and the crib would rise again, and the car would slow down, and the crib would settle, and the car would speed up, until suddenly there was the sound of ripping metal and a wild surge forward, and in the rear-view I saw slats and springs and the mattress and splinters of Troy's crib and bent-double roof-rack strips twisting and elevating higher and higher into the air and many cars in slow motion swerving long before the debris started to rain down.

Troy was with us at the time, gazing out the back window. 'That's my crib,' he said in a voice of awe.

'The wind resistance will slow us down,' Dave now complained about the box.

'Isn't too much wind resistance against the law?' I asked.

This was not a question Dave considered worth even a glance.

As we pulled onto the ring road, he said he never wanted to see the Gunns again as long as he lived.

I told him I could appreciate how he felt, but it was just a box and I'd make the call.

I spent that whole drive thinking about the Gunns. At one point I asked Dave what he thought it was about Rolf and Big Elspeth.

'Pride,' he said.

I thought about that for a while, and then I said, 'So how could we stand them ten years ago?'

'Immaturity, stupidity, drugs.'

'What?' Troy said from the back seat. '*Drugs? What?*'

The more I thought about Big Elspeth, the more I wondered how I could have been her friend for so long. I thought about my parents and how their friends weren't friends so much as people who amused them, very theatrical or neurotic, witty people, and after a while they'd get bored and take up with new ones. I wondered if I was like that, only slower to let go. Dave, I knew, wasn't like that at all. The way Dave thinks about people, it's a miracle he's not a hermit. For Dave there are the few dozen who will speak out when innocent people are herded into prison camps, and then there are the millions who say nothing.

We didn't get back until after ten.

Dave squeezed the garage door opener the way he likes to do, from halfway down the block, like Batman, and we were tired but otherwise alert, or so we'd have said if nothing had happened. Even after the crunch and the car not able to enter the garage, Dave and I could only look at each other until Troy cried, '*The box!*'

Immediately our neighbours Joan and Ernie were pressed up against the windows telling us how they'd been out for a walk and seen it coming and screamed at the top of their lungs but we didn't hear. It's funny how people will tell you something over and over until they calm down.

Fortunately the roof rack had peeled back as with Troy's crib, so the box was hardly damaged, only our car. Ernie helped Dave carry the box into the house.

'What is it?' I heard Ernie ask.

'Relief,' Dave told him.

Meanwhile Ralph the dog was beside himself. You would think that after fifteen years of unremitting human love, even a dog with an inferiority complex as big as Ralph's would be able to grasp the fact that he has not been abandoned. The kids were wired, it was a restless night, and the little boy I dropped off at soccer practice in the morning was the colour of chalk.

The next day Jessica didn't crash until noon. Counting on an hour for myself, I went down to throw in a wash. That's when I found out where Dave and Ernie had put the box. On top of the dryer. Good thinking, men. It was too heavy for me, and anyways where would I move it to? My laundry room is, like, eight by six. I was still standing there staring at the box when Jess woke up, and that was it for my Me time. When Dave got home I complained about his choice of location for the box, but he just went on eating his spaghetti.

The rest of the week was no improvement. The box was on my list, but I ran out of space, so I copied everything onto another piece of paper, everything except *Phone about box.* Not that I believe these things just happen. And then, as I was half expecting, Troy came down with a flu that was going around at school, and twenty-four hours later Becky and Jess were taking their turns on the porcelain phone. For three days it was three sick kids. For two more, one sick mum.

Dave never gets sick. And then a long stretch of a week or possibly more and nothing done about the box. I think what happened was, the nuisance of the thing on my dryer eclipsed the nuisance of making the call. It was like when you're carrying four or five things and you pick up something extra. The extra bumps one of the originals, which you immediately lose.

But I did finally act.

First I called the operator, because aside from a Sudan box number, there was just a name and address in this city, an apartment in the north end. The operator gave me the number. I called it. No answer. Over the next four days I called that number fifteen, maybe twenty times. Whenever I got a chance I called it. By this time I was starting to feel guilty, because more than two weeks had passed and I was afraid the people had already left for the Sudan.

And then one day a man answered. 'Yeah, what is it.'

'Is that Adrian Zignash?'

'It might be.'

'Well, this might be Aileen Nakamura.' Dave's Japanese Canadian.

I told Adrian Zignash I had a box for him and when would he like to come by and pick it up?

'I would not like to come by and pick it up,' Adrian Zignash replied. 'The trip's off. Any box is your problem.' And Adrian Zignash hung up.

When Dave came in from work I told him about this call, and he said we should drive over to Adrian Zignash's and throw the box through the front window.

'He's on the twelfth floor.'

'In that case we push it off the roof.'

I laughed and gave Dave a punch in the arm. As for the box, it went on sitting on my dryer. For eight months. By then I could reach around and set the heat mode by feel.

But the box did weigh on me. It may not have been constantly in the forefront of my mind, but at any time of the day I was liable to find myself worrying about it, and when I woke up in the night it was not so much an item on the list—like Becky's asthma, the cuts at Dave's work, my mum's circulation—as a night symptom of all that needed to be done and *let's be very clear about this here in the stark lucidness of three a.m.* was damn well not being done. But daylight smears focus, mine anyway, and what might be absolutely critical at three a.m., twelve hours later is just another nagging worry, and this one seemed to have a lot less to do with the possibility of any kind of practical action than with my totally unresolved thing about Big Elspeth, that other major weight on the clothes dryer of my soul.

And then suddenly it was spring, and one day I was gathering up assorted junk for the people at Mental Retardation, and my eyes fell on the box. Why not? I couldn't budge it, but the MR guy hoisted it onto his belly and carried it up the stairs and out the door as if this was something he did twenty times a day. So the box was gone, my laundry room was suddenly almost spacious, and I felt ruthless and efficient but only briefly, because really the box was the kind of problem that retreats to nothing as soon as it's solved.

Two weeks later, when I had more or less forgotten about the box, the call came, from a Mrs Zombo. Mrs Zombo had the voice of a person who has been living on Camels and antidepressants for twenty years. She called to say that she and her husband were missionaries and that their colleagues in the Sudan had not yet received the box. When exactly had we sent it?

I told her we hadn't sent it. Nobody told us to send it. Nobody gave us any money to send it. I said I had just given it to the MR.

This information met with a long pause, and I imagined Mrs Zombo slumped over with a coronary from the shock. When she came back she came back robotic, like voice mail. 'You gave, that box, to Muscular Research.'

'No. The Mental Retardation Society. Or whatever they're calling themselves now. Institute for the Chronically Challenged. I don't know.'

'Mrs Nakamura, I must say I fail to find such remarks amusing. Your attitude has me wondering if you fully realize what you have done.'

'Sure I realize. I gave a box that sat on our dryer for eight months to the mentally handicapped.'

Here Mrs Zombo's voice went flat and dead, like doom. 'That box contained twenty, thousand, dollars' worth of desperately required, medical equipment.'

I swallowed.

'Do you, appreciate, Mrs Nakamura, how many people, primarily children, are dead and dying at this moment because of your unbelievable thoughtlessness?'

'Nobody told—'

'That box was entrusted to your care.'

'I didn't know!'

There was an exhalation of smoke. 'You knew that the box had been placed in your care. You knew that Mr Zignash was unable to take it, as previously arranged. You knew that if there was any problem you could always speak to your friends, the Gunns. Exactly what else did you need to know?'

'I didn't know it was important!'

'But you *assumed* it was unimportant. In effect you chose not to know whether it was or it was not important.'

After a while I started apologizing. When that didn't make any difference I started promising. I told Mrs Zombo I'd do everything I could to get the box back from the MR.

'The name and address of the purchaser or purchasers will be on the receipt. Anything in the range of twenty thousand dollars will be appropriate.'

'Pardon?'

'Twenty thousand dollars. To buy back the equipment from the purchaser or purchasers.'

'Are you serious?'

'You do accept responsibility for the loss of these instruments?'

'You think I have twenty thousand dollars?'

Mrs Zombo didn't say anything then, and in the silence, my heart louder than my words, I asked, 'What are these instruments, anyways?'

'My husband will be able to tell you as much about that as you need to know.'

'Well, could you put your husband on, please?'

'He's not here. My husband is an extremely busy man.'

I told Mrs Zombo I'd do what I could. I told her it was an innocent mistake.

'The innocents, Mrs Nakamura, are the ones who are dying as we speak.'

'So I'm sorry,' I said and hung up and right away started feeling just terrible to have come across snippy about this.

And then I got mad.

By the time Dave arrived home I'd called the MR three times, but it was after five and I kept getting their machine. When I told Dave about Mrs Zombo's call, he clutched his head like Desi Arnaz.

'Call Big Elspeth! Get this Mrs Zamboni's number! I want to speak to her myself!'

So I called Big Elspeth, who went into one of her *not so deeply hurt as to be spared perplexity numbers*. After a while she came right out and said, 'Why on earth didn't you call me sooner?'

'Because we've been hoping that you and your stuffed-shirt dolt husband would pass quietly out of our lives,' I might have replied, but not at the time. What I did was I grovelled. I told Big Elspeth, I know, I know, I should have, and I was really sorry now that I hadn't. And then I asked for the Zombos' number.

Big Elspeth said that what I should do was give the Zombos a chance to calm down, and the whole thing would blow over.

I said she was right, it probably would, but Dave did want to talk to Mrs Zombo.

Big Elspeth didn't say anything.

I asked her again for the Zombos' number.

Big Elspeth said she didn't have the Zombos' number.

When I had understood this I said, 'You do know this woman, don't you, Elspeth?'

'Bernice? Yes, of course. But not as a person.'

'No? As what then? A tuna?'

Big Elspeth had covered the receiver, and I heard her call, 'Rolf, we don't have the Zombos' number, do we.' It wasn't a question.

'Whose?' Rolf shouted from somewhere deep inside the house, or possibly the tub.

'The Zombos'!'

'No! Why should we?'

Elspeth came back, and I said, 'You accepted the box from people you didn't even have a number for?'

'Well, they were very pushy. If they gave us their number I'm sure we threw it out. After they left we talked about how it had been for us, and we agreed they're pigs. You know how it is with weekend guests. There's no chance to compare notes until you can see their backs.'

I told Big Elspeth I'd call her later.

The next day Jess and I paid a visit to the MR depot, a bare fluorescent space in an industrial strip mall on a service road. Fields to the south and west. A thin woman in a faded print dress was sorting a big pile of clothes in the middle of the floor. It was a warm day, the front door was propped open, and she didn't hear us come in for traffic noise. When I touched her shoulder she looked up with a complete lack of surprise. You really have to wonder how some people survive. Straight on she was narrow like a wolfhound, with thin colourless hair and a look of ageless exhaustion. I explained my problem, and she told me she didn't know about a box.

I asked her about medical equipment.

She didn't know about medical equipment.

I asked her where the stuff went from here.

She brightened. To the stores.

I asked her how many stores.

She wasn't sure.

She said she used to have a husband, but he drove into a tunnel and it took off his head.

As Jess and I were coming down the side of our house to the back door, she said, 'Teh-phone!' and then I could hear it too. With Jess balanced on one arm, I thought I'd never find my keys.

'Mrs Nakamura, *hi*.' A voice like butter and cream, silk and fur. A talker's voice, the kind of voice Dave means when he says he doesn't like talk and he doesn't like talkers.

'This is Paul Zombo,' the voice said. 'How are you today?'

'Okay.'

'That's great, that's just great. You people wouldn't be enjoying the same magnificent spring weather up there that we are here?'

'It's a nice day.'

'Good, good. Mrs Nakamura, I guess you'll know why I'm calling.'

'I've got a fair idea.'

It's funny how sometimes a person will be locked into behaving one way while inside she's going berserk with totally other feelings. I couldn't wait to tell Paul Zombo what I'd been up to on behalf of his box. As soon as I got the chance, I did.

'Excellent,' Paul Zombo said when I had finished. 'I just knew you'd be doing your best.'

'Next I'm checking the stores,' I said in a businesslike voice.

'Terrific.'

'There's just one thing.'

'What's that, Mrs Nakamura?'

'What exactly was in the box?'

'Relief, basically.'

'Well, could you send me a list or something?'

'Absolutely. Well, Mrs Nakamura, this is a Christian Relief Canada dime, so I won't keep you. But before I hang up I just want you to know how much we here at CRC appreciate your efforts. We're all praying very hard for your success.'

'Why, thank you,' I said.

I finished feeding Jess and checked the phone book. There were two MR shops, north- and southside. We drove out to both.

Nothing. Everybody seemed to have just taken about five aspirins. At the southside branch I made myself so obnoxious I had them begging me to call the director, a nice lady with her mouth full of old money, and she said I should get in touch with the driver. She gave me another number, and from them I got the home number for Wes, with the belly.

That night when Dave came home I told him about my day, and he was not the least bit impressed. He said I should not be running all over town behaving like a person who thought the box was her fault.

I didn't say anything. But as soon as I heard the shower and the yank of the shower curtain I called Wes, who had just got in and remembered right away. 'Steel banded? Name Zignash?'

Don't you love the way some people really know their jobs? I asked Wes where the box was now, and he told me it would be divided up and at one or both stores. By now maybe some of it already sold.

So what could I do?

Not much, unless I knew what was in the box.

'I'm waiting to find that out.'

Here I looked up to see Dave standing in the middle of the living room in a towel. I said goodbye to Wes, and Dave and I had a big fight that ended in the following agreement: a free hand for me, provided that no money changed hands and Dave would hear about the box only at his own request.

All the next week I didn't know what to do without knowing what had been in the box, so I didn't do anything except check the mail. Then another call came from Paul Zombo.

'Mrs Nakamura, how goes the search?'

'It hasn't. You never sent me the list.'

'Oh dear. Didn't we do that?'

'*Do what?*' I heard a woman's voice with an edge say, right next to the phone.

'I can't do anything more without the list,' I said.

'I understand. Mrs Nakamura, would you mind if we came in?'

Now, it happened at that moment I was looking out the window at a car parked out front, and in the passenger seat a man was talking on a car phone, and I was half thinking that this was who I was talking to.

'I won't pay,' I said. 'This hasn't been only my fault.'

'No, Mrs Nakamura. It isn't about that. If we could come in, I'll explain.'

I told him the baby was asleep and when she woke up I'd have to feed her.

'Of course,' Paul Zombo said.

Three minutes later the baby was no longer asleep, because the bell woke Ralph, whose dreams are from hell, and he went into panicky barking.

Paul Zombo was unusually tall and narrow, with wavy orange hair and an enormous tanned baby face like a hubcap. The woman was slim in a slit skirt. She had false nails and a look of permanent dissatisfaction that pulled down one corner of her mouth in the manner of a mild stroke. They seemed to be carrying a lot of things, and I thought of salespeople.

'Mrs Nakamura, this is Dixie. Dixie's our rock at headquarters.'

'I am headquarters,' Dixie said, looking not at me but at the case she was setting down on the floor.

'Make yourselves comfortable,' I told them, 'while I fix something for Twinkletoes here.'

I had never called Jess that and had no idea why I did it now. She stiffened both legs and studied her toes.

'No hurry,' Paul Zombo said. 'It'll take us a couple of minutes to set up.'

'Set up?'

'Just a few slides.'

'Of what?'

'Mrs Nakamura, may I call you Aileen?'

He was untelescoping a tube of some kind. A screen. I said he could call me Aileen. 'Technology,' I said and went to make Jess's lunch. In the kitchen I refused to think what would happen if Dave came home early, whereas a story about this I could shape and time for his less troubled consumption.

I stuck my head around the door. 'Coffee?'

Paul Zombo was crouched over a small projector. Dixie was standing at the window with her arms folded, looking out.

'That would be wonderful,' Paul Zombo said.

So I made a fresh pot and moved Jess's high chair to the entrance from the kitchen, away from the rug, and brought the coffee and some cookies on a tray, and by that time he was all set up. With my permission he pulled the drapes and used a couple of *Reader's Digests* to prop the projector, which he set on the coffee table, with the screen right up against the mantelpiece. It's not such a big living room, really. I poured the coffee, Jess was happy with her peanut butter sandwich and apple juice, and I sat on the end of the chesterfield handy to her while Paul Zombo hung over the projector and Dixie sat beside him in Dave's recliner with her legs crossed at the knees, looking cheesed off.

'Aileen,' Paul Zombo said. 'Dixie and I would like to share with you a little bit of what Christian Relief Canada is doing for the people of the Sudan.'

The projector light came on and the fan started up. The tray rotated a notch, and we were looking at a green-blue sea dotted with sailboats. A blue sky.

'Now, this is the Red Sea, from the beach at Port Sudan.'

'It's so *blue*,' I said.

There was a sort of embarrassed pause, and Paul Zombo said, 'It's never actually been red, you know.'

At this point I noticed Dixie scowling at him, and I liked her then.

The tray rotated. We were looking down a beach. It was amazingly lush, so lush that Dixie seemed to jolt slightly in her chair.

'I never imagined the Sudan would be so lush,' I said.

'It's the wrong tray,' Dixie said.

'I don't think so, Dixie,' Paul Zombo replied kindly. 'Port Sudan was remarkably green. This is still the coast, remember.'

The tray rotated. Another view of the sea. Very blue.

'Wrong tray,' Dixie said and stood up.

'The Red Sea,' Paul Zombo replied quickly but firmly. 'The coastline really is quite low, but the Red Sea isn't shallow at all. Scholars now believe the Israelites crossed farther up, Aileen, at the Gulf of Suez. See those boats? Crafts very much like the ones you see here have been in continuous use since the days of the Pharoahs.'

'Wake up and smell the coffee, Paul,' Dixie said. 'Those are windsurfers.'

'Of course today, with the Suez Canal,' Paul Zombo continued, raising his voice a little, 'the Red Sea has become a major shipping route. It's a wonder there isn't an international tanker perched somewhere on the horizon.'

The tray rotated. A white hotel, taken from the street. *El Cid.*

The tray rotated. A sun setting into the sea.

The tray rotated, and a block-faced woman in a lavender mumu, a cigarette in one hand, stood looking uncomfortable against a whitewashed wall.

'How'd this get in here?' Paul Zombo wanted to know.

Dixie plunked back down in Dave's chair. In a singsong she said, 'Looks like the Yucatan tray to me.'

'Must be strays. That's my wife Bernice, Aileen. This is one from our holiday last winter, in Mexico.'

The tray rotated, and we saw American tourists walking on a beach.

'Paul, this is dumb. The lady is not interested in your holiday in Mexico.'

Paul Zombo turned to me. 'Aileen, looks like somehow we've grabbed the wrong slides here. But what say, now that we're all set up, we just go ahead?'

I glanced around at Jess, and she seemed game. 'Fine with us,' I said.

'Okay, Dixie?' Paul Zombo said. 'Why don't we just?'

'Just what, Paul? Just exactly what? Just sit here and look at your fucking holiday slides?' Dixie turned suddenly to me. 'Look, can I smoke?'

'Actually, Dixie, there's the baby.' I knew with Dave's nose he'd pick up cigarette right away. 'Would the front step be okay?'

'Forget it.'

The tray rotated to a market scene. 'Now this one,' Paul Zombo said, 'could have been taken anywhere.' He crossed to the screen. 'That is, racial type and costume aside. And produce. The wares, on the other hand, are fairly similar. And a Sudanese market would be just as crowded, easily, as what you see here. Of course, the vendors have less to sell, what with the drought and the famine and the social chaos—the country's been in a state of civil war for almost thirty years, you realize—but the people do come. Of course, they don't have a lot of choice. The whole operation is a drabber, dustier, dingier matter altogether.'

Paul Zombo returned to the projector. The tray rotated.

'Ah yes. Now, this is the view from our hotel room. See how that point of land sort of embraces the bay? It really is a natural harbour. You don't get the big breakers there that you get farther along in either direction. Still, hey—' He was back at the screen, pointing. 'What's this?'

'Surfers,' I said.

'Now, surfers you definitely won't see a lot of in the Sudan.'

'Well *duh*,' Dixie said.

Paul Zombo was looking at me. 'The most heart-breaking thing about the Sudan, Aileen, I mean aside from the West doing nothing, is the kids in the south. For years now, thousands of homeless Dinka children have been wandering the countryside from camp to camp. When the government bombs come they move on. These are children, Aileen. Living worse than cattle, like *hunted* cattle—' Here Paul Zombo's voice broke. He took a handkerchief from his pocket and wiped his eyes.

Dixie had twisted around in her chair. 'It's not right what's happening in that godforsaken shit hole,' she told me.

The tray rotated. A hotel room.

Paul Zombo cleared his throat. 'Nothing at all like our quarters in Khartoum, believe me. Khartoum is the capital of Sudan, Aileen. It and the north are ruled by Muslim fundamentalists. Quite the extremists, in fact. Ethnic cleansers, if you're familiar with that term. Anyway, it was forty in the shade, a merciless sun. But the worst part, worse than the heat and the dust, was the nervous kids with AK-47s, and I do mean kids, thirteen-, fourteen-year-olds, it was incredible, waking us in the night.'

The tray rotated to a picture of two couples, one of them definitely Paul and Bernice Zombo, with their arms around each other's shoulders. The woman on the end was doing a spiritless chorus-line kick. The Zombos looked abject and sozzled.

'This is just some people we met,' Paul Zombo said.

The tray rotated to an alarming one of Mrs Zombo foreshortened, taken from the foot of the bed. She was on her back, buck naked, with her legs slightly parted and her eyes closed. In her left hand was a hair dryer, directed at the shifted mass of her left breast.

'I don't believe this,' Dixie said.

'How'd that one get in here?' Paul Zombo wondered. He seemed to reflect a moment. 'Bernice uses a hair dryer on her body to get herself to sleep, Aileen. When she was little her parents fought all the time. The blower also shut out the sound of that. I thought it would make a cute picture.'

'Awful cute,' Dixie said.

Jessica wanted out of her chair. I went to unclip her.

The tray rotated then rotated again fast before I could look around. When I did I saw a young Mexican in the bow of a boat, grinning wildly.

'For God's sake, Paul. Haven't we seen enough?'

'This is good old Amerigo,' Paul Zombo said. 'He took a gang of us out in his boat one day to do a bit of snorkeling. Ever since I was a kid, Aileen, I've had this thing about how many fingers people have. Paintings, real life—well, to make a long story short, Amerigo had six! Number six was growing out the side of his baby finger, like a little sausage—'

Paul Zombo was pointing at the edge of his hand and looking at me as if I should say something—but what?

'You know, here, Aileen, the doctors would whip that finger off within hours. Not there.' He shook his head, remembering.

The tray rotated, and we were back to the first slide. Paul Zombo switched off the projector. 'That's it, everyone.'

'Already?' Dixie went out to the front step for a smoke.

As Paul Zombo was packing up, I asked him what had been in the box.

'Relief!' Dixie called through the screen door.

Paul Zombo held up his hands. 'Aileen, you've done enough. I'd say the box is now back in our court.'

He stepped closer, confidential. 'Listen, I'm sorry about Dixie. She's got a good heart, but she can be a little rough sometimes. Poor kid hasn't had an easy life.'

'That's enough, Paul!' Dixie called. 'You can stop talking about me any time!' She had one of those voices that go harsh when they're raised.

A few minutes later they were back in the car, and Paul Zombo called to thank me again for the twenty dollars I'd given towards Christian Relief Canada's work in the Sudan. I told him he was welcome. He waved goodbye, but I don't think he could see me for the reflection off our window, because he turned immediately to say something to Dixie as she pulled away.

Three days later a short guy with a Beatle haircut and an unfinished child's face cherry red with eczema rang the bell.

'Hello, I'm looking for an Aileen Nakamura. She a tenant of yours?'

I get this all the time. When I told him she was me, his brow darkened as if this was impossible. 'I'm Craig Storch,' he said. 'I represent an organization called Christian Relief Canada. My clients have instructed me to give you this.' He produced an envelope.

I told Craig Storch to slide his envelope under the screen door.

What it was was a notice, signed by Bernice Zombo and copied to me with the compliments of Paul Zombo, informing Rolf and Elspeth Gunn of 4167 Spruceway Blvd., etc., that Christian Relief Canada was suing them for $5,145.00, the estimated value of the goods that had been entrusted to their care.

The next day I got a call from Big Elspeth, a vile torrent that surged down the line like a sewer back-up. Normally I'd have gone to jelly on springs and worked away to smooth everything over. This time I just listened. In Grade Seven I had a teacher who said you don't know a thing until you can say it, but he must have been thinking of something else. I couldn't explain Big Elspeth, not then, not now, couldn't begin to, but since that one time I listened to her I don't have any more confusion. I'm sure there'll be reasons for how she is, good reasons, but fuck her, you know what I mean? And I don't have any negative feelings at all when I say that.

So anyways, on Saturday night Dave and I stayed home, and after I got the kids down, he made popcorn and opened a couple of beers, and when I thought he was ready for it I told him the story of Paul Zombo and Dixie and Craig Storch and the call from Big Elspeth, and he asked the kinds of questions he asks when he's interested, good questions, and we had a high old time. Since Big Elspeth's call the Gunns aren't speaking to us, and the other good thing that's come of the box is, it's got our asses in gear about adopting a child overseas, the way you can, for so much a month. It may not be a lot in the scheme of things, but as Dave says you do what you can do.

1995

Barbara Gowdy

Brief Biography

- Born in 1950.
- Characters in stories include Siamese twins, a two-headed man, and a four-legged woman.
- The title of 'We So Seldom Look on Love' is a line from Frank O'Hara's poem 'Ode On Necrophilia.' The story is based on an article about a woman who stole a body from a hearse.
- 'We So Seldom Look on Love' becomes movie *Kissed* (1997), starring Molly Parker.
- Travels and does extensive research on African elephants in Kenya to write *The White Bone* (1998).
- Works have been published in twenty-four countries.

Born in Windsor, ON, Gowdy was raised in Canada's first planned community, Don Mills; the intended English Garden City instead became a conventional, middle-class Toronto suburb. Conforming to stereotypes of women, especially by downplaying her intelligence, was difficult. After graduating from York University in her twenties, Gowdy studied piano for eight years at the Royal Conservatory of Music. A self-confessed perfectionist, she felt she could not succeed as a professional performer. She quit the piano and worked at a variety of jobs: intern stockbroker, managing editor for a book publishing company, creative writing teacher, and interviewer for a TV literary program.

But her conventional life disguised an interest in unconventional fictions with vulnerable characters, deformed in body and soul. Gowdy considers 'normality' and 'conformity' as restrictive. Many of her characters are inversions of the well-ordered universe of the Canadian literary tradition. Her first book, *Through the Green Valley* (1988), is a historical romance, but she soon pushed the boundaries of narrative. Much like Sinclair Ross, who saw Prairie landscapes as hostile, she perceived Ontario suburbs as menacing, repressed, and miserable. Not an autobiographical writer, she told a reporter from *Quill & Quire*, 'I like imagining lives other than my own.' Her novel *Falling Angels* (1989) portrays a dysfunctional family that holidays in a bomb shelter instead of at Disneyland. *Helpless* (2007) portrays a sympathetic pedophile. She is critical of bad parenting and absent fathers. Fascinated by animals, she wrote *The White Bone*, a complex quest novel narrated by elephants escaping ivory poachers.

Despite Gowdy's disregard for convention, her work descends from a long tradition. Some scholars, such as Justin D. Edwards in *Gothic Canada: Reading the Spectre of a National Literature* (2005), argue that three centuries of Canadian writing involves ghosts, monsters, and deformities. He concludes that Canada is 'haunted as a nation' by the 'imaginative interactions' of all cultures and traditions. In this way Gowdy, like Alice Munro, is a Southern Ontario Gothic writer, though her unusual perspective on the abnormal, body anxiety, and physical alterations is much different from Munro's. More like Angela Carter, Gowdy explores obsession, desire, gender identity, and cultural taboos. Because of fashion pressures, she once said she believed all women were female impersonators.

The stories in *We So Seldom Look on Love* (1992), her only short story collection, originated from 'strange but true' anecdotes or accounts in magazines. In Gowdy's retelling they challenge feminine ideals, concepts of normality, theology of the perverse, and ideas of what is monstrous and what is permissible. In the spirit of Edgar Allan Poe, or per-

haps the Marquis de Sade, she deals with sexuality among marginal, often outcast, characters, exploring the boundaries between *eros* and *thanatos*, love and death. In a 2000 interview, she stated she 'was not interested in the mind of the sociopath, or even the creep,' that her stories were explorations of the 'so-called abnormal.' As a first-person narrative, 'We So Seldom Look on Love' enables Gowdy to sympathetically view her character's emotional disconnection and strange behaviour. When her character says 'making love to a corpse was like being burned by a white light,' libido and spirit are mysteriously linked.

We So Seldom Look on Love

When you die, and your earthly self begins turning into your disintegrated self, you radiate an intense current of energy. There is always energy given off when a thing turns into its opposite, when love, for instance, turns into hate. There are always sparks at those extreme points. But life turning into death is the most extreme of extreme points. So just after you die, the sparks are really stupendous. Really magical and explosive.

I've seen cadavers shining like stars. I'm the only person I've ever heard of who has. Almost everyone senses something, though, some vitality. That's why you get resistance to the idea of cremation or organ donation. 'I want to be in one piece,' people say. Even Matt, who claimed there was no soul and no afterlife, wrote a PS in his suicide note that he be buried intact.

As if it would have made any difference to his energy emission. No matter what you do—slice open the flesh, dissect everything, burn everything—you're in the path of a power way beyond your little interferences.

I grew up in a nice, normal, happy family outside a small town in New Jersey. My parents and my brother are still living there. My dad owned a flower store. Now my brother owns it. My brother is three years older than I am, a serious, remote man. But loyal. When I made the headlines he phoned to say that if I needed money for a lawyer, he would give it to me. I was really touched. Especially as he was standing up to Carol, his wife. She got on the extension and screamed, 'You're sick! You should be put away!'

She'd been wanting to tell me that since we were thirteen years old.

I had an animal cemetery back then. Our house was beside a woods and we had three outdoor cats, great hunters who tended to leave their kills in one piece. Whenever I found a body, usually a mouse or a bird, I took it into my bedroom and hid it until midnight. I didn't know anything about the ritual significance of the midnight hour. My burials took place then because that's when I woke up. It no longer happens, but I was such a sensitive child that I think I must have been aroused by the energy given off as day clicked over into the dead of night and, simultaneously, as the dead of night clicked over into the next day.

In any case, I'd be wide awake. I'd get up and go to the bathroom to wrap the body in toilet paper. I felt compelled to be so careful, so respectful. I whispered a chant. At each step of the burial I chanted. 'I shroud the body, shroud the body, shroud little sparrow with broken wing.' Or 'I lower the body, lower the body . . .' And so on.

Climbing out the bathroom window was accompanied by: 'I enter the night, enter the night . . .' At my cemetery I set the body down on a special flat rock and took my pyjamas off. I was behaving out of pure inclination. I dug up four or five graves and unwrapped the animals from their shrouds. The rotting smell was crucial. So was the cool air. Normally I'd be so keyed up at this point that I'd burst into a dance.

I used to dance for dead men, too. Before I climbed on top of them, I'd dance all around the prep room. When I told Matt about this he said that I was shaking my personality out of my body so that the sensation of participating in the cadaver's energy eruption would be intensified. 'You're trying to imitate the disintegration process,' he said.

Maybe—on an unconscious level. But what I was aware of was the heat, the heat of my danced-out body, which I cooled by lying on top of the cadaver. As a child I'd gently wipe my skin with two of the animals I'd just unwrapped. When I was covered all over with their scent, I put them aside, unwrapped the new corpse and did the same with it. I called this the Anointment. I can't describe how it felt. The high, high rapture. The electricity that shot through me.

The rest, wrapping the bodies back up and burying them, was pretty much what you'd expect.

It astonishes me now to think how naive I was. I thought I had discovered something that certain other people, if they weren't afraid to give it a try, would find just as fantastic as I did. It was a dark and forbidden thing, yes, but so was sex. I really had no idea that I was jumping across a vast behavioural gulf. In fact, I couldn't see that I was doing anything wrong. I still can't, and I'm including what happened with Matt. Carol said I should have been put away, but I'm not bad-looking, so if offering my body to dead men is a crime, I'd like to know who the victim is.

Carol has always been jealous of me. She's fat and has a wandering eye. Her eye gives her a dreamy, distracted quality that I fell for (as I suppose my brother would eventually do) one day at a friend's thirteenth birthday party. It was the beginning of the summer holidays, and I was yearning for a kindred spirit, someone to share my secret life with. I saw Carol standing alone, looking everywhere at once, and I chose her.

I knew to take it easy, though. I knew not to push anything. We'd search for dead animals and birds, we'd chant and swaddle the bodies, dig graves, make popsicle-stick crosses. All by daylight. At midnight I'd go out and dig up the grave and conduct a proper burial.

There must have been some chipmunk sickness that summer. Carol and I found an incredible number of chipmunks, and a lot of them had no blood on them, no sign of cat. One day we found a chipmunk that evacuated a string of foetuses when I picked it up. The foetuses were still alive, but there was no saving them, so I took them into the house and flushed them down the toilet.

A mighty force was coming from the mother chipmunk. It was as if, along with her own energy, she was discharging all the energy of her dead brood. When Carol and I began to dance for her, we both went a little crazy. We stripped down to our underwear, screamed, spun in circles, threw dirt up into the air. Carol has always denied it, but she took off her bra and began whipping trees with it. I'm sure the sight of her doing this is what inspired me to take off my undershirt and underpants and to perform the Anointment.

Carol stopped dancing. I looked at her, and the expression on her face stopped me dancing, too. I looked down at the chipmunk in my hand. It was bloody. There were streaks of blood all over my body. I was horrified. I thought I'd squeezed the chipmunk too hard.

But what had happened was, I'd begun my period. I figured this out a few minutes after Carol ran off. I wrapped the chipmunk in its shroud and buried it. Then I got dressed and lay down on the grass. A little while later my mother appeared over me.

'Carol's mother phoned,' she said. 'Carol is very upset. She says you made her perform some disgusting witchcraft dance. You made her take her clothes off, and you attacked her with a bloody chipmunk.'

'That's a lie,' I said. 'I'm menstruating.'

After my mother had fixed me up with a sanitary napkin, she told me she didn't think I should play with Carol any more. 'There's a screw loose in there somewhere,' she said.

I had no intention of playing with Carol any more, but I cried at what seemed like a cruel loss. I think I knew that it was all loneliness from that moment on. Even though I was only thirteen, I was cutting any lines that still drifted out toward normal eroticism. Bosom friends, crushes, pyjama-party intimacy, I was cutting all those lines off.

A month or so after becoming a woman I developed a craving to perform autopsies. I resisted doing it for almost a year, though. I was frightened. Violating the intactness of the animal seemed sacrilegious and dangerous. Also unimaginable—I couldn't imagine what would happen.

Nothing. Nothing would happen, as I found out. I've read that necrophiles are frightened of getting hurt by normal sexual relationships, and maybe there's some truth in that (although my heart's been broken plenty of times by cadavers, and not once by a live man), but I think that my attraction to cadavers isn't driven by fear, it's driven by excitement, and that one of the most exciting things about a cadaver is how dedicated it is to dying. Its will is all directed to a single intention, like a huge wave heading for shore, and you can ride along on the wave if you want to, because no matter what you do, because with you or without you, that wave is going to hit the beach.

I felt this impetus the first time I worked up enough nerve to cut open a mouse. Like anyone else, I balked a little at slicing into the flesh, and I was repelled for a few seconds when I saw the insides. But something drove me to go through these compunctions. It was as if I were acting solely on instinct and curiosity, and anything I did was all right, provided it didn't kill me.

After the first few times, I started sticking my tongue into the incision. I don't know why. I thought about it, I did it, and I kept on doing it. One day I removed the organs and cleaned them with water, then put them back in, and I kept on doing that, too. Again, I couldn't tell you why except to say that any provocative thought, if you act upon it, seems to set you on a trajectory.

By the time I was sixteen I wanted human corpses. Men. (That way I'm straight.) I got my chauffeur's licence, but I had to wait until I was finished high school before Mr Wallis would hire me as a hearse driver at the funeral home.

Mr Wallis knew me because he bought bereavement flowers at my father's store. Now *there* was a weird man. He would take a trocar, which is the big needle you use to draw out a cadaver's fluids, and he would push it up the penises of dead men to make them look semi-erect, and then he'd sodomize them. I caught him at it once, and he tried to tell me that he'd been urinating in the hopper. I pretended to believe him. I was upset though, because I knew that dead men were just dead flesh to him. One minute he'd be locked up with a young male corpse, having his way with him, and the next minute he'd be embalming him as if nothing had happened, and making sick jokes about him, pretending to find evidence of rampant homosexuality—colons stalagmited with dried semen, and so on.

None of this joking ever happened in front of me. I heard about it from the crazy old man who did the mopping up. He was also a necrophile, I'm almost certain, but no longer active. He called dead women Madonnas. He rhapsodized about the beautiful Madonnas he'd had the privilege of seeing in the 1940s, about how much more womanly and feminine the Madonnas were twenty years before.

I just listened. I never let on what I was feeling, and I don't think anyone suspected. Necrophiles aren't supposed to be blond and pretty, let alone female. When I'd been working at the funeral home for about a year, a committee from the town council tried to get me to enter the Milk Marketer's Beauty Pageant. They knew about my job, and they knew I was studying embalming at night, but I had told people I was preparing myself for medical school, and I guess the council believed me.

For fifteen years, ever since Matt died, people have been asking me how a woman makes love to a corpse.

Matt was the only person who figured it out. He was a medical student, so he knew that if you apply pressure to the chest of certain fresh corpses, they purge blood out of their mouths.

Matt was smart. I wish I could have loved him with more than sisterly love. He was tall and thin. My type. We met at the doughnut shop across from the medical library, got to talking, and liked each other immediately, an unusual experience for both of us. After about an hour I knew that he loved me and that his love was unconditional. When I told him where I worked and what I was studying, he asked why.

'Because I'm a necrophile,' I said.

He lifted his head and stared at me. He had eyes like high-resolution monitors. Almost too vivid. Normally I don't like looking people in the eye, but I found myself staring back. I could see that he believed me.

'I've never told anyone else,' I said.

'With men or women?' he asked.

'Men. Young men.'

'How?'

'Cunnilingus.'

'Fresh corpses?'

'If I can get them.'

'What do you do, climb on top of them?'

'Yes.'

'You're turned on by blood.'

'It's a lubricant,' I said. 'It's colourful. Stimulating. It's the ultimate bodily fluid.'

'Yes,' he said, nodding. 'When you think about it. Sperm propagates life. But blood sustains it. Blood is primary.'

He kept asking questions, and I answered them as truthfully as I could. Having confessed what I was, I felt myself driven to testing his intellectual rigour and the strength of his love at first sight. Throwing rocks at him without any expectation that he'd stay standing. He did, though. He caught the whole arsenal and asked for more. It began to excite me.

We went back to his place. He had a basement apartment in an old rundown building. There were books in orange-crate shelves, in piles on the floor, all over the bed. On the wall above his desk was a poster of Doris Day in the movie *Tea for Two*. Matt said she looked like me.

'Do you want to dance first?' he asked, heading for his record player. I'd told him about how I danced before climbing on corpses.

'No.'

He swept the books off the bed. Then he undressed me. He had an erection until I told him I was a virgin. 'Don't worry,' he said, sliding his head down my stomach. 'Lie still.'

The next morning he phoned me at work. I was hungover and blue from the night before. After leaving his place I'd gone straight to the funeral home and made love to an autopsy case. Then I'd got drunk in a seedy country-and-western bar and debated going back to the funeral home and suctioning out my own blood until I lost consciousness.

It had finally hit me that I was incapable of falling in love with a man who wasn't dead. I kept thinking, 'I'm not normal.' I'd never faced this before. Obviously, making love to corpses isn't normal, but while I was still a virgin I must have been assuming that I could give it up any time I liked. Get married, have babies. I must have been banking on a future that I didn't even want let alone have access to.

Matt was phoning to get me to come around again after work.

'I don't know,' I said.

'You had a good time. Didn't you?'

'Sure, I guess.'

'I think you're fascinating,' he said.

I sighed.

'Please,' he said. 'Please.'

A few nights later I went to his apartment. From then on we started to meet every Tuesday and Thursday evening after my embalming class, and as soon as I left his place, if I knew there was a corpse at the mortuary—any male corpse, young or old—I went straight there and climbed in a basement window.

Entering the prep room, especially at night when there was nobody else around, was like diving into a lake. Sudden cold and silence, and the sensation of penetrating a new element where the rules of other elements don't apply. Being with Matt was like lying on the beach of the lake. Matt had warm, dry skin. His apartment was overheated and noisy. I lay on Matt's bed and soaked him up, but only to make the moment when I entered the prep room even more overpowering.

If the cadaver was freshly embalmed, I could usually smell him from the basement. The smell is like a hospital and old cheese. For me, it's the smell of danger and permission, it used to key me up like amphetamine, so that by the time I reached the prep room, tremors were running up and down my legs. I locked the door behind me and broke into a wild dance, tearing my clothes off, spinning around, pulling at my hair. I'm not sure what this was all about, whether or not I was trying to take part in the chaos of the corpse's disintegration, as Matt suggested. Maybe I was prostrating myself, I don't know.

Once the dancing was over I was always very calm, almost entranced. I drew back the sheet. This was the most exquisite moment. I felt as if I were being blasted by white light. Almost blinded, I climbed onto the table and straddled the corpse. I ran my hands over his skin. My hands and the insides of my thighs burned as if I were touching dry ice. After a few minutes I lay down and pulled the sheet up over my head. I began to kiss his mouth. By now he might be drooling blood. A corpse's blood is thick, cool and sweet. My head roared.

I was no longer depressed. Far from it, I felt better, more confident, than I had ever felt in my life. I had discovered myself to be irredeemably abnormal. I could either slit my throat or surrender—wholeheartedly now—to my obsession. I surrendered. And what happened was that obsession began to storm through me, as if I were a tunnel. I became the medium of obsession as well as both ends of it. With Matt, when we made love, I was the receiving end, I was the cadaver. When I left him and went to the funeral home, I was the lover. Through me Matt's love poured into the cadavers at the funeral home, and through me the cadavers filled Matt with explosive energy.

He quickly got addicted to this energy. The minute I arrived at his apartment, he had to hear every detail about the last corpse I'd been with. For a month or so I had him pegged as a latent homosexual necrophile voyeur, but then I began to see that it wasn't the corpses themselves that excited him, it was my passion for them. It was the power that went into that passion and that came back, doubled, for his pleasure. He kept asking, 'How did you feel? Why do you think you felt that way?' And then, because the source of all this power disturbed him, he'd try to prove that my feelings were delusory.

'A corpse shows simultaneous extremes of character,' I told him. 'Wisdom and innocence, happiness and grief, and so on.'

'Therefore all corpses are alike,' he said. 'Once you've had one you've had them all.'

'No, no. They're all different. Each corpse contains his own extremes. Each corpse is only as wise and as innocent as the living person could have been.'

He said, 'You're drafting personalities onto corpses in order to have power over them.'

'In that case,' I said, 'I'm pretty imaginative, since I've never met two corpses who were alike.'

'You *could* be that imaginative,' he argued. 'Schizophrenics are capable of manufacturing dozens of complex personalities.'

I didn't mind these attacks. There was no malice in them, and there was no way they could touch me, either. It was as if I were luxuriously pouring my heart out to a very clever, very concerned, very tormented analyst. I felt sorry for him. I understood his twisted desire to turn me into somebody else (somebody who might love him). I used to fall madly in love with cadavers and then cry because they were dead. The difference between Matt and me was that I had become philosophical. I was all right.

I thought that he was, too. He was in pain, yes, but he seemed confident that what he was going through was temporary and not unnatural. 'I am excessively curious,' he said. 'My fascination is any curious man's fascination with the unusual.' He said that by feeding his lust through mine, he would eventually saturate it, then turn it to disgust.

I told him to go ahead, give it a try. So he began to scour the newspapers for my cadavers' obituaries and to go to their funerals and memorial services. He made charts of my preferences and the frequency of my morgue encounters. He followed me to the morgue at night and waited outside so that he could get a replay while I was still in an erotic haze. He sniffed my skin. He pulled me over to streetlights and examined the blood on my face and hands.

I suppose I shouldn't have encouraged him. I can't really say why I did, except that in the beginning I saw his obsession as the outer edge of my own obsession, a place I didn't have to visit as long as he was there. And then later, and despite his increasingly erratic behaviour, I started to have doubts about an obsession that could come on so suddenly and that could come through me.

One night he announced that he might as well face it, he was going to have to make love to corpses, male corpses. The idea nauseated him, he said, but he said that secretly, deep down, unknown even to himself, making love to male corpses was clearly the target of his desire. I blew up. I told him that necrophilia wasn't something you forced yourself to do. You longed to do it, you needed to do it. You were born to do it.

He wasn't listening. He was glued to the dresser mirror. In the last weeks of his life he stared at himself in the mirror without the least self-consciousness. He focused on his face, even though what was going on from the neck down was the arresting part. He had begun to wear incredibly weird outfits. Velvet capes, pantaloons, high-heeled red boots. When we made love, he kept these outfits on. He stared into my eyes, riveted (it later occurred to me) by his own reflection.

Matt committed suicide, there was never any doubt about that. As for the necrophilia, it wasn't a crime, not fifteen years ago. So even though I was caught in the act, naked and straddling an unmistakably dead body, even though the newspapers found out about it and made it front-page news, there was nothing the police could charge me with.

In spite of which I made a full confession. It was crucial to me that the official report contain more than the detective's bleak observations. I wanted two things on record: one, that Matt was ravished by a reverential expert; two, that his cadaver blasted the energy of a star.

'Did this energy blast happen before or after he died?' the detective asked.

'After,' I said, adding quickly that I couldn't have foreseen such a blast. The one tricky area was why I hadn't stopped the suicide. Why I hadn't talked, or cut, Matt down.

I lied. I said that as soon as I entered Matt's room, he kicked away the ladder. Nobody could prove otherwise. But I've often wondered how much time actually passed between when I opened the door and when his neck broke. In crises, a minute isn't a minute. There's the same chaos you get at the instant of death, with time and form breaking free, and everything magnifying and coming apart.

Matt must have been in a state of crisis for days, maybe weeks before he died. All that staring in mirrors, thinking, 'Is this my face?' Watching as his face separated into its infinitesimal particles and reassembled into a strange new face. The night before he died, he had a mask on. A Dracula mask, but he wasn't joking. He wanted to wear the mask while I made love to him as if he were a cadaver. No way, I said. The whole point, I reminded him, was that I played the cadaver. He begged me, and I laughed because of the mask and with relief. If he wanted to turn the game around, then it was over between us, and I was suddenly aware of how much I liked that idea.

The next night he phoned me at my parents' and said, 'I love you,' then hung up.

I don't know how I knew, but I did. A gun, I thought. Men always use guns. And then I thought, no, poison, cyanide. He was a medical student and had access to drugs. When I arrived at his apartment, the door was open. Across from the door, taped to the wall, was a note: 'DEAD PERSON IN BEDROOM.'

But he wasn't dead. He was standing on a stepladder. He was naked. An impressively knotted noose, attached to a pipe that ran across the ceiling, was looped around his neck.

He smiled tenderly. 'I knew you'd come,' he said.

'So why the note?' I demanded.

'Pull away the ladder,' he crooned. 'My beloved.'

'Come on. This is stupid. Get down.' I went up to him and punched his leg.

'All you have to do,' he said, 'is pull away the ladder.'

His eyes were even darker and more expressive than usual. His cheekbones appeared to be highlighted. (I discovered minutes later he had make-up on.) I glanced around the room for a chair or a table that I could bring over and stand on. I was going to take the noose off him myself.

'If you leave,' he said, 'if you take a step back, if you do anything other than pull away the ladder, I'll kick it away.'

'I love you,' I said. 'Okay.'

'No, you don't,' he said.

'I do!' To sound like I meant it I stared at his legs and imagined them lifeless. 'I do!'

'No, you don't,' he said softly. 'But,' he said, 'you will.'

I was gripping the ladder. I remember thinking that if I held tight to the ladder, he wouldn't be able to kick it away. I was gripping the ladder, and then it was by the wall, tipped over. I have no memory of transition between these two events. There was a loud crack, and gushing water. Matt dropped gracefully, like a girl fainting. Water poured on him from the broken pipe. There was a smell of excrement. I dragged him by the noose.

In the living room I pulled him onto the green shag carpet. I took my clothes off. I knelt over him. I kissed the blood at the corner of his mouth.

True obsession depends on the object's absolute unresponsiveness. When I used to fall for a particular cadaver, I would feel as if I were a hollow instrument, a bell or a flute. I'd empty out. I would clear out (it was involuntary) until I was an instrument for the cadaver to swell into and be amplified. As the object of Matt's obsession how could I be other than impassive, while he was alive?

He was playing with fire, playing with me. Not just because I couldn't love him, but because I was irradiated. The whole time that I was involved with Matt, I was making love to corpses, absorbing their energy, blazing it back out. Since that energy came from the act of life alchemizing into death, there's a possibility that it was alchemical itself. Even if it wasn't, I'm sure it gave Matt the impression that I had the power to change him in some huge and dangerous way.

I now believe that his addiction to my energy was really a craving for such a transformation. In fact, I think that all desire is desire for transformation, and that all transformation—all movement, all process—happens because life turns into death.

I am still a necrophile, occasionally, and recklessly. I have found no replacement for the torrid serenity of a cadaver.

1996

Haruki Murakami

Brief Biography

- Born in Kyoto, Japan, in 1949 and raised in Kobe.
- Fascinated by music, he operates a Tokyo jazz club for seven years; his sentences have jazz rhythms.
- His novel *Norwegian Wood* (1987) is named for a Beatles' song; another novel is titled *Kafka on the Shore* (2005).
- To quit smoking, he runs his first marathon—has now run about thirty (his best time is 3.27 in New York); in 2007 publishes *What I Talk About When I Talk About Running*.
- Has written non-fiction about Japanese earthquakes and the Tokyo subway terrorist attack, which he says represents the violence beneath Japanese society.
- Lives in Tokyo and, to avoid constant publicity, also in New York City.

Haruki Murakami is one of the most popular Japanese writers in history. Paradoxically, his intertextual references often combine Japanese culture with American subject matter. He has translated into Japanese Western writers such as F. Scott Fitzgerald, J.D. Salinger, John Irving, and the complete works of his friend Raymond Carver, who influenced his style (Carver's stories of 'small humiliations' have found a receptive audience in Japan). Murakami's fiction epitomizes the contradictions of modern cross-culture with its clash between collective values and transcendent personal ones. A US reviewer commented that 'his stories move so effortlessly between the surface reality of materialistic yuppie life and the horrors of a sensitized imagination.'

Murakami frequently recalls how he gave no thought to a writing career until one day lying on the grass and sipping a beer at a baseball game. Yakult Swallows player Dave Hinton hit a double, and Murakami, at age twenty-nine, inexplicably realized he would write novels. Known as 'the Rat trilogy,' his first three coming-of-age novels describe alienated students, not baseball. In Japan these books are used as English primers. Following the success of these works, he decided to write full-time. He sold his jazz club, Peter Cat (named after a family pet), but continued to add to his jazz and rock record collection, estimated at over 6,000 albums. As the most popular contemporary Japanese author in the world, a dozen of his novels, three non-fiction works, and three volumes of his stories have been translated into English and thirty-eight other languages.

In his best-known novel, *The Wind-Up Bird Chronicle* (1994), his non-fiction, and his interviews, Murakami addresses controversial issues of Japan's past. Similar to Heinrich Böll in his consideration of post-war reconstruction, he cautions against 'historical amnesia' and takes direct aim at capitalistic Japan as disillusioned, cold, and unforgiving. Repressed desires and historical loss lurk beneath the surface of his well-honed stories. He claims that storytelling is both redemptive and a common global language. Though he has been criticized in Japan for attacking traditions, undermining history, diluting the language, and celebrating pop culture, his books have sold more than eight million copies in his homeland. His complex use of pop music, such as works by the Beatles, the Beach Boys, and Van Halen, often illuminates inter-generational conflict in Japan and acts as a bridge between Japanese and Western readers. (*Village Voice* notes: 'Murakami was accused of being *batakusai*, or "stinking of butter," too American to be purely Japanese,' though his works often denounce the Americanization of Japan's culture.) A self-confessed loner, he considers himself 'an individualist' who has never fit in with the Japanese literary establishment. In one satirical story, vicious, eyeless birds known as 'Sharpie Crows' repre-

sent the traditional conformist Japanese literary scene against which the narrator rebels.

Other Murakami stories include man-eating cats, a living man made out of ice, nameless characters or some named after himself, and unemployed loners: one character refuses ever-present corporate culture and manages by making endless vats of pasta. Murakami's fiction often blends realism and the surreal using non-traditional forms. 'The Seventh Man,' from *Blind Willow, Sleeping Woman* (2006), employs a frame narrative with the actual tale related by a man identified simply as the evening's seventh speaker. Though it is essentially realistic in details, like a Poe story elements of the horrific and a growing sense of dread suggest an obsessive psychological state: the story explores the precarious hold of a past trauma on the individual.

The Seventh Man

'A huge wave nearly swept me away,' said the seventh man, almost whispering. 'It happened one September afternoon when I was ten years old.'

The man was the last one to tell his story that night. The hands of the clock had moved past ten. The small group that huddled in a circle could hear the wind tearing through the darkness outside, heading west. It shook the trees, set the windows to rattling, and moved past the house with one final whistle.

'It was the biggest wave I had ever seen in my life,' he said. 'A strange wave. An absolute giant.'

He paused.

'It just barely missed me, but in my place it swallowed everything that mattered most to me and swept it off to another world. I took years to find it again and to recover from the experience—precious years that can never be replaced.'

The seventh man appeared to be in his midfifties. He was a thin man, tall, with a mustache, and next to his right eye he had a short but deep-looking scar that could have been made by the stab of a small blade. Stiff, bristly patches of white marked his short hair. His face had the look you see on people when they can't quite find the words they need. In his case, though, the expression seemed to have been there from long before, as though it were part of him. The man wore a simple blue shirt under a gray tweed coat, and every now and then he would bring his hand to his collar. None of those assembled there knew his name or what he did for a living.

He cleared his throat, and for a moment or two his words were lost in silence. The others waited for him to go on.

'In my case, it was a wave,' he said. 'There's no way for me to tell, of course, what it will be for each of you. But in my case it just happened to take the form of a gigantic wave. It presented itself to me all of a sudden one day, without warning, in the shape of a giant wave. And it was devastating.'

I grew up in a seaside town in S—— Prefecture. It was such a small town, I doubt that any of you would recognize the name if I were to mention it. My father was the local doctor, and so I had a rather comfortable childhood. Ever since I could remember, my best friend was a boy I'll call K. His house was close to ours, and he was a grade behind me in school. We were like brothers, walking to and from school together, and always playing together when we got home. We never once fought during our long friendship. I did have a brother, six years older, but what with the age difference and differences in our personalities, we were never very close. My real brotherly affection went to my friend K.

K was a frail, skinny little thing, with a pale complexion and a face almost pretty enough to be a girl's. He had some kind of speech impediment, though, which might have made him seem retarded to anyone who didn't know him. And because he was so frail, I always played his protector, whether at school or at home. I was kind of big and athletic, and the other kids all looked up to me. But the main reason I enjoyed spending time with K was that he was such a sweet, pure-hearted boy. He was not the least bit retarded, but because of his impediment, he didn't do too well at school. In most subjects, he could barely keep up. In art class, though, he was great. Just give him a pencil or paints and he would make pictures that were so full of life that even the teacher was amazed. He won prizes in one contest after another, and I'm sure he would have become a famous painter if he had continued with his art into adulthood. He liked to do seascapes. He'd go out to the shore for hours, painting. I would often sit beside him, watching the swift, precise movements of his brush, wondering how, in a few seconds, he could possibly create such lively shapes and colors where, until then, there had been only blank white paper. I realize now that it was a matter of pure talent.

One year, in September, a huge typhoon hit our area. The radio said it was going to be the worst in ten years. The schools were closed, and all the shops in town lowered their shutters in preparation for the storm. Starting early in the morning, my father and brother went around the house nailing shut all the storm doors, while my mother spent the day in the kitchen cooking emergency provisions. We filled bottles and canteens with water, and packed our most important possessions in rucksacks for possible evacuation. To the adults, typhoons were an annoyance and a threat they had to face almost annually, but to the kids, removed as we were from such practical concerns, it was just a great big circus, a wonderful source of excitement.

Just after noon the color of the sky began to change all of a sudden. There was something strange and unreal about it. I stayed outside on the porch, watching the sky, until the wind began to howl and the rain began to beat against the house with a weird dry sound, like handfuls of sand. Then we closed the last storm door and gathered together in one room of the darkened house, listening to the radio. This particular storm did not have a great deal of rain, it said, but the winds were doing a lot of damage, blowing roofs off houses and capsizing ships. Many people had been killed or injured by flying debris. Over and over again, they warned people against leaving their homes. Every once in a while, the house would creak and shudder as if a huge hand were shaking it, and sometimes there would be a great crash of some heavy-sounding object against a storm door. My father guessed that these were tiles blowing off the neighbors' houses. For lunch we ate the rice and omelets my mother had cooked, listening to the radio and waiting for the typhoon to blow past.

But the typhoon gave no sign of blowing past. The radio said it had lost momentum almost as soon as it came ashore at S—— Prefecture, and now it was moving northeast at the pace of a slow runner. The wind kept up its savage howling as it tried to uproot everything that stood on land and carry it to the far ends of the earth.

Perhaps an hour had gone by with the wind at its worst like this when a hush fell over everything. All of a sudden it was so quiet, we could hear a bird crying in the distance. My father opened the storm door a crack and looked outside. The wind had stopped, and the rain had ceased to fall. Thick, gray clouds edged across the sky, and patches of blue showed here and there. The trees in the yard were still dripping their heavy burden of rainwater.

'We're in the eye of the storm,' my father told me. 'It'll stay quiet like this for a while, maybe fifteen, twenty minutes, kind of like an intermission. Then the wind'll come back the way it was before.'

I asked him if I could go outside. He said I could walk around a little if I didn't go far. 'But I want you to come right back here at the first sign of wind.'

I went out and started to explore. It was hard to believe that a wild storm had been blowing there until a few minutes before. I looked up at the sky: I felt the storm's great 'eye' up there, fixing its cold stare on all of us below. No such 'eye' existed, of course: we were just in that momentary quiet spot at the center of the pool of whirling air.

While the grown-ups checked for damage to the house, I went down to the beach. The road was littered with broken tree branches, some of them thick pine boughs that would have been too heavy for an adult to lift alone. There were shattered roof tiles everywhere, cars with cracked windshields, and even a doghouse that had tumbled into the middle of the street. A big hand might have swung down from the sky and flattened everything in its path.

K saw me walking down the road and came outside.

'Where are you going?' he asked.

'Just down to look at the beach,' I said.

Without a word, he came along with me. He had a little white dog that followed after us.

'The minute we get any wind, though, we're going straight back home,' I said, and K gave me a silent nod.

The shore was a two-hundred-yard walk from my house. It was lined with a concrete breakwater—a big dike that stood as high as I was tall in those days. We had to climb a short stairway to reach the water's edge. This was where we came to play almost every day, so there was no part of it we didn't know well. In the eye of the typhoon, though, it all looked different: the color of the sky and of the sea, the sound of the waves, the smell of the tide, the whole expanse of the shore. We sat atop the breakwater for a time, taking in the view without a word to each other. We were supposedly in the middle of a great typhoon, and yet the waves were strangely hushed. And the point where they washed against the beach was much farther away than usual, even at low tide. The white sand stretched out before us as far as we could see. The whole, huge space felt like a room without furniture, except for the band of flotsam that lined the beach.

We stepped down to the other side of the breakwater and walked along the broad beach, examining the things that had come to rest there. Plastic toys, sandals, chunks of wood that had probably once been parts of furniture, pieces of clothing, unusual bottles, broken crates with foreign writing on them, and other, less recognizable items: it was like a big candy store. The storm must have carried these things from very far away. Whenever something unusual caught our attention, we would pick it up and look at it every which way, and when we were done, K's dog would come over and give it a good sniff.

We couldn't have been doing this more than five minutes when I realized that the waves had come up right next to me. Without any sound or other warning, the sea had suddenly stretched its long, smooth tongue out to where I stood on the beach. I had never seen anything like it before. Child though I was, I had grown up on the shore and knew how frightening the ocean could be—the savagery with which it could strike unannounced. And so I had taken care to keep well back from the waterline. In spite of that, the waves had slid up to within inches of where I stood. And then, just as soundlessly, the water drew back—and stayed back. The waves that had approached me were as unthreatening as waves can be—a gentle washing of the sandy beach. But something ominous about them—something like the touch of a reptile's skin—had sent a chill down my spine. My fear was totally groundless—and totally real. I knew instinctively that they were alive. The waves were alive. They knew I was here and they were planning to grab me. I felt as if some huge man-eating beast were lying somewhere on a grassy plain, dreaming of the moment it would pounce and tear me to pieces with its sharp teeth. I had to run away.

'I'm getting out of here!' I yelled to K. He was maybe ten yards down the beach, squatting with his back to me, and looking at something. I was sure I had yelled loud enough, but my voice did not seem to have reached him. He might have been so absorbed in whatever it was he had found that my call made no impression on him. K was like that. He would get involved with things to the point of forgetting everything else. Or possibly I had not yelled as loudly as I thought. I do recall that my voice sounded strange to me, as though it belonged to someone else.

Then I heard a deep rumbling sound. It seemed to shake the earth. Actually, before I heard the rumble I heard another sound, a weird gurgling as though a lot of water was surging up through a hole in the ground. It continued for a while, then stopped, after which I heard the strange rumbling. Even that was not enough to make K look up. He was still squatting, looking down at something at his feet, in deep concentration. He probably did not hear the rumbling. How he could have missed such an earthshaking sound, I don't know. This may seem odd, but it might have been a sound that only I could hear—some special kind of sound. Not even K's dog seemed to notice it, and you know how sensitive dogs are to sound.

I told myself to run over to K, grab hold of him, and get out of there. It was the only thing to do. I *knew* that the wave was coming, and K didn't know. As clearly as I knew what I ought to be doing, I found myself running the other way—running full speed toward the dike, alone. What made me do this, I'm sure, was fear, a fear so overpowering it took my voice away and set my legs to running on their own. I ran stumbling along the soft sand beach to the breakwater, where I turned and shouted to K.

'Hurry, K! Get out of there! The wave is coming!' This time my voice worked fine. The rumbling had stopped, I realized, and now, finally, K heard my shouting and looked up. But it was too late. A wave like a huge snake with its head held high, poised to strike, was racing toward the shore. I had never seen anything like it in my life. It had to be as tall as a three-story building. Soundlessly (in my memory, at least, the image is soundless), it rose up behind K to block out the sky. K looked at me for a few seconds, uncomprehending. Then, as if sensing something, he turned toward the wave. He tried to run, but now there was no time to run. In the next instant, the wave had swallowed him. It hit him full on, like a locomotive at full speed.

The wave crashed onto the beach, shattering into a million leaping waves that flew through the air and plunged over the dike where I stood. I was able to dodge its impact by ducking behind the breakwater. The spray wet my clothes, nothing more. I scrambled back up onto the wall and scanned the shore. By then the wave had turned and, with a wild cry, it was rushing back out to sea. It looked like part of a gigantic rug that had been yanked by someone at the other end of the earth. Nowhere on the shore could I find any trace of K, or of his dog. There was only the empty beach. The receding wave had now pulled so much water out from the shore it seemed to expose the entire ocean bottom. I stood alone on the breakwater, frozen in place.

The silence came over everything again—a desperate silence, as though sound itself had been ripped from the earth. The wave had swallowed K and disappeared into the far distance. I stood there, wondering what to do. Should I go down to the beach? K might be down there somewhere, buried in the sand. . . . But I decided not to leave the dike. I knew from experience that big waves often came in twos and threes.

I'm not sure how much time went by—maybe ten or twenty seconds of eerie emptiness—when, just as I had guessed, the next wave came. Another gigantic roar shook the beach, and again, after the sound had faded, another huge wave raised its head to strike. It towered before me, blocking out the sky, like a deadly cliff. This time, though, I didn't run. I stood rooted to the seawall, entranced, waiting for it to attack. What good would it do to run, I thought, now that K had been taken? Or perhaps I simply froze, overcome with fear. I can't be sure what it was that kept me standing there.

The second wave was just as big as the first—maybe even bigger. From far above my head it began to fall, losing its shape, like a brick wall slowly crumbling. It was so huge that it no longer looked like a real wave. It seemed to be some other thing, something from another, far-off world, that just happened to assume the shape of a wave. I readied myself for the moment the darkness would take me. I didn't even close my eyes. I remember hearing my heart pound with incredible clarity.

The moment the wave came before me, however, it stopped. All at once it seemed to run out of energy, to lose its forward motion and simply hover there, in space, crumbling in stillness. And in its crest, inside its cruel, transparent tongue, what I saw was K.

Some of you may find this impossible to believe, and if so, I don't blame you. I myself have trouble accepting it even now. I can't explain what I saw any better than you can, but I know it was no illusion, no hallucination. I am telling you as honestly as I can what happened at that moment—what really happened. In the tip of the wave, as if enclosed in some kind of transparent capsule, floated K's body, reclining on its side. But that is not all. K was looking straight at me, smiling. There, right in front of me, close enough so that I could have reached out and touched him, was my friend, my friend K who, only moments before, had been swallowed by the wave. And he was smiling at me. Not with an ordinary smile—it was a big, wide-open grin that literally stretched from ear to ear. His cold, frozen eyes were locked on mine. He was no longer the K I knew. And his right arm was stretched out in my direction, as if he were trying to grab my hand and pull me into that other world where he was now. A little closer, and his hand would have caught mine. But, having missed, K then smiled at me one more time, his grin wider than ever.

I seem to have lost consciousness at that point. The next thing I knew, I was in bed in my father's clinic. As soon as I awoke, the nurse went to call my father, who came running. He took my pulse, studied my pupils, and put his hand on my forehead. I tried to move my arm, but I couldn't lift it. I was burning with fever, and my mind was clouded. I had been wrestling with a high fever for some time, apparently. 'You've been asleep for three days,' my father said to me. A neighbor who had seen the whole thing had picked me up and carried me home. They had not been able to find K. I wanted to say something to my father. I *had* to say something to him. But my numb and swollen tongue could not form words. I felt as if some kind of creature had taken up residence in my mouth. My father asked me to tell him my name, but before I could remember what it was, I lost consciousness again, sinking into darkness.

Altogether, I stayed in bed for a week on a liquid diet. I vomited several times, and had bouts of delirium. My father told me afterward I was so bad that he had been afraid that I might suffer permanent neurological damage from the shock and high fever. One way or another, though, I managed to recover— physically, at least. But my life would never be the same again.

They never found K's body. They never found his dog, either. Usually when someone drowned in that area, the body would wash up a few days later on the shore of a small inlet to the east. K's body never did. The big waves probably carried it far out to sea—too far for it to reach the shore. It must have sunk to the ocean bottom to be eaten by the fish. The search went on for a very long time, thanks to the cooperation of the local fishermen, but eventually it pe- tered out. Without a body, there was never any funeral. Half-crazed, K's parents would wander up and down the beach every day, or they would shut themselves up at home, chanting sutras.

As great a blow as this had been for them, though, K's parents never chided me for having taken their son down to the shore in the midst of a typhoon. They knew how I had always loved and protected K as if he had been my own little brother. My parents, too, made a point of never mentioning the incident in my presence. But I knew the truth. I knew that I could have saved K if I had tried. I probably could have run over and dragged him out of the reach of the wave. It would have been close, but as I went over the timing of the events in memory, it always seemed to me that I could have made it. As I said before, though, over- come with fear, I abandoned him there and saved only myself. It pained me all the more that K's parents failed to blame me and that everyone else was so careful never to say anything to me about what had happened. It took me a long time to recover from the emotional shock. I stayed away from school for weeks. I hardly ate a thing, and spent each day in bed, staring at the ceiling.

K was always there, lying in the wave tip, grinning at me, his hand out- stretched, beckoning. I couldn't get that searing image out of my mind. And when I managed to sleep, it was there in my dreams—except that, in my dreams, K would hop out of his capsule in the wave and grab my wrist to drag me back inside with him.

And then there was another dream I had. I'm swimming in the ocean. It's a beautiful summer afternoon, and I'm doing an easy breaststroke far from shore. The sun is beating down on my back, and the water feels good. Then, all of a sudden, someone grabs my right leg. I feel an ice-cold grip on my ankle. It's strong, too strong to shake off. I'm being dragged down under the surface. I see K's face there. He has the same huge grin, split from ear to ear, his eyes locked on mine. I try to scream, but my voice will not come. I swallow water, and my lungs start to fill.

I wake up in the darkness, screaming, breathless, drenched in sweat.

At the end of the year, I pleaded with my parents to let me move to another town. I couldn't go on living in sight of the beach where K had been swept away, and my nightmares wouldn't stop. If I didn't get out of there, I'd go crazy. My parents understood and made arrangements for me to live elsewhere. I moved to Nagano Prefecture in January to live with my father's family in a mountain village near Komoro. I finished elementary school in Nagano and stayed on through junior and senior high school there. I never went home, even for holidays. My parents came to visit me now and then.

I live in Nagano to this day. I graduated from a college of engineering in the city of Nagano and went to work for a precision toolmaker in the area. I still work for them. I live like anybody else. As you can see, there's nothing unusual about me. I'm not very sociable, but I have a few friends I go mountain climbing with. Once I got away from my hometown, I stopped having nightmares all the time. They remained a part of my life, though. They would come to me now and then, like bill collectors at the door. It happened whenever I was on the verge of forgetting. And it was always the same dream, down to the smallest detail. I would wake up screaming, my sheets soaked with sweat.

This is probably why I never married. I didn't want to wake someone sleeping next to me with my screams in the middle of the night. I've been in love with several women over the years, but I never spent a night with any of them. The terror was in my bones. It was something I could never share with another person.

I stayed away from my hometown for over forty years. I never went near that seashore—or any other. I was afraid that, if I did, my dream might happen in reality. I had always enjoyed swimming, but after that day I never even went to a pool. I wouldn't go near deep rivers or lakes. I avoided boats and wouldn't take a plane to go abroad. Despite all these precautions, I couldn't get rid of the image of myself drowning. Like K's cold hand, this dark premonition caught hold of my mind and refused to let go.

Then, last spring, I finally revisited the beach where K had been taken by the wave.

My father had died of cancer the year before, and my brother had sold the old house. In going through the storage shed, he had found a cardboard carton crammed with childhood things of mine, which he sent to me in Nagano. Most of it was useless junk, but there was one bundle of pictures that K had painted and given to me. My parents had probably put them away for me as a keepsake of K, but the pictures did nothing but reawaken the old terror. They made me feel as if K's spirit would spring back to life from them, and so I quickly returned them to their paper wrapping, intending to throw them away. I couldn't make myself do it, though. After several days of indecision, I opened the bundle again and forced myself to take a long, hard look at K's watercolors.

Most of them were landscapes, pictures of the familiar stretch of ocean and sand beach and pine woods and the town, and all done with that special clarity and coloration I knew so well from K's hand. They were still amazingly vivid despite the years, and had been executed with even greater skill than I recalled. As I leafed through the bundle, I found myself steeped in warm memories. The deep feelings of the boy K were there in his pictures—the way his eyes were opened on the world. The things we did together, the places we went together began to come back to me with great intensity. And I realized that his eyes were my eyes, that I myself had looked upon the world back then with the same lively, unclouded vision as the boy who had walked by my side.

I made a habit after that of studying one of K's pictures at my desk each day when I got home from work. I could sit there for hours with one painting. In each I found another of those soft landscapes of childhood that I had shut out of my memory for so long. I had a sense, whenever I looked at one of K's works, that something was permeating my very flesh.

Perhaps a week had gone by like this when the thought suddenly struck me one evening: I might have been making a terrible mistake all those years. As he lay there in the tip of the wave, surely, K had not been looking at me with hatred or resentment; he had not been trying to take me away with him. And that terrible grin he had fixed me with: that, too, could have been an accident of angle or light and shadow, not a conscious act on K's part. He had probably already lost consciousness, or perhaps he had been giving me a gentle smile of eternal parting. The intense look of hatred I had thought I saw on his face had been nothing but a reflection of the profound terror that had taken control of me for the moment.

The more I studied K's watercolor that evening, the greater the conviction with which I began to believe these new thoughts of mine. For no matter how long I continued to look at the picture, I could find nothing in it but a boy's gentle, innocent spirit.

I went on sitting at my desk for a very long time. There was nothing else I could do. The sun went down, and the pale darkness of evening began to envelop the room. Then came the deep silence of night, which seemed to go on forever. At last, the scales tipped, and dark gave way to dawn. The new day's sun tinged the sky with pink, and the birds awoke to sing.

It was then I knew I must go back.

I threw a few things in a bag, called the company to say I would not be in, and boarded a train for my old hometown.

I did not find the same quiet little seaside town that I remembered. An industrial city had sprung up nearby during the rapid development of the sixties, bringing great changes to the landscape. The one little gift shop by the station had grown into a mall, and the town's only movie theater had been turned into a supermarket. My house was no longer there. It had been demolished some months before, leaving only a scrape on the earth. The trees in the yard had all been cut down, and patches of weeds dotted the black stretch of ground. K's old house had disappeared as well, having been replaced by a concrete parking lot full of commuters' cars and vans. Not that I was overcome by sentiment. The town had ceased to be mine long before.

I walked down to the shore and climbed the steps of the breakwater. On the other side, as always, the ocean stretched off into the distance, unobstructed, huge, the horizon a single straight line. The shoreline, too, looked the same as it had before: the long beach, the lapping waves, people strolling at the water's edge. The time was after four o'clock, and the soft sun of late afternoon embraced everything below as it began its long, almost meditative, descent to the west. I lowered my bag to the sand and sat down next to it in silent appreciation of the gentle seascape. Looking at this scene, it was impossible to imagine that a great typhoon had once raged here, that a massive wave had swallowed my best friend in all the world. There was almost no one left now, surely, who remembered those terrible events. It began to seem as if the whole thing were an illusion that I had dreamed up in vivid detail.

And then I realized that the deep darkness inside me had vanished. Suddenly. As suddenly as it had come. I raised myself from the sand and, without bothering either to take off my shoes or roll up my cuffs, walked into the surf to let the waves lap at my ankles. Almost in reconciliation, it seemed, the same waves that had washed up on the beach when I was a boy were now fondly washing my feet, soaking black my shoes and pant cuffs. There would be one slow-moving wave, then a long pause, and then another wave would come and go. The people passing by gave me odd looks, but I didn't care. I had found my way back again, at last.

I looked up at the sky. A few gray cotton chunks of cloud hung there, motionless. They seemed to be there for me, though I'm not sure why I felt that way. I remembered having looked up at the sky like this in search of the 'eye' of the typhoon. And then, inside me, the axis of time gave one great heave. Forty long years collapsed like a dilapidated house, mixing old time and new time together in a single swirling mass. All sounds faded, and the light around me shuddered. I lost my balance and fell into the waves. My heart throbbed at the back of my throat, and my arms and legs lost all sensation. I lay that way for a long time, face in the water, unable to stand. But I was not afraid. No, not at all. There was no longer anything for me to fear. Those days were gone.

I stopped having my terrible nightmares. I no longer wake up screaming in the middle of the night. And I am trying now to start life over again. No, I know it's probably too late to start again. I may not have much time left to live. But even if it comes too late, I am grateful that, in the end, I was able to attain a kind of salvation, to effect some sort of recovery. Yes, grateful: I could have come to the end of my life unsaved, still screaming in the dark, afraid.

The seventh man fell silent and turned his gaze upon each of the others. No one spoke or moved or even seemed to breathe. All were waiting for the rest of his story. Outside, the wind had fallen, and nothing stirred. The seventh man brought his hand to his collar once again, as if in search of words.

'They tell us that the only thing we have to fear is fear itself, but I don't believe that,' he said. Then, a moment later, he added: 'Oh, the fear is there, all right. It comes to us in many different forms, at different times, and overwhelms us. But the most frightening thing we can do at such times is to turn our backs on it, to close our eyes. For then we take the most precious thing inside us and surrender it to something else. In my case, that something was the wave.'

1996   Translated by Jay Rubin

Timothy Taylor

Brief Biography

- Born in 1963 in Venezuela.
- Youngest of five, is raised in Horseshoe Bay (near West Vancouver) and Edmonton.
- Like Sinclair Ross, is a banker turned author. An economist with an MBA from Queen's University, he works as a commercial loans banker and later in private practice as a consultant to the fisheries industry.
- He imagines being a writer by reading Mordecai Richler's 1980 autobiographical novel, *Joshua Then and Now*. His first stories were encouraged by the Toronto literary magazine *Descant* and a supportive agent.
- After a decade-long apprenticeship, in 2000 is the first writer to place three stories in the *Journey Prize Anthology*.

Although his studies and banking career took him across Canada, Timothy Taylor felt most at home in Vancouver. To leave Toronto, where he had a secure job as a commercial loans banker, to become a writer was a perilous career decision. But Taylor thrives on the uneasy tension between urban trends and natural surroundings and is committed to writing about Vancouver as a literary setting. He told Linda Richards of *January Magazine* that he admired the symbolism of the sockeye salmon, its connection to the home stream, and the importance of local communities. In an interview with *Quill & Quire*, he spoke of working in a twelfth-floor Vancouver office, his day a 'business model' divided evenly among fiction, articles, and documentary film scripts.

A thorough researcher, Taylor masters the 'job language' of his characters— from chefs' culinary arts to the jargon of architects. He learned to calculate mathematical probabilities at a race track for the title story of his only collection, *Silent Cruise* (2002). For other stories,

he gained insights into cheese making, antique watches, exotic knives, and junkyards. Fascinated by the phenomenon of 'consumer behaviour,' he describes foods, fashions, and leisure activities in his fiction. Many of his stories also expose disturbing disparities between wealth and poverty, a feature influenced by his work as chairperson of a non-profit agency for mentally ill and homeless addicts.

Taylor's first novel, *Stanley Park* (2001), was shortlisted for many awards, including the Giller Prize. Based on a fifty-year-old unsolved crime, the novel is a murder mystery of two children called 'the babes in the wood.' It is a creative blend of many short stories, with characters including a father researching the homeless in Stanley Park and a son operating a gourmet restaurant spookily named 'The Monkey's Paw' (recalling the title of a classic horror story by W.W. Jacobs).

His second novel, *Story House* (2006) —the title refers to a decaying Haida longhouse—is a story of two feuding half-brothers set in a contemporary milieu of architectural restoration, boxing, and reality TV. Critic Brandon McFarlane notes how Taylor's writings might define Canadian literature's emerging characteristics in the twenty-first century—'globalized urbanism, characters defined by their profession, and conservative literary aesthetics' based on psychological realism instead of postmodern experimentation. Taylor's approach to 'literary urbanism' recalls such forerunners as J.G. Sime, Morley Callaghan, and Mavis Gallant.

Like all traditional short stories, 'Smoke's Fortune' contains an outer and an inner conflict that contribute to the rising tension. Although the minor conflict shows two friends hunting a rabid Doberman in a junkyard, Taylor uses voice and imagery to make us question the true feelings of the nameless narrator towards his older friend, Smoke. The result is a suspenseful story that reaches a peak of chilling intensity as the narrator keeps Smoke in his telescopic sights.

Smoke's Fortune

After some talking, Fergie offered us forty dollars to shoot the dog. Smoke haggled with him, standing in that little screened porch tacked onto the front of Fergie's house, but he just said the dog was dying anyhow and swatted at a fly. Smoke said we wanted forty dollars each, and that we knew the dog had bitten a kid, and that the RCMP said kill it. But Fergie didn't budge even though we said we'd bury it and all. He said, 'I know I can't kill the bastard anyway. Here's your forty dollars. You boys take it.'

So we took it, Smoke and I. Then we got my Ruger 30-06 out of Smoke's truck and went to the shack by the yard where Fergie kept all his wrecks and parts of cars. He kept two dogs in there. They were fenced, but I guess there was one kid smarter than that fence. When Fergie found the kid, and then the dog with blood in her mouth even he knew what had to happen. And Fergie was a guy crazy for his dogs.

Frank Hall was in the shack propping up the desk with his feet, and he laughed when we came in.

'Here come the hunters,' he said, and came over to the counter. 'Don't get bit now, you hear?'

That was Frank, always winking and ribbing, but Smoke flipped a bit. He grabbed Frank's jacket and pulled him hard up into the counter so some coffee spilled. I was glad I was carrying the rifle so nothing went off or anything. Frank just laughed again like he couldn't care, and got a fresh toothpick out.

The yard was set out like a football field. Blocks on the fifteen-yard line, exhaust units on the forty, stacks of bodies on the forty-five. All with some roads for the trucks running out into the junk and then back into the corner by the Haffreys' land.

The dogs knew Smoke, but since I'd only started with Fergie in July, I carried a deer steak. This was Smoke's idea. I wasn't too sure really. If they didn't recognize me I figured the steak might give them the wrong idea. So I hung back a bit while Smoke went ahead looking for the dog.

'This fucking heat,' I heard him say.

'What,' I said.

'I can't see through this heat,' he said.

'It's hot, all right,' I said swinging the steak.

We kept on walking through the blocks. There was about a half acre of them I guessed. Up ahead I could see the stacks of pipes, then the rads, bodies, and smaller parts all grown up with weeds and grass. Fergie kept a yard for certain, everything neat and separated and lined with rosehips.

'Smoke,' I said.

'What.'

'Listen, I shouldn't be carrying the steak and the rifle. I mean, I can't shoot her one-handed. I figured maybe . . .'

But Smoke came back to where I stood and said to me slowly, like it didn't need saying, 'We find her, you throw the steak, then you shoot her. It's easy.'

I looked at him.

'I'm here to do the finding,' he said. 'They like me.'

This was how Smoke got you to do things. He made it real obvious, and then kept on telling you anyway. So by the end of his telling, you were wishing he'd be quiet and let you do it.

We went on walking, through some trucks and into more blocks. I guess there might have been a thousand old engines there, all black and rust-coloured. Right where we were, the grass grew up through some of the cylinders. They looked pretty in all that junk, which was mostly just oily.

Smoke was poking on ahead, into the big stacks of bodies. It was well-known junkyard knowledge that you watched yourself in the stacks. Frank always told about Marcel, who came out from Quebec and was crushed under a stack. He was tugging at some piece of dirty junk and pulled about three trucks down on himself. Right out from Quebec, had a job for maybe three weeks, and pulling on something he was probably barely curious about and boom. So I was watching Smoke a bit because he would tug on stuff even though he'd probably been in a junkyard as long as Frank, or even Fergie. That was Smoke's way, tugging on things even when he was in the stacks.

'Here, here, here,' I heard him say, like he was coaxing something, and then I saw him back out from under a big cab-over with his hand out. I stayed back near the blocks, holding the steak, ready to throw.

Smoke came back further and a dog came out of the grass. I could hear it panting and breathing all hanging with saliva the way they do when it's hot. This was all the sound, next to Smoke saying, 'Here, here, here. Yes, yes. Easy boy.'

When they were right in front of me Smoke just held his hand out, dangled it in the dog's face and waited. Then I'll be damned if the dog didn't start smiling, only all I saw was that whole face change, and the eyes squint back and tight, and the teeth drop out of the black lips, and the mouth crease back along the sides. I have to admit I dropped the steak and brought the Ruger right up fast thinking about squeezing not jerking the trigger, and letting the bastard move at you before you fire.

Smoke turned his hand over and cupped the dog under the muzzle and said, 'Just show them slow, like that, see?'

Jesus, I was like a stone. I think I even turned grey-coloured.

'Hey, that's great Smoke,' I said.

'What are you going to do? Shoot me or what?'

'No, hey,' I said lowering the rifle and stooping to pick up the steak. 'No.'

'This here's the one that likes me,' Smoke said, all grins.

'Yeah, well, I guess I can see you've met.'

'Here, I'll go put this one in the pen so's we don't have to catch him another four times. Give me some steak.'

I propped the rifle between my knees and managed to get my knife out. I hacked off a bit and tossed it.

'OK, I'll be back. Have a smoke or something. Don't wander around and get lost.'

'Right.' I said. And I sat down on the nearest block and smoked. It was too hot to smoke actually, but I was feeling like having one. Sometimes when I want a smoke the worst, I don't even like it when I light up. It'll even make me feel sick sometimes. I figure that's just like me to feel sick about something when you want it the most.

Smoke came back patting dust out of his pants, looking all keyed up again. He was glad to find the one dog. Now he was thinking about finding the bitch, and it wasn't getting any cooler.

'OK, OK, OK, huphuphup. Move it out!' he started shouting like a crazy person. 'Here pup, here pup!'

'Jesus, Smoke, you'll get her all riled.'

'Relax on the trigger, old son. I'm finding dogs. Come here, dog!'

So we went off further, looking. Right into the back parts of the yard where the real junk was. Some of Fergie's stuff back here didn't move too often, I figured. The back of some old Seville was rusting off to one side, fins slanting up through the weeds.

Smoke was poking, pulling on things like nothing could ever hurt him. Under a pile of fenders twenty, thirty feet high, he pulls up a piece of a radio or something and says, 'Well, shit, look at this.' I think a fender even fell off about a foot away and he just shuffled over and said, 'Hey, easy now.'

'Smoke.'

'Yeah.'

We had stopped again, I was getting dust down my shirt.

'Smoke, we're getting way the hell back here.'

Smoke came over and took a drag off my cigarette and then took one out of the package in my shirt pocket, and lit it off an old Zippo he carried around. I've seen Smoke use about three of his own cigarettes over the years and that includes the one he keeps behind his ear. He's never without the Zippo though, he loves that old thing.

'Well, she's out there, son,' he said.

Then, as he dragged on the cigarette, Smoke got to thinking and he sat down on the grass, quiet, and I slid down so my neck could crook between the manifold and the block on this old motor. There were clouds floating by really peacefully. Maybe forty clouds across the whole sky.

'Smoke, you figure that cloud's a hundred miles across?'

'Where?'

'There. That one that looks like a couch or something.'

Smoke started craning his neck all around, trying to think of an answer.

'Well,' he said finally, 'you know, I think they're actually a whole lot smaller than people think. The sky's actually smaller than people think too. You take Fergie, say, thinks he's a smart guy. Now he'll tell you that this sky's so big you can't even start to understand it. But it isn't. It's really quite small to some scientists. And getting smaller every year.'

Smoke kept on talking. I was remembering about last Saturday at the Tudor. There was a lady there I'd never seen before. Really pretty, in a skirt, looking around her like she was a little scared or something. Like maybe she got a flat going through town on her way to Red Deer and ended up here. Sitting at this bar, sipping a Coors, waiting for someone from the garage.

Well, Smoke caught one sight of her and went right up to her like she was waiting for him in particular. 'Are you the lady with the flat?' he said, like Magnum PI or something. You know, here's a time when I'm thinking, Maybe this lady had a flat. Smoke, he's thinking, Maybe, maybe not, no difference. And I get to wondering sometimes why it is that Smoke thinks he can ask people right on if they have a flat just because they're pretty.

Then Smoke shifted over in the weeds and looked down at me. I noticed he had stopped talking.

'You entirely comfortable, son?' he said.

'Why yes, Smoke,' I said. The exhaust manifold felt smooth and cool on my neck.

'Well, don't you wake up if you can kill that bitch sleeping.'

'Oh, I'm not sleeping.'

'Well, what do you think?'

I stalled a bit, wondering what I might have missed. I pulled myself up a bit, looking around for the steak. It was all ground with dirt and I wondered if a rabid dog would still like it.

'What about this steak?' I asked Smoke finally.

Smoke looked at it.

'Doesn't look too good, does it?'

'Not to me,' I said.

Smoke shrugged and looked around.

'Say, I'm going to beat the brush around here a bit, maybe drive her back toward you so you can get a shot at her.' He squinted a bit into the weeds.

'Uh, well, Smoke, I'm not too sure here . . .'

He was on his feet, gliding into the grass.

'Smoke, Jesus!' I jumped up. Smoke stopped and turned slowly, following his nose around like he was finding me by smell.

'Listen, I mean, why don't we fan out together?' The idea of wandering around these stacks with both Smoke and a rabid dog cut loose seemed like craziness.

Smoke looked disgusted for a second, like I was about twelve years old for being spooked by a dog. 'You got the fucking gun,' he said. 'You just use it when the time seems right.'

I stood there for about a minute after he left. Not moving. Swearing quietly and keeping my breathing even and shallow. The grass stretched out around me, yellow and burnt, stained with oil so the heat made your head swim with fumes. The sun kept rising higher overhead like it wasn't planning to set that day.

I backed up, holding the Ruger against my thigh, feeling the rough patterned grip on the stock grab little tufts of my jeans. I was feeling backward with my left hand, until I felt the big stack of radiators behind me. I crouched down, watching the dry weeds and thinking.

The rads had a lot of sharp edges so I stopped and pulled on my hunting gloves, which let your trigger finger hang out. Then I slung the rifle flat across my shoulders and began looking for a place to start climbing. The rads were stacked in a huge pyramid, maybe forty feet high. I put my boot up on one and pushed, knocking one off higher up. It came sliding down the stack, and I rolled to one side. It hit my shoulder and then the ground.

I started again. Trying to stay on top of the metal pieces as I climbed. My boots gripped on the rough edges all right, but as I got higher I was knocking them off left and right, kicking twisted chunks of metal down into the lane. I kept thinking, Fergie will kill us if we don't clean this up.

When I got to the top, I was afraid to look down for a while. I pinched my eyes almost shut and wormed my way onto a flat area at the top of the stack. Here I shifted around and got myself cross-legged. Then I slung the Ruger off my back carefully, trying not to shake too much. I sat like that, with the rifle up, stock up against my cheek, elbows on my knees. Then I opened my eyes wider and started looking around the yard.

Smoke was pretty small from up there. He was moving up and down the lanes, cutting across the grassy bits between the bodies and the blocks, trying to sweep through the yard toward me, and flush her out. It was kind of hypnotic, like watching a spider wait out a fly. Only now I wondered whether Smoke was the spider or the fly or what.

He was right up to the exhaust pipes, all jumbled with the weeds. He was bobbing his head again like he was smelling something, taking a quiet step or two every so often. I nestled the rifle into my cheek. The wood was oily and hot from the sun. Through the scope I could see Smoke and about two feet all around him. With my other eye open, though, I could still see the rest of the yard. My dad taught me that. A lot of people think your scope eye stops working if you do that, but it doesn't. You start seeing better. As you stare and you don't blink, you suddenly start getting every little movement all over the yard. And in the middle, this circle of larger detail.

I could see Smoke breathing slowly, his cheek sucking in and out. I could see the brick-red sunburn across his neck and the line of dirt around his collar. Across the top of my sight, I could see a truck on the highway, maybe a mile away. You could barely hear it growling, but I could see it moving and see the black exhaust jump out the pipe every time he took another gear. I could see them both, Smoke and the truck.

Smoke kept on crawling through those pipes. Near the far side of the pile he slowed right down and froze. His one hand was up hanging over a tailpipe, the other behind his back, his nose pointing. I tracked the crosshairs of the scope over his shoulders into the grass, then back into his open hand. His hand went into a fist, my left eye was shaking, trying to see all over the yard and concentrate on Smoke at the same time.

Suddenly he jumped to the left, swinging his hand down and pulling the pipe with it. They crashed and rolled across the dirt and he leaped backwards and rolled on one shoulder, coming up in a squat with his hunting knife hovering in front of him, blade up. The crosshairs hung in open air for a moment, a foot in front of his face.

In that second when Smoke was still, I saw her. In my left eye, in the big picture. She was there, where we'd dropped the steak, maybe twenty yards from Smoke. She was muzzling the meat, pawing it. Trying to figure out why it smelled so good and looked so bad, I guess.

She wasn't looking too good herself. All matted and caked around the mouth, dripping drool on herself when she shook her black head. Her sharp snout had flecks of grey, her chest was muddy and her legs shook badly. Her hair was dull, and she panted as she pawed the meat, then jumped back and shook her head from side to side. Just a half-crazy old Doberman, mad at the world and hungry.

When she heard Smoke dump the exhaust pipes, she stopped and listened. She turned and thrashed on her back in the dust then stood up again. I didn't move the rifle too much, just let it coast over as Smoke started out down the lane again and cut into the weeds towards her. I was dead still except for that,

that tiny movement of the barrel; Smoke walked along slowly, whistling softly, wondering where I was, maybe, crosshairs on his shoulder. When he crouched down, I'd freeze entirely. No breathing, both eyes locked open, I think my heart stopped even.

I guess I kept meaning to do something, but I didn't want to. I felt almost sleepy except for my face smeared into the Ruger. Pretty soon they were both moving again. Smoke in the scope. The bitch in the yard. I was seeing them both, eyes running with tears. When she saw Smoke through the weeds she went still and tight, low to the ground, like a piece of steel sitting with the others. I was thinking about shooting her then, but I was afraid the bullet would skip right off her, ricochet around, maybe hurt someone. Her lips went back into a grin; her teeth hung with dirt and saliva.

Smoke was batting at some weeds with an old antenna. I was looking at his scalp with my right eye, thinking I could feel the itch of the dirt and grass in it. I scratched it lightly with the crosshairs. From the back up across the top where it was tangled, down into the slick sideburns and the tuft in the ear.

And I was watching these two tangled bits of hair and dirt and saliva get closer together and thinking about how my finger, soft on the trigger, was going to do something soon, very small, and stop them from hurting each other, which seemed a shame, although also very natural.

And then she moved up fast, coming off the ground like a jet, real low at first and then wide and high. Her front legs in and close to her chest, her head forward, brows over and down to protect her eyes, her mouth lipless, showing every tooth and every rib on her black gums. Streaming saliva. And I just sat there until I saw her pass from my left eye into the right, and when she burst into my scope I shot her.

And then she seemed to vanish, and I lowered the Ruger, and Smoke had spun around like a drunken wrestler and was sitting in the grass, his knife still in his belt, his face blank, his mouth open a bit.

I climbed down and walked into the lane past the broken dog. Smoke was on his feet again, grinning. As we stood there he took a cigarette out of my pocket, lit it off the Zippo, and said, 'Nice piece of shooting, son.' And I guess I knew he'd say something like that.

2002

Richard Van Camp

Brief Biography

- Born in 1971; half white, half Dogrib (Tlicho).
- His parents are taxidermists.
- Is raised in the Métis community of Fort Smith, NWT, where residents speak Cree, English, French, and Chippewayan.
- Plans on becoming a land claims negotiator for the Dogrib.
- At age twenty-five, publishes *The Lesser Blessed*, a 'coming-of-age' novel and the first book written by a member of the Dogrib nation.
- 'Sky Burial,' starring Cree actor Ben Cardinal, is broadcast as CBC radio drama.
- Fan of graphic fiction, science fiction, and fantasy; edits comics for the Healthy Aboriginal Network.
- A successful children's author, his *Welcome Song for Baby: A Lullaby for Newborns* is given to every newborn baby in BC in 2008 as part of the Books for Babies initiative.

Richard Van Camp is a member of the Dogrib nation, whose lands lie between Great Slave Lake and Great Bear Lake in the Northwest Territories. As a vocal spokesperson for the 'second generation' of Aboriginal writers in Canada, he participates in workshops and readings across the country, as well as in the United States and Australia. He told an interviewer, 'Stories for us are the best medicine. Where I'm from, storytelling is how we honour one another.' Van Camp, who has written scripts for the TV show *North of 60*, has criticized the 'atrocious' portrayal of Aboriginal stereotypes in comics, countless TV programs, and movies. He points out that his is the second generation that writes in English and is free from the repressive impositions of residential schools. He says, 'I dislike the term First Nations, because that term excludes the Métis, non-Status people, the Inuit, and children who were adopted out and are trying really hard to reclaim their identities. That's why I love the word "Aboriginal": it includes everybody.'

Van Camp published his short story collection, *Angel Wing Splash Pattern* (2002), with the small Aboriginal publisher Kegedonce Press. With six Canadian Aboriginal publishers and the increasing prominence of Native perspectives in universities and colleges, young Aboriginal authors are now able to reach a larger audience. With the UN declaring 1993 The Year of Indigenous Peoples, these authors began to see themselves as part of a larger body of indigenous peoples. Like Thomas King challenging issues of borders, boundaries, and national identity, Canada's Aboriginal writers and publishers are 'crossing borders' in global co-operative ventures with Australian and New Zealand publishers as the so-called 'Fourth World' (after Grand Chief George Manuel's definition).

A graduate of the Creative Writing Program at the University of Victoria and the En'owkin International School of Writing, Van Camp now teaches creative writing for Aboriginal students at the University of British Columbia. His well-received novel, *The Lesser Blessed* (1996), is set in a small town in the Northwest Territories and uses unsparing realism to portray social problems—alcoholism, violence, sexual and substance abuse—affecting Aboriginal youth.

In much of his short fiction, Van Camp fashions the oral tradition of storytelling into clipped vignettes of contemporary life, revealing its tragedy and despair as well as its energies and redemptive promise. The stories in *Angel Wing Splash Pattern* compose a 'photo album,' a 'braid-ing' of traditional stories, reminiscences, observations, and personal history. Some stories focus solely on Aboriginal characters and are set in the area around Fort Smith, while others include non-Natives and are set in British Columbia or else-where in Canada. 'Sky Burial,' which takes place in Edmonton, originated in a Victoria, BC, food court where Van Camp saw a beautiful Native girl eating with an older white woman and started thinking, 'What if a dying medicine man saw her in the mall and gave her everything he had?' The pathos in the story derives partly from Icabus's need to pass on his ancestral gift, received from animal-spirit beings, to a young Cree girl.

Sky Burial

Pain seared up Icabus' leg forcing him to stop and wince. He wheezed through one lung, and the mall blurred around him. He coughed and his chest sounded and felt as if it were stuffed with the broken glass of gray light bulbs. This was it: he was dying. The Cree medicine had him.

In his reflection, Icabus hated what he saw. I'm not that skinny, am I? He was bleeding inside and felt so weak. 'I seen better lookin' corpses.' Something had blown behind his left eye earlier that morning, causing his ears to ring.

The bird. It was dying in front of him. He didn't know what the bird was called but was awed at how bright and blue the feathers were.

Parakeet? Parrot? No, he knew it wasn't the true name of the bird's tribe, and he wished he knew. He thought of all the shampoo bottles his daughter Augustine used and chose the one that smelled the best.

'Papaya,' he said. 'That's your Dogrib name now: Papaya.'

The pet store, which showcased the bird, had it in a cage. The bird measured three feet from black beak to bright blue tail, yet the cage only offered four. A sign read: 'Do Not Tap Cage.' The bird was upside down, shitting on itself and biting at the chain that sliced into its leg.

The bird deserved something far better than this.

Oh, how Icabus wished to be around fire. He was sure the bird was a woman. She panted; her black tongue licked at her swollen ankle. She hung awkwardly, rested, shivered, tried to bite at the chain, fell back, shivered again. It looked as if she were drowning. Icabus watched the bird and felt under his shirt where he was bleeding inside. It was if he had been force-fed thousands of porcupine quills that were growing with each breath. He pressed into his left rib cage as he strained to open the cage.

'Macaw,' a voice said suddenly behind him.

'Huh?'

'It's a Macaw.'

Icabus turned to look at the wielder of such a firm voice. It was a child. An Indian girl. Tall, slim. She was beautiful. Her eyes were large and round. She wore a T-shirt with a huge white owl with yellow eyes on it. A younger white boy with a runny nose came up and started banging on the cage. The girl left as fast as she had appeared. Icabus wanted to talk to her, but he was hit again with pain. He coughed and coughed and coughed. He held himself up against the glass and looked down until the reddest blood dripped from his mouth. He had to hurry, but where was the sign?

Icabus bought a coffee and a doughnut at Grandma Lee's. As he sat, the pain bit again as if the quills inside him were starting to burrow and grind inside his guts, shredding everything inside him. He put his head down and focused on his shoes. He took a breath, biting the tip of his tongue. 'Chinaman did a good job on polishing them up,' he wiggled his toes. 'Too bad the bitches got me.'

Any other man, he coughed, any other man would not have woken up from last night's sleep. Each heartbeat drove a long hot metal blade through his skull over and over. This was not the flu. It was a death sentence for what he and the boy had done to the sweat lodges in Rae.

Together he and Morris had burned them all. Icabus wanted to teach the Crees not to charge money for their sweat lodges on Dogrib soil, but the lesson had cost him everything—or had it? Was there still time? He'd thought last night about passing on his medicine to Morris, but Icabus had seen black around him before he left, and he knew Morris' days were numbered.

If he thought about it, he'd start to cry and if he started to cry here he'd never stop. The boy would have to look after himself. Their time was getting closer, and he knew it.

No more sunrises, no more northern lights, no more snow or cold or anything . . . and it had to be here, in a mall of strangers. All he could do was look down and think. His shoes were so polished they looked like black ice. In the reflection he watched the shadows and saw a man walking towards him. Morris? He wanted to ask. My adopted son?

'There you are,' Harold said and sat beside him.

The pain struck again. Icabus bit into his doughnut. The dough would soak up the blood inside him. The noise of the mall rose around him: the metal-whine of blenders, children hollering for toys. Harold had a tray of Cokes and tacos and the smell was thick and sweet.

'We were looking for you. God, you look sick.'

Icabus stared out the window to the mall parking lot. His ear began to ring again. A blonde child stood crying in the middle of the pavement, her red balloon flying away. One of her shoes was off. Behind her, the Edmonton sunset tore the sky in half. Icabus squinted but couldn't see a parent for the girl. He leaned forward, tracking the balloon as far as he could, and he wanted so desperately to follow it.

'I see you got your shoes fixed.' Harold took the paper bag and looked inside. 'What else?'

Icabus glared at him for not asking first. 'Safes,' he grumbled. 'Suzy Muktuck's in town.' He studied Harold's throat and hated how white it was.

'Icabus,' Harold blushed. 'Nobody calls them safes anymore. Did Augy say you could afford these?'

Icabus ignored the question and wiped cold sweat from his forehead. *I'm dying. They got me bleeding to death inside.*

'I don't understand why you got those fixed up,' Harold scoffed. 'You don't even have enough money for next week. Christ, you've been eating at our place the last four days . . .'

'Gotta look good at my funeral,' Icabus explained.

Harold missed it. 'If I hear another trapping story, I don't know what I'll do.'

'Our family comes from the land. You need to remember this.'

Harold rolled his eyes and bit into the taco. Tomato sauce gushed out the bottom. Icabus closed his eyes. The sauce was blood. Augustine's blood every time she tried to have a baby. The blood of his son who had killed himself. The blood in his piss and spit.

Harold went on talking with a full mouth. Icabus nodded, pretending to pay attention. He sipped his coffee and waited for a sign. 'Where's Augy?' He asked.

'Looking for you.' Harold bit into the taco again and Icabus looked for the little girl. She was gone.

'There you are,' an exhausted voice heaved. Augustine huffed towards them: her bad perm, pink track pants, Jean jacket, dusty runners. She sat down, grabbed the other taco, and elbowed Harold. 'And you!' she scolded, 'this is cold.' She bit into it anyway. Icabus studied his daughter and her husband. He looked into her black and dying hair, her dreadful perm, and thought, 'Spider legs, thousands of spider legs.'

The couple gabbed. Food toppled out of their mouths. Their noise was muffled and lost to the crowd. It will be okay, he thought. He'd left his wedding band by his bed. The day before, when Harold had assumed he was at the dentist's, he'd emptied his account and left his money in his wallet under his pillow. Three thousand dollars in thirty 100 dollar bills would go far for them. As for his clothes, they would all be burned once he left. Icabus looked around.

To his right, a table away, sat a family of ruined Indians. They had all let themselves go. They fed on burgers, fries, shakes. The mother had cut her hair.

The kids were pudgy. The man was soft. Where are the warriors? Icabus had been waiting for a nod or a sign of acknowledgment, but the Indians wouldn't meet his eyes. What's happened to us? he thought. What the hell has happened to all of us?

'Oh,' a breath lit from his mouth. It was the young girl he saw, the one with the owl shirt. Augy and Harold kept talking, taking turns sucking the straw, biting into more tacos.

Her long black hair was what caught him. She was as slender as a diamond willow. She moved with a white woman across the perimeter. What the hell was she doing with a white woman? They carried hot dogs and drinks. The girl sat down quickly out of his view. He shifted to see her better.

'... and the lady, Dad. The lady said we could visit Sundays and we could bring you home cooked food. It'll be good for you to be with others your own age.' Augy ate while Harold listened and nodded. 'You'll love it.'

'The move will be good for you.' Harold added. 'Think of all the French Safes you could use over there.'

Icabus nodded again and looked for the young girl. A young couple was in his way. They had their lower lips pierced and whenever they kissed Icabus could hear metals clicking, clicking. 'Savages,' he thought. He squinted and saw her. She was nodding, listening to the white woman speak.

Icabus sat straight up and almost spilled his drink. He brought his hand up over his lip and caressed the whiskers on his chin. She's the one, he thought. It was her shirt that did it. The white owl was the sign he'd been looking for.

'I'm Stan the man with the nine!' Stan would yell to the women who drank with them. 'When I die, there's gonna be two boxes: one for Stan and one for the nine!' The women would giggle and Stan would always throw Icabus a wink.

It was the winter of '79. They were drinking at Stan's. Icabus was taking a leak outside a party when he looked up and saw a huge white owl looking down at him. What he remembered most was the eyes. Yellow eyes. With fire and power behind them. They were eyes he couldn't lie to. Eyes he couldn't tame. The eyes saw him for what he really was: a drunk.

The owl hissed at him as he ran back to his shack. He grabbed his .410 and Stan ran after him.

'Lookit' this fuckin' owl!' Icabus hooted. 'Look!'

They were both drunk and Stan made the sign of the cross when he saw the owl.

Stan yelled, 'Someone's gonna die! Don't shoot it!' but Icabus aimed and fired. *I didn't mean to hit it*, he would say later, but they saw an explosion of white feathers. Stan punched him hard, catching his ear. Icabus fell down. Stan ran into the snow to help the bird. It was dead.

Neither of them buried the bird, and Icabus never spoke to Stan ever again.

The next time Icabus saw the owl, it was in a dream. He dreamt he was walking in the snow to the old trapline he and Stan shared when they were kids when the owl landed in front of him. The eyes of the owl had changed. They were Stan's.

Icabus woke as Augy ran into his room saying that Stan had died. Family had called from Rae. A stroke had taken Stan during the night.

The pain hit again. Icabus bit his cheek so he wouldn't scream. 'It's gettin' closer,' he whispered. He thought of his wife who had died far too young from the cancer. Delphine. He thought of her grace, her elegance. The community thought she was so shy, but Icabus knew that she saved the very best of herself for him. Oh, they had argued; they had yelled, but the passion and the peace between them grew every year they had together. He missed her love and was sad at the thought of losing her. God took you, he thought, and I never got to hear everything you had to say.

After her funeral, whenever he saw a butterfly, he would call her name. And whenever he saw a red fox, he would whisper his son's name and weep with guilt because his son died alone and ashamed. It will be something, he thought, to see you both again: young, alive, and radiant. In his dreams, Icabus walked into the Great Slave Lake by his home in Rae as he died, releasing himself to it, and disappearing.

On CBC, before he left Rae, the Dogrib leaders were telling everybody to boil the water twice before drinking it. They never said why.

He shook his head. 'We can't drink it, but we bathe in it.' He took a long breath. Using the table, he pulled himself up slowly and stood still as the blood roared in his ears. He could taste blood in his saliva.

'Where are you goin'?' Harold asked.

'To sing for the last time,' Icabus answered.

'What?'

Icabus began to sing under his breath. He walked carefully, cautiously. His lips moved and he felt the wind gather around him. He walked slowly in his polished shoes, almost as if making a deal with the pain to give him just a little more time, just a little more, and there she was. She and the white woman were eating their hot dogs. The girl was the first to see him. 'Mommy,' she said. 'Look at the Indian.'

The mother gawked towards him and warned, 'Now, honey . . .'

'Scuse me,' Icabus said, all the while hoping he'd have enough time. The mother looked around, perhaps for Security, but the girl watched him. 'There's something in your daughter's hair.'

'What!' the mother squawked. 'Where?' She went through her daughter's hair. 'Oh, Mindy . . .'

Mindy wouldn't stop looking at him.

Icabus tried to smile through all of the pain inside of him. 'I'm a Dogrib Indian. Have you ever heard of us?'

The mother stopped briefly looking through Mindy's hair and watched him. 'Please have a seat. My daughter is Cree.'

He held his back, leaned into the table, careful of his knees, and sat slowly across from them. He winced and bit his lip. 'It's okay if you haven't.'

'But your hair is short,' Mindy said.

Icabus laughed, surprised with the observation. 'Our hair is short. We're different, that way, from the Crees, but we pray the same way.'

Icabus began singing inside and could feel the power rising around him. He ran his fingers through his hair and pulled three hairs from his scalp. From the inside of his jacket, he pulled out his gift for the girl.

'Well,' Mindy's mother exhaled, 'I can't find anything.'

'It's right here.' Icabus explained. He leaned forward, passing the gift from one hand to the other, before feeling through Mindy's hair. He felt the waves of a hot lake, the down on a duck's belly, the under-flesh of a thousand petals.

'Can I give you something?' he asked.

She smiled and nodded.

'Look!' he said and brought back a bright blue feather. He pulled a few hairs from her head when he pulled back the feather.

'Oh my,' the mother grinned. 'Oh my!'

'Oh, Mommy,' Mindy clapped, 'it's beautiful!'

'For you.' Icabus offered to Mindy. 'From the bird.'

'The Macaw!' Mindy beamed.

'When a woman gives birth to a girl,' he offered, 'the girl is the father's teacher.'

Under the table, he wrapped her hair around his fingers.

'I'm my daddy's teacher?' Mindy asked.

'You're the one,' he finished. Yes, he would teach her. He sang. He called it forth and it came. The young girl giggled and covered her mouth. A hand grabbed onto Icabus' shoulder almost snapping the song.

'Here he is!' Harold called. 'Over here, Augy!'

Icabus looked down.

'Dye aye kae khlee nee,' he whispered and looked over to Mindy. 'Remember me.'

'Can I keep the feather?' she asked.

He coughed and nodded. 'Do you like cats?'

Mindy shook her head. 'I'm allergic.'

'You can't use your medicine around cats,' he said. 'They'll steal it.'

'What do you mean?' the mother asked.

'In your life, you need to listen with the deepest part of you for what to do. You need to listen with you blood.'

'That is good advice,' the mother pulled out her purse. 'What tribe are you from again?'

'Dogrib,' he answered and when he spoke, he smiled. This was it.

The mother wrote this down. 'Is that one word or two?'

'Thank you,' Mindy smiled and held the feather up to the light.

Icabus was pleased.

'Dad!' Augy said and came over. 'I'm so sorry,' she apologized to the woman. 'My father wanders.' She cleared her throat and lowered her voice. 'He's . . . confused.'

Icabus sang louder now and began moving his lips. Maybe the girl would one day visit Rae with questions about him, questions that were asked by her blood and his medicine.

Icabus felt the song push against the back of his teeth and run its fingers through her hair. He thought of the lake and looked into Mindy's eyes. He sent part of himself: the best part. Mindy's eyes registered his power. She wasn't scared and that was good.

He sang and twisted her hair with his under the table. He remembered the song as best he could. It was the same song his grandmother had sung to him. He looked down to make sure his shadow covered Mindy's. The pain sliced again. He sang her name with a breath and all she heard was: 'Deeeee . . .'

He pulled the braid of their hair until it snapped, and Icabus left his body. It was like falling skyward. Mindy received him: the Macaw's blue feather in her hand; her mother pulling Mindy close; Augy, her bad perm blocking out the sun.

'Dad? Dad!'

Icabus flew with an explosion of white feathers and was swallowed by the hottest lake. He could hear the most beautiful songs being sung by thousands of voices, and there was peace. He became it. Everything was so blue, and he noticed that the colors red and black were nowhere to be seen. He could see Delphine waiting for him. She was radiant, standing in her tanned moosehide dress, and beside her stood Justin, who stood so proud. Morris wasn't here, and that was a good sign. Icabus looked to his left. Stan walked beside him, smiled, placed his hand on Icabus' shoulder, guided him home . . .

2002

Thomas King

Brief Biography

- Born 1943 in Sacramento, CA to a Cherokee father and German-Greek mother.
- Works as professional photojournalist; in one witty series, Native children wear Lone Ranger masks and in another, Native tourists pose in front of tourist monuments.
- Immigrates to Canada in 1980, teaching English and Native Literature at the University of Guelph.
- Writes stories to impress a professor, now his wife.
- First novel, *Medicine River* (1990), becomes a CBC movie in 1993, starring Graham Greene.
- In 2003, becomes the first person of Native descent to deliver the Massey Lectures; named member of the Order of Canada in 2004.
- Like Haruki Murakami, King compares writing to music.
- Finishes fourth as NDP candidate for Guelph in 2008 federal election.

As heir to a legacy of questioning cultural identity established by Pauline Johnson, Thomas King is now probably Canada's best-known Native writer, his stories and novels often taught in literature and Native Studies courses. King has said, 'The truth about stories is that that's all we are,' and the storyteller is a prominent figure in King's fiction, underscoring the importance of the oral tradition in transmitting the history, sense of community, and values of Aboriginal cultures.

King's works, many of them set on a fictional Blackfoot reserve in Alberta, have been praised for their accessibility and their ability to evoke the dilemma of the marginalized Indian without overtly politicizing or alienating non-Native readers. King's mixed ancestry and his vocation as a university professor have made him an ideal mediator, one who seeks to raise awareness more than militantly declaim. Seemingly innocuous situations, realistic dialogue, and satirical humour combine in his fiction to create plausible contexts that highlight the precariousness of white–Native relationships and show Native characters tentatively exploring their identity. In a book-length study of King's work, *Border Crossings: Thomas King's Cultural Inversions* (2003), Arnold E. Davidson, Priscilla L. Walton, and Jennifer Andrews explain the way that King's humour 'takes on a life of its own in a Native North American context by bringing communities together, facilitating conflict resolution, and establishing a common bond between otherwise divided nations.'

Yet King has said that he would rather 'annoy than placate,' and beneath the genial exterior of much of his fictional world lurks a host of tensions and hostilities. The central characters in his first two novels, *Medicine River* (1990) and *Green Grass, Running Water* (1993), are caught between two worlds. They attempt but fail to fit into mainstream society where they are often viewed stereotypically or as exotic commodities before being urged by elders, friends, and family to reclaim their Aboriginal heritage. Like Bharati Mukherjee, King seeks a new definition of ethnicity, not colonial definitions. In his radical essay 'Godzilla vs Post-Colonial' (1990), he objects to the term 'post-colonialism' as ethnocentric, a 'construct of oppression' that separates Native writers from their traditions.

Green Grass, Running Water, a post-modern blend of realism, fantasy, and myth, represents King's break with the realism of his first novel: he employs a non-linear narrative with four remarkable Natives named Lone Ranger, Hawkeye, Ishmael, and Robinson Crusoe, plus the traditional trickster figure, Coyote. Critics note elements of magic realism in his fiction, including 'A Short History of Indians

in Canada,' the title story of his most recent collection (2005). King inserts magically improbable elements into an ordinary situation, that of an insomniac businessman looking for some 3 a.m. excitement in the big city. Brief and composed almost entirely of dialogue, the story maintains the devices of a conventional story with identifiable characters, plot, setting, and point of view.

Besides his writing output—three novels, two story collections, children's fiction, and essays—King is an editor, photographer, film director, and creator of the CBC radio series *The Dead Dog Café Comedy Hour*. He has also edited two anthologies of contemporary Native fiction (*All My Relations*, 1992; *First Voices, First Words*, 2001).

See Thomas King, from Introduction to *All My Relations: An Anthology of Contemporary Canadian Native Fiction*, p. 445.

A Short History of Indians in Canada

Can't sleep, Bob Haynie tells the doorman at the King Eddie. Can't sleep, can't sleep.

First time in Toronto? says the doorman.

Yes, says Bob.

Businessman?

Yes.

Looking for some excitement?

Yes.

Bay Street, sir, says the doorman.

Bob Haynie catches a cab to Bay Street at three in the morning. He loves the smell of concrete. He loves the look of city lights. He loves the sound of skyscrapers.

Bay Street.

Smack!

Bob looks up just in time to see a flock of Indians fly into the side of the building.

Smack! Smack!

Bob looks up just in time to get out of the way.

Whup!

An Indian hits the pavement in front of him.

Whup! Whup!

Two Indians hit the pavement behind him.

Holy Cow! shouts Bob, and he leaps out of the way of the falling Indians.

Whup! Whup! Whup!

Bob throws his hands over his head and dashes into the street. And is almost hit by a city truck.

Honk!

Two men jump out of the truck. Hi, I'm Bill. Hi, I'm Rudy.

Hi, I'm Bob.

Businessman? says Bill.

Yes.

First time in Toronto? says Rudy.

Yes.

Whup! Whup! Whup!

Look out! Bob shouts. There are Indians flying into the skyscrapers and falling on the sidewalk.

Whup!

Mohawk, says Bill.

Whup! Whup!

Couple of Cree over here, says Rudy.

Amazing, says Bob. How can you tell?

By the feathers, says Bill. We got a book.

It's our job, says Rudy.

Whup!

Bob looks around. What's this one? he says.

Holy! says Bill. Holy! says Rudy.

Check the book, says Bill. Just to be sure.

Flip, flip, flip.

Navajo!

Bill and Rudy put their arms around Bob. A Navajo! Don't normally see Navajos this far north. Don't normally see Navajos this far east.

Is she dead? says Bob.

Nope, says Bill. Just stunned.

Most of them are just stunned, says Rudy.

Some people never see this, says Bill. One of nature's mysteries. A natural phenomenon.

They're nomadic you know, says Rudy. And migratory.

Toronto's in the middle of the flyway, says Bill. The lights attract them.

Bob counts the bodies. Seventy-three. No. Seventy-four. What can I do to help?

Not much that anyone can do, says Bill. We tried turning off the lights in the buildings.

We tried broadcasting loud music from the roofs, says Rudy.

Rubber owls? asks Bob.

It's a real problem this time of the year, says Bill.

Whup! Whup! Whup!

Bill and Rudy pull green plastic bags out of their pockets and try to find the open ends.

The dead ones we bag, says Rudy.

The lives ones we tag, says Bill. Take them to the shelter. Nurse them back to health. Release them in the wild.

Amazing, says Bob.

A few wander off dazed and injured. If we don't find them right away, they don't stand a chance.

Amazing, says Bob.

You're one lucky guy, says Bill. In another couple of weeks, they'll be gone.

A family from Alberta came through last week and didn't even see an Ojibway, says Rudy.

Your first time in Toronto? says Bill.

It's a great town, says Bob. You're doing a great job.

Whup!

Don't worry, says Rudy. By the time the commuters show up, you'll never even know the Indians were here.

Bob catches a cab back to the King Eddie and shakes the doorman's hand. I saw the Indians, he says.

Thought you'd enjoy that, sir, says the doorman.

Thank you, says Bob. It was spectacular.

Not like the old days. The doorman sighs and looks up into the night. In the old days, when they came through, they would black out the entire sky.

2005

Shyam Selvadurai

Brief Biography

- Born in 1965 in Colombo, Sri Lanka (formerly British-ruled Ceylon), to a Tamil father and Sinhalese mother; his origins mirror conflicts between minority Hindu Tamils and majority Buddhist Sinhalese.
- In 1983, moves to Canada after Sri Lankan civil war begins.
- Earns BFA in Creative Writing from York University; resides in Toronto.
- Edits the first anthology of South Asian diaspora writers, *Story-Wallah* (2005), which describes shift in Asian-Canadian writing from 'immigrant' to 'diasporic' narratives.
- His first novel for young adults, *Swimming in the Monsoon Sea* (2005), addresses gay issues.
- 'The Demoness Kali' wins Gold Prize at National Magazine awards, 2006.

A significant writer in post-colonial and queer studies, Shyam Selvadurai represents a new wave of South Asian writers. He is virtually alone in Sri Lanka as an openly gay cultural figure. His realistic fiction portrays a hybrid multiculturalism, not only depicting layers of conflict as a legacy of British colonialism between the Ceylonese and English, but also the post-independence ethnic and religious differences between the Sinhalese and Tamils.

Though his writing reveals conflicts within generations and family secrets in Sri Lankan, English-speaking upper-middle classes, it more importantly breaks the silence around sexuality, especially gay men.

Selvadurai's award-winning *Funny Boy: A Novel in Six Stories* (1994) tells both the story of a gay man in Sri Lanka and the historical background of the civil war. In Sri Lanka, homosexuality is illegal, punishable by twelve years' imprisonment. Though the novel, a best-seller in Sri Lanka, was read by the country's

president and instigated a public debate on gay rights, the laws dating from Victorian times have not yet been repealed. His article 'Coming Out,' published in *Time Asia* (1998), describes his fears living with a gay partner in Sri Lanka.

The ancient Greek term 'diaspora' means 'a scattering of seeds,' and now refers to refugees, exiles, asylum-seekers, immigrants, or any large population forced to relocate due to war, genocide, persecution, slavery, or natural disaster. Selvadurai's anthology *Story-Wallah* includes displaced or expatriate Indian and Sri Lankan writers from every continent. In his editorial he notes, 'my identity . . . as a writer, . . . my creativity comes not from "Sri Lankan" or "Canadian" but precisely from the space between, that marvelous open space represented by the hyphen, in which the two parts of my identity jostle and rub up against each other like tectonic plates.'

In her scholarly study, *Impossible Desires: Queer Diasporas and South Asian Public Cultures* (2005), Gayatri Gopinath notes that 'queer diaspora' both challenges Euro-American notions of hetero- and homosexuality and colonialism while offering alternative imaginings of nation and family. Touching on this theme, Selvadurai's *Cinnamon Gardens* (1999), inspired in part by Jane Austen's *Pride and Prejudice* (1813), is set in colonial Ceylon in the 1920s. The novel (the title refers to a wealthy quarter of Colombo) describes, among other incidents, how British homosexuals became involved with local men. Recalling stories told by his liberated grandmother, who rode horses and drove cars at a time when women were chaperoned, Selvadurai researched archives for the beginnings of modern Sri Lanka. He became fascinated with the 1920s, the women's movement, the labour movement, and the realization that the British governing system could not work in a multicultural society, asking what political system should replace it. Catching a society at a moment of change and shifting social order, his work portrays psychic anxiety and nostalgia as expression of loss.

'The Demoness Kali' is an initiation story that recalls a time of familial betrayal and a loss of innocence. It is a traditional narrative that questions traditions. Though the story reveals the cruelty of the grandmother as well as the school system (and indirectly alludes to cruelties of class and caste war), it also has a tone of nostalgia, a longing for beauty and a permanent home.

See Shyam Selvadurai, from 'Introducing Myself in the Diaspora,' p. 449.

The Demoness Kali

I often have a dream, inspired by a Buddhist Jataka story I was told as a child. In the dream, I am my mother and I run in panic through a landscape that resembles the Dry Zone of Sri Lanka, the soil sandy, the parched riverbed rutted; thorn bushes rip at my clothes, leaving bloody scratches on my body. In my arms, I carry an infant. I am being pursued by something fearsome and, looking back, I see that it is my grandmother, incarnated as the demoness Kali. Her face resembles one of those Sri Lankan devil masks: a snout of a nose, bulging red eyes, matted black hair, small tusks protruding from the corners of her mouth, pulled back in a hideous grin.

I am no match for my grandmother, who is fleet of foot, and she easily overcomes me and bars my way. I clutch my child to my chest, pleading, but I am helpless against my grandmother, who snatches the infant from my arms and opens her mouth wide to consume him.

For the first six years of my life, I did not know my grandmother because she and my mother had a falling out when my parents married. My mother was just eighteen years old when she met my father. He was twenty-five and a boarder in a neighbour's house, having come to Colombo for a junior executive post at an insurance company. My grandmother opposed the marriage because my father was Christian and Tamil, my mother's family Buddhist and Sinhalese. But perhaps she also sensed the great weakness in my father, even though he had a good position at the time, with a prestigious company.

My father might have been willing to back away, but my mother, who had inherited her will from my grandmother, had made up her mind. It was she who masterminded the elopement, arranging everything from the quick ceremony in a magistrate's office to their brief honeymoon in Kandy. By the time they returned to Colombo, my grandmother had disowned her daughter.

Within a year of their marriage, my father's weakness showed itself. He made a mistake at work, losing the company a great deal of money; he was fired for his incompetence. Over the next few years, my parents, my two older sisters, and I moved continually as my father's ineptitude cost him job after job. With each sacking, he fell to a lower level of employment until finally, by the time I was six years old, he had sunk to manager of a little rest house in Wellawaya.

It was a rundown place with light green walls that had not been painted in years and dusty, shabby furniture with upholstery that smelled of damp and mould. The seven bedrooms were in no better state. The toilets were particularly awful, with cracked cisterns and leaking rusty taps, the walls dark with fungi. Behind the rooms, an open drain carried water and sewage from the bathrooms to an underground cesspit.

The rooms, when they were occupied, were usually taken by travelling salesmen and low-level government servants. From our quarters, we would often hear their drunken carousing late into the night, the same tired baila songs with their lewd lyrics. In typical Sri Lankan form, the men would not eat until they were good and tight, and so the staff was kept up well past midnight before dinner was served. My father would return to our rooms in the small hours of the morning, bleached with fatigue.

To my sisters and I, who knew no better, the rest house in Wellawaya had its charms. There was a vast back garden with fruit trees that we would feast off all year round. There were goats and cows, which we named and treated as our personal pets. The waiters and cook were our friends, and they would often make us treats for tea like halvah, kawun, kokis, or pol toffee.

To my mother, raised in a wealthy home in Colombo, this rest house must have been intolerable. I remember her pacing our quarters at night, as the ribaldry grew in the dining room. She would also sit for hours in a plastic lawn chair outside our quarters, staring in a stupor at the sporadic traffic on the Wellawaya Road. I strangely don't have any memory of her crying during this period, nor of any fits of anger. I think that she was beyond tears—that, as she sat sprawled in the plastic chair, she was coldly contemplating her life and planning how and when she would act.

One morning, she woke me before dawn, calling my name softly and nudging my ear with her lips. When I opened my eyes, she beckoned me outside. She was already dressed in a sari, and in the living room, she had laid out a set of clothes for me. 'We're going to Colombo,' she said as she helped me into my shorts and shirt. 'We're going to visit your aachi.'

'I have an aachi?' I asked in surprise.

She smiled and buttoned up my shirt.

'How long are we going to be gone?'

'Just overnight, son.'

The trip to Colombo took eight hours, and by the time we arrived at the Fort bus terminal, it was late afternoon. I was woken by my mother, and even before I sat up, my ears were assaulted by the sounds outside. I stared out at the terminal, jammed with buses honking and reversing and belching out diesel fumes, drivers yelling and cursing as they tried to get in or out. Streams of people jostled and pushed against each other as they boarded or left buses, bought tickets, saw loved ones off. Vendors, shrieking their wares to drown out their competitors, sold lottery tickets, garish plastic flowers, and cheap toys. They held aloft basins of cashews wrapped in banana leaves, sliced pineapple sprinkled with chili powder and salt, and roasted peanuts. My mother clutched my hand tightly and led me off the bus. The moment we stepped out, I felt myself stifled by all the crowds and smells and noise. 'Ammi,' I cried, pulling on her hand, wanting to get back in the bus, 'Ammi, I'm scared.'

'Nonsense, son,' she said. 'There's nothing to be scared about at all. This is just Colombo.'

After some fierce haggling over fare, we boarded a taxi. Soon we had left the cacophony of the Fort behind us and were driving along a splendid esplanade that sloped down to the sea. 'Look, Shivan,' my mother said in an awed voice as she hugged me, 'it's Galle Face Green. Isn't it lovely? When I was your age, I would come here for morning sea baths with my ayah Rosalind. We would bring a hamper with us that had hot-hot hoppers in it.'

'Will we do that too, Ammi?'

'I hope so, son. I hope so.'

My grandmother's house was in Thimbirigasyaya, a relatively affluent area of Colombo. There was a tall wall around it. Through the iron bars of the front gate, I could see the driveway curving around the front garden, ending under the portico. The house was a sprawling bungalow with a high, gabled red-tiled roof that had wooden fretwork along the edge of it, and a front veranda with carved pillars and latticework. The walls had been newly whitewashed. My mother did not ring the bell, but stood at the gate waiting. Soon an old servant woman in a sarong and blouse came around the back of the house, looking toward the gate as if she was expecting someone. My mother raised her arm and the woman, who was wiping her hands on a tea towel, became still. She began to walk down the driveway. Her pace quickened and soon she was running. When she got to the gate, she let out a tremendous choked sob and struggled with the latch. She opened the gate and, stepping out, cried, '*Aney*, babba, the Gods have been good to grant me this sight of you.' She began to weep, touching my mother's face, her hair, her shoulders, her arms. Soon my mother was crying, too, saying, 'I never thought I would see you again, Rosalind, I never did.'

Rosalind held my mother's head against her capacious bosom. '*Aiyo*, babba, don't cry, don't cry. You are home now.'

She noticed me and, letting go of my mother, knelt on the ground and gently took my hand in hers. 'He is beautiful,' she whispered to my mother, 'just like you were as a child.'

'Don't tell him that,' my mother said with a laugh and a sob. 'He's already spoiled enough.' She wiped her eyes, then straightened the palu of her sari and squared her shoulders. 'I suppose I should go in and face her.'

Rosalind rose to her feet. 'I told Loku-Nona you were coming, babba. I thought it was best.'

'And?' my mother asked anxiously.

'Loku-Nona acted like she hadn't heard me, but then she yelled at me, saying the stringhoppers were not steamed long enough.' Rosalind gave my mother a wry grimace. 'Just keep your temper.'

The old ayah led us to the kitchen. It was in the back courtyard and, like most Sri Lankan kitchens, was a shed with half walls and a tin roof over it for protection from the rain. There was a brick hearth and a long, scarred, blackened table with a kerosene stove on it and a coconut scraper attached at one end. The pots and pans were on a free-standing shelf.

'Shivan,' my mother said, 'you stay here with Rosalind.' She patted her hair, pushed her handbag over her shoulder and went into the house.

Rosalind beckoned me to a low stool, then put a plate of banana fritters soaked in kitul treacle in front of me. 'I made these especially for you, baby-mahataya,' she said.

As I tucked into them, she sat on a low stool across from me, watching with great satisfaction, every so often stroking my arm or pushing back the hair from my forehead.

After what seemed a long time, my mother came out. Her eyes were red and her cheeks stained. 'She says she will never forgive me,' my mother said.

Rosalind drew in her breath. 'No, no, babba, you cannot give in so easily. Let her see her own grandson.'

Rosalind took away my plate of fritters and brought me to my feet. She smoothed out my hair and straightened my collar. 'Let her see him.'

'There's no point,' my mother said.

Rosalind grabbed my hand. I pulled away, terrified, but she held on and took me into the pantry, with its spice safe and ancient refrigerator, and from there into the main part of the house.

The house was built in the old Sinhalese style with a central room, vast and high-ceilinged, that was called the saleya and served as both the living and dining room. Doors led into bedrooms on either side. Rosalind walked me firmly to a curtained doorway and pushed me through.

My grandmother snorted like a startled horse.

I stood by the curtain, sniffling. Then I fearfully raised my eyes to her.

Seated in bed was a tall, thin woman with pronounced tendons in her neck and knotty arms. She had long grey hair that lay on her shoulders and down her back in stringy, sparse strands. Her features were patrician and haughty. She was wearing an ankle-length white cotton nightdress with a pattern of delicate little rosebuds on it and a matching long-sleeved housecoat with white and pink ribbon appliquéd on the yoke. She had just woken up from her afternoon rest, and there was a cup of tea on her side table.

She was staring at me, appalled, and I saw that she had no idea, until this moment, that I had accompanied my mother. I began to cry in earnest now, whimpering, 'Ammi, I want my Ammi. I want to go home.'

After a moment, when my grandmother said nothing, I sneaked a glance at her. She was busily polishing a silver box, and I saw that on her bed were a number of porcelain ornaments and silver objects. Her bedroom was lined with glass-fronted cabinets crammed with bric-a-brac.

My grandmother suddenly yelled in a shrill voice, 'Ro-salind, Ro-salind. Come here!' She spoke in Sinhalese, and despite my fear, I was slightly shocked that she used the derogatory verb 'vareng' and ended her sentence with the rude 'bung.'

Even though the old ayah was probably standing right outside the door, she took her time presenting herself.

My grandmother gave her a stern frown. 'Have you given the boy something to eat?' She had called Rosalind by the lowest form of 'you,' 'oomba,' but the ayah seemed unfazed.

Rosalind sucked in her breath in dismay. 'I never thought to do so, Loku-Nona.'

'Why not?' my grandmother suddenly shrieked, flinging her polishing cloth down on the bed. 'Is your head full of cow dung?' She held one arm out in my direction. 'The boy has probably not had a meal since breakfast. Can you see the way he is crying from hunger? *Aiyo!* If I turn my eyes away for one minute, this house goes to pieces. Take him away, take him away and give him a meal, for goodness' sake.'

With that, she picked up her cloth and began to clean another ornament, muttering under her breath.

Rosalind took my hand and we left.

My legs were trembling from witnessing my grandmother's tantrum, but Rosalind looked pleased with herself. This time, she set me up at the dining table with another plate of fritters, which I greedily set about consuming, being ravenously hungry, in that way one is after a fright.

As I ate, my mother sat at the table watching me with a small smile on her face. She glanced every so often in the direction of my grandmother's bedroom, from which we could now hear much activity.

After some time, my grandmother came out. She was wearing a white Kandyan sari and had knotted her hair neatly into a bun at the nape of her neck. She barely gave us a glance as she flapped into the dining room. 'Ro-salind, Ro-salind,' she called as she made her way past us. This time Rosalind presented herself right away. 'I'm going to the temple for the evening pooja,' my grandmother said. 'Tomorrow, when you go to Sathiya Stores, buy three plastic school lunch boxes. One blue and two pink.'

'Yes, Loku-Nona.' Rosalind shot my mother a triumphant look.

My grandmother saw this, but she did not say anything. She walked past the dining table, checking her handbag to see if she had everything she wanted. Then taking out her change purse, she let it fall to the ground, the coins scattering in all directions. Rosalind made to go forward, but my mother lifted her hand to stop her. My mother rose from her chair. Getting down on her hands and knees, she began to crawl around the saleya retrieving the coins. She collected every one, and when the change purse was full again, she crawled over to my grandmother and handed it to her. My grandmother took the purse without a word and continued toward the portico where her car was waiting. My mother stayed on her knees looking after her. She was twenty-nine years old and her life was over.

I don't know what passed between my parents when we returned to the rest house the next day, but the following morning, my mother told my sisters and me to get dressed and pack for our trip to Colombo. While we did so, we could see our father sitting in the living room, staring out a window, his face numb. When we were done, my mother led us out. 'Children, go kiss your father and say goodbye.'

We went toward him reluctantly. He stared at us for a moment as if we were strangers, then he began to cry. '*Aiyo*, Hema,' he looked pleadingly at her. 'Don't take them away from me. I could not bear it.'

'How can you be so selfish?' my mother screamed at him. 'Don't you love them at all? Is this the future you want for them? In this stinking hellhole of a place, without a proper education?'

'Please, Hema, please give me one more chance.'

'No, Hector.' My mother ran her hand over her forehead. 'No more chances.'

My father put his head in his hands and wept, his shoulders shaking.

My sisters and I stared at him with the contempt and fear of contamination that children, so weak themselves, have for weakness in others.

During the first few days in my grandmother's house, we hardly saw her at all. She was a restless woman and could not stay home long. She was often out on errands to the Thimbirigasyaya Market or to the Fort or to visit the temple. My grandmother was widowed very early, her husband being twenty years older than her, and she had used the money he had left to build quite a fortune. She had invested in numerous rental properties, and she was frequently going out to inspect them or to evict tenants or to see her lawyer about land deeds and land transfers. When she was home, she stayed in her bedroom, running the household from there. Though she had taken us into her home, she had not forgiven my mother and so refused to have meals with us.

I don't remember missing the rest house or my father, and if I have any memory of our arrival and settling down, it is that we had no school for those first few days and relished the unexpected vacation. My grandmother's vast front and back gardens presented even more possibilities than the one in Wellawaya. My mother was not home very much, either. She was busy visiting principals of the schools she wanted us in and begging to have us taken on as charity students. She was also looking up old school friends, who might help her find employment through their fathers or husbands.

One evening, my sisters and I got into a fight in the front garden over a bowl of billing fruit. Renu, my oldest sister, claimed they were all hers because she had climbed the billing tree to pluck them, but Kamala and I staunchly held onto the bowl in which we had collected the fruit she threw down at us, saying that if not for our dexterous catching, the fruit would be all bruised and inedible. We were shrieking at each other, our hands on our hips, when we became aware of our grandmother watching us from the front veranda. We fell silent. She beckoned us to her, and once we were standing in front of her, not daring to look up, she said in Sinhalese, 'This is not some thuppai rest house in Wellawaya. No shouting and screaming. Do you understand?'

My sisters said nothing, but I, fearing her anger, whispered, 'Yes, Aachi.'

This was the first time any of us had called her 'aachi,' and the instant I did so, a mixture of emotions passed over her face. She gave a startled snort.

When she went back inside, my sisters looked at each other and giggled.

They decided to make our grandmother a bouquet, and I followed them about the garden as they picked flowers and leaves and arranged them. Renu got a piece of string from Rosalind and tied the bunch together. Then she held it out to me. 'Shivan must take it to Aachi.'

I looked at her, dismayed. I had just assumed that one of my sisters, being older, would do so. 'No,' I cried and hurriedly folded my arms to my chest. 'No, I won't.'

'Yes you will,' said Renu, gripping my arm so tightly it hurt. 'You are the grandson.'

'Yes, Kamala said, 'the grandson is the most important.'

I shook my head and looked away stubbornly.

Renu lifted her fist. 'If you don't, I'll give you tokkas every day for one week.'

Faced with the hard crack of Renu's knuckles on my skull for a week, I grabbed the bunch ungraciously.

My sisters led me into the saleya, holding me by the arms in case I thought to bolt. When we were in front of my grandmother's bedroom, Kamala pulled the curtain aside and Renu shoved me through. My grandmother was seated on her bed reading a newspaper, and she lowered it, startled.

'For … for you, Aachi,' I said in Sinhalese, my throat dry, parroting what my sisters wanted me to say. 'Thank you very much for allowing us to be in your house. You are very kind.'

I held out the bouquet. My grandmother stared at it and then at me. Finally, my courage deserting me, I put the flowers on her bed and ran out.

We crept around the side of the house to her bedroom window, wanting to see if she had accepted our gift. There was a half curtain across it, and we carefully lifted up the bottom edge and peered in. She had picked up the bouquet and was smelling it, a thoughtful look on her face.

We grinned at each other. I was delighted with myself, as if I alone had thought up and executed this feat of daring.

In our innocence, we had no idea what we had unleashed.

My mother, wanting to bring us up to the standard of Colombo schools, had dug up her old English, math, and science primers. Every morning and afternoon, we had to do the exercise she had assigned us, and she would mark them when she got home. Rosalind had set up a table on the back veranda, so she could keep an eye on us from the kitchen and stop us bickering and quarrelling with each other.

The next morning, we were bent over our work when my grandmother came out. I grinned at her and kicked my legs against the side of my chair, feeling that I had won a new status with her. She gave me a frosty glare and I hurriedly looked down at my work.

After a moment, I felt her standing behind me, her shadow falling across my page. My task for that morning was to develop my English handwriting by copying out sentences from the Grade 1 Radiant Way Primer—*See Pat Run. Run Pat Run. Pat runs to Mother*. My writing, always a weak point with me, was ill formed and I had made numerous errors. With my grandmother looming over me, my hand began to shake and my scrawl grew worse, my errors plentiful. She clamped her hand on my shoulder, her fingernails digging into my flesh. 'Erase that. Start again.' Her voice was deathly quiet.

I hurriedly rubbed out the words I had written. In doing so, I erased the line above that was correct.

My grandmother sucked her tongue against her teeth in a prolonged *tttttch*. 'Look at this child,' she said indignantly to no one in particular. 'Cow dung in his brain.'

I glanced quickly at my sisters, but they kept their heads bent over their work, dreading they might be next.

Rosalind, as she grated a coconut, looked over as much as she dared.

I began to write my line again, but this time, in my nervousness, I pressed too hard and the point of my pencil broke.

'You did that on purpose, *nah*?' My grandmother cried. 'Trying to waste time and not do your work, lazy, dirty fellow.' She gave me a sharp slap on the side of my head.

I whimpered and rubbed my nose.

My grandmother snatched my pencil away from me. 'Where is the pencil cutter?'

Renu held it out to her, keeping her head bent. My grandmother took it and sharpened the pencil. Then she thrust the pencil at me and flung the cutter on the table.

I began to write the line again. My grandmother had over-sharpened the pencil and the point was wobbly. I wrote out the words cautiously, but there was only so far I could go before the point broke.

My grandmother drew in her breath. I quickly put down my pencil and clasped my hands tightly in my lap.

'You did that on purpose.' I could feel her breath hot on the top of my head.

Kamala, not raising her head, slid the pencil cutter over to me, but before I could take it, my grandmother snatched the cutter and flung it into the back courtyard. 'You think you can just do what you want in this house, you savage child?' Her voice rose shrilly. 'You think that, because I'm an old woman, you can hoodwink me?'

She slapped the back of my head and dragged me to my feet.

'No, Aachi, no,' I cried. 'I'm sorry. I promise I won't do it again.'

Rosalind had come out of the kitchen and was watching helplessly.

My grandmother grabbed me by the ear and dragged me into the saleya and through to her room. She let go of me and went to an almirah in a corner. After fumbling around in the space between the almirah and the wall, she drew out a long, thin bamboo cane covered in dust. She brushed it against the side of her housecoat and then tapped the cane on her hand as if to check its strength.

I stared at her in horror, unable to believe what was about to happen.

She crooked her finger and indicated for me to bend over her bed. I shook my head and refused to do so.

'Come,' my grandmother ordered, using the verb 'vareng.'

'No,' I cried, 'I won't. You're not my Ammi. I hate you, you old woman.'

I had used the word 'gaani,' the rudest form of 'woman,' and my grandmother's face grew red with fury. 'You wicked boy,' she cried, and rushed at me with the cane raised.

She began to beat me. I tried to fend off her blows with my arms and run away, but she gripped my arm tightly. As the blows rained down, I writhed and twisted and, finally, collapsed on the floor, curled up, my hands protecting my head and face.

My grandmother only stopped when her strength wore out. Then she flung the cane across the room and sat on the edge of her bed, panting. After a while, she stood up and, stepping over my body, went out of her room.

Rosalind hurried inside, followed by my sisters. They helped me to my feet and led me away to my room. In the bathroom, as I sat on the toilet seat, Rosalind knelt in front of me and checked my body. Then she applied gentian violet to my cuts. I yelled at each sting.

The old ayah put me to bed and, while my sisters sat vigil, went to the kitchen. As I lay under the coverlet, the shock of what had happened wore off and I began to cry great hiccupping sobs. Kamala held my hand and stroked my head, but Renu paced the room, a fierce look on her face.

After a while, Rosalind returned with a cup of hot milk laced with vanilla and sugar. She propped my pillows and I sat up and sipped on the drink, sniffling and hiccupping. Once I was sufficiently calmed down, Rosalind patted the bed for my sisters to come and sit on it. Then she looked at us all gravely. 'Your mother must never find out about this.'

'But why?' Kamala cried. 'I'm definitely telling Ammi,' Renu added.

Rosalind sighed. 'Your mother has enough on her plate. I don't think she could bear anything else.' She took my hand in hers. 'I know this is difficult for you to understand, but what your grandmother did to you, she did out of affection. She has singled you out, her grandson.'

We stared at her in disbelief.

'Yes,' she nodded. 'She is just a woman from a different time, a different way of doing things. She does not know how to show love in any other way. So,' she looked around at us, 'can we make a pact not to tell your mother?'

After a moment my sisters nodded reluctantly, but I ducked my head, drinking from my cup.

I lay in bed for the rest of the day, and by late afternoon, I heard my mother return. She came into the house calling to us. The girls rushed into the saleya to greet her, followed by Rosalind.

I began to cry. 'Ammi,' I bawled, 'Amm-i!'

'What's going on?' my mother asked Rosalind.

'Oh, nothing, babba, he just fell and hurt himself.'

My mother's footsteps drew near and she pulled aside the curtain to my room.

I held out my arms to her, to show my bruises, and she dropped her handbag on a table and came to me. 'What happened, son? What did you do?'

My sisters and Rosalind had also come into the room. 'He just fell from the billing tree.' Rosalind said.

'Is that true?'

My sisters and I glanced at each other. 'Renu? Kamala?'

My sisters said nothing.

I began to sniffle. I suddenly wanted justice, and I cried out, 'Aachi did this to me.'

My mother became very still. She looked at Rosalind, who glanced down at her feet.

'It's nothing, babba, you know how your mother is, she—'

'*Aah*, that wretched witch.' My mother rushed out of the room. We all followed.

She darted across the saleya and pulled back the curtain of my grandmother's room.

'How dare you touch my child?' she cried.

My grandmother was getting dressed to go to temple, and she turned from the mirror where she was examining herself. 'Get out of my room.'

My mother stood her ground. The cane was lying on the side table.

She grabbed it, snapped it across her knee and flung the pieces on the floor. 'You will not do to my children what you did to me.'

My grandmother advanced on my mother, raising a shaking finger at her. 'Just remember your place in this house. You're lucky I have allowed you to stay.'

'You allow me to stay because you don't want to lose face with your friends and our relatives,' my mother replied.

'You're wrong there, my daughter. I let you stay because I shudder to think of what disgrace you would bring on our family name if I allowed you to live on your own.'

'What do you mean?'

'I mean that you're a common whore who would open your legs for any man who showed you the least affection.'

My mother looked at her as if she had been slapped.

'You ran away with that thuppai Tamil dog like a bitch in heat.'

My mother began to cry. 'Why would you say that? Why?' She turned to Rosalind, 'Look at the way she speaks to her own daughter.'

'I wish you were not my daughter. Every day I wish for that. But I accept that this is my karma, that I have done something terrible in my previous life to have deserved you. Through meritorious deeds at the temple, I am trying hard to work off the ill effects of that karma.' My grandmother pushed past my mother and left.

My mother continued to weep, her face in her hands. She had accidentally banged her arm against something and cut it. Blood trickled down to her elbow; drops falling to stain her sari.

Rosalind went to her with soothing murmurs and led her away. We heard my grandmother's car start in the portico and go down the driveway.

Renu came up to me. 'See what you have done to Amma?' she hissed. 'You sneaker.' She gave me a tokka on the head.

Even Kamala glared at me.

I crept away to my room and lay on my bed curled up, listening to my mother still sobbing on the back veranda.

The next day, instead of sitting with my sisters, I took my copy book and the Radiant Way to my grandmother's room. She was going through some accounts that were spread over her coverlet. She looked up at me, surprised. Lowering my eyes, I sat on the floor by her bed and began to work on my exercises.

Despite my terror of her, I was determined that my mother would never cry like that again.

My mother never found out about this ritual between my grandmother and me, which continued for the next seven years until I turned thirteen. My grandmother was often cruel, slapping the side of my head or giving me a couple of strokes with a new cane she had purchased. But I took it quietly, and I sensed her respect for me because of that.

In the end, it was not the beatings that greatly affected me. The school I went to believed, as did all elite boys' schools, that corporal punishment was necessary to make a boy into the sort of man who could run the politics and commerce of this country. And the beatings of those burly masters easily surpassed my grandmother's. What did affect me was having to keep those afternoons with my grandmother hidden from my mother. They caused a crushing loneliness within, a separation from the person I loved most. And this exile pressed down on all my emotions, making me withdrawn and solitary, trapped inside myself, shaping me into the person I have become today.

On the day I turned thirteen, my grandmother invited me to go for a drive with her. She directed the driver to take us to what she called her Turret Road property.

It was a large two-storey house set in a vast garden. The property was much grander than the one we lived in, and this address in Colombo 7, was the finest. An American couple who worked in the embassy was renting it, and we did not go in. Instead, my grandmother stood with me at the gate and pointed out various features of the house. Then she told me how much she was charging them in rupees and I was staggered. She tossed her head. 'Of course, I'm no fool. They don't pay me in our useless rupees that are devaluing-devaluing every day. They remit dollars to a secret account I have in England.' She squeezed my elbow tight, her breath stale as she leaned into me. 'Or course, you must never tell anyone that, puthey, not even your mother. The money is for your foreign education.'

This was the first time she had called me 'puthey,' the affectionate diminutive for 'putha,' or 'son.' She was beaming, and even the way she spoke to me was different, a new intimacy, a new equality to her tone.

As we drove through Colombo to her Pettah property, I glanced occasionally at her. She sat with her arms folded beneath her breasts, her lips pursed in satisfaction. Having turned thirteen, my status with her had suddenly changed, as if I had passed from childhood to manhood. I felt curiously oppressed by this sudden elevation of my status—unprepared and frightened of what its challenges might be. My apprehension only grew when we arrived at her Pettah property.

It was nothing more than a dilapidated row house that was only one step up from a slum dwelling. The outside wall had not been whitewashed in years and was covered with black and green fungus and rot. The roof was patched with rusted takaran where the red tiles had fallen off; the front veranda had sagging eaves and pillars that were cracked and leaned precariously. My grandmother walked up the front steps to the veranda and rapped sharply on the front door.

After a little while, a child called out from the other side asking who it was. 'Who do you think?' my grandmother replied.

The child, as if parroting something he was being prompted to say, replied, 'Amma is not home.'

My grandmother made a contemptuous sound. 'Of course she is. Where would she go, ah?' She rapped on the door. 'Siriyawathy, open the door. Otherwise I will have it kicked in.'

The door slowly opened and a woman in a soiled, faded dress, her hair in an untidy plait, stood there, her head bent.

'What is this, hiding-hiding from me?' my grandmother replied, sounding grimly amused.

The woman glanced up at us. Her face was thin from hunger. There were large circles around her eyes that made them seem enormous. The child, who was half hiding behind her legs, was dressed only in a pair of shorts, and his belly was distended from malnutrition. My grandmother pushed past them and led me in. She went from room to room, showing me various features and problems and telling me how much more money she could make if she rented this house as a chummery for factory girls, which she was thinking of doing. The house was cramped and dark, the rooms sparsely furnished, the paint on the walls peeling, the floors cracked. The woman and child had disappeared, and when we left, my grandmother called out before she shut the door, 'Siriyawathy, you can come out of hiding now.' She gave me another smile.

As we went down the veranda steps, she took my arm for support. 'That Siriyawathy must have done something very bad in her past life. Look at her, recently widowed with a small child to raise. It's a terrible thing to be living out the effects of bad karma, *nah.*' She sighed and shook her head. 'But what is to be done, *ah?*'

That day, my grandmother took me all over Colombo and showed me her properties. There were fifteen in all, and with the exception of the grand house in Colombo 7, they were middle-class bungalows and poor little houses. With each visit, I felt a heaviness and panic growing in my chest. This was my birth-right, and my grandmother was showing me the properties because she ex-pected I would take them over someday. I could not shake away the feeling that something was going to be expected of me soon, some display of manliness that I feared I would fail.

A few days later, my grandmother invited me to come for a ride with her. We were going to see someone called the Kotahena Mudalali.

Kotahena, which was just past the Fort and Pettah, abutted the bay of Colombo and was the rougher, uglier, mundane side that all ports have just beyond the more scenic sections. Once we left the main road and turned down a narrow side street, we were in nothing more than an extended slum. The car came to a stop in front of a house that was far better than any of the others around it. Set back a little from the street, it was a well-kept bungalow. The cemented front garden had a garish marble fountain in the middle, with an arrangement of plastic flamingos and penguins around it. The windows had heavy bars across them, and even the front door had an extra door of iron bars in front of it. My grandmother did not get out; instead she had the driver toot his horn imperiously. A woman stepped out of the front door, and when she saw the car, she immediately nodded and smiled and went back inside. After a moment, a man came out of the house, buttoning up his shirt as he hurried down to the front gate.

'Ah, nona, how nice to see you,' he said as he leaned in the car window.

His face was pitted with acne scars, and there was a long gash that ran down one cheek to his jawline.

'How is the business, Chandralal?'

'Thanks to your generous loan, doing very well, nona.'

'I'm always pleased to hear that, Chandralal. I know how to back a good man.' My grandmother opened her bag and drew out a piece of paper and an envelope of money. She handed it to the man. 'Something I need taken care of. A tenant problem.'

'You don't have to say another word, nona.'

'Shall we do it now? It's always better to get these things taken care of im-mediately, *nah?* Are your golayas around?'

He straightened up and gave a piercing whistle through his teeth. After a moment, various doors on the street opened and men stuck their heads out. 'Come,' he called out. 'We have a job.'

Chandralal sat in the front with the driver, and his golayas followed in trishaws. I knew what was going to happen and I was terrified.

Our car stopped some distance from the Pettah property. Chandralal got out and led his golayas toward the house. They went up to the front veranda, and Chandralal hammered on the door. No one answered. He hammered again and yelled, 'Are you going to come out or do you want me to break down this door?'

Along the street, other women came out to see what was going on. One of the golayas came to the edge of the veranda and glared at them. 'What are you looking at? Do you want me to show you something, *ah*?'

He began to unbutton his fly and the women quickly went inside their homes. The other golayas hooted and laughed.

Chandralal signalled to his men and they gathered around him. He nodded to one who was huge, his red eyes buried in layers of fat. The man went back a few steps and then took a run at the door, crashing into it sideways. The door flew open, cracking against the wall behind, a shower of plaster falling to the ground. The men charged inside. There was much shouting, and suddenly a woman's scream pierced the air, followed by the wail of a child.

Chandralal emerged dragging the woman by her plait. Her face was contorted with pain and she clutched onto his hands to prevent him from yanking her hair any further. He pulled her down the steps and flung her into the street.

'Amma, Amma,' her child wailed from inside, and the woman leapt to her feet, shrieking, 'Leave my child, don't hurt him.'

One of the men brought out her child, unharmed, and put him by her. She clung to him, sobbing, 'Don't cry, don't cry, everything is going to be okay.'

The men, under Chandralal's supervision, took out the furniture and flung it into the street. When one of the golayas brought out a garlanded photograph of a man, the woman scrambled to her feet and cried, '*Aney*, please, please, don't damage my husband's photograph.'

But he threw it into the street and the glass shattered, ripping through the portrait.

I became aware that my grandmother was watching me. I turned to her. 'The truth is, puthey, with our rental laws it is almost impossible to get rid of a tenant. It would take years in court, *nah*? You understand, don't you?'

She was searching my face, and there was a tremendous need in her eyes that I had never seen before.

'*Um*, yes, Aachi,' I replied, not knowing what else to say.

She patted my arm.

That night, after dinner, my grandmother called me to her bedroom. She was getting ready for bed, brushing her hair in front of the toilet table. '*Ah*, puthey.' She put down her brush and beckoned me forward. From a drawer, she took out a thin box. 'A gift for you.'

I opened the box. Inside there was a gold chain with a cylindrical gold pendant that contained a scroll blessed by the Buddhist monks.

As I stood in front of the mirror, my grandmother fastened the clasp at the back of my neck. I had passed her test, which I saw now was one of loyalty, not manliness. I had not protested, I had not judged her, and so I was completely hers. And yet, she was curiously, completely mine.

2006

Part II

Documents & Dialogues

A. Prologue:
The Need for Narrative

Fourteen Ways of Looking at a Classic

Writers are inevitably readers before they become writers. In 'Why Read the Classics?' Italian author Italo Calvino canvasses diverse works of Western literature from the Ancient world of Homer, Ovid, and Xenophon to that of twentieth-century writers such as Conrad, Hemingway, and Borges.

'A classic never exhausts all it has to say to its readers.'

Italo Calvino, from 'Why Read the Classics?'

1. The classics are those books about which you usually hear people saying: 'I'm rereading . . .', never 'I'm reading . . .'
2. The classics are those books which constitute a treasured experience for those who have read and loved them; but they remain just as rich an experience for those who reserve the chance to read them for when they are in the best condition to enjoy them.
3. The classics are books which exercise a particular influence, both when they imprint themselves on our imagination as unforgettable, and when they hide in the layers of memory disguised as the individual's or the collective unconscious.
4. A classic is a book which with each rereading offers as much of a sense of discovery as the first reading.
5. A classic is a book which even when we read it for the first time gives the sense of rereading something we have read before.
6. A classic is a book which has never exhausted all it has to say to its readers.
7. The classics are those books which come to us bearing the aura of previous interpretations, and trailing behind them the traces they have left in the culture or cultures (or just in the languages and customs) through which they have passed.
8. A classic is a work which constantly generates a pulviscular cloud of critical discourse around it, but which always shakes the particles off.
9. Classics are books which, the more we think we know them through hearsay, the more original, unexpected, and innovative we find them when we actually read them.

10. A classic is the term given to any book which comes to represent the whole universe, a book on a par with ancient talismans.
11. 'Your' classic is a book to which you cannot remain indifferent, and which helps you define yourself in relation or even in opposition to it.
12. A classic is a work that comes before other classics; but those who have read other classics first immediately recognize its place in the genealogy of classic works.
13. A classic is a work which relegates the noise of the present to a background hum, which at the same time the classics cannot exist without.
14. A classic is a work which persists as background noise even when a present that is totally incompatible with it holds sway.

1981

The Need for Narrative

Robert Fulford (b. 1932) is an award-winning Canadian journalist and essayist who was selected to deliver the Massey Lecture Series in 1999. He is the former editor of Saturday Night *magazine and is currently a regular contributor to the* Globe and Mail *and* Toronto Life, *as well as a columnist for the* National Post. *In the selection below, from the Massey Lectures, Fulford argues that in spite of competing media, stories—from gossip to 'master narratives'—endure because they satisfy our universal quest to know ourselves.*

'A story that matters to us . . . becomes a bundle in which we wrap truth, hope, and dread.'

Robert Fulford, from 'Gossip, Literature, and the Fictions of the Self'

. . . There is no such thing as *just a story*. A story is always charged with meaning; otherwise it is not a story, merely a sequence of events. It may be possible, as social scientists imagine, to create value-free sociology, but there is no such thing as a value-free story. And we can be sure that if we know a story well enough to tell it, then it carries meaning for us. We can say about stories what W.H. Auden said about books—some stories may be unjustly forgotten, but no stories are unjustly remembered. They do not survive through the vagaries of whim. If a story has been swimming in the vast ocean of human consciousness for decades or centuries or even millennia, it has earned its place.

This goes some distance towards explaining what I call the triumph of narrative. In our time, narrative has come under severe attack. The 'master narratives' by which our society traditionally guided itself, from the Bible to the agreed-upon stories of beneficial British imperialism and European ascendancy, have been challenged and largely discredited. The Cold War, a narrative that organized the way many people saw the world for more than four decades, has dissolved. Popular narrative on television has come to be seen as the opiate of the masses, the way religion was described long ago. Serious fiction writers are nervous about introducing too-obvious narratives into their books. And yet humanity clings to narrative. We may mistrust large-scale narratives that attempt to shape society, but our narrative drive persists. For all the reasons that fill this book, we cannot do without it.

Stories survive partly because they remind us of what we know and partly because they call us back to what we consider significant. *Hansel and Gretel* reminds us how helpless we felt as children. *Anne of Green Gables* reminds us of the power of imagination in a world that tries to deny its value. *Huckleberry Finn* reminds us of the individual's duty to defy the rules of an unjust world. Orwell's *1984* reminds us of our century's darkest moments, when the individual spirit itself became a crime; conversely, it helps us to remember why we think individualism is central to our way of life.

Stories, however valuable, may be puzzling as well as engaging. Often, even the greatest story may fail at the task it sets for itself—and this applies as much to movies and plays and novels as it does to folk tales handed down from our ancestors. Stories ostensibly begin in order to explain something, or to make an event clear. They turn an incident this way and that, throw several kinds of light on it, surround it with a certain mood—and then put it back in its place, still unexplained. The father of the modern short story, Anton Chekhov, wrote 'The Lady with the Dog' a century ago, in 1899. It has since been translated and published again and again all over the world, but no one would claim that it solves the problem it presents—a cold and promiscuous man finds himself falling in love for the first time when it is both inconvenient and too late. At the end, we have no idea what the characters will do or even what they should do. In a few pages, Chekhov leads us to the core of a complex and excruciating dilemma and leaves us there.

Among those who produce films and TV shows, and try to shape novels for the mass market, there's a tendency to make every story explain itself clearly and conclude neatly. It has become a kind of rule that neatness counts in narrative: don't leave the audience wondering. Sometimes we express resentment when this rule is broken. But if that rule actually applied, the Book of Job, to take one spectacular case, would have disappeared from our consciousness long ago. Certainly it makes no ordinary sense. The Book of Job concerns a prosperous man whose faith in God is tested by terrible acts committed against him with the agreement of God. It describes draconian punishments whose rationale we cannot begin to understand, permitted by a god we cannot admire, recounted to us by an author whose identity we cannot know. Yet it remains with us, more than 2,000 years after it was first set down; there's something that makes Job's hideous story, with his boils and his murdered children, more appealing than almost any equivalent in the Western tradition. It lives in daily conversation as much as in the Bible and in literature; people know Job who can't remember anything much about Joshua or Saul. What accounts for its power?

It deals with the most painful human situation—arbitrary suffering—yet to those who are afflicted it offers neither consolation nor understanding. Perhaps that's the very reason it maintains its large place in our collective imagination: implicitly, it tells us that the ways of God, or nature, or whatever force governs life, are unknowable—and it is presumptuous of us to try to know them. Perhaps we return to the Book of Job to remind ourselves that whatever we do, our fate may well be determined by incomprehensible forces.

A story that matters to us, whether it's an ancient story like Job's or a modern story like Herzog's, becomes a bundle in which we wrap truth, hope, and dread. Stories are how we explain, how we teach, how we entertain ourselves, and how we often do all three at once. They are the juncture where facts and feelings meet. And for those reasons, they are central to civilization—in fact, civilization takes form in our minds, as a series of narratives. . . .

The anthropologist Clifford Geertz says that humans are 'symbolizing, conceptualizing, meaning-seeking' animals. In our species, he says, 'The drive to make sense out of experience, to give it form and order, is evidently as real and as pressing as the more familiar biological needs.' To Geertz, a human being is an organism 'which cannot live in a world it is unable to understand.' But if it is understanding we yearn for, why isn't analysis good enough? Why can't we simply *study* our experience rather than recounting it chronologically?

The answer is that narrative, as opposed to analysis, has the power to mimic the unfolding of reality. Narrative is selective, and may be untrue, but it can produce the feeling of events occurring in time; it seems to be rooted in reality. This is also the reason for the triumph of narrative, its penetration and in some ways its dominance of our collective imagination: with a combination of ancient devices and up-to-the-minute technology, it can appear to replicate life. . . .

1999

The Qualities of an Outstanding Story

Short story scholar Thomas A. Gullason answers this question and supports his thesis by analyzing three stories: Chekhov's 'The Lady with the Dog', Hemingway's 'Big Two-Hearted River', and Crane's 'An Illusion in Red and White.' Gullason claims that the first criterion of a great story is a sense 'of freshness, of newness.'

'It has an uncharacteristic—not a characteristic—slant on the world.'

Thomas A. Gullason, from 'What Makes a "Great" Short Story Great?'

... Other qualities need to be added to freshness of style and subject for a short story to achieve greatness, to have 'force' and power, to be kept alive and perennially new. Generally, it does have an uncharacteristic—not a characteristic—slant on the world and on human values; generally, it is unrepresentative—not representative—in the chronicle of story development. In their own time, great short stories have typically been considered unorthodox, out of the mainstream; and they have been instrumental in creating a new mainstream.

In testing and validating the idea of greatness in any short story, the reader can quickly come to one conclusion: there is no absolute set of criteria for a great short story; each has its own special imprint. But any great short story must have staying power, depth, range or scope, where its form and content merge to produce a highly individualized, living, and vital portrait from life. It either entices or forces the reader to come back to it—as though it were a strong magnet—for further profit. In the end, it may still remain a mystery or open-ended, offering 'everything and confirming nothing.' Not singly but in combination—whether in subject, style, setting, mood, tone, plot, character, action, or theme—the great short story evolves, and as it strikes out in new directions, it makes a case (often unconsciously) for its own immortality. ...

A great short story is inevitably a 'long' short story. It makes many demands of its reading audience, which often must be a captive one drawn from the college and university classroom. The popular short story, meanwhile, is indeed 'short'; it makes few demands of the reader's imagination and time. Popular short stories by skilled practitioners such as Guy de Maupassant, O. Henry, and W. Somerset Maugham still have a large following. Though they can be 'summed up' in a few lines, they are entertaining, and they will continue to entertain. O. Henry's chestnuts, 'The Gift of the Magi' and 'The Cop and the Anthem,' have already become part of folklore.

With an eye on his audience, the popular short-story writer is overly conscious of and dependent on the mechanics of plot, cause and effect, unity, and completeness, including the trick-ending dividend; he is cornered and confined by the reality he is trying to explore and reflect. The result is that he often turns out formula stories (not always intentionally), which are one-dimensional, static, predictable, and transitory in value.

The great short-story writer—normally free of the restraints and demands of mechanical plots and attending formulas—corners reality, and experiments with and explores new horizons and new depths; therefore, his stories are three-dimensional (sometimes more), dynamic, unpredictable, and permanent in value. He draws on and maintains a close relationship with the novel, poetry, drama, music, and painting, as he pursues and elevates one's consciousness, as he creates indelible portraits from life. Even though he may always have a small audience, the great short-story writer, with his great short story—and not the popular writer, with his popular story—keeps the form alive, brings it prestige, and makes it a worthy competitor with the other arts.

1990

B. The Art of the Short Story

The Single Effect

Although Poe did not rate the 'tale' as highly as the poem, he did favour it over the novel. In his review of fellow American writer Nathaniel Hawthorne's first collection of tales, Poe deductively established the principles for the short story. Poe's dictum about the tale's single effect and the economy needed to bring it about became the starting point for short story theorists well into the twentieth century. In particular, Poe praised Hawthorne's originality.

'If his very initial sentence tend[s] not to the out-bringing of this effect, then he has failed in his first step.'

Edgar Allan Poe, from 'Review of *Twice-Told Tales*'

. . . Were we called upon, however, to designate that class of composition which, next to such a poem as we have suggested, should best fulfil the demands of high genius—should offer it the most advantageous field of exertion—we should unhesitatingly speak of the prose tale, as Mr Hawthorne has here exemplified it. We allude to the short prose narrative, requiring from a half-hour to one or two hours in its perusal. The ordinary novel is objectionable, from its length, for reasons already stated in substance. As it cannot be read at one sitting, it deprives itself, of course, of the immense force derivable from *totality*. Worldly interests intervening during the pauses of perusal, modify, annul, or counteract, in a greater or less degree, the impressions of the book. But simple cessation in reading, would, of itself, be sufficient to destroy the true unity. In the brief tale, however, the author is enabled to carry out the fullness of his intention, be it what it may. During the hour of perusal the soul of the reader is at the writer's control. There are no external or extrinsic influences—resulting from weariness or interruption.

A skilful literary artist has constructed a tale. If wise, he has not fashioned his thoughts to accommodate his incidents; but having conceived, with deliberate care, a certain unique or single *effect* to be wrought out, he then invents such incidents—he then combines such events as may best aid him in establishing this preconceived effect. If his very initial sentence tend not to the out-bringing of this effect, then he has failed in his first step. In the whole composition there should be no word written, of which the tendency, direct or indirect, is not to the one preestablished design. And by such means, with such care and skill, a picture is at length painted which leaves in the mind of him who contemplates it with a kindred art, a sense of the fullest satisfaction. The idea of the tale has been presented unblemished, because undisturbed; and this is an end unattainable by the novel. Undue brevity is just as exceptionable here as in the poem; but undue length is yet more to be avoided.

We have said that the tale has a point of superiority even over the poem. In fact, while the *rhythm* of this latter is an essential aid in the development of the poet's highest idea—the idea of the Beautiful—the artificialities of this rhythm are an inseparable bar to the development of all points of thought or expression which have their basis in *Truth*. But Truth is often, and in very great degree, the aim of the tale. Some of the finest tales are tales of ratiocination. Thus the field of this species of composition, if not in so elevated a region on the mountain of Mind, is a table-land of far vaster extent than the domain of the mere poem. Its products are never so rich, but infinitely more numerous, and more appreciable by the mass of mankind. The writer of the prose tale, in short, may bring to his theme a vast variety of modes or inflections of thought and expression—(the ratiocinative, for example, the sarcastic, or the humorous) which are not only antagonistical to the nature of the poem, but absolutely forbidden by one of its most peculiar and indispensable adjuncts; we allude, of course, to rhythm. It may be added here, *par parenthèse*, that the author who aims at the purely beautiful in a prose tale is laboring at great disadvantage. For Beauty can be better treated in a poem. Not so with terror, or passion, or horror, or a multitude of such other points. And here it will be seen how full of prejudice are the usual animadversions against those *tales of effect*, many fine examples of which were found in the earlier numbers of *Blackwood's Magazine*. The impressions produced were wrought in a legitimate sphere of action, and constituted a legitimate although sometimes an exaggerated interest. They were relished by every man of genius; although there were found many men of genius who condemned them without just ground. The true critic will but demand that the design intended be accomplished, to the fullest extent, by the means most advantageously applicable. . . .

1842

Rendering 'Reality'

Known for his treatment of 'the international theme,' which juxtaposed naive Americans and sophisticated Europeans, Henry James (1843–1916) brought a new self-consciousness to fiction. To the New York edition of his novels (1909), he appended eighteen prefaces that introduced readers to pertinent topics in his own work, such as point of view and the 'central intelligence.' He wrote many other critical essays, including 'The Art of Fiction,' which is among the best known. In this excerpt, James discusses the essential quality of the fiction writer as one 'on whom nothing is lost.'

'Experience . . . is a kind of huge spiderweb of the finest silken threads suspended in the chamber of consciousness.'

Henry James, from 'The Art of Fiction'

The characters, the situation, which strike one as real will be those that touch and interest one most, but the measure of reality is very difficult to fix. The reality of [Miguel de Cervantes'] Don Quixote or of [Charles Dickens'] Mr Micawber is a very delicate shade; it is a reality so coloured by the author's vision that, vivid as it may be, one would hesitate to propose it as a model; one would expose one's self to some very embarrassing questions on the part of a pupil. It goes without saying that you will not write a good novel unless you possess the sense of reality; but it will be difficult to give you a recipe for calling that sense into being. Humanity is immense and reality has a myriad [of] forms; the most one can affirm is that some of the flowers of fiction have the odour of it, and others have not; as for telling you in advance how your nosegay should be composed, that is another affair. It is equally excellent and inconclusive to say that one must write from experience; to our supposititious aspirant such a declaration might savour of mockery. What kind of experience is intended, and where does it begin and end? Experience is never limited and it is never complete; it is an immense sensibility, a kind of huge spiderweb, of the finest silken threads, suspended in the chamber of consciousness and catching every airborne particle in its tissue. It is the very atmosphere of the mind; and when the mind is imaginative—much more when it happens to be that of a man of genius—it takes itself to the faintest hints of life, it converts the very pulses of the air into revelations. The young lady living in the village has only to be a damsel upon whom nothing is lost to make it quite unfair (as it seems to me) to declare to her that she shall have nothing to say about the military. Greater miracles have been seen than that, imagination assisting, she should speak the truth about some of these gentlemen. I remember an English novelist, a woman of genius, telling me that she was much commended for the impression she had managed to give in one of her tales of the nature and way of life of the French Protestant youth. She had been asked where she learned so much about this recondite being, she had been congratulated on her peculiar opportunities. These opportunities consisted in her having once, in Paris, as she ascended a staircase, passed an open door where, in the household of a *pasteur*, some of the young Protestants were seated at a table round a finished meal. The glimpse made a picture; it lasted only a moment, but the moment was experience. She had got her impression, and she evolved her type. She knew what youth was, and what Protestantism; she also had the advantage of having seen what it was to be French, so that she converted these ideas into a concrete image and produced a reality. Above all, however, she was blessed with the faculty which when you give it an inch takes an ell, and which for the artist is a much greater source of strength than any accident of residence or place in the social scale. The power to guess the unseen from the seen, to trace the implication of things, to judge the whole piece by the pattern, the condition of feeling life, in general, so completely that you are well on your way to knowing any particular corner of it—this cluster of gifts may almost be said to constitute experience, and they occur in country and in town, and in the most differing stages of education. If experience consists of impressions, it may be said that impressions *are* experience, just as (have we not seen it?) they are the very air we breathe. Therefore, if I should certainly say to a novice, 'Write from experience and experience only,' I should feel that this was rather a tantalizing monition if I were not careful immediately to add, 'Try to be one of the people on whom nothing is lost!'

1884

Codifying the Short Story

Though known primarily as a drama critic, Brander Matthews (1852–1929) extended Poe's brief comments on the short story into the realm of scholarship in The Philosophy of the Short-Story—*the title echoes one of Poe's major critical works,* 'The Philosophy of Composition.' *With Poe, Matthews declared, the short story* 'became conscious of itself.'

'It is a *genre* . . . as individual as the Lyric itself and as various.'

Brander Matthews, from The Philosophy of the Short-Story

. . . A true Short-story is something other and something more than a mere story which is short. A true Short-story differs from the Novel chiefly in its essential unity of impression. In a far more exact and precise use of the word, a Short-story has unity as a Novel cannot have it. Often, it may be noted by the way, the Short-story fulfils the three false unities of the French classic drama: it shows one action, in one place, on one day. A Short-story deals with a single character, a single event, a single emotion, or the series of emotions called forth by a single situation. Poe's paradox that a poem cannot greatly exceed a hundred lines in length under penalty of ceasing to be one poem and breaking into a string of poems, may serve to suggest the precise difference between the Short-story and the Novel. The Short-story is the single effect, complete and self-contained, while the Novel is of necessity broken into a series of episodes. Thus the Short-story has, what the Novel cannot have, the effect of 'totality,' as Poe called it, the unity of impression.

Of a truth the Short-story is not only not a chapter out of a Novel, or an incident or an episode extracted from a longer tale, but at its best it impresses the reader with the belief that it would be spoiled if it were made larger, or if it were incorporated into a more elaborate work. . . .

The novelist may take his time; he has abundant room to turn about. The writer of Short-stories must be concise, and compression, a vigorous compression, is essential. For him, more than for anyone else, the half is more than the whole. Again, the novelist may be commonplace, he may bend his best energies to the photographic reproduction of the actual; if he show[s] us a cross-section of real life we are content; but the writer of Short-stories must have originality and ingenuity. If to compression, originality, and ingenuity he add[s] also a touch of fantasy, so much the better. . . .

Perhaps the difference between a Short-story and a Sketch can best be indicated by saying that, while a Sketch may be still-life, in a Short-story something always happens. A Sketch may be an outline of character, or even a picture of a mood of mind, but in a Short-story there must be something done, there must be an action. . . .

1901

Fiction's Appeal

Although he was Polish by birth and didn't learn English until his early twenties, Joseph Conrad (1857–1924) became a key figure in English modernism. At age thirty-six, he gave up a sea-faring life, devoting himself to writing novels and short stories. He is known as one of the language's finest stylists, as can be seen in this paean to art's mystery and timelessness.

'To make you hear, to make you feel—it is, before all, to make you see.'

Joseph Conrad, from Preface to *The Nigger of the Narcissus*

A work that aspires, however humbly, to the condition of art should carry its justification in every line. And art itself may be defined as a single-minded attempt to render the highest kind of justice to the visible universe, by bringing to light the truth, manifold and one, underlying its every aspect. It is an attempt to find in its forms, in its colours, in its light, in its shadows, in the aspects of matter and in the facts of life what of each is fundamental, what is enduring and essential—their one illuminating and convincing quality—the very truth of their existence. The artist, then, like the thinker or the scientist, seeks the truth and makes his appeal. Impressed by the aspect of the world the thinker plunges into ideas, the scientist into facts—whence, presently, emerging they make their appeal to those qualities of our being that fit us best for the hazardous enterprise of living. They speak authoritatively to our common-sense, to our intelligence, to our desire of peace or to our desire of unrest; not seldom to our prejudices, sometimes to our fears, often to our egoism—but always to our credulity. And their words are heard with reverence, for their concern is with weighty matters: with the cultivation of our minds and the proper care of our bodies, with the attainment of our ambitions, with the perfection of the means and the glorification of our precious aims.

It is otherwise with the artist.

Confronted by the same enigmatical spectacle the artist descends within himself, and in that lonely region of stress and strife, if he be deserving and fortunate, he finds the terms of his appeal. His appeal is made to our less obvious capacities: to that part of our nature which, because of the warlike conditions of existence, is necessarily kept out of sight within the more resisting and hard qualities—like the vulnerable body within a steel armour. His appeal is less loud, more profound, less distinct, more stirring—and sooner forgotten. Yet its effect endures forever. The changing wisdom of successive generations discards ideas, questions facts, demolishes theories. But the artist appeals to that part of our being which is not dependent on wisdom: to that in us which is a gift and not an acquisition—and, therefore, more permanently enduring. He speaks to our capacity for delight and wonder, to the sense of mystery surrounding our lives; to our sense of pity, and beauty, and pain; to the latent feeling of fellowship with all creation—and to the subtle but invincible conviction of solidarity that knits together the loneliness of innumerable hearts, to the solidarity in dreams, in joy, in sorrow, in aspirations, in illusions, in hope, in fear, which binds men to each other, which binds together all humanity—the dead to the living and the living to the unborn. . . .

Fiction—if it at all aspires to be art—appeals to temperament. And in truth it must be, like painting, like music, like all art, the appeal of one temperament to all the other innumerable temperaments whose subtle and resistless power endows passing events with their true meaning, and creates the moral, the emotional atmosphere of the place and time. Such an appeal to be effective must be an impression conveyed through the senses; and, in fact, it cannot be made in any other way, because temperament, whether individual or collective, is not amenable to persuasion. All art, therefore, appeals primarily to the senses, and the artistic aim when expressing itself in written words must also make its appeal through the senses, if its high desire is to reach the secret spring of responsive emotions. It must strenuously aspire to the plasticity of sculpture, to the colour of painting, and to the magic suggestiveness of music—which is the art of arts. And it is only through complete, unswerving devotion to the perfect blending of form and substance; it is only through an unremitting never-discouraged care for the shape and ring of sentences that an approach can be made to plasticity, to colour, and that the light of magic suggestiveness may be brought to play for an evanescent instant over the commonplace surface of words: of the old, old words, worn thin, defaced by ages of careless usage.

The sincere endeavour to accomplish that creative task, to go as far on that road as his strength will carry him, to go undeterred by faltering, weariness, or reproach, is the only valid justification for the worker in prose. And if his conscience is clear, his answer to those who in the fulness of a wisdom which looks for immediate profit demand specifically to be edified, consoled, amused; who demand to be promptly improved, or encouraged, or frightened, or shocked, or charmed, must run thus:—My task which I am trying to achieve is, by the power of the written word to make you hear, to make you feel—it is, before all, to make you *see*. That—and no more, and it is everything. If I succeed, you shall find there according to your deserts: encouragement, consolation, fear, charm—all you demand—and, perhaps, also that glimpse of truth for which you have forgotten to ask.

To snatch in a moment of courage, from the remorseless rush of time, a passing phase of life, is only the beginning of the task. The task approached in tenderness and faith is to hold up unquestioningly, without choice and without fear, the rescued fragment before all eyes in the light of a sincere mood. It is to show its vibration, its colour, its form; and through its movement, its form, and its colour, reveal the substance of its truth—disclose its inspiring secret: the stress and passion within the core of each convincing moment. In a single-minded attempt of that kind, if one be deserving and fortunate, one may perchance attain to such clearness of sincerity that at last the presented vision of regret or pity, of terror or mirth, shall awaken in the hearts of the beholders that feeling of unavoidable solidarity; of the solidarity in mysterious origin, in toil, in joy, in hope, in uncertain fate, which binds men to each other and all mankind to the visible world. . . .

1898

Rendering Experience

In her critical writings, Virginia Woolf (1882–1941) railed against literary tradi-
tionalism while advocating an art based on inner experience. In her fiction, she of-
ten replaced conventional plots with stream-of-consciousness narratives to convey
the fluctuations of the perceiving mind. Her essay 'Modern Fiction,' like Conrad's
preface, can be seen as a manifesto of the impressionistic method.

'Life is a luminous halo.'

Virginia Woolf, from 'Modern Fiction'

... Examine for a moment an ordinary mind on an ordinary day. The mind
receives a myriad [of] impressions—trivial, fantastic, evanescent, or engraved
with the sharpness of steel. From all sides they come, an incessant show of innumerable atoms; and as they fall, as they shape themselves into the life of
Monday or Tuesday, the accents falls differently from of old; the moment of
importance came not here but there; so that, if a writer were a free man and not
a slave, if he could write what he chose, not what he must, if he could base his
work upon his own feeling and not upon convention, there would be no plot,
no comedy, no tragedy, no love interest or catastrophe in the accepted style,
and perhaps not a single button sewn on as the Bond Street tailors would have
it. Life is not a series of gig lamps symmetrically arranged; life is a luminous
halo, a semi-transparent envelope surrounding us from the beginning of consciousness to the end. Is it not the task of the novelist to convey this varying,
this unknown and uncircumscribed spirit, whatever aberration or complexity
it may display, with as little mixture of the alien and external as possible? We are
not pleading merely for courage and sincerity; we are suggesting that the proper
stuff of fiction is little other than custom would have us believe it.

It is, at any rate, in some such fashion as this that we seek to define the quality which distinguishes the work of several young writers, among whom Mr
James Joyce is the most notable, from that of their predecessors. They attempt
to come closer to life, and to preserve more sincerely and exactly what interests
and moves them, even if to do so they must discard most of the conventions
which are commonly observed by the novelist. Let us record the atoms as they
fall upon the mind in the order in which they fall, let us trace the pattern,
however disconnected and incoherent in appearance, which each sight or incident scores upon the consciousness. Let us not take it for granted that life
exists more fully in what is commonly thought big than in what is commonly
thought small. Anyone who has read *A Portrait of the Artist as a Young Man*
or, what promises to be a far more interesting work, *Ulysses*, now appearing
in *The Little Review*, will have hazarded some theory of this nature as to Mr

Joyce's intention. On our part, with such a fragment before us, it is hazarded rather than affirmed; but whatever the intention of the whole, there can be no question but that it is of the utmost sincerity and that the result, difficult or unpleasant as we may judge it, is undeniably important. In contrast with those whom we have called materialists, Mr Joyce is spiritual; he is concerned at all costs to reveal the flickerings of that innermost flame which flashes its messages through the brain, and in order to preserve it he disregards with complete courage whatever seems to him adventitious, whether it be probability, or coherence, or any other of these signposts which for generations have served to support the imagination of a reader when called upon to imagine what he can neither touch nor see. . . .

1919

The Morality of the Short Story

In this excerpt Anglo-Irish writer Elizabeth Bowen (1899–1973) elevates the short story to a major art form, touching on its lyricism and its freedom from the complexity and conclusiveness of the novel.

'[I]t may more nearly than the novel approach aesthetic and moral truth.'

Elizabeth Bowen, from Introduction to *The Faber Book of Modern Short Stories*

. . . The story should have the valid central emotion and inner spontaneity of the lyric; it should magnetize the imagination and give pleasure—of however disturbing, painful, or complex a kind. The story should be as composed, in the plastic sense, and as visual as a picture. It must have tautness and clearness; it must contain no passage not aesthetically relevant to the whole. The *necessary* subject dictates its own relevance. However plain or lively or unpretentious be the manner of the story, the central emotion—emotion however remotely involved or hinted at—should be austere, major. The subject must have implicit dignity. If in the writer half-conscious awe of his own subject be lacking, the story becomes flooded with falseness, mawkishness, whimsicality, or some ulterior spite. The plot, whether or not it be ingenious or remarkable, for however short a way it is to be pursued, ought to raise some issue, so that it may continue in the mind. The art of the short story permits a break at what in the novel would be the crux of the plot: the short story, free from the *longueurs* of the novel, is also exempt from the novel's conclusiveness—too often forced and false: it may thus more nearly than the novel approach aesthetic and moral truth. It can, while remaining rightly prosaic and circumstantial, give scene, action, event, character a poetic new actuality. It must have had, to the writer, moments of unfamiliarity, where it imposed itself.

The writer's imagination must operate in the world, whether factual or fantastic, that is most natural to it. The one nineteenth-century writer, in English, of the short story proper, Edgar Allan Poe, dealt almost wholly in fantasy: in England, in the same century, the much humbler F. Anstey, with a few little-known stories, followed. Since Poe's day, it has been the English rather than the Americans who have occupied the fantastic domain. Pure, objectified, or projected fantasy (as opposed to private, escapist fantasy, or to *Bovaryisme)* stays, on the whole, with our older writers, or writers early in time, such as Richard Middleton, who died young by his own act. Rudyard Kipling and H.G. Wells, with some of their greatest stories, Walter de la Mare, E.M. Forster, Algernon Blackwood, and M.R. James have each added to a terribly likely world, whose oddness has a super-rationality, which is waiting just at the edge of normal experience. Younger writers have, now and then, each projected his own ray into it. The fantasy story has often a literary beauty that is disarming; the one test one can apply is: does the *imagination* find this credible? Any crazy house against moonlight might, like the House of Usher, split right down to show the moon: there is assent at once, but no way to check up. Fancy has an authority reason cannot challenge. The pure fantasy writer works in a free zone: he has not to reconcile inner and outer images.

There is only one pure (or externalized) fantasy story in this book: the separate nature and problems of the fantasy story set it apart; also, the general trend of the short story has been, lately, towards inward, or, as it were, applied and functional fantasy, which does not depart from life but tempers it. Pure (as opposed to applied) fantasy has, it is true, reappeared in the apocalyptic writing of Dylan Thomas: the delirium or the dream. This may be another beginning. Up to now, however, and during most of the period this collection covers, writers have, rather, tended to explore and annotate different kinds of escape or of compensation. The retreat from fact that private fantasy offers has been as grateful in life as its variations are fascinating to art. Man has to live how he can: overlooked and dwarfed he makes himself his own theatre. Is the drama inside heroic or pathological? Outward acts have often an inside magnitude. The short story, within its shorter span than the novel's, with its freedom from forced complexity, its possible lucidness, is able, like the poetic drama, to measure man by his aspirations and dreads and place him alone on that stage which, inwardly, every man is conscious of occupying alone.

1939

Exploring 'Storyness' through Metaphor

Julio Cortázar (1914–1984) was raised in Buenos Aires, Argentina, but immigrated to Paris at age thirty-seven, where he worked as a translator for thirty-three years (he translated all of Poe's works). His friend Borges was his first publisher, though Cortázar (unlike Borges) was an ardent supporter of leftist causes. Drawing on astronomy, photography, and boxing, Cortázar identifies the 'secret alchemy' of the short story.

'[In a] short story . . . life and the written expression of life engage in a fraternal battle, and the result of that battle is the story itself.'

Julio Cortázar, from 'Some Aspects of the Short Story'

Almost all the stories I have written belong to the genre known as 'fantastic' for lack of a better term, and they are opposed to that false realism which consists of believing that everything can be described and explained as it was accepted by the scientific and philosophical optimism of the eighteenth century; that is, within a world directed more or less harmoniously by a system of laws, principles, cause-and-effect relations, defined psychologies, and well-mapped geographies. In my case, the suspicion of another order, more secret and less communicable, and the rich discovery of Alfred Jarry, for whom the true study of reality lay not in its laws, but in the exceptions to those laws, have been some of the orienting principles of my personal search for a literature beyond all ingenuous realism. I am certain that there exist certain constants, certain values which hold for all short stories, fantastic or realistic, dramatic or humorous. And I think that perhaps it is possible to show here those invariable elements which give a good short story its peculiar atmosphere and make it a work of art.

A discussion of the short story should interest us especially, since almost all the Spanish-speaking countries of America give the story great importance, which it has never had in other Latin countries like France or Spain. As is natural among younger literatures, in our countries spontaneous creation almost always precedes critical examination, and that is as it should be. No one can claim that short stories should be written only after learning their rules. In the first place, there are no such rules; at most one can speak of points of view, of certain constants which give a structure to this genre which is hard to pigeonhole. In the second place, the short-story writers themselves don't have to be theoreticians and critics, and it is natural that the latter enter the scene only when there exists a body of literature which permits inquiry and clarification of its development and its qualities. In America, in Cuba, just as in Mexico or Chile or Argentina, a great number of short-story writers worked from the beginning of this century on, without knowing each other, discovering each other almost posthumously. But someday definitive anthologies will be made, as they are in Anglo-Saxon countries, for example, and we will all know just how far we've come. For the moment, I will speak of the short story in the abstract, as a literary genre.

A short story, in the final analysis, moves in that projection of man where life and the written expression of life engage in a fraternal battle, and the result of that battle is the story itself, a live synthesis as well as a synthesis of life, something like the shimmering water in a glass, the fleeting within the permanent.

Only images can transmit that secret alchemy which explains the profound resonance which a great story has within us, which in turn explains why there are so few truly great stories. To understand the peculiar character of the short story, it must be compared to the novel, a much more popular genre about which there are many options and ideas. It has been pointed out, for instance, that the novel develops on paper, and therefore in the time taken to read it, with no limits other than the exhaustion of the artistic material. For its part, the short story begins with the notion of limits—in the first place, of physical limits, so that in France, when a story exceeds twenty pages, it is called a *nouvelle*, something between the short story and the proper novel. In this sense, the novel and the short story can be compared analogically with the film and the photograph, since the film is, essentially, an 'open order' like the novel, while a successful photo presupposes a circumscribed limitation, imposed in part by the reduced field which the camera captures and also by the way in which the photographer uses that limitation aesthetically. I don't know if you have heard a professional photographer talk about his art; I have always been surprised by the fact that, in many cases, they talk much as a short-story writer might. Photographers like Cartier-Bresson or Brassai define their art as an apparent paradox: that of cutting off a fragment of reality, giving it certain limits, but in such a way that this segment acts like an explosion which fully opens a much more ample reality, like a dynamic vision which spiritually transcends the space reached by the camera. While in films, as in the novel, a more ample and multi-faceted reality is captured through the development of partial and accumulative elements, which do not exclude, of course, a synthesis which will give a climax to the work. A high quality photograph or story proceeds inversely; that is, the photographer or the story writer finds himself obliged to choose and delimit an image or an event which must be meaningful, which is meaningful not only in itself, but rather is capable of acting on the viewer or the reader as a kind of opening, an impetus which projects the intelligence and the sensibility toward something which goes well beyond the visual or literary anecdote contained in the photograph or the story. An Argentine writer who is a boxing fan told me that in the struggle between an emotive text and its reader, the novel always wins on points, while the story must win by a knockout. This is true in the sense that the novel progressively accumulates effects upon the reader while a good short story is incisive, biting, giving no quarter from the first sentence. Don't take this too literally, because a good short-story writer is a very clever boxer, and many of his early blows can seem harmless when really they are undermining his adversary's most solid resistance. Take whatever great story you like and analyze its first page. I would be surprised if you found any gratuitous, merely decorative elements. The short-story writer knows he can't proceed cumulatively, that time is not his ally. His only solution is to work deeply, vertically, heading up or down in literary space. This, which seems like a metaphor, nevertheless expresses the essential aspects of the method. The story's time and space must be condemned entities, submitted to a high spiritual and formal pressure to bring about that opening I spoke of. Ask yourself why a certain story is bad. It is not bad because of the subject, because in literature there are no good or bad subjects, there is only a good or bad treatment of the subject. Nor is it bad because the characters are uninteresting, since even a stone is interesting when a Henry James or a Franz Kafka deals with it.

We said that the short-story writer works with material which we term meaningful. The story's significant element seems to reside mainly *in its subject*, in the act of choosing a real or imaginary happening which has that mysterious property of illuminating something beyond itself, to the extent that a common domestic occurrence, such as we have in so many admirable stories of a Katherine Mansfield or of a Sherwood Anderson, is converted into an implacable summary of a certain human condition or the burning symbol of a social or historical order. A story is meaningful when it ruptures its own limits with that explosion of spiritual energy which suddenly illuminates something far beyond that small and sometimes sordid anecdote which is being told. I think, for instance, of the themes of the majority of the admirable stories of Anton Chekhov. What is there in them which is not sadly ordinary, mediocre, often conformist or uselessly rebellious? What is told in these stories is almost like what we, as children, shared with our elders in boring gatherings; we heard our grandparents or our aunts tell the little insignificant family tales of frustrated ambitions, of local dramas, of living-room anguish, of a piano, of tea and cakes. But nevertheless, the stories of Katherine Mansfield, of Chekhov, are significant; something explodes in them while we read them, and it offers us a kind of break in daily routine which goes well beyond the anecdote described. You will have realized by now that the mysterious significance does not lie only in the subject of the story, because really, the majority of the bad stories which we have all read contain episodes like those treated by the authors we've mentioned. The idea of significance is worthless if we do not relate it to the ideas of intensity and tension, which refer to the technique used to develop the subject. And this is where the sharp distinction is made between the good and the bad short-story writer.

A story writer is a man who, surrounded by the din and clamor of the world, and bound, to a greater or lesser degree, to the historical reality which holds him, suddenly chooses a certain subject and makes a story out of it, and this choosing of a subject is not so simple. Sometimes the story writer elects his subject and other times he feels as if it were imposed on him irresistibly; it forces him to write it. In my case, the great majority of my stories were written outside my will, above or below my conscious reasoning, as if I were no more than a medium through which an alien force passed and took shape. But this, which can depend on the individual temperament, does not change the essential fact, that in a certain moment, there is a subject, be it invented, chosen voluntarily, or strangely imposed from a plane where nothing is definable.

It seems to me that the subject from which a good story will emerge is always exceptional, but I don't mean by this that a subject must be extraordinary, uncommon, mysterious, or singular. On the contrary, it can be about a perfectly trivial and everyday occurrence. It is exceptional in that it is like a magnet: a good subject attracts an entire system of connected stories, it solidifies in the author, and later in the reader, many notions, glimpses, sentiments, and even ideas which virtually were floating in his memory or his sensibility. A good subject is like a good sun, a star with a planetary system around it of which, many times, we were unaware until the story writer, an astronomer of words, revealed it to us. Or rather, to be more modest and more up to date at the same time, a good subject has something of the atomic about it, a nucleus around which the electrons whirl; and, when all is said and done, isn't this a proposal of life, a dynamic which urges us to get outside ourselves and enter a more complex and more beautiful system of relations? . . .

1963   Translated by Aden W. Haye

C. Genre and the Short Story

*Many short story critics have attempted to define the short prose
narrative by comparing it to another genre or form, especially the
long prose narrative, the novel.*

The Novel and the Short Story

*American writer Edith Wharton set out to explain the art of the novel and the
short story in* The Writing of Fiction.

'Situation is the main concern of the short story, character of the novel.'

Edith Wharton, from *The Writing of Fiction*

. . . A curious distinction between the successful tale and the successful novel at
once presents itself. It is safe to say (since the surest way of measuring achievement in art is by survival) that the test of the novel is that its people should be
alive. No subject in itself, however fruitful, appears to be able to keep a novel
alive; only the characters in it can. Of the short story the same cannot be said.
Some of the greatest stories owe their vitality entirely to the dramatic rendering
of a situation. Undoubtedly the characters engaged must be a little more than
puppets; but apparently, also, they may be a little less than individual human
beings. In this respect the short story, rather than the novel, might be called the
direct descendant of the old epic or ballad—of those earlier forms of fiction
in all of which action was the chief affair, and the characters, if they did not
remain mere puppets, seldom or never became more than types—such as the
people, for instance, in Molière. The reason of the difference is obvious. Type,
general character, may be set forth in a few strokes, but the progression, the
unfolding of personality, of which the reader instinctively feels the need if the
actors in the tale are to retain their individuality for him through a succession
of changing circumstances—this slow but continuous growth requires space,
and therefore belongs by definition to a larger, a symphonic plan.

The chief technical difference between the short story and the novel may
therefore be summed up by saying that situation is the main concern of the short
story, character of the novel; and it follows that the effect produced by the short
story depends almost entirely on its form, or presentation. Even more—yes, and
much more—than in the construction of the novel, the impression of vividness,

of *presentness*, in the affair narrated, has to be sought, and made sure of beforehand, by that careful artifice which is the real carelessness of art. The short-story writer must not only know from what angle to present his anecdote if it is to give out all its fires, but must understand just *why* that particular angle and no other is the right one. He must therefore have turned his subject over and over, walked around it, so to speak, and applied to it those laws of perspective which Paolo Uccello called 'so beautiful,' before it can be offered to the reader as a natural unembellished fragment of experience, detached like a ripe fruit from the tree.

The moment the writer begins to grope in the tangle of his 'material,' to hesitate between one and another of the points that any actual happening thrusts up in such disorderly abundance, the reader feels a corresponding hesitancy, and the illusion of reality vanishes. The nonobservance of the optics of the printed page results in the same failure to make the subject 'carry' as the nonobservance of the optics of the stage in presenting a play. By all means let the writer of short stories reduce the technical trick to its minimum—as the cleverest actresses put on the least paint; but let him always bear in mind that the surviving minimum is the only bridge between the reader's imagination and his. . . .

1924

The author of both short stories and novels, American Steven Millhauser (b. 1943) is an innovative stylist who won a Pulitzer Prize for his 1996 novel Martin Dressler. *In this essay he personifies both forms, suggesting that the self-effacing story harbours secret ambitions.*

'The short story concentrates on its grain of sand. . .'

Steven Millhauser, 'The Ambition of the Short Story'

The short story—how modest in bearing! How unassuming in manner! It sits there quietly, eyes lowered, almost as if trying not to be noticed. And if it should somehow attract your attention, it says quickly, in a brave little self-deprecating voice alive to all the possibilities of disappointment: 'I'm not a novel, you know. Not even a short one. If that's what you're looking for, you don't want me.' Rarely has one form so dominated another. And we understand, we nod our heads knowingly: here in America, size is power. The novel is the Wal-Mart, the Incredible Hulk, the jumbo jet of literature. The novel is insatiable—it wants to devour the world. What's left for the poor short story to do? It can cultivate its garden, practice meditation, water the geraniums in the window box. It can take a course in creative nonfiction. It can do whatever it likes, so long as it doesn't forget its place—so long as it keeps quiet and stays out of the way. 'Hoo ha!' cries the novel. 'Here ah come!' The short story is always ducking for cover. The novel buys up the land, cuts down the trees, puts up the condos. The short story scampers across a lawn, squeezes under a fence.

Of course there are virtues associated with smallness. Even the novel will grant as much. Large things tend to be unwieldy, clumsy, crude; smallness is the realm of elegance and grace. It's also the realm of perfection. The novel is exhaustive by nature; but the world is inexhaustible; therefore the novel, that Faustian striver, can never attain its desire. The short story by contrast is inherently selective. By excluding almost everything, it can give perfect shape to what remains. And the short story can even lay claim to a kind of completeness that eludes the novel—after the initial act of radical exclusion, it can include all of the little that's left. The novel, when it remembers the short story at all, is pleased to be generous. 'I admire you,' it says, placing its big rough hand over its heart. 'No kidding. You're so—you're so—' So pretty! So svelte! So high class! And smart, too. The novel can hardly contain itself. After all, what difference does it make? It's nothing but talk. What the novel cares about is vastness, is power. Deep in its heart, it disdains the short story, which makes do with so little. It has no use for the short story's austerity, its suppression of appetite, its refusals and renunciations. The novel wants things. It wants territory. It wants the whole world. Perfection is the consolation of those who have nothing else.

So much for the short story. Modest in its pretensions, shyly proud of its petite virtues, a trifle anxious in relation to its brash rival, it contents itself with sitting back and letting the novel take on the big world. And yet, and yet. That modest pose—am I mistaken, or is it a little overdone? Those glancing-away looks—do they contain a touch of slyness? Can it be that the little short story dares to have ambitions of its own? If so, it will never admit them openly, because of a sharp instinct for self-protection, a long habit of secrecy bred by oppression. In a world ruled by swaggering novels, smallness has learned to make its way cautiously. We will have to intuit its secret. I imagine the short story harboring a wish. I imagine the short story saying to the novel: You can have everything—everything—all I ask is a single grain of sand. The novel, with a careless shrug, a shrug both cheerful and contemptuous, grants the wish.

But that grain of sand is the story's way out. That grain of sand is the story's salvation. I take my cue from William Blake: 'To see a world in a grain of sand.' Think of it: the world in a grain of sand; which is to say, every part of the world, however small, contains the world entirely. Or to put it another way: if you concentrate your attention on some apparently insignificant portion of the world, you will find, deep within it, nothing less than the world itself. In that single grain of sand lies the beach that contains the grain of sand. In that single grain of sand lies the ocean that dashes against the beach, the ship that sails the ocean, the sun that shines down on the ship, the interstellar winds, a teaspoon in Kansas, the structure of the universe. And there you have the ambition of the short story, the terrible ambition that lies behind its fraudulent modesty: to body forth the whole world. The short story believes in transformation. It believes in hidden powers. The novel prefers things in plain view. It has no patience with individual grains of sand, which glitter but are difficult to see. The novel wants to sweep everything into its mighty embrace—shores, mountains, continents. But it can never succeed, because the world is vaster than a novel, the world rushes away at every point. The novel leaps restlessly from place to place, always hungry, always dissatisfied, always fearful of coming to an end—because when it stops, exhausted but never at peace, the world will have escaped it. The short story concentrates on its grain of sand, in the fierce belief that there—right there, in the palm of its hand—lies the universe. It seeks to know that grain of sand the way a lover seeks to know the face of the beloved. It looks for the moment when the grain of sand reveals its true nature. In that moment of mystic expansion, when the macrocosmic flower bursts from the microcosmic seed, the short story feels its power. It becomes bigger than itself. It becomes bigger than the novel. It becomes as big as the universe. Therein lies the immodesty of the short story, its secret aggression. Its method is revelation. Its littleness is the agency of its power. The ponderous mass of the novel strikes it as the laughable image of weakness. The short story apologizes for nothing. It exults in its shortness. It wants to be shorter still. It wants to be a single word. If it could find that word, if it could utter that syllable, the entire universe would blaze up out of it with a roar. That is the outrageous ambition of the short story, that is its deepest faith, that is the greatness of its smallness.

2008

Canadian writer Greg Hollingshead, who has written both short stories and novels, sees contrastive principles at work in each, the novel expanding outward, the short story drawing inward to its centre.

'A point of perfect, drunken poise. . .'

Greg Hollingshead, from 'Short Story vs Novel'

. . . The primary difference between the short story and the novel is not word length. A novel is not a short story that kept going, though every short story writer dreams of writing such a story. Neither is a novel a string of stories with discursive and other connective tissue and padding. One of the first things the writer learns is how amazingly little room there is in a good novel for extraneousness, or noise. The primary difference between the short story and the novel is not length but the larger, more conceptual weight of meaning that the longer narrative must carry on its back from page to page, scene to scene. It's not baggy wordage that causes the diffusiveness of the novel, it's this long-distance haul of meaning. In a good short story the meaning is not so abstractable, so portable, as it must be in a novel, but is rather more tightly and ineffably embodied in the formal details of the text. A scene in a short story—and there may be only one—operates with a centripetal force of concentration. But a scene in a novel spins off a good deal of its energy looking not only backward and forward in the text but also sideways, outside the text, towards the material world, to that set of common assumptions considered ordinary life. That energy is centrifugal, opening out, not constantly seeking to revolve upon its own still centre.

Consider the difference in terms of time. Dr Johnson said, 'No man is ever happy in the present unless he is drunk.' The seeking of happiness in the present is a spiritual impulse, and also an artistic one (the other kind of happiness), and nowhere in literature is it so purely expressed as in lyric poetry and the short story. In a good short story the crisis exists in present time, it is a point of perfect, drunken poise between past and future, and every word of the text, every nuance of rhythm, every piece of shading and point of light, has been brought to bear upon it. As Frank O'Connor said, in a short story the crisis is the story. In a novel, by contrast, the crisis is only our destination, it occurs as a point in an unfolding of time; it is the logical result of what has come before it, which is as good as to say, of the moral qualities of the hero's choices to date, and it indicates what the future has in store for one who, by having acted this way, has come to this. So while the short story, like poetry, seeks to focus time, the novel, being more like history, being the most secular of forms, seeks to survey it.

This is why when other than market forces are allowed to prevail, the novel is a form best suited to older writers. The minds of older writers have slowed down and stopped jumping around so uncontrollably, they have grown familiar if not necessarily easy with their own contents, their spiritual hunger has been dulled by time and its accommodations, and they are now interested more in the inexorable laws of moral implication than in perfect artistic moments of drunken poise. Also, of course, having more personal history to survey, they have more to work with. They have the material. Young writers are rarely able to maintain the perspective necessary to write good novels, but they do often write good short stories, and they do often write good strange hybrid longer fictions that poeticize the modes of the novel and novelize poetry. Unfortunately, by the time they're writing good novels, they are often no longer writing with the spiritual force of poets. But every once in a while, to the salvation of literary fiction, there appears a mature writer of short stories—someone like Chekhov, or Munro—whose handling of the form at its best is so undulled, so poised, so capacious, so intelligent, that the short in short story is once again revealed as the silly adjective it is, for suddenly here are simply stories, spiritual histories, narratives amazingly porous yet concentrated and undiffused, grave without weight, ordinary but strange, and the unhappy bifurcation of poetry and history is once again revealed as the pernicious cultural illusion it is.

1999

The Lyric and the Short Story

Eileen Baldeshwiler defines the 'lyrical' short story in contrast to the 'epical,' tracing its development from Russians Ivan Turgenev and Anton Chekhov to contemporary practitioners such as Katherine Mansfield, D.H. Lawrence, Virginia Woolf, Eudora Welty, and others.

'The record of a moment of intense feeling or perception which contains its own significant form.'

Eileen Baldeshwiler, from 'The Lyric Short Story: The Sketch of a History'

When the history of the modern short story is written, it will have to take into account two related developments, tracing the course of the larger mass of narratives that, for purposes of clarification we could term 'epical,' and the smaller group which, to accentuate differences, we might call 'lyrical.' The larger group of narratives is marked by external action developed 'syllogistically' through characters fabricated mainly to forward plot, culminating in a decisive ending that sometimes affords a universal insight, and expressed in the serviceably inconspicuous language of prose realism. The other segment of stories concentrates on internal changes, moods, and feelings, utilizing a variety of structural patterns depending on the shape of the emotion itself, relies for the most part on the open ending, and is expressed in the condensed, evocative, often figured language of the poem. In present day literary theory, the term 'lyric' refers of course not so much to structure as to subject and tone, and it is mainly to these aspects of the brief narrative that the adjective is meant to call attention in the phrase 'lyrical' story. Obviously, the distinction between prose narrative and verse remains absolute: the 'lyrical' story, like any other, includes the essentials of storytelling—persons with some degree of verisimilitude engaged in a unified action in time—and the medium remains prose. . . .

When Chekhov, like Turgenev, raises tone to the level of a major device, we see an important step away from the conventional tale of reported action (the 'epical' story) toward a condition approaching that of the lyric poem. Besides freeing the short story from the limitations of conventional plot, Turgenev and Chekhov consciously exploited language itself to express more sharply states of feeling and subtle changes in emotion. With these authors, the locus of narrative art has moved from external action to internal states of mind, and the plot line will hereafter consist, in this mode, of tracing complex emotions to a closing cadence utterly unlike the reasoned resolution of the conventional cause-and-effect narrative. It is here that we observe the birth of the 'open' story. Besides the use of the emotional curve, other new patterns of story organization are beginning to emerge, such as the alternation of scenes and moods for a 'surrealistic' effect, the circling around a central dilemma or set of feelings, the record of a moment of intense feeling or perception which contains its own significant form. . . .

1969

D. Epiphany and the Short Story

The Joycean Epiphany

In Stephen Hero *(the draft of Joyce's autobiographical novel* A Portrait of the Artist as a Young Man, *1916), the main character, Stephen Dedalus, articulates some components of his aesthetic theory. Stephen describes a chance conversation between a young lady and a young gentleman, and in the dialogue that follows with his schoolmate Cranly expands on the mechanics of the epiphany, a sudden manifestation of truth. Joyce collected these truths in a 'book of epiphanies' and called on them in writing fictional scenes, such as those in* Dubliners. *While other modernists have viewed the 'moment of recognition' in a different light, the concept of the epiphany remains central to the study of the modernist short story.*

'The gropings of a spiritual eye which seeks to adjust its vision to an exact focus.'

James Joyce, from *Stephen Hero*

. . . A young lady was standing on the steps of one of those brown brick houses which seem the very incarnation of Irish paralysis. A young gentleman was leaning on the rusty railings of the area. Stephen as he passed on his quest heard the following fragment of colloquy out of which he received an impression keen enough to afflict his sensitiveness very severely.

The Young Lady—(drawling discreetly) . . . O, yes . . . I was . . . at the . . . cha . . . pel . . .

The Young Gentleman—(inaudibly) . . . I . . . (again inaudibly) . . . I . . .

The Young Lady—(softly) . . . O . . . but you're . . . ve . . . ry . . . wick . . . ed . . .

This triviality made him think of collecting many such moments together in a book of epiphanies. By an epiphany he meant a sudden spiritual manifestation, whether in the vulgarity of speech or of gesture or in a memorable phase of the mind itself. He believed that it was for the man of letters to record these epiphanies with extreme care, seeing that they themselves are the most delicate and evanescent of moments. He told Cranly that the clock of the Ballast Office was capable of an epiphany. Cranly questioned the inscrutable dial of the Ballast Office with his no less inscrutable countenance:

—Yes, said Stephen. I will pass it time after time, allude to it, refer to it, catch a glimpse of it. It is only an item in the catalogue of Dublin's street furniture. Then all at once I see it and I know at once what it is: epiphany.

—What?

—Imagine my glimpses at that clock as the gropings of a spiritual eye which seeks to adjust its vision to an exact focus. The moment the focus is reached the object is epiphanised. . . .

1908

The three critics below argue that recent—and many modernist— stories don't include a character insight at all, substituting another pattern truer to the modern or postmodern experience.

Against Epiphany

In this introduction to his book, Philip Stevick argues that contemporary writers studiously avoid epiphanies.

'What we start with is pretty much what we have in the end.'

Philip Stevick, from Introduction to *Anti-Story: An Anthology of Experimental Fiction*

To tell what recent fiction is, we must tell what recent fiction is not. And the place to begin is with the word 'epiphany.' The word was first applied to literature by Joyce, who borrowed it from its religious usage in which it means the showing forth specifically of Christ's divinity; Joyce chose to apply the word to certain very brief recorded moments in an artistic journal, events, sensations, visual observations that Joyce thought exhibited a sort of luminous intensity. From that usage Joyce carried it over so as to apply it to the moment of insight at the structural heart of his shorter fiction, that image or event near the end of a story which makes possible for at least one of the characters, and for us as readers, an intuitive act of understanding. Since Joyce, the word has been widely used, its usage extended, and it has been made to apply to insights quite unJoycean and to writers who would have been horrified to find themselves in Joyce's company. The word was none too precise as Joyce used it; it has become less precise since. Still, for all of its imprecision, the word does signify a structural feature of hundreds of modern stories of the kind that now seems conservative. The whole significance of such stories, their whole justification for being, is invested in that moment of insight around which the rest of the story deploys itself. The epiphany, in the extended sense I have indicated, is the single feature of the modern classic story most repeated and consistently characteristic. Conversely, there is no feature of the classic twentieth-century story so carefully avoided by writers who wish to do something new with short fiction. Characters in the works that follow do not learn. There are no insights. Relationships are not grasped in an instant. Structurally, the stories are flat, or circular, or cyclic, or mosaic constructions, or finally indeterminate or incomprehensible in their shape—they are not climactic. What we start with is pretty much what we have at the end. No epiphanies. . . .

1971

Moving Toward Disillusionment

After identifying two common structures of short stories, 'anecdotal' (plotted) and 'epiphanic' (plotless) stories, Thomas M. Leitch proposes a contrary or 'antithetical' rhythm in American short stories, tracing this pattern in the works of Stephen Crane, Edgar Allan Poe, Herman Melville, and Flannery O'Connor.

'Many American short stories . . . constitute essentially a means of unknowing rather than a means to knowledge.'

Thomas M. Leitch, from 'The Debunking Rhythm of the American Short Story'

. . . Particularly in the American short story, the reader's movement from bewilderment to authoritative revelation, from ignorance to knowledge, is complemented by what we might call the debunking rhythm of the short story, a rhythm that depends on a special use of antithesis. . . .

The revelation with which short stories end can simultaneously provide a stable sense of closure and adumbrate a new order that displaces the assumptions of the exposition. Often, however, this displacement does not correspond to a movement from ignorance to knowledge but simply indicates a debunking or unknowing of the illusions that the story began by encouraging. Paco in [Hemingway's] 'The Capital of the World' and the older waiter in 'A Clean, Well-Lighted Place' undergo experiences which do not so much enlighten audiences by means of authoritative revelations as disabuse them of their illusions about the world the story presents and represents without substituting any positive or more comprehensive wisdom. In Henry James's 'The Figure in the Carpet' and 'In the Cage,' the audience moves again not so much from ignorance to knowledge as from a false sense of certainty to a more authentic sense of uncertainty about the revelations James persistently withholds.

It is clearly impossible for a story to chart a progression from ignorance to knowledge—either the character's progression or the audience's—without presenting a complementary movement from false illusions to disillusionment, a movement based on the antithetical structure I have been describing. But it is quite possible to challenge the character's, and the audience's, assumptions about the world without substituting any more-authoritative knowledge, so that such stories constitute not a form of knowledge but a challenge to knowledge, that is, a way of debunking assumptions which are not really true. A great many American short stories, whose antithetical structures indicate movements toward disillusionment rather than teleological movements toward revelation and reintegration, constitute essentially a means of unknowing rather than a means to knowledge. To borrow the terminology of Susan Lohafer's *Coming to Terms with the Short Story*, I would suggest that each of these stories, whether or not it includes a homecoming, is preeminently a story of departure, of movement away from the known. More specifically, these stories commonly debunk a particular subject: the concept of a public identity, a self that acts in such a knowable, deliberate way as to assert a stable, discrete identity. The American short story as a genre presents a critique of the notion of a stable and discrete personal identity constituted by an individual's determinate actions—a means to the author's unmaking, and the audience's unknowing, an active, determinate self that was only an illusion to begin with.

Stephen Crane's characters, like Melville's in 'The Encantadas,' are constantly attempting to establish identities their worlds do not support. Fred Collins, in 'A Mystery of Heroism,' acts heroically in crossing a battlefield for a bucket of water and, finally, in giving water to a dying officer, but feels certain that his deed, the response to a dare, does not make him a hero. Although he remains convinced that there is such a thing as a hero, the story, as its title indicates, serves to debunk the very possibility of heroism. . . .

1989

Significant Omissions

Observing that both the short story and minimalism are 'governed by an aesthetic of exclusion,' Cynthia J. Hallett concludes that it is the characteristics and objectives of minimalist writing that distinguish the story from the novel and the poem.

'The blunt, uncomplicated prose mirrors empty lives.'

Cynthia J. Hallett, from 'Minimalism and the Short Story'

... The seeds of art and artifice that inform both literary minimalism in general and the short story in particular can be traced to such otherwise diverse writers as Edgar Allan Poe, Anton Chekhov, James Joyce, Samuel Beckett, and Ernest Hemingway—all of whose conscious codes of omission are designed to make audiences feel more than they understand: Poe's notion of unity and singleness of effect; Chekhov's maxim that he must focus on the end of a short story and artfully concentrate there an impression of the total work; Joyce's minimal dependence on the traditional notion of plot, particularly renouncing highly plotted stories in favor of seemingly static episodes and 'slices' of reality; Beckett's efforts, in the words of William Hutchings, 'to present the ultimate distillation of his inimitable world-view...'; and Hemingway's communication of complex emotional states by the ostensibly simple patterning of concrete details—his 'tip of the iceberg' effect.

In the minimalist short story, subject matter and writing style often combine for singular effect. The blunt, uncomplicated prose mirrors empty lives, and the lack of narrator commentary demands extensive reader participation. For the most part, the characters of minimalist fiction are ordinary people, neither heroes nor larger than life, just people who appear to inhabit the 'real world,' where doing and/or saying nothing is often easier than the alternative. In their silence and paralysis they appear to be hyper-Hemingway-heroes, that is, not so much less-heroic as *even more* not-heroic—Hemingway-heroes[2] (squared)—but different from Hemingway, whose characters often respond to *their* inability to communicate by/with some form of action; on the other hand, the postmodern, minimalist writer creates characters more like those in Joyce's *Dubliners*, whose inarticulation so often leads to paralysis. This inability to act or to move also evokes images of those characters that people so many works by Samuel Beckett. These literary characteristics combine to generate a type of fiction that reflects the evolution of not only a certain breed of American prose, but also a particular strain of aesthetics in literature now often genetically, and by some generically, associated with the short story....

As a rule, writers of the minimalist short story manipulate figurative speech to present what appears to be a single event, a mere incident, a nothing-is-happening-here story that is actually an intricate figurative pattern that reflects or signifies the human condition and capacity. With this technique these writers create a mathematical relationship, a ratio, between the singular and universal, the part and the whole, the trifle and the significant: the singular is to the universal as the part is to the whole, and so the trifle is the significant. As a result of this figurative polarity, in these stories what appears to be a trifle is potently significant. In addition, much of what is omitted becomes significant by its absence. This conscious use of poetic trope as a vehicle for expanding image and meaning in a story is what makes these short stories lyrical. This method of story reflects what Charles May sees as the 'Chekhovian uniting of the lyrical and the realistic . . . a basic characteristic of the modern short story' ('Reality in the Modern Short Story' 371). A. Walton Litz suggests that in the United States, the early fiction writers 'were led to the short story in part by . . . the 'thinness' of American life, its lack of a rich and complex social texture: the brief poetic tale . . . seemed the natural form for their intense but isolated experiences' (4). If Litz is correct, then today, this 'thinness' is reflected in minimalist fiction, which displays a particular vision of contemporary American life, a social milieu characterized by a certain lack of emotion and an inability to verbalize, to communicate, or to connect with others. Eugene Current-García sees it as a 'problem of alienation and the individual's quest for self-fulfillment—and the results [of] their efforts . . . (499)'. Contemporary depictions of these efforts, so reminiscent of Joyce's *Dubliners* are found more recently in Carver's 'blue-collar' fiction. Repressed or compressed emotion is a key function to minimalism—emotion resounding below a deceptively mute surface.

As neo-realists, minimalist writers seem to share with postmodernists the conviction that the world is random and contingent rather than defined and governed by some stable set of rules, truths, and laws; they view language with much the same conviction. The consequences of this typically postmodern outlook endorsed by the minimalist writers are visible in their style and themes. Their short stories 'cut to the quick' of the characters' lives and 'to the quick' of the implied human condition, evoking the pain that so often accompanies these penetrations. Many of the characters appear to be in psychic or emotional pain and then behave as if this pain is simply Muzak in their lives—elevator music that has no bearing on, or connection to, the event, or non-event, of their daily condition; but rather, it serves to drown out other kinds of noises—thought, or awareness perhaps. This apparent desensitization to all kinds of pain is a central issue of the human condition as portrayed in much of the fiction of the latter half of the twentieth-century, and the abbreviated responses innate to this 'numbness' are especially reflected in the condensed structure and detached narrative tone of minimalist short stories. . . .

1996

E. Reality, Fantasy, and the Short Story

The Grotesque

Flannery O'Connor (1925–1964) was born in Georgia and is often identified as a 'Southern Gothic' writer. She wrote two novels, along with many short stories and essays. Her characters are outcasts, misfits, or religious zealots who undergo crises in faith, enacting patterns of violence in an attempt to achieve redemption. In this excerpt, O'Connor distinguishes between two kinds of realism, that which accurately 'reproduces' human concerns and that which uses distortion to explore the limits of the unknowable.

'Their fictional qualities lean away from the typical social patterns, toward mystery and the unexpected.'

Flannery O'Connor, from 'Aspects of the Grotesque in Southern Fiction'

. . . In these grotesque works [of Southern writers], we find that the writer has made alive some experience which we are not accustomed to observe every day, or which the ordinary man may never experience in his ordinary life. We find that connections which we would expect in the customary kind of realism have been ignored, that there are strange skips and gaps which anyone trying to describe manners and customs would certainly not have left. Yet the characters have an inner coherence, if not always a coherence to their social framework. Their fictional qualities lean away from typical social patterns, toward mystery and the unexpected. It is this kind of realism that I want to consider.

All novelists are fundamentally seekers and describers of the real but the realism of each novelist will depend on his view of the ultimate reaches of reality. Since the eighteenth century, the popular spirit of each succeeding age has tended more and more to the view that the ills and mysteries of life will eventually fall before the scientific advances of man, a belief that is still going strong even though this is the first generation to face total extinction because of these advances. If the novelist is in tune with this spirit, if he believes that actions are predetermined by psychic make-up or the economic situation or some other determinable factor, then he will be concerned above all with an accurate reproduction of the things that most immediately concern man, with the natural forces that he feels control his destiny. Such a writer may produce a great tragic naturalism, for by his responsibility to the things he sees, he may transcend the limitations of his narrow vision.

On the other hand, if the writer believes that our life is and will remain essentially mysterious, if he looks upon us as beings existing in a created order to whose laws we freely respond, then what he sees on the surface will be of interest to him only as he can go through it into an experience of mystery itself. His kind of fiction will always be pushing its own limits outward toward the limits of mystery, because for this kind of writer, the meaning of a story does not begin except at a depth where adequate motivation and adequate psychology and the various determinations have been exhausted. Such a writer will be interested in what we don't understand rather than in what we do. He will be interested in possibility rather than in probability. He will be interested in characters who are forced out to meet evil and grace and who act on a trust beyond themselves—whether they know very clearly what it is they act upon or not. To the modern mind, this kind of character, and his creator, are typical Don Quixotes, tilting at what is not there.

I would not like to suggest that this kind of writer, because his interest is predominantly in mystery, is able in any sense to slight the concrete. Fiction begins where human knowledge begins—with the senses—and every fiction writer is bound by this fundamental aspect of his medium. I do believe, however, that the kind of writer I am describing will use the concrete in a more drastic way. His way will much more obviously be the way of distortion....

1960

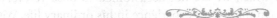

The Fantastic

Tzvetan Todorov (b. 1939), who was born in Bulgaria and lives in France, is a leading critical theorist whose more than twenty books explore such fields as history, semiotics, ethics, and literature. His exhaustive study of the fantastic classifies many writers, including Kafka and Poe, according to the definitions he formulates in his book.

'That hesitation experienced by a person who knows only the laws of nature, confronting an apparently supernatural event.'

Tzvetan Todorov, from *The Fantastic: A Structural Approach to a Literary Genre*

... In a world which is indeed our world, the one we know, a world without devils, sylphides, or vampires, there occurs an event which cannot be explained by the laws of this same familiar world. The person who experiences the event must opt for one of two possible solutions: either he is the victim of an illusion of the senses, of a product of the imagination—and laws of the world then remain what they are; or else the event has indeed taken place, it is an integral part of reality—but then this reality is controlled by laws unknown to us. Either the devil is an illusion, an imaginary being; or else he really exists, precisely like other living beings—with this reservation, that we encounter him infrequently.

The fantastic occupies the duration of this uncertainty. Once we choose one answer or the other, we leave the fantastic for a neighboring genre, the uncanny or the marvelous. The fantastic is that hesitation experienced by a person who knows only the laws of nature, confronting an apparently supernatural event....

The fantastic requires the fulfillment of three conditions. First, the text must oblige the reader to consider the world of the characters as a world of living persons and to hesitate between a natural and a supernatural explanation of the events described. Second, this hesitation may also be experienced by a character; thus the reader's role is so to speak entrusted to a character, and at the same time the hesitation is represented, it becomes one of the themes of the work—in the case of naive reading, the actual reader identifies himself with the character. Third, the reader must adopt a certain attitude with regard to the text: he will reject allegorical as well as 'poetic' interpretations. These three requirements do not have an equal value. The first and the third actually constitute the genre; the second may not be fulfilled. Nonetheless, most examples satisfy all three conditions....

1975

The 'Tale'

Drawing some distinctions between short and extended prose and, importantly, between the 'tale' and the 'short story,' English writer Angela Carter explains why the 'tale' speaks to our deeper human nature.

'Provoking unease . . . '

Angela Carter, from Afterword to *Fireworks: Nine Stories in Various Disguises*

I started to write short pieces when I was living in a room too small to write a novel in. So the size of my room modified what I did inside it and it was the same with the pieces themselves. The limited trajectory of the short narrative concentrates its meaning. Sign and sense can fuse to an extent impossible to achieve among the multiplying ambiguities of an extended narrative. I found that, though the play of surfaces never ceased to fascinate me, I was not so much exploring them as making abstractions from them. I was writing, therefore, tales.

Though it took me a long time to realize why I liked them, I'd always been fond of Poe, and Hoffman—Gothic tales, cruel tales, tales of wonder, tales of terror, fabulous narratives that deal directly with the imagery of the unconscious—mirrors; the externalized self; forsaken castles; haunted forests; forbidden sexual objects. Formally, the tale differs from the short story in that it makes few pretences at the imitation of life. The tale does not log everyday experience, as the short story does; it interprets everyday experience through a system of imagery derived from subterranean areas behind everyday experience, and therefore the tale cannot betray its readers into a false knowledge of everyday experience.

The Gothic tradition in which Poe writes grandly ignores the value systems of our institutions; it deals entirely with the profane. Its great themes are incest and cannibalism. Character and events are exaggerated beyond reality, to become symbols, ideas, passions. Its style will tend to be ornate, unnatural—and thus operate against the perennial human desire to believe the word as fact. Its only humour is black humour. It retains a singular moral function—that of provoking unease.

The tale has relations with sub-literary forms of pornography, ballad, and dream, and it has not been dealt with kindly by literati. And is it any wonder? Let us keep the unconscious in a suitcase, as Père Ubu did with his conscience, and flush it down the lavatory when it gets too troublesome.

So I worked on tales. I was living in Japan; I came back to England in 1972. I found myself in a new country. It was like waking up, it was a rude awakening. We live in Gothic times. Now, to understand and to interpret is the main thing; but my method of investigation is changing. . . .

1974

Magic Realism

Geoff Hancock, editor-in-chief of the short story quarterly Canadian Fiction Magazine *(1974–1998), has published numerous anthologies of innovative and experimental fiction, as well as Quebec Gothic fiction in translation, and interviews with Canadian writers. He is considered a pioneering theorist in Canadian magic realism. The following excerpt considers various difficulties in defining the term.*

'Magic Realism raises for the fiction writer the same problems as always: Can we know the truth, and, if so, how will we tell it?'

Geoff Hancock, from Magic Realism and Canadian Literature: Essays and Stories

What exactly is Magic Realism? Part of the problem of definition is that the subject is wider than literature. But a few features can be identified: exaggerated comic effects; hyperbole treated as fact; liberation from a boring world; dramatic settings treated as extraordinary; a labyrinthine awareness of other books that highlights concerns of other writers; the use of fantasy to cast assumption on the nature of reality; an absurd recreation of 'history'; a parody of government and politicians' unusual perceptions based on biased or distorted points of view; a metafictional awareness of the process of fiction-making; a reminder of the mysteriousness of the literary imagination at work; a collective sense of the folkloric past; a concern with the structures of fiction and the imagination; and profound implications for readers of books, be those books history, fact, or fiction.

Alejo Carpentier has gone so far as to suggest that the marvellous is not universal, but something exclusively Latin-American. He called the marvellous the subconscious of Latin America. He writes that the marvellous reveals itself only to those who believe in it; he adds that the narrative force of the marvellous comes from those places most difficult to reach, such as the Amazon hideaway of *The Lost Steps*, his most famous novel. For Carpentier, the marvellous Latin-American reality is based on a 'primitive faith' that includes an acceptance of the superstitious as part of daily life. Fantasy and reality, he suggests, merge 'by virtue of the exultation of spirit.'

Yet as I look at my shelf filled with Canadian examples, I see that miracles are not found just in Latin America. Perhaps we have to define our terms in a different context: perhaps we need a different set of premises. The Latin-American examples are useful for Canadian writers looking for a different means of self-expression, if only as a place to start. But as I thought about the idea of magic realism, I realized I had many questions.

Does Magic Realism have at its base a religious nature found in mythology and beliefs? If so, can only the religious believe in such fictions? Does magic in a technological society provide a distancing effect? How can we prove the marvellous to be 'true' in an emotional or psychic sense? Is there a link, through magic, to a wider universe? Are writers really like shamans, existing somewhere between a community and the cosmic forces? Between affirmation and denial? Between order and disorder?

Carpentier notes, as a self-criticism, that he was always on the outside looking in. A space needed 'intrusion' to be discovered. The Indians and places of his marvellous America became objects of discovery, and he as writer, a self-conscious intellectual conquistador who failed to become part of what he recorded.

Magic Realism has a philosophical awkwardness. We cannot come up with a definition. Magic Realists do not distinguish between moments in writing where any effort is made to integrate myth with history and where myth is complete and satisfactory in itself. Critics of Carpentier, such as Juan Carlos Onetti, a confirmed urban writer, complain there should be a division between the real and the fiction. Magic Realism is a reminder, Onetti argues, that the product of language is human-made and not natural. Other critics of fantastic and marvellous writers in Latin America complain that art is placed before social commitment. Social realists argue that Magic Realist characters are caricatures, non-problematic character types, rather than fully formed psychological creations. Such critics further argue that hyperbole and literary gamesmanship replace political perspectives in nations ruled by dictatorships.

To put these arguments another way, Magic Realism raises for the fiction writer the same problems as always: Can we know the truth, and, if so, how will we tell it?

1986

Fantasy, Reality, and Metafiction

Linda Hutcheon, a specialist in postmodern culture and critical theory, is a Canadian feminist who teaches at the University of Toronto. The following excerpt from her book Narcissistic Narrative: The Metafictional Paradox *considers similarities between fantasy and 'realistic' fiction and the way a reader's imagination co-operates with or co-creates fictions by Italo Calvino.*

'From the point of view of the reader, it is no easier to create and believe in the well-documented world of Zola than it is for him to imagine hobbits or elves.'

Linda Hutcheon, from 'Actualizing Narrative Structures: Detective Plot, Fantasy, Games, and the Erotic'

. . . *All* literature could be said to be 'escape' literature: readers as well as authors want to create worlds as real as, but other than, the world that is, to use the narrator's terms in *The French Lieutenant's Woman*. In fact, all reading (whether of novels, history, or science) is a kind of 'escape' in that it involves a temporary transfer of consciousness from the reader's empirical surroundings to things imagined rather than perceived. Perhaps it is the imposed order and coherence, as well as the fictiveness, of the worlds created by the imagination that separate them from other linguistic constructs. The act of reading partakes of man's lived life: what he reads competes, during that act, with the empirical world he inhabits. If this is seen as desirable, then one speaks of the freedom, the liberation of the mind through art; if it is not, then one talks of literature as 'escape' in derogatory terms. Theoreticians of the *nouveau roman* were quick to claim the freedom-inducing properties of the new fiction; because of its linguistic and fictive natures, the novelistic universe can and does compete with the empirical. And its paradigm is the world of fantasy.

The reader's act of forming the universe of fantasy (or of metafiction using fantasy as a model) is like that of forming all novelistic worlds in that it provides the freedom—or the 'escape'—of an ordered vision, perhaps a kind of 'vital' consolation for living in a world whose order one usually perceives and experiences only as chaos. That the order here is of a fictive universe does not matter; the need and desire for such order is real, as is the need for freedom, for the liberation of the imagination from the bondage of empirical fact.

Not only have works of metafiction and fantasy become simultaneously plentiful recently (the Tolkien fad being only one manifestation of the latter), but they have both often been denied the critical treatment allowed to 'serious' literature. However, neither represents a current outside the central mode of literature or fiction (that is, realism), as some have claimed. Fantasy is indeed the 'other side of realism' and represents historically a parallel and equally valid literary tradition. The most extreme autonomous universes of fantasy are still referential; if they were not the reader could not imagine their existence. This has always been the case. In diachronic terms, the same external and internal forces and concerns that spawned traditional realistic fiction could be said to have created Science Fiction. Did the interest and curiosity in exploration promote only true travel tales (and so *Robinson Crusoe)* or can one include Gulliver's imaginary voyages? The positivistic, scientific materialism of the last century brought both *L'Assomoir* and *Frankenstein*.

From the point of view of the reader it is no easier to create and believe in the well-documented world of Zola than it is for him to imagine hobbits or elves: the imaginative leap into the novel's world of time and space must be made in both cases. Any literary landscapes, inhabitants or events can be made credible. 'A dream world may be full of inexplicable gaps and logical inconsistencies;' explained Auden, 'an imaginary world may not, for it is a world of law, not of wish. Its laws may be different from those which govern our own, but they must be as intelligible and inviolable.' Like Tolkien's Middle Earth, Borges' self-reflective world in 'Tlön, Uqbar, Orbis Tertius' has its own history, geography, culture, its own inhabitants, myths, and language.

The invented autonomous cosmos of fantasy becomes a model in metafiction for the temporal and spatial structuration of both the universe of the work and its very narration—and this is so from the perspectives of both writer and reader. . . .

In [the stories in *t zero*], the author becomes intrigued with the imaginative possibilities for narrative which lie latent in scientific theories of creation (of the universe, the earth, the body) and in mathematical and logical concepts of time and space. In most of the tales the narrator, one Qfwfq, tells of the time when he was only consciousness, straining to achieve bodily form. The referents of the scientific theory are real enough, but in the context of Qfwfq's narration they become fictive, the fuel for imaginative flight.

Taking the human reader into account, Qfwfq tries to explain his pre-human state as consciousness straining to perceive the new forms of nature by assembling sensations which allow a visual or aural image to form. Then, of course, comes the problem of naming objects and states. Fantasy, Calvino reveals, shares with science the burden of inadequate linguistic resources which threaten to block actual perception; Qfwfq's situation differs in that he can express his states *afterwards* without the danger of language guiding or tyrannizing what he actually perceives. In metafictional terms, the interest is in the structural similarity between the efforts of the humanoid consciousness toward perception, meaning, and naming and the imaginative processes of the reader of fiction who must not—once the text has established itself—allow real referents to blind him to what is really a fictive world. The naming process is done anew in each work.

Qfwfq is content to allow his reader liberties with his story: the process of narration, though guided by him, is open. In *Ti con zero*, in a story about the origin of the birds, the narrator tells the reader, if he does not like the far-fetched (and textually self-conscious) means by which Qfwfq has arrived at the land of the birds, that he can make up another. The important thing is to have him arrive there somehow. . . .

1980

F. The Writer's Tools

Character

Frank O'Connor (1903–66), one of Ireland's most respected writers, published his highly influential full-length study of the short story in 1962. Though O'Connor's thesis that the short story writer—not the novelist—wrote primarily about the marginalized can be challenged, his study brought attention to a neglected art. To support his thesis, O'Connor analyzed the stories of Chekhov, Joyce, Mansfield, Lawrence, and Hemingway, among others.

'. . . An intense awareness of human loneliness.'

Frank O'Connor, from Introduction to *The Lonely Voice*

. . . [T]he short story has never had a hero.

What it has instead is a submerged population group—a bad phrase which I have had to use for want of a better. That submerged population changes its character from writer to writer, from generation to generation. It may be Gogol's officials, Turgenev's serfs, Maupassant's prostitutes, Chekhov's doctors and teachers, Sherwood Anderson's provincials, always dreaming of escape. . . .

Always in the short story there is this sense of outlawed figures wandering about the fringes of society, superimposed sometimes on symbolic figures whom they caricature and echo—Christ, Socrates, Moses. It is not for nothing that there are famous short stories called 'Lady Macbeth of the Mtsensk District' and 'A Lear of the Steppes' and—in reverse—one called 'An Akoulina of the Irish Midlands.' As a result there is in the short story at its most characteristic something we do not often find in the novel—an intense awareness of human loneliness. Indeed, it might be truer to say that while we often read a familiar novel again for companionship, we approach the short story in a very different mood. It is more akin to the mood of Pascal's saying: *Le silence éternel de ces espaces infinis m'effraie* [The eternal silence of the infinite spaces frightens me].

I have admitted that I do not profess to understand the idea fully: it is too vast for a writer with no critical or historical training to explore by his own inner light, but there are too many indications of its general truth for me to ignore it altogether. When I first dealt with it I had merely noticed the peculiar geographical distribution of the novel and the short story. For some reason Czarist Russia and modern America seemed to be able to produce both great novels and great short stories, while England, which might be called without exaggeration the homeland of the novel, showed up badly when it came to the short story. On the other hand my own country, which had failed to produce a single novelist, had produced four or five storytellers who seemed to me to be first-rate.

I traced these differences very tentatively, but—on the whole, as I now think, correctly—to a difference in the national attitude toward society. In America as in Czarist Russia one might describe the intellectual's attitude to society as 'It may work,' in England as 'It must work,' and in Ireland as 'It can't work.' A young American of our own time or a young Russian of Turgenev's might look forward with a certain amount of cynicism to a measure of success and influence; nothing but bad luck could prevent a young Englishman's achieving it, even today; while a young Irishman can still expect nothing but incomprehension, ridicule, and injustice. Which is exactly what the author of *Dubliners* got.

The reader will have noticed that I left out France, of which I know little, and Germany, which does not seem to have distinguished itself in fiction. But since those days I have seen fresh evidence accumulating that there was some truth in the distinctions I made. I have seen the Irish crowded out by Indian storytellers, and there are plenty of indications that they in their turn, having become respectable, are being out-written by West Indians like Samuel Selvon.

Clearly, the novel and the short story, though they derive from the same sources, derive in a quite different way, and are distinct literary forms; and the difference is not so much formal (though, as we shall see, there are plenty of formal differences) as ideological. I am not, of course, suggesting that for the future the short story can be written only by Eskimos and American Indians: without going so far afield, we have plenty of submerged population groups. I am suggesting strongly that we can see in it an attitude of mind that is attracted by submerged population groups, whatever these may be at any given time— tramps, artists, lonely idealists, dreamers, and spoiled priests. The novel can still adhere to the classical concept of civilized society, of man as an animal who lives in a community, as in Jane Austen and Trollope it obviously does; but the short story remains by its very nature remote from the community—romantic, individualistic, and intransigent. . . .

1962

Language

Raymond Carver, one of the most influential short story writers of the late twentieth century, writes here in the forceful, deceptively simple style that is his fictional trademark.

'The words can be so precise they may even sound flat, but they can still carry.'

Raymond Carver, from 'On Writing'

... It's possible, in a poem or a short story, to write about commonplace things and objects using commonplace but precise language, and to endow those things—a chair, a window curtain, a fork, a stone, a woman's earring—with immense, even startling power. It is possible to write a line of seemingly innocuous dialogue and have it send a chill along the reader's spine—the source of artistic delight, as Nabokov would have it. That's the kind of writing that most interests me. I hate sloppy or haphazard writing whether it flies under the banner of experimentation or else is just clumsily rendered realism. ...

That's all we have, finally, the words, and they had better be the right ones, with the punctuation in the right places so that they can best say what they are meant to say. If the words are heavy with the writer's own unbridled emotions, or if they are imprecise and inaccurate for some other reason—if the words are in any way blurred—the reader's eyes will slide right over them and nothing will be achieved. The reader's own artistic sense will simply not be engaged. ...

I like it when there is some feeling of threat or sense of menace in short stories. I think a little menace is fine to have in a story. For one thing, it's good for the circulation. There has to be tension, a sense that something is imminent, that certain things are in relentless motion, or else, most often, there simply won't be a story. What creates tension in a piece of fiction is partly the way the concrete words are linked together to make up the visible action of the story. But it's also the things that are left out, that are implied, the landscape just under the smooth (but sometimes broken and unsettled) surface of things.

V.S. Pritchett's definition of a short story is 'something glimpsed from the corner of the eye, in passing.' Notice the 'glimpse' part of this. First the glimpse. Then the glimpse given life, turned into something that illuminates the moment and may, if we're lucky—that word again—have even further-ranging consequences and meaning. The short story writer's task is to invest the glimpse with all that is in his power. He'll bring his intelligence and literary skill to bear (his talent), his sense of proportion and sense of the fitness of things: of how things out there really are and how he sees those things—like no one else sees them. And this is done through the use of clear and specific language, language used so as to bring to life the details that will light up the story for the reader. For the details to be concrete and convey meaning, the language must be accurate and precisely given. The words can be so precise they may even sound flat, but they can still carry; if used right, they can hit all the notes.

1983

Plot and Form

Eudora Welty (1909–2001), a Mississippi writer influenced by William Faulkner, was known for her mastery of short story technique and form. She wrote many works on writing, including A Writer's Beginning, *which traced her fictional impulse to family and community while stressing the need to preserve the ultimate mystery of artistic creation: 'There is no explanation outside fiction for what the writer is learning to do,' she said.*

'Plots are what we see with.'

Eudora Welty, from 'The Reading and Writing of Short Stories'

... As we all have observed, plot can throw its weight in any of several ways, varying in their complexity, flexibility, and interest: onto the narrative, or situation; onto the character; onto the interplay of characters; and onto some higher aspects of character, emotional states, and so on, which is where the rules leave off, if they've come with us this far, and the uncharted country begins. ...

In outward semblance, many stories have plots in common—which is of no more account than that many people have blue eyes. Plots are, indeed, what we see with. What's seen is what we're interested in.

On some level all stories are stories of search—which isn't surprising at all. From the intense wild penetration of the hunter in 'The Bear' by William Faulkner to the gentle Sunday excursion of Katherine Mansfield's 'Miss Brill'; from the cruel errand of Nick's father to the Indian camp in Ernest Hemingway's story to the fantasy of soaring into the realm of the poetic imagination in E.M. Forster's 'Celestial Omnibus'; from the fireman seeking the seat of the fire in William Sansom's 'Fireman Flower' to the Henry James man in 'The Jolly Corner' seeking, with infinite pains and wanderings, the image of himself and what he might have been, through the corridors of a haunted house—in any group of stories we might name as they occur to us, the plot is search. It is the ancient Odyssey and the thing that was ancient when first the Odyssey was sung. Joyce's *Ulysses* is the titan modern work on the specific subject, but when Miss Brill sits in the park, we feel an old key try at an old lock again—she too is looking. Our most ancient dreams help to convince us that her timid Sunday afternoon is the adventure of her life, and measure for us her defeat.

Corresponding to the search involved is always the other side of the coin. On one side of James's coin is search, on the other side is blight. Faulkner is concerned with doom and history, Hemingway with career, ritual, and fate—and so on. Along with search go the rise and fall of life, pride, and the dust. And Virginia Woolf sees errand and all alike dissolving in a surpassing mystery.

When plot, whatever it does or however it goes, becomes the outward manifestation of the very germ of the story, then it is purest—then the narrative thread is least objectionable, then it is not in the way. When it is identifiable in every motion and progression of its own with the motion and progression of simple revelation, then it is at its highest use. Plot can be made so beautifully to reveal character, reveal atmosphere and the breathing of it, reveal the secrets of hidden, inner (that is, 'real') life, that its very unfolding is a joy. It is a subtle satisfaction—that comes from where? Probably it comes from a deep-seated perception we all carry in us of the beauty of organization—of that less strictly definable thing, of form.

Where does form come from—how do you 'get it'? My guess is that form is evolved. It is the residue, the thrown-off shape, of the very act of writing, as I look at it. It is the work, its manifestation in addition to the characters, the plot, the sensory impressions—it is the result of these which comes to more than their mathematical total. It is these plus something more. This something more springs from the whole. It pertains to the essence of the story. From the writer's point of view we might say that form is somehow connected with the process of the story's work—that form *is* the work. From the reader's point of view, we might say that form is connected with recognition; it is what makes us know, in a story, what we are looking at, what unique thing we are for a length of time intensely contemplating. It does seem that the part of the mind which form speaks to and reaches is the memory. . . .

1949

Style

Mavis Gallant is a Canadian short story writer who has lived in Paris since 1950. Paris Notebooks, from which this excerpt is taken, contains essays and reviews. Gallant argues that an authentic style cannot be separated from other elements of an artistic work.

'Style in writing, as in painting, is the author's thumbprint, his mark.'

Mavis Gallant, from 'What Is Style?'

. . . Leaving aside the one analysis closed to me, of my own writing, let me say what style is *not*: it is not a last-minute addition to prose, a charming and universal slipcover, a coat of paint used to mask the failings of a structure. Style is inseparable from structure, part of the conformation of whatever the author has to say. What he says—this is what fiction is about—is that something is taking place and that nothing lasts. Against the sustained tick of a watch, fiction takes the measure of a life, a season, a look exchanged, the turning point, desire as brief as a dream, the grief and terror that after childhood we cease to express. The lie, the look, the grief are without permanence. The watch continues to tick where the story stops.

A loose, a wavering, a slipshod, an affected, a false way of transmitting even a fragment of this leaves the reader suspicious: What is this too elaborate or too simple language hiding? What is the author trying to disguise? Probably he doesn't know. He has shown the works of the watch instead of its message. He may be untalented, just as he may be a gifted author who for some deeply private reason (doubt, panic, the pressures of a life unsuited to writing) has taken to rearranging the works in increasingly meaningless patterns. All this is to say that content, meaning, intention, and form must make up a whole, and must above all have a reason to be.

There are rules of style. By applying them doggedly any literate, ambitious, and determined person should be able to write like Somerset Maugham. Maugham was conscious of his limitations and deserves appreciation on that account: 'I knew that I had no lyrical quality, I had a small vocabulary ... I had little gift for metaphors; the original or striking simile seldom occurred to me. Poetic flights and the great imaginative sweep were beyond my powers.' He decided, sensibly, to write 'as well as my natural defects allowed' and to aim at 'lucidity, simplicity, and euphony.' The chance that some other indispensable quality had been overlooked must have been blanketed by a lifetime of celebrity. Now, of course, first principles are there to be heeded or, at the least, considered with care; but no guided tour of literature, no commitment to the right formula or to good taste (which is changeable anyway), can provide, let alone supplant, the inborn vitality and tension of living prose.

Like every other form of art, literature is no more and nothing less than a matter of life and death. The only question worth asking about a story—or a poem, or a piece of sculpture, or a new concert hall—is, 'Is it dead or alive?' If a work of the imagination needs to be coaxed into life, it is better scrapped and forgotten. Working to rule, trying to make a barely breathing work of fiction simpler and more lucid and more euphonious merely injects into the desperate author's voice a tone of suppressed hysteria, the result of what E.M. Forster called 'confusing order with orders.' And then, how reliable are the rules? Listen to Pablo Picasso's rejection of a fellow-artist: 'He looks up at the sky and says, "Ah, the sky is blue," and he paints a blue sky. Then he takes another look and says, "The sky is mauve, too," and he adds some mauve. The next time he looks he notices a trace of pink, and he adds a little pink.' It sounds a proper mess, but Picasso was talking about Pierre Bonnard. As soon as we learn the names, the blues, mauves, and pinks acquire a meaning, a reason to be. Picasso was right, but only in theory. In the end, everything depends on the artist himself.

Style in writing, as in painting, is the author's thumbprint, his mark. I do not mean that it establishes him as finer or greater than other writers, though that can happen too. I am thinking now of prose style as a writer's armorial bearings, his name and address. In a privately printed and libellous pamphlet, Colette's first husband, Willy, who had fraudulently signed her early novels, tried to prove she had gone on to plagiarize and plunder different things he had written. As evidence he offered random sentences from work he was supposed to have influenced or inspired. Colette's manner, robust and personal, seems to leap from the page. Willy believed he had taught Colette 'everything,' and it may have been true—'everything,' that is, except her instinct for language, her talent for perceiving the movement of life, and a faculty for describing it. He was bound to have influenced her writing; it couldn't be helped. But by the time he chose to print a broadside on the subject, his influence had been absorbed, transmuted, and—most humbling for the teacher—had left no visible trace.

There is no such a thing as a writer who has escaped being influenced. I have never heard a professional writer of any quality or standing talk about 'pure' style, or say he would not read this or that for fear of corrupting or affecting his own; but I have heard it from would-be writers and amateurs. Corruption—if that is the word—sets in from the moment a child learns to speak and to hear language used and misused. A young person who does not read, and read widely, will never write anything—at least, nothing of interest. From time to time, in France, a novel is published purporting to come from a shepherd whose only influence has been the baaing of lambs on some God-forsaken slope of the Pyrenees. His artless and untampered-with mode of expression arouses the hope that there will be many more like him, but as a rule he is never heard from again. For 'influences' I would be inclined to substitute 'acquisitions.' What they consist of, and amount to, are affected by taste and environment, preferences and upbringing (even, and sometimes particularly, where the latter has been rejected), instinctive selection. The beginning writer has to choose, tear to pieces, spit out, chew up, and assimilate as naturally as a young animal—as naturally and as ruthlessly. Style cannot be copied, except by the untalented. It is, finally, the distillation of a lifetime of reading and listening, of selection and rejection. But if it is not a true voice, it is nothing.

1986

Symbol and Theme

See Flannery O'Connor, 'The Grotesque,' p. 423. In the following excerpt, O'Connor demystifies symbol and theme.

'Many students confuse the *process* of understanding a thing with understanding it.'

Flannery O'Connor, from 'The Nature and Aim of Fiction'

... The novel works by a slower accumulation of detail than the short story does. The short story requires more drastic procedures than the novel because more has to be accomplished in less space. The details have to carry more immediate weight. In good fiction, certain of the details will tend to accumulate meaning from the story itself, and when this happens, they become symbolic in their action.

Now the word *symbol* scares a good many people off, just as the word *art* does. They seem to feel that a symbol is some mysterious thing put in arbitrarily by the writer to frighten the common reader—sort of a literary Masonic grip that is only for the initiated. They seem to think that it is a way of saying something that you aren't actually saying, and so if they can be got to read a reputedly symbolic work at all, they approach it as if it were a problem in algebra. Find *x*. And when they do find or think they find this abstraction, *x*, then they go off with an elaborate sense of satisfaction and the notion that they have 'understood' the story. Many students confuse the *process* of understanding a thing with understanding it.

I think that for the fiction writer himself, symbols are something he uses simply as a matter of course. You might say that these are details that, while having their essential place in the literal level of the story, operate in depth as well as on the surface, increasing the story in every direction.

I think the way to read a book is always to see what happens, but in a good novel, more always happens than we are able to take in at once, more happens than meets the eye. The mind is led on by what it sees into the greater depths that the book's symbols naturally suggest. This is what is meant when critics say that a novel operates on several levels. The truer the symbol, the deeper it leads you, the more meaning it opens up. To take an example from my own book, *Wise Blood*, the hero's rat-colored automobile is his pulpit and his coffin as well as something he thinks of as a means of escape. He is mistaken in thinking that it is a means of escape, of course, and does not really escape his predicament until the car is destroyed by the patrolman. The car is a kind of death-in-life symbol, as his blindness is a life-in-death symbol. The fact that these meanings are there makes the book significant. The reader may not see them but they have their effect on him nonetheless. This is the way the modern novelist sinks, or hides, his theme.

The kind of vision the fiction writer needs to have, or to develop, in order to increase the meaning of his story is called anagogical vision, and that is the kind of vision that is able to see different levels of reality in one image or one situation. The medieval commentators on Scripture found three kinds of meaning in the literal level of the sacred text: one they called allegorical, in which one fact pointed to another; one they called tropological, or moral, which had to do with what should be done; and one they called anagogical, which had to do with the Divine life and our participation in it. Although this was a method applied to biblical exegesis, it was also an attitude toward all of creation, and a way of reading nature which included most possibilities, and I think it is this enlarged view of the human scene that the fiction writer has to cultivate if he is ever going to write stories that have any chance of becoming a permanent part of our literature. It seems to be a paradox that the larger and more complex the personal view, the easier it is to compress it into fiction.

People have a habit of saying, 'What is the theme of your story?' and they expect you to give them a statement: 'the theme of my story is the economic pressure of the machine on the middle class'—or some such absurdity. And when they've got a statement like that, they go off happy and feel it is no longer necessary to read the story.

Some people have the notion that you read the story and then climb out of it into the meaning, but for the fiction writer himself the whole story is the meaning, because it is an experience, not an abstraction. . . .

1969

Voice

In this brief letter, Katherine Mansfield describes her characteristic method of matching style to the voice of a character.

'I chose . . . even the sound of every sentence.'

Katherine Mansfield, Letter to Richard Murry

It's a very queer thing how *craft* comes into writing. I mean down to details. Par exemple. In 'Miss Brill' I choose not only the length of every sentence, but even the sound of every sentence. I choose the rise and fall of every paragraph to fit her, and to fit her on that day at that very moment. After I'd written it I read it aloud—numbers of times—just as one would *play over* a musical composition—trying to get it nearer and nearer to the expression of Miss Brill—until it fitted her.

Don't think I'm vain about the little sketch. It's only the method I wanted to explain. I often wonder whether other writers do the same—If a thing has really come off it seems to me there mustn't be one single word out of place, or one word that could be taken out. That's how I AIM at writing. It will take some time to get anywhere near there.

But you know, Richard, I was only thinking last night people have hardly begun to write yet. Put poetry out of it for a moment and leave out Shakespeare—now I mean prose. Take the very best of it. Aren't they still cutting up sections rather than tackling the whole of a mind? I had a moment of absolute terror in the night. I suddenly thought of *a living mind*—a whole mind—with absolutely nothing left out. With *all* that one knows how much does one not know? I used to fancy one knew all but some kind of mysterious core (or one could). But now I believe just the opposite. The unknown is far, far greater than the known. The known is only a mere shadow. This is a fearful thing and terribly hard to face. But it must be faced.

17 January 1921

G. The Short Story and Its Practitioners

Charlotte Perkins Gilman

Twenty years after 'The Yellow Wallpaper' was published, Charlotte Perkins Gilman wrote a short essay about the story's origins.

'It was not intended to drive people crazy, but to save people from being driven crazy.'

Charlotte Perkins Gilman, 'Why I Wrote "The Yellow Wallpaper"'

Many and many a reader has asked that. When the story first came out, in the *New England Magazine* about 1891, a Boston physician made protest in *The Transcript*. Such a story ought not to be written, he said; it was enough to drive anyone mad to read it.

Another physician, in Kansas I think, wrote to say that it was the best description of incipient insanity he had ever seen, and—begging my pardon— had I been there?

Now the story of the story is this:

For many years I suffered from a severe and continuous nervous breakdown tending to melancholia—and beyond. During about the third year of this trouble I went, in devout faith and some faint stir of hope, to a noted specialist in nervous diseases, the best known in the country. This wise man put me to bed and applied the rest cure, to which a still-good physique responded so promptly that he concluded there was nothing much the matter with me, and sent me home with solemn advice to 'live as domestic a life as far as possible,' to 'have but two hours' intellectual life a day,' and 'never to touch pen, brush, or pencil again' as long as I lived. This was in 1887.

I went home and obeyed those directions for some three months, and came so near the borderline of utter mental ruin that I could see over.

Then, using the remnants of intelligence that remained, and helped by a wise friend, I cast the noted specialist's advice to the winds and went to work again—work, the normal life of every human being; work, in which is joy and growth and service, without which one is a pauper and a parasite—ultimately recovering some measure of power.

Being naturally moved to rejoicing by this narrow escape, I wrote *The Yellow Wallpaper*, with its embellishments and additions, to carry out the ideal (I never had hallucinations or objections to my mural decorations) and sent a copy to the physician who so nearly drove me mad. He never acknowledged it.

The little book is valued by alienists and as a good specimen of one kind of literature. It has, to my knowledge, saved one woman from a similar fate—so terrifying her family that they let her out into normal activity and she recovered.

But the best result is this. Many years later I was told that the great specialist had admitted to friends of his that he had altered his treatment of neurasthenia since reading *The Yellow Wallpaper*.

It was not intended to drive people crazy, but to save people from being driven crazy, and it worked.

1913

Anton Chekhov

The letters of Anton Chekhov (1860–1904) are full of advice for younger writers; they also reveal his rigorous practices as one of the forebears of the modern short story.

'In planning a story one is bound to think first about its framework: from a crowd of leading or subordinate characters one selects one person only . . .'

Anton Chekhov, from *Letters* 1888–99

30 May 1888: 'The artist must be not the judge of his characters.'
It seems to me it is not for writers of fiction to solve such questions as that of God, of pessimism, etc. The writer's business is simply to describe who has been speaking about God or about pessimism, how, and in what circumstances. The artist must be not the judge of his characters and of their conversations, but merely an impartial witness. I have heard a desultory conversation of two Russians about pessimism—a conversation which settles nothing—and I must report that conversation as I heard it; it is for the jury, that is, for the readers, to decide on the value of it. My business is merely to be talented—i.e., to know how to distinguish important statements from unimportant, how to throw light on the characters, and to speak their language. Shtcheglov-Leontyev blames me for finishing the story with the words, 'There's no making out anything in this world.' He thinks a writer who is a good psychologist ought to be able to make it out—that is what he

is a psychologist for. But I don't agree with him. It is time that writers, especially those who are artists, recognized that there is no making out anything in this world, as once Socrates recognized it, and Voltaire, too. The mob thinks it knows and understands everything; and the more stupid it is the wider it imagines its outlook to be. And if a writer whom the mob believes in has the courage to say that he does not understand anything of what he sees, that alone will be something gained in the realm of thought and a great step in advance.

27 October 1888: Character and the short story
... And so in planning a story one is bound to think first about its framework: from a crowd of leading or subordinate characters one selects one person only—wife or husband; one puts him on the canvas and paints him alone, making him prominent, while the others one scatters over the canvas like small coin, and the result is something like the vault of heaven: one big moon and a number of very small stars around it. But the moon is not a success because it can only be understood if the stars too are intelligible, and the stars are not worked out. And so what I produce is not literature, but something like the patching of Trishka's coat. What am I to do? I don't know, I don't know. I must trust to time which heals all things.

6 February 1898: Politics and the writer
Let Dreyfus be guilty, and Zola is still right, since it is the duty of writers not to accuse, not to prosecute, but to champion even the guilty once they have been condemned and are enduring punishment. I shall be told: 'What of the political position? The interests of the State?' But great writers and artists ought to take part in politics only so far as they have to protect themselves from politics. There are plenty of accusers, prosecutors, and gendarmes without them, and in any case, the role of Paul suits them better than that of Saul. Whatever the verdict may be, Zola will anyway experience a vivid delight after the trial, his old age will be a fine old age, and he will die with a conscience at peace, or at any rate greatly solaced.

3 September 1899: Good writing
[advice to Russian writer Maxim Gorky] When reading the proofs, cross out a host of concrete nouns and other words. You have so many such nouns that the reader's mind finds it a task to concentrate on them, and he soon grows tired. You understand it at once when I say, 'The man sat on the grass'; you understand it because it is clear and makes no demands on the attention. On the other hand, it is not easily understood, and it is difficult for the mind, if I write, 'A tall, narrow-chested, middle-sized man, with a red beard, sat on the green grass, already trampled by pedestrians, sat silently, shyly, and timidly looked about him.' That is not immediately grasped by the mind, whereas good writing should be grasped at once,—in a second.

I wrote to you once that you must be unconcerned when you write pathetic stories. And you did not understand me. You may weep and moan over your stories, you may suffer together with your heroes, but I consider one must do this so that the reader does not notice it. The more objective, the stronger will be the effect.... The more sensitive the matter in hand, the more calmly one should describe it—and the more touching it will be at last.

Stephen Crane

After Crane's death at age twenty-eight, journalist John N. Hilliard published these letters in the New York Times: *the first was written when Crane and Hilliard worked as reporters in New York City, the second, which appears below, after the publication of Crane's acclaimed Civil War novel,* The Red Badge of Courage *(1895). In spite of literary success, Crane was often unfairly attacked for his unconventional lifestyle. The letters helped to promote the legacy of a modest, sincere man who took quiet pride in his work.*

'[T]he cut-and-dried curriculum of the college did not appeal to me. Humanity was a much more interesting study.'

Stephen Crane, from 'Letters to a Friend About His Ambition, His Art, and His Views of Life'

As far as myself and my own meagre success are concerned, I began the battle of life with no talent, no equipment, but with an ardent admiration and desire. I did little work at school, but confined my abilities, such as they were, to the diamond. Not that I dislike books, but the cut-and-dried curriculum of the college did not appeal to me. Humanity was a much more interesting study. When I ought to have been at recitations I was studying faces on the streets, and when I ought to have been studying my next day's lessons I was watching the trains roll in and out of the Central Station. So, you see, I had, first of all, to recover from college. I had to build up, so to speak. And my chiefest desire was to write plainly and unmistakably, so that all men (and some women) might read and understand.

I have only one pride—and may it be forgiven me. This single pride is that the English edition of *The Red Badge of Courage* has been received with praise by the English reviewers ..., and the big reviews here praise it for just what I intended it to be, a psychological portrayal of fear. They all insist that I am a veteran of the civil war, whereas the fact is, as you know, I never smelled even the powder of a sham battle. I know what the psychologists say, that a fellow can't comprehend a condition that he has never experienced, and I argued that many times with the Professor. Of course, I have never been in a battle, but I believe that I got my sense of the rage of conflict on the football field, or else fighting is a hereditary instinct, and I wrote intuitively, for the Cranes were a family of fighters in the old days, and in the Revolution every member did his duty. But be that as it may, I endeavoured to express myself in the simplest and [most] concise way. If I failed, the fault is not mine. I have been very careful not to let any theories or pet ideas of my own creep into my work. Preaching is fatal to art in literature. I try to give to readers a slice out of life; and if there is any moral or lesson in it, I do not try to point it out. I let the reader find it for himself. The result is more satisfactory to both the reader and myself. As Emerson said, 'There should be a long logic beneath the story, but it should be kept carefully out of sight.' Before *The Red Badge of Courage* was published, I found it difficult to make both ends meet. The book was written during this period. It was an effort born of pain, and I believe it was beneficial to it as a piece of literature. It seems a pity that this should be so—that art should be a child of suffering; and yet such seems to be the case. Of course there are fine writers who have good incomes and live comfortably and contentedly; but if the conditions of their life were harder, I believe that their work would be better.

1900

Native Fiction

As oral storytelling expanded to include written forms, Native literature has been able to reach large Native and non-Native audiences. In his introduction to All My Relations, *Thomas King addresses central issues about contemporary Native literature. He grapples with the problem of defining Native literature and considers some of its challenges for non-Native readers. He notes commonalities between Native and non-Native writing.*

'The appearance of Native stories in a written form has opened up new worlds of imagination for a non-Native audience.'

Thomas King, from Introduction to *All My Relations: An Anthology of Contemporary Canadian Native Fiction*

'All my relations' is the English equivalent of a phrase familiar to most Native peoples in North America. It may begin or end a prayer or a speech or a story, and, while each tribe has its own way of expressing this sentiment in its own language, the meaning is the same.

'All my relations' is at first a reminder of who we are and of our relationship with both our family and our relatives. It also reminds us of the extended relationship we share with all human beings. But the relationships that Native people see go further, the web of kinship extending to the animals, to the birds, to the fish, to the plants, to all the animate and inanimate forms that can be seen or imagined. More than that, 'all my relations' is an encouragement for us to accept the responsibilities we have within this universal family by living our lives in a harmonious and moral manner (a common admonishment is to say of someone that they act as if they have no relations).

Within Native cultures, as within other cultures, this world of relationships is shared through language and literature. As long as the languages remained oral, the literature was available to a particular audience. But, as Native storytellers have become bilingual—telling and writing their stories in English, French, Spanish—they have created both a more pan-Native as well as a non-Native audience.

For Native audiences, the twentieth-century phenomenon of Native storytellers from different tribes sharing their stories in a common language —through the contemporary and non-traditional forms of written poetry, prose, and drama—has helped to reinforce many of the beliefs that tribes have held individually, beliefs that tribes are now discovering they share mutually. While this has not, as yet, created what might be called a pan-Native literature, the advent of written Native literature has provided Native writers with common structures, themes, and characters which can effectively express traditional and contemporary concerns about the world and the condition of living things.

It should be said at this point that when we talk about contemporary Native literature, we talk as though we already have a definition for this body of literature when, in fact, we do not. And, when we talk about Native writers, we talk as though we have a process for determining who is a Native writer and who is not, when, in fact, we don't. What we do have is a collection of literary works by individual authors who are Native by ancestry, and our hope, as writers and critics, is that if we wait long enough, the sheer bulk of this collection, when it reaches some sort of critical mass, will present us with a matrix within which a variety of patterns can be discerned.

This waiting is neither timidity nor laziness on our part. There are a great many difficulties in trying to squeeze definitions out of what we currently have. We could simply say that Native literature is literature produced by Natives. This is a competent enough definition in that it covers both contemporary written literature and oral tribal literature, and, at the same time, insists that Native literature is literature produced by Natives and not by non-Natives, recognizing that being Native is a matter of race rather than something more transitory such as nationality. One can become a Canadian and a Canadian writer, for example, without having been born in Canada, but one is either born an Indian or one is not.

This definition—on the basis of race—however, makes a rather large assumption, a type of *dicto simpliciter*. It assumes that the matter of race imparts to the Native writer a tribal understanding of the universe, access to a distinct culture, and a literary perspective that is unattainable by non-Natives. In our discussions of Native literature, we try to imagine that there is a racial denominator which full-bloods raised in cities, half-bloods raised on farms, quarter-bloods raised on reservations, Indians adopted and raised by white families, Indians who speak their tribal language, Indians who speak only English, traditionally educated Indians, university-trained Indians, Indians with little education, and the like all share. We know, of course, that there is not. We know that this is a romantic, mystical, and, in many instances, a self-serving notion that the sheer number of cultural groups in North America, the variety of Native languages, and the varied conditions of the various tribes should immediately belie.

All of which leaves us with these questions: What, for example, do we do with writers who are not Native by birth but whose experience and knowledge may make them more perceptive writers and commentators than many writers who are Native by birth? And what do we do with writers who are Native and who have few ties to a culture or tribe and who do not write about Natives or Native culture? The most vivid examples might involve whites who were adopted or raised as Indians within an Indian community. Nationalism manages this dilemma well enough because it does not insist on the accident of birth as a *sine qua non*.

Perhaps our simple definition that Native literature is literature produced by Natives will suffice for the while providing we resist the temptation of trying to define a Native, for, as Wallace Black Elk reminds us in *Black Elk: The Sacred Ways of a Lakota*, 'You know straight across the board, hardly anyone really knows what is Indian. The word *Indian* in itself really doesn't mean anything. That's how come nobody knows anything about Indians.'

Whatever definitions we decide on (if we ever do), the appearance of Native stories in a written form has opened up new worlds of imagination for a non-Native audience. Most Canadians have only seen Natives through the eyes of non-Native writers, and, while many of these portrayals have been sympathetic, they have also been limited in their variety of characters, themes, structures, and images.

In large part, the majority of these works are set in the nineteenth century, a period that Native writers assiduously avoid. Some of the reasons for this avoidance are obvious. The literary stereotypes and clichés for which the period is famous have been, I think, a deterrent to many of us. Feathered warriors on Pinto ponies, laconic chiefs in full regalia, dusky, raven-haired maidens, demonic shamans with eagle-claw rattles and scalping knives are all pictur-esque and exciting images, but they are, more properly, servants of a non-Native imagination. Rather than try to unravel the complex relationship between the nineteenth-century Indian and the white mind, or to craft a new set of images that still reflects the time but avoids the flat, static depiction of the Native and the two-dimensional quality of the culture, most of us have consciously set our literature in the present, a period that is reasonably free of literary monoliths and which allows for greater latitude in the creation of characters and situa-tions, and, more important, allows us the opportunity to create for ourselves and our respective cultures both a present and a future. In many ways, I remain amazed at the extent of this particular division between non-Native writers and Native writers, though perhaps we will begin to write historical novels once we discover ways to make history our own.

I said that Native literature—that is, written Native literature—has opened up new worlds of imagination for a non-Native audience. It is not that we have consciously set out to do this. It is, rather, a by-product of the choices (i.e. not writing historical novels) we have made as writers and as Natives. The two ma-jor choices that we have made so far are concerned with the relationship be-tween oral literature and written literature and with the relationship between Native people and the idea of community, and the stories in this volume, to a great extent, reflect these choices.

There is the misconception that Native oral literature is an artifact, some-thing that vanished as an art form in the last century. Though virtually invisible outside a tribal setting, oral literature remains a strong tradition and is one of the major influences on many Native writers. . . .

While their stories are different, each possesses a timeless quality that speaks to some of the essential relationships that exist in traditional cultures—the re-lationship between humans and the animals, the relationship between humans and the land, and the relationship between reality and imagination.

A most important relationship in Native cultures is the relationship which humans share with each other, a relationship that is embodied within the idea of community. Community, in a Native sense, is not simply a place or a group of people, rather it is, as novelist Louise Erdrich describes it, a place that has been 'inhabited for generations,' where 'the landscape becomes enlivened by a sense of group and family history.' . . .

There is, I think, the assumption that contemporary Indians will write about Indians. At the same time, there is danger that if we do not centre our literature on Indians, our work might be seen as inauthentic. Authenticity can be a slip-pery and limiting term when applied to Native literature for it suggests cultural and political boundaries past which we should not let our writing wander. And, if we wish to stay within these boundaries, we must not only write about Indian people and Indian culture, we must also deal with the concept of 'Indian-ness,' a nebulous term that implies a set of expectations that are used to mark out that which is Indian and that which is not.

Of course there is no such standard, and at least three of the writers in this collection have already begun to wander past these boundaries. Beth Brant in her story, 'Turtle Gal,' Richard Green in 'The Last Crow,' and Jordan Wheeler in 'The Seventh Wave' do not use traditional Native characters, nor do they make use of elements from oral literature, or create a strong sense of Native community. Instead, these writers imagine Native people engaged in a broad range of activities which do not, in and of themselves, satisfy the expectations conjured up by the notion of 'Indian-ness.' Beth Brant's fine story of an Indian girl who is befriended by an old, black man after her mother dies, Richard Green's slightly sardonic tale of a crow hunt, and Jordan Wheeler's humorous piece on surfing and seaside romance, do not concern themselves with 'authenticity,' rather they are concerned with the range of human emotions and experience that all people share. Wheeler's description of a Cree trying to learn to surf is a particularly satiric and pointed reminder that the limitations placed on us by non-Native expectations are simply cultural biases that will change only when they are ignored. . . .

1990

Literature of the South Asian Diaspora

In his introduction to Story-Wallah! A Celebration of South Asian Fiction, *a collection of twenty-six stories by South Asian diasporic writers, Shyam Selvadurai traces his evolving identity from his childhood in Sri Lanka, where it was embedded in family and outside influences, including Western music and books. After arriving in Canada at age nineteen, though, he began questioning his 'Sri Lankanness' and the assumptions of a fixed cultural identity that masks or ignores difference. Exploring the concept of diaspora, Selvadurai uncovered an identity that is transformative and diverse.*

'The idea of diaspora acknowledges the act, the trauma, of migration.'

Shyam Selvadurai, from 'Introducing Myself in the Diaspora'

. . . For the first nineteen years of my life, questions of cultural identity never troubled me. I was born and raised in Sri Lanka, and it was clear to me who I was. That 'I' was manifested in being a member of my immediate and extended family, the generations before us lying in the graveyard. It was manifested in my school. Various grand-uncles, older cousins, and even my older brother had gone there before me and the teachers saw me in the context of this continuity (though negatively, always expressing their disappointment at my lack of sportiness, compared to my forbearers). This 'I' was embodied in the landscape, the place names, rivers, lakes, stretches of beach that were tied to the narrative of, not just my life, but that of my parents and grandparents before me. This sense of identity remained curiously unshaken by the fact that, growing up, I listened exclusively to Western pop music and read Western books. The rise of ethnic nationalism and tensions between the majority Sinhalese and the minority Tamils (of whom I am a member because of my father, even though my mother is Sinhalese) did not shake my identity. Even the growing violence, the spilling over of that violence into our lives, which would ultimately force us to leave Sri Lanka, did not disturb that sense of who I was.

It was the arrival in Canada that shook it. Here, for the first time, I found myself forced, like almost all new immigrants, to ask myself those questions about who I was: What did it mean to be Sri Lankan? What aspects of my culture made me Sri Lankan, what aspects didn't? What was the essence of Sri Lankanness?

The answers readily furnished themselves and had actually been with me all along through my life in Sri Lanka. I had just not known it.

All colonial societies, in their struggle for independence and the forming of a new nation, reshape and redefine their identity. This drive for a cultural identity involves the establishment of a collective, essential self that is shared by people with a common ancestry and common history. This essential identity is seen to be unchanging, eternal; it provides a common frame of reference to a newly emerged nation. The goal of these new nations, released from colonialism, is to bring to light this identity that has been suppressed and distorted and disfigured by the colonial masters; to express this identity through a retelling of the past. At the core of this restored identity lies the idea that, beyond the mess and contradictions of today, is a resplendent past whose existence, when it is discovered, will restore a people as a culture, as a society.

My problem in embracing this notion of an essential, pure cultural identity was that its contradictions almost immediately bedevilled me. Where, for example, did someone like me, with a Sinhalese mother and a Tamil father, fit in? And what to do with that much-adored grandmother of mine with her blue eyes and white skin who never thought of herself as anything but, well, Sri Lankan? What also to do with the pesky fact that a piece of pop music by the Bee Gees or Olivia Newton-John could take me back to my teenage years, and those long tropical afternoons spent lying on my bed, listening to the radio, in a way no Sri Lankan song could?

In the quest for my cultural identity, I was also discovering that, within Sri Lanka itself, opposition had been mounted by writers and thinkers against this notion of a pure, eternal, fixed Sri Lankan identity. Through reading these writers, I became aware that it was the very idea of a pure, essential culture that had led to the rise of both Sinhalese and Tamil nationalism and violence—the inability of both communities to accept that they shared a crossbred culture where there was more in common than different; the insistence by each that their culture was superior; the refusal by each to acknowledge that we are a little island nation to whose shores, over the centuries, have come the winds of other cultures that have been integrated into what was now being hailed as a pure culture. I could not ignore that it was this very notion of purity that had ultimately brought such violence to my family and forced us out of Sri Lanka.

On a personal level, I was also beginning to come to terms with being gay, beginning to live out another very important part of my identity. It was very clear to me that the pure sense of being Sri Lankan was based on rigid heterosexual and gender roles. Where did someone like me belong then? By being gay, was I no longer Sri Lankan? And if that was not the case, what did it mean to be both Sri Lankan and gay; how to live out this combination of identities?

Some of the answers to these questions came through my understanding the concept of diaspora.

The word 'diaspora' (a term unfamiliar to many who are diasporic themselves) comes from Greek and implies a 'scattering of seeds.' In its most classical sense, diaspora was used to define the experience of Jews expelled from Palestine and forced to disperse to the various parts of the earth. It is now broadly used to define other groups that have, through forced or voluntary migration, taken up abode in places other than the original centre. The Chinese, Irish, Turkish, Armenian, South Asian, and Greek diasporas are examples of this dispersal.

'Immigrant' is often used to identify these groups (and, indeed, the writers coming from these groups). The problem with this term is that the emphasis is on the act of arrival in a new land; it conveys a sense that someone is a perpetual newcomer, a perpetual outsider. The term 'immigrant' does not leave much room for the process of becoming and changing and the dynamic cultural mixing that 'diaspora' suggests. 'Diaspora' also allows for the encompassing of a wider range of people and experiences.

On the one hand, the idea of diaspora acknowledges that the history and culture from which we have come is not an illusion. Histories are real, they have produced concrete and symbolic results. The past still informs who we are. And the truth is that the discovery of hidden histories has played a very important function in many social movements of our time—feminist, gay, anti-colonial, anti-racist. As such, it should not be dismissed outright. A collective identity can be very effective as a tool of resistance and empowerment and freedom.

On the other hand, the idea of diaspora acknowledges the act, the trauma, of migration and the fact that one cannot but be transformed in the new land. The emphasis must shift to a sense of cultural identity that is eclectic and diverse, a sense of cultural identity that is transforming itself, making itself new over and over again. A continuous work in progress. This sense of cultural identity, while taking into account that a group or a culture might have many important points of similarity, also acknowledges that there are many points of difference between its people, and that these differences, such as sexuality and gender and class, also define who we are. This sense of cultural identity stresses not just who one was in the past, but who one might be in the process of becoming.

In embracing the idea of diaspora, South Asian diaspora in my case, I am not blind to its shortcomings.

To start with, the notion of a South Asian diaspora is very questionable really when you take into account the differences, not to mention strife, between India, Pakistan, Bangladesh, and Sri Lanka, which constitute South Asia (yet one cannot deny that it is a useful concept that has been effectively employed in the West to lobby for political and social change, for creating venues and spaces for artistic expression).

While in theory diasporic identity is supposed to be fluid and encompassing of difference, in practice it is often quite the opposite, as we see in the violent expression of purity by some members of the South Asian diaspora to Salman Rushdie's *The Satanic Verses*. Another problem with the idea of diaspora is that despite its best intentions it tends to homogenize a group on a global level, whereas in practice, within that very group, immigration or expulsion might have taken place at different points in history and under different circumstances. Then, depending on the country of destination and interaction with the cultures there, these groups might have evolved in very different ways. In the South Asian context, this is seen clearly in the cultural difference between South Asians who migrated to the Caribbean in the nineteenth century as indentured labourers and South Asians who migrated directly from the subcontinent to the West in the latter half of the twentieth century. The former group, through cultural interaction with the emancipated African slave population, has evolved a very distinct culture. In Shani Mootoo's short story 'Out on Main Street,' this difference is played out with great humour in the clash between an Indo-Caribbean woman in Canada and more recent immigrants from Asia. In the story, the woman is referred to as a 'bastardized Indian,' which points to another problem with the concept of diaspora—privileging the point of origin in forming a diasporic identity at the expense of cross-cultural experiences. . . .

2005

Dialogues

The following interview took place in 1982.

Interview with Alice Munro, from *Canadian Writers at Work: Interviews with Geoff Hancock*

HANCOCK: I see you as a lyricist, as a songwriter. You give voice to our secret selves.

MUNRO: That's absolutely what I think a short story can do. . . .

HANCOCK: Are you a compulsive story writer? You couldn't stop yourself.

MUNRO: I don't suppose so, no. For a long time I didn't want to go on writing stories. And even now, I've got a book of stories coming out this fall and I will have to go out and face all these people who say 'Well, how come you're still writing stories and do you think your next book . . .' Half the people who say 'What about your next book?' say 'Is it a novel?' and when I say no they say 'Oh, well is it connected short stories?' and I say no. And then everything just falls away. 'Well, I mean, she didn't even connect them?'

And yet, I think the most attractive kind of writing of all is just the single story. It satisfies me the way nothing else does. I will probably, from now on, just go on writing books of short stories which are not connected as long as my publisher will consent to publish them. Of course, you know you are not very popular with a publisher if you do this. For years and years I would convince myself that I really had a novel there and I would take these ideas I had and bloat them up and I would start writing them and they would go all—they would just fall. It was just a total waste of time. And I'd become very depressed. So it took me a long time to reconcile myself to being a short-story writer. . . .

HANCOCK: Don't artists unify the creative impulses of humanity to make this world a better place?

MUNRO: No. As far as I am a normal political person, the kind of person who contributes money and gets involved in causes and thinks about things, I would say I was trying to make a better world. But as a writer, I don't think that way at all. I just get excited by looking at bits of the world here and there and trying to pull a story out of them. Take the story that begins *Who Do You Think You Are?* 'Royal Beatings' contains, among many other things, a child being beaten by her father. There is *no* way I started out to write a story to alleviate the lot of children who are beaten by fathers. As a person this is a cause that would concern me very much. As a writer I just want to look at the situation to see what's going on. I just want to see what's there. I just want to write about it. Then, when

I transform back into my ordinary liberal, maternal self, I would immediately want such things stopped. So, do you see what I mean?

Now, it's very hard to say in that sense I want to make a better world. I just have no time for thinking about anything like that because the writing is so hard. I think that's why I don't have answers to a lot of questions. Many writers know exactly what they're doing and have thought things out. Whereas I go into this peculiar limbo and this kind of shady area to look for the story and this takes up a lot of my time and I don't think very clearly about it. And I always think, when I finish this story, I'm going to take—What do I mean?—take a rest where I use my mind. Because I feel I never have. And there'll be time for it someday. Sometimes I will try to put everything aside, try to put this whole queer occupation aside and become a thinking person. And I've never done that. I've never been able to do it. . . .

HANCOCK: There's also a global vision that's starting to creep into your stories. You've moved away from Ontario. You're writing about other continents. Australia, in 'Bardon Bus.'

MUNRO: Yes, I have a bit but, to me, that kind of geography is very unimportant. I don't think that a story in which the characters go through their actions in, say, Tokyo, is somehow a deeper story with a kind of meaning in it you can't have if the characters do those things in Moose Jaw. I don't think the setting matters at all. A lot of people think I'm a regional writer. And I use the region where I grew up a lot. But I don't have any idea of writing to show the kind of things that happen in a certain place. These things happen and the place is part of it. But in a way, it's incidental.

HANCOCK: One of the things that I have noticed in your work, which, I think for me, underlines a lot of it, is the way time passes. There's a very strong sense that your stories are about how time is remembered. There are gaps. It's not just chronological time. It's 'felt time.' The story isn't realistic in its time. But it's realistic in the way time is felt to be real. And often, you use time as a catalyst.

You like to open up a character's old life. A beginning might be 'Many years later, as Rose sat in a cafeteria, she remembered . . .'

MUNRO: That sounds pretty heavy-handed, doesn't it? Well, I like doing that a lot. I like looking at people's lives over a number of years, without continuity. Like catching them in snapshots. And I like the way people relate, or don't relate, to the people they were earlier. This is the sense of life that interests me a lot.

HANCOCK: Do you like the feeling that something happens in the gaps between the scenes?

MUNRO: Yes. Something happens that you can't know about. And that the person themself doesn't know about. I think this is why I'm not drawn to writing novels. Because I don't see that people develop and arrive somewhere. I just see people living in flashes. From time to time. And this is something you do become aware of as you go into middle age. Before that you really haven't got enough time experience. But you meet people who were a certain kind of character ten years ago and they're someone completely different today. They may tell you a story of what their life was like ten years ago that is different again from what you saw at the time. None of these stories will seem to connect. There are all these realities. The reality a person presents in the narrative we all tell about our own lives. And there's the reality that you observe in the person as a character in your life. And then there's God knows what else. . . .

HANCOCK: The feminine side of myself reacts very strongly to certain aspects of your work. Especially how women survive in a patriarchal society. . . . Is that a message coming across? Do you embed lessons in the stories?

MUNRO: Ahhhh! No lessons. No lessons *ever*. I didn't even think, when I began writing, that I was writing about women, at all. I just wrote these stories. When I wrote *Lives of Girls and Women,* it didn't cross my mind that I was writing a feminist book. Because I didn't know what I was doing. It just occurred to me once that I wanted to write the kind of thing about a young girl's sexual experience that had often been written about boys'. I was doing it when I thought of this. I thought, I'm glad this is what I am doing. But I didn't think, then, that I was writing about women and their ways of survival.

I just wrote it because I know a great deal about that. In that same society there are men surviving. But I haven't written about that, yet. I don't know as much about it. But in *that* society of the fairly poor people, I don't think of it exactly as a patriarchal society. I think of our society as a whole that way. But on those lower levels, often, women have a considerable degree of power. That's something I'm very interested in. In the way women, for instance who are waitresses, or who have jobs like that, often feel quite strong though they will have very conventional opinions. They will probably believe there are all sorts of things women shouldn't do but in their actual behavior with men, they can often be pretty tough characters. And in a way I grew up with women who were like that. There was no sense in that community of the women being victims of society or the men. Now, I am consciously interested in the way women live. The way things are different for men and women at middle age, and so on. The particular conflicts between men and women seem to me to be so much more articulate at a middle-class, educated level. I see them now in a way that I never saw them when I was growing up. You know, in *Lives,* the grandmother and aunts have very definite views about the role of women and the things women shouldn't do. But the thing is, those people have very definite views about *everybody*. Everybody is in this structured society. In the actual society I grew up in, if anyone had asked me 'Would you rather be a boy or girl?,' I would have opted to be a girl. And for the very reason of more freedom. . . .

The following interview took place in 1987.

Interview with Bharati Mukherjee, from *Canadian Writers at Work: Interviews with Geoff Hancock*

HANCOCK: . . . Details, gestures work forcefully together in your characterizations. Do you see the characters?

MUKHERJEE: It depends on the work. Yes, definitively, with the two novels. I was mesmerized by the main characters, Tara and Dimple, in those novels. They became companions; I felt that they had lives almost independent of me. Most North American writers start with short fiction, then go on to novels. I started with novels.

Short stories don't always occur to me as being about a character. Sometimes a line or a possible title will set me going. 'The Lady From Lucknow,' for instance, began with the title. In stories, the hard thing is to find the right 'voice,' by which I mean locating a centre. Once I find the 'voice,' I don't seem to need to revise drastically. When I wrote novels, I found myself doing three drafts—the first to find out what the novel was *really* about; the second to sharpen the narrative; the third to catch any infelicities. But nowadays the short stories usually come to me at one sitting. I believe in revision, though. Or rather, I believe that good writing consists of decisions and calculations. One must know why one chooses this word instead of that. I share Isaac Babel's belief that the well-placed comma can stab the heart. I try to make my writing students sensitive to how a word looks and sounds. . . .

HANCOCK: Do you find there's a difference between the Canadian and the American story?

MUKHERJEE: Yes. I think there's a measurable difference between contemporary Canadian and American fiction. I believe that culture, national mythologies, literary traditions shape both the 'inside' and the 'outside' of a work. One can detect in choice of syntax, for instance, some cultural assumptions. In the 1980s writers from traditional societies, for example India-based Indian novelists writing in English about India, are more likely to feel comfortable using an omniscient point of view than are American writers.

By the way, in my World Literature course at Montclair State College in New Jersey, I always use a novel by a Canadian author. Timothy Findley's *The Wars* works very well in the course. My students certainly feel that in *The Wars* they are encountering a society and a mode of processing that are very different from theirs. They realize that the First World War is central to the English Canadians in a way that it isn't to Americans.

HANCOCK: You said somewhere that Canada 'fired up your rage.'

MUKHERJEE: Yes. My experience with racism in Canada unleashed an anger that eventually led to potent fiction. But initially I expended my energies addressing civil-rights problems. Writing 'An Invisible Woman'—the essay for *Saturday Night*—was very painful.

HANCOCK: Do you see that your work is equally concerned with form and language as it is with the particular issues of your content?

MUKHERJEE: I'm a careful writer. I am alert to the potency of, and possibilities in, language. English is a language that I have appropriated. At age three, I was sent to an English-medium school in Calcutta. Perhaps we who appropriate English are more aware of the language's powers than are native-speakers. Language gives me my identity. I am the writer I am because I write in North American English about immigrants in the New World. . . .

HANCOCK: Do you see yourself as a Canadian writer, or a North American, or an international writer? Do you see that there's been changes in the Canadian publishing community as well? A new generation of publishers, editors, readers is more receptive to your work now than when it was first published.

MUKHERJEE: I remember some years ago reading about Cynthia Good, the senior editor at Penguin Books, in *Quill & Quire*. The article quoted her as saying —I am paraphrasing what I remember after all these years—that she was looking for Canadian writers who were also international. I remember thinking to myself with relief that finally, thanks to editors like her, Canadian literature has come of age, that it has moved away from the fiercely parochial nationalism of the late 1960s and of the 1970s, that it can now accommodate writers who write of the 'other' Canada.

Clark [Blaise] and I came to live in Montreal in 1966, as you know. I taught fiction-writing at McGill and, for a longish time, directed McGill's Creative Writing program, and my first novel, which was published in the States in 1972, did rather well.

What I'm saying is that I got started as a writer—in 1972 I was a Canadian novelist with an 'international' reputation—at a time when nationalist Canadian writers were defining Canadian literature by exclusion rather than by inclusion. . . .

HANCOCK: Does [the 'fiction of the marvellous'] appeal to you as a writer?

MUKHERJEE: In Hindu story-telling—I am talking about the ancient tales from the *Puranasa* and the two epics of the *Ramayana* and the *Mahabharata*—the magical is the norm. All Hindu children, especially children in villages, are told the ancient stories again and again. Shape-changes are common in these tales. Birds talk. Animals practise ethics. It was colonialism that derailed Indian writers from continuing that convention of 'magic.' I am not eager to use the term 'magic realism' because it doesn't precisely convey what I mean about this Hindu oral literature. Colonialism forced generations of Indian writers to value British models and to look down on the native. The British managed to convince Indians that British literature was rational, realistic, and superior, and that Indian literature with its magical qualities was childish. Do I write magic realism? I include 'the marvellous' in my fiction, especially in my first novel. My fiction clearly inhabits a space in which there are extra-rational presences. . . .

HANCOCK: You said that *Darkness* came about as a result of your second trip to the United States to live.

MUKHERJEE: Moving out of Canada gave me back my voice. The last seven years or so in Canada I felt I was constantly being forced to see myself as part of an unwanted 'visible minority.' All I say about the move and its effects on my fiction I have said in the Introduction to that book.

HANCOCK: Ironically, in Canada, you won a National Magazine Award for your honest invective.

MUKHERJEE: In my acceptance speech I said that only in Canada would someone win a prize for indicting the society. I couldn't have written 'An Invisible Woman' if I hadn't left Canada, though.

The following interview with Shani Mootoo took place in 2007.

Interview with Shani Mootoo, from Maya Khankoje, 'To Bend but not to Bow'

You use the Caribbean vernacular and standard English with great ease. How about Canadian, eh?

I beg to quibble: There is no Caribbean vernacular—not even a Trinidadian one. Draw a grid using horizontal and vertical lines. Imagine this as Trinidad society stratified. You could fill each block with the different speech inflections of the various social corners of the island. There are race-based differences in speech, class nuances, too. But there is a manner common to all on the street. I tried to suggest this in *He Drown She in the Sea*. I am fascinated by how and when various individuals and groups use the several hybrid forms of this English we love to bend.

I have been in Canada for 25 years, and I hear that finally I am picking up some phrases and a bit of an accent. My mother, who lives in Trinidad, comments that 'a bit of' is a typical Canadian phrase. Perhaps it might replace the tired stereotype of 'eh?'—eh? And which accent? In Canada there are many, many accents.

In *He Drown She*, I wanted to write the BC landscape from the view of this Trinidadian immigrant—me—and also from my protagonist's—an immigrant of Guanagaspar, a fictional island based on Trinidad. I wanted to talk about wine drinking, too. I wanted to bring the various influences of my Trinidad past to bear on a literary interpretation of two subjects dear to me. To attempt to render these in a Canadian accent might have reduced both to stereotypes, as in *eh?* I thought it might have more value, as an immigrant writer of colour, to try putting into literary language not feelings of trepidation or awe for this landscape, but feelings of desire.

Harry, the protagonist, is in awe, but I wrote with an intimacy and deep love for those peaks, lakes, mountain roads, the flora there. He sees with my eyes, not with those of someone wary of them. For me, writing these parts meant not to try to speak like a Canadian or write like a wine connoisseur, but to unearth how my own already hybridized experiences bore on them, and so to interpret them. . . .

Do you believe in national identity?
I wonder what you mean by 'believe' and by 'national identity.' These days, we are made to feel that this thing is a truth and it must be bowed to. There are many of us who have several geographical identities at once, so a single national identity makes no sense whatsoever.

Flag waving may have its place in moments, but in general it worries me. It seems to require—for those of us who have come from elsewhere—a public giving up and letting go of aspects of what made us who we are. For me, national identity implies the unspoken language of strangers, aliens, other, outsider, and is a precursor to racism.

Funny thing is, if racism foments at the border, it swallows those within. Many of us are a mirror of those on the other side. The essentialist nature of national identity is divisive, hateful, and exclusionary. I want to say, thank heaven we live in a country that lets us revere our multiple heritages and that these are not seen as symbolic of anti-Canadian sentiment; but I won't, because there are moments when these parts of our lives are being watched and tagged as possible indicators of treason-in-the-making. There is little room for conversation in the notion of belief.

National identity is an idea that needs to be scrutinized, shaken loose, discussed constantly. It is not a truth or an absolute. It is not something to be believed in or not believed in.

Are gender and sexuality predetermined at birth or social constructs? Or are they of no consequence at all?
Evidence shows they are sometimes predetermined at birth by the medical profession and caregivers, all with vested interests in conformity. In the case of the individual who is being determined, it matters. Why the hurtful, hateful

policing? Of course, one knows why—the petty, small-world, small-view details of why. In a more humanitarian, universal, and loving world, would the specifics of a person's gender and sexuality need to matter? Only to be celebrated however, whenever, and in whichever of its multitude of variations it manifests.

You depict the oppression of males under patriarchal society. How do you reconcile your tenderness for them with your loathing of the violence inflicted by men on some of your female characters?
Precisely by recognizing that oppression breeds oppression. A question that a writer asks is why? I can't accept that human beings are inherently oppressive or violent. Here is a question we may, rather, ask: Are males naturally oppressive? Is male violence predetermined at birth? Or is it a social construct?

Colonialism, class, gender, ethnicity, marginality, dislocation, and unconditional love are some of the themes you touch upon. Anything else?
I am pleased and amused when others make lists of what I write. I don't have such a list myself. But it is interesting to see, from the point of view of others, what I write about. This suggests to me some consistency, and this pleases me. It also suggests certain obsessions, but I won't worry about it.

Your poetry is redolent of tropical sensuality. Have Canadian winters put a damper on it?
It suits me well that the comment part of your question in fact answers the question itself.

Are feminist struggles incompatible with social struggles at large?
Ideally, feminist struggles are not for the cause of one group of people—and a hugely amorphous one at that—but are for the amelioration of all personkind. Ideally, social struggles are everyone's business. Ideally, there should be no conflict here.

On the other hand, social struggles can be a front for causes that have at their lead, in some instances, feminism's antithesis: patriarchy. Also, as opportunities increase to meddle in the affairs of communities other than our very own, it must be recognized that one region's manner of doing feminism might differ from those of another. There is no altruistic feminism. The same goes for social struggles. When to meddle and when not to meddle is a tricky business worth worrying about.

What is your mission as a writer?
To work at writing. To ask why? To ask it again and again. To try to understand. To have conversations through storytelling—conversations like this.

H. Epilogue: Writer and Reader

How to Read Well

Vladimir Nabokov (1899–1977) is the author of seventeen novels, including Lolita *(1955), and dozens of stories. Born in St. Petersburg, Russia, he lived his adult life outside Russia, including almost twenty years in the United States, where he taught at Cornell University from 1948 to 1959.* Lectures on Literature, *published three years after his death, includes his notes on teaching such works as Kafka's 'The Metamorphosis' and Joyce's* Ulysses. *In the excerpt below, reprinted from the Introduction, Nabokov considers what makes a good reader.*

'[L]iterature was born on the day when a boy came crying wolf, wolf and there was no wolf behind him.'

Vladimir Nabokov, from 'Good Readers and Good Writers'

... In reading, one should notice and fondle details. There is nothing wrong about the moonshine of generalization when it comes *after* the sunny trifles of the book have been lovingly collected. If one begins with a ready-made generalization, one begins at the wrong end and travels away from the book before one has started to understand it. Nothing is more boring or more unfair to the author than starting to read, say, *Madame Bovary*, with the preconceived notion that it is a denunciation of the bourgeoisie. We should always remember that the work of art is invariably the creation of a new world, so that the first thing we should do is to study that new world as closely as possible, approaching it as something brand new, having no obvious connection with the worlds we already know. When this new world has been closely studied, then and only then let us examine its links with other worlds, other branches of knowledge.

Another question: Can we expect to glean information about places and times from a novel? Can anybody be so naive as to think he or she can learn anything about the past from those buxom best-sellers that are hawked around by book clubs under the heading of historical novels? But what about the masterpieces? Can we rely on Jane Austen's picture of landowning England with baronets and landscaped grounds when all she knew was a clergyman's parlor? And *Bleak House*, that fantastic romance within a fantastic London, can we call it a study of London a hundred years ago? Certainly not. And the same holds for other such novels in this series. The truth is that great novels are great fairy tales—and the novels in this series are supreme fairy tales.

Time and space, the colors of the seasons, the movements of muscles and minds, all these are for writers of genius (as far as we can guess and I trust we guess right) not traditional notions which may be borrowed from the circulating library of public truths but a series of unique surprises which master artists have learned to express in their own unique way. To minor authors is left the ornamentation of the commonplace: these do not bother about any reinventing of the world; they merely try to squeeze the best they can out of a given order of things, out of traditional patterns of fiction. The various combinations these minor authors are able to produce within these set limits may be quite amusing in a mild ephemeral way because minor readers like to recognize their own ideas in a pleasing disguise. But the real writer, the fellow who sends planets spinning and models a man asleep and eagerly tampers with the sleeper's rib, that kind of author has no given values at his disposal: he must create them himself. The art of writing is a very futile business if it does not imply first of all the art of seeing the world as the potentiality of fiction. The material of this world may be real enough (as far as reality goes) but does not exist at all as an accepted entirety: it is chaos, and to this chaos the author says 'go!' allowing the world to flicker and to fuse. It is now recombined in its very atoms, not merely in its visible and superficial parts. The writer is the first man to map it and to form the natural objects it contains. Those berries there are edible. That speckled creature that bolted across my path might be tamed. That lake between those trees will be called Lake Opal or, more artistically, Dishwater Lake. That mist is a mountain—and that mountain must be conquered. Up a trackless slope climbs the master artist, and at the top, on a windy ridge, whom do you think he meets? The panting and happy reader, and there they spontaneously embrace and are linked forever if the book lasts forever.

One evening at a remote provincial college through which I happened to be jogging on a protracted lecture tour, I suggested a little quiz—ten definitions of a reader, and from these ten the students had to choose four definitions that would combine to make a good reader. I have mislaid the list, but as far as I remember the definitions went something like this. Select four answers to the question what should a reader be to be a good reader:

1. The reader should belong to a book club.
2. The reader should identify himself or herself with the hero or heroine.
3. The reader should concentrate on the social-economic angle.
4. The reader should prefer a story with action and dialogue to one with none.
5. The reader should have seen the book in a movie.
6. The reader should be a budding author.
7. The reader should have imagination.
8. The reader should have memory.
9. The reader should have a dictionary.
10. The reader should have some artistic sense.

The students leaned heavily on emotional identification, action, and the social-economic or historical angle. Of course, as you have guessed, the good reader is one who has imagination, memory, a dictionary, and some artistic sense—which sense I propose to develop in myself and in others whenever I have the chance.

Incidentally, I use the word *reader* very loosely. Curiously enough, one cannot *read* a book: one can only reread it. A good reader, a major reader, an active and creative reader is a rereader. And I shall tell you why. When we read a book for the first time the very process of laboriously moving our eyes from left to right, line after line, page after page, this complicated physical work upon the book, the very process of learning in terms of space and time what the book is about, this stands between us and artistic appreciation. When we look at a painting we do not have to move our eyes in a special way even if, as in a book, the picture contains elements of depth and development. The element of time does not really enter in a first contact with a painting. In reading a book, we must have time to acquaint ourselves with it. We have no physical organ (as we have the eye in regard to a painting) that takes in the whole picture and then can enjoy its details. But at a second, or third, or fourth reading we do, in a sense, behave towards a book as we do towards a painting. However, let us not confuse the physical eye, that monstrous masterpiece of evolution, with the mind, an even more monstrous achievement. A book, no matter what it is—a work of fiction or a work of science (the boundary line between the two is not as clear as is generally believed)—a book of fiction appeals first of all to the mind. The mind, the brain, the top of the tingling spine, is, or should be, the only instrument used upon a book.

Now, this being so, we should ponder the question how does the mind work when the sullen reader is confronted by the sunny book. First, the sullen mood melts away, and for better or worse the reader enters into the spirit of the game. The effort to begin a book, especially if it is praised by people whom the young reader secretly deems to be too old-fashioned or too serious, this effort is often difficult to make; but once it is made, rewards are various and abundant. Since the master artist used his imagination in creating his book, it is natural and fair that the consumer of a book should use his imagination too.

There are, however, at least two varieties of imagination in the reader's case. So let us see which one of the two is the right one to use in reading a book. First, there is the comparatively lowly kind which turns for support to the simple emotions and is of a definitely personal nature. (There are various subvarieties here, in this first section of emotional reading.) A situation in a book is intensely felt because it reminds us of something that happened to us or to someone we know or knew. Or, again, a reader treasures a book mainly because it evokes a country, a landscape, a mode of living which he nostalgically recalls as part of his own past. Or, and this is the worst thing a reader can do, he identifies himself with a character in the book. This lowly variety is not the kind of imagination I would like readers to use.

So what is the authentic instrument to be used by the reader? It is impersonal imagination and artistic delight. What should be established, I think, is an artistic harmonious balance between the reader's mind and the author's mind. We ought to remain a little aloof and take pleasure in this aloofness while at the same time we keenly enjoy—passionately enjoy, enjoy with tears and shivers—the inner weave of a given masterpiece. To be quite objective in these matters is of course impossible. Everything that is worthwhile is to some extent subjective. For instance, you sitting there may be merely my dream, and I may be your nightmare. But what I mean is that the reader must know when and where to curb his imagination and this he does by trying to get clear the specific world the author places at his disposal. We must see things and hear things, we must visualize the rooms, the clothes, the manners of an author's people. The color of Fanny Price's eyes in *Mansfield Park* and the furnishing of her cold little room are important.

We all have different temperaments, and I can tell you right now that the best temperament for a reader to have, or to develop, is a combination of the artistic and the scientific one. The enthusiastic artist alone is apt to be too subjective in his attitude towards a book, and so a scientific coolness of judgment will temper the intuitive heat. If, however, a would-be reader is utterly devoid of passion and patience—of an artist's passion and a scientist's patience—he will hardly enjoy great literature.

Literature was born not the day when a boy crying wolf, wolf came running out of the Neanderthal valley with a big gray wolf at his heels: literature was born on the day when a boy came crying wolf, wolf and there was no wolf behind him. That the poor little fellow because he lied too often was finally eaten up by a real beast is quite incidental. But here is what is important. Between the wolf in the tall grass and the wolf in the tall story there is a shimmering go-between. That go-between, that prism, is the art of literature.

Literature is invention. Fiction is fiction. To call a story a true story is an insult to both art and truth. Every great writer is a great deceiver, but so is that arch-cheat Nature. Nature always deceives. From the simple deception of propagation to the prodigiously sophisticated illusion of protective colors in butterflies or birds, there is in Nature a marvelous system of spells and wiles. The writer of fiction only follows Nature's lead.

Going back for a moment to our wolf-crying woodland little woolly fellow, we may put it this way: the magic of art was in the shadow of the wolf that he deliberately invented, his dream of the wolf; then the story of his tricks made a good story. When he perished at last, the story told about him acquired a good lesson in the dark around the campfire. But he was the little magician. He was the inventor.

There are three points of view from which a writer can be considered: he may be considered as a storyteller, as a teacher, and as an enchanter. A major writer combines these three—storyteller, teacher, enchanter—but it is the enchanter in him that predominates and makes him a major writer.

To the storyteller we turn for entertainment, for mental excitement of the simplest kind, for emotional participation, for the pleasure of traveling in some remote region in space or time. A slightly different though not necessarily higher mind looks for the teacher in the writer. Propagandist, moralist, prophet—this is the rising sequence. We may go to the teacher not only for moral education but also for direct knowledge, for simple facts. Alas, I have known people whose purpose in reading the French and Russian novelists was to learn something about life in gay Paree or in sad Russia. Finally, and above all, a great writer is always a great enchanter, and it is here that we come to the really exciting part when we try to grasp the individual magic of his genius and to study the style, the imagery, the pattern of his novels or poems.

The three facets of the great writer—magic, story, lesson—are prone to blend in one impression of unified and unique radiance, since the magic of art may be present in the very bones of the story, in the very marrow of thought. There are masterpieces of dry, limpid, organized thought which provoke in us an artistic quiver quite as strongly as a novel like *Mansfield Park* does or as any rich flow of Dickensian sensual imagery. It seems to me that a good formula to test the quality of a novel is, in the long run, a merging of the precision of poetry and the intuition of science. In order to bask in that magic a wise reader reads the book of genius not with his heart, not so much with his brain, but with his spine. It is there that occurs the telltale tingle even though we must keep a little aloof, a little detached when reading. Then with a pleasure which is both sensual and intellectual we shall watch the artist build his castle of cards and watch the castle of cards become a castle of beautiful steel and glass.

1980

In Praise of Reading

An Argentinian-born Canadian who resides in France (he once read to the blind Borges), Alberto Manguel (b. 1948) has published numerous anthologies of short stories on gay or erotic themes, the fantastic, fabulous, and imaginary, as well as several books on libraries. He dismisses descriptions of himself as a writer. He is only a 'reader' with all the doubt that implies, as he discusses in this conclusion to his award-winning A History of Reading.

'[I]n the end I will better understand who I, the reader, am.'

Alberto Manguel, from 'Endpaper Pages'

In Hemingway's celebrated story 'The Snows of Kilimanjaro,' the protagonist, who is dying, recalls all the stories he will now never write. 'He knew at least twenty good stories from out there and he had never written one. Why?' He mentions a few but the list, of course, must be endless. The shelves of books we haven't written, like those of books we haven't read, stretches out into the darkness of the universal library's farthest space. We are always at the beginning of the beginning of the letter *A*.

Among the books I haven't written—among the books I haven't read but would like to read—is *The History of Reading*. I can see it, just there, at the exact point where the light of this section of the library ends and the darkness of the next section begins. I know exactly what it looks like. I can picture its cover and imagine the feel of its rich cream pages. I can guess, with prurient accuracy, the sensual dark cloth binding beneath the jacket, and the embossed golden letters. I know its sober title page, and its witty epigraph and moving dedication. I know it possesses a copious and curious index which will give me intense delight, with headings such as (I fall by chance on the letter T) *Tantalus for readers, Tarzan's library, Tearing pages, Toes (reading with), Tolstoy's canon, Tombstones, Torment by recitation, Tortoise (see Shells and animal skins), Touching books, Touchstone and censorship, Transmigration of readers' souls (see Lending books)*. I know the book has, like veins in marble, signatures of illustrations that I have never seen before: a seventh-century mural depicting the Library of Alexandria as seen by a contemporary artist; a photograph of the poet Sylvia Plath reading out loud in a garden, in the rain; a sketch of Pascal's room at Port-Royal, showing the books he kept on his desk; a photograph of the sea-sodden books saved by one of the passengers on the *Titanic*, without which she would not abandon ship; Greta Garbo's Christmas list for 1933, drawn up in her own hand, showing that among the books she was going to buy was Nathanael West's *Miss Lonelyhearts*; Emily Dickinson in bed, a frilly bonnet tied snugly under her chin and six or seven books lying around her, whose titles I can just barely make out.

I have the book open in front of me, on my table. It is amicably written (I have an exact sense of its tone), accessible and yet erudite, informative and yet reflective. The author, whose face I've seen in the handsome frontispiece, is smiling agreeably (I can't tell if it's a man or a woman; the clean-shaven face could be either, and so could the initials of the name) and I feel I'm in good hands. I know that as I proceed through the chapters I will be introduced to that ancient family of readers, some famous, many obscure, to which I belong. I will learn of their manners, and the changes in those manners, and the transformation they underwent as they carried with them, like the magi of old, the power of transforming dead signs into living memory. I will read of their triumphs and persecutions and almost secret discoveries. And in the end I will better understand who I, the reader, am.

That a book does not exist (or does not yet exist) is not a reason to ignore it any more than we would ignore a book on an imaginary subject. There are volumes written on the unicorn, on Atlantis, on gender equality, on the Dark Lady of the Sonnets and the equally dark Youth. But the history this book records has been particularly difficult to grasp; it is made, so to speak, of its digressions. One subject calls to another, an anecdote brings a seemingly unrelated story to mind, and the author proceeds as if unaware of logical causality or historical continuity, as if defining the reader's freedom in the very writing about the craft.

And yet, in this apparent randomness, there is a method: this book I see before me is the history not only of reading but also of common readers, the individuals who, through the ages, chose certain books over others, accepted in a few cases the verdict of their elders, but at other times rescued forgotten titles from the past, or put upon their library shelves the elect among their contemporaries. This is the story of their small triumphs and their secret sufferings, and of the manner in which these things came to pass. How it all happened is minutely chronicled in this book, in the daily life of a few ordinary people discovered here and there in family memoirs, village histories, accounts of life in distant places long ago. But it is always individuals who are spoken of, never vast nationalities or generations whose choices belong not to the history of reading but to that of statistics. Rilke once asked, 'Is it possible that the whole history of the world has been misunderstood? Is it possible that the past is false, because we've always spoken about its masses, as if we were telling about a gathering of people, instead of talking about the one person they were standing around, because he was a stranger and was dying? Yes, it's possible.' This misunderstanding the author of *The History of Reading* has surely recognized.

Here then, in Chapter Fourteen, is Richard de Bury, Bishop of Durham and treasurer and chancellor to King Edward II, who was born on 24 January 1287, in a little village near Bury St Edmund's, in Suffolk, and who, on his fifty-eighth birthday, completed a book, explaining that 'because it principally treats of the love of books, we have chosen after the fashion of the ancient Romans fondly to name it by a Greek word, *Philobiblon*.' Four months later, he died. De Bury had collected books with a passion; he had, it was said, more books than all the other bishops of England put together, and so many lay piled around his bed that it was hardly possible to move in his room without treading on them. De Bury, thank the stars, was not a scholar, and just read what he liked. He thought the *Hermes Trismegistus* (a Neoplatonic volume of Egyptian alchemy from around the third century AD) an excellent scientific book 'from before the Flood,' attributed the wrong works to Aristotle, and quoted some terrible verses as if they were by Ovid. It didn't matter. 'In books,' he wrote, 'I find the dead as if they were alive; in books I foresee things to come; in books warlike affairs are set forth; from books come forth the laws of peace. All things are corrupted and decay in time; Saturn ceases not to devour the children that he generates: all the glory of the world would be buried in oblivion, unless God had provided mortals with the remedy of books.' (Our author doesn't mention it, but Virginia Woolf, in a paper read at school, echoed de Bury's contention: 'I have sometimes dreamt,' she wrote, 'that when the Day of Judgement dawns and the great conquerors and lawyers and statesmen come to receive their rewards—their crowns, their laurels, their names carved indelibly upon imperishable marble—the Almighty will turn to Peter and will say, not without a certain envy when He sees us coming with our books under our arms, "Look, these need no reward. We have nothing to give them. They have loved reading."')

Chapter Eight is devoted to an almost forgotten reader whom Saint Augustine, in one of his letters, praises as a formidable scribe and to whom he dedicated one of his books. Her name was Melania the Younger (to distinguish her from her grandmother, Melania the Elder) and she lived in Rome, in Egypt, and in North Africa. She was born around 385 and died in Bethlehem in 439. She was passionately fond of books, and copied out for herself as many as she could find, thereby collecting an important library. The scholar Gerontius, writing in the fifth century, described her as 'naturally gifted' and so fond of reading that 'she would go through the *Lives of the Fathers* as if she were eating dessert.' 'She read books that were bought, as well as books she chanced upon with such diligence that no word or thought remained unknown to her. So overwhelming was her love of learning, that when she read in Latin, it seemed to everyone that she did not know Greek and, on the other hand, when she read in Greek, it was thought that she did not know Latin.' Brilliant and transient, Melania the Younger drifts through *The History of Reading* as one of the many who sought comfort in books.

From a century closer to us (but the author of *The History of Reading* doesn't care for these arbitrary conventions, and invites him into Chapter Six) another eclectic reader, the genial Oscar Wilde, makes his appearance. We follow his reading progress, from the Celtic fairy-tales given to him by his mother to the scholarly volumes he read at Magdalen College in Oxford. It was here at Oxford that, for one of his examinations, he was asked to translate from the Greek version of the story of the Passion in the New Testament, and since he did so easily and accurately the examiners told him it was enough. Wilde continued, and once again the examiners told him to stop. 'Oh, do let me go on,' Wilde said, 'I want to see how it ends.'

For Wilde, it was as important to know what he liked as it was to know what he should avoid. For the benefit of the subscribers to the *Pall Mall Gazette* he issued, on 8 February 1886, these words of advice on what 'To Read, or Not to Read':

Books not to read at all, such as Thomson's *Seasons*, Rogers' *Italy*, Paley's *Evidences*, all the Fathers, except St Augustine, all John Stuart Mill, except the essay on Liberty, all Voltaire's plays without any exception, Butler's *Analogy*, Grant's *Aristotle*, Hume's *England*, Lewes' *History of Philosophy*, all argumentative books, and all books that try to prove anything. . . . To tell people what to read is as a rule either useless or harmful, for the true appreciation of literature is a question of temperament not of teaching, to Parnassus there is no primer, and nothing that one can learn is ever worth learning. But to tell people what not to read is a very different matter, and I venture to recommend it as a mission to the University Extension Scheme.

Private and public reading tastes are discussed quite early in the book, in Chapter Four. The role of reader as anthologist is considered, as collector of material either for oneself (the commonplace book of Jean-Jacques Rousseau is the example given) or for others (Palgrave's *Golden Treasury*), and our author very amusingly shows how concepts of audience modify the choice of an anthologist's texts. To support this 'micro-history of anthologies' our author quotes Professor Jonathan Rose on the 'five common fallacies to reader response':

- first, all literature is political, in the sense that it always influences the political consciousness of the reader;
- second, the influence of a given text is directly proportional to its circulation;
- third, 'popular' culture has a much larger following than 'high' culture, and therefore it more accurately reflects the attitudes of the masses;
- fourth, 'high' culture tends to reinforce acceptance of the existing social and political order (a presumption widely shared by both the left and the right); and
- fifth, the canon of 'great books' is defined solely by social elites. Common readers either do not recognize that canon, or else they accept it only out of deference to elite opinion.

As our author makes quite clear, we the readers are commonly guilty of subscribing to at least some, if not all, of these fallacies. The chapter also mentions 'ready-made' anthologies collected and come upon by chance, such as the ten thousand texts assembled in a curious Jewish archive in Old Cairo, called the Geniza and discovered in 1890 in the sealed lumber-room of a medieval synagogue. Because of the Jewish reverence for the name of God, no paper was thrown away for fear it might bear His name, and therefore everything from marriage contracts to grocery lists, from love poems to booksellers' catalogues (one of which included the first known reference to *The Arabian Nights*), was assembled here for a future reader.

Not one but three chapters (Thirty-one, Thirty-two, and Thirty-three) are devoted to what our author calls 'The Invention of the Reader.' Every text assumes a reader. When Cervantes begins his introduction to the first part of *Don Quixote* with the invocation 'Leisured reader,' it is I who from the first words become a character in the fiction, a person with time enough to indulge in the story that is about to begin. To me Cervantes addresses the book, to me he explains the facts of its composition, to me he confesses the book's shortcomings. Following the advice of a friend, he has written himself a few laudatory poems recommending the book (today's less inspired version is to ask well-known personalities for praise and stick their panegyrics on the book's jacket). Cervantes undermines his own authority by taking me into his confidence. I, the reader, am put on my guard and, by that very action, disarmed. How can I protest what has been explained to me so clearly? I agree to play the game. I accept the fiction. I don't close the book. . . .

The History of Reading, fortunately, has no end. After the final chapter and before the already-mentioned copious index, our author has left a number of blank pages for the reader to add further thoughts on reading, subjects obviously missed, apposite quotations, events and characters still in the future. There is some consolation in that. I imagine leaving the book by the side of my bed, I imagine opening it up tonight, or tomorrow night, or the night after that, and saying to myself, 'It's not finished.'

1996

The Need for a Reader

This excerpt is from one of six lectures on writing that Margaret Atwood delivered at the University of Cambridge in England, exploring the nature of the relationships among writers, their works, and their audience.

'[T]he act of reading is just as singular—always—as the act of writing.'

Margaret Atwood, from 'Communion: Nobody to Nobody'

I would like to begin by talking about messengers. Messengers always exist in a triangular situation—the one who sends the message, the message-bearer, whether human or inorganic, and the one who receives the message. Picture, therefore, a triangle, but not a complete triangle: something more like an upside-down V. The writer and the reader are at the two lateral corners, but there's no line joining them. Between them—whether above or below—is a third point, which is the written word, or the text, or the book, or the poem, or the letter, or whatever you would like to call it. This third point is the only point of contact between the other two. As I used to say to my writing students in the distant days when I had some, 'Respect the page. It's all you've got.'

The writer communicates with the page. The reader also communicates with the page. The writer and the reader communicate only through the page. This is one of the syllogisms of writing as such. Pay no attention to the facsimiles of the writer that appear on talk shows, in newspaper interviews, and the like—they ought not to have anything to do with what goes on between you, the reader, and the page you are reading, where an invisible hand has previously left some marks for you to decipher, much as one of John Le Carré's dead spies has left a waterlogged shoe with a small packet in it for George Smiley. I know this is a far-fetched image, but it is also curiously apt, since the reader is—among other things—a sort of spy. A spy, a trespasser, someone in the habit of reading other people's letters and diaries. As Northrop Frye has implied, the reader does not hear, he overhears.

So far I've spoken primarily about writers. Now it's the turn of readers, more or less. . . .

For whom does the writer write? The question poses itself most simply in the case of the diary-writer or journal-keeper. Only very occasionally is the answer specifically *no one*, but this is a misdirection, because we couldn't hear it unless a writer had put it in a book and published it for us to read. Here for instance is diary-writer Doctor Glas, from Hjalmar Söderberg's astonishing 1905 Swedish novel of the same name:

> Now I sit at my open window, writing—for whom? Not for any friend or mistress. Scarcely for myself, even. I do not read today what I wrote yesterday; nor shall I read this tomorrow. I write simply so my hand can move, my thoughts move of their own accord. I write to kill a sleepless hour.

A likely story, and it *is* a likely story—we, the readers, believe it easily enough. But the truth—the real truth, the truth behind the illusion—is that the writing is not by Doctor Glas, and it's not addressed to no one. It's by Hjalmar Söderberg, and it's addressed to us.

The fictional writer who writes to no one is rare. More usually, even fictional writers writing fictional journals wish to suppose a reader. Here is a passage from George Orwell's *Nineteen Eighty-Four*, a book I read as a young person, shortly after it first came out in 1949. As we know, *Nineteen Eighty-Four* takes place in a grimy totalitarian future ruled by Big Brother. The hero, Winston Smith, has seen in a junk-store window a forbidden object: 'a thick, quarto-sized blank book with a red back and a marbled cover' and 'smooth creamy paper.' He has been seized by the desire to possess this book, despite the dangers that owning it would entail. Who among writers has not been overcome by a similar desire? And who has not been aware, too, of the dangers—specifically, the dangers of self-revelation? Because if you get hold of a blank book, especially one with creamy pages, you will be driven to write in it. And this is what Winston Smith does, with a real pen and real ink, because the lovely paper deserves these. But then a question arises:

> For whom, it suddenly occurred to him to wonder, was he writing this diary? For the future, for the unborn . . . For the first time the magnitude of what he had undertaken came home to him. How could you communicate with the future? It was of its nature impossible. Either the future would resemble the present, in which case it would not listen to him: or it would be different from it, and his predicament would be meaningless.

A common writerly dilemma: who's going to read what you write, now or ever? Who do you want to read it? Winston Smith's first readership is himself—it gives him satisfaction to write his forbidden thoughts in his diary. When I was a teenager, this account of Winston Smith's blank book was intensely attractive to me. I too attempted to keep such a diary, without result. My failure was my failure to imagine a reader. I didn't want anybody else to read my diary—only I should have access to it. But I myself already knew the sorts of things I might put into it, and mawkish things they were, so why bother writing them down? It seemed a waste of time. But many have not found it so. Countless are the diaries and journals, most obscure, some famous, that have been faithfully kept through the centuries, or the centuries of pen and paper, at least. For whom was Samuel Pepys writing? Or Saint-Simon? Or Anne Frank? There is something magical about such real-life documents. The fact that they have survived, have reached our hands, seems like the delivery of an unexpected treasure; or else like a resurrection.

These days I do manage to keep a journal of sorts, more in self-defense than anything else, because I know who the reader will be: it will be myself, in about three weeks, because I can no longer remember what I might have been doing at any given time. The older one gets, the more relevant Beckett's play *Krapp's Last Tape* comes to be. In this play, Krapp is keeping a journal on tape, from year to year. His only reader—or auditor—is himself, as he plays back bits of the tapes from his earlier lives. As time goes on, he has a harder and harder time identifying the person he is now with his former selves. It's like that bad stockbrokers' joke about Alzheimer's Disease—at least you keep meeting new people—but in Krapp's case, and increasingly in mine, you yourself are those new people.

The private diary is about as minimalist as you can get, in the writer-to-reader department, because writer and reader are assumed to be the same. It is also about as intimate, as a form. Next comes, I suppose, the private letter: one writer, one reader, and a shared intimacy. 'This is my letter to the World / That never wrote to me,' said Emily Dickinson. Of course she might have got more replies if she'd mailed it. But she did intend a reader, or more than one, at least in the future: she saved her poems up very carefully, and even sewed them into little booklets. Her faith in the existence, indeed the attentiveness, of the future reader was the opposite of Winston Smith's despair.

Writers have of course made copious use of the letter as a form, inserting letters into the narrative, and in some cases building whole novels out of them, as Richardson did in *Pamela, Clarissa Harlowe,* and *Sir Charles Grandison,* and as Laclos did in *Les Liaisons dangereuses.* For the reader, the fictional exchange of letters among several individuals provides the delight of the secret agent listening in on a wire: letters have an immediacy that the past tense cannot provide, and the lies and manipulations of the characters can be caught *in flagrante delicto.* Or this is the idea.

A few words about letter-writing and the anxieties specific to it. When I was a child, there was a game that was popular at little girls' birthday parties. It went like this:

The children stood in a circle. One of them was It, and walked around the outside of the circle holding a handkerchief, while the others sang:

I wrote a letter to my love
And on the way I dropped it,
A little doggie picked it up
And put it in his pocket.

Then there was talk of dog-bites, and a moment when the handkerchief was dropped behind someone, followed by a chase around the outside of the circle. None of this part interested me. I was still worrying about the letter. How terrible that it had been lost, and that the person to whom it was written would never get it! How equally terrible that someone else had found it! My only consolation was that dogs can't read.

Ever since writing was invented, such accidents have been a distinct possibility. Once the words have been set down they form part of a material object, and as such must take their chances. The letter from the king that is exchanged, unknown to the messenger, causing an innocent person to be condemned to death—this is not merely an old folktale motif. Forged letters, letters gone astray and never received, letters that are destroyed, or that fall into the wrong hands—not only that, forged manuscripts, entire books that are lost and never read, books that are burned, books that fall into the hands of those who don't read them in the spirit in which they are written, or who do, but still resent them deeply—all these confusions and mistakes and acts of misapprehension and malice have taken place many times over, and continue to take place. In the lists of those targeted and imprisoned and killed by any dictatorship, there are always quite a few writers whose works have reached—self-evidently—the wrong readers. A bullet in the neck is a very bad review.

But for every letter and every book, there is an intended reader, a true reader. How then to deliver the letter or book into the right hands? Winston Smith, writing his diary, finds he cannot be content with himself as his only reader. He chooses an ideal reader—a party official called O'Brien, in whom he believes he detects the signs of a subversiveness equal to his own. O'Brien, he feels, will understand him. He's right about this: his intended reader does understand him. O'Brien has already thought the thoughts that Winston Smith is thinking, but he's thought them in order to be prepared with the counter-moves, because O'Brien is a member of the secret police, and what he understands is that Winston is a traitor to the regime. He proceeds to arrest poor Winston, and then to destroy both his diary and his mind.

O'Brien is a negative or demonic version of Writer-to-Dear Reader, that ideal one-to-one relationship in which the person reading is exactly the person who ought to be reading. A more recent variation of the Demon Reader has been created by Stephen King, who specializes in extreme paranoia—and since he has a different kind of paranoia for every taste, he has a special one just for writers. The book is *Misery*, and in it a writer of suffering-heroine romances featuring a hapless maiden called Misery falls into the hands of a deranged nurse who styles herself 'your biggest fan.' Veterans of book-signings would know right then to run for the washroom and escape out the window, but our hero can't do that, because he's been incapacitated in a car crash. What his 'biggest fan' wants is to force him to write a book about Misery, just for her. Then, he realizes, she plans to bump him off so that this book will only ever have one reader—herself. It's a version of the sultan's-maze motif—used, among other places, in *The Phantom of the Opera*—in which the patron of a work of art wishes to murder its maker so only he will possess its secrets. The hero of *Misery* escapes with his life after the required amount of guck has messed up the furniture, leaving us to reflect that the one-to-one Writer-to-Dear-Reader relationship can get altogether too close for comfort.

It is altogether too close for comfort as well when the reader confuses the writer with the text: such a reader wants to abolish the middle term, and to get hold of the text by getting hold of the writer, in the flesh. We assume too easily that a text exists to act as a communication between the writer and the reader. But doesn't it also act as a disguise, even a shield—a protection? The play *Cyrano de Bergerac* features a large-nosed poet who expresses his love for the heroine by pretending to be someone else—but it is he who writes the eloquent letters that win her heart. Thus the book, as a form, expresses its own emotions and thoughts, while concealing from view the person who has concocted them. The difference between Cyrano and the book in general is that Cyrano gives vent to his own emotions, but the thoughts and emotions in a book are not necessarily those of the writer of it.

Despite the hazards a reader may pose, a reader must be postulated by a writer, and always is. Postulated, but rarely visualized in any exact, specific form—apart that is from the primary readers, who may be those named on the dedication page—'Mr. W.H.,' or 'my wife,' and so forth—or the group of friends and editors thanked in the acknowledgments. But beyond that, the reader is the great unknown. Here is Emily Dickinson on the subject:

> I'm Nobody! Who are you?
> Are you—Nobody—Too?
> Then there's a pair of us!
> Don't tell!—they'd advertise—you know!
>
> How dreary—to be—Somebody!
> How public—like a Frog—
> To tell one's name—the livelong June—
> To an admiring Bog!!

'Nobody' is the writer, and the reader is also Nobody. In that sense, all books are anonymous, and so are all readers. Reading and writing—unlike, for instance, acting and theatre-going—are both activities that presuppose a certain amount of solitude, even a certain amount of secrecy. I expect Emily Dickinson is using 'Nobody' in both of its senses—in the sense of an insignificant person, a nobody, but also in the sense of the invisible and never-to-be-known writer, addressing the invisible and never-to-be-known reader.

If the writer is Nobody addressing the reader, who is another Nobody—that hypocrite reader who is his likeness and his brother, as Baudelaire remarked—where do the dreary Somebody and the admiring Bog come into it?

Publication changes everything. 'They'd advertise,' warns Emily Dickinson, and how right she was. Once the catalog is out of the bag, the assumed readership cannot consist of just one person—a friend or a lover, or even a single unknown Nobody. With publication, the text replicates itself, and the reader is no longer an intimate, a one to your one. Instead the reader too multiplies, just like the copies of the book, and all those nobodies add up to the reading public. If the writer has a success, he becomes a Somebody, and the mass of readers becomes his admiring Bog. But turning from a nobody into a somebody is not without its traumas. The nobody-writer must throw off the cloak of invisibility and put on the cloak of visibility. As Marilyn Monroe is rumored to have said, 'If you're nobody you can't be somebody unless you're somebody else.' . . .

[W]here is the writer when the reader is reading? There are two answers to that. First, the writer is nowhere. In his small piece called 'Borges and I,' Jorge Luis Borges inserts a parenthetical aside about his own existence. '(If it is true that I am someone)' he says. By the time we, the readers, come to read those lines, that's a very big *if*, because by the time the reader is reading, the writer may not even exist. The writer is thus the original invisible man: not there at all but also very solidly there, at one and the same time, because the second answer to the question—*Where is the writer when the reader is reading?*—is, 'Right here.' At least we have the impression that he or she is right here, in the same room with us—we can hear the voice. Or we can almost hear the voice. Or we can hear *a* voice. Or so it seems. As the Russian writer Abram Tertz says in his story 'The Icicle,' 'Look, I'm smiling at you, I'm smiling in you, I'm smiling through you. How can I be dead if I breathe in every quiver of your hand?'

In Carol Shields's novel *Swann: A Mystery*, about a murdered woman poet and also about her readers, we find out that the original versions of the dead woman's poems are no longer fully legible—they were written on scraps of old envelopes and got thrown into the garbage by mistake, which blurred them quite a bit. Not only that, a resentful connoisseur has gone around destroying the few remaining copies of the first edition. But several readers have luckily memorized the poems, or parts of them, and at the end of the book they create—or recreate one of these poems before our very eyes, by reciting the fragments. 'Isis keeps Osiris alive by remembering him,' says Dudley Young. 'Remembering' as a pun may of course have two senses—it is the act of memory, but it is also the opposite of dismembering. Or this is what the ear hears. Any reader creates by assembling the fragments of a read book—we can read, after all, only in fragments—and making them into an organic whole in her mind.

Perhaps you will remember the end of Ray Bradbury's futuristic nightmare, *Fahrenheit 451*. All the books are being burnt, in favor of wraparound TV screens that allow for more complete social control. Our hero, who begins as a fireman helping to destroy the books, becomes a convert to the secret resistance movement dedicated to preserving books and, along with them, human history and thought. At length he finds himself in a forest where the insurgents are hiding out. Each has *become* a book, by memorizing it. The fireman is introduced to Socrates, Jane Austen, Charles Dickens, and many more, all of them reciting the books they have assimilated, or 'devoured.' The reader has in effect eliminated the middle point of the triangle—the text in its paper version—and has actually become the book, or vice versa.

With this circuit complete, I will go back to the first question—for whom does the writer write? And I will give two answers. The first is a story about my first real reader.

When I was nine, I was enrolled in a secret society, complete with special handshakes, slogans, rituals, and mottoes. The name of this was the Brownies, and it was quite bizarre. The little girls in it pretended to be fairies, gnomes, and elves, and the grownup leading it was called Brown Owl. Sadly, she did not wear an owl costume, nor did the little girls wear fairy outfits. This was a disappointment to me, but not a fatal one.

I did not know the real name of Brown Owl, but I thought she was wise and fair, and as I needed someone like that in my life at the time, I adored this Brown Owl. Part of the program involved completing various tasks, for which you might collect badges to sew on to your uniform, and in aid of various badge-collecting projects—needlework stitches, seeds of autumn, and so forth—I made some little books, in the usual way: I folded the pages, and sewed them together with sock-darning wool. I then inserted text and illustrations. I gave these books to Brown Owl, and the fact that she liked them was certainly more important to me than the badges. This was my first real writer–reader relationship. The writer, me; the go-between, my books; the recipient, Brown Owl; the result, pleasure for her, and gratification for me.

Many years later, I put Brown Owl into a book. There she is, still blowing her whistle and supervising the knot tests, in my novel *Cat's Eye*, for the same reason that a lot of things and people are put into books. That was in the 1980s, and I was sure the original Brown Owl must have been long dead by then.

Then a few years ago a friend said to me, 'Your Brown Owl is my aunt.' 'Is?' I said. 'She can't possibly be alive!' But she was, so off we went to visit her. She was well over ninety, but Brown Owl and I were very pleased to see each other. After we'd had tea, she said, 'I think you should have these,' and she took out the little books I had made fifty years before—which for some reason she'd kept—and gave them back to me. She died three days later.

That's my first answer: the writer writes for Brown Owl, or for whoever the equivalent of Brown Owl may be in his or her life at the time. A real person, then: singular, specific.

Here's my second answer. At the end of Isak Dinesen's 'The Young Man With the Carnation,' God's voice makes itself heard to the young writer Charlie, who has been so despairing about his work. '"Come," said the Lord. "I will make a covenant between Me and you. I, I will not measure you out any more distress than you need to write your books . . . But you are to write the books. For it is I who want them written. Not the public, not by any means the critics, but Me, Me!" "Can I be certain of that?" asked Charlie. "Not always," said the Lord.'

So that is who the writer writes for: for the reader. For the reader who is not Them, but You. For the Dear Reader. For the ideal reader, who exists on a continuum somewhere between Brown Owl and God. And this ideal reader may prove to be anyone at all—any *one* at all— because the act of reading is just as singular—always—as the act of writing.

2002

Part III

A Brief Handbook of Short Fiction Terms and Concepts

The following terms are common to the study and analysis of short fiction, though many also apply to other literary genres. Bolded words indicate additional terms that are briefly defined within the entry or defined elsewhere in the handbook.

(the) Absurd: Worldview or perspective in which the breakdown of political order or religious faith conveys meaninglessness. The absurdist view, though often comic, stresses human haplessness or irrationality. Characteristics of absurd stories often include non-realistic characters, circular plots, lack of exposition or motivation, incoherence, miscommunication, contradiction, inconsistency, and randomness. Anton Chekhov's and Nikolai Gogol's stories, forerunners of the modernist tradition, portray futile existences. A reaction to World War II, the 'theatre of the absurd' of the 1950s reinvigorated European theatre. Elements of the absurd are present in Kafka's 'A Report to an Academy' and Böll's 'My Sad Face.' See also **(the) Surreal**.

Allegory: Narrative in which characters, actions, places, and objects are given abstract qualities, resulting in two meanings, the literal and the symbolic. To avoid censorship, many writers have resorted to allegory to suggest meanings outside the narrative. Poe's 'The Masque of the Red Death' has sometimes been read as allegory, with the rooms in the abbey representing the stages of life. The search for unattainable beauty in Calvino's 'The Origin of the Birds' also suggests an allegorical dimension.

Allusion: Brief references to historical, religious, mythic, literary, or other outside sources. Allusions from the Bible, Shakespeare, classic myths, or historic events may broaden a work's theme or reveal character. Sime's 'An Irregular Union' alludes to Edward Carpenter, a nineteenth-century social reformer whose radical ideas Phyllis, the story's protagonist, has dutifully absorbed. Allusions may often clarify a writer's intentions, though Joyce scholars have never fully penetrated his dense allusions. Some writers, like Poe and Borges, may allude to works that don't exist. See also **Intertext(uality)**; **Symbol**.

Ambiguity: Textual qualities or properties that make a specific interpretation uncertain or unstable or suggest many possible meanings derived through re-reading. In general, 'ambiguous' or 'open-ended' modern stories stimulate the reader's imagination. Stories often reveal many levels of insight, enhancing the need for literary criticism, which suggests a variety of perspectives towards artistic creation. A similar term, **indeterminacy**, refers to a text's resistance to definitive readings. See also **Author–Reader relationship**.

Antagonist: See **Protagonist**.

Archetype: 'Primordial image' that, according to psychologist Carl Jung, represents part of the collective unconscious of humans. Contemporary Jungian depth psychologists, like James Hillman and Madeline Sonik, suggest that archetypes are basic psychic structures that unite authors, characters, and readers. Often used by writers to give depth and resonance to literature, archetypal images appear in myths, dreams, rituals, and other collective experiences. Examples include the shadow or 'other' self (Callaghan's 'A Predicament'); the animal guide (Van Camp's

'Sky Burial'); the journey, quest, or the descent to the underworld (Wharton's 'A Journey'); the devil (Ross's 'The Runaway'); and the old man, the wise mother, and other cross-cultural images, characters, settings, and occurrences. See also **Motif**.

Atmosphere: See **Mood**.

Author–Reader relationship: A set of potentialities that exist between the author and reader of a text. Research in the last forty years has shown that authors often have specific expectations of their readers; for example, the **implied reader** is one who possesses the 'competencies' to respond to cues in a literary text. Although **reader-response criticism** suggests that competent readers are never completely passive, writers (usually through their **narrators**) may directly evoke reader involvement in the creation of a text or its meaning. For example, the narrator of Calvino's 'The Origin of the Birds' asks the reader to imagine the story as a comic strip. In Atwood's 'Happy Endings,' the narrator begins by inviting the reader to choose between alternate endings. More generally, readers might need to fill in 'gaps' in a story or make other inferences, such as the order of events or the narrator's **tone**. See Hallett, from 'Minimalism and the Short Story,' page 420; Hutcheon, from 'Actualizing Narrative Structures: Detective Plot, Fantasy, Games, and the Erotic,' page 428; Nabokov, from 'Good Readers and Good Writers,' page 461; Alberto Manguel, from 'Endpaper Pages,' page 465; and Atwood, from 'Communion: Nobody to Nobody,' page 470.

Character: A combination of attributes that make up a completed being and which a reader is capable of imagining. There is usually, though not always, one main character in a short story (see **Protagonist**). Although E.M. Forster's definition of 'round or flat characters' applies mostly to longer fiction, it is also useful here. **Round** characters are complex and may embody inconsistencies in their thoughts or actions, whereas **flat** characters are distinguished by only one quality, displayed consistently in a work. **Dynamic** characters are capable of growth or development, whereas **static** characters do not evolve. The narrator of Hollingshead's 'The People of the Sudan' is a round character whose thoughts and actions suggest internal complexity. Mr Willy in Wilson's 'The Window' is an example of a dynamic character who undergoes development through the course of a story and/or comes to a vital realization, a new or changed perception (see **Epiphany**).

    Postmodern characters are elusive by definition, neither flat nor round, but 'empty'—isolated, individual identities lost in a dehumanized world. As authors reject or subvert the **mimetic** traditions of realism, characters may become unrealistic, 'human-like' if improbable, talking birds, insects, or animals, such as the reborn ape in Kafka's 'A Report to an Academy' or even concepts, like Qwfwq, the math equation in Calvino's 'The Origin of the Birds.' In Hempel's 'Nashville Gone to Ashes,' animals remain animals but are given distinguishing characteristics. Authors may appear as characters in their own fiction, as Murakami and Borges sometimes do. Unlike modernist characters with free will who struggle to reach goals, postmodern characters are frequently victims in a stylized world, such as King's flying Indians in 'A Short History of Indians in Canada.' Their stories can have no epiphany, no conclusions, no awareness, and no insights because their precarious world has no meaning. (See Hallett, from 'Minimalism and the Short Story,' page 420; and Leitch, from 'The Debunking Rhythm of the American Short Story,' page 419.)

Character may be revealed through direct (**description, exposition**) or indirect means (**dialogue,** action/**plot**). Character **stereotyping** occurs when a character (either intentionally or unintentionally) is made to represent a predictable collective trait. A **caricature** is exaggerated or distorted in some way to reveal a limited human aspect, often for humorous or satiric purposes. Aymé's 'The Walker-Through-Walls' and Boll's My Sad Face employ caricatures. See James, from 'The Art of Fiction,' page 396; Frank O'Connor, from 'Introduction' to *The Lonely Voice,* page 431; and Chekhov, from *Letters,* page 442.

Chronology: From the Greek for 'logic of time,' the arrangement of events. While the traditional story is linear in its temporal arrangements, other basic chronological tools include **flashbacks** or **foreshadowing**. A typical linear dramatic story begins near the climax and moves towards a resolution. A non-linear chronology, such as that of Gallant's 'Between Zero and One,' reveals a character through associative events. Munro's 'Pictures of the Ice' presents the **dénouement** first, then arranges the chronology to suggest to readers how it came to be. As the attempt to portray experience became more complex, fiction writers skeptical of 'beginnings' and fearful of apocalyptic 'ends' broke traditional patterns. Since disrupting linear time affects causality, reader coherence is sometimes also disturbed. Even so, the connection of incidents reveals 'a unity of action,' as defined by Poe. See also **Flashback; Foreshadowing**.

Climax: See **Dramatic Structure**.

Closure: Refers to the ending of literary works. A **closed dénouement** satisfies aesthetic and all dramatic requirements. A character moves through a dramatic arc, solves a problem, or returns full circle to his or her origins. By contrast, **open-endedness** (**open dénouement**) refers to the lack of resolution of one or more elements. The open-ended nature of short fiction is one of its distinctive features, in contrast to the novel. As a rich area for research, scholars continue to explore complexities of closure in fiction and the reader's need for explanation. By avoiding any sense of completeness, a minimalist story has no closure; the reader's experience of certain words, phrases, or tones of the story determines possible meanings. Spencer's 'The Girl Who Loved Horses' has a clear sense of closure; Blaise's 'Eyes' and Hempel's 'Nashville Gone to Ashes' are less certain.

Dénouement: See **Dramatic Structure**.

Dialogue: Representation of a character's speech in literature typically used to reveal character and/or plot. Dialogue shows what characters *say* as opposed to what they *do* (action).

Diaspora (dī ás pur ah): Literally, 'a scattering of seeds,' the dispersal of ethnic, racial, or cultural groups from their homeland due to natural disaster, persecution, or other forms of political, social, or economic oppression. The diaspora (sometimes capitalized) is more than simply the *subject* of much post-colonial writing; it encompasses the personal and collective search for identity and legitimacy in a world where the distributions of power are unequal or arbitrary. Writers of the diaspora include Bharati Mukherjee, Shani Mootoo, Edwidge Danticat, and Shyam

Selvadurai. See Hancock, from 'Interview with Bharati Mukherjee,' page 456; Khankoje, 'To Bend but not to Bow' [Interview with Shani Mootoo], page 458; and Selvadurai, from 'Introducing Myself in the Diaspora,' page 449.

Diction: Word choice, either specific words or the level of language used throughout a work (e.g., elevated, colloquial, formal, abstract, concrete). The formal diction in Kafka's 'A Report to an Academy' is appropriate for the audience being addressed; however, it also suggests an ironic **tone**. Diction may also reveal something about the character or world he or she inhabits—for example, the Trinidadian English of the narrator in Mootoo's 'Out on Main Street'—or be a feature of a particular writer and thus be associated with **style**. See also **Impressionism**; **Minimalism**. See Carver, from 'On Writing,' page 432.

Dramatic structure: Originates from drama. The phases of a plot include **exposition** (explanation), **rising action** (beginning with the incident that introduces the conflict), **climax** (high point of conflict), and **falling action**, leading to the **dénouement** (resolution). Spencer's 'The Girl Who Loved Horses' has such a structure. This durable form, sometimes called 'well made' or 'formula fiction,' lends itself to many works of fiction, as well as TV scripts and films. However, many literary writers abandoned dramatic structures as misleading or misrepresentative of reality. Such writers rely on emotional complexity, precise details, and thematic imagery.

Epiphany: Literally, a 'showing forth,' a manifestation of a spiritual truth. In Greek drama, the epiphany was marked by the appearance of a god who imposed order and harmony on the human-created disorder; the Christian Feast of the Epiphany celebrates the revelation of Christ's divinity to the Three Wise Men. In fiction, an epiphany is a discovery or realization made by the main character, resulting in a change in his or her perception or producing a new way of looking at something. Many modernist short stories employ a form of epiphany, though there is considerable debate about the term's meaning and its applicability to short fiction in general. For Joyce, an epiphany was the recognition in an ordinary event of an extraordinary meaning not perceived before. (See Joyce, from *Stephen Hero*, page 417.) In terms of a story's dramatic structure, the epiphany is a **climax of recognition**.

Exposition: The part of the narrative that gives background information or other necessary detail before the initiating incident. In a fairy tale like *Cinderella*, exposition would include everything from the 'Once upon a time' opening to the invitation to the royal ball (i.e., the incident that begins the conflict). In the traditional linear structure, the exposition occurs at the beginning, but it could occur at any point in the narrative where explanation is needed. Stories as diverse as Johnson's 'The Derelict' and Dougan's 'Black Cherry' use exposition to set the scene and reveal character. However, not all stories begin with exposition. Mansfield's 'The Stranger,' for example, begins **in medias res** (literally, 'in the middle of things') with background information provided through action and dialogue. See also **Dramatic Structure**.

(the) Fantastic: Generally refers to incidents, settings, or characters that are not 'true to life' or that could not take place in a cause–effect world; in other words, they defy rational explanation. Literary theorist Tzvetan Todorov stressed the role of the reader when he identified the fantastic as a dividing line that causes us to hesitate in our confrontation with 'an apparently supernatural event.' Borges's 'Shakespeare's Memory' and Murakami's 'The Seventh Man' comprise elements of the Fantastic. See also **(the) Gothic**; **(the) Grotesque**; **Magic realism**. See Todorov, from *The Fantastic: A Structural Approach to a Literary Genre*, page 424.

Figurative language/Figure of speech: See **Imagery**; **Metaphor and Metonymy**.

Flashback: Technique of recalling a past action or event in order to illuminate the present situation. Van Camp's 'Sky Burial' uses both flashbacks and **foreshadowing** (see below). By contrast, the entire story of some first-person narratives, such as a childhood memory, is told in the past from the vantage of the adult perspective (Laurence's 'The Loons'; Selvadurai's 'The Demoness Kali').

Foregrounding: An element of a text that is highlighted or stands out is said to be foregrounded. For example, Trinidadian speech patterns are foregrounded in Mootoo's 'Out on Main Street,' and Gilman foregrounds the diary form in 'The Yellow Wallpaper.' Foregrounding points to the way stories are constructed by the **principle of selection**, whereby an author chooses specific techniques and details to create a desired aesthetic effect, some of which will be more important than others.

Foreshadowing: Technique of anticipating a future action or result. Although foreshadowing may create suspense and keep the reader interested, it can also serve more complex goals, such as drawing attention to character flaws (Ross's 'The Runaway') or evoking sympathy or **pathos** (Danticat's 'Children of the Sea').

Frame (tale/narrative): Among the oldest of literary devices, a form of structural repetition in which a text begins and ends in the same way: it is 'framed' by similar or identical phrasing, by its setting, or by its narrator. In Murakami's 'The Seventh Man,' the narrator introduces the character who relates the story, then returns at the end to describe its effect on its listeners. The **embedded narrative** is thus given special prominence, suggesting its significance to its listeners (including the reader).

Genre: Flexible system originating with Aristotle of classifying literary works by their shared characteristics. For example, literature can be grouped into poems, plays, novels, short stories, and non-fiction prose (essays). Smaller divisions, or **sub-genres**, are sometimes made—short stories might be classified as myths, fairy tales, fantasies, mysteries, westerns, horror, or science fiction, each of which might be further subdivided.

(the) Gothic: Drawn from architecture, refers to a subgenre of the novel popular in England from 1790 to 1820. Characteristics of the gothic—gloomy atmosphere, images of decay and death, supernatural occurrences, enclosed spaces, and domineering male characters—were later incorporated into the Victorian novel (for example, novels by the Brontë sisters and Charles Dickens) while other Victorian and Edwardian writers, like Sheridan Le Fanu and W.W. Jacobs continued the Gothic tradition in the short story. Since the 1970s some have claimed a 'Gothic revival' or a **new Gothic** (neo-Gothic) that reflects the dark anxieties, fears, and preoccupations of today's world. The Gothic foregrounds plot, subject matter, and setting over character, striving to create a terrifying or portentous mood. The Gothic has been studied as a subversive form that questions prevailing assumptions, such as the subjugation of women. Poe's 'The Masque of the Red Death,' Gilman's 'The Yellow Wallpaper,' Wharton's 'A Journey,' Spencer's 'The Girl Who Loved Horses,' Blaise's 'Eyes,' Munro's 'Pictures of the Ice,' Carter's 'The Company of Wolves,' and Gowdy's 'We So Seldom Look on Love' all employ gothic elements. See also **(the) Grotesque**. See Carter, from Afterword to *Fireworks: Nine Stories in Various Disguises*, p. 425.

Graphic Literature/Fiction/Narrative: Form in which plot, setting, character, and other narrative elements are conveyed through successive frames and gutters containing visual images as well as dialogue (in speech balloons) and exposition (in captions). Graphic literature is usually distinguished from comic books by its higher levels of seriousness and sophistication, as well as by its replacing of superheroes with flawed characters. Graphic novels are the most common form of graphic literature. Dougan's 'Black Cherry' is an example of graphic fiction.

(the) Grotesque: Associated with comedy and/or satire, a form that evokes the abnormal, animalistic, or freakish through a style of exaggeration or distortion. American writers Edgar Allan Poe, Nathanael West, Flannery O'Connor, Eudora Welty, and Katherine Dunn are known for their use of the grotesque. Carter employs the grotesque in 'The Company of Wolves,' as does Kafka in his description of the sailors and the ape's attempts to mimic them in 'A Report to an Academy'. See Flannery O'Connor, from 'Aspects of the Grotesque in Southern Fiction,' page 423.

Humour (the comic): A complex and often underrated quality in fiction that can be differentiated in its kind, purpose, effects, and underlying mechanisms. Verbal humour, such as puns and **word play**, operates at the level of language, whereas situational humour is inherent in a specific situation. In drama, low comedy, with its pratfalls, mistaken identities, and misunderstandings, is different from high comedy, a sophisticated form that appeals more to the intellect and stresses **wittiness**. In its purpose, humour can range from primarily entertainment to a sustained critique on human institutions to bring about change (see **Satire**). Humour can be mild, moderate, or harsh, producing different effects in its audience, from approval to censure. It can also unleash emotions as divergent as rage or sadness.

Humour of the incongruous is based on a contrast between expectation and the unexpected, what shouldn't happen but does. **Humour of the familiar** is based on similarity, occurrences that we recognize. In TV comedies, this humour might take the form of a character behaving in a predictable way, being 'true to type.' Kafka's 'A Report to an Academy' and King's 'A Short History of Indians in Canada' rely on humour of the incongruous, while Hollingshead's 'The People of the Sudan' uses both humour of the incongruous (Paul Zombo's slide show) and the familiar (the narrator's attempts to dispose of the box, then deny her responsibility). In fiction, humour is often mixed with other forms to produce a complex response. In Hempel's 'Nashville Gone to Ashes,' for example, it underscores an unsatisfying relationship between a wife and husband. **Black humour** can produce unease or nervous laughter as the reader acknowledges an aspect of the human condition. See also **Irony**.

Imagery: Words that convey sense impressions, particularly sight, used in almost all literary writing. Images may occur as precise objects in descriptive passages where their primary focus is on the physical world, or they may become symbols in **figurative** (non-literal) language. Thinking in unlikely imagery is an important aspect of 'non-realistic' fiction, such as the talking ape in Kafka's 'A Report to an Academy'. By using non-traditional imagery in fiction, as Aboriginal writers King ('A Short History of Indians in Canada') and Van Camp ('Sky Burial') do, understanding also changes. Distinctive or contrasting image patterns may highlight a story's theme. See also **Motif**.

Impressionism: An elusive term, as both a movement within modernism (originating in painting as a form that broke up the picture surface with dabs of colour) and a general term that can apply to the qualities of a writer's style, especially in the modernist era. Instead of the static descriptions of traditional **realism**, impressionistic techniques reveal a character's constantly changing thoughts, feelings, sensations, and impressions. Literary modernists used impressionistic techniques, such as broken speech and rapid shifts in thought, to show the mind in flux and the complexity of the subjective self. Mansfield ('The Stranger') and Crane ('A Mystery of Heroism') often used these techniques to portray the immediate perceptions and spontaneous intuitions of their characters. See Conrad, from Preface to *The Nigger of the Narcissus*, page 399; and Woolf, from 'Modern Fiction,' page 402.

Indirection: The use of techniques, devices, and strategies that enable readers to infer meanings/significance. Literary works do not usually state their themes or describe their characters directly but use types of indirection to get them across. Thus, what is stated may be different from what is implied. The use of **dialogue** to reveal character is an example of indirection; similarly, **irony** is an indirect technique because it reveals a more significant meaning under the surface one. Allusions, metaphors, personification, and other forms of figurative language are also examples of indirection.

Initiation story: Narrative pattern in which the central character, usually young and naive, undergoes a test or trial that prepares him or her for entry into the adult world. The dramatic arc then follows a curve from ignorance to knowledge. Because initiation into a group has a social dimension, each incident or event may comment on some aspect of society. Fables and folktales often focus on an initiation process. In 'The Company of Wolves,' Carter utilizes the initiation pattern, though her protagonist is far from the conventional innocent. In Hemingway's 'The Capital of the World,' a naive protagonist tragically fails in his initiation.

Intertext(uality): Reliance of a text on other texts (not necessarily written ones) or the incorporation of other texts within the primary text. A writer might use an intertext to enrich, **parody**, or revise the original text—for example, Carter's revision of the fairy tale 'Little Red Riding Hood' in 'The Company of Wolves.' In general, the use of intertexts acknowledges a writer's debt to other writers and their texts, as Lawrence's 'Tickets, Please' does to Euripides' drama *The Bacchae*. Intertextuality challenges or resists **closure** since these stories demand re-reading and discussion. See also **Allusion; Text**.

Irony: Device of **indirection** usually revealed through a work's **tone**. Irony involves two levels of meaning, the apparent (literal or surface) meaning and another (non-literal or deeper) meaning. It may differ in degree according to its purpose and traditionally is divided into **verbal**, **dramatic**, and **situational** types.

In **verbal irony**, the true meaning of the words contradicts their surface meaning. For example, when the narrator of Munro's 'Pictures of the Ice' states that Brent became 'more religious than Austin,' we know that he merely *pretended* to be more religious.

In **dramatic irony**, the reader possesses an awareness about a character or situation that the character doesn't. Writers often use innocent or naive first-person narrators who lack the experience to interpret their actions correctly (Selvadurai's 'The Demoness Kali'). A character's blindness may also prevent him or her from seeing the significance of an action, as in Johnson's 'The Derelict,' where Cragstone cannot see how his disclosures have compromised his moral judgment. See also **Narrator: reliability**.

In **situational irony**, a situation appears to point to a particular outcome but results in a different or opposite one. The endings of Poe's 'The Masque of the Red Death,' Mansfield's 'The Stranger,' Borges's 'Shakespeare's Memory,' and Aymé's 'The Walker-Through-Walls' are ironic because the outcome is unexpected, or 'ironically fitting.'

Literary Criticism/Theory: Literary writers and scholars have tried to systematically analyze literature and/or explicate its uses and functions, thereby developing 'schools' or 'movements' with specific approaches or tools for analysis. Such approaches, typically, are concerned more with analysis (breaking down) than with evaluation (assigning merit); however, the organization of specific works or authors into a 'canon'—for example, the **Traditional Canon** (see below)—has meant that some works were elevated over others or judged more favourably according to the literary standards that prevailed at the time.

Several important critical approaches to short fiction have evolved in the last century. While they haven't completely supplanted **Formalism** (**New Criticism**), dominant from the 1920s to the early 1970s, they have broadened its focus and challenged many of its assumptions—for example, that isolating a text from the author's life and culture is the best way to analyze it. Formalist critics from the southern United States focused their study on a limited number of works thought to exemplify the highest artistic standards (and detract attention from the Deep South's poverty and racism), most written by male, white writers. Their initially effective explication was later criticized for religious conservatism, bias, ignoring changing values, separating books and authors from historical context, and ignoring or misrepresenting women. Since their so-called **Western** or **Traditional Canon** was never fixed or fully agreed upon, a later generation of scholars claimed it excluded contradictions and diversity within the tradition, such as works of 'minority' writers (e.g., women of colour), an author's political stance, and even ambiguities in language. Yet text-centred criticism was here to stay. The term **Deconstruction**, originating in the 1960s theories of Jacques Derrida, is a more recent **text-centred** approach to the study of literature. Deconstructionists probe for gaps and incon-sistencies in a text to encourage variant readings.

By contrast, **context-centred** approaches consider texts as embedded in social, historical, and cultural forces. **Post-colonialism** centres on the literature of former European colonies, critiquing Eurocentric perspectives while exploring the theme of collective and personal identity. Beginning as a critique of patriarchal structures, **Feminist Literary Criticism** expanded to focus on the study of gender itself, em-bracing such areas as race and class, anthropology, psychology, ecology, and eco-nomics. **New Historicism** stresses the historical time the text was written while **Reader-Response Criticism** addresses issues relating to the act of reading. Other important critical approaches, such as **Gay/Lesbian Studies** and **Ecocriticism**, have evolved within the last twenty years in response to changing social and envi-ronmental awareness.

Lyric: A short poem that expresses strong feeling or spontaneous emotion. Some com-mentators believe stories are closer to poetry than are other prose forms, due to their compression and intensity. Narrative fiction tends towards cause and effect; lyric fiction may aspire to dreamlike evocation, with poetic devices such as alliteration or even rhyme. Sometimes the epiphany is presented lyrically. Thus, literary critics often explore the **lyricism** (lyrical qualities) of short fiction. See Baldeshwiler, from 'The Lyric Short Story: The Sketch of a History,' page 414; and Hollingshead, from 'Short Story vs Novel,' page 412.

Magic realism: A loosely defined term, which originated in painting and became well known through Borges, Cortázar, and other Latin American writers. Rejecting rational explanations of reality, magic realists foreground magical or 'impossible' elements in an otherwise realistic narrative to produce what early practitioner Alejo Carpentier termed a 'heightened reality.' Magic realism differs from the **fantastic** and **the surreal** since its effects are found in reality. Magic realism jolts us out of our accepted and static patterns of experience, to **defamiliarize**, or make uncertain, these patterns. Because magic realism refers to the unknowable (be it shamanism or organized religion) or conflicting perspectives of reality (such as indigenous views versus the conqueror's), it has found favour with post-colonial writers. Aymé's 'The Walker-Through-Walls' and King's 'A Short History of Indians in Canada' use magic realist techniques. See Hancock, from *Magic Realism and Canadian Literature: Essays and Stories*, page 426.

Metafiction: Created by American author William Gass in a 1970 essay, an enigmatic and contested term describing a phase of experimental writing prominent in the 1960s. The term called attention to the conventions and artifices involved in mak-ing fiction as a reaction against post–World War II literary realism. Common de-vices include directly commenting on or questioning the way the story is told. One of the themes in a metafictional work is the status of fiction and fiction-making. Metafiction uses the work itself to explore this status and thus is some-times called a 'self-conscious' fictional form. Because of its confused definitions, as well as writers creating many short-lived variant names, such as 'superfiction,' 'surfiction,' or 'self-reflexive fiction,' to describe their work, the term now generally describes a wide range of narratives as old as the tradition of written fiction. Critic Linda Hutcheon created the phrase 'historiographic metafiction,' which blends factual history and creative fiction, questions 'historical truth,' and redefines 'suppressed histories.' Atwood's 'Happy Endings' and Schoemperlen's 'The Antonyms of Fiction' are examples of metafiction; Calvino's 'The Origin of the Birds' also contains metafictional elements. See Hutcheon, from 'Actualizing Narrative Structures: Detective Plot, Fantasy, Games, and the Erotic,' page 428.

Metaphor and Metonymy: Literary devices that make connections between objects. Philosophers, poets, and fiction writers have debated since Aristotle the merits of metaphor and metonymy as basic to concepts of language. A metaphor is a figure of speech involving a comparison between two objects not usually associated or considered alike; a **simile** is a more explicit comparison that uses 'like,' 'as,' or a similar word/phrase to introduce the second object. Metaphors and similes are features of lyrical writing. Original metaphors have force and power. Metonymy, a feature of realistic fiction, makes logical connections between objects by substituting one object for another with which it is associated. The opening of Crane's 'A Mystery of Heroism' provides examples of a metaphor (first italics), a simile (second italics), and metonymy: 'On the ground was the crimson terror of an exploding shell, with *fibres of flame* that seemed *like lances*.' Metonymy is illustrated in the following where 'battery' and 'guns' refer to those who are firing them: 'On the top of the hill a battery was arguing in tremendous roars with some other guns.' See also **Style**.

Mimesis: From the Greek for 'to imitate,' originated in ancient rhetoric and was applied to the arts. In fiction, mimesis is the attempt to imitate life or draw on lifelike attributes of a person, object, setting, etc.

Minimalism: Much-debated term referring to a style of writing that is pared to the essence with few modifiers or descriptive words. A minimalist story dismisses plot, has average characters, suggests life is a continuum with little meaning, is open to multiple interpretations, and eliminates narrative conventions. Minimalism can also be narrated in a detached, banal, or ironic tone. The essence of minimalism, whether applied to a style or form, is in its omissions and what the reader is left to infer by a close reading of the story. Hemingway, Carver, and Hempel are frequently cited as minimalists. See Hallett, from 'Minimalism and the Short Story,' page 420; and Carver, from 'On Writing,' page 432.

Modernism: Period (1895–1945) of artistic innovation and renewal in literature as well as in the other arts. Characteristics of modernists include 1) reaction against Victorian values, morality, and sense of order; 2) emphasis on subjective rather than objective experience; 3) experimentation in styles and techniques, such as non-linear narratives and multiple perspectives; 4) interest in psychology and rejection of religion; 5) creation of a new artistic self-consciousness, resulting in theorizing about art and in movements like **Impressionism**, Imagism, and **Surrealism**. Key modernists include Joseph Conrad, Stephen Crane, William Faulkner, Ernest Hemingway, James Joyce, D.H. Lawrence, Katherine Mansfield, and Virginia Woolf. Other important modernists, such as T.S. Eliot, Ezra Pound, Gertrude Stein, and W.B. Yeats, were primarily poets.

Monologue: Meaning 'single' (mono) plus 'speech' (logos), form of first-person narration that records uninterrupted the thoughts and/or feelings of the narrator. Though a monologue reveals the inner world of the speaker, it is usually directed to one or more listeners (Kafka's 'A Report to an Academy'). **Inner (Interior) Monologue** is a more extreme form that presents unedited the character's thoughts and feelings, sometimes unpunctuated and in the present tense. By contrast, **epistolary fiction** takes the form of letters—not speech—that reveal a character's inner world (Danticat's 'Children of the Sea'). See also **Point of View**.

Mood: Emotional response or complexity of responses generated by the elements of a work, for example, calm, terror, empathy, sadness, humour, suspense. Mood and **atmosphere** are closely related, but atmosphere is usually evoked by setting, whereas mood could arise from other elements, including dialogue, character, imagery, diction, or situation. The mood of pathos and, perhaps, desperation in Van Camp's 'Sky Burial' is evoked partly by the setting (a doughnut shop), character (a dying Native man), and situation (the man's desire to pass his gift on to a Cree girl). See also **Tone**.

Motif: Originating from music, where it means a repeated note or phrase, refers to a distinctive narrative element, such as an image, action, incident, or concept, that becomes significant through repetition and its connection to a work's theme. An example is the chiming of the clock in the seventh room in Poe's 'The Masque of the Red Death.' See also **Imagery; Symbol**.

Motivation: Factor or, more likely, complexity of psychological factors that help determine characters' behaviours or account for their thoughts or words. Motivation is often the focus of **psychological realism**.

Myth: The oldest creative use of language, a tale told by a narrator. The storyteller's art is to share an experience or explain spiritual and natural phenomena, such as the origins of the world. It forms part of a group's oral tradition and is passed down from generation to generation. Sometimes the word 'mythic' is applied to an event or situation of collective or archetypal significance. For example, the journey of a character in Danticat's 'Children of the Sea' recalls the journey of African slaves to America and the Caribbean (known as the 'Middle Passage'). A related form, **legends** unify members of a community by describing the heroic exploits of its individuals, like the heroes of Homer's epics, the *Iliad* and the *Odyssey*.

Narrative: Originating from the same root as 'story,' means 'to know' the world of experience. Theorists suggest Western narrative is framed by two world views, Biblical narratives and mythological epics. Critics have suggested narrative is a series of at least four layers between a writer and a reader such as author and **implied author** (the author as he or she appears to the reader), or reader and **implied reader** (the reader as envisioned by the author). Although cultural differences affect interpretation, all stories in all cultures tend to have the same basic patterns despite form or content. See also **Narrator**.

Narrator: Person or voice (which may not be human) telling the story. Narrators vary in their **presence** (third-person narrators), **involvement** (first-person), and **reliability** (first-person). Closely related concepts include **Point of View** and **Voice**.

Third-person narrators differ in their degree of presence in or absence from the narrative. Until the twentieth century, **intrusive narrators** (who, for example, interrupted the narrative flow when they wished to comment on a character's action) were common. The narrator of Sime's 'An Irregular Union' occasionally intrudes, principally to generalize or universalize the protagonist's situation. With the exception of narrators of metafiction intruding to comment on the story or its artifice, such interventions are rare in today's fiction. A narrator's distance, or detachment, can often be determined by **tone** or **voice**. Distance can be used to help create **irony**. Even the most detached narrator, however, is not the same as the author. Examples of detached narrators are those of Joyce's 'A Painful Case' and Hemingway's 'The Capital of the World.'

Involved narrators are main characters in their stories, often revealing their actions, motivations, and feelings directly; however, they do not have access to the inner worlds of other characters, so their viewpoint is limited by their subjectivity. Some first-person narrators are primarily **observers** or combine involvement with observation (Ross's 'The Runaway'). In Murakami's 'The Seventh Man,' the story is introduced by an uninvolved narrator, who is followed by an involved narrator.

A **reliable narrator** can be trusted to give a truthful or accurate picture of events and character. Most third-person narrators are reliable. However, first-person narrators may be **unreliable** not only because they are limited by their subjectivity but also because they may consciously or unconsciously distort, deceive, or minimize their role or responsibility. In such cases, readers may have to decide whether this unreliability is due to the narrator's limited perspective or intentional deceptiveness. The device of an unreliable narrator can serve to draw a reader into the story in an effort to sort out the truth—for example, in Gilman's 'The Yellow Wallpaper,' Mukherjee's 'The Lady from Lucknow,' Hollingshead's 'The People of the Sudan,' and Gowdy's 'We So Seldom Look on Love.'

Naturalism: Outgrowth of realistic writing in the late nineteenth and early twentieth centuries. Unlike its predecessor, Romanticism, naturalism uses scientific methods of observation and stresses a character's helplessness before external forces, like society, nature, or heredity. Yet naturalism often contains symbolist elements. Naturalistic writers, such as French novelist Émile Zola and North American writers Frank Norris, Theodore Dreiser, Stephen Crane, and Sinclair Ross, often portray their protagonists as victims of fate. Wharton's 'A Journey' and Joyce's 'A Painful Case' employ naturalistic elements.

Parody: Generally involves an imitation of another work or style, using exaggeration or distortion to make fun of its dominant characteristics. Many contemporary short fiction writers consider the conventions of traditional stories, concepts of character, and manipulation of language to be well worn and use parody in order to renew fiction. Kafka's 'A Report to an Academy' and Carter's 'The Company of Wolves' use parody.

Plot: As described by E.M. Forster, the best arrangement or sequence of incidents within a narrative. Stories are how we shape experience, be it through direct chronology or rearranged elements. Traditionally, the plot focuses on the external actions of characters; however, it could also focus on the inner world. A century of film, painting, collage, montage, photography, and later TV and the Internet, suggested innovative ways to shape short fiction. See Welty, from 'The Reading and Writing of Short Stories,' page 434. See also **Chronology**.

Point of View (POV): The angle of vision from which the story is told, which affects the reader's reaction to the characters. The reduced use of both omniscient narrators and traditional dramatic structures and resolutions after the nineteenth century led to the significance of the narrating mind and a new way to experience character and meaning for the reader.

If the **first-person** POV is used ('I,' 'we'), the narrator will have limited access to characters and incidents other than what is personally experienced or witnessed. Authors may use first-person narrators to establish an intimate bond with the reader. Approximately half of the stories in this anthology use first-person POV.

Second-person POV ('you') is less common, though first-person narrators may occasionally address their audience as 'you.' Blaise's 'Eyes' uses second-person POV.

Third-person POV ('she,' 'he,' 'they,' 'them') offers greater variety, from wide to narrow angle. A narrator capable of moving from one character's perspective to another's and from one scene to the next is essentially **omniscient**, or all-knowing. More common are third-person narrators who are restricted to the consciousness of one character (**restrictive omniscient**), usually the **protagonist**. American writer Henry James called the character who did the seeing the 'central intelligence' (though James often used a less important character in this role). Still other narrators can move in and out of the minds of more than one character in a scene but otherwise lack the range of the omniscient narrator. Sime's 'An Irregular Union' and Hemingway's 'The Capital of the World' use the omniscient POV while the remaining use some form of restrictive POV. See also **Narrator; Voice**.

Postmodern(ism) (PM): Emerging in the 1980s, literary movement that incorporates diverse aspects of contemporary culture. Although notoriously difficult to define, postmodernism in literature may reflect—and even pursue—some of the goals of modernism, but rejects such assumptions as the authority of the author, univocal (one-voice) perspectives, unifying narratives, and other 'absolutes.' In their place, the postmodern often stresses plurality, possibility, and play. PM short fiction tends to focus on the intense 'moment' or 'instant' (for a contrastive view of the intense moment, see **Epiphany**) since the future is uncertain. Because this moment is constantly changing, writers simultaneously balance uncertainty, disruption, and innovation with new images and clever wordplay. See also **Modernism**.

Protagonist: Meaning 'first actor,' the main character in a fictional work. The **antagonist** opposes the main character, though this opposition isn't necessarily conscious or intentional. Not all stories include an antagonist. In Ross's 'The Runaway,' the protagonist is the narrator's father, and their neighbour, Luke Taylor, is the antagonist. The antagonist in Callaghan's 'A Predicament' is the drunken man who wanders into the confessional. In both cases, the antagonist provokes the story's central conflict.

Realism: With its roots in the works of French novelists Gustav Flaubert and Honoré de Balzac, realism spread to North America in the late nineteenth century, depicting the lives of ordinary, usually middle-class characters using everyday language.

Realism began as a response to **Romanticism**'s larger-than-life characters and exotic settings. The spirit of realism was boosted by the scientific advances in the mid-nineteenth century and the rise of rational inquiry. As realism developed, writers sought to incorporate its basic characteristics by applying them to specific subjects and settings.

The focus also shifted from nature to mass culture, often presented as threatening or incomprehensible. With the distrust of or loss of faith in knowledge, the omniscient narrators of Leo Tolstoy's or Charles Dickens's times tended to be replaced by those with limited perspectives and narrowed points of view. The research of Charles Darwin, Sigmund Freud, and Albert Einstein shattered long-held views about 'reality,' while World War I tore apart cultures, audiences, and identities. Many writers no longer tried to present 'objective reality.' Realistic places were presented as fragments of character consciousness, and realistic characters were often presented as paranoid, brooding, alienated, or distrustful. The after-effects of propaganda and mass advertising meant even language could no longer be trusted. Postmodern characters may even be aware they are fictional creations. See also **Metafiction**.

Given the many permutations of realism, it has been argued that most literary writing in the last 100 years is realistic writing despite the growth of apparently 'non-realistic' genres such as **(the) Fantastic** and **magic realism**, especially in Latin America and parts of Europe. There are various types of realism: **Psychological realism** focuses on characters' motivation and other aspects of their psychological makeup; **social realism** shows characters at odds with society's institutions; **moral realism** centres on the ethical choices confronting characters; **urban realism** portrays characters adapting to or victims of dehumanized urban landscapes; and **documentary realism** combines factual rigour with invention to produce a 'life-like' recreation. Some critics apply the term **neo-realism** to European writers such as Calvino or Americans such as Hempel who seem to present strict documentary reportage but have many interpretative levels 'to make the real seem strange.'

The range and diversity of realistic approaches can be seen in many stories in this anthology. For example, in spite of many differences, Crane in 'A Mystery of Heroism,' Lawrence in 'Tickets, Please,' and Spencer in 'The Girl Who Loved Horses' could be considered psychological realists. Social realism is evident in Sime's 'An Irregular Union,' Gallant's 'Between Zero and One,' and Mootoo's 'Out on Main Street.' Moral issues are critical in Johnson's 'The Derelict,' Callaghan's 'A Predicament,' and Dalisay's 'Heartland,' while the modern city is a focus in Callaghan's 'A Predicament,' Mootoo's 'Out on Main Street,' Dougan's 'Black Cherry,' and Taylor's 'Smoke's Fortune.' Carver's 'Feathers' exemplifies neo-realism. See also **Naturalism**.

Satire: Genre that mocks or criticizes institutions or commonly held beliefs by using **humour**, **irony**, or ridicule. The purpose behind satire can vary from the desire to raise awareness or institute change to the simple need to make people laugh at themselves (for example, much satire in TV comedies, like *The Simpsons*, has no moral function). The degree of satire can range from poking fun to harsh condemnation. Satire often has one or more specific targets, such as academic discourse and human pride (Kafka's 'A Report to an Academy') or the totalitarian state (Böll's 'My Sad Face'). Other stories with satiric elements include Aymé's 'The Walker-Through-Walls,' King's 'A Short History of Indians in Canada,' and Hollingshead's 'The People of the Sudan.' See also **Humour; Irony; Parody**.

Setting: The time and place of the story. Unlike novels, stories are often restricted to one setting. Details of the setting need not be specific. For example, Crane's 'A Mystery of Heroism' is set during the American Civil War, but the precise place is not given; by contrast, Wilson's 'The Window' is set in downtown Vancouver, but no time is mentioned.

(Short) Story Cycle: Series of linked stories usually collected in book form, similar to a **novel in stories**, but stories in story cycles do not always use the same characters. Instead, they may have the same setting or interweave common issues or themes, like the stories in Sime's *Sister Woman* that collectively explore the oppression of working women in Montreal around the turn of the twentieth century. Similarly, the stories in Joyce's *Dubliners*, including 'A Painful Case,' show inhabitants of Dublin clinging to outdated traditions and conventions. One character, such as Linnet Muir in Gallant's 'Between Zero and One,' can unify several stories. In *Krik? Krak!* Danticat uses a variety of characters and settings (many stories, including 'Children of the Sea,' refer to the town of Ville Rose, Haiti) to explore Haiti's tragic past.

Simile: See **Metaphor**.

Structure: Arrangements of parts into an aesthetic whole. A structural approach to a work emphasizes the interrelation of parts. See also **Plot; Chronology**.

(the) Surreal: Literary movement partly a reaction against World War I and partly a continuation of **Romanticism**. The surrealists held lofty mystical ambitions to transform reality through the power of the imagination. While the **absurd** generally focuses on the outer, the surrealist intellectual adventure surrenders the ego and focuses on dreams, sensory confusion, symbolism, the occult, and visions. Surrealism was an influential precursor to **magic realism**, modern art, and new wave cinema. Surrealistic writing deliberately blurs the boundaries between the outer and the inner through a dreamlike atmosphere, which surrealists call *le merveilleux* or 'revelation.' Poe's 'The Masque of the Red Death' and Aymé's 'The Walker-Through-Walls' contain surreal elements.

Style: 1) The distinctive way an author uses words and other linguistic or textual elements, such as **diction**, rhythm, **tone**, sentence structure, **syntax**, punctuation, **figures of speech**, **allusions**, etc. The term can be applied to one work or to various works throughout a writer's career. For example, many have seen Elizabeth Spencer's style as markedly 'Southern' with its breathless rhythms and syntactic inversions. The style of a story will usually be connected with larger structural elements, such as character or theme. For example, the style of Joyce's 'A Painful Case' conveys distance and objectivity; by contrast, the style of Gallant's 'Between Zero and One' is sophisticated yet intimate, drawing the reader into the world being described. 2) Forms or structures with distinctive features, such as the diary form in Gilman's 'The Yellow Wallpaper.' See Gallant, from 'What Is Style?' page 435.

Symbol: Image referring to a person, place, thing, or action that is given importance in a work due to the way the author uses it or because of its associations. Unlike **figures of speech**, a symbol resonates and cannot be 'pinned down' to one specific meaning. A **traditional symbol**, such as the sea, star, or heart, has recognizable cross-cultural associations (see **Archetype**). The importance of a **contextual symbol** depends on context, the way the author uses it throughout the work. Symbols are sometimes announced in a story's title: Wharton's 'A Journey,' Wilson's 'The Window,' and Laurence's 'The Loons.' See Flannery O'Connor, from 'The Nature and Aim of Fiction,' page 438.

Syntax: Word order; the arrangement of words in a sentence or larger unit. **Inverted** or **disrupted syntax** refers to a style that departs from normal word order.

Tale: Of more ancient lineage than the short story, a brief, entertaining narrative that stresses plot at the expense of (often stereotypical) character. Not dependent on the laws of everyday reality, the tale may include supernatural elements. Poe called his stories 'tales,' as did his contemporary Nathaniel Hawthorne. Carter said she preferred the tale because it represented a deeper reality behind everyday experience. See Carter, Afterword to *Fireworks: Nine Stories in Various Disguises*, page 425.

Text: Production—not necessarily a literary one—that encodes one or more messages or meanings, that lends itself to interpretation, and/or that provides aesthetic pleasure to a reader or viewer. The meaning of texts is often embedded in cultural expectations and/or conventions. Examples of written texts include essays, books (such as novels), articles in newspapers, poems, short stories, weblogs, e-mails; examples of visual texts include plays and other performances, movies, video games, and advertising.

Theme: Overarching meaning or universal qualities manifested in a work. A story's theme, however, cannot be studied in isolation: plot, setting, character, point of view, tone, style, and other elements can contribute to a theme.

Tone: The emotional or intellectual register of the work—that is, the way the author conveys his or her attitude towards subject matter and/or audience (e.g., solemn, reverent, exalted, comic, ironic, mocking, intimate, or contemplative). The tone of Gallant's 'Between Zero and One' could be called, among other things, 'irreverent,' while that of Laurence's 'The Loons' could be termed 'elegiac.'

Understatement: Figure of speech in which something is stated as less (important) than it really is. Crane, Hemingway, and Hempel often use understatement. See also **Irony**.

Voice (or **narrative voice**): Filtering of what the narrator sees through use of linguistic or textual devices. A fiction entangles multiple perspectives of an author, a narrator, and the speaking characters. How an author uses voice(s) has become a specialized area of scholarship with various branches called **narratology**. The attributes of **reliable** and **unreliable narrators** direct or misdirect readers as they emerge through language, tone, diction, dialect, emphasis, style, rhythm, and other features. Voice is to narrator as speech is to speaker—that is, you can isolate different attributes of an author, narrator, or character by his or her tone, vocabulary, speech patterns, and the like. See also **Narrator**.

ACKNOWLEDGEMENTS

Margaret Atwood, 'Happy Endings,' from *Good Bones and Simple Murders*. Copyright © 1983, 1992, 1994. Published by McClelland & Stewart Ltd. Used with permission of the publisher. Excerpt from 'Communion: Nobody to Nobody—The Eternal Triangle: The Writer, the Reader, and the Book as Go-Between,' from *Negotiating with the Dead: A Writer on Writing*.

Marcel Aymé, 'The Walker-Through-Walls,' from *Walker-Through-Walls and Other Stories*, published by The Bodley Head, 1972. Reprinted by permission of The Random House Group Ltd.

Eileen Baldeshwiler, excerpt from 'The Lyric Short Story: The Sketch of a History,' *Studies in Short Fiction* (1969).

Clark Blaise, 'Eyes,' from *A North American Education*.

Heinrich Böll, 'My Sad Face,' from *The Stories of Heinrich Boll*, trans. Leila Vennewitz. Reprinted by permission of Northwestern University Press.

Jorge Luis Borges, 'Shakespeare's Memory,' from *Collected Fictions* by Jorge Luis Borges, trans. Andrew Hurley. Copyright © 1998 by Maria Kodama; translation copyright © 1998 by Penguin Putnam Inc. Used by permission of Viking Penguin, a division of Penguin Group (USA) Inc.

Elizabeth Bowen, from Introduction to *The Faber Book of Modern Short Stories*. Reprinted by permission of Faber & Faber Ltd.

Morley Callaghan, 'A Predicament,' appears in *The Complete Stories, Volume One*, by Morley Callaghan, pages 53-57, published by Exile Editions, © 2003.

Italo Calvino, 'The Origin of the Birds,' from *t zero*, trans. William Weaver. Copyright © 1969 by Italo Calvino. Reprinted in Canada with permission of The Wylie Agency LLC. Excerpts from *Why Read the Classics?* Copyright © 1999 by The Estate of Italo Calvino, reprinted in Canada with permission of The Wylie Agency LLC.

Angela Carter, 'The Company of Wolves,' from *The Bloody Chamber* and excerpt from Afterword to *Fireworks: Nine Stories in Various Disguises*. Copyright © Angela Carter. Reproduced by permission of the author c/o Rogers, Coleridge & White Ltd., 20 Powis Mews, London W11 1JN.

Raymond Carver, 'Feathers,' from *Where I'm Calling From*. Copyright © 1986, 1987, 1988 by Raymond Carver, reprinted in Canada with permission of The Wylie Agency LLC. Excerpt from 'On Writing,' Copyright © 1981 by Raymond Carver, reprinted in Canada with permission of The Wylie Agency LLC. A version of this essay was first published in *The New York Times Book Review*.

Julio Cortázar, excerpt from 'Some Aspects of the Short Story,' *The Arizona Quarterly* Spring (1982): 5–17. Reprinted by permission of the publisher.

Stephen Crane, 'A Mystery of Heroism'; excerpt from 'Letters to a Friend About His Ambition, His Art, and His Views of Life,' published in *The New York Times*, 14 July 1900.

Jose Dalisay, Jr, 'Heartland.' Reprinted by permission of the author.

Edwidge Danticat, 'Children of the Sea,' from *Krik? Krak!* Copyright © 1993, 1995 by Edwidge Danticat, excerpted by permission of Soho Press, Inc. All rights reserved.

Michael Dougan, 'Black Cherry,' from *I Can't Tell You Anything*. Reprinted by permission of the author.

Café Productions Inc. with permission of the author. Excerpt from Introduction from *All My Relations: An Anthology of Contemporary Canadian Native Fiction*.

Margaret Laurence, 'The Loons,' from *A Bird in the House*. Copyright © 1963, 1964, 1965, 1966, 1967, 1970. Published by McClelland & Stewart Ltd. Used with permission of the publisher.

Thomas M. Leitch, excerpt from 'The Debunking Rhythm of the American Short Story,' in Lohafer and Clarey, eds, *Short Story Theory at a Crossroads*. Reprinted by permission of Louisiana State University Press.

Alberto Manguel, excerpt from 'Endpaper Pages,' in *A History of Reading*. Copyright © 1996 by Alberto Manguel. Reprinted by permission of Knopf Canada.

Katharine Mansfield, excerpt from *The Critical Writings of Katherine Mansfield*, ed. Clare Hanson. Reprinted by permission of Palgrave Macmillan.

Steven Millhauser, excerpt from 'The Ambition of the Short Story,' *New York Times* 5 Oct. 2008. Copyright © 2008 *The New York Times*. All rights reserved. Used by permission and protected by the Copyright Laws of the United States. The printing, copying, redistribution, or retransmission of the material without express written permission is prohibited.

Shani Mootoo, 'Out on Main Street,' from *Out on Main Street and Other Stories*. Reprinted by permission of the author.

Bharati Mukherjee, 'The Lady from Lucknow.' Copyright © 1985 by Bharati Mukherjee. Originally published in *Darkness*. Reprinted by permission of the author.

Alice Munro, 'Pictures of the Ice,' from *Friend of My Youth*. Copyright © 1990. Published by McClelland & Stewart Ltd. Used with permission of the publisher.

Haruki Murakami, 'The Seventh Man,' trans. Jay Rubin, copyright © 2006 by Haruki Murakami, from *Blind Willow, Sleeping Woman: Twenty-Four Stories* by Haruki Murakami, trans. by Philip Gabriel and Jay Rubin. Used by permission of Alfred A. Knopf, a division of Random House, Inc.

Vladimir Nabokov, 'Good Readers and Good Writers,' from *Lectures on Literature*. Copyright © 1980 by the Estate of Vladimir Nabokov. Reprinted by permission of Houghton Mifflin Harcourt Publishing Company.

Flannery O'Connor, excerpts from 'Aspects of the Grotesque in Southern Fiction' and 'The Nature and Aim of Fiction' from *Mystery and Manners* by Flannery O'Connor, edited by Sally and Robert Fitzgerald. Copyright © 1969 by the Estate of Mary Flannery O'Connor. Reprinted by permission of Farrar, Straus and Giroux, LLC.

Frank O'Connor, excerpt from Introduction to *The Lonely Voice: A Study of the Short Story* (Cleveland: World Publishing Company, 1963). Copyright © 1963 by Frank O'Connor. Used by permission of The Jennifer Lyons Literary Agency, LLC.

Sinclair Ross, 'The Runaway,' from *The Lamp at Noon and Other Stories*. Copyright © 1968. Published by McClelland & Stewart Ltd. Used with permission of the publisher.

Diane Schoemperlen, 'Antonyms of Fiction' from *Red Plaid Shirt*. Copyright © 2002 by Diane Schoemperlen. A Phyllis Bruce Book. Published by HarperCollins Publishers Ltd. All rights reserved.

Shyam Selvadurai, 'The Demoness Kali,' first published *Toronto Life*, August 2006. Copyright © Shyam Selvadurai. With permission of the author. Excerpt from 'Introducing Myself in the Diaspora,' in *Story-Wallah! A Celebration of South Asian Fiction*.

Elizabeth Spencer, 'The Girl Who Loved Horses,' from *The Stories of Elizabeth Spencer*. Copyright © by Elizabeth Spencer 1979. Reprinted with permission of McIntosh & Otis, Inc. All rights reserved.

Philip Stevik, excerpt from Introduction to *Anti-Story: An Anthology of Experimental Fiction*. Reprinted with permission of The Free Press, a Division of Simon & Schuster, Inc. Introduction, Copyright © 1971 by The Free Press. All rights reserved.

Timothy Taylor, 'Smoke's Fortune,' from *Silent Cruise*. Copyright © 2002 by Timothy Taylor. Reprinted by permission of Knopf Canada.

Tzvetan Todorov, excerpt from *The Fantastic: A Structural Approach to a Literary Genre*, trans. Richard Howard. English translation © 1973 by The Press of Case Western Reserve University. Originally published in French as *Introduction à la littérature Fantastique*. Copyright © 1970 by Editions du Seuil. Reprinted by permission of Georges Borchardt, Inc., for Editions du Seuil.

Richard Van Camp, 'Sky Burial,' from *Angel Wing Splash Pattern*, 2nd edn. Reprinted by permission of the author. The second part of this story—Morris's account of what happened next—is called 'Snow White Nothing for Miles' in *Angel Wing Splash Pattern*.

Eudora Welty, excerpt from 'The Reading and Writing of Short Stories,' *Atlantic* (Apr. 1949). Reprinted by permission of Russell & Volkening, Inc., as agents for the author. Copyright © 1949 by Eudora Welty, renewed in 1977 by Eudora Welty. Originally published by *The Atlantic Monthly*.

Ethel Wilson, 'The Window,' from *Mrs Golightly and Other Stories*.